EVERYMAN'S LIBRARY

435

HISTORY

Everyman, I will go with thee, and be thy guide,
In thy most need to go by thy side

GIBBON'S DECLINE AND FALL OF THE ROMAN EMPIRE

IN SIX VOLUMES . VOLUME TWO

INTRODUCTION BY
CHRISTOPHER DAWSON

LONDON J. M. DENT & SONS LTD
NEW YORK E. P. DUTTON & CO INC

CONTENTS.

THE
HISTORY OF THE DECLINE AND FALL
OF THE
ROMAN EMPIRE

CHAPTER XVI

The Conduct of the Roman Government towards the Christians, from the Reign of Nero to that of Constantine

IF we seriously consider the purity of the Christian religion, the sanctity of its moral precepts, and the innocent as well as austere lives of the greater number of those who during the first ages embraced the faith of the Gospel, we should naturally suppose that so benevolent a doctrine would have been received with due reverence even by the unbelieving world; that the learned and the polite, however they might deride the miracles, would have esteemed the virtues of the new sect; and that the magistrates, instead of persecuting, would have protected an order of men who yielded the most passive obedience to the laws, though they declined the active cares of war and government. If, on the other hand, we recollect the universal toleration of Polytheism, as it was invariably maintained by the faith of the people, the incredulity of philosophers, and the policy of the Roman senate and emperors, we are at a loss to discover what new offence the Christians had committed, what new provocation could exasperate the mild indifference of antiquity, and what new motives could urge the Roman princes, who beheld without concern a thousand forms of religion subsisting in peace under their gentle sway, to inflict a severe punishment on any part of their subjects who had chosen for themselves a singular but an inoffensive mode of faith and worship.

The religious policy of the ancient world seems to have assumed a more stern and intolerant character to oppose the progress of Christianity. About fourscore years after the death of Christ, his innocent disciples were punished with death by the sentence of a proconsul of the most amiable and philosophic character, and according to the laws of an emperor distinguished by the wisdom and justice of his general administration. The apologies which were repeatedly addressed to the successors of Trajan are filled with the most pathetic complaints that the Christians, who obeyed the dictates and solicited the liberty of conscience, were alone, among all the subjects of the Roman empire, excluded from the common benefits of their auspicious government. The deaths of a few eminent martyrs have been recorded with care; and from the time that Christianity was invested with the supreme power, the governors of the church have been no less diligently employed in displaying the cruelty, than in imitating the conduct, of their Pagan adversaries. To separate (if it be possible) a few authentic as well as interesting facts from an undigested mass of fiction and error, and to relate, in a clear and rational manner, the causes, the extent, the duration, and the most important circumstances of the persecutions to which the first Christians were exposed, is the design of the present chapter.

The sectaries of a persecuted religion, depressed by fear, animated with resentment, and perhaps heated by enthusiasm, are seldom in a proper temper of mind calmly to investigate, or candidly to appreciate, the motives of their enemies, which often escape the impartial and discerning view even of those who are placed at a secure distance from the flames of persecution. A reason has been assigned for the conduct of the emperors towards the primitive Christians, which may appear the more specious and probable as it is drawn from the acknowledged genius of Polytheism. It has already been observed that the religious concord of the world was principally supported by the implicit assent and reverence which the nations of antiquity expressed for their respective traditions and ceremonies. It might therefore be expected that they would unite with indignation against any sect or people which should separate itself from the communion of mankind, and, claiming the exclusive possession of divine knowledge, should disdain every form of worship except its own as impious and idolatrous. The rights of toleration were held by mutual indulgence: they were justly forfeited by a refusal of the accustomed tribute. As the payment of this tribute was inflexibly refused by the Jews, and by them alone, the consideration of the treatment which they experienced from the Roman magistrates will serve to explain how far these speculations are justified by facts, and will lead us to discover the true causes of the persecution of Christianity.

Without repeating what has been already mentioned of the reverence of the Roman princes and governors for the temple of Jerusalem, we shall only observe that the destruction of the temple and city was accompanied and followed by every circumstance that could exasperate the minds of the conquerors, and authorise religious persecutions by the most specious arguments of political justice and the public safety. From the reign of Nero to that of Antoninus Pius, the Jews discovered a fierce impatience of the dominion of Rome, which repeatedly broke out in the most furious massacres and insurrections. Humanity is shocked at the recital of the horrid cruelties which they committed in the cities of Egypt, of Cyprus, and of Cyrene, where they dwelt in treacherous friendship with the unsuspecting natives;[1] and we are tempted to applaud the severe retaliation which was exercised by the arms of the legions against a race of fanatics whose dire and credulous superstition seemed to render them the implacable enemies not only of the Roman government, but of human kind.[2] The enthusiasm of the Jews was supported by the opinion that it was unlawful for them to pay taxes to an idolatrous master, and by the flattering promise which they derived from their ancient oracles, that a conquering Messiah would soon arise, destined to break their fetters, and to invest the favourites of heaven with the empire of the earth. It was by announcing himself as their long-expected deliverer, and by calling on all the descendants of Abraham to assert the hope of Israel, that the famous Barchochebas collected a formidable army, with which he resisted during two years the power of the emperor Hadrian.[3]

Notwithstanding these repeated provocations, the resentment of the Roman princes expired after the victory, nor were their apprehensions continued beyond the period of war and danger. By the general indulgence of Polytheism, and by the mild temper of Antoninus Pius, the Jews were restored to their ancient

[1] In Cyrene they massacred 220,000 Greeks; in Cyprus, 240,000; in Egypt a very great multitude. Many of these unhappy victims were sawn asunder, according to a precedent to which David had given the sanction of his example. The victorious Jews devoured the flesh, licked up the blood, and twisted the entrails like a girdle round their bodies. See Dion Cassius, l. lxviii. [c. 32] p. 1145.

[2] Without repeating the well-known narratives of Josephus, we may learn from Dion (l. lxix. [c. 14] p. 1162), that in Hadrian's war 580,000 Jews were cut off by the sword, besides an infinite number which perished by famine, by disease, and by fire.

[3] For the sect of the Zealots, see Basnage, Histoire des Juifs, l. i. c. 17; for the characters of the Messiah, according to the Rabbis, l. v. c. 11, 12, 13; for the actions of Barchochebas, l. vii. c. 12. [Hist. of Jews, iii. 115, etc.—M.]

privileges, and once more obtained the permission of circumcising their children, with the easy restraint that they should
never confer on any foreign proselyte that distinguishing mark
of the Hebrew race.[1] The numerous remains of that people,
though they were still excluded from the precincts of Jerusalem,
were permitted to form and to maintain considerable establishments both in Italy and in the provinces, to acquire the freedom
of Rome, to enjoy municipal honours, and to obtain at the same
time an exemption from the burdensome and expensive offices
of society. The moderation or the contempt of the Romans
gave a legal sanction to the form of ecclesiastical police which
was instituted by the vanquished sect. The patriarch, who had
fixed his residence at Tiberias, was empowered to appoint his
subordinate ministers and apostles, to exercise a domestic jurisdiction, and to receive from his dispersed brethren an annual
contribution.[2] New synagogues were frequently erected in the
principal cities of the empire; and the sabbaths, the fasts, and
the festivals, which were either commanded by the Mosaic law
or enjoined by the traditions of the Rabbis, were celebrated in the
most solemn and public manner.[3] Such gentle treatment insensibly assuaged the stern temper of the Jews. Awakened
from their dream of prophecy and conquest, they assumed the
behaviour of peaceable and industrious subjects. Their irreconcilable hatred of mankind, instead of flaming out in acts of
blood and violence, evaporated in less dangerous gratifications.
They embraced every opportunity of overreaching the idolaters
in trade, and they pronounced secret and ambiguous imprecations against the haughty kingdom of Edom.[4]

[1] It is to Modestinus, a Roman lawyer (l. vi. regular.), that we are indebted for a distinct knowledge of the edict of Antoninus. See Casaubon
ad Hist. August. p. 27.

[2] See Basnage, Histoire des Juifs, l. iii. c. 2, 3. The office of Patriarch
was suppressed by Theodosius the younger.

[3] We need only mention the Purim, or deliverance of the Jews from the
rage of Haman, which, till the reign of Theodosius, was celebrated with
insolent triumph and riotous intemperance. Basnage, Hist. des Juifs,
l. vi. c. 17, l. viii. c. 6.

[4] According to the false Josephus, Tsepho, the grandson of Esau, conducted into Italy the army of Æneas, king of Carthage. Another colony
of Idumæans, flying from the sword of David, took refuge in the dominions
of Romulus. For these, or for other reasons of equal weight, the name of
Edom was applied by the Jews to the Roman empire.

[The false Josephus is a forger and fabulist of comparatively modern
times, though some of the legends he tells may be of ancient date. Milman
throws out the suggestion that some of the stories in the Talmud may be
history in a figurative disguise. The Jews may dare to say many things
of Rome, under the significant appellation of Edom, which they feared
to utter publicly.—O. S.]

Since the Jews, who rejected with abhorrence the deities adored by their sovereign and by their fellow-subjects, enjoyed, however, the free exercise of their unsocial religion, there must have existed some other cause which exposed the disciples of Christ to those severities from which the posterity of Abraham was exempt. The difference between them is simple and obvious, but, according to the sentiments of antiquity, it was of the highest importance. The Jews were a *nation*, the Christians were a *sect :* and if it was natural for every community to respect the sacred institutions of their neighbours, it was incumbent on them to persevere in those of their ancestors. The voice of oracles, the precepts of philosophers, and the authority of the laws, unanimously enforced this national obligation. By their lofty claim of superior sanctity the Jews might provoke the Polytheists to consider them as an odious and impure race. By disdaining the intercourse of other nations they might deserve their contempt. The laws of Moses might be for the most part frivolous or absurd; yet, since they had been received during many ages by a large society, his followers were justified by the example of mankind, and it was universally acknowledged that they had a right to practise what it would have been criminal in them to neglect. But this principle, which protected the Jewish synagogue, afforded not any favour or security to the primitive church. By embracing the faith of the Gospel the Christians incurred the supposed guilt of an unnatural and unpardonable offence. They dissolved the sacred ties of custom and education, violated the religious institutions of their country, and presumptuously despised whatever their fathers had believed as true or had reverenced as sacred. Nor was this apostasy (if we may use the expression) merely of a partial or local kind; since the pious deserter who withdrew himself from the temples of Egypt or Syria would equally disdain to seek an asylum in those of Athens or Carthage. Every Christian rejected with contempt the superstitions of his family, his city, and his province. The whole body of Christians unanimously refused to hold any communion with the gods of Rome, of the empire, and of mankind. It was in vain that the oppressed believer asserted the inalienable rights of conscience and private judgment. Though his situation might excite the pity, his arguments could never reach the understanding, either of the philosophic or of the believing part of the Pagan world. To their apprehensions it was no less a matter of surprise that any individuals should entertain scruples against complying with the established mode of worship than if they had conceived a sudden abhorrence to the manners, the dress, or the language of their native country.[1]

The surprise of the Pagans was soon succeeded by resentment, and the most pious of men were exposed to the unjust but dangerous imputation of impiety. Malice and prejudice concurred in representing the Christians as a society of atheists, who, by the most daring attack on the religious constitution of the empire, had merited the severest animadversion of the civil magistrate. They had separated themselves (they gloried in the confession) from every mode of superstition which was received in any part of the globe by the various temper of Polytheism: but it was not altogether so evident what deity, or what form of worship, they had substituted to the gods and temples of antiquity. The pure and sublime idea which they entertained of the Supreme Being escaped the gross conception of the Pagan multitude, who were at a loss to discover a spiritual and solitary God, that was neither represented under any corporeal figure or visible symbol, nor was adored with the accustomed pomp of libations and festivals, of altars and sacrifices.[2] The sages of Greece and Rome, who had elevated their minds to the contemplation of the existence and attributes of the First Cause, were induced by reason or by vanity to reserve for themselves and their chosen disciples the privilege of this philosophical devotion,[3] They were far from admitting the prejudices of mankind as the standard of truth, but they considered them as flowing from the original disposition of human nature; and they supposed that any popular mode of faith and worship which presumed to disclaim the assistance of the senses would, in proportion as it receded from superstition, find itself incapable of restraining the wonderings of the fancy and the visions of fanaticism. The careless glance which men of wit and learning condescended to cast on the Christian revelation served only to

---

[1] From the arguments of Celsus, as they are represented and refuted by Origen (l. v. [c. 59] p. 247-259), we may clearly discover the distinction that was made between the Jewish *people* and the Christian *sect*. See in the Dialogue of Minucius Felix (p. 5, 6) a fair and not inelegant description of the popular sentiments with regard to the desertion of the established worship.

[2] Cur nullas aras habent? templa nulla? nulla nota simulacra? . . . Unde autem, vel quis ille, aut ubi, Deus unicus, solitarius, destitutus? Minucius Felix, p. 10. The Pagan interlocutor goes on to make a distinction in favour of the Jews, who had once a temple, altars, victims, etc.

[3] It is difficult (says Plato) to attain, and dangerous to publish, the knowledge of the true God. See the Théologie des Philosophes, in the Abbé d'Olivet's French translation of Tully de Naturâ Deorum, tom. i. p. 275.

confirm their hasty opinion, and to persuade them that the principle, which they might have revered, of the Divine Unity, was defaced by the wild enthusiasm, and annihilated by the airy speculations, of the new sectaries. The author of a celebrated dialogue, which has been attributed to Lucian, whilst he affects to treat the mysterious subject of the Trinity in a style of ridicule and contempt, betrays his own ignorance of the weakness of human reason, and of the inscrutable nature of the Divine perfections.[1]

It might appear less surprising that the founder of Christianity should not only be revered by his disciples as a sage and a prophet, but that he should be adored as a God. The Polytheists were disposed to adopt every article of faith which seemed to offer any resemblance, however distant or imperfect, with the popular mythology; and the legends of Bacchus, of Hercules, and of Æsculapius had, in some measure, prepared their imagination for the appearance of the Son of God under a human form.[2] But they were astonished that the Christians should abandon the temples of those ancient heroes who, in the infancy of the world, had invented arts, instituted laws, and vanquished the tyrants or monsters who infested the earth; in order to choose for the exclusive object of their religious worship an obscure teacher, who, in a recent age, and among a barbarous people, had fallen a sacrifice either to the malice of his own countrymen, or to the jealousy of the Roman government. The Pagan multitude, reserving their gratitude for temporal benefits alone, rejected the inestimable present of life and immortality which was offered to mankind by Jesus of Nazareth. His mild constancy in the midst of cruel and voluntary sufferings, his universal benevolence, and the sublime simplicity of his actions and character, were insufficient, in the opinion of those carnal

---

[1] The author of the Philopatris perpetually treats the Christians as a company of dreaming enthusiasts, δαιμόνιοι αἰθέριοι, αἰθεροβατοῦντες, ἀεροβατοῦντες, etc.; and in one place manifestly alludes to the vision in which St. Paul was transported to the third heaven. In another place, Triephon, who personates a Christian, after deriding the gods of Paganism, proposes a mysterious oath:—

Ὑψιμέδοντα θεὸν, μέγαν, ἄμβροτον, οὐρανίωνα,
Υἱὸν πατρὸς, πνεῦμα ἐκ πατρὸς ἐκπορευόμενον,
Ἕν ἐκ τριῶν, καὶ ἐξ ἑνὸς τρία.

Ἀριθμέειν με διδάσκεις (is the profane answer of Critias), καὶ ὅρκος ἡ ἀριθμητική· οὐκ οἶδα γάρ τι λέγεις· ἓν τρία, τρία ἕν !

[2] According to Justin Martyr (Apolog. Major, c. 70-85), the dæmon, who had gained some imperfect knowledge of the prophecies, purposely contrived this resemblance, which might deter, though by different means, both the people and the philosophers from embracing the faith of Christ.

men, to compensate for the want of fame, of empire, and of success; and whilst they refused to acknowledge his stupendous triumph over the powers of darkness and of the grave, they misrepresented, or they insulted, the equivocal birth, wandering life, and ignominious death, of the divine Author of Christianity.[1]

The personal guilt which every Christian had contracted, in thus preferring his private sentiment to the national religion, was aggravated in a very high degree by the number and union of the criminals. It is well known, and has been already observed, that Roman policy viewed with the utmost jealousy and distrust any association among its subjects; and that the privileges of private corporations, though formed for the most harmless or beneficial purposes, were bestowed with a very sparing hand.[2] The religious assemblies of the Christians, who had separated themselves from the public worship, appeared of a much less innocent nature: they were illegal in their principle, and in their consequences might become dangerous; nor were the emperors conscious that they violated the laws of justice, when, for the peace of society, they prohibited those secret and sometimes nocturnal meetings.[3] The pious disobedience of the Christians made their conduct, or perhaps their designs, appear in a much more serious and criminal light; and the Roman princes, who might perhaps have suffered themselves to be disarmed by a ready submission, deeming their honour concerned in the execution of their commands, sometimes attempted, by rigorous punishments, to subdue this independent spirit, which boldly acknowledged an authority superior to that of the magistrate. The extent and duration of this spiritual conspiracy seemed to render it every day more deserving of his animadversion. We have already seen that the active and successful zeal of the Christians had insensibly diffused them through every province and almost every city of the empire. The new converts seemed to renounce their family and country, that they might connect themselves in an indissoluble band of union with a peculiar society, which everywhere assumed a different character

[1] In the first and second books of Origen, Celsus treats the birth and character of our Saviour with the most impious contempt. The orator Libanius praises Porphyry and Julian for confuting the folly of a sect which style a dead man of Palestine, God, and the Son of God. Socrates, Hist. Ecclesiast. iii. 23.

[2] The emperor Trajan refused to incorporate a company of 150 firemen for the use of the city of Nicomedia. He disliked all associations. See Plin. Epist. x. 42, 43.

[3] The proconsul Pliny had published a general edict against unlawful meetings. The prudence of the Christians suspended their Agapæ; but it was impossible for them to omit the exercise of public worship.

from the rest of mankind. Their gloomy and austere aspect, their abhorrence of the common business and pleasures of life, and their frequent predictions of impending calamities,[1] inspired the Pagans with the apprehension of some danger which would arise from the new sect, the more alarming as it was the more obscure. "Whatever," says Pliny, "may be the principle of their conduct, their inflexible obstinacy appeared deserving of punishment."[2]

The precautions with which the disciples of Christ performed the offices of religion were at first dictated by fear and necessity; but they were continued from choice. By imitating the awful secrecy which reigned in the Eleusinian mysteries, the Christians had flattered themselves that they should render their sacred institutions more respectable in the eyes of the Pagan world.[3] But the event, as it often happens to the operations of subtile policy, deceived their wishes and their expectations. It was concluded that they only concealed what they would have blushed to disclose. Their mistaken prudence afforded an opportunity for malice to invent, and for suspicious credulity to believe, the horrid tales which described the Christians as the most wicked of human kind, who practised in their dark recesses every abomination that a depraved fancy could suggest, and who solicited the favour of their unknown God by the sacrifice of every moral virtue. There were many who pretended to confess or to relate the ceremonies of this abhorred society. It was asserted, "that a new-born infant, entirely covered over with flour, was presented, like some mystic symbol of initiation, to the knife of the proselyte, who unknowingly inflicted many a secret and mortal wound on the innocent victim of his error; that as soon as the cruel deed was perpetrated, the sectaries drank up the blood, greedily tore asunder the quivering members, and pledged themselves to eternal secrecy, by a mutual consciousness of guilt. It was as confidently affirmed that this inhuman sacrifice was succeeded by a suitable entertainment, in which intemperance served as a provocative to brutal lust; till, at the appointed moment, the lights were suddenly extin-

---

[1] As the prophecies of the Antichrist, approaching conflagration, etc., provoked those Pagans whom they did not convert, they were mentioned with caution and reserve; and the Montanists were censured for disclosing too freely the dangerous secret. See Mosheim, p. 413.

[2] Neque enim dubitabam, qualecunque esset quod faterentur (such are the words of Pliny), pervicaciam certe et inflexibilem obstinationem debere puniri. [Epist. x. 97.]

[3] See Mosheim's Ecclesiastical History, vol. i. p. 101, and Spanheim, Remarques sur les Césars de Julien, p. 468, etc.

guished, shame was banished, nature was forgotten; and, as accident might direct, the darkness of the night was polluted by the incestuous commerce of sisters and brothers, of sons and of mothers." [1]

But the perusal of the ancient apologies was sufficient to remove even the slightest suspicion from the mind of a candid adversary. The Christians, with the intrepid security of innocence, appeal from the voice of rumour to the equity of the magistrates. They acknowledge that, if any proof can be produced of the crimes which calumny has imputed to them, they are worthy of the most severe punishment. They provoke the punishment, and they challenge the proof. At the same time they urge, with equal truth and propriety, that the charge is not less devoid of probability than it is destitute of evidence; they ask whether any one can seriously believe that the pure and holy precepts of the Gospel, which so frequently restrain the use of the most lawful enjoyments, should inculcate the practice of the most abominable crimes; that a large society should resolve to dishonour itself in the eyes of its own members; and that a great number of persons, of either sex, and every age and character, insensible to the fear of death or infamy, should consent to violate those principles which nature and education had imprinted most deeply in their minds. [2] Nothing, it should seem, could weaken the force or destroy the effect of so unanswerable a justification, unless it were the injudicious conduct of the apologists themselves, who betrayed the common cause of religion, to gratify their devout hatred to the domestic enemies of the church. It was sometimes faintly insinuated, and sometimes boldly asserted, that the same bloody sacrifices, and the same incestuous festivals, which were so falsely ascribed to the orthodox believers, were in reality celebrated by the Marcionites, by the Carpocratians, and by several other sects of the Gnostics, who, notwithstanding they might deviate into the paths of heresy, were still actuated by the sentiments of men, and still governed by the precepts of Christianity. [3] Accusations of a

[1] See Justin Martyr, Apolog. i. 35 [c. 27? ed. Ben.], ii. 14 [c. 12, p. 97, ed. Ben.]. Athenagoras, in Legation. c. 27. Tertullian, Apolog. c. 7, 8, 9. Minucius Felix, p. 9, 10, 30, 31. The last of these writers relates the accusation in the most elegant and circumstantial manner. The answer of Tertullian is the boldest and most vigorous.

[2] In the persecution of Lyons, some Gentile slaves were compelled, by the fear of tortures, to accuse their Christian master. The church of Lyons, writing to their brethren of Asia, treat the horrid charge with proper indignation and contempt. Euseb. Hist. Eccles. v. i.

[3] See Justin Martyr, Apolog. i. 35 [c. 27? ed. Ben.]. Irenæus adv. Hæres. i. 24. Clemens Alexandrin. Stromat. l. iii. p. 438 [c. 2, p. 514, ed.

similar kind were retorted upon the church by the schismatics who had departed from its communion,[1] and it was confessed on all sides that the most scandalous licentiousness of manners prevailed among great numbers of those who affected the name of Christians. A Pagan magistrate, who possessed neither leisure nor abilities to discern the almost imperceptible line which divides the orthodox faith from heretical pravity, might easily have imagined that their mutual animosity had extorted the discovery of their common guilt. It was fortunate for the repose, or at least for the reputation, of the first Christians, that the magistrates sometimes proceeded with more temper and moderation than is usually consistent with religious zeal, and that they reported, as the impartial result of their judicial inquiry, that the sectaries who had deserted the established worship appeared to them sincere in their professions and blameless in their manners, however they might incur, by their absurd and excessive superstition, the censure of the laws.[2]

History, which undertakes to record the transactions of the past, for the instruction of future ages, would ill deserve that honourable office if she condescended to plead the cause of tyrants, or to justify the maxims of persecution. It must, however, be acknowledged that the conduct of the emperors who appeared the least favourable to the primitive church is by no means so criminal as that of modern sovereigns who have employed the arm of violence and terror against the religious opinions of any part of their subjects. From their reflections, or even from their own feelings, a Charles V. or a Louis XIV. might have acquired a just knowledge of the rights of conscience, of the obligation of faith, and of the innocence of error. But the princes and magistrates of ancient Rome were strangers to those principles which inspired and authorised the inflexible obstinacy of the Christians in the cause of truth, nor could they

---

Oxon. 1715]. Euseb. iv. 8. It would be tedious and disgusting to relate all that the succeeding writers have imagined, all that Epiphanius has received, and all that Tillemont has copied. M. de Beausobre (Hist. du Manichéisme, l. ix. c. 8, 9) has exposed, with great spirit, the disingenuous arts of Augustin and Pope Leo I.

[1] When Tertullian became a Montanist, he aspersed the morals of the church which he had so resolutely defended. " Sed majoris est Agape, quia per hanc adolescentes tui cum sororibus dormiunt. Appendices scilicet gulæ lascivia et luxuria." De Jejuniis, c. 17. The 35th canon of the council of Illiberis provides against the scandals which too often polluted the vigils of the church, and disgraced the Christian name in the eyes of unbelievers.

[2] Tertullian (Apolog. c. 2) expatiates on the fair and honourable testimony of Pliny, with much reason, and some declamation.

themselves discover in their own breasts any motive which would have prompted them to refuse a legal, and as it were a natural, submission to the sacred institutions of their country.   The same reason which contributes to alleviate the guilt, must have tended to abate the rigour, of their persecutions. As they were actuated, not by the furious zeal of bigots, but by the temperate policy of legislators, contempt must often have relaxed, and humanity must frequently have suspended, the execution of those laws which they enacted against the humble and obscure followers of Christ.   From the general view of their character and motives we might naturally conclude: I. That a considerable time elapsed before they considered the new sectaries as an object deserving of the attention of government.   II. That in the conviction of any of their subjects who were accused of so very singular a crime, they proceeded with caution and reluctance.   III. That they were moderate in the use of punishments; and IV. That the afflicted church enjoyed many intervals of peace and tranquillity.   Notwithstanding the careless indifference which the most copious and the most minute of the Pagan writers have shown to the affairs of the Christians,[1] it may still be in our power to confirm each of these probable suppositions by the evidence of authentic facts.

I. By the wise dispensation of Providence a mysterious veil was cast over the infancy of the church, which, till the faith of the Christians was matured, and their numbers were multiplied, served to protect them not only from the malice but even from the knowledge of the Pagan world.   The slow and gradual abolition of the Mosaic ceremonies afforded a safe and innocent disguise to the more early proselytes of the Gospel.   As they were for the greater part of the race of Abraham, they were distinguished by the peculiar mark of circumcision, offered up their devotions in the Temple of Jerusalem till its final destruction, and received both the Law and the Prophets as the genuine inspirations of the Deity.   The Gentile converts who by a spiritual adoption had been associated to the hope of Israel, were likewise confounded under the garb and appearance of Jews;[2] and as the

[1] In the various compilation of the Augustan History (a part of which was composed under the reign of Constantine) there are not six lines which relate to the Christians; nor has the diligence of Xiphilin discovered their name in the large history of Dion Cassius.

[The greater part of the Augustan History is dedicated to Diocletian. This may account for the silence of its authors concerning Christianity.— O. S.]

[2] An obscure passage of Suetonius (in Claud. c. 25) may seem to offer a proof how strangely the Jews and Christians of Rome were confounded with each other.

Polytheists paid less regard to articles of faith than to the external worship, the new sect, which carefully concealed, or faintly announced, its future greatness and ambition, was permitted to shelter itself under the general toleration which was granted to an ancient and celebrated people in the Roman empire. It was not long, perhaps, before the Jews themselves, animated with a fiercer zeal and a more jealous faith, perceived the gradual separation of their Nazarene brethren from the doctrine of the synagogue: and they would gladly have extinguished the dangerous heresy in the blood of its adherents. But the decrees of Heaven had already disarmed their malice; and though they might sometimes exert the licentious privilege of sedition, they no longer possessed the administration of criminal justice; nor did they find it easy to infuse into the calm breast of a Roman magistrate the rancour of their own zeal and prejudice. The provincial governors declared themselves ready to listen to any accusation that might affect the public safety; but as soon as they were informed that it was a question not of facts but of words, a dispute relating only to the interpretation of the Jewish laws and prophecies, they deemed it unworthy of the majesty of Rome seriously to discuss the obscure differences which might arise among a barbarous and superstitious people. The innocence of the first Christians was protected by ignorance and contempt; and the tribunal of the Pagan magistrate often proved their most assured refuge against the fury of the synagogue.[1] If, indeed, we were disposed to adopt the traditions of a too credulous antiquity, we might relate the distant peregrinations, the wonderful achievements, and the various deaths of the twelve apostles: but a more accurate inquiry will induce us to doubt whether any of those persons who had been witnesses to the miracles of Christ were permitted, beyond the limits of Palestine, to seal with their blood the truth of their testimony.[2] From the ordinary term of human life, it may very naturally be presumed that most of them were deceased before the discontent of the Jews broke out into that furious war which was terminated only by the ruin of Jerusalem. During a long period, from the death of Christ

[1] See, in the eighteenth and twenty-fifth chapters of the Acts of the Apostles, the behaviour of Gallio, proconsul of Achaia, and of Festus, procurator of Judæa.

[2] In the time of Tertullian and Clemens of Alexandria the glory of martyrdom was confined to St. Peter, St. Paul, and St. James. It was gradually bestowed on the rest of the apostles by the more recent Greeks, who prudently selected for the theatre of their preaching and sufferings some remote country beyond the limits of the Roman empire. See Mosheim, p. 81; and Tillemont, Mémoires Ecclésiastiques, tom. i. part. iii.

to that memorable rebellion, we cannot discover any traces of Roman intolerance, unless they are to be found in the sudden, the transient, but the cruel persecution, which was exercised by Nero against the Christians of the capital, thirty-five years after the former, and only two years before the latter, of those great events. The character of the philosophic historian, to whom we are principally indebted for the knowledge of this singular transaction, would alone be sufficient to recommend it to our most attentive consideration.

In the tenth year of the reign of Nero the capital of the empire was afflicted by a fire which raged beyond the memory or example of former ages.[1] The monuments of Grecian art and of Roman virtue, the trophies of the Punic and Gallic wars, the most holy temples, and the most splendid palaces were involved in one common destruction. Of the fourteen regions or quarters into which Rome was divided, four only subsisted entire, three were levelled with the ground, and the remaining seven, which had experienced the fury of the flames, displayed a melancholy prospect of ruin and desolation. The vigilance of government appears not to have neglected any of the precautions which might alleviate the sense of so dreadful a calamity. The Imperial gardens were thrown open to the distressed multitude, temporary buildings were erected for their accommodation, and a plentiful supply of corn and provisions was distributed at a very moderate price.[2] The most generous policy seemed to have dictated the edicts which regulated the disposition of the streets and the construction of private houses; and, as it usually happens in an age of prosperity, the conflagration of Rome, in the course of a few years, produced a new city, more regular and more beautiful than the former. But all the prudence and humanity affected by Nero on this occasion were insufficient to preserve him from the popular suspicion. Every crime might be imputed to the assassin of his wife and mother; nor could the prince who prostituted his person and dignity on the theatre be deemed incapable of the most extravagant folly. The voice of rumour accused the emperor as the incendiary of his own capital; and, as the most incredible stories are the best adapted to the genius of an enraged people, it was gravely reported, and firmly believed, that Nero, enjoying the calamity which he had occasioned,

[1] Tacit. Annal. xv. 38-44. Sueton. in Neron. c. 38. Dion Cassius, l. lxii. [c. 16] p. 1014. Orosius, vii. 7.

[2] The price of wheat (probably of the *modius*) was reduced as low as *terni Nummi*; which would be equivalent to about fifteen shillings the English quarter.

amused himself with singing to his lyre the destruction of ancient Troy.[1] To divert a suspicion which the power of despotism was unable to suppress, the emperor resolved to substitute in his own place some fictitious criminals. " With this view (continues Tacitus) he inflicted the most exquisite tortures on those men who, under the vulgar appellation of Christians, were already branded with deserved infamy. They derived their name and origin from Christ, who, in the reign of Tiberius, had suffered death by the sentence of the procurator Pontius Pilate.[2] For a while this dire superstition was checked, but it again burst forth; and not only spread itself over Judæa, the first seat of this mis-chievous sect, but was even introduced into Rome, the common asylum which receives and protects whatever is impure, what-ever is atrocious. The confessions of those who were seized discovered a great multitude of their accomplices, and they were all convicted, not so much for the crime of setting fire to the city as for their hatred of human kind.[3] They died in torments, and their torments were embittered by insult and derision. Some were nailed on crosses; others sewn up in the skins of wild beasts, and exposed to the fury of dogs; others again, smeared over with combustible materials, were used as torches to illumi-nate the darkness of the night. The gardens of Nero were destined for the melancholy spectacle, which was accompanied with a horse-race, and honoured with the presence of the emperor,

[1] We may observe that the rumour is mentioned by Tacitus with a very becoming distrust and hesitation, whilst it is greedily transcribed by Suetonius, and solemnly confirmed by Dion.

[2] This testimony is alone sufficient to expose the anachronism of the Jews, who place the birth of Christ near a century sooner. (Basnage, Histoire des Juifs, l. v. c. 14, 15.) We may learn from Josephus (Anti-quitat. xviii. 3 [c. 2, § 2, ed. Oxon. 1720]) that the procuratorship of Pilate corresponded with the last ten years of Tiberius, A.D. 27-37. As to the particular time of the death of Christ, a very early tradition fixed it to the 25th of March, A.D. 29, under the consulship of the two Gemini (Tertullian adv. Judæos, c. 8). This date, which is adopted by Pagi, Cardinal Norris, and Le Clerc, seems at least as probable as the vulgar era, which is placed (I know not from what conjectures) four years later.

[3] *Odio humani generis convicti.* These words may either signify the hatred of mankind towards the Christians, or the hatred of the Christians towards mankind. I have preferred the latter sense, as the most agreeable to the style of Tacitus, and to the popular error, of which a precept of the Gospel (see Luke xiv. 26) had been, perhaps, the innocent occasion. My interpretation is justified by the authority of Lipsius; of the Italian, the French, and the English translators of Tacitus; of Mosheim (p. 102), of Le Clerc (Historia Ecclesiast. p. 427), of Dr. Lardner (Testimonies, vol. i. p. 345), and of the Bishop of Gloucester (Divine Legation, vol. iii. p. 38). But as the word *convicti* does not unite very happily with the rest of the sentence, James Gronovius has preferred the reading of *conjuncti*, which is authorised by the valuable MS. of Florence.

who mingled with the populace in the dress and attitude of a charioteer. The guilt of the Christians deserved indeed the most exemplary punishment, but the public abhorrence was changed into commiseration, from the opinion that those unhappy wretches were sacrificed, not so much to the public welfare as to the cruelty of a jealous tyrant." [1] Those who survey with a curious eye the revolutions of mankind may observe that the gardens and circus of Nero on the Vatican, which were polluted with the blood of the first Christians, have been rendered still more famous by the triumph and by the abuse of the persecuted religion. On the same spot [2] a temple, which far surpasses the ancient glories of the Capitol, has been since erected by the Christian Pontiffs, who, deriving their claim of universal dominion from an humble fisherman of Galilee, have succeeded to the throne of the Cæsars, given laws to the barbarian conquerors of Rome, and extended their spiritual jurisdiction from the coast of the Baltic to the shores of the Pacific Ocean.

But it would be improper to dismiss this account of Nero's persecution till we have made some observations that may serve to remove the difficulties with which it is perplexed, and to throw some light on the subsequent history of the church.

1. The most sceptical criticism is obliged to respect the truth of this extraordinary fact, and the integrity of this celebrated passage of Tacitus. The former is confirmed by the diligent and accurate Suetonius, who mentions the punishment which Nero inflicted on the Christians, a sect of men who had embraced a new and criminal superstition. [3] The latter may be proved by the consent of the most ancient manuscripts; by the inimitable character of the style of Tacitus; by his reputation, which guarded his text from the interpolations of pious fraud; and by the purport of his narration, which accused the first Christians of the most atrocious crimes, without insinuating that they possessed any miraculous or even magical powers above the rest of mankind. [4] 2. Notwithstanding it is probable that Tacitus

[1] Tacit. Annal. xv. 44.
[2] Nardini Roma Antica, p. 487. Donatus de Româ Antiquâ, l. iii. p. 449.
[3] Sueton. in Nerone, c. 16. The epithet of *malefica*, which some sagacious commentators have translated *magical*, is considered by the more rational Mosheim as only synonymous to the *exitiabilis* of Tacitus.
[4] The passage concerning Jesus Christ which was inserted into the text of Josephus between the time of Origen and that of Eusebius, may furnish an example of no vulgar forgery. The accomplishment of the prophecies, the virtues, miracles, and resurrection of Jesus, are distinctly related. Josephus acknowledges that he was the Messiah, and hesitates whether he should call him a man. If any doubt can still remain concerning this celebrated passage, the reader may examine the pointed objections of Le

was born some years before the fire of Rome,[1] he could derive only from reading and conversation the knowledge of an event which happened during his infancy. Before he gave himself to the public he calmly waited till his genius had attained its full maturity, and he was more than forty years of age when a grateful regard for the memory of the virtuous Agricola extorted from him the most early of those historical compositions which will delight and instruct the most distant posterity. After making a trial of his strength in the life of Agricola, and the description of Germany, he conceived, and at length executed, a more arduous work, the history of Rome, in thirty books, from the fall of Nero to the accession of Nerva. The administration of Nerva introduced an age of justice and prosperity, which Tacitus had destined for the occupation of his old age;[2] but when he took a nearer view of his subject, judging, perhaps, that it was a more honourable or a less invidious office to record the vices of past tyrants than to celebrate the virtues of a reigning monarch, he chose rather to relate, under the form of annals, the actions of the four immediate successors of Augustus. To collect, to dispose, and to adorn a series of fourscore years in an immortal work, every sentence of which is pregnant with the deepest observations and the most lively images, was an undertaking sufficient to exercise the genius of Tacitus himself during the greatest part of his life. In the last years of the reign of Trajan, whilst the victorious monarch extended the power of Rome beyond its ancient limits, the historian was describing, in the second and fourth books of his Annals, the tyranny of Tiberius;[3] and the emperor Hadrian must have succeeded to the throne before Tacitus, in the regular prosecution of his work, could relate the fire of the capital and the cruelty of Nero

Fevre (Havercamp. Joseph. tom. ii. p. 267-273), the laboured answers of Daubuz (p. 187-232), and the masterly reply (Bibliothèque Ancienne et Moderne, tom. vii. p. 237-288) of an anonymous critic, whom I believe to have been the learned Abbé de Longuerue.

[The Palatine Codex of Josephus does not contain the eighteenth book of the Antiquities. It is a mistake to regard the passage as wholly spurious, and I am inclined to agree with Heinichen, Ewald, Bury, and others in regarding the passage as only tainted by interpolations, but not wholly spurious. Bury calls attention to another passage in which reference is made to the death of " St. James, brother of Jesus called the Christ."—O. S.]

[1] See the lives of Tacitus by Lipsius and the Abbé de la Bleterie, Dictionnaire de Bayle à l'article TACITE, and Fabricius, Biblioth. Latin. tom. ii. p. 386, edit. Ernest.

[2] Principatum Divi Nervæ, et imperium Trajani, uberiorem securioremque materiam, senectuti seposui. Tacit. Hist. i. l.

[3] See Tacit. Annal. ii. 61, iv. 4.

towards the unfortunate Christians. At the distance of sixty
years it was the duty of the annalist to adopt the narratives of
contemporaries; but it was natural for the philosopher to
indulge himself in the description of the origin, the progress, and
the character of the new sect, not so much according to the knowledge or prejudices of the age of Nero, as according to those of
the time of Hadrian. 3. Tacitus very frequently trusts to the
curiosity or reflection of his readers to supply those intermediate
circumstances and ideas which, in his extreme conciseness, he
has thought proper to suppress. We may therefore presume to
imagine some probable cause which could direct the cruelty of
Nero against the Christians of Rome, whose obscurity, as well as
innocence, should have shielded them from his indignation, and
even from his notice. The Jews, who were numerous in the
capital and oppressed in their own country, were a much fitter
object for the suspicions of the emperor and of the people: nor
did it seem unlikely that a vanquished nation, who already
discovered their abhorrence of the Roman yoke, might have
recourse to the most atrocious means of gratifying their implacable revenge. But the Jews possessed very powerful
advocates in the palace, and even in the heart of the tyrant; his
wife and mistress, the beautiful Poppæa, and a favourite player
of the race of Abraham, who had already employed their intercession on behalf of the obnoxious people.[1] In their room it
was necessary to offer some other victims, and it might easily be
suggested that, although the genuine followers of Moses were
innocent of the fire of Rome, there had arisen among them a new
and pernicious sect of GALILÆANS, which was capable of the
most horrid crimes. Under the appellation of GALILÆANS two
distinctions of men were confounded, the most opposite to each
other in their manners and principles; the disciples who had
embraced the faith of Jesus of Nazareth,[2] and the zealots who
had followed the standard of Judas the Gaulonite.[3] The former
were the friends, the latter were the enemies, of human kind;

---

[1] The player's name was Aliturus. Through the same channel, Josephus
(de Vitâ suâ, c. 3), about two years before, had obtained the pardon and
release of some Jewish priests who were prisoners at Rome.

[2] The learned Dr. Lardner (Jewish and Heathen Testimonies, vol. ii. p.
102, 103) has proved that the name of Galilæans was a very ancient, and
perhaps the primitive, appellation of the Christians.

[3] Joseph. Antiquitat. xviii. 1, 2. Tillemont, Ruine des Juifs, p. 742.
The sons of Judas were crucified in the time of Claudius. His grandson
Eleazar, after Jerusalem was taken, defended a strong fortress with 960
of his most desperate followers. When the battering-ram had made a
breach, they turned their swords against their wives, their children, and at
length against their own breasts. They died to the last man.

and the only resemblance between them consisted in the same inflexible constancy which, in the defence of their cause, rendered them insensible of death and tortures. The followers of Judas, who impelled their countrymen into rebellion, were soon buried under the ruins of Jerusalem; whilst those of Jesus, known by the more celebrated name of Christians, diffused themselves over the Roman empire. How natural was it for Tacitus, in the time of Hadrian, to appropriate to the Christians the guilt and the sufferings [1] which he might, with far greater truth and justice, have attributed to a sect whose odious memory was almost extinguished! 4. Whatever opinion may be entertained of this conjecture (for it is no more than a conjecture), it is evident that the effect, as well as the cause, of Nero's persecution, were confined to the walls of Rome; [2] that the religious tenets of the Galilæans, or Christians, were never made a subject of punishment, or even of inquiry; and that, as the idea of their sufferings was, for a long time, connected with the idea of cruelty and injustice, the moderation of succeeding princes inclined them to spare a sect oppressed by a tyrant whose rage had been usually directed against virtue and innocence.

It is somewhat remarkable that the flames of war consumed almost at the same time the Temple of Jerusalem and the Capitol of Rome; [3] and it appears no less singular that the tribute which devotion had destined to the former should have been converted by the power of an assaulting victor to restore and adorn the splendour of the latter. [4] The emperors levied a general capitation tax on the Jewish people; and although the

[1] [This supposition of Gibbon's concerning the appropriation to the Christians by Tacitus in the reign of Hadrian of the guilt and sufferings in question, is quite erroneous. It is not even possible, far less probable. Tacitus, as Guizot says, could not be deceived in attributing to the Christians of Rome the guilt and sufferings which with greater truth he might have attributed to the followers of Judas the Gaulonite. It may well be doubted whether the followers of Judas were ever known, as a sect, under the name of Galileans.—O. S.]

[2] See Dodwell. Paucitat. Mart. l. xiii. The Spanish Inscription in Gruter, p. 238, No. 9, is a manifest and acknowledged forgery, contrived by that noted impostor Cyriacus of Ancona to flatter the pride and prejudices of the Spaniards. See Ferreras, Histoire d'Espagne, tom. i. p. 192.

[3] The Capitol was burnt during the civil war between Vitellius and Vespasian, the 19th of December, A.D. 69. On the 10th of August, A.D. 70, the Temple of Jerusalem was destroyed by the hands of the Jews themselves, rather than by those of the Romans.

[4] The new Capitol was dedicated by Domitian. Sueton. in Domitian. c. 5. Plutarch in Poplicola [c. 15], tom. i. p. 230, edit. Bryant. The gilding alone cost 12,000 talents (above two millions and a half). It was the opinion of Martial (l. ix. Epigram 4), that, if the emperor had called in his debts, Jupiter himself, even though he had made a general auction of Olympus would have been unable to pay two shillings in the pound.

sum assessed on the head of each individual was inconsiderable, the use for which it was designed, and the severity with which it was exacted, were considered as an intolerable grievance.[1] Since the officers of the revenue extended their unjust claim to many persons who were strangers to the blood or religion of the Jews, it was impossible that the Christians, who had so often sheltered themselves under the shade of the synagogue, should now escape this rapacious persecution. Anxious as they were to avoid the slightest infection of idolatry, their conscience forbade them to contribute to the honour of that dæmon who had assumed the character of the Capitoline Jupiter. As a very numerous though declining party among the Christians still adhered to the law of Moses, their efforts to dissemble their Jewish origin were detected by the decisive test of circumcision;[2] nor were the Roman magistrates at leisure to inquire into the difference of their religious tenets. Among the Christians who were brought before the tribunal of the emperor, or, as it seems more probable, before that of the procurator of Judæa, two persons are said to have appeared, distinguished by their extraction, which was more truly noble than that of the greatest monarchs. These were the grandsons of St. Jude the apostle, who himself was the brother of Jesus Christ.[3] Their natural pretensions to the throne of David might perhaps attract the respect of the people, and excite the jealousy of the governor; but the meanness of their garb and the simplicity of their answers soon convinced him that they were neither desirous nor capable of disturbing the peace of the Roman empire. They frankly confessed their royal origin, and their near relation to the Messiah, but they disclaimed any temporal views, and professed that his kingdom, which they devoutly expected, was purely of a spiritual and angelic nature. When they were examined concerning

[1] With regard to the tribute, see Dion Cassius, l. lxvi. [c. 7] p. 1082, with Reimarus's notes; Spanheim, de Usu Numismatum, tom. ii. p. 571; and Basnage, Histoire des Juifs, l. vii. c. 2.

[2] Suetonius (in Domitian. c. 12) had seen an old man of ninety publicly examined before the procurator's tribunal. This is what Martial calls Mentula tributis damnata.

[3] This appellation was at first understood in the most obvious sense, and it was supposed that the brothers of Jesus were the lawful issue of Joseph and Mary. A devout respect for the virginity of the mother of God suggested to the Gnostics, and afterwards to the orthodox Greeks, the expedient of bestowing a second wife on Joseph. The Latins (from the time of Jerome) improved on that hint, asserted the perpetual celibacy of Joseph, and justified by many similar examples that Jude, as well as Simon and James, who are styled the brothers of Jesus Christ, were only his first-cousins. See Tillemont, Mém. Ecclésiast. tom. i. part iii.; and Beausobre, Hist. Critique du Manichéisme, l. ii. c. 2.

their fortune and occupation, they showed their hands hardened with daily labour, and declared that they derived their whole subsistence from the cultivation of a farm near the village of Cocaba, of the extent of about twenty-four English acres,[1] and of the value of nine thousand drachms, or three hundred pounds sterling. The grandsons of St. Jude were dismissed with compassion and contempt.[2]

But although the obscurity of the house of David might protect them from the suspicions of a tyrant, the present greatness of his own family alarmed the pusillanimous temper of Domitian, which could only be appeased by the blood of those Romans whom he either feared, or hated, or esteemed. Of the two sons of his uncle Flavius Sabinus,[3] the elder was soon convicted of treasonable intentions, and the younger, who bore the name of Flavius Clemens, was indebted for his safety to his want of courage and ability.[4] The emperor for a long time distinguished so harmless a kinsman by his favour and protection, bestowed on him his own niece Domitilla, adopted the children of that marriage to the hope of the succession, and invested their father with the honours of the consulship. But he had scarcely finished the term of his annual magistracy, when on a slight pretence he was condemned and executed; Domitilla was banished to a desolate island on the coast of Campania;[5] and sentences either of death or of confiscation were pronounced against a great number of persons who were involved in the same accusation. The guilt imputed to their charge was that of *Atheism* and *Jewish manners ;*[6] a singular association of ideas, which cannot with any propriety be applied except to the Chris-

---

[1] Thirty-nine πλέθρα, squares of an hundred feet each, which, if strictly computed, would scarcely amount to nine acres. But the probability of circumstances, the practice of other Greek writers, and the authority M. de Valois, incline me to believe that the πλέθρον is used to express the Roman jugerum.

[2] Eusebius, iii. 20. The story is taken from Hegesippus.

[3] See the death and character of Sabinus in Tacitus (Hist. iii. 74, 75). Sabinus was the elder brother, and, till the accession of Vespasian, had been considered as the principal support of the Flavian family.

[4] Flavium Clementem patruelem suum *contemptissimæ inertiæ* . . . ex tenuissimâ suspicione interemit. Sueton. in Domitan. c. 15.

[5] The isle of Pandataria, according to Dion. Bruttius Præsens (apud Euseb. iii. 18) banishes her to that of Pontia, which was not far distant from the other. That difference, and a mistake, either of Eusebius or of his transcribers, have given occasion to suppose two Domitillas, the wife and the niece of Clemens. See Tillemont, Mémoires Ecclésiastiques, tom. ii. p. 224.

[6] Dion, l. lxvii. [c. 14] p. 1112. If the Bruttius Præsens, from whom it is probable that he collected this account, was the correspondent of Pliny (Epistol. vii. 3), we may consider him as a contemporary writer.

tians, as they were obscurely and imperfectly viewed by the
magistrates and by the writers of that period. On the strength
of so probable an interpretation, and too eagerly admitting the
suspicions of a tyrant as an evidence of their honourable crime,
the church has placed both Clemens and Domitilla among its
first martyrs, and has branded the cruelty of Domitian with the
name of the second persecution. But this persecution (if it
deserves that epithet) was of no long duration. A few months
after the death of Clemens and the banishment of Domitilla,
Stephen, a freedman belonging to the latter, who had enjoyed the
favour, but who had not surely embraced the faith, of his
mistress, assassinated the emperor in his palace.[1] The memory
of Domitian was condemned by the senate; his acts were
rescinded; his exiles recalled; and under the gentle administration of Nerva, while the innocent were restored to their rank and
fortunes, even the most guilty either obtained pardon or escaped
punishment.[2]

II. About ten years afterwards, under the reign of Trajan,
the younger Pliny was intrusted by his friend and master with
the government of Bithynia and Pontus. He soon found himself at a loss to determine by what rule of justice or of law he
should direct his conduct in the execution of an office the most
repugnant to his humanity. Pliny had never assisted at any
judicial proceedings against the Christians, with whose name
alone he seems to be acquainted; and he was totally uninformed
with regard to the nature of their guilt, the method of their conviction, and the degree of their punishment. In this perplexity
he had recourse to his usual expedient, of submitting to the
wisdom of Trajan an impartial, and, in some respects, a favourable account of the new superstition, requesting the emperor
that he would condescend to resolve his doubts and to instruct
his ignorance.[3] The life of Pliny had been employed in the
acquisition of learning, and in the business of the world. Since
the age of nineteen he had pleaded with distinction in the

---

[1] Suet. in Domit. c. 17. Philostratus in Vit. Apollon. l. viii.

[2] Dion, l. lxviii. [c. 1] p. 1118. Plin. Epistol. iv. 22.

[3] Plin. Epistol. x. 97. The learned Mosheim expresses himself (p. 147,
232) with the highest approbation of Pliny's moderate and candid temper.
Notwithstanding Dr. Lardner's suspicions (see Jewish and Heathen Testimonies, vol. ii. p. 46), I am unable to discover any bigotry in his language
or proceedings.

[Yet according to Milman, the humane Pliny put two female attendants,
probably deaconesses, to the torture, in order to ascertain the real nature
of these suspicious meetings.—O. S.]

tribunals of Rome,[1] filled a place in the senate, had been invested with the honours of the consulship, and had formed very numerous connections with every order of men, both in Italy and in the provinces. From *his* ignorance therefore we may derive some useful information. We may assure ourselves that when he accepted the government of Bithynia there were no general laws or decrees of the senate in force against the Christians; that neither Trajan nor any of his virtuous predecessors, whose edicts were received into the civil and criminal jurisprudence, had publicly declared their intentions concerning the new sect; and that, whatever proceedings had been carried on against the Christians, there were none of sufficient weight and authority to establish a precedent for the conduct of a Roman magistrate.

The answer of Trajan, to which the Christians of the succeeding age have frequently appealed, discovers as much regard for justice and humanity as could be reconciled with his mistaken notions of religious policy.[2] Instead of displaying the implacable zeal of an Inquisitor, anxious to discover the most minute particles of heresy, and exulting in the number of his victims, the emperor expresses much more solicitude to protect the security of the innocent than to prevent the escape of the guilty. He acknowledges the difficulty of fixing any general plan; but he lays down two salutary rules, which often afforded relief and support to the distressed Christians. Though he directs the magistrates to punish such persons as are legally convicted, he prohibits them, with a very humane inconsistency, from making any inquiries concerning the supposed criminals. Nor was the magistrate allowed to proceed on every kind of information. Anonymous charges the emperor rejects, as too repugnant to the equity of his government; and he strictly requires, for the conviction of those to whom the guilt of Christianity is imputed, the positive evidence of a fair and open accuser. It is likewise probable that the persons who assumed so invidious an office were obliged to declare the grounds of their suspicions, to specify (both in respect to time and place) the secret assemblies which their Christian adversary had frequented, and to disclose a great number of circumstances which were

[1] Plin. Epist. v. 8. He pleaded his first cause A.D. 81; the year after the famous eruptions of Mount Vesuvius, in which his uncle lost his life.

[2] Plin. Epist. x. 98. Tertullian (Apolog. c. 5) considers this rescript as a relaxation of the ancient penal laws, " quas Trajanus ex parte frustratus est: " and yet Tertullian, in another part of his Apology, exposes the inconsistency of prohibiting inquiries and enjoining punishments.

concealed with the most vigilant jealousy from the eye of the profane. If they succeeded in their prosecution, they were exposed to the resentment of a considerable and active party, to the censure of the more liberal portion of mankind, and to the ignominy which, in every age and country, has attended the character of an informer. If, on the contrary, they failed in their proofs, they incurred the severe and perhaps capital penalty which, according to a law published by the emperor Hadrian, was inflicted on those who falsely attributed to their fellow-citizens the crime of Christianity. The violence of personal or superstitious animosity might sometimes prevail over the most natural apprehensions of disgrace and danger; but it cannot surely be imagined that accusations of so unpromising an appearance were either lightly or frequently undertaken by the Pagan subjects of the Roman empire.[1]

The expedient which was employed to elude the prudence of the laws affords a sufficient proof how effectually they disappointed the mischievous designs of private malice or superstitious zeal. In a large and tumultuous assembly the restraints of fear and shame, so forcible on the minds of individuals, are deprived of the greatest part of their influence. The pious Christian, as he was desirous to obtain, or to escape, the glory of martyrdom, expected, either with impatience or with terror, the stated returns of the public games and festivals. On those occasions the inhabitants of the great cities of the empire were collected in the circus or the theatre, where every circumstance of the place, as well as of the ceremony, contributed to kindle their devotion and to extinguish their humanity. Whilst the numerous spectators, crowned with garlands, perfumed with incense, purified with the blood of victims, and surrounded with the altars and statues of their tutelar deities, resigned themselves to the enjoyment of pleasures which they considered as an essential part of their religious worship, they recollected that the Christians alone abhorred the gods of mankind, and, by their

---

[1] Eusebius (Hist. Ecclesiast. l. iv. c. 9) has preserved the edict of Hadrian. He has likewise (c. 13) given us one still more favourable under the name of Antoninus, the authenticity of which is not so universally allowed. The second Apology of Justin contains some curious particulars relative to the accusations of Christians.

[The enactment of this law of Hadrian's creates the supposition that accusations of " the crime of Christianity " were not so uncommon or received with such mistrust as Gibbon would have us believe. As Bury aptly says, the difference between the rescripts of Hadrian and Antoninus was that the former protected the Christians against calumnious accusations; the latter against the accusation of atheism in general.—O. S.]

absence and melancholy on these solemn festivals, seemed to insult or to lament the public felicity. If the empire had been afflicted by any recent calamity, by a plague, a famine, or an unsuccessful war; if the Tiber had, or if the Nile had not, risen beyond its banks; if the earth had shaken, or if the temperate order of the seasons had been interrupted, the superstitious Pagans were convinced that the crimes and the impiety of the Christians, who were spared by the excessive lenity of the government, had at length provoked the Divine justice. It was not among a licentious and exasperated populace that the forms of legal proceedings could be observed; it was not in an amphitheatre, stained with the blood of wild beasts and gladiators, that the voice of compassion could be heard. The impatient clamours of the multitude denounced the Christians as the enemies of gods and men, doomed them to the severest tortures, and, venturing to accuse by name some of the most distinguished of the new sectaries, required with irresistible vehemence that they should be instantly apprehended and cast to the lions.[1] The provincial governors and magistrates who presided in the public spectacles were usually inclined to gratify the inclinations, and to appease the rage of the people, by the sacrifice of a few obnoxious victims. But the wisdom of the emperors protected the church from the danger of these tumultuous clamours and irregular accusations, which they justly censured as repugnant both to the firmness and to the equity of their administration. The edicts of Hadrian and of Antoninus Pius expressly declared that the voice of the multitude should never be admitted as legal evidence to convict or to punish those unfortunate persons who had embraced the enthusiasm of the Christians.[2]

III. Punishment was not the inevitable consequence of conviction, and the Christians whose guilt was the most clearly proved by the testimony of witnesses, or even by their voluntary confession, still retained in their own power the alternative of life or death. It was not so much the past offence, as the actual resistance, which excited the indignation of the magistrate. He was persuaded that he offered them an easy pardon, since, if they consented to cast a few grains of incense upon the altar, they were dismissed from the tribunal in safety and with applause. It was esteemed the duty of a humane judge to endeavour to

---

[1] See Tertullian (Apolog. c. 40). The Acts of the Martyrdom of Polycarp exhibit a lively picture of these tumults, which were usually fomented by the malice of the Jews.

[2] These regulations are inserted in the above-mentioned edicts of Hadrian and Pius. See the Apology of Melito (apud Euseb. l. iv. c. 26).

reclaim, rather than to punish, those deluded enthusiasts.
Varying his tone according to the age, the sex, or the situation
of the prisoners, he frequently condescended to set before their
eyes every circumstance which could render life more pleasing,
or death more terrible; and to solicit, nay to intreat them, that
they would show some compassion to themselves, to their
families, and to their friends.[1] If threats and persuasions
proved ineffectual, he had often recourse to violence; the scourge
and the rack were called in to supply the deficiency of argument,
and every art of cruelty was employed to subdue such inflexible,
and, as it appeared to the Pagans, such criminal obstinacy.
The ancient apologists of Christianity have censured, with equal
truth and severity, the irregular conduct of their persecutors,
who, contrary to every principle of judicial proceeding, admitted
the use of torture, in order to obtain, not a confession, but a
denial, of the crime which was the object of their inquiry.[2] The
monks of succeeding ages, who, in their peaceful solitudes, entertained themselves with diversifying the deaths and sufferings of
the primitive martyrs, have frequently invented torments of a
much more refined and ingenious nature. In particular, it has
pleased them to suppose that the zeal of the Roman magistrates,
disdaining every consideration of moral virtue or public decency,
endeavoured to seduce those whom they were unable to vanquish, and that by their orders the most brutal violence was
offered to those whom they found it impossible to seduce. It is
related that pious females, who were prepared to despise death,
were sometimes condemned to a more severe trial, and called
upon to determine whether they set a higher value on their
religion or on their chastity. The youths to whose licentious
embraces they were abandoned received a solemn exhortation
from the judge to exert their most strenuous efforts to maintain
the honour of Venus against the impious virgin who refused
to burn incense on her altars. Their violence, however, was
commonly disappointed, and the seasonable interposition of
some miraculous power preserved the chaste spouses of Christ
from the dishonour even of an involuntary defeat. We should
not indeed neglect to remark that the more ancient as well as

[1] See the rescript of Trajan, and the conduct of Pliny. The most
authentic Acts of the Martyrs abound in these exhortations.

[The usual test put by Pliny before a suspected Christian was to worship
the gods, to present offerings to the statue of the emperor, and to blaspheme
the name of Christ.—O. S.]

[2] In particular, see Tertullian (Apolog. c. 2, 3) and Lactantius (Institut.
Divin. v. 9). Their reasonings are almost the same; but we may discover
that one of these apologists had been a lawyer, and the other a rhetorician.

authentic memorials of the church are seldom polluted with these extravagant and indecent fictions.[1]

The total disregard of truth and probability in the representation of these primitive martyrdoms was occasioned by a very natural mistake. The ecclesiastical writers of the fourth or fifth centuries ascribed to the magistrates of Rome the same degree of implacable and unrelenting zeal which filled their own breasts against the heretics or the idolaters of their own times. It is not improbable that some of those persons who were raised to the dignities of the empire might have imbibed the prejudices of the populace, and that the cruel disposition of others might occasionally be stimulated by motives of avarice or of personal resentment.[2] But it is certain, and we may appeal to the grateful confessions of the first Christians, that the greatest part of those magistrates who exercised in the provinces the authority of the emperor or of the senate, and to whose hands alone the jurisdiction of life and death was intrusted, behaved like men of polished manners and liberal education, who respected the rules of justice, and who were conversant with the precepts of philosophy. They frequently declined the odious task of persecution, dismissed the charge with contempt, or suggested to the accused Christian some legal evasion by which he might elude the severity of the laws.[3] Whenever they were invested with a discretionary power,[4] they used it much less for the oppression than for the relief and benefit of the afflicted church. They were far from condemning all the Christians who were accused before their tribunal, and very far from punishing with death all those who were convicted of an obstinate adherence to the new superstition. Contenting themselves, for the most part, with the milder chastisements of imprisonment, exile, or slavery in the mines,[5] they

[1] See two instances of this kind of torture in the Acta Sincera Martyrum, published by Ruinart, p. 160, 399. Jerome, in his Legend of Paul the Hermit, tells a strange story of a young man who was chained naked on a bed of flowers, and assaulted by a beautiful and wanton courtesan. He quelled the rising temptation by biting off his tongue.

[2] The conversion of his wife provoked Claudius Herminianus, governor of Cappadocia, to treat the Christians with uncommon severity. Tertullian ad Scapulam, c. 3.

[3] Tertullian, in his epistle to the governor of Africa, mentions several remarkable instances of lenity and forbearance which had happened within his knowledge.

[4] Neque enim in universum aliquid quod quasi certam formam habeat, constitui potest: an expression of Trajan, which gave a very great latitude to the governors of provinces.

[5] In metalla damnamur, in insulas relegamur. Tertullian, Apolog. c. 12. The mines of Numidia contained nine bishops, with a proportionable number of their clergy and people, to whom Cyprian addressed a pious epistle of praise and comfort. See Cyprian. Epistol. 76, 77.

left the unhappy victims of their justice some reason to hope
that a prosperous event, the accession, the marriage, or the
triumph of an emperor, might speedily restore them by a general
pardon to their former state. The martyrs, devoted to immediate execution by the Roman magistrates, appear to have
been selected from the most opposite extremes. They were
either bishops and presbyters, the persons the most distinguished
among the Christians by their rank and influence, and whose
example might strike terror into the whole sect;[1] or else they were
the meanest and most abject among them, particularly those of
the servile condition, whose lives were esteemed of little value,
and whose sufferings were viewed by the ancients with too careless an indifference.[2] The learned Origen, who, from his experience as well as reading, was intimately acquainted with the
history of the Christians, declares, in the most express terms,
that the number of martyrs was very inconsiderable.[3] His
authority would alone be sufficient to annihilate that formidable
army of martyrs, whose relics, drawn for the most part from
the catacombs of Rome, have replenished so many churches,[4]
and whose marvellous achievements have been the subject of
so many volumes of holy romance.[5]   But the general assertion

[1] Though we cannot receive with entire confidence either the epistles or
the acts of Ignatius (they may be found in the second volume of the
Apostolic Fathers), yet we may quote that bishop of Antioch as one of
these *exemplary* martyrs.   He was sent in chains to Rome as a public
spectacle; and when he arrived at Troas he received the pleasing intelligence that the persecution of Antioch was already at an end.

[2] Among the martyrs of Lyons (Euseb. l. v. c. 1) the slave Blandina was
distinguished by more exquisite tortures.   Of the five martyrs so much
celebrated in the Acts of Felicitas and Perpetua, two were of a servile, and
two others of a very mean, condition.

[3] Origen. advers. Celsum. l. iii. p. 116 [c. 8, tom. i. p. 452, ed. Bened.].
His words deserve to be transcribed:—"'Ολίγοι κατὰ καιροὺς, καὶ σφόδρα
εὐαρίθμητοι ὑπὲρ τῆς Χριστιανῶν θεοσεβείας τεθνήκασι."

[4] If we recollect that all the Plebeians of Rome were not Christians, and
that all the Christians were not saints and martyrs, we may judge with
how much safety religious honours can be ascribed to bones or urns indiscriminately taken from the public burial-place.   After ten centuries of a
very free and open trade some suspicions have arisen among the more
learned Catholics.   They now require, as a proof of sanctity and martyrdom, the letters B. M., a vial full of red liquor supposed to be blood, or the
figure of a palm-tree.   But the two former signs are of little weight, and
with regard to the last, it is observed by the critics—1. That the figure, as
it is called, of a palm, is perhaps a cypress, and perhaps only a stop, the
flourish of a comma used in the monumental inscriptions.   2. That the
palm was the symbol of victory among the Pagans.   3. That among the
Christians it served as the emblem, not only of martyrdom, but in general
of a joyful resurrection.   See the epistle of P. Mabillon on the worship of
unknown saints, and Muratori sopra le Antichità Italiane, Dissertat. lviii.

[5] As a specimen of these legends, we may be satisfied with 10,000 Christian soldiers crucified in one day, either by Trajan or Hadrian, on Mount

of Origen may be explained and confirmed by the particular testimony of his friend Dionysius, who, in the immense city of Alexandria, and under the rigorous persecution of Decius, reckons only ten men and seven women who suffered for the profession of the Christian name.[1]

During the same period of persecution, the zealous, the eloquent, the ambitious Cyprian governed the church, not only of Carthage, but even of Africa. He possessed every quality which could engage the reverence of the faithful, or provoke the suspicions and resentment of the Pagan magistrates. His character as well as his station seemed to mark out that holy prelate as the most distinguished object of envy and of danger.[2] The experience, however, of the life of Cyprian is sufficient to prove that our fancy has exaggerated the perilous situation of a Christian bishop; and that the dangers to which he was exposed were less imminent than those which temporal ambition is always prepared to encounter in the pursuit of honours. Four Roman emperors, with their families, their favourites, and their adherents, perished by the sword in the space of ten years, during which the bishop of Carthage guided by his authority and eloquence the councils of the African church. It was only in the third year of his administration that he had reason, during a few months, to apprehend the severe edicts of Decius, the vigilance of the magistrate, and the clamours of the multitude, who loudly demanded that Cyprian, the leader of the Christians, should be thrown to the lions. Prudence suggested the necessity of a temporary retreat, and the voice of prudence was obeyed. He withdrew himself into an obscure solitude, from whence he could maintain a constant correspondence with the clergy and people of Carthage; and, concealing himself till the tempest was past, he preserved his life, without relinquishing either his power or his reputation. His extreme caution did not however escape the censure of the more rigid Christians, who lamented, or the reproaches of his personal enemies, who insulted, a conduct

---

Ararat. See Baronius ad Martyrologium Romanum; Tillemont, Mém. Ecclésiast. tom. ii. part ii. p. 438; and Geddes's Miscellanies, vol. ii. p. 203. The abbreviation of MIL., which may signify either *soldiers* or *thousands*, is said to have occasioned some extraordinary mistakes.

[1] Dionysius ap. Euseb. l. vi. c. 41. One of the seventeen was likewise accused of robbery.

[2] The letters of Cyprian exhibit a very curious and original picture both of the *man* and of the *times*. See likewise the two Lives of Cyprian, composed with equal accuracy, though with very different views; the one by Le Clerc (Bibliothèque Universelle, tom. xii. p. 208-378), the other by Tillemont, Mémoires Ecclésiastiques, tom. iv. part i. p. 76-459.

which they considered as a pusillanimous and criminal desertion
of the most sacred duty.[1] The propriety of reserving himself for
the future exigencies of the church, the example of several holy
bishops,[2] and the divine admonitions which, as he declares himself, he frequently received in visions and ecstasies, were the
reasons alleged in his justification.[3] But his best apology may
be found in the cheerful resolution with which, about eight
years afterwards, he suffered death in the cause of religion. The
authentic history of his martyrdom has been recorded with
unusual candour and impartiality. A short abstract therefore
of its most important circumstances will convey the clearest
information of the spirit and of the forms of the Roman persecutions.[4]

When Valerian was consul for the third, and Gallienus for the
fourth time, Paternus, proconsul of Africa, summoned Cyprian
to appear in his private council-chamber. He there acquainted
him with the imperial mandate which he had just received,[5]
that those who had abandoned the Roman religion should immediately return to the practice of the ceremonies of their
ancestors. Cyprian replied without hesitation that he was a
Christian and a bishop, devoted to the worship of the true and
only Deity, to whom he offered up his daily supplications for the
safety and prosperity of the two emperors, his lawful sovereigns.
With modest confidence he pleaded the privilege of a citizen in
refusing to give any answer to some invidious and indeed illegal
questions which the proconsul had proposed. A sentence of
banishment was pronounced as the penalty of Cyprian's disobedience; and he was conducted without delay to Curubis,
a free and maritime city of Zeugitana, in a pleasant situation, a
fertile territory, and at the distance of about forty miles from

---

[1] See the polite but severe epistle of the clergy of Rome to the bishop of
Carthage (Cyprian. Epist. 8, 9). Pontius labours with the greatest care
and diligence to justify his master against the general censure.

[2] In particular those of Dionysius of Alexandria, and Gregory Thauma-
turgus of Neo-Cæsarea. See Euseb. Hist. Ecclesiast. l. vi. c. 40; and
Mémoires de Tillemont, tom. iv. part ii. p. 685.

[3] See Cyprian. Epist. 16, and his Life by Pontius.

[4] We have an original Life of Cyprian by the deacon Pontius, the companion of his exile and the spectator of his death; and we likewise possess
the ancient proconsular Acts of his martyrdom. These two relations are
consistent with each other, and with probability; and what is somewhat
remarkable, they are both unsullied by any miraculous circumstances.

[5] It should seem that these were circular orders, sent at the same time to
all the governors. Dionysius (ap. Euseb. l. vii. c. 11) relates the history of
his own banishment from Alexandria almost in the same manner. But as
he escaped and survived the persecution, we must account him either more
or less fortunate than Cyprian.

Carthage.[1] The exiled bishop enjoyed the conveniences of life
and the consciousness of virtue. His reputation was diffused
over Africa and Italy; an account of his behaviour was published
for the edification of the Christian world; [2] and his solitude was
frequently interrupted by the letters, the visits, and the con-
gratulations of the faithful. On the arrival of a new proconsul
in the province the fortune of Cyprian appeared for some time
to wear a still more favourable aspect. He was recalled from
banishment, and, though not yet permitted to return to Carthage,
his own gardens in the neighbourhood of the capital were assigned
for the place of his residence.[3]

At length, exactly one year [4] after Cyprian was first apprehended, Galerius Maximus, proconsul of Africa, received the
imperial warrant for the execution of the Christian teachers.
The bishop of Carthage was sensible that he should be singled out
for one of the first victims, and the frailty of nature tempted him
to withdraw himself, by a secret flight, from the danger and the
honour of martyrdom; but, soon recovering that fortitude which
his character required, he returned to his gardens, and patiently
expected the ministers of death. Two officers of rank, who were
intrusted with that commission, placed Cyprian between them
in a chariot, and, as the proconsul was not then at leisure, they
conducted him, not to a prison, but to a private house in Carthage,
which belonged to one of them. An elegant supper was provided
for the entertainment of the bishop, and his Christian friends were
permitted for the last time to enjoy his society, whilst the streets
were filled with a multitude of the faithful, anxious and alarmed
at the approaching fate of their spiritual father.[5] In the morn-

---

[1] See Plin. Hist. Natur. v. 3; Cellarius, Geograph. Antiq. part iii. p. 96;
Shaw's Travels, p. 90; and for the adjacent country (which is terminated
by Cape Bona, or the promontory of Mercury) l'Afrique de Marmol. tom.
ii. p. 494. There are the remains of an aqueduct near Curubis, or Curbis,
at present altered into Gurbes; and Dr. Shaw read an inscription which
styles that city *Colonia Fulvia*. The deacon Pontius (in Vit. Cyprian. c.
12) calls it " Apricum et competentem locum, hospitium pro voluntate
secretum, et quicquid apponi eis ante promissum est, qui regnum et justi-
tiam Dei quærunt."

[2] See Cyprian. Epistol. 77, edit. Fell.

[3] Upon his conversion he had sold those gardens for the benefit of the
poor. The indulgence of God (most probably the liberality of some
Christian friend) restored them to Cyprian. See Pontius, c. 15.

[4] When Cyprian, a twelvemonth before, was sent into exile, he dreamt
that he should be put to death the next day. The event made it necessary
to explain that word as signifying a year. Pontius, c. 12.

[5] Pontius (c. 15) acknowledges that Cyprian, with whom he supped,
passed the night custodiâ delicatâ. The bishop exercised a last and very
proper act of jurisdiction, by directing that the younger females, who

ing he appeared before the tribunal of the proconsul, who, after informing himself of the name and situation of Cyprian, commanded him to offer sacrifice, and pressed him to reflect on the consequences of his disobedience. The refusal of Cyprian was firm and decisive, and the magistrate, when he had taken the opinion of his council, pronounced, with some reluctance, the sentence of death. It was conceived in the following terms: " That Thascius Cyprianus should be immediately beheaded, as the enemy of the gods of Rome, and as the chief and ring-leader of a criminal association, which he had seduced into an impious resistance against the laws of the most holy emperors Valerian and Gallienus." [1] The manner of his execution was the mildest and least painful that could be inflicted on a person convicted of any capital offence: nor was the use of torture admitted to obtain from the bishop of Carthage either the recantation of his principles or the discovery of his accomplices.

As soon as the sentence was proclaimed, a general cry of " We will die with him " arose at once among the listening multitude of Christians who waited before the palace gates. The generous effusions of their zeal and affection were neither serviceable to Cyprian nor dangerous to themselves. He was led away under a guard of tribunes and centurions, without resistance and without insult, to the place of his execution, a spacious and level plain near the city, which was already filled with great numbers of spectators. His faithful presbyters and deacons were permitted to accompany their holy bishop. They assisted him in laying aside his upper garment, spread linen on the ground to catch the precious relics of his blood, and received his orders to bestow five-and-twenty pieces of gold on the executioner. The martyr then covered his face with his hands, and at one blow his head was separated from his body. His corpse remained during some hours exposed to the curiosity of the Gentiles, but in the night it was removed, and transported, in a triumphal procession and with a splendid illumination, to the burial-place of the Christians. The funeral of Cyprian was publicly celebrated without receiving any interruption from the Roman magistrates;

watched in the street, should be removed from the dangers and temptations of a nocturnal crowd. Act. Proconsularia, c. 2.

[The motive of fear was not the one which induced Cyprian to conceal himself for a short period. He was threatened with being transported to Utica, but it was his earnest desire to die in Carthage, that his martyrdom there might conduce to the edification of those whom he had guided during life.—O. S.]

[1] See the original sentence in the Acts, c. 4; and in Pontius, c. 17. The latter expresses it in a more rhetorical manner.

and those among the faithful who had performed the last offices to his person and his memory were secure from the danger of inquiry or of punishment. It is remarkable that, of so great a multitude of bishops in the province of Africa, Cyprian was the first who was esteemed worthy to obtain the crown of martyrdom.[1]

It was in the choice of Cyprian either to die a martyr or to live an apostate, but on that choice depended the alternative of honour or infamy. Could we suppose that the bishop of Carthage had employed the profession of the Christian faith only as the instrument of his avarice or ambition, it was still incumbent on him to support the character which he had assumed,[2] and, if he possessed the smallest degree of manly fortitude, rather to expose himself to the most cruel tortures than by a single act to exchange the reputation of a whole life for the abhorrence of his Christian brethren and the contempt of the Gentile world. But if the zeal of Cyprian was supported by the sincere conviction of the truth of those doctrines which he preached, the crown of martyrdom must have appeared to him as an object of desire rather than of terror. It is not easy to extract any distinct ideas from the vague though eloquent declamations of the Fathers, or to ascertain the degree of immortal glory and happiness which they confidently promised to those who were so fortunate as to shed their blood in the cause of religion.[3] They inculcated with becoming diligence that the fire of martyrdom supplied every defect and expiated every sin; that, while the souls of ordinary Christians were obliged to pass through a slow and painful purification, the triumphant sufferers entered into the immediate fruition of eternal bliss, where, in the society of the patriarchs, the apostles, and the prophets, they reigned with Christ, and acted as his assessors in the universal judgment of mankind. The assurance of a lasting reputation upon earth, a motive so congenial to the vanity of human nature, often served to animate the courage of the martyrs. The honours which Rome or Athens bestowed on those citizens who had fallen in the cause of their

[1] Pontius, c. 19. M. de Tillemont (Mémoires, tom. iv. part i. p. 450, note 50) is not pleased with so positive an exclusion of any former martyrs of the episcopal rank.

[2] Whatever opinion we may entertain of the character or principles of Thomas Becket, we must acknowledge that he suffered death with a constancy not unworthy of the primitive martyrs. See Lord Lyttelton's History of Henry II., vol. ii. p. 592, etc.

[3] See in particular the treatise of Cyprian de Lapsis, p. 87-98, edit. Fell. [p. 121.] The learning of Dodwell (Dissertat. Cyprianic. xii. xiii.), and the ingenuity of Middleton (Free Inquiry, p. 162, etc.), have left scarcely anything to add concerning the merit, the honours, and the motives of the martyrs.

country were cold and unmeaning demonstrations of respect, when compared with the ardent gratitude and devotion which the primitive church expressed towards the victorious champions of the faith. The annual commemoration of their virtues and sufferings was observed as a sacred ceremony, and at length terminated in religious worship. Among the Christians who had publicly confessed their religious principles, those who (as it very frequently happened) had been dismissed from the tribunal or the prisons of the Pagan magistrates obtained such honours as were justly due to their imperfect martyrdom and their generous resolution. The most pious females courted the permission of imprinting kisses on the fetters which they had worn, and on the wounds which they had received. Their persons were esteemed holy, their decisions were admitted with deference, and they too often abused, by their spiritual pride and licentious manners, the pre-eminence which their zeal and intrepidity had acquired.[1] Distinctions like these, whilst they display the exalted merit, betray the inconsiderable number, of those who suffered and of those who died for the profession of Christianity.

The sober discretion of the present age will more readily censure than admire, but can more easily admire than imitate, the fervour of the first Christians, who, according to the lively expression of Sulpicius Severus, desired martyrdom with more eagerness than his own contemporaries solicited a bishopric.[2] The epistles which Ignatius composed as he was carried in chains through the cities of Asia breathe sentiments the most repugnant to the ordinary feelings of human nature. He earnestly beseeches the Romans that, when he should be exposed in the amphitheatre, they would not, by their kind but unseasonable intercession, deprive him of the crown of glory; and he declares his resolution to provoke and irritate the wild beasts which might be employed as the instruments of his death.[3] Some stories are related of the courage of martyrs who actually performed what Ignatius had

[1] Cyprian. Epistol. 5, 6, 7, 22, 24; and de Unitat. Ecclesiæ. The number of pretended martyrs has been very much multiplied by the custom which was introduced of bestowing that honourable name on confessors.

[2] Certatim gloriosa in certamina ruebatur; multoque avidius tum martyria gloriosis mortibus quærebantur, quam nunc Episcopatus pravis ambitionibus appetuntur. Sulpicius Severus, l. ii. [p. 385, ed. Lugd. Bat. 1647.] He might have omitted the word *nunc*.

[3] See Epist. ad Roman. c. 4, 5, ap. Patres Apostol. tom. ii. p. 27. It suited the purpose of Bishop Pearson (see Vindiciæ Ignatianæ, part ii. c. 9) to justify, by a profusion of examples and authorities, the sentiments of Ignatius.

intended, who exasperated the fury of the lions, pressed the executioner to hasten his office, cheerfully leaped into the fires which were kindled to consume them, and discovered a sensation of joy and pleasure in the midst of the most exquisite tortures. Several examples have been preserved of a zeal impatient of those restraints which the emperors had provided for the security of the church. The Christians sometimes supplied by their voluntary declaration the want of an accuser, rudely disturbed the public service of paganism,[1] and, rushing in crowds round the tribunal of the magistrates, called upon them to pronounce and to inflict the sentence of the law. The behaviour of the Christians was too remarkable to escape the notice of the ancient philosophers, but they seem to have considered it with much less admiration than astonishment. Incapable of conceiving the motives which sometimes transported the fortitude of believers beyond the bounds of prudence or reason, they treated such an eagerness to die as the strange result of obstinate despair, of stupid insensibility, or of superstitious frenzy.[2] "Unhappy men!" exclaimed the proconsul Antoninus to the Christians of Asia, "unhappy men! if you are thus weary of your lives, is it so difficult for you to find ropes and precipices?"[3] He was extremely cautious (as it is observed by a learned and pious historian) of punishing men who had found no accusers but themselves, the imperial laws not having made any provisions for so unexpected a case; condemning therefore a few as a warning to their brethren, he dismissed the multitude with indignation and contempt.[4] Notwithstanding this real or affected disdain, the intrepid constancy of the faithful was productive of more salutary effects on those minds which nature or grace had disposed for the easy reception of religious truth. On these melancholy occasions there were many among the Gentiles who pitied, who admired, and who were converted. The generous enthusiasm was communicated from the sufferer to the spectators, and the blood of

[1] The story of Polyeuctes, on which Corneille has founded a very beautiful tragedy, is one of the most celebrated, though not perhaps the most authentic, instances of this excessive zeal. We should observe that the 60th canon of the council of Illiberis refuses the title of martyrs to those who exposed themselves to death by publicly destroying the idols.
[2] See Epictetus, l. iv. c. 7 (though there is some doubt whether he alludes to the Christians); Marcus Antoninus de Rebus suis, l. xi. c. 3; Lucian in Peregrin.
[3] Tertullian ad Scapul. c. 5. The learned are divided between three persons of the same name, who were all proconsuls of Asia. I am inclined to ascribe this story to Antoninus Pius, who was afterwards emperor; and who may have governed Asia under the reign of Trajan.
[4] Mosheim, de Rebus Christ. ante Constantin. p. 235.

martyrs, according to a well-known observation, became the seed of the church.

But although devotion had raised, and eloquence continued to inflame, this fever of the mind, it insensibly gave way to the more natural hopes and fears of the human heart, to the love of life, the apprehension of pain, and the horror of dissolution. The more prudent rulers of the church found themselves obliged to restrain the indiscreet ardour of their followers, and to distrust a constancy which too often abandoned them in the hour of trial.[1] As the lives of the faithful became less mortified and austere, they were every day less ambitious of the honours of martyrdom; and the soldiers of Christ, instead of distinguishing themselves by voluntary deeds of heroism, frequently deserted their post, and fled in confusion before the enemy whom it was their duty to resist. There were three methods, however, of escaping the flames of persecution, which were not attended with an equal degree of guilt: the first indeed was generally allowed to be innocent; the second was of a doubtful, or at least of a venial, nature; but the third implied a direct and criminal apostacy from the Christian faith.

I. A modern Inquisitor would hear with surprise, that, whenever an information was given to a Roman magistrate of any person within his jurisdiction who had embraced the sect of the Christians, the charge was communicated to the party accused, and that a convenient time was allowed him to settle his domestic concerns, and to prepare an answer to the crime which was imputed to him.[2] If he entertained any doubt of his own constancy, such a delay afforded him the opportunity of preserving his life and honour by flight, of withdrawing himself into some obscure retirement or some distant province, and of patiently expecting the return of peace and security. A measure so consonant to reason was soon authorised by the advice and example of the most holy prelates; and seems to have been censured by few, except by the Montanists, who deviated into heresy by their strict and obstinate adherence to the rigour of ancient discipline.[3] II. The provincial governors, whose zeal

[1] See the Epistle of the Church of Smyrna, ap. Euseb. Hist. Eccles. l. iv. c. 15.

[2] In the second Apology of Justin there is a particular and very curious instance of this legal delay. The same indulgence was granted to accused Christians in the persecution of Decius: and Cyprian (de Lapsis) expressly mentions the " Dies negantibus præstitutus."

[3] Tertullian considers flight from persecution as an imperfect, but very criminal, apostasy, as an impious attempt to elude the will of God, etc. etc. He has written a treatise on this subject (see p. 536-544, edit. Rigalt.),

was less prevalent than their avarice, had countenanced the practice of selling certificates (or libels as they were called), which attested that the persons therein mentioned had complied with the laws, and sacrificed to the Roman deities. By producing these false declarations, the opulent and timid Christians were enabled to silence the malice of an informer, and to reconcile in some measure their safety with their religion. A slight penance atoned for this profane dissimulation.[1] III. In every persecution there were great numbers of unworthy Christians who publicly disowned or renounced the faith which they had professed; and who confirmed the sincerity of their abjuration by the legal acts of burning incense or of offering sacrifices. Some of these apostates had yielded on the first menace or exhortation of the magistrate; whilst the patience of others had been subdued by the length and repetition of tortures. The affrighted countenances of some betrayed their inward remorse, while others advanced with confidence and alacrity to the altars of the gods.[2] But the disguise which fear had imposed subsisted no longer than the present danger. As soon as the severity of the persecution was abated, the doors of the churches were assailed by the returning multitude of penitents, who detested their idolatrous submission, and who solicited with equal ardour, but with various success, their readmission into the society of Christians.[3]

IV. Notwithstanding the general rules established for the con-

which is filled with the wildest fanaticism and the most incoherent declamation. It is, however, somewhat remarkable that Tertullian did not suffer martyrdom himself.

[1] The *Libellatici*, who are chiefly known by the writings of Cyprian, are described with the utmost precision in the copious commentary of Mosheim, p. 483-489.

[2] Plin. Epistol. x. 97. Dionysius Alexandrin. ap. Euseb. l. vi. c. 41. Ad prima statim verba minantis inimici maximus fratrum numerus fidem suam prodidit: nec prostratus est persecutionis impetu, sed voluntario lapsu seipsum prostravit. Cyprian. Opera, p. 89. Among these deserters were many priests and even bishops.

[3] It was on this occasion that Cyprian wrote his treatise De Lapsis, and many of his epistles. The controversy concerning the treatment of penitent apostates does not occur among the Christians of the preceding century. Shall we ascribe this to the superiority of their faith and courage, or to our less intimate knowledge of their history?

[Pliny expressly says that the greater part of the Christians persisted in avowing themselves to be so. The number of those who renounced their faith was infinitely below the number of those who boldly confessed it. The prefect and his assessors present at the council (says Eusebius) were alarmed at seeing the crowd of Christians, and the judges themselves trembled. Lastly, St. Cyprian informs us that the greater part of those who had appeared weak brethren in the persecution of Decius, made glorious proof of their courage in that of Gallus.—O. S.]

viction and punishment of the Christians, the fate of those
sectaries, in an extensive and arbitrary government, must still,
in a great measure, have depended on their own behaviour, the
circumstances of the times, and the temper of their supreme as
well as subordinate rulers. Zeal might sometimes provoke, and
prudence might sometimes avert or assuage, the superstitious
fury of the Pagans. A variety of motives might dispose the
provincial governors either to enforce or to relax the execution
of the laws; and of these motives the most forcible was their
regard not only for the public edicts, but for the secret intentions
of the emperor, a glance from whose eye was sufficient to kindle
or to extinguish the flames of persecution. As often as any
occasional severities were exercised in the different parts of the
empire, the primitive Christians lamented and perhaps magnified
their own sufferings; but the celebrated number of *ten* persecutions has been determined by the ecclesiastical writers of the
fifth century, who possessed a more distinct view of the prosperous
or adverse fortunes of the church from the age of Nero to that of
Diocletian. The ingenious parallels of the *ten* plagues of Egypt,
and of the *ten* horns of the Apocalypse, first suggested this calculation to their minds; and in their application of the faith
of prophecy to the truth of history they were careful to select
those reigns which were indeed the most hostile to the Christian
cause.[1] But these transient persecutions served only to revive
the zeal and to restore the discipline of the faithful; and the
moments of extraordinary rigour were compensated by much
longer intervals of peace and security. The indifference of some
princes and the indulgence of others permitted the Christians to
enjoy, though not perhaps a legal, yet an actual and public
toleration of their religion.

The Apology of Tertullian contains two very ancient, very
singular, but at the same time very suspicious instances of
Imperial clemency; the edicts published by Tiberius and by
Marcus Antoninus, and designed not only to protect the innocence of the Christians, but even to proclaim those stupendous
miracles which had attested the truth of their doctrine. The
first of these examples is attended with some difficulties which
might perplex a sceptical mind.[2] We are required to believe

[1] See Mosheim, p. 97. Sulpicius Severus was the first author of this
computation; though he seemed desirous of reserving the tenth and
greatest persecution for the coming of the Antichrist.
[2] The testimony given by Pontius Pilate is first mentioned by Justin.
The successsive improvements which the story acquired (as it has passed
through the hands of Tertullian, Eusebius, Epiphanius, Chrysostom, Orosius,

that Pontius Pilate informed the emperor of the unjust sentence
of death which he had pronounced against an innocent, and, as
it appeared, a divine person; and that, without acquiring the
merit, he exposed himself to the danger, of martyrdom; *that*
Tiberius, who avowed his contempt for all religion, immediately
conceived the design of placing the Jewish Messiah among the
gods of Rome; *that* his servile senate ventured to disobey the
commands of their master; *that* Tiberius, instead of resenting
their refusal, contented himself with protecting the Christians
from the severity of the laws, many years before such laws were
enacted or before the church had assumed any distinct name or
existence; and lastly, *that* the memory of this extraordinary transaction was preserved in the most public and authentic records,
which escaped the knowledge of the historians of Greece and
Rome, and were only visible to the eyes of an African Christian,
who composed his Apology one hundred and sixty years after
the death of Tiberius. The edict of Marcus Antoninus is supposed to have been the effect of his devotion and gratitude for
the miraculous deliverance which he had obtained in the Mar-
comannic war. The distress of the legions, the seasonable
tempest of rain and hail, of thunder and of lightning, and the
dismay and defeat of the barbarians, have been celebrated by
the eloquence of several Pagan writers. If there were any
Christians in that army, it was natural that they should ascribe
some merit to the fervent prayers which, in the moment of
danger, they had offered up for their own and the public safety.
But we are still assured by monuments of brass and marble, by
the Imperial medals, and by the Antonine column, that neither
the prince nor the people entertained any sense of this signal
obligation, since they unanimously attribute their deliverance
to the providence of Jupiter, and to the interposition of Mercury.
During the whole course of his reign Marcus despised the Christians as a philosopher, and punished them as a sovereign.[1]

By a singular fatality, the hardships which they had endured
under the government of a virtuous prince immediately ceased
on the accession of a tyrant; and as none except themselves had
experienced the injustice of Marcus, so they alone were protected
by the lenity of Commodus. The celebrated Marcia, the most
favoured of his concubines, and who at length contrived the

Gregory of Tours, and the authors of the several editions of the Acts of
Pilate), are very fairly stated by Dom Calmet, Dissertat. sur l'Ecriture
tom. iii. p. 651, etc.

[1] On this miracle, as it is commonly called, of the Thundering Legion, see
the admirable criticism of Mr. Moyle, in his Works, vol. ii. p. 81-390.

murder of her Imperial lover, entertained a singular affection
for the oppressed church; and though it was impossible that
she could reconcile the practice of vice with the precepts of the
Gospel, she might hope to atone for the frailties of her sex and
profession by declaring herself the patroness of the Christians.[1]
Under the gracious protection of Marcia they passed in safety the
thirteen years of a cruel tyranny; and when the empire was
established in the house of Severus, they formed a domestic but
more honourable connection with the new court.   The emperor
was persuaded that, in a dangerous sickness, he had derived some
benefit, either spiritual or physical, from the holy oil with which
one of his slaves had anointed him.   He always treated with
peculiar distinction several persons of both sexes who had embraced the new religion.   The nurse as well as the preceptor of
Caracalla were Christians; and if that young prince ever betrayed
a sentiment of humanity, it was occasioned by an incident which,
however trifling, bore some relation to the cause of Christianity.[2]
Under the reign of Severus the fury of the populace was checked;
the rigour of ancient laws was for some time suspended; and the
provincial governors were satisfied with receiving an annual
present from the churches within their jurisdiction, as the price,
or as the reward, of their moderation.[3]   The controversy concerning the precise time of the celebration of Easter armed the
bishops of Asia and Italy against each other, and was considered as the most important business of this period of leisure
and tranquillity.[4]   Nor was the peace of the church interrupted
till the increasing numbers of proselytes seem at length to have
attracted the attention, and to have alienated the mind, of
Severus.   With the design of restraining the progress of Christianity, he published an edict, which, though it was designed to
affect only the new converts, could not be carried into strict
execution without exposing to danger and punishment the most
zealous of their teachers and missionaries.   In this mitigated
persecution we may still discover the indulgent spirit of Rome

[1] Dion Cassius, or rather his abbreviator Xiphilin, l. lxxii. [c. 4] p. 1206.
Mr. Moyle (p. 266) has explained the condition of the church under the
reign of Commodus.

[2] Compare the Life of Caracalla, in the Augustan History, with the
epistle of Tertullian to Scapula.   Dr. Jortin (Remarks on Ecclesiastical History, vol. ii. p. 5, etc.) considers the cure of Severus, by the means of holy
oil, with a strong desire to convert it into a miracle.

[3] Tertullian de Fugâ, c. 13.   The present was made during the feast of
the Saturnalia; and it is a matter of serious concern to Tertullian that the
faithful should be confounded with the most infamous professions which
purchased the connivance of the government.

[4] Euseb. l. v. c. 23, 24.   Mosheim, p. 435-447.

and of Polytheism, which so readily admitted every excuse in favour of those who practised the religious ceremonies of their fathers.[1]

But the laws which Severus had enacted soon expired with the authority of that emperor; and the Christians, after this accidental tempest, enjoyed a calm of thirty-eight years.[2] Till this period they had usually held their assemblies in private houses and sequestered places. They were now permitted to erect and consecrate convenient edifices for the purpose of religious worship;[3] to purchase lands, even at Rome itself, for the use of the community; and to conduct the elections of their ecclesiastical ministers in so public, but at the same time in so exemplary a manner, as to deserve the respectful attention of the Gentiles.[4] This long repose of the church was accompanied with dignity. The reigns of those princes who derived their extraction from the Asiatic provinces proved the most favourable to the Christians; the eminent persons of the sect, instead of being reduced to implore the protection of a slave or concubine, were admitted into the palace in the honourable characters of priests and philosophers; and their mysterious doctrines, which were already diffused among the people, insensibly attracted the curiosity of their sovereign. When the empress Mamæa passed through Antioch, she expressed a desire of conversing with the celebrated Origen, the fame of whose piety and learning was spread over the East. Origen obeyed so flattering an invitation, and, though he could not expect to succeed in the conversion of an artful and ambitious woman, she listened with pleasure to his eloquent exhortations, and honourably dismissed him to his retirement in Palestine.[5] The sentiments of Mamæa were adopted by her son Alexander, and the philosophic devotion

---

[1] Judæos fieri sub gravi pœnâ vetuit. Idem etiam de Christianis sanxit. Hist. August. p. 70. [Spart. Sever. c. 17.]

[2] Sulpicius Severus, l. ii. p. 384 [ed. Lugd. Bat. 1647]. This computation (allowing for a single exception) is confirmed by the History of Eusebius and by the writings of Cyprian.

[3] The antiquity of Christian churches is discussed by Tillemont (Mémoires Ecclésiastiques, tom. iii. part ii. p. 68-72) and by Mr. Moyle (vol. i. p. 378-398). The former refers the first construction of them to the peace of Alexander Severus; the latter, to the peace of Gallienus.

[4] See the Augustan History, p. 130. [Lamprid. Alex. Sever. c. 45.] The emperor Alexander adopted their method of publicly proposing the names of those persons who were candidates for ordination. It is true that the honour of this practice is likewise attributed to the Jews.

[5] Euseb. Hist. Ecclesiast. l. vi. c. 21. Hieronym. de Script. Eccles. c. 54 [vol. ii. p. 879, ed. Vallars.]. Mamæa was styled a holy and pious woman, both by the Christians and the Pagans. From the former, therefore, it was impossible that she should deserve that honourable epithet.

of that emperor was marked by a singular but injudicious regard
for the Christian religion.   In his domestic chapel he placed the
statues of Abraham, of Orpheus, of Apollonius, and of Christ,
as an honour justly due to those respectable sages who had instructed mankind in the various modes of addressing their
homage to the supreme and universal Deity.[1]   A purer faith, as
well as worship, was openly professed and practised among his
household.   Bishops, perhaps for the first time, were seen at
court; and, after the death of Alexander, when the inhuman
Maximin discharged his fury on the favourites and servants of
his unfortunate benefactor, a great number of Christians, of
every rank, and of both sexes, were involved in the promiscuous
massacre, which, on their account, has improperly received the
name of Persecution.[2]

Notwithstanding the cruel disposition of Maximin, the effects
of his resentment against the Christians were of a very local and
temporary nature, and the pious Origen, who had been proscribed as a devoted victim, was still reserved to convey the
truths of the Gospel to the ear of monarchs.[3]   He addressed
several edifying letters to the emperor Philip, to his wife, and to
his mother, and as soon as that prince, who was born in the
neighbourhood of Palestine, had usurped the Imperial sceptre,
the Christians acquired a friend and a protector.   The public
and even partial favour of Philip towards the sectaries of the new
religion, and his constant reverence for the ministers of the
church, gave some colour to the suspicion, which prevailed in
his own times, that the emperor himself was become a convert

[1] See the Augustan History, p. 123.   [Lampr. Alex. Sever. c. 29.]
Mosheim (p. 465) seems to refine too much on the domestic religion of
Alexander.   His design of building a public temple to Christ (Hist. August.
p. 129 [Lampr. Alex. Sever. c. 43]), and the objection which was suggested
either to him, or in similar circumstances to Hadrian, appear to have no
other foundation than an improbable report, invented by the Christians,
and credulously adopted by an historian of the age of Constantine.

[2] Euseb. l. vi. c. 28.   It may be presumed that the success of the Christians had exasperated the increasing bigotry of the Pagans.   Dion Cassius,
who composed his history under the former reign, had most probably
intended for the use of his master those counsels of persecution which he
ascribes to a better age, and to the favourite of Augustus.   Concerning
this oration of Mæcenas, or rather of Dion, I may refer to my own unbiassed opinion (vol. i. p. 55, note 25), and to the Abbé de la Bléterie
(Mémoires de l'Académie, tom. xxiv. p. 303; tom. xxv. p. 432).
[This massacre, which lasted during the whole reign of the emperor
Maximin, has every right to be called a persecution, much more so in fact
than many of the others to which Gibbon applies the term.—O. S.]

[3] Orosius, l. vii. c. 19, mentions Origen as the object of Maximin's
resentment; and Firmilianus, a Cappadocian bishop of that age, gives a
just and confined idea of this persecution (apud Cyprian. Epist. 75).

to the faith;[1] and afforded some grounds for a fable which was afterwards invented, that he had been purified by confession and penance from the guilt contracted by the murder of his innocent predecessor.[2] The fall of Philip introduced, with the change of masters, a new system of government, so oppressive to the Christians, that their former condition, ever since the time of Domitian, was represented as a state of perfect freedom and security, if compared with the rigorous treatment which they experienced under the short reign of Decius.[3] The virtues of that prince will scarcely allow us to suspect that he was actuated by a mean resentment against the favourites of his predecessor; and it is more reasonable to believe that, in the prosecution of his general design to restore the purity of Roman manners, he was desirous of delivering the empire from what he condemned as a recent and criminal superstition. The bishops of the most considerable cities were removed by exile or death: the vigilance of the magistrates prevented the clergy of Rome during sixteen months from proceeding to a new election; and it was the opinion of the Christians that the emperor would more patiently endure a competitor for the purple than a bishop in the capital.[4] Were it possible to suppose that the penetration of Decius had discovered pride under the disguise of humility, or that he could foresee the temporal dominion which might insensibly arise from the claims of spiritual authority, we might be less surprised that he should consider the successors of St. Peter as the most formidable rivals to those of Augustus.

The administration of Valerian was distinguished by a levity and inconstancy ill suited to the gravity of the *Roman Censor*

[1] The mention of those princes who were publicly supposed to be Christians, as we find it in an epistle of Dionysius of Alexandria (ap. Euseb. l. vii. c. 10), evidently alludes to Philip and his family; and forms a contemporary evidence that such a report had prevailed; but the Egyptian bishop, who lived at an humble distance from the court of Rome, expresses himself with a becoming diffidence concerning the truth of the fact. The epistles of Origen (which were extant in the time of Eusebius, see l. vi. c. 36) would most probably decide this curious, rather than important, question.

[2] Euseb. l. vi. c. 34. The story, as is usual, has been embellished by succeeding writers, and is confuted, with much superfluous learning, by Frederick Spanheim (Opera Varia, tom. ii. p. 400, etc.).

[3] Lactantius, de Mortibus Persecutorum, c. 3, 4. After celebrating the felicity and increase of the church under a long succession of good princes, he adds, " Extitit post annos plurimos, execrabile animal, Decius, qui vexaret Ecclesiam."

[4] Euseb. l. vi. c. 39. Cyprian. Epistol. 55. The see of Rome remained vacant from the martyrdom of Fabianus, the 20th of January, A.D. 250, till the election of Cornelius, the 4th of June, A.D. 251. Decius had probably left Rome, since he was killed before the end of that year.

In the first part of his reign he surpassed in clemency those princes who had been suspected of an attachment to the Christian faith. In the last three years and a half, listening to the insinuations of a minister addicted to the superstitions of Egypt, he adopted the maxims, and imitated the severity, of his predecessor Decius.[1] The accession of Gallienus, which increased the calamities of the empire, restored peace to the church; and the Christians obtained the free exercise of their religion by an edict addressed to the bishops, and conceived in such terms as seemed to acknowledge their office and public character.[2] The ancient laws, without being formally repealed, were suffered to sink into oblivion; and (excepting only some hostile intentions which are attributed to the emperor Aurelian [3]) the disciples of Christ passed above forty years in a state of prosperity, far more dangerous to their virtue than the severest trials of persecution.

The story of Paul of Samosata, who filled the metropolitan see of Antioch while the East was in the hands of Odenathus and Zenobia, may serve to illustrate the condition and character of the times. The wealth of that prelate was a sufficient evidence of his guilt, since it was neither derived from the inheritance of his fathers, nor acquired by the arts of honest industry. But Paul considered the service of the church as a very lucrative profession.[4] His ecclesiastical jurisdiction was venal and rapacious; he extorted frequent contributions from the most opulent of the faithful, and converted to his own use a considerable part of the public revenue. By his pride and luxury the Christian religion was rendered odious in the eyes of the Gentiles. His council chamber and his throne, the splendour with which he appeared in public, the suppliant crowd who solicited his

---

[1] Euseb. l. vii. c. 10. Mosheim (p. 548) has very clearly shown that the præfect Macrianus, and the Egyptian *Magus*, are one and the same person.

[2] Eusebius (l. vii. c. 13) gives us a Greek version of this Latin edict, which seems to have been very concise. By another edict he directed that the *Cæmeteria* should be restored to the Christians.

[3] Euseb. l. vii. c. 30. Lactantius de M. P. c. 6. Hieronym. in Chron. p. 177 [Anno ab. Abr. 2290, tom. viii. p. 757, ed. Vallars.]. Orosius, l. vii. c. 23. Their language is in general so ambiguous and incorrect, that we are at a loss to determine how far Aurelian had carried his intentions before he was assassinated. Most of the moderns (except Dodwell, Dissertat. Cyprian. xi. 64) have seized the occasion of gaining a few extraordinary martyrs.

[4] Paul was better pleased with the title of *Ducenarius* than with that of bishop. The *Ducenarius* was an imperial procurator, so called from his salary of two hundred *Sestertia*, or £1600 a year. (See Salmasius ad Hist. August. p. 124.) Some critics suppose that the bishop of Antioch had actually obtained such an office from Zenobia, while others consider it only as a figurative expression of his pomp and insolence.

attention, the multitude of letters and petitions to which he dictated his answers, and the perpetual hurry of business in which he was involved, were circumstances much better suited to the state of a civil magistrate [1] than to the humility of a primitive bishop. When he harangued his people from the pulpit, Paul affected the figurative style and the theatrical gestures of an Asiatic sophist, while the cathedral resounded with the loudest and most extravagant acclamations in the praise of his divine eloquence. Against those who resisted his power, or refused to flatter his vanity, the prelate of Antioch was arrogant, rigid, and inexorable; but he relaxed the discipline, and lavished the treasures of the church on his dependent clergy, who were permitted to imitate their master in the gratification of every sensual appetite. For Paul indulged himself very freely in the pleasures of the table, and he had received into the episcopal palace two young and beautiful women, as the constant companions of his leisure moments.[2]

Notwithstanding these scandalous vices, if Paul of Samosata had preserved the purity of the orthodox faith, his reign over the capital of Syria would have ended only with his life; and had a seasonable persecution intervened, an effort of courage might perhaps have placed him in the rank of saints and martyrs. Some nice and subtle errors, which he imprudently adopted and obstinately maintained, concerning the doctrine of the Trinity, excited the zeal and indignation of the Eastern churches.[3] From Egypt to the Euxine Sea, the bishops were in arms and in motion. Several councils were held, confutations were published, excommunications were pronounced, ambiguous explanations were by turns accepted and refused, treaties were concluded and violated,

---

[1] Simony was not unknown in those times; and the clergy sometimes bought what they intended to sell. It appears that the bishopric of Carthage was purchased by a wealthy matron, named Lucilla, for her servant Majorinus. The price was 400 *Folles*. (Monument. Antiq. ad calcem Optati, p. 263.) Every *Follis* contained 125 pieces of silver, and the whole sum may be computed at about £2400.

[2] If we are desirous of extenuating the vices of Paul, we must suspect the assembled bishops of the East of publishing the most malicious calumnies in circular epistles addressed to all the churches of the empire (ap. Euseb. l. vii. c. 30).

[3] His heresy (like those of Noetus and Sabellius, in the same century) tended to confound the mysterious distinction of the divine persons. See Mosheim, p. 702, etc.

[Paul entertained an idea of attempting a union between Judaism and Christianity. Both parties, however, rejected the unnatural alliance, and Milman says the continued protection of Paul by the severe and virtuous Zenobia is the only circumstance that might raise a doubt concerning the notorious immorality of Paul.—O. S.]

and at length Paul of Samosata was degraded from his episcopal character by the sentence of seventy or eighty bishops who assembled for that purpose at Antioch, and who, without consulting the rights of the clergy or people, appointed a successor by their own authority. The manifest irregularity of this proceeding increased the numbers of the discontented faction; and as Paul, who was no stranger to the arts of courts, had insinuated himself into the favour of Zenobia, he maintained above four years the possession of the episcopal house and office. The victory of Aurelian changed the face of the East, and the two contending parties, who applied to each other the epithets of schism and heresy, were either commanded or permitted to plead their cause before the tribunal of the conqueror. This public and very singular trial affords a convincing proof that the existence, the property, the privileges, and the internal policy of the Christians, were acknowledged, if not by the laws, at least by the magistrates of the empire. As a Pagan and as a soldier, it could scarcely be expected that Aurelian should enter into the discussion, whether the sentiments of Paul or those of his adversaries were most agreeable to the true standard of the orthodox faith. His determination, however, was founded on the general principles of equity and reason. He considered the bishops of Italy as the most impartial and respectable judges among the Christians and, as soon as he was informed that they had unanimously approved the sentence of the council, he acquiesced in their opinion, and immediately gave orders that Paul should be compelled to relinquish the temporal possessions belonging to an office, of which, in the judgment of his brethren, he had been regularly deprived. But while we applaud the justice, we should not overlook the policy of Aurelian, who was desirous of restoring and cementing the dependence of the provinces on the capital, by every means which could bind the interest or prejudices of any part of his subjects.[1]

Amidst the frequent revolutions of the empire the Christians still flourished in peace and prosperity; and notwithstanding a celebrated era of martyrs has been deduced from the accession of Diocletian,[2] the new system of policy, introduced and maintained by the wisdom of that prince, continued, during more

---

[1] Euseb. Hist. Ecclesiast. l. vii. c. 30. We are entirely indebted to him for the curious story of Paul of Samosata.

[2] The era of martyrs, which is still in use among the Copts and the Abyssinians, must be reckoned from the 29th of August, A.D. 284; as the beginning of the Egyptian year was nineteen days earlier than the real accession of Diocletian. See Dissertation Préliminaire à l'Art de vérifier les Dates.

than eighteen years, to breathe the mildest and most liberal spirit of religious toleration. The mind of Diocletian himself was less adapted indeed to speculative inquiries than to the active labours of war and government. His prudence rendered him averse to any great innovation, and, though his temper was not very susceptible of zeal or enthusiasm, he always maintained an habitual regard for the ancient deities of the empire. But the leisure of the two empresses, of his wife Prisca, and of Valeria his daughter, permitted them to listen with more attention and respect to the truths of Christianity, which in every age has acknowledged its important obligations to female devotion.[1] The principal eunuchs, Lucian [2] and Dorotheus, Gorgonius and Andrew, who attended the person, possessed the favour, and governed the household of Diocletian, protected by their powerful influence the faith which they had embraced. Their example was imitated by many of the most considerable officers of the palace, who, in their respective stations, had the care of the Imperial ornaments, of the robes, of the furniture, of the jewels, and even of the private treasury; and, though it might some-times be incumbent on them to accompany the emperor when he sacrificed in the temple,[3] they enjoyed, with their wives, their children, and their slaves, the free exercise of the Christian religion. Diocletian and his colleagues frequently conferred the most important offices on those persons who avowed their abhorrence for the worship of the gods, but who had displayed abilities proper for the service of the state. The bishops held an honourable rank in their respective provinces, and were treated with distinction and respect, not only by the people, but by the magistrates themselves. Almost in every city the ancient churches were found insufficient to contain the increasing multitude of proselytes; and in their place more stately and capacious edifices were erected for the public worship of the faithful. The corruption of manners and principles, so forcibly lamented by Eusebius,[4] may be considered, not only as a

---

[1] The expression of Lactantius (de M. P. c. 15), "sacrificio pollui coegit," implies their antecedent conversion to the faith; but does not seem to justify the assertion of Mosheim (p. 912), that they had been privately baptised.

[2] M. de Tillemont (Mémoires Ecclésiastiques, tom. v. part i. p. 11, 12) has quoted from the Spicilegium of Dom Luc d'Archeri a very curious instruc-tion which bishop Theonas composed for the use of Lucian.

[3] Lactantius de M. P. c. 10.

[4] Eusebius, Hist. Ecclesiast. l. viii. c. 1. The reader who consults the original will not accuse me of heightening the picture. Eusebius was about sixteen years of age at the accession of the emperor Diocletian.

consequence, but as a proof, of the liberty which the Christians enjoyed and abused under the reign of Diocletian. Prosperity had relaxed the nerves of discipline. Fraud, envy, and malice prevailed in every congregation. The presbyters aspired to the episcopal office, which every day became an object more worthy of their ambition. The bishops, who contended with each other for ecclesiastical pre-eminence, appeared by their conduct to claim a secular and tyrannical power in the church; and the lively faith which still distinguished the Christians from the Gentiles was shown much less in their lives than in their controversial writings.

Notwithstanding this seeming security, an attentive observer might discern some symptoms that threatened the church with a more violent persecution than any which she had yet endured. The zeal and rapid progress of the Christians awakened the Polytheists from their supine indifference in the cause of those deities whom custom and education had taught them to revere. The mutual provocations of a religious war, which had already continued above two hundred years, exasperated the animosity of the contending parties. The Pagans were incensed at the rashness of a recent and obscure sect, which presumed to accuse their countrymen of error, and to devote their ancestors to eternal misery. The habits of justifying the popular mythology against the invectives of an implacable enemy, produced in their minds some sentiments of faith and reverence for a system which they had been accustomed to consider with the most careless levity. The supernatural powers assumed by the church inspired at the same time terror and emulation. The followers of the established religion intrenched themselves behind a similar fortification of prodigies; invented new modes of sacrifice, of expiation, and of initiation;[1] attempted to revive the credit of their expiring oracles;[2] and listened with eager credulity to every impostor who flattered their prejudices by a tale of wonders.[3] Both

[1] We might quote, among a great number of instances, the mysterious worship of Mithras and the Taurobolia; the latter of which became fashionable in the time of the Antonines (see a Dissertation of M. de Boze, in the Mémoires de l'Académie des Inscriptions, tom. ii. p. 443). The romance of Apuleius is as full of devotion as of satire.

[2] The impostor Alexander very strongly recommended the oracle of Trophonius at Mallos, and those of Apollo at Claros and Miletus (Lucian, tom. ii. p. 236, edit. Reitz [Alexand. c. 29]). The last of these, whose singular history would furnish a very curious episode, was consulted by Diocletian before he published his edicts of persecution (Lactantius de M. P. c. 11).

[3] Besides the ancient stories of Pythagoras and Aristeas, the cures performed at the shrine of Æsculapius, and the fables related of Apollonius of

parties seemed to acknowledge the truth of those miracles which were claimed by their adversaries; and while they were contented with ascribing them to the arts of magic, and to the power of dæmons, they mutually concurred in restoring and establishing the reign of superstition.[1] Philosophy, her most dangerous enemy, was now converted into her most useful ally. The groves of the Academy, the gardens of Epicurus, and even the portico of the Stoics, were almost deserted, as so many different schools of scepticism or impiety;[2] and many among the Romans were desirous that the writings of Cicero should be condemned and suppressed by the authority of the senate.[3] The prevailing sect of the new Platonicians judged it prudent to connect themselves with the priests, whom perhaps they despised, against the Christians, whom they had reason to fear. These fashionable philosophers prosecuted the design of extracting allegorical wisdom from the fictions of the Greek poets; instituted mysterious rites of devotion for the use of their chosen disciples; recommended the worship of the ancient gods as the emblems or ministers of the Supreme Deity, and composed against the faith of the Gospel many elaborate treatises,[4] which have since been committed to the flames by the prudence of orthodox emperors.[5]

Although the policy of Diocletian and the humanity of Constantius inclined them to preserve inviolate the maxims of toleration, it was soon discovered that their two associates, Maximian

Tyana, were frequently opposed to the miracles of Christ; though I agree with Dr. Lardner (see Testimonies, vol. iii. p. 253, 352), that, when Philostratus composed the Life of Apollonius, he had no such intention.

[1] It is seriously to be lamented that the Christian fathers, by acknowledging the supernatural, or, as they deem it, the infernal part of Paganism, destroy with their own hands the great advantage which we might otherwise derive from the liberal concessions of our adversaries.

[2] Julian ([tom. i.] p. 301, edit. Spanheim) expresses a pious joy that the providence of the gods had extinguished the impious sects, and for the most part destroyed the books of the Pyrrhonians and Epicureans, which had been very numerous, since Epicurus himself composed no less than 300 volumes. See Diogenes Laertius, l. x. c. 26.

[3] Cumque alios audiam mussitare indignanter, et dicere opportere statui per Senatum, aboleantur ut hæc scripta, quibus Christiana Religio comprobetur, et vetustatis opprimatur auctoritas. Arnobius adversus Gentes, l. iii. p. 103, 104, [p. 98, 99, ed. Ant. 1604]. He adds very properly, Erroris convincite Ciceronem . . . nam intercipere scripta, et publicatam velle submergere lectionem, non est Deum [Deos] defendere sed veritatis testificationem timere.

[4] Lactantius (Divin. Institut. l. v. c. 2, 3) gives a very clear and spirited account of two of these philosophic adversaries of the faith. The large treatise of Porphyry against the Christians consisted of thirty books, and was composed in Sicily about the year 270.

[5] See Socrates, Hist. Ecclesiast, l. i. c. 9, and Codex Justinian. l. i. tit i. l. 3.

and Galerius, entertained the most implacable aversion for the
name and religion of the Christians. The minds of those princes
had never been enlightened by science; education had never
softened their temper. They owed their greatness to their
swords, and in their most elevated fortune they still retained their
superstitious prejudices of soldiers and peasants. In the general
administration of the provinces they obeyed the laws which their
benefactor had established; but they frequently found occasions
of exercising within their camp and palaces a secret persecution,[1]
for which the imprudent zeal of the Christians sometimes offered
the most specious pretences. A sentence of death was executed
upon Maximilianus, an African youth, who had been produced
by his own father before the magistrate as a sufficient and legal
recruit, but who obstinately persisted in declaring that his conscience would not permit him to embrace the profession of a
soldier.[2] It could scarcely be expected that any government
should suffer the action of Marcellus the centurion to pass with
impunity. On the day of a public festival, that officer threw
away his belt, his arms, and the ensigns of his office, and exclaimed with a loud voice that he would obey none but Jesus
Christ the eternal King, and that he renounced for ever the use
of carnal weapons, and the service of an idolatrous master. The
soldiers, as soon as they recovered from their astonishment,
secured the person of Marcellus. He was examined in the city
of Tingi by the president of that part of Mauritania; and as he
was convicted by his own confession, he was condemned and
beheaded for the crime of desertion.[3] Examples of such a
nature savour much less of religious persecution than of martial
or even civil law: but they served to alienate the mind of the
emperors, to justify the severity of Galerius, who dismissed a
great number of Christian officers from their employments; and to

---

[1] Eusebius, l. viii. c. 4, c. 17. He limits the number of military martyrs,
by a remarkable expression (σπανίως τούτων εἶς που καὶ δεύτερος), of
which neither his Latin nor French translator have rendered the energy.
Notwithstanding the authority of Eusebius, and the silence of Lactantius,
Ambrose, Sulpicius, Orosius, etc., it has been long believed that the
Thebæan legion, consisting of 6000 Christians, suffered martyrdom by the
order of Maximian, in the valley of the Pennine Alps. The story was first
published about the middle of the fifth century, by Eucherius bishop of
Lyons, who received it from certain persons, who received it from Isaac
bishop of Geneva, who is said to have received it from Theodore bishop of
Octodurum. The abbey of St. Maurice still subsists, a rich monument of
the credulity of Sigismund, king of Burgundy. See an excellent Dissertation in the thirty-sixth volume of the Bibliothèque Raisonnée, p. 427-454.
[2] See the Acta Sincera, p. 299. The accounts of his martyrdom, and of
that of Marcellus, bear every mark of truth and authenticity.
[3] Acta Sincera, p. 302.

authorise the opinion that a sect of enthusiasts, which avowed principles so repugnant to the public safety, must either remain useless, or would soon become dangerous subjects of the empire.

After the success of the Persian war had raised the hopes and the reputation of Galerius, he passed a winter with Diocletian in the palace of Nicomedia; and the fate of Christianity became the object of their secret consultations.[1] The experienced emperor was still inclined to pursue measures of lenity; and though he readily consented to exclude the Christians from holding any employments in the household or the army, he urged in the strongest terms the danger as well as cruelty of shedding the blood of those deluded fanatics. Galerius at length extorted from him the permission of summoning a council, composed of a few persons the most distinguished in the civil and military departments of the state. The important question was agitated in their presence, and those ambitious courtiers easily discerned that it was incumbent on them to second, by their eloquence, the importunate violence of the Cæsar. It may be presumed that they insisted on every topic which might interest the pride, the piety, or the fears, of their sovereign in the destruction of Christianity. Perhaps they represented that the glorious work of the deliverance of the empire was left imperfect, as long as an independent people was permitted to subsist and multiply in the heart of the provinces. The Christians (it might speciously be alleged), renouncing the gods and the institutions of Rome, had constituted a distinct republic, which might yet be suppressed before it had acquired any military force; but which was already governed by its own laws and magistrates, was possessed of a public treasure, and was intimately connected in all its parts by the frequent assemblies of the bishops, to whose decrees their numerous and opulent congregations yielded an implicit obedience. Arguments like these may seem to have determined the reluctant mind of Diocletian to embrace a new system of persecution: but though we may suspect, it is not in our power to relate, the secret intrigues of the palace, the private views and resentments, the jealousy of women or eunuchs, and all those trifling but decisive causes which so often influence the fate of empires and the councils of the wisest monarchs.[2]

[1] De M. P. c. 11. Lactantius (or whoever was the author of this little treatise) was, at that time, an inhabitant of Nicomedia; but it seems difficult to conceive how he could acquire so accurate a knowledge of what passed in the Imperial cabinet.

[2] The only circumstance which we can discover is the devotion and jealousy of the mother of Galerius. She is described by Lactantius as

The pleasure of the emperors was at length signified to the Christians, who, during the course of this melancholy winter, had expected, with anxiety, the result of so many secret consultations. The twenty-third of February, which coincided with the Roman festival of the Terminalia,[1] was appointed (whether from accident or design) to set bounds to the progress of Christianity. At the earliest dawn of day the Prætorian præfect,[2] accompanied by several generals, tribunes, and officers of the revenue, repaired to the principal church of Nicomedia, which was situated on an eminence in the most populous and beautiful part of the city. The doors were instantly broke open; they rushed into the sanctuary; and as they searched in vain for some visible object of worship, they were obliged to content themselves with committing to the flames the volumes of Holy Scripture. The ministers of Diocletian were followed by a numerous body of guards and pioneers, who marched in order of battle, and were provided with all the instruments used in the destruction of fortified cities. By their incessant labour, a sacred edifice, which towered above the Imperial palace, and had long excited the indignation and envy of the Gentiles, was in a few hours levelled with the ground.[3]

The next day the general edict of persecution was published;[4] and though Diocletian, still averse to the effusion of blood, had moderated the fury of Galerius, who proposed that every one refusing to offer sacrifice should immediately be burnt alive, the penalties inflicted on the obstinacy of the Christians might be deemed sufficiently rigorous and effectual. It was enacted that their churches, in all the provinces of the empire, should be demolished to their foundations; and the punishment of death was denounced against all who should presume to hold any secret assemblies for the purpose of religious worship. The philosophers, who now assumed the unworthy office of directing the blind zeal of persecution, had diligently studied the nature and

Deorum montium cultrix; mulier admodum superstitiosa. She had a great influence over her son, and was offended by the disregard of some of her Christian servants.

[1] The worship and festival of the god Terminus are elegantly illustrated by M. de Boze, Mém. de l'Académie des Inscriptions, tom. i. p. 50.

[2] In our only MS. of Lactantius we read *profectus* ; but reason, and the authority of all the critics, allow us, instead of that word, which destroys the sense of the passage, to substitute *præfectus*.

[3] Lactantius, de M. P. c. 12, gives a very lively picture of the destruction of the church.

[4] Mosheim (p. 922-926), from many scattered passages of Lactantius and Eusebius, has collected a very just and accurate notion of this edict; though he sometimes deviates into conjecture and refinement.

genius of the Christian religion; and as they were not ignorant that the speculative doctrines of the faith were supposed to be contained in the writings of the prophets, of the evangelists, and of the apostles, they most probably suggested the order that the bishops and presbyters should deliver all their sacred books into the hands of the magistrates; who were commanded, under the severest penalties, to burn them in a public and solemn manner. By the same edict, the property of the church was at once confiscated; and the several parts of which it might consist were either sold to the highest bidder, united to the Imperial domain, bestowed on the cities and corporations, or granted to the solicitations of rapacious courtiers. After taking such effectual measures to abolish the worship and to dissolve the government of the Christians, it was thought necessary to subject to the most intolerable hardships the condition of those perverse individuals who should still reject the religion of nature, of Rome, and of their ancestors. Persons of a liberal birth were declared incapable of holding any honours or employments; slaves were for ever deprived of the hopes of freedom; and the whole body of the people were put out of the protection of the law. The judges were authorised to hear and to determine every action that was brought against a Christian. But the Christians were not permitted to complain of any injury which they themselves had suffered; and thus those unfortunate sectaries were exposed to the severity, while they were excluded from the benefits, of public justice. This new species of martyrdom, so painful and lingering, so obscure and ignominious, was, perhaps, the most proper to weary the constancy of the faithful: nor can it be doubted that the passions and interest of mankind were disposed on this occasion to second the designs of the emperors. But the policy of a well-ordered government must sometimes have interposed in behalf of the oppressed Christians; nor was it possible for the Roman princes entirely to remove the apprehension of punishment, or to connive at every act of fraud and violence, without exposing their own authority and the rest of their subjects to the most alarming dangers.[1]

This edict was scarcely exhibited to the public view, in the most conspicuous place of Nicomedia, before it was torn down by the hands of a Christian, who expressed at the same time, by the bitterest invectives, his contempt as well as abhorrence for

[1] Many ages afterwards Edward I. practised, with great success, the same mode of persecution against the clergy of England. See Hume's History of England, vol. ii. p. 300, last 4to edition.

such impious and tyrannical governors. His offence, according to the mildest laws, amounted to treason, and deserved death. And if it be true that he was a person of rank and education, those circumstances could serve only to aggravate his guilt. He was burnt, or rather roasted, by a slow fire; and his executioners, zealous to revenge the personal insult which had been offered to the emperors, exhausted every refinement of cruelty, without being able to subdue his patience, or to alter the steady and insulting smile which, in his dying agonies, he still preserved in his countenance. The Christians, though they confessed that his conduct had not been strictly conformable to the laws of prudence, admired the divine fervour of his zeal; and the excessive commendations which they lavished on the memory of their hero and martyr contributed to fix a deep impression of terror and hatred in the mind of Diocletian.[1]

His fears were soon alarmed by the view of a danger from which he very narrowly escaped. Within fifteen days the palace of Nicomedia, and even the bedchamber of Diocletian, were twice in flames; and though both times they were extinguished without any material damage, the singular repetition of the fire was justly considered as an evident proof that it had not been the effect of chance or negligence. The suspicion naturally fell on the Christians; and it was suggested, with some degree of probability, that those desperate fanatics, provoked by their present sufferings, and apprehensive of impending calamities, had entered into a conspiracy with their faithful brethren, the eunuchs of the palace, against the lives of two emperors whom they detested as the irreconcilable enemies of the church of God. Jealousy and resentment prevailed in every breast, but especially in that of Diocletian. A great number of persons, distinguished either by the offices which they had filled or by the favour which they had enjoyed, were thrown into prison. Every mode of torture was put in practice, and the court, as well as city, was polluted with many bloody executions.[2] But as it was found impossible to extort any discovery of this

---

[1] Lactantius only calls him quidam, etsi non recte, magno tamen animo, etc., M. P. c. 13. Eusebius (l. viii. c. 5) adorns him with secular honours. Neither have condescended to mention his name; but the Greeks celebrate his memory under that of John. See Tillemont, Mémoires Ecclésiastiques, tom. v. part ii. p. 320.

[2] Lactantius de M. P. c. 13, 14 [14, 15]. Potentissimi quondam Eunuchi necati, per quos Palatium et ipse constabat. Eusebius (l. viii. c 6) mentions the cruel executions of the eunuchs Gorgonius and Dorotheus, and of Anthimus bishop of Nicomedia; and both those writers describe, in a vague but tragical manner, the horrid scenes which were acted even in the Imperial presence.

mysterious transaction, it seems incumbent on us either to presume the innocence, or to admire the resolution, of the sufferers. A few days afterwards Galerius hastily withdrew himself from Nicomedia, declaring that, if he delayed his departure from that devoted palace, he should fall a sacrifice to the rage of the Christians. The ecclesiastical historians, from whom alone we derive a partial and imperfect knowledge of this persecution, are at a loss how to account for the fears and danger of the emperors. Two of these writers, a prince and a rhetorician, were eye-witnesses of the fire of Nicomedia. The one ascribes it to lightning and the divine wrath, the other affirms that it was kindled by the malice of Galerius himself.[1]

As the edict against the Christians was designed for a general law of the whole empire, and as Diocletian and Galerius, though they might not wait for the consent, were assured of the concurrence, of the Western princes, it would appear more consonant to our ideas of policy that the governors of all the provinces should have received secret instructions to publish, on one and the same day, this declaration of war within their respective departments. It was at least to be expected that the convenience of the public highways and established posts would have enabled the emperors to transmit their orders with the utmost despatch from the palace of Nicomedia to the extremities of the Roman world; and that they would not have suffered fifty days to elapse before the edict was published in Syria, and near four months before it was signified to the cities of Africa.[2] This delay may perhaps be imputed to the cautious temper of Diocletian, who had yielded a reluctant consent to the measures of persecution, and who was desirous of trying the experiment under his more immediate eye before he gave way to the disorders and discontent which it must inevitably occasion in the distant provinces. At first, indeed, the magistrates were restrained from the effusion of blood; but the use of every other severity was permitted, and even recommended to their zeal; nor could the Christians, though they cheerfully resigned the ornaments of

---

[1] See Lactantius, Eusebius, and Constantine, ad Cœtum Sanctorum, c. xxv. Eusebius confesses his ignorance of the cause of this fire.

[There is no instance in the history of these times of the Christians turning on their persecutors; we have therefore not the slightest reason to attribute to them the fire in the palace of Diocletian in Nicomedia. Had it been done by a Christian, says M. de Tillemont, it would probably have been a fanatic who would have gloried in the deed and published it. The fire was doubtless caused by lightning, and was fed and increased by the malice of Galerius.—O. S.]

[2] Tillemont, Mémoires, Ecclésiast. tom. v. part i. p. 43.

their churches, resolve to interrupt their religious assemblies, or
to deliver their sacred books to the flames. The pious obstinacy
of Felix, an African bishop, appears to have embarrassed the
subordinate ministers of the government. The curator of his
city sent him in chains to the proconsul. The proconsul transmitted him to the Prætorian præfect of Italy; and Felix, who
disdained even to give an evasive answer, was a length beheaded
at Venusia, in Lucania, a place on which the birth of Horace has
conferred fame.[1] This precedent, and perhaps some Imperial
rescript, which was issued in consequence of it, appeared to
authorise the governors of provinces in punishing with death
the refusal of the Christians to deliver up their sacred books.
There were undoubtedly many persons who embraced this opportunity of obtaining the crown of martyrdom; but there were
likewise too many who purchased an ignominious life by dis-
covering and betraying the Holy Scripture into the hands of
infidels. A great number even of bishops and presbyters
acquired, by this criminal compliance, the opprobrious epithet
of *Traditors ;* and their offence was productive of much present
scandal and of much future discord in the African church.[2]

The copies as well as the versions of Scripture were already so
multiplied in the empire, that the most severe inquisition could
no longer be attended with any fatal consequences; and even
the sacrifice of those volumes which, in every congregation, were
preserved for public use, required the consent of some treacherous
and unworthy Christians. But the ruin of the churches was
easily effected by the authority of the government and by the
labour of the Pagans. In some provinces, however, the magistrates contented themselves with shutting up the places of
religious worship. In others they more literally complied with
the terms of the edict; and, after taking away the doors, the
benches, and the pulpit, which they burnt as it were in a funeral
pile, they completely demolished the remainder of the edifice.[3]
It is perhaps to this melancholy occasion that we should apply

[1] See the Acta Sincera of Ruinart, p. 353; those of Felix of Thibara, or
Tibiur, appear much less corrupted than in the other editions, which afford
a lively specimen of legendary licence.

[2] See the first book of Optatus of Milevis against the Donatists. Paris,
1700, edit. Dupin. He lived under the reign of Valens.

[3] The ancient monuments, published at the end of Optatus, p. 261, etc.,
describe, in a very circumstantial manner, the proceedings of the governors
in the destruction of churches. They made a minute inventory of the plate,
etc., which they found in them. That of the church of Cirta, in Numidia,
is still extant. It consisted of two chalices of gold and six of silver; six
urns, one kettle, seven lamps, all likewise of silver; besides a large quantity
of brass utensils and wearing apparel.

a very remarkable story, which is related with so many circumstances of variety and improbability that it serves rather to excite than to satisfy our curiosity. In a small town in Phrygia, of whose name as well as situation we are left ignorant, it should seem that the magistrates and the body of the people had embraced the Christian faith; and as some resistance might be apprehended to the execution of the edict, the governor of the province was supported by a numerous detachment of legionaries. On their approach the citizens threw themselves into the church, with the resolution either of defending by arms that sacred edifice or of perishing in its ruins. They indignantly rejected the notice and permission which was given them to retire, till the soldiers, provoked by their obstinate refusal, set fire to the building on all sides, and consumed, by this extraordinary kind of martyrdom, a great number of Phrygians, with their wives and children.[1]

Some slight disturbances, though they were suppressed almost as soon as excited, in Syria and the frontiers of Armenia, afforded the enemies of the church a very plausible occasion to insinuate that those troubles had been secretly fomented by the intrigues of the bishops, who had already forgotten their ostentatious professions of passive and unlimited obedience.[2] The resentment, or the fears, of Diocletian at length transported him beyond the bounds of moderation which he had hitherto preserved, and he declared, in a series of cruel edicts, his intention of abolishing the Christian name. By the first of these edicts the governors of the provinces were directed to apprehend all persons of the ecclesiastical order; and the prisons destined for the vilest criminals were soon filled with a multitude of bishops, presbyters, deacons, readers, and exorcists. By a second edict the magistrates were commanded to employ every method of severity which might reclaim them from their odious super-

---

[1] Lactantius (Institut. Divin. v. 11) confines the calamity to the *conventiculum*, with its congregation. Eusebius (viii. 11) extends it to a whole city, and introduces something very like a regular siege. His ancient Latin translator, Rufinus, adds the important circumstance of the permission given to the inhabitants of retiring from thence. As Phrygia reached to the confines of Isauria, it is possible that the restless temper of those independent barbarians may have contributed to this misfortune.

[2] Eusebius, l. viii. c. 6. M. de Valois (with some probability) thinks that he has discovered the Syrian rebellion in an oration of Libanius; and that it was a rash attempt of the tribune Eugenius, who with only five hundred men seized Antioch, and might perhaps allure the Christians by the promise of religious toleration. From Eusebius (l. ix. c. 8), as well as from Moses of Chorene (Hist. Armen. l. ii. 77, etc.), it may be inferred that Christianity was already introduced into Armenia.

stition, and oblige them to return to the established worship of the gods. This rigorous order was extended, by a subsequent edict, to the whole body of Christians, who were exposed to a violent and general persecution.[1] Instead of those salutary restraints which had required the direct and solemn testimony of an accuser, it became the duty as well as the interest of the Imperial officers to discover, to pursue, and to torment the most obnoxious among the faithful. Heavy penalties were denounced against all who should presume to save a proscribed sectary from the just indignation of the gods and of the emperors. Yet, notwithstanding the severity of this law, the virtuous courage of many of the Pagans, in concealing their friends or relations, affords an honourable proof that the rage of superstition had not extinguished in their minds the sentiments of nature and humanity.[2]

Diocletian had no sooner published his edicts against the Christians than, as if he had been desirous of committing to other hands the work of persecution, he divested himself of the Imperial purple. The character and situation of his colleagues and successors sometimes urged them to enforce, and sometimes inclined them to suspend, the execution of these rigorous laws; nor can we acquire a just and distinct idea of this important period of ecclesiastical history unless we separately consider the state of Christianity, in the different parts of the empire, during the space of ten years which elapsed between the first edicts of Diocletian and the final peace of the church.

The mild and humane temper of Constantius was averse to the oppression of any part of his subjects. The principal offices of his palace were exercised by Christians. He loved their persons, esteemed their fidelity, and entertained not any dislike to their religious principles. But as long as Constantius remained in the subordinate station of Cæsar, it was not in his power openly to reject the edicts of Diocletian, or to disobey the commands of Maximian. His authority contributed, however, to alleviate the sufferings which he pitied and abhorred. He consented with reluctance to the ruin of the churches, but he ventured to protect the Christians themselves from the fury of the populace and from the rigour of the laws. The provinces of Gaul (under which we may probably include those of Britain)

---

[1] See Mosheim, p. 938; the text of Eusebius very plainly shows that the governors, whose powers were enlarged, not restrained, by the new laws, could punish with death the most obstinate Christians as an example to their brethren.

[2] Athanasius, p. 833, ap. Tillemont, Mém. Ecclésiast. tom. v. part i. p. 90.

were indebted for the singular tranquillity which they enjoyed
to the gentle interposition of their sovereign.[1] But Datianus,
the president or governor of Spain, actuated either by zeal or
policy, chose rather to execute the public edicts of the emperors
than to understand the secret intentions of Constantius; and it
can scarcely be doubted that his provincial administration was
stained with the blood of a few martyrs.[2] The elevation of Con
stantius to the supreme and independent dignity of Augustus
gave a free scope to the exercise of his virtues, and the shortness
of his reign did not prevent him from establishing a system of
toleration of which he left the precept and the example to his
son Constantine. His fortunate son, from the first moment of
his accession declaring himself the protector of the church, at
length deserved the appellation of the first emperor who publicly
professed and established the Christian religion. The motives
of his conversion, as they may variously be deduced from benevolence, from policy, from conviction, or from remorse, and the
progress of the revolution, which, under his powerful influence
and that of his sons, rendered Christianity the reigning religion
of the Roman empire, will form a very interesting and important
chapter in the second volume of this history. At present it may
be sufficient to observe that every victory of Constantine was
productive of some relief or benefit to the church.

The provinces of Italy and Africa experienced a short but
violent persecution. The rigorous edicts of Diocletian were
strictly and cheerfully executed by his associate Maximian, who
had long hated the Christians, and who delighted in acts of blood
and violence. In the autumn of the first year of the persecution
the two emperors met at Rome to celebrate their triumph;
several oppressive laws appear to have issued from their secret
consultations, and the diligence of the magistrates was animated
by the presence of their sovereigns. After Diocletian had divested
himself of the purple, Italy and Africa were administered under

[1] Eusebius, l. viii. c. 13. Lactantius de M. P. c. 15. Dodwell (Dissertat.
Cyprian. xi. 75) represents them as inconsistent with each other. But the
former evidently speaks of Constantius in the station of Cæsar, and the
latter of the same prince in the rank of Augustus.

[2] Datianus is mentioned in Gruter's Inscriptions as having determined
the limits between the territories of Pax Julia and those of Ebora, both
cities in the southern part of Lusitania. If we recollect the neighbourhood
of those places to Cape St. Vincent, we may suspect that the celebrated
deacon and martyr of that name has been inaccurately assigned by Prudentius, etc., to Saragossa or Valentia. See the pompous history of his sufferings, in the Mémoires de Tillemont, tom. v. part ii. p. 58-85. Some
critics are of opinion that the department of Constantius, as Cæsar, did
not include Spain, which still continued under the immediate jurisdiction
of Maximian.

the name of Severus, and were exposed, without defence, to the
implacable resentment of his master Galerius. Among the
martyrs of Rome, Adauctus deserves the notice of posterity.
He was of a noble family in Italy, and had raised himself,
through the successive honours of the palace, to the important
office of treasurer of the private demesnes. Adauctus is the
more remarkable for being the only person of rank and distinction who appears to have suffered death during the whole course
of this general persecution.[1]

The revolt of Maxentius immediately restored peace to the
churches of Italy and Africa, and the same tyrant who oppressed
every other class of his subjects showed himself just, humane,
and even partial, towards the afflicted Christians. He depended
on their gratitude and affection, and very naturally presumed
that the injuries which they had suffered, and the dangers which
they still apprehended, from his most inveterate enemy, would
secure the fidelity of a party already considerable by their
numbers and opulence.[2] Even the conduct of Maxentius
towards the bishops of Rome and Carthage may be considered
as the proof of his toleration, since it is probable that the most
orthodox princes would adopt the same measures with regard to
their established clergy. Marcellus, the former of those prelates,
had thrown the capital into confusion by the severe penance
which he imposed on a great number of Christians who, during
the late persecution, had renounced or dissembled their religion.
The rage of faction broke out in frequent and violent seditions;
the blood of the faithful was shed by each other's hands; and
the exile of Marcellus, whose prudence seems to have been less
eminent than his zeal, was found to be the only measure capable
of restoring peace to the distracted church of Rome.[3] The

[1] Eusebius, l. viii. c. 11.   Gruter, Inscrip. p. 1171, No. 18.   Rufinus has
mistaken the office of Adauctus, as well as the place of his martyrdom.

[2] Eusebius, l. viii. c. 14.   But as Maxentius was vanquished by Constantine, it suited the purpose of Lactantius to place his death among those
of the persecutors.

[3] The epitaph of Marcellus is to be found in Gruter, Inscrip. p. 1172,
No. 3, and it contains all that we know of his history.   Marcellinus and
Marcellus, whose names follow in the list of popes, are supposed by many
critics to be different persons; but the learned Abbé de Longuerue was
convinced that they were one and the same.

> Veridicus rector lapsis quia crimina flere
> Prædixit miseris, fuit omnibus hostis amarus.
> Hinc furor, hinc odium; sequitur discordia, lites,
> Seditio, cædes; solvuntur fœdera pacis.
> Crimen ob alterius, Christum qui in pace negavit
> Finibus expulsus patriæ est feritate Tyranni.
> Hæc breviter Damasus voluit comperta referre:
> Marcelli populus meritum cognoscere posset.

We may observe that Damasus was made bishop of Rome A.D. 366.

behaviour of Mensurius, bishop of Carthage, appears to have been still more reprehensible. A deacon of that city had published a libel against the emperor. The offender took refuge in the episcopal palace, and, though it was somewhat early to advance any claims of ecclesiastical immunities, the bishop refused to deliver him up to the officers of justice. For this treasonable resistance Mensurius was summoned to court, and, instead of receiving a legal sentence of death or banishment, he was permitted, after a short examination, to return to his diocese.[1] Such was the happy condition of the Christian subjects of Maxentius, that, whenever they were desirous of procuring for their own use any bodies of martyrs, they were obliged to purchase them from the most distant provinces of the East. A story is related of Aglae, a Roman lady, descended from a consular family, and possessed of so ample an estate that it required the management of seventy-three stewards. Among these Boniface was the favourite of his mistress, and, as Aglae mixed love with devotion, it is reported that he was admitted to share her bed. Her fortune enabled her to gratify the pious desire of obtaining some sacred relics from the East. She intrusted Boniface with a considerable some of gold and a large quantity of aromatics, and her lover, attended by twelve horsemen and three covered chariots, undertook a remote pilgrimage as far as Tarsus in Cilicia.[2]

The sanguinary temper of Galerius, the first and principal author of the persecution, was formidable to those Christians whom their misfortunes had placed within the limits of his dominions; and it may fairly be presumed that many persons of a middle rank, who were not confined by the chains either of wealth or of poverty, very frequently deserted their native country, and sought a refuge in the milder climate of the West. As long as he commanded only the armies and provinces of Illyricum, he could with difficulty either find or make a considerable number of martyrs in a warlike country which had entertained the missionaries of the Gospel with more coldness and reluctance than any other part of the empire.[3] But when

[1] Optatus contr. Donatist. l. i. c. 17, 18.
[2] The Acts of the Passion of St. Boniface, which abound in miracles and declamation, are published by Ruinart (p. 283-291), both in Greek and Latin, from the authority of very ancient manuscripts.
[3] During the four first centuries there exist few traces of either bishops or bishoprics in the western Illyricum. It has been thought probable that the primate of Milan extended his jurisdiction over Sirmium, the capital of that great province. See the Geographia Sacra of Charles de St. Paul, p. 68-76, with the observations of Lucas Holstenius.

Galerius had obtained the supreme power and the government of the East, he indulged in their fullest extent his zeal and cruelty, not only in the provinces of Thrace and Asia, which acknowledged his immediate jurisdiction, but in those of Syria, Palestine, and Egypt, where Maximin gratified his own inclination by yielding a rigorous obedience to the stern commands of his benefactor.[1]

The frequent disappointments of his ambitious views, the experience of six years of persecution, and the salutary reflections which a lingering and painful distemper suggested to the mind of Galerius, at length convinced him that the most violent efforts of despotism are insufficient to extirpate a whole people, or to subdue their religious prejudices. Desirous of repairing the mischief that he had occasioned, he published in his own name, and in those of Licinius and Constantine, a general edict, which, after a pompous recital of the Imperial titles, proceeded in the following manner:

" Among the important cares which have occupied our mind for the utility and preservation of the empire, it was our intention to correct and re-establish all things according to the ancient laws and public discipline of the Romans. We were particularly desirous of reclaiming into the way of reason and nature the deluded Christians who had renounced the religion and ceremonies instituted by their fathers, and, presumptuously despising the practice of antiquity, had invented extravagant laws and opinions according to the dictates of their fancy, and had collected a various society from the different provinces of our empire. The edicts which we have published to enforce the worship of the gods having exposed many of the Christians to danger and distress, many having suffered death, and many more, who still persist in their impious folly, being left destitute of *any* public exercise of religion, we are disposed to extend to those unhappy men the effects of our wonted clemency. We permit them, therefore, freely to profess their private opinions, and to assemble in their conventicles without fear or molestation, provided always that they preserve a due respect to the established laws and government. By another rescript we shall signify our intentions to the judges and magistrates, and we hope that our indulgence will engage the Christians to offer up their prayers to the Deity whom they adore for our safety and pros-

[1] The eighth book of Eusebius, as well as the supplement concerning the martyrs of Palestine, principally relate to the persecution of Galerius and Maximin. The general lamentations with which Lactantius opens the fifth book of his Divine Institutions allude to their cruelty.

perity, for their own, and for that of the republic." [1] It is not usually in the language of edicts and manifestos that we should search for the real character of the secret motives of princes; but as these were the words of a dying emperor, his situation, perhaps, may be admitted as a pledge of his sincerity.

When Galerius subscribed this edict of toleration, he was well assured that Licinius would readily comply with the inclinations of his friend and benefactor, and that any measures in favour of the Christians would obtain the approbation of Constantine. But the emperor would not venture to insert in the preamble the name of Maximin, whose consent was of the greatest importance, and who succeeded a few days afterwards to the provinces of Asia. In the first six months, however, of his new reign, Maximin affected to adopt the prudent counsels of his predecessor; and though he never condescended to secure the tranquillity of the church by a public edict, Sabinus, his Prætorian præfect, addressed a circular letter to all the governors and magistrates of the provinces, expatiating on the Imperial clemency, acknowledging the invincible obstinacy of the Christians, and directing the officers of justice to cease their ineffectual prosecutions, and to connive at the secret assemblies of those enthusiasts. In consequence of these orders, great numbers of Christians were released from prison, or delivered from the mines. The confessors, singing hymns of triumph, returned into their own countries, and those who had yielded to the violence of the tempest, solicited with tears of repentance their re-admission into the bosom of the church. [2]

But this treacherous calm was of short duration; nor could the Christians of the East place any confidence in the character of their sovereign. Cruelty and superstition were the ruling passions of the soul of Maximin. The former suggested the means, the latter pointed out the objects, of persecution. The emperor was devoted to the worship of the gods, to the study of magic, and to the belief of oracles. The prophets or philosophers, whom he revered as the favourites of Heaven, were frequently raised to the government of provinces, and admitted into his most secret councils. They easily convinced him that the Christians had been indebted for their victories to their regular discipline, and that the weakness of polytheism had

---

[1] Eusebius (l. viii. c. 17) has given us a Greek version, and Lactantius (de M. P. c. 34) the Latin original, of this memorable edict. Neither of these writers seems to recollect how directly it contradicts whatever they have just affirmed of the remorse and repentance of Galerius.

[2] Eusebius, l. ix. c. 1. He inserts the epistle of the præfect.

principally flowed from a want of union and subordination among the ministers of religion. A system of government was therefore instituted, which was evidently copied from the policy of the church. In all the great cities of the empire, the temples were repaired and beautified by the order of Maximin, and the officiating priests of the various deities were subjected to the authority of a superior pontiff destined to oppose the bishop, and to promote the cause of paganism. These pontiffs acknowledged, in their turn, the supreme jurisdiction of the metropolitans or high priests of the province, who acted as the immediate vicegerents of the emperor himself. A white robe was the ensign of their dignity; and these new prelates were carefully selected from the most noble and opulent families. By the influence of the magistrates, and of the sacerdotal order, a great number of dutiful addresses were obtained, particularly from the cities of Nicomedia, Antioch, and Tyre, which artfully represented the well-known intentions of the court as the general sense of the people; solicited the emperor to consult the laws of justice rather than the dictates of his clemency; expressed their abhorrence of the Christians, and humbly prayed that those impious sectaries might at least be excluded from the limits of their respective territories. The answer of Maximin to the address which he obtained from the citizens of Tyre is still extant. He praises their zeal and devotion in terms of the highest satisfaction, descants on the obstinate impiety of the Christians, and betrays, by the readiness with which he consents to their banishment, that he considered himself as receiving, rather than as conferring, an obligation. The priests as well as the magistrates were empowered to enforce the execution of his edicts, which were engraved on tables of brass; and though it was recommended to them to avoid the effusion of blood, the most cruel and ignominious punishments were inflicted on the refractory Christians.[1]

The Asiatic Christians had everything to dread from the severity of a bigoted monarch who prepared his measures of violence with such deliberate policy. But a few months had scarcely elapsed before the edicts published by the two Western emperors obliged Maximin to suspend the prosecution of his designs: the civil war which he so rashly undertook against Licinius employed all his attention; and the defeat and death

[1] See Eusebius, l. viii. c. 14, l. ix. c. 2-8. Lactantius de M. P. c. 36. These writers agree in representing the arts of Maximin: but the former relates the execution of several martyrs, while the latter expressly affirms, occidi servos Dei vetuit.

of Maximin soon delivered the church from the last and most implacable of her enemies.[1]

In this general view of the persecution which was first authorised by the edicts of Diocletian, I have purposely refrained from describing the particular sufferings and deaths of the Christian martyrs. It would have been an easy task, from the history of Eusebius, from the declamations of Lactantius, and from the most ancient acts, to collect a long series of horrid and disgusting pictures, and to fill many pages with racks and scourges, with iron hooks and red-hot beds, and with all the variety of tortures which fire and steel, savage beasts, and more savage executioners, could inflict on the human body. These melancholy scenes might be enlivened by a crowd of visions and miracles destined either to delay the death, to celebrate the triumph, or to discover the relics of those canonised saints who suffered for the name of Christ. But I cannot determine what I ought to transcribe, till I am satisfied how much I ought to believe. The gravest of the ecclesiastical historians, Eusebius himself, indirectly confesses that he has related whatever might redound to the glory, and that he has suppressed all that could tend to the disgrace, of religion.[2] Such an acknowledgment will naturally excite a suspicion that a writer who has so openly violated one of the fundamental laws of history has not paid a very strict regard to the observance of the other; and the suspicion will derive additional credit from the character of Eusebius, which was less tinctured with credulity, and more practised in the arts of courts, than that of almost any of his contemporaries. On some particular occasions, when the magistrates were exasperated by some personal motives of interest or resentment, when the zeal of the martyrs urged them to forget the rules of prudence, and perhaps of decency, to overturn the altars, to pour out imprecations against the emperors, or to strike the judge as he sat on his tribunal, it may be presumed that every mode of torture which cruelty could invent, or constancy could endure, was

[1] A few days before his death he published a very ample edict of toleration, in which he imputes all the severities which the Christians suffered to the judges and governors, who had misunderstood his intentions. See the edict in Eusebius, l. ix. c. 10.

[2] Such is the *fair* deduction from two remarkable passages in Eusebius, l. viii. c. 2, and de Martyr. Palestin. c. 12. The prudence of the historian has exposed his own character to censure and suspicion. It was well known that he himself had been thrown into prison; and it was suggested that he had purchased his deliverance by some dishonourable compliance. The reproach was urged in his lifetime, and even in his presence, at the council of Tyre. See Tillemont, Mémoires Ecclésiastiques, tom. viii. part i. p. 67

exhausted on those devoted victims.[1]   Two circumstances, however, have been unwarily mentioned, which insinuate that the
general treatment of the Christians who had been apprehended
by the officers of justice was less intolerable than it is usually
imagined to have been.   1. The confessors who were condemned
to work in the mines were permitted by the humanity or the
negligence of their keepers to build chapels, and freely to profess
their religion in the midst of those dreary habitations.[2]   2. The
bishops were obliged to check and to censure the forward zeal
of the Christians, who voluntarily threw themselves into the
hands of the magistrates.   Some of these were persons oppressed
by poverty and debts, who blindly sought to terminate a miserable existence by a glorious death.   Others were allured by the
hope that a short confinement would expiate the sins of a whole
life; and others again were actuated by the less honourable
motive of deriving a plentiful subsistence, and perhaps a considerable profit, from the alms which the charity of the faithful
bestowed on the prisoners.[3]   After the church had triumphed
over all her enemies, the interest as well as vanity of the captives
prompted them to magnify the merit of their respective suffering.
A convenient distance of time or place gave an ample scope to
the progress of fiction; and the frequent instances which might
be alleged of holy martyrs whose wounds had been instantly
healed, whose strength had been renewed, and whose lost
members had miraculously been restored, were extremely convenient for the purpose of removing every difficulty, and of

[1] The ancient, and perhaps authentic, account of the sufferings of
Tarachus and his companions (Acta Sincera Ruinart, p. 419-448) is filled
with strong expressions of resentment and contempt, which could not fail
of irritating the magistrate.   The behaviour of Ædesius to Hierocles,
præfect of Egypt, was still more extraordinary. λόγοις τε καὶ ἔργοις τὸν
δικαστὴν . . . περιβαλὼν.   Euseb. de Martyr. Palestin. c. 5.
[The pagan historians justify in many places the details transmitted
regarding the tortures endured by the Christians. Celsus, for example,
reproaches the Christians with holding their assemblies in secret on
account of the fear inspired by their sufferings, for he adds, " When you
are arrested you are dragged to punishment, and before you are put to
death you have to suffer all kinds of tortures." Origen Contra Celsum.
Libanius, also the panegyrist of Julian says, speaking of the Christians,
" Those who followed a corrupt religion were in continual apprehensions;
they feared lest Julian should invent tortures still more refined than those
to which they had been exposed before, mutilation, burning alive, etc., for
the emperor had inflicted on them all these barbarities." Liban. Parent
in Julian.—O. S.]
[2] Euseb. de Martyr. Palestin. c. 13.
[3] Augustin. Collat. Carthagin. Dei, iii. c. 13, ap. Tillemont, Mémoires
Ecclésiastiques, tom. v. part i. p. 46.   The controversy with the Donatists
has reflected some, though perhaps a partial, light on the history of the
African church.

silencing every objection. The most extravagant legends, as they conduced to the honour of the church, were applauded by the credulous multitude, countenanced by the power of the clergy, and attested by the suspicious evidence of ecclesiastical history.

The vague descriptions of exile and imprisonment, of pain and torture, are so easily exaggerated or softened by the pencil of an artful orator, that we are naturally induced to inquire into a fact of a more distinct and stubborn kind; the number of persons who suffered death in consequence of the edicts published by Diocletian, his associates, and his successors. The recent legendaries record whole armies and cities which were at once swept away by the undistinguishing rage of persecution. The more ancient writers content themselves with pouring out a liberal effusion of loose and tragical invectives, without condescending to ascertain the precise number of those persons who were permitted to seal with their blood their belief of the Gospel. From the history of Eusebius it may however be collected that only nine bishops were punished with death; and we are assured, by his particular enumeration of the martyrs of Palestine, that no more than ninety-two Christians were entitled to that honourable appellation.[1] As we are unacquainted with the degree of episcopal zeal and courage which prevailed at that time, it is not in our power to draw any useful inferences from the former of these facts: but the latter may serve to justify a very important and probable conclusion. According to the distribution of Roman provinces, Palestine may be considered as the sixteenth

---

[1] Eusebius de Martyr. Palestin. c. 13. He closes his narration by assuring us that these were the martyrdoms inflicted in Palestine during the *whole* course of the persecution. The ninth chapter of his eighth book, which relates to the province of Thebais in Egypt, may seem to contradict our moderate computation; but it will only lead us to admire the artful management of the historian. Choosing for the scene of the most exquisite cruelty the most remote and sequestered country of the Roman empire, he relates that in Thebais from ten to one hundred persons had frequently suffered martyrdom in the same day. But when he proceeds to mention his own journey into Egypt, his language insensibly becomes more cautious and moderate. Instead of a large but definite number, he speaks of many Christians (πλείους), and most artfully selects two ambiguous words (ἱστορήσαμεν and ὑπομείναντας) which may signify either what he had seen or what he had heard; either the expectation or the execution of the punishment. Having thus provided a secure evasion, he commits the equivocal passage to his readers and translators; justly conceiving that their piety would induce them to prefer the most favourable sense. There was perhaps some malice in the remark of Theodorus Metochita, that all who, like Eusebius, had been conversant with the Egyptians, delighted in an obscure and intricate style. (See Valesius ad loc.)

part of the Eastern empire:[1] and since there were some governors who, from a real or affected clemency, had preserved their hands unstained with the blood of the faithful,[2] it is reasonable to believe that the country which had given birth to Christianity produced at least the sixteenth part of the martyrs who suffered death within the dominions of Galerius and Maximin; the whole might consequently amount to about fifteen hundred, a number which, if it is equally divided between the ten years of the persecution, will allow an annual consumption of one hundred and fifty martyrs. Allotting the same proportion to the provinces of Italy, Africa, and perhaps Spain, where, at the end of two or three years, the rigour of the penal laws was either suspended or abolished, the multitude of Christians in the Roman empire, on whom a capital punishment was inflicted by a judicial sentence, will be reduced to somewhat less than two thousand persons. Since it cannot be doubted that the Christians were more numerous, and their enemies more exasperated, in the time of Diocletian than they had ever been in any former persecution, this probable and moderate computation may teach us to estimate the number of primitive saints and martyrs who sacrificed their lives for the important purpose of introducing Christianity into the world.

We shall conclude this chapter by a melancholy truth which obtrudes itself on the reluctant mind; that, even admitting, without hesitation or inquiry, all that history has recorded, or devotion has feigned, on the subject of martyrdoms, it must still be acknowledged that the Christians, in the course of their intestine dissensions, have inflicted far greater severities on each other than they had experienced from the zeal of infidels. During the ages of ignorance which followed the subversion of the Roman empire in the West, the bishops of the Imperial city extended their dominion over the laity as well as clergy of the Latin church. The fabric of superstition which they had erected, and which might long have defied the feeble efforts of reason, was at length assaulted by a crowd of daring fanatics, who, from the twelfth to the sixteenth century, assumed the popular character of reformers. The church of Rome defended

---

[1] When Palestine was divided into three, the præfecture of the East contained forty-eight provinces. As the ancient distinctions of nations were long since abolished, the Romans distributed the provinces according to a general proportion of their extent and opulence.

[2] Ut gloriari possint nullum se innocentium peremisse, nam et ipse audivi aliquos gloriantes, quia administratio sua, in hac parte, fuerit incruenta. Lactant. Institut. Divin. v. 11.

by violence the empire which she had acquired by fraud; a system of peace and benevolence was soon disgraced by the proscriptions, wars, massacres, and the institution of the holy office. And as the reformers were animated by the love of civil as well as of religious freedom, the Catholic princes connected their own interest with that of the clergy, and enforced by fire and the sword the terrors of spiritual censures. In the Netherlands alone more than one hundred thousand of the subjects of Charles V. are said to have suffered by the hand of the executioner; and this extraordinary number is attested by Grotius,[1] a man of genius and learning, who preserved his moderation amidst the fury of contending sects, and who composed the annals of his own age and country at a time when the invention of printing had facilitated the means of intelligence and increased the danger of detection. If we are obliged to submit our belief to the authority of Grotius, it must be allowed that the number of Protestants who were executed in a single province and a single reign far exceeded that of the primitive martyrs in the space of three centuries and of the Roman empire. But if the improbability of the fact itself should prevail over the weight of evidence; if Grotius should be convicted of exaggerating the merit and sufferings of the reformers;[2] we shall be naturally led to inquire what confidence can be placed in the doubtful and imperfect monuments of ancient credulity; what degree of credit can be assigned to a courtly bishop and a passionate declaimer, who, under the protection of Constantine, enjoyed the exclusive privilege of recording the persecutions inflicted on the Christians by the vanquished rivals or disregarded predecessors of their gracious sovereign.

[1] Grot. Annal. de Rebus Belgicis, l. i. p. 12, edit. fol.
[2] Fra Paolo (Istoria del Concilio Tridentino, l. iii.) reduces the number of the Belgic martyrs to 50,000. In learning and moderation Fra Paolo was not inferior to Grotius. The priority of time gives some advantage to the evidence of the former, which he loses on the other hand by the distance of Venice from the Netherlands.

CHAPTER XVII

Foundation of Constantinople—Political System of Constantine and his
Successors—Military Discipline—The Palace—The Finances

THE unfortunate Licinius was the last rival who opposed the
greatness, and the last captive who adorned the triumph, of
Constantine. After a tranquil and prosperous reign the conqueror bequeathed to his family the inheritance of the Roman
empire; a new capital, a new policy, and a new religion; and
the innovations which he established have been embraced and
consecrated by succeeding generations. The age of the great
Constantine and his sons is filled with important events; but
the historian must be oppressed by their number and variety,
unless he diligently separates from each other the scenes which
are connected only by the order of time. He will describe the
political institutions that gave strength and stability to the
empire before he proceeds to relate the wars and revolutions
which hastened its decline. He will adopt the division unknown
to the ancients of civil and ecclesiastical affairs: the victory of
the Christians, and their intestine discord, will supply copious
and distinct materials both for edification and for scandal.

After the defeat and abdication of Licinius his victorious rival
proceeded to lay the foundations of a city destined to reign in
future times the mistress of the East, and to survive the empire
and religion of Constantine. The motives, whether of pride or of
policy, which first induced Diocletian to withdraw himself from
the ancient seat of government, had acquired additional weight
by the example of his successors and the habits of forty years.
Rome was insensibly confounded with the dependent kingdoms
which had once acknowledged her supremacy; and the country
of the Cæsars was viewed with cold indifference by a martial
prince, born in the neighbourhood of the Danube, educated in
the courts and armies of Asia, and invested with the purple by
the legions of Britain. The Italians, who had received Constantine as their deliverer, submissively obeyed the edicts which
he sometimes condescended to address to the senate and people
of Rome; but they were seldom honoured with the presence of
their new sovereign. During the vigour of his age Constantine,
according to the various exigencies of peace and war, moved
with slow dignity or with active diligence along the frontiers of
his extensive dominions; and was always prepared to take the

field either against a foreign or a domestic enemy. But as he gradually reached the summit of prosperity and the decline of life, he began to meditate the design of fixing in a more permanent station the strength as well as majesty of the throne. In the choice of an advantageous situation he preferred the confines of Europe and Asia; to curb with a powerful arm the barbarians who dwelt between the Danube and the Tanais; to watch with an eye of jealousy the conduct of the Persian monarch, who indignantly supported the yoke of an ignominious treaty. With these views Diocletian had selected and embellished the residence of Nicomedia: but the memory of Diocletian was justly abhorred by the protector of the church; and Constantine was not insensible to the ambition of founding a city which might perpetuate the glory of his own name. During the late operations of the war against Licinius he had sufficient opportunity to contemplate, both as a soldier and as a statesman, the incomparable position of Byzantium; and to observe how strongly it was guarded by nature against an hostile attack, whilst it was accessible on every side to the benefits of commercial intercourse. Many ages before Constantine, one of the most judicious historians of antiquity [1] had described the advantages of a situation from whence a feeble colony of Greeks derived the command of the sea, and the honours of a flourishing and independent republic.[2]

If we survey Byzantium in the extent which it acquired with the august name of Constantinople, the figure of the Imperial city may be represented under that of an unequal triangle. The obtuse point, which advances towards the east and the shores of Asia, meets and repels the waves of the Thracian Bosphorus. The northern side of the city is bounded by the harbour, and the southern is washed by the Propontis or Sea of Marmora. The basis of the triangle is opposed to the west, and terminates the continent of Europe. But the admirable form and division of

---

[1] Polybius, l. iv. [c. 45] p. 423, edit. Casaubon. He observes that the peace of the Byzantines was frequently disturbed, and the extent of their territory contracted, by the inroads of the wild Thracians.

[2] The navigator Byzas, who was styled the son of Neptune, founded the city 656 [rather 667—S.] years before the Christian era. His followers were drawn from Argos and Megara. Byzantium was afterwards rebuilt and fortified by the Spartan general Pausanias. See Scaliger, Animadvers. ad Euseb. p. 81. Ducange, Constantinopolis, l. i. part i. cap. 15, 16. With regard to the wars of the Byzantines against Philip, the Gauls, and the kings of Bithynia, we should trust none but the ancient writers who lived before the greatness of the Imperial city had excited a spirit of flattery and fiction.

the circumjacent land and water cannot, without a more ample explanation, be clearly or sufficiently understood.

The winding channel through which the waters of the Euxine flow with a rapid and incessant course towards the Mediterranean received the appellation of Bosphorus, a name not less celebrated in the history than in the fables of antiquity.[1] A crowd of temples and of votive altars, profusely scattered along its steep and woody banks, attested the unskilfulness, the terrors, and the devotion of the Grecian navigators who, after the example of the Argonauts, explored the dangers of the inhospitable Euxine. On these banks tradition long preserved the memory of the palace of Phineus, infested by the obscene harpies;[2] and of the sylvan reign of Amycus, who defied the son of Leda to the combat of the Cestus.[3] The straits of the Bosphorus are terminated by the Cyanean rocks, which, according to the description of the poets, had once floated on the face of the waters, and were destined by the gods to protect the entrance of the Euxine against the eye of profane curiosity.[4] From the Cyanean rocks to the point and harbour of Byzantium the winding length of the Bosphorus extends about sixteen miles,[5] and its most ordinary breadth may be computed at about one mile and a half. The *new* castles of Europe and Asia are constructed, on either continent, upon the foundations of two celebrated temples, of Serapis and of Jupiter Urius. The *old* castles, a work of the Greek emperors, command the narrowest part of the channel, in a place where the opposite banks advance within five hundred paces of each other. These fortresses were restored and

[1] The Bosphorus has been very minutely described by Dionysius of Byzantium, who lived in the time of Domitian (Hudson, Geograph. Minor. tom. iii.), and by Gilles or Gyllius, a French traveller of the sixteenth century. Tournefort (Lettre XV.) seems to have used his own eyes, and the learning of Gyllius. [Add Von Hammer, Constantinopolis und der Bosporos, 8vo.—M.]

[2] There are very few conjectures so happy as that of Le Clerc (Bibliothèque Universelle, tom. i. p. 148), who supposes that the harpies were only locusts. The Syriac or Phœnician name of those insects, their noisy flight, the stench and devastation which they occasion, and the north wind which drives them into the sea, all contribute to form the striking resemblance.

[3] The residence of Amycus was in Asia, between the old and the new castles, at a place called Laurus Insana. That of Phineus was in Europe, near the village of Mauromole and the Black Sea. See Gyllius de Bosph. l. ii. c. 23. Tournefort, Lettre XV.

[4] The deception was occasioned by several pointed rocks, alternately covered and abandoned by the waves. At present there are two small islands, one towards either shore; that of Europe is distinguished by the column of Pompey.

[5] The ancients computed one hundred and twenty stadia, or fifteen Roman miles. They measured only from the new castles, but they carried the straits as far as the town of Chalcedon.

strengthened by Mahomet the Second when he meditated the siege of Constantinople: [1] but the Turkish conqueror was most probably ignorant that, near two thousand years before his reign, Darius had chosen the same situation to connect the two continents by a bridge of boats.[2] At a small distance from the old castles we discover the little town of Chrysopolis, or Scutari, which may almost be considered as the Asiatic suburb of Constantinople. The Bosphorus, as it begins to open into the Propontis, passes between Byzantium and Chalcedon. The latter of those cities was built by the Greeks a few years before the former; and the blindness of its founders, who overlooked the superior advantages of the opposite coast, has been stigmatised by a proverbial expression of contempt.[3]

The harbour of Constantinople, which may be considered as an arm of the Bosphorus, obtained, in a very remote period, the denomination of the *Golden Horn*. The curve which it describes might be compared to the horn of a stag, or as it should seem, with more propriety, to that of an ox.[4] The epithet of *golden* was expressive of the riches which every wind wafted from the most distant countries into the secure and capacious port of Constantinople. The river Lycus, formed by the conflux of two little streams, pours into the harbour a perpetual supply of fresh water, which serves to cleanse the bottom and to invite the periodical shoals of fish to seek their retreat in that convenient recess. As the vicissitudes of tides are scarcely felt in those seas, the constant depth of the harbour allows goods to be landed on the quays without the assistance of boats; and it has been observed that, in many places, the largest vessels may rest their prows against the houses while their sterns are floating in

---

[1] Ducas. Hist. c. 34 [p. 136, ed. Paris; p. 108, ed. Ven.; p. 242, ed. Bonn]. Leunclavius Hist. Turcica Mussulmanica, l. xv. p. 577. Under the Greek empire these castles were used as state prisons, under the tremendous name of Lethe, or towers of oblivion.

[2] Darius engraved in Greek and Assyrian letters, on two marble columns, the names of his subject nations, and the amazing numbers of his land and sea forces. The Byzantines afterwards transported these columns into the city, and used them for the altars of their tutelar deities. Herodotus, l. iv. c. 87.

[3] Namque artissimo inter Europam Asiamque divortio Byzantium in extremâ Europâ posuere Græci, quibus, Pythium Apollinem consulentibus ubi conderent urbem, redditum oraculum est, quærerent sedem *cæcorum* terris adversam. Eâ ambage Chalcedonii monstrabantur, quod priores illuc advecti, prævisâ locorum utilitate pejora legissent. Tacit. Annal. xii. 63.

[4] Strabo, l. vii. p. 492 [320, ed. Casaubon]. Most of the antlers are now broken off; or, to speak less figuratively, most of the recesses of the harbour are filled up. See Gyllius de Bosphoro Thracio, l. i. c. 5.

the water.[1] From the mouth of the Lycus to that of the harbour this arm of the Bosphorus is more than seven miles in length. The entrance is about five hundred yards broad, and a strong chain could be occasionally drawn across it to guard the port and city from the attack of an hostile navy.[2]

Between the Bosphorus and the Hellespont, the shores of Europe and Asia receding on either side inclose the Sea of Marmora, which was known to the ancients by the denomination of Propontis. The navigation from the issue of the Bosphorus to the entrance of the Hellespont is about one hundred and twenty miles. Those who steer their westward course through the middle of the Propontis may at once descry the high lands of Thrace and Bithynia, and never lose sight of the lofty summit of Mount Olympus, covered with eternal snows.[3] They leave on the left a deep gulf, at the bottom of which Nicomedia was seated, the imperial residence of Diocletian; and they pass the small islands of Cyzicus and Proconnesus before they cast anchor at Gallipoli, where the sea, which separates Asia from Europe, is again contracted into a narrow channel.

The geographers who, with the most skilful accuracy, have surveyed the form and extent of the Hellespont, assign about sixty miles for the winding course, and about three miles for the ordinary breadth, of those celebrated straits.[4] But the narrowest part of the channel is found to the northward of the old Turkish castles, between the cities of Sestus and Abydus.

[1] Procopius de Ædificiis, l. i. c. 5. His description is confirmed by modern travellers. See Theyenot. part i. l. i. c. 15. Tournefort, Lettre XII. Niebuhr, Voyage d'Arabie, p. 22.
   [The river Lycus really discharges itself into the Propontis, which in view of what follows may be said to measure in length about 40 miles, by one mile in breadth.—O. S.]
[2] See Ducange, C. P. l. i. part i. c. 16, and his Observations sur Ville-hardouin, p. 289. The chain was drawn from the Acropolis near the modern Kiosk to the tower of Galata, and was supported at convenient distances by large wooden piles.
[3] Thevenot (Voyages au Levant, part i. l. i. c. 14) contracts the measure to 125 small Greek miles. Belon (Observations, l. ii. c. 1) gives a good description of the Propontis, but contents himself with the vague expression of one day and one night's sail. When Sandys (Travels, p. 21) talks of 150 furlongs in length as well as breadth, we can only suppose some mistake of the press in the text of that judicious traveller.
[4] See an admirable dissertation of M. d'Anville upon the Hellespont or Dardanelles, in the Mémoires de l'Académie des Inscriptions, tom. xxviii. p. 318-346. Yet even that ingenious geographer is too fond of supposing new, and perhaps imaginary *measures*, for the purpose of rendering ancient writers as accurate as himself. The stadia employed by Herodotus in the description of the Euxine, the Bosphorus, etc. (l. iv. c. 85), must undoubtedly be all of the same species; but it seems impossible to reconcile them either with truth or with each other.

It was here that the adventurous Leander braved the passage
of the flood for the possession of his mistress.[1]   It was here likewise, in a place where the distance between the opposite banks
cannot exceed five hundred paces, that Xerxes imposed a
stupendous bridge of boats, for the purpose of transporting into
Europe a hundred and seventy myriads of barbarians.[2]   A sea
contracted within such narrow limits may seem but ill to deserve
the singular epithet of *broad*, which Homer, as well as Orpheus,
has frequently bestowed on the Hellespont.   But our ideas of
greatness are of a relative nature: the traveller, and especially
the poet, who sailed along the Hellespont, who pursued the
windings of the stream, and contemplated the rural scenery,
which appeared on every side to terminate the prospect, insensibly lost the remembrance of the sea; and his fancy painted
those celebrated straits with all the attributes of a mighty river,
flowing with a swift current, in the midst of a woody and inland
country, and at length, through a wide mouth, discharging itself
into the Ægean or Archipelago.[3]   Ancient Troy,[4] seated on an
eminence at the foot of Mount Ida, overlooked the mouth of the
Hellespont, which scarcely received an accession of waters from
the tribute of those immortal rivulets the Simois and Scamander.
The Grecian camp had stretched twelve miles along the shore,
from the Sigean to the Rhœtean promontory; and the flanks of

[1] The oblique distance between Sestus and Abydus was thirty stadia.
The improbable tale of Hero and Leander is exposed by M. Mahudel, but
is defended on the authority of poets and medals by M. de la Nauze.   See
the Académie des Inscriptions, tom. vii. Hist. p. 74, Mem. p. 240.
[Gibbon will not admit great width to exist between the two nearest
points of the Hellespont than between those of the Bosphorus; yet (as
Milman says) all the ancient writers speak of the Hellespontic strait as
being broader than the other.   They agree, in fact, in giving it a width of
seven stadia at its narrowest point (cf. Herod. iv. c. 85; vii. c. 34; Plin. b.
iv. c. 12), which would represent about 875 paces.   Gibbon's measurement
is incorrect, owing to his adopting the theory of D'Anville that the ancients
had a stadium of 51 toises.—O. S.]
[2] See the seventh book of Herodotus, who has erected an elegant trophy
to his own fame and to that of his country.   The review appears to have
been made with tolerable accuracy; but the vanity, first of the Persians,
and afterwards of the Greeks, was interested to magnify the armament
and the victory.   I should much doubt whether the *invaders* have ever
outnumbered the *men* of any country which they attacked.
[3] See Wood's Observations on Homer, p. 320.   I have, with pleasure,
selected this remark from an author who in general seems to have disappointed the expectation of the public as a critic, and still more as a traveller.
He had visited the banks of the Hellespont; he had read Strabo; he ought
to have consulted the Roman itineraries.   How was it possible for him to
confound Ilium and Alexandria Troas (Observations, p. 340, 341), two
cities which were sixteen miles distant from each other?
[4] Demetrius of Scepsis wrote sixty books on thirty lines of Homer's
catalogue.   The thirteenth Book of Strabo is sufficient for *our* curiosity.

the army were guarded by the bravest chiefs who fought under
the banners of Agamemnon. The first of those promontories
was occupied by Achilles with his invincible myrmidons, and the
dauntless Ajax pitched his tents on the other. After Ajax had
fallen a sacrifice to his disappointed pride and to the ingratitude
of the Greeks, his sepulchre was erected on the ground where he
had defended the navy against the rage of Jove and of Hector;
and the citizens of the rising town of Rhœteum celebrated his
memory with divine honours.[1] Before Constantine gave a just
preference to the situation of Byzantium, he had conceived the
design of erecting the seat of empire on this celebrated spot, from
whence the Romans derived their fabulous origin. The extensive plain which lies below ancient Troy, towards the Rhœtean
promontory and the tomb of Ajax, was first chosen for his new
capital; and, though the undertaking was soon relinquished,
the stately remains of unfinished walls and towers attracted the
notice of all who sailed through the straits of the Hellespont.[2]

We are at present qualified to view the advantageous position
of Constantinople, which appears to have been formed by nature
for the centre and capital of a great monarchy. Situated in the
forty-first degree of latitude, the Imperial city commanded, from
her seven hills,[3] the opposite shores of Europe and Asia; the
climate was healthy and temperate, the soil fertile, the harbour
secure and capacious, and the approach on the side of the continent was of small extent and easy defence. The Bosphorus
and the Hellespont may be considered as the two gates of Constantinople, and the prince who possessed those important passages could always shut them against a naval enemy and open
them to the fleets of commerce. The preservation of the eastern
provinces may, in some degree, be ascribed to the policy of Constantine, as the barbarians of the Euxine, who in the preceding
age had poured their armaments into the heart of the Mediter-

[1] Strabo, l. xiii. p. 595. The disposition of the ships, which were drawn
up on dry land, and the posts of Ajax and Achilles, are very clearly described by Homer. See Iliad, vii. 220.

[2] Zosim. l. ii. [c. 30] p. 105. Sozomen, l. ii. c. 3. Theophanes, p. 18
[p. 14, ed. Ven.; vol. i. p. 34, ed. Bonn]. Nicephorus Callistus, l. vii. p. 48.
Zonaras, tom. ii. l. xiii. [c. 3] p. 6. Zosimus places the new city between
Ilium and Alexandria, but this apparent difference may be reconciled by
the large extent of its circumference. Before the foundation of Constantinople, Thessalonica is mentioned by Cedrenus (p. 283) [vol. i. p. 496, ed.
Bonn], and Sardica by Zonaras, as the intended capital. They both
suppose, with very little probability, that the emperor, if he had not been
prevented by a prodigy, would have repeated the mistake of the *blind*
Chalcedonians.

[3] Pocock's Description of the East, vol. ii. part ii. p. 127. His plan of
the seven hills is clear and accurate. That traveller is seldom so satisfactory.

ranean, soon desisted from the exercise of piracy, and despaired
of forcing this insurmountable barrier. When the gates of the
Hellespont and Bosphorus were shut, the capital still enjoyed
within their spacious enclosure every production which could
supply the wants or gratify the luxury of its numerous inhabitants. The sea-coasts of Thrace and Bithynia, which languish
under the weight of Turkish oppression, still exhibit a rich
prospect of vineyards, of gardens, and of plentiful harvests;
and the Propontis has ever been renowned for an inexhaustible
store of the most exquisite fish, that are taken in their stated
seasons, without skill, and almost without labour.[1] But when
the passages of the straits were thrown open for trade, they
alternately admitted the natural and artificial riches of the north
and south, of the Euxine and of the Mediterranean. Whatever
rude commodities were collected in the forests of Germany and
Scythia, as far as the sources of the Tanais and the Borysthenes;
whatsoever was manufactured by the skill of Europe or Asia;
the corn of Egypt, and the gems and spices of the farthest India,
were brought by the varying winds into the port of Constantinople, which, for many ages, attracted the commerce of the
ancient world.[2]

The prospect of beauty, of safety, and of wealth, united in a
single spot, was sufficient to justify the choice of Constantine.
But as some decent mixture of prodigy and fable has, in every
age, been supposed to reflect a becoming majesty on the origin
of great cities,[3] the emperor was desirous of ascribing his resolution not so much to the uncertain counsels of human policy as
to the infallible and eternal decrees of divine wisdom. In one
of his laws he has been careful to instruct posterity that, in
obedience to the commands of God, he laid the everlasting foundations of Constantinople;[4] and though he has not condescended
to relate in what manner the celestial inspiration was communicated to his mind, the defect of his modest silence has been
liberally supplied by the ingenuity of succeeding writers, who

[1] See Belon, Observations, c. 72-76. Among a variety of different
species, the Pelamides, a sort of Thunnies, were the most celebrated. We
may learn from Polybius, Strabo, and Tacitus, that the profits of the
fishery constituted the principal revenue of Byzantium.

[2] See the eloquent description of Busbequius, epistol. i. p. 64. Est in
Europa; habet in conspectu Asiam, Egyptum, Africamque à dextrâ: quæ
tametsi contiguæ non sunt, maris tamen navigandique commoditate veluti
junguntur. A sinistrâ vero Pontus est Euxinus, etc.

[3] Datur hæc venia antiquitati, ut miscendo humana divinis, primordia
urbium augustiora faciat. T. Liv. in procœm.

[4] He says, in one of his laws, pro commoditate Urbis quam æterno
nomine, jubente Deo, donavimus. Cod. Theodos. l. xiii. tit. v. leg. 7.

describe the nocturnal vision which appeared to the fancy of
Constantine as he slept within the walls of Byzantium. The
tutelar genius of the city, a venerable matron sinking under the
weight of years and infirmities, was suddenly transformed into
a blooming maid, whom his own hands adorned with all the
symbols of Imperial greatness.[1] The monarch awoke, interpreted
the auspicious omen, and obeyed, without hesitation, the will of
Heaven. The day which gave birth to a city or colony was
celebrated by the Romans with such ceremonies as had been
ordained by a generous superstition;[2] and though Constantine
might omit some rites which savoured too strongly of their
Pagan origin, yet he was anxious to leave a deep impression of
hope and respect on the minds of the spectators. On foot, with
a lance in his hand, the emperor himself led the solemn procession, and directed the line which was traced as the boundary of
the destined capital, till the growing circumference was observed
with astonishment by the assistants, who, at length, ventured
to observe that he had already exceeded the most ample measure
of a great city. "I shall still advance," replied Constantine,
"till HE, the invisible guide who marches before me, thinks
proper to stop."[3] Without presuming to investigate the nature
or motives of this extraordinary conductor, we shall content
ourselves with the more humble task of describing the extent
and limits of Constantinople.[4]

In the actual state of the city, the palace and gardens of the
Seraglio occupy the eastern promontory, the first of the seven
hills, and cover about one hundred and fifty acres of our own
measure. The seat of Turkish jealousy and despotism is erected
on the foundations of a Grecian republic; but it may be supposed
that the Byzantines were tempted by the conveniency of the

[1] The Greeks, Theophanes, Cedrenus, and the author of the Alexandrian
Chronicle, confine themselves to vague and general expressions. For a
more particular account of the vision we are obliged to have recourse to
such Latin writers as William of Malmesbury. See Ducange, C. P. l. i.
p. 24, 25.
[2] See Plutarch in Romul. [c. 11] tom. i. p. 49, edit. Bryan. Among other
ceremonies, a large hole, which had been dug for that purpose, was filled
up with handfuls of earth, which each of the settlers brought from the place
of his birth, and thus adopted his new country.
[3] Philostorgius, l. ii. c. 9. This incident, though borrowed from a suspected writer, is characteristic and probable.
[4] See in the Mémoires de l'Académie, tom. xxxv. p. 747-758, a dissertation of M. d'Anville on the extent of Constantinople. He takes the plan
inserted in the Imperium Orientale of Banduri as the most complete; but
by a series of very nice observations he reduces the extravagant proportion
of the scale, and, instead of 9500, determines the circumference of the city
as consisting of about 7800 French *toises*.

harbour to extend their habitations on that side beyond the modern limits of the Seraglio. The new walls of Constantine stretched from the port to the Propontis across the enlarged breadth of the triangle, at the distance of fifteen stadia from the ancient fortification, and with the city of Byzantium they enclosed five of the seven hills which, to the eyes of those who approach Constantinople, appear to rise above each other in beautiful order.[1] About a century after the death of the founder, the new buildings, extending on one side up the harbour, and on the other along the Propontis, already covered the narrow ridge of the sixth and the broad summit of the seventh hill. The necessity of protecting those suburbs from the incessant inroads of the barbarians engaged the younger Theodosius to surround his capital with an adequate and permanent enclosure of walls.[2] From the eastern promontory to the golden gate, the extreme length of Constantinople was about three Roman miles,[3] the circumference measured between ten and eleven, and the surface might be computed as equal to about two thousand English acres. It is impossible to justify the vain and credulous exaggerations of modern travellers, who have sometimes stretched the limits of Constantinople over the adjacent villages of the European and even of the Asiatic coast.[4] But the suburbs of Pera and Galata, though situate beyond the harbour, may deserve to be considered as a part of the city;[5] and this addition may

[1] Codinus, Antiquitat. Const. p. 12 [p. 25, ed. Bonn]. He assigns the church of St. Anthony as the boundary on the side of the harbour. It is mentioned in Ducange, l. iv. c. 6; but I have tried, without success, to discover the exact place where it was situated.

[2] The new wall of Theodosius was constructed in the year 413. In 447 it was thrown down by an earthquake, and rebuilt in three months by the diligence of the præfect Cyrus. The suburb of the Blachernæ was first taken into the city in the reign of Heraclius. Ducange, Const. l. i. c. 10, 11.

[3] The measurement is expressed in the Notitia by 14,075 feet. It is reasonable to suppose that these were Greek feet; the proportion of which has been ingeniously determined by M. d'Anville. He compares the 180 feet with 78 Hashemite cubits, which in different writers are assigned for the heights of St. Sophia. Each of these cubits was equal to 27 French inches.

[4] The accurate Thevenot (l. i. c. 15) walked in one hour and three-quarters round two of the sides of the triangle, from the Kiosk of the Seraglio to the seven towers. D'Anville examines with care, and receives with confidence, this decisive testimony, which gives a circumference of ten or twelve miles. The extravagant computation of Tournefort (Lettre XI.) of thirty-four or thirty miles, without including Scutari, is a strange departure from his usual character.

[5] The sycæ, or fig-trees, formed the thirteenth region, and were very much embellished by Justinian. It has since borne the names of Pera and Galata. The etymology of the former is obvious; that of the latter is unknown. See Ducange, Const. l. i. c. 22, and Gyllius de Byzant. l. iv. c. 10.

perhaps authorise the measure of a Byzantine historian, who
assigns sixteen Greek (about fourteen Roman) miles for the circumference of his native city.[1]   Such an extent may seem not
unworthy of an Imperial residence.   Yet Constantinople must
yield to Babylon and Thebes,[2] to ancient Rome, to London, and
even to Paris.[3]

The master of the Roman world, who aspired to erect an
eternal monument of the glories of his reign, could employ in the
prosecution of that great work the wealth, the labour, and all
that yet remained of the genius, of obedient millions.   Some
estimate may be formed of the expense bestowed with Imperial
liberality on the foundation of Constantinople by the allowance
of about two millions five hundred thousand pounds for the construction of the walls, the porticoes, and the aqueducts.[4]   The
forests that overshadowed the shores of the Euxine, and the
celebrated quarries of white marble in the little island of Proconnesus, supplied an inexhaustible stock of materials, ready to
be conveyed, by the convenience of a short water-carriage, to
the harbour of Byzantium.[5]   A multitude of labourers and artificers urged the conclusion of the work with incessant toil; but
the impatience of Constantine soon discovered that, in the decline
of the arts, the skill as well as numbers of his architects bore a
very unequal proportion to the greatness of his designs.   The
magistrates of the most distant provinces were therefore directed
to institute schools, to appoint professors, and, by the hopes of
rewards and privileges, to engage in the study and practice of
architecture a sufficient number of ingenious youths who had
received a liberal education.[6]   The buildings of the new city

[1] One hundred and eleven stadia, which may be translated into modern
Greek miles each of seven stadia, or 660, sometimes only 600, French
toises.   See D'Anville, Mesures Itinéraires, p. 53.
[2] When the ancient texts, which describe the size of Babylon and Thebes,
are settled, the exaggerations reduced, and the measures ascertained, we
find that those famous cities filled the great but not incredible circumference of about twenty-five or thirty miles.   Compare D'Anville, Mém. de
l'Académie, tom. xxviii. p. 235, with his Description de l'Egypte, p. 201, 202.
[3] If we divide Constantinople and Paris into equal squares of 50 French
toises (fathoms), the former contains 850, and the latter 1160, of those
divisions.
[4] Six hundred centenaries, or sixty thousand pounds' weight of gold.
This sum is taken from Codinus, Antiquit. Const. p. 11 [p. 23, ed. Bonn];
but unless that contemptible author had derived his information from some
purer sources, he would probably have been unacquainted with so obsolete
a mode of reckoning.
[5] For the forests of the Black Sea, consult Tournefort, Lettre XVI.; for
the marble quarries of Proconnesus, see Strabo, I. xiii, p. 588.   The latter
had already furnished the materials of the stately buildings of Cyzicus
[6] See the Codex Theodos. I. xiii. tit. iv. leg. 1.   This law is dated in the

were executed by such artificers as the reign of Constantine could afford; but they were decorated by the hands of the most celebrated masters of the age of Pericles and Alexander. To revive the genius of Phidias and Lysippus surpassed indeed the power of a Roman emperor; but the immortal productions which they had bequeathed to posterity were exposed without defence to the rapacious vanity of a despot. By his commands the cities of Greece and Asia were despoiled of their most valuable ornaments.[1] The trophies of memorable wars, the objects of religious veneration, the most finished statues of the gods and heroes, of the sages and poets of ancient times, contributed to the splendid triumph of Constantinople; and gave occasion to the remark of the historian Cedrenus,[2] who observes, with some enthusiasm, that nothing seemed wanting except the souls of the illustrious men whom these admirable monuments were intended to represent. But it is not in the city of Constantine, nor in the declining period of an empire, when the human mind was depressed by civil and religious slavery, that we should seek for the souls of Homer and of Demosthenes.

During the siege of Byzantium the conqueror had pitched his tent on the commanding eminence of the second hill. To perpetuate the memory of his success, he chose the same advantageous position for the principal Forum,[3] which appears to have been of a circular or rather elliptical form. The two opposite entrances formed triumphal arches; the porticoes, which enclosed it on every side, were filled with statues, and the centre of the Forum was occupied by a lofty column, of which a mutilated fragment is now degraded by the appellation of the *burnt pillar*. This column was erected on a pedestal of white marble twenty feet high, and was composed of ten pieces of porphyry,

year 334, and was addressed to the præfect of Italy, whose jurisdiction extended over Africa. The commentary of Godefroy on the whole title well deserves to be consulted.

[1] Constantinopolis dedicatur pœne omnium urbium nuditate. Hieronym. Chron. p. 181. See Codinus, p. 8, 9 [p. 16 *sqq.* ed. Bonn]. The author of the Antiquitat. Const. l. iii. (apud Banduri Imp. Orient. tom. i. p. 41) enumerates Rome, Sicily, Antioch, Athens, and a long list of other cities. The provinces of Greece and Asia Minor may be supposed to have yielded the richest booty.

[2] Hist. Compend. p. 369 [vol. i. p. 648, ed. Bonn]. He describes the statue, or rather bust, of Homer with a degree of taste which plainly indictates that Cedrenus copied the style of a more fortunate age.

[3] Zosim. l. ii. [c. 30] p. 106. Chron. Alexandrin. vel Paschal. p. 284. Ducange, Const. l. i. c. 24. Even the last of those writers seems to confound the Forum of Constantine with the Augusteum, or court of the palace. I am not satisfied whether I have properly distinguished what belongs to the one and the other.

each of which measured about ten feet in height, and about
thirty-three in circumference.[1]   On the summit of the pillar,
above one hundred and twenty feet from the ground, stood the
colossal statue of Apollo.   It was of bronze, had been transported
either from Athens or from a town of Phrygia, and was supposed
to be the work of Phidias.   The artist had represented the god
of day, or, as it was afterwards interpreted, the emperor Constantine himself, with a sceptre in his right hand, the globe of the
world in his left, and a crown of rays glittering on his head.[2]
The Circus, or Hippodrome, was a stately building about four
hundred paces in length, and one hundred in breadth.[3]   The
space between the two *metæ* or goals was filled with statues and
obelisks; and we may still remark a very singular fragment of
antiquity, the bodies of three serpents twisted into one pillar of
brass.   Their triple heads had once supported the golden tripod
which, after the defeat of Xerxes, was consecrated in the temple
of Delphi by the victorious Greeks.[4]   The beauty of the Hippo-

---

[1] The most tolerable account of this column is given by Pocock, Description of the East, vol. ii. part ii. p. 131.   But it is still in many instances
perplexed and unsatisfactory.

[2] Ducange, Const. l. i. c. 24, p. 76, and his notes ad Alexiad. p. 382.   The
statue of Constantine or Apollo was thrown down under the reign of
Alexius Comnenus.

[On this column Constantine with singular shamelessness placed his own
statue, to which were attributed the qualities of Apollo and Christ.   He
substituted the nails of the Passion for the rays of the sun.   In A.D. 1412
the keystone was loosened by an earthquake, and the statue fell in the
reign of Alexius Comnenus, being replaced by the Cross.—O. S.]

[3] Tournefort (Lettre XII.) computes the Atmeidan at four hundred
paces.   If he means geometrical paces of five feet each, it was three
hundred *toises* in length, about forty more than the great circus of Rome.
See d'Anville, Mesures Itinéraires, p. 73.

[According to the measurements of M. Paspatés (says Professor Bury)
the length was 320 yards, the breadth 79 yards.—O. S.]

[4] The guardians of the most holy relics would rejoice if they were able to
produce such a chain of evidence as may be alleged on this occasion.   See
Banduri ad Antiquitat. Const. p. 668.   Gyllius de Byzant. l. ii. c. 13.   1.
The original consecration of the tripod and pillar in the temple of Delphi
may be proved from Herodotus and Pausanias.   2. The Pagan Zosimus
agrees with the three ecclesiastical historians, Eusebius, Socrates, and Sozomen, that the sacred ornaments of the temple of Delphi were removed to
Constantinople by the order of Constantine; and among these the serpen-
tine pillar of the Hippodrome is particularly mentioned.   3. All the
European travellers who have visited Constantinople, from Buondelmonte
to Pocock, describe it in the same place, and almost in the same manner;
the differences between them are occasioned only by the injuries which it
has sustained from the Turks.   Mahomet the Second broke the under jaw
of one of the serpents with a stroke of his battle-axe.   Thevenot, l. i. c. 17.

[In 1808 the Janissaries revolted against the vizier, Mustapha Baisactar,
who wished to introduce a new system of military organisation, besieged
the quarter of the Hippodrome in which stood the palace of the viziers, and
the Hippodrome was consumed in the conflagration.—O. S.]

drome has been long since defaced by the rude hands of the
Turkish conquerors, but, under the similar appellation of
Atmeidan, it still serves as a place of exercise for their horses.
From the throne, whence the emperor viewed the Circensian
games, a winding staircase [1] descended to the palace; a magnificent edifice, which scarcely yielded to the residence of Rome
itself, and which, together with the dependent courts, gardens,
and porticoes, covered a considerable extent of ground upon the
banks of the Propontis, between the Hippodrome and the church
of St. Sophia.[2] We might likewise celebrate the baths, which
still retained the name of Zeuxippus, after they had been enriched
by the munificence of Constantine, with lofty columns, various
marbles, and above threescore statues of bronze.[3] But we should
deviate from the design of this history if we attempted minutely
to describe the different buildings or quarters of the city. It may
be sufficient to observe that whatever could adorn the dignity
of a great capital, or contribute to the benefit or pleasure of its
numerous inhabitants, was contained within the walls of Constantinople. A particular description, composed about a century
after its foundation, enumerates a capitol or school of learning,
a circus, two theatres, eight public and one hundred and fifty-
three private baths, fifty-two porticoes, five granaries, eight
aqueducts or reservoirs of water, four spacious halls for the
meetings of the senate or courts of justice, fourteen churches,
fourteen palaces, and four thousand three hundred and eighty-
eight houses which, for their size or beauty, deserved to be distinguished from the multitude of plebeian habitations.[4]

[1] The Latin name *Cochlea* was adopted by the Greeks, and very frequently occurs in the Byzantine history. Ducange, Const. l. ii. c. 1, p. 104.

[2] There are three topographical points which indicate the situation of the
palace. 1. The staircase which connected it with the Hippodrome or
Atmeidan. 2. A small artificial port on the Propontis, from whence there
was an easy ascent, by a flight of marble steps, to the gardens of the palace.
3. The Augusteum was a spacious court, one side of which was occupied by
the front of the palace, and another by the church of St. Sophia.

[3] Zeuxippus was an epithet of Jupiter, and the baths were a part of old
Byzantium. The difficulty of assigning their true situation has not been
felt by Ducange. History seems to connect them with St. Sophia and the
palace; but the original plan inserted in Banduri places them on the other
side of the city, near the harbour. For their beauties see Chron. Paschal,
p. 285, and Gyllius de Byzant. l. ii. c. 7. Christodorus (see Antiquitat.
Const. l. vii.) composed inscriptions in verse for each of the statues. He
was a Theban poet in genius as well as in birth:—

Bœotum in crasso jurares aëre natum.

[4] See the Notitia. Rome only reckoned 1780 large houses, *domus ;* but
the word must have had a more dignified signification. No *insulæ* are
mentioned at Constantinople. The old capital consisted of 424 streets,
the new of 322.

The populousness of his favoured city was the next and most
serious object of the attention of its founder. In the dark ages
which succeeded the translation of the empire, the remote and
the immediate consequences of that memorable event were
strangely confounded by the vanity of the Greeks and the
credulity of the Latins.[1] It was asserted and believed that all
the noble families of Rome, the senate, and the equestrian order,
with their innumerable attendants, had followed their emperor
to the banks of the Propontis; that a spurious race of strangers
and plebeians was left to possess the solitude of the ancient
capital; and that the lands of Italy, long since converted into
gardens, were at once deprived of cultivation and inhabitants.[2]
In the course of this history such exaggerations will be reduced to
their just value; yet, since the growth of Constantinople cannot
be ascribed to the general increase of mankind and of industry,
it must be admitted that this artificial colony was raised at the
expense of the ancient cities of the empire. Many opulent
senators of Rome and of the eastern provinces were probably
invited by Constantine to adopt for their country the fortunate
spot which he had chosen for his own residence. The invitations
of a master are scarcely to be distinguished from commands, and
the liberality of the emperor obtained a ready and cheerful
obedience. He bestowed on his favourites the palaces which
he had built in the several quarters of the city, assigned them
lands and pensions for the support of their dignity,[3] and alienated
the demesnes of Pontus and Asia to grant hereditary estates
by the easy tenure of maintaining a house in the capital.[4]   But

[1] Liutprand Legatio ad Imp. Nicephorum, p. 153. The modern Greeks
have strangely disfigured the antiquities of Constantinople. We might
excuse the errors of the Turkish or Arabian writers; but it is somewhat
astonishing that the Greeks, who had access to the authentic materials
preserved in their own language, should prefer fiction to truth, and loose
tradition to genuine history. In a single page of Codinus we may detect
twelve unpardonable mistakes: the reconciliation of Severus and Niger,
the marriage of their son and daughter, the siege of Byzantium by the
Macedonians, the invasion of the Gauls which recalled Severus to Rome,
the *sixty* years which elapsed from his death to the foundation of Constantinople, etc.

[2] Montesquieu, Grandeur et Décadence des Romains, c. 17.

[3] Themist. Orat. iii. p. 48, edit. Hardouin. Sozomen, l. ii. c. 3. Zosim.
l. ii. [c. 31] p. 107. Anonym. Valesian. p. 715. If we could credit Codinus
(p. 10) [p. 20, *sq.*, ed. Bonn], Constantine built houses for the senators on
the exact model of their Roman palaces, and gratified them, as well as
himself, with the pleasure of an agreeable surprise; but the whole story is
full of fictions and inconsistencies.

[4] The law by which the younger Theodosius, in the year 438, abolished
this tenure, may be found among the Novellæ of that emperor at the end of
the Theodosian Code, tom. vi. nov. 12. M. de Tillemont (Hist. des

these encouragements and obligations soon became superfluous, and were gradually abolished. Wherever the seat of government is fixed, a considerable part of the public revenue will be expended by the prince himself, by his ministers, by the officers of justice, and by the domestics of the palace. The most wealthy of the provincials will be attracted by the powerful motives of interest and duty, of amusement and curiosity. A third and more numerous class of inhabitants will insensibly be formed, of servants, of artificers, and of merchants, who derive their subsistence from their own labour, and from the wants or luxury of the superior ranks. In less than a century Constantinople disputed with Rome itself the pre-eminence of riches and numbers. New piles of buildings, crowded together with too little regard to health or convenience, scarcely allowed the intervals of narrow streets for the perpetual throng of men, of horses, and of carriages. The allotted space of ground was insufficient to contain the increasing people, and the additional foundations, which on either side were advanced into the sea, might alone have composed a very considerable city.[1]

The frequent and regular distributions of wine and oil, of corn or bread, of money or provisions, had almost exempted the poorer citizens of Rome from the necessity of labour. The magnificence of the first Cæsars was in some measure imitated by the founder of Constantinople:[2] but his liberality, however it might excite the applause of the people, has incurred the censure of posterity. A nation of legislators and conquerors might assert their claim to the harvests of Africa, which had been purchased

Empereurs, tom. iv. p. 371) has evidently mistaken the nature of these estates. With a grant from the Imperial demesnes, the same condition was accepted as a favour, which would justly have been deemed a hardship if it had been imposed upon private property.

[1] The passages of Zosimus, of Eunapius, of Sozomen, and of Agathias, which relate to the increase of buildings and inhabitants at Constantinople, are collected and connected by Gyllius de Byzant l. i. c. 3. Sidonius Apollinaris (in Panegyr. Anthem. 56, p. 279, edit. Sirmond) describes the moles that were pushed forwards into the sea; they consisted of the famous Puzzolan sand, which hardens in the water.

[2] Sozomen, l. ii. c. 3. Philostorg. l. ii. c. 9. Codin. Antiquitat. Const. p. 8 [p. 16, ed. Bonn]. It appears by Socrates, l. ii. c. 13, that the daily allowance of the city consisted of eight myriads of σίτου, which we may either translate, with Valesius, by the words modii of corn, or consider as expressive of the number of loaves of bread.

[This must not be taken to mean 80,000 *medimni* as Naudet supposes, or 80,000 *modii* as Finlay believes. It is probable the reference is to 80,000 loaves of bread. In fact this is stated by the author of the Life of Paul, Bishop of Constantinople, and it is confirmed by the fact that, from the time of Aurelian, bread was daily distributed to the people at Rome instead of corn every month as formerly.—O. S.]

with their blood; and it was artfully contrived by Augustus,
that, in the enjoyment of plenty, the Romans should lose the
memory of freedom. But the prodigality of Constantine could
not be excused by any consideration either of public or private
interest; and the annual tribute of corn imposed upon Egypt
for the benefit of his new capital was applied to feed a lazy and
insolent populace, at the expense of the husbandmen of an industrious province.[1] Some other regulations of this emperor
are less liable to blame, but they are less deserving of notice. He
divided Constantinople into fourteen regions or quarters,[2]
dignified the public council with the appellation of senate,[3] communicated to the citizens the privileges of Italy,[4] and bestowed
on the rising city the title of Colony, the first and most favoured
daughter of ancient Rome. The venerable parent still maintained
the legal and acknowledged supremacy, which was due to her age,

[1] See Cod. Theodos. l. xiii. and xiv. and Cod. Justinian. Edict. xii. tom.
ii. p. 648, edit. Genev. See the beautiful complaint of Rome in the poem
of Claudian de Bell. Gildonico, ver. 60-62:—

> Cum subiit par Roma mihi, divisaque sumsit
> Æquales Aurora togas; Ægyptia rura
> In partem cessere novam.

[2] The regions of Constantinople are mentioned in the Code of Justinian,
and particularly described in the Notitia of the younger Theodosius; but
as the four last of them are not included within the wall of Constantine, it
may be doubted whether this division of the city should be referred to the
founder.

[3] Senatum constituit secundi ordinis; *Claros* vocavit. Anonym. Valesian. p. 715. The senators of old Rome were styled *Clarissimi.* See
a curious note of Valesius ad Ammian. Marcellin. xxii. 9. From the
eleventh epistle of Julian it should seem that the place of senator was
considered as a burthen rather than as an honour; but the Abbé de la
Bléterie (Vie de Jovien, tom. ii. p. 371) has shown that this epistle could
not relate to Constantinople. Might we not read, instead of the celebrated
name of Βυζαντίοις, the obscure but more probable word Βισανθήνοις?
Bisanthe or Rhœdestus, now Rhodosto, was a small maritime city of
Thrace. See Stephan. Byz. de Urbibus, p. 225 [ed. Lugd. B. 1694], and
Cellar. Geograph. tom. i. p. 849.

[4] Cod. Theodos. l. xiv. 13. [Add Cod. Just. xi. 20.—S.] The commentary of Godefroy (tom. v. p. 220) is long, but perplexed; nor indeed is it
easy to ascertain in what the Jus Italicum could consist after the freedom
of the city had been communicated to the whole empire.

[The Jus Italicum consisted in, first, the right of having a free constitution; secondly, the exemption from taxes; and thirdly, the title of the land
to be regarded as Quiritarian property. Down to the time of Diocletian,
Italy was free from both the land-tax and the poll-tax, but when she lost
this exemption the privilege was still retained by many of the provincial
towns, and continued to bear the name of the Jus Italicum, though no
longer appropriate. This is the only way in which the mention of the Jus
Italicum in the code of Justinian can be accounted for at the time when
the free constitution of the towns, and the institution of Quiritarian property
had been put an end to.—O. S.]

to her dignity, and to the remembrance of her former greatness.[1]

As Constantine urged the progress of the work with the impatience of a lover, the walls, the porticoes, and the principal edifices were completed in a few years, or, according to another account, in a few months:[2] but this extraordinary diligence should excite the less admiration, since many of the buildings were finished in so hasty and imperfect a manner, that, under the succeeding reign, they were preserved with difficulty from impending ruin.[3] But while they displayed the vigour and freshness of youth, the founder prepared to celebrate the dedication of his city.[4] The games and largesses which crowned the pomp of this memorable festival may easily be supposed; but there is one circumstance of a more singular and permanent nature, which ought not entirely to be overlooked. As often as the birthday of the city returned, the statue of Constantine, framed by his order, of gilt wood, and bearing in its right hand a small image of the genius of the place, was erected on a triumphal car. The guards, carrying white tapers, and clothed in their richest apparel, accompanied the solemn procession as it moved through the Hippodrome. When it was opposite to the throne of the reigning emperor, he rose from his seat, and

[1] Julian (Orat. i. p. 8) celebrates Constantinople as not less superior to all other cities than she was inferior to Rome itself. His learned commentator (Spanheim, p. 75, 76) justifies this language by several parallel and contemporary instances. Zosimus, as well as Socrates and Sozomen, flourished after the division of the empire between the two sons of Theodosius, which established a perfect *equality* between the old and the new capital.

[2] Codinus (Antiquitat. p. 8 [p. 17, ed. Bonn]) affirms that the foundations of Constantinople were laid in the year of the world 5837 (A.D. 329), on the 26th of September, and that the city was dedicated the 11th of May, 5838 (A.D. 330). He connects these dates with several characteristic epochs, but they contradict each other; the authority of Codinus is of little weight, and the space which he assigns must appear insufficient. The term of ten years is given us by Julian (Orat. i. p. 8); and Spanheim labours to establish the truth of it (p. 69-75), by the help of two passages from Themistius (Orat. iv. p. 58) and of Philostorgius (l. ii. c. 9), which form a period from the year 324 to the year 334. Modern critics are divided concerning this point of chronology, and their different sentiments are very accurately described by Tillemont, Hist. des Empereurs, tom. iv. p. 619-625.

[3] Themistius, Orat. iii. p. 47. Zosim. l. ii. [c. 32] p. 108. Constantine himself, in one of his laws (Cod. Theod. l. xv. tit. i. [leg. 23?]), betrays his impatience.

[4] Cedrenus and Zonaras, faithful to the mode of superstition which prevailed in their own times, assure us that Constantinople was consecrated to the virgin Mother of God.

[The city was dedicated on the 11th May, A.D. 330.—O. S.]

with grateful reverence adored the memory of his predecessor.[1]
At the festival of the dedication, an edict, engraved on a column
of marble, bestowed the title of SECOND or NEW ROME on the
city of Constantine.[2] But the name of Constantinople[3] has
prevailed over that honourable epithet, and after the revolution
of fourteen centuries still perpetuates the fame of its author.[4]

The foundation of a new capital is naturally connected with
the establishment of a new form of civil and military administration. The distinct view of the complicated system of policy
introduced by Diocletian, improved by Constantine, and completed by his immediate successors, may not only amuse the
fancy by the singular picture of a great empire, but will tend
to illustrate the secret and internal causes of its rapid decay.
In the pursuit of any remarkable institution, we may be frequently led into the more early or the more recent times of the
Roman history; but the proper limits of this inquiry will be
included within a period of about one hundred and thirty years,
from the accession of Constantine to the publication of the
Theodosian code;[5] from which, as well as from the *Notitia* of
the East and West,[6] we derive the most copious and authentic
information of the state of the empire. This variety of objects
will suspend, for some time, the course of the narrative; but
the interruption will be censured only by those readers who are
insensible to the importance of laws and manners, while they

[1] The earliest and most complete account of this extraordinary ceremony
may be found in the Alexandrian Chronicle, p. 285. Tillemont, and the
other friends of Constantine, who are offended with the air of Paganism
which seems unworthy of a Christian prince, had a right to consider it as
doubtful, but they were not authorised to omit the mention of it.

[2] Sozomen, l. ii. c. 3. Ducange, C. P. l. i. c. 6. Velut ipsius Romæ
filiam, is the expression of Augustin. de Civitat. Dei, l. v. c. 25.

[3] Eutropius, l. x. c. 8. Julian. Orat. i. p. 8. Ducange, C. P. l. i. c. 5.
The name of Constantinople is extant on the medals of Constantine.

[4] The lively Fontenelle (Dialogues des Morts, xii.) affects to deride the
vanity of human ambition, and seems to triumph in the disappointment of
Constantine, whose immortal name is now lost in the vulgar appellation of
Istambol, a Turkish corruption of εἰς τὴν πόλιν. Yet the original name is
still preserved, 1. By the nations of Europe. 2. By the modern Greeks.
3. By the Arabs, whose writings are diffused over the wide extent of their
conquests in Asia and Africa. See d'Herbelot, Bibliothèque Orientale,
p. 275. 4. By the more learned Turks, and by the emperor himself in
his public mandates. Cantemir's History of the Othman Empire, p. 51.

[5] The Theodosian code was promulgated A.D. 438. See the Prolegomena
of Godefroy, c. i. p. 185.

[6] Pancirolus, in his elaborate Commentary, assigns to the Notitia a date
almost similar to that of the Theodosian Code; but his proofs, or rather
conjectures, are extremely feeble. I should be rather inclined to place this
useful work between the final division of the empire (A.D. 395) and the
successful invasion of Gaul by the barbarians (A.D. 407). See Histoire des
Anciens Peuples de l'Europe, tom. vii. p. 40.

peruse, with eager curiosity, the transient intrigues of a court, or the accidental event of a battle.

The manly pride of the Romans, content with substantial power, had left to the vanity of the East the forms and ceremonies of ostentatious greatness.[1] But when they lost even the semblance of those virtues which were derived from their ancient freedom, the simplicity of Roman manners was insensibly corrupted by the stately affectation of the courts of Asia. The distinctions of personal merit and influence, so conspicuous in a republic, so feeble and obscure under a monarchy, were abolished by the despotism of the emperors; who substituted in their room a severe subordination of rank and office, from the titled slaves who were seated on the steps of the throne, to the meanest instruments of arbitrary power. This multitude of abject dependents was interested in the support of the actual government, from the dread of a revolution which might at once confound their hopes and intercept the reward of their services. In this divine hierarchy (for such it is frequently styled) every rank was marked with the most scrupulous exactness, and its dignity was displayed in a variety of trifling and solemn ceremonies, which it was a study to learn, and a sacrilege to neglect.[2] The purity of the Latin language was debased, by adopting, in the intercourse of pride and flattery, a profusion of epithets which Tully would scarcely have understood, and which Augustus would have rejected with indignation. The principal officers of the empire were saluted, even by the sovereign himself, with the deceitful titles of your *Sincerity*, your *Gravity*, your *Excellency*, your *Eminence*, your *sublime and wonderful Magnitude*, your *illustrious and magnificent Highness*.[3] The codicils or patents of their office were curiously emblazoned with such emblems as were best adapted to explain its nature and high dignity—the image or portrait of the reigning emperors; a triumphal car; the book of mandates placed on a table, covered with a rich carpet, and illuminated by four tapers; the allegorical figures of the pro-

---

[1] Scilicet externæ superbiæ sueto, non inerat notitia nostri (perhaps *nostræ*); apud quos vis Imperii valet, inania transmittuntur. Tacit. Annal. xv. 31. The gradation from the style of freedom and simplicity to that of form and servitude may be traced in the Epistles of Cicero, of Pliny, and of Symmachus.

[2] The emperor Gratian, after confirming a law of precedency published by Valentinian, the father of his *Divinity*, thus continues: Siquis igitur indebitum sibi locum usurpaverit, nullâ se ignorantiâ defendat; sitque plane *sacrilegii* reus, qui *divina* præcepta neglexerit. Cod. Theod. l. vi. tit. v. leg. 2.

[3] Consult the *Notitia Dignitatum* at the end of the Theodosian Code, tom. vi. p. 316.

vinces which they governed; or the appellations and standards
of the troops whom they commanded. Some of these official
ensigns were really exhibited in their hall of audience; others
preceded their pompous march whenever they appeared in
public; and every circumstance of their demeanour, their dress,
their ornaments, and their train, was calculated to inspire a
deep reverence for the representatives of supreme majesty. By
a philosophic observer the system of the Roman government
might have been mistaken for a splendid theatre, filled with
players of every character and degree, who repeated the language,
and imitated the passions, of their original model.[1]

All the magistrates of sufficient importance to find a place in
the general state of the empire were accurately divided into
three classes—1, The *Illustrious ;* 2, The *Spectabiles,* or *Respectable ;* and, 3, The *Clarissimi,* whom we may translate by the
word *Honourable.* In the times of Roman simplicity, the last-
mentioned epithet was used only as a vague expression of
deference, till it became at length the peculiar and appropriated
title of all who were members of the senate,[2] and consequently
of all who, from that venerable body, were selected to govern
the provinces. The vanity of those who, from their rank and
office, might claim a superior distinction above the rest of the
senatorial order, was long afterwards indulged with the new
appellation of *Respectable :* but the title of *Illustrious* was
always reserved to some eminent personages who were obeyed
or reverenced by the two subordinate classes. It was communicated only, I. To the consuls and patricians; II. To the
Prætorian præfects, with the præfects of Rome and Constantinople; III. To the masters general of the cavalry and the
infantry; and, IV. To the seven ministers of the palace, who
exercised their *sacred* functions about the person of the emperor.[3]
Among those illustrious magistrates who were esteemed co-
ordinate with each other, the seniority of appointment gave
place to the union of dignities.[4] By the expedient of honorary

---

[1] Pancirolus ad Notitiam utriusque Imperii, p. 39. But his explanations are obscure, and he does not sufficiently distinguish the painted
emblems from the effective ensigns of office.

[2] In the Pandects, which may be referred to the reigns of the Antonines,
Clarissimus is the ordinary and legal title of a senator.

[Another title of importance that must be noted was *Vir Consularis,* for
those holding provincial governorships.—O. S.]

[3] Pancirol. p. 12-17. I have not taken any notice of the two inferior
ranks, *Perfectissimus* and *Egregius,* which were given to many persons who
were not raised to the senatorial dignity.

[4] Cod. Theodos. l. vi. tit. vi. The rules of precedency are ascertained
with the most minute accuracy by the emperors, and illustrated with equal
prolixity by their learned interpreter.

codicils, the emperors, who were fond of multiplying their favours, might sometimes gratify the vanity, though not the ambition, of impatient courtiers.[1]

I. As long as the Roman consuls were the first magistrates of a free state, they derived their right to power from the choice of the people. As long as the emperors condescended to disguise the servitude which they imposed, the consuls were still elected by the real or apparent suffrage of the senate. From the reign of Diocletian even these vestiges of liberty were abolished, and the successful candidates, who were invested with the annual honours of the consulship, affected to deplore the humiliating condition of their predecessors. The Scipios and the Catos had been reduced to solicit the votes of plebeians, to pass through the tedious and expensive forms of a popular election, and to expose their dignity to the shame of a public refusal; while their own happier fate had reserved them for an age and government in which the rewards of virtue were assigned by the unerring wisdom of a gracious sovereign.[2] In the epistles which the emperor addressed to the two consuls elect, it was declared that they were created by his sole authority.[3] Their names and portraits, engraved on gilt tablets of ivory, were dispersed over the empire as presents to the provinces, the cities, the magistrates, the senate, and the people.[4] Their solemn inauguration was performed at the place of the Imperial residence; and during a period of one hundred and twenty years Rome was constantly deprived of the presence of her ancient magistrates.[5] On the

---

[1] Cod. Theodos. l. vi. tit. xxii.

[2] Ausonius (in Gratiarum Actione) basely expatiates on this unworthy topic, which is managed by Mamertinus (Panegyr. Vet. xi. [x.] 16, 19) with somewhat more freedom and ingenuity.

[3] Cum de Consulibus in annum creandis, solus mecum volutarem . . . te Consulem et designavi, et declaravi, et priorem nuncupavi; are some of the expressions employed by the emperor Gratian to his preceptor the poet Ausonius.

[4] Immanesque . . . dentes
Qui secti ferro in tabulas auroque micantes,
Inscripti rutilum cælato Consule nomen
Per proceres et vulgus eant.
                    Claud. de Cons. Stilichon. iii. 346.

Montfaucon has represented some of these tablets or dypticks [diptychs, δίπτυχα.—S.]; see Supplément à l'Antiquité, tom. iii. p. 220.

[5] Consule lætatur post plurima sæcula viso
Pallanteus apex: agnoscunt rostra curules
Auditas quondam proavis: desuetaque cingit
Regius auratis fora fascibus Ulpia lictor.
                    Claud. in vi. Cons. Honorii, 643.

From the reign of Carus to the sixth consulship of Honorius there was an interval of one hundred and twenty years, during which the emperors were

morning of the first of January the consuls assumed the ensigns
of their dignity. Their dress was a robe of purple, embroidered
in silk and gold, and sometimes ornamented with costly gems.[1]
On this solemn occasion they were attended by the most eminent
officers of the state and army in the habit of senators; and the
useless fasces, armed with the once formidable axes, were borne
before them by the lictors.[2] The procession moved from the
palace [3] to the Forum or principal square of the city; where the
consuls ascended their tribunal, and seated themselves in the
curule chairs, which were framed after the fashion of ancient
times. They immediately exercised an act of jurisdiction, by
the manumission of a slave who was brought before them for
that purpose; and the ceremony was intended to represent the
celebrated action of the elder Brutus, the author of liberty and
of the consulship, when he admitted among his fellow-citizens
the faithful Vindex, who had revealed the conspiracy of the
Tarquins.[4] The public festival was continued during several
days in all the principal cities; in Rome, from custom; in
Constantinople, from imitation; in Carthage, Antioch, and
Alexandria, from the love of pleasure and the superfluity of
wealth.[5] In the two capitals of the empire the annual games of

always absent from Rome on the first day of January. See the Chrono-
logie de Tillemont, tom. iii., iv. and v.

[1] See Claudian in Cons. Prob. et Olybrii, 178, etc.; and in iv. Cons.
Honorii, 585, etc.; though in the latter it is not easy to separate the
ornaments of the emperor from those of the consul. Ausonius received
from the liberality of Gratian a *vestis palmata*, or robe of state, in which the
figure of the emperor Constantius was embroidered.

> [2] Cernis ut armorum proceres legumque potentes
> Patricios sumunt habitus, et more Gabino
> Discolor incedit legio, positisque parumper
> Bellorum signis, sequitur vexilla Quirini?
> Lictori cedunt aquilæ, ridetque togatus
> Miles, et in mediis effulget curia castris?
>
> Claud. in iv. Cons. Honorii, 5.
>
> —— *strictasque* procul radiare *secures.*
>
> In Cons. Prob. 231.

[3] See Valesius ad Ammian. Marcellin. l. xxii. c. 7.

> [4] Auspice mox lætum sonuit clamore tribunal,
> Te fastos ineunte quater; solemnia ludit
> Omina Libertas: deductum Vindice morem
> Lex servat, famulusque jugo laxatus herili
> Ducitur, et grato remeat securior ictu.
>
> Claud. in iv. Cons. Honorii, 611.

[5] Celebrant quidem solemnes istos dies omnes ubique urbes quæ sub
legibus agunt; et Roma de more, et Constantinopolis de imitatione, et
Antiochia pro luxu, et discincta Carthago, et domus fluminis Alexandria,
sed Treviri Principis beneficio. Ausonius in Grat. Actione [p. 715, ed.
Amst. 1671].

the theatre, the circus, and the amphitheatre [1] cost four thousand pounds of gold, (about) one hundred and sixty thousand pounds sterling; and if so heavy an expense surpassed the faculties or the inclination of the magistrates themselves, the sum was supplied from the Imperial treasury.[2] As soon as the consuls had discharged these customary duties, they were at liberty to retire into the shade of private life, and to enjoy during the remainder of the year the undisturbed contemplation of their own greatness. They no longer presided in the national councils; they no longer executed the resolutions of peace or war. Their abilities (unless they were employed in more effective offices) were of little moment; and their names served only as the legal date of the year in which they had filled the chair of Marius and of Cicero. Yet it was still felt and acknowledged, in the last period of Roman servitude, that this empty name might be compared, and even preferred, to the possession of substantial power. The title of consul was still the most splendid object of ambition, the noblest reward of virtue and loyalty. The emperors themselves, who disdained the faint shadow of the republic, were conscious that they acquired an additional splendour and majesty as often as they assumed the annual honours of the consular dignity.[3]

The proudest and most perfect separation which can be found in any age or country between the nobles and the people is perhaps that of the Patricians and the Plebeians, as it was established in the first age of the Roman republic. Wealth and honours, the offices of the state, and the ceremonies of religion, were almost exclusively possessed by the former; who, preserving the purity of their blood with the most insulting jealousy,[4]

---

[1] Claudian (in Cons. Mall. Theodori, 279-331) describes, in a lively and fanciful manner, the various games of the circus, the theatre, and the amphitheatre, exhibited by the new consul. The sanguinary combats of gladiators had already been prohibited.

[It must be noted that 20 centenaria equal 2000 pounds in gold, not 4000. Procopius says 20 centenaria were equal to 144,000 solidi, and from the time of Constantine there were 72 solidi to the pound. Supposing the solidus to be worth 10s. English, the sum expended would be £72,000.—O. S.]

[2] Procopius in Hist. Arcana, c. 26.

[3] In Consulatu honos sine labore suscipitur. (Mamertin. in Panegyr. Vet. xi. [x.] 2). This exalted idea of the consulship is borrowed from an Oration (iii. p. 107) pronounced by Julian in the servile court of Constantius. See the Abbé de la Bléterie (Mémoires de l'Académie, tom. xxiv p. 289), who delights to pursue the vestiges of the old constitution, and who sometimes finds them in his copious fancy.

[4] Intermarriages between the Patricians and Plebeians were prohibited by the laws of the XII Tables; and the uniform operations of human nature may attest that the custom survived the law. See in Livy (iv. 1-6)

held their clients in a condition of specious vassalage. But these distinctions, so incompatible with the spirit of a free people, were removed, after a long struggle, by the persevering efforts of the Tribunes. The most active and successful of the Plebeians accumulated wealth, aspired to honours, deserved triumphs, contracted alliances, and, after some generations, assumed the pride of ancient nobility.[1] The Patrician families, on the other hand, whose original number was never recruited till the end of the commonwealth, either failed in the ordinary course of nature, or were extinguished in so many foreign and domestic wars, or, through a want of merit or fortune, insensibly mingled with the mass of the people.[2] Very few remained who could derive their pure and genuine origin from the infancy of the city, or even from that of the republic, when Cæsar and Augustus, Claudius and Vespasian, created from the body of the senate a competent number of new Patrician families, in the hope of perpetuating an order which was still considered as honourable and sacred.[3] But these artificial supplies (in which the reigning house was always included) were rapidly swept away by the rage of tyrants, by frequent revolutions, by the change of manners, and by the intermixture of nations.[4] Little more was left when Constantine ascended the throne than a vague and imperfect the pride of family urged by the consul, and the rights of mankind asserted by the tribune Canuleius.

[1] See the animated picture drawn by Sallust, in the Jugurthine war, of the pride of the nobles, and even of the virtuous Metellus, who was unable to brook the idea that the honour of the consulship should be bestowed on the obscure merit of his lieutenant Marius (c. 64). Two hundred years before, the race of the Metelli themselves were confounded among the Plebeians of Rome; and from the etymology of their name of *Cæcilius*, there is reason to believe that those haughty nobles derived their origin from a sutler.

[2] In the year of Rome 800 very few remained, not only of the old Patrician families, but even of those which had been created by Cæsar and Augustus. (Tacit. Annal. xi. 25.) The family of Scaurus (a branch of the Patrician Æmilii) was degraded so low that his father, who exercised the trade of a charcoal merchant, left him only ten slaves and somewhat less than three hundred pounds sterling. (Valerius Maximus, l. iv. c. 4, n. 11. Aurel. Victor in Scauro. [De Viris Ill. 72]). The family was saved from oblivion by the merit of the son.

[3] Tacit. Annal. xi. 25. Dion Cassius, l. lii. [c. 42] p. 693. The virtues of Agricola, who was created a Patrician by the emperor Vespasian, reflected honour on that ancient order; but his ancestors had not any claim beyond an Equestrian nobility.

[4] This failure would have been almost impossible if it were true, as Casaubon compels Aurelius Victor to affirm (ad Sueton. in Cæsar. c. 42; see Hist. August. p. 203 [Trebell. Poll. Claud. c. 3], and Casaubon Comment. p. 220), that Vespasian created at once a thousand Patrician families. But this extravagant number is too much even for the whole Senatorial order, unless we should include all the Roman knights who were distinguished by the permission of wearing the laticlave.

tradition that the Patricians had once been the first of the Romans. To form a body of nobles, whose influence may restrain while it secures the authority of the monarch, would have been very inconsistent with the character and policy of Constantine; but, had he seriously entertained such a design, it might have exceeded the measure of his power to ratify by an arbitrary edict an institution which must expect the sanction of time and of opinion. He revived, indeed, the title of PATRICIANS, but he revived it as a personal, not as an hereditary distinction. They yielded only to the transient superiority of the annual consuls; but they enjoyed the pre-eminence over all the great officers of state, with the most familiar access to the person of the prince. This honourable rank was bestowed on them for life; and, as they were usually favourites and ministers who had grown old in the Imperial court, the true etymology of the word was perverted by ignorance and flattery; and the Patricians of Constantine were reverenced as the adopted *Fathers* of the emperor and the republic.[1]

II. The fortunes of the Prætorian præfects were essentially different from those of the consuls and Patricians. The latter saw their ancient greatness evaporate in a vain title. The former, rising by degrees from the most humble condition, were invested with the civil and military administration of the Roman world. From the reign of Severus to that of Diocletian, the guards and the palace, the laws and the finances, the armies and the provinces, were intrusted to their superintending care; and, like the vizirs of the East, they held with one hand the seal, and with the other the standard, of the empire. The ambition of the præfects, always formidable, and sometimes fatal to the masters whom they served, was supported by the strength of the Prætorian bands; but, after those haughty troops had been weakened by Diocletian and finally suppressed by Constantine, the præfects, who survived their fall, were reduced without difficulty to the station of useful and obedient ministers. When they were no longer responsible for the safety of the emperor's person, they resigned the jurisdiction which they had hitherto claimed and exercised over all the departments of the palace. They were deprived by Constantine of all military command as soon as they had ceased to lead into the field, under their immediate orders, the flower of the Roman troops; and, at length, by a singular revolution, the captains of the guards were transformed into the civil magistrates of the provinces. According to the

[1] Zosimus, l. ii [c. 40] p. 118; and Godefroy ad Cod. Theodos. l. vi. tit. vi.

plan of government instituted by Diocletian, the four princes had each their Prætorian præfect; and after the monarchy was once more united in the person of Constantine, he still continued to create the same number of FOUR PRÆFECTS, and intrusted to their care the same provinces which they already administered. 1. The præfect of the East stretched his ample jurisdiction into the three parts of the globe which were subject to the Romans, from the cataracts of the Nile to the banks of the Phasis, and from the mountains of Thrace to the frontiers of Persia. 2. The important provinces of Pannonia, Dacia, Macedonia, and Greece once acknowledged the authority of the præfect of Illyricum. 3. The power of the præfect of Italy was not confined to the country from whence he derived his title; it extended over the additional territory of Rhætia as far as the banks of the Danube, over the dependent islands of the Mediterranean, and over that part of the continent of Africa which lies between the confines of Cyrene and those of Tingitania. 4. The præfect of the Gauls comprehended under that plural denomination the kindred provinces of Britain and Spain, and his authority was obeyed from the wall of Antoninus to the foot of Mount Atlas.[1]

After the Prætorian præfects had been dismissed from all military command, the civil functions which they were ordained to exercise over so many subject nations were adequate to the ambition and abilities of the most consummate ministers. To their wisdom was committed the supreme administration of justice and of the finances, the two objects which, in a state of peace, comprehend almost all the respective duties of the sovereign and of the people; of the former, to protect the citizens who are obedient to the laws; of the latter, to contribute the share of their property which is required for the expenses of the state. The coin, the highways, the posts, the granaries, the manufactures, whatever could interest the public prosperity, was moderated by the authority of the Prætorian præfects. As the immediate representatives of the Imperial majesty, they were empowered to explain, to enforce, and on some occasions to modify, the general edicts by their discretionary proclamations. They watched over the conduct of the provincial governors,

---

[1] Zosimus, l. ii. [c. 33] p. 109, 110. If we had not fortunately possessed this satisfactory account of the division of the power and provinces of the Prætorian præfects, we should frequently have been perplexed amidst the copious details of the Code, and the circumstantial minuteness of the Notitia.

[The Præfects still provided supplies for the soldiers, collected the inland revenue, and appointed as well as watched over the conduct of the provincial governors.—O. S.]

removed the negligent, and inflicted punishments on the guilty. From all the inferior jurisdictions an appeal in every matter of importance, either civil or criminal, might be brought before the tribunal of the præfect: but *his* sentence was final and absolute; and the emperors themselves refused to admit any complaints against the judgment or the integrity of a magistrate whom they honoured with such unbounded confidence.[1] His appointments were suitable to his dignity;[2] and, if avarice was his ruling passion, he enjoyed frequent opportunities of collecting a rich harvest of fees, of presents, and of perquisites. Though the emperors no longer dreaded the ambition of their præfects, they were attentive to counterbalance the power of this great office by the uncertainty and shortness of its duration.[3]

From their superior importance and dignity, Rome and Constantinople were alone excepted from the jurisdiction of the Prætorian præfects. The immense size of the city, and the experience of the tardy, ineffectual operation of the laws, had furnished the policy of Augustus with a specious pretence for introducing a new magistrate, who alone could restrain a servile and turbulent populace by the strong arm of arbitrary power.[4] Valerius Messalla was appointed the first præfect of Rome, that his reputation might countenance so invidious a measure; but at the end of a few days that accomplished citizen[5] resigned his

---

[1] See a law of Constantine himself. A præfectis autem prætorio provocare, non sinimus. Cod. Justinian. l. vii. tit. lxii. leg. 19. Charisius, a lawyer of the time of Constantine (Heinec. Hist. Juris Romani, p. 349), who admits this law as a fundamental principle of jurisprudence, compares the Prætorian præfects to the masters of the horse of the ancient dictators. Pandect. l. i. tit. xi.

[2] When Justinian, in the exhausted condition of the empire, instituted a Prætorian præfect for Africa, he allowed him a salary of one hundred pounds of gold. Cod. Justinian. l. i. tit. xxvii. leg. i.

[3] For this, and the other dignities of the empire, it may be sufficient to refer to the ample commentaries of Pancirolus and Godefroy, who have diligently collected and accurately digested in their proper order all the legal and historical materials. From those authors Dr. Howell (History of the World, vol. ii. p. 24-77) has deduced a very distinct abridgment of the state of the Roman empire.

[4] Tacit. Annal. vi. 11. Euseb. in Chron. p. 155. Dion Cassius, in the oration of Mæcenas (l. lii. [c. 21] p. 675), describes the prerogatives of the præfect of the city as they were established in his own time.

[5] The fame of Messalla has been scarcely equal to his merit. In the earliest youth he was recommended by Cicero to the friendship of Brutus. He followed the standard of the republic till it was broken in the fields of Philippi: he then accepted and deserved the favour of the most moderate of the conquerors; and uniformly asserted his freedom and dignity in the court of Augustus. The triumph of Messalla was justified by the conquest of Aquitain. As an orator he disputed the palm of eloquence with Cicero himself. Messalla cultivated every muse, and was the patron of

office, declaring, with a spirit worthy of the friend of Brutus, that he found himself incapable of exercising a power incompatible with public freedom.[1] As the sense of liberty became less exquisite, the advantages of order were more clearly understood; and the præfect, who seemed to have been designed as a terror only to slaves and vagrants, was permitted to extend his civil and criminal jurisdiction over the equestrian and noble families of Rome. The prætors, annually created as the judges of law and equity, could not long dispute the possession of the Forum with a vigorous and permanent magistrate who was usually admitted into the confidence of the prince. Their courts were deserted; their number, which had once fluctuated between twelve and eighteen,[2] was gradually reduced to two or three; and their important functions were confined to the expensive obligation [3] of exhibiting games for the amusement of the people. After the office of Roman consuls had been changed into a vain pageant, which was rarely displayed in the capital, the præfects assumed their vacant place in the senate, and were soon acknowledged as the ordinary presidents of that venerable assembly. They received appeals from the distance of one hundred miles; and it was allowed as a principle of jurisprudence that all municipal authority was derived from them alone.[4] In the discharge of his laborious employment the governor of Rome was assisted by fifteen officers, some of whom had been originally his equals, or even his superiors. The principal departments were relative to the command of a numerous watch, established as a safeguard against fires, robberies, and nocturnal disorders; the custody and distribution of the public allowance of corn and provisions; the care of the port, of the aqueducts, of the common sewers, and of the navigation and bed of the Tiber; the inspection of the markets, the theatres, and of the private as well as public works.

every man of genius. He spent his evenings in philosophic conversation with Horace; assumed his place at table between Delia and Tibullus; and amused his leisure by encouraging the poetical talents of young Ovid.

[1] Incivilem esse potestatem contestans, says the translator of Eusebius. Tacitus expresses the same idea in other words: quasi nescius exercendi.

[2] See Lipsius, Excursus D. ad 1 lib. Tacit. Annal.

[3] Heineccii Element. Juris Civilis secund. ordinem Pandect. tom. i. p. 70. See likewise Spanheim de Usu Numismatum, tom. ii. dissertat. x. p. 119. In the year 450 Marcian published a law that *three* citizens should be annually created prætors of Constantinople by the choice of the senate, but with their own consent. Cod. Justinian. l. i. tit. xxxix. leg. 2.

[4] Quidquid igitur intra urbem admittitur, ad P. U. videtur pertinere; sed et siquid intra centesimum milliarium. Ulpian in Pandect. l. i. tit. xii. n. 1. He proceeds to enumerate the various offices of the præfect, who, in the code of Justinian (l. i. tit. xxxix. leg. 3), is declared to precede and command all city magistrates sine injuriâ ac detrimento honoris alieni.

Their vigilance ensured the three principal objects of a regular police—safety, plenty, and cleanliness; and, as a proof of the attention of government to preserve the splendour and ornaments of the capital, a particular inspector was appointed for the statues; the guardian, as it were, of that inanimate people, which, according to the extravagant computation of an old writer, was scarcely inferior in number to the living inhabitants of Rome. About thirty years after the foundation of Constantinople a similar magistrate was created in that rising metropolis, for the same uses and with the same powers. A perfect equality was established between the dignity of the *two* municipal and that of the *four* Prætorian præfects.[1]

Those who in the Imperial hierarchy were distinguished by the title of *Respectable* formed an intermediate class between the *illustrious* præfects and the *honourable* magistrates of the provinces. In this class the proconsuls of Asia, Achaia, and Africa claimed a pre-eminence, which was yielded to the remembrance of their ancient dignity; and the appeal from their tribunal to that of the præfects was almost the only mark of their dependence.[2] But the civil government of the empire was distributed into thirteen great DIOCESES, each of which equalled the just measure of a powerful kingdom. The first of these dioceses was subject to the jurisdiction of the *count* of the East; and we may convey some idea of the importance and variety of his functions by observing that six hundred apparitors, who would be styled at present either secretaries, or clerks, or ushers, or messengers, were employed in his immediate office.[3] The place of *Augustal præfect* of Egypt was no longer filled by a Roman knight, but the name was retained; and the extraordinary powers which the situation of the country and the temper of the inhabitants had once made indispensable were still continued to the governor. The eleven remaining dioceses —of Asiana, Pontica, and Thrace; of Macedonia, Dacia, and Pannonia, or Western Illyricum; of Italy and Africa; of Gaul, Spain, and Britain—were governed by twelve *vicars* or *vice-*

---

[1] Besides our usual guides, we may observe that Felix Cantelorius has written a separate treatise, De Præfecto Urbis; and that many curious details concerning the police of Rome and Constantinople are contained in the fourteenth book of the Theodosian Code.

[2] Eunapius affirms that the proconsul of Asia was independent of the præfect; which must, however, be understood with some allowance: the jurisdiction of the vice-præfect he most assuredly disclaimed. Pancirolus, p. 161.

[3] The proconsul of Africa had four hundred apparitors; and they all received large salaries, either from the treasury or the province. See Pancirol, p. 26, and Cod. Justinian. l. xii. tit. lvi. lvii.

præfects,[1] whose name sufficiently explains the nature and dependence of their office. It may be added that the lieutenant-generals of the Roman armies, the military counts and dukes, who will be hereafter mentioned, were allowed the rank and title of *Respectable.*

As the spirit of jealousy and ostentation prevailed in the councils of the emperors, they proceeded with anxious diligence to divide the substance and to multiply the titles of power. The vast countries which the Roman conquerors had united under the same simple form of administration were imperceptibly crumbled into minute fragments, till at length the whole empire was distributed into one hundred and sixteen provinces, each of which supported an expensive and splendid establishment. Of these, three were governed by *proconsuls,* thirty-seven by *consulars,* five by *correctors,* and seventy-one by *presidents.*[2] The appellations of these magistrates were different; they ranked in successive order, the ensigns of their dignity were curiously varied, and their situation, from accidental circumstances, might be more or less agreeable or advantageous. But they were all (excepting only the proconsuls) alike included in the class of *honourable* persons; and they were alike intrusted, during the pleasure of the prince, and under the authority of the præfects or their deputies, with the administration of justice and the finances in their respective districts. The ponderous volumes of the Codes and Pandects[3] would furnish ample materials for a

---

[1] In Italy there was likewise the *Vicar of Rome.* It has been much disputed whether his jurisdiction measured one hundred miles from the city, or whether it stretched over the ten southern provinces of Italy.
[The Vicar of Rome was styled " Vicar of the Prætorian Prefect of Italy," and he had authority over that officer, but not over the prefect of the city (Prefectus Urbis). The Vicar of Rome governed the ten southern provinces, forwarding the income to Rome. The northern provinces were under the " Vicar of Italy." Thus the name Italia, by a singular change, came to be specially applied (in official language at least) to those northern provinces which, in the time of the Republic, were excluded from Italy proper, being styled Gallia Cisalpina (Gaul on this side of the Alps) in contradiction to Gallia Transalpina. By the later arrangement the provinces, to which the name Italia was in republican days confined, were now excluded from it. Diocletian distributed all the provinces of the empire into twelve large vicariates or dioceses. This arrangement was subsequently enlarged to thirteen, Egypt, which was at first part of the vicariate of the east, being promoted to be a separate vicariate towards the end of the fourth century.—O. S.]
[2] The Table on pp. 102-103, taken from Marquardt (Becker's Handbuch der Römischen Alterthümer, vol. iii. part i. p. 240), shows the division of the empire under the four Prætorian præfects.
[3] Among the works of the celebrated Ulpian there was one, in ten books, concerning the office of a proconsul, whose duties in the most essential articles were the same as those of an ordinary governor of a province.

minute inquiry into the system of provincial government, as in the space of six centuries it was improved by the wisdom of the Roman statesmen and lawyers. It may be sufficient for the historian to select two singular and salutary provisions, intended to restrain the abuse of authority. 1. For the preservation of peace and order, the governors of the provinces were armed with the sword of justice. They inflicted corporal punishments, and they exercised, in capital offences, the power of life and death. But they were not authorised to indulge the condemned criminal with the choice of his own execution or to pronounce a sentence of the mildest and most honourable kind of exile. These prerogatives were reserved to the præfects, who alone could impose the heavy fine of fifty pounds of gold: their vicegerents were confined to the trifling weight of a few ounces.[1] This distinction, which seems to grant the larger while it denies the smaller degree of authority, was founded on a very rational motive. The smaller degree was infinitely more liable to abuse. The passions of a provincial magistrate might frequently provoke him into acts of oppression, which affected only the freedom or the fortunes of the subject; though, from a principle of prudence, perhaps of humanity, he might still be terrified by the guilt of innocent blood. It may likewise be considered that exile, considerable fines, or the choice of an easy death, relate more particularly to the rich and the noble; and the persons the most exposed to the avarice or resentment of a provincial magistrate were thus removed from his obscure persecution to the more august and impartial tribunal of the Prætorian præfect. 2. As it was reasonably apprehended that the integrity of the judge might be biassed, if his interest was concerned or his affections were engaged, the strictest regulations were established to exclude any person, without the special dispensation of the emperor, from the government of the province where he was born;[2] and to prohibit the governor or his son from contracting

---

[1] The presidents, or consulars, could impose only two ounces; the vice-præfects, three; the proconsuls, count of the East, and præfect of Egypt, six. See Heineccii Jur. Civil. tom. i. p. 75. Pandect. l. xlviii. tit. xix. n. 8. Cod Justinian. l. i. tit. liv. leg. 4, 6.

[The term Præsides was adopted when Gallienus excluded senators from governorships of imperial provinces and appointed knights.—O. S.]

[2] Ut nulli patriæ suæ administratio sine speciali principis permissu permittatur. Cod. Justinian. l. i. tit. xli. This law was first enacted by the emperor Marcus, after the rebellion of Cassius (Dion, l. lxxi. [c. 31, p. 1195]). The same regulation is observed in China, with equal strictness, and with equal effect.

I. Præfectus Prætorio Galliarum.	II. Præfectus Prætorio Italiæ.

I. Præfectus Prætorio Galliarum.

A. *Vicarius Hispaniæ.*
1. Consularis Bæticæ.
2.   ,,   Lusitaniæ.
3.   ,,   Gallæciæ.
4. Præses Tarraconensis.
5.   ,,   Carthaginiensis.
6.   ,,   Tingitaniæ.
7.   ,,   Insularum Balearium.

B. *Vicarius Septem Provinciarum.*
1. Consularis Viennensis.
2.   ,,   Lugdunensis.
3.   ,,   Germaniæ I
4.   ,,   Germaniæ II.
5.   ,,   Belgicæ I.
6.   ,,   Belgicæ II.
7. Præses Alpium Maritimarum.
8.   ,,   Pœninarum et Graiarum.
9.   ,,   Maximæ Sequanorum.
10.   ,,   Aquitanicæ I.
11.   ,,   Aquitanicæ II.
12.   ,,   Novempopulanæ.
13.   ,,   Narbonensis I.
14.   ,,   Narbonensis II.
15.   ,,   Lugdunensis II.
16.   ,,   Lugdunensis III.
17.   ,,   Lugdunensis Senoniæ.

C. *Vicarius Britanniarum.*
1. Consularis Maximæ Cæsariensis
2.   ,,   Valentiæ
3. Præses Britanniæ I
4.   ,,   Britanniæ II.
5.   ,,   Flaviæ Cæsariensis.
    (Together 29.)

II. Præfectus Prætorio Italiæ.

A. *Vicarius Urbis Romæ.*
1. Consularis Campaniæ.
2.   ,,   Tusciæ et Umbriæ.
3.   ,,   Piceni Suburbicarii.
4.   ,,   Siciliæ.
5. Corrector Apuliæ et Calabriæ.
6.   ,,   Bruttiorum et Lucaniæ.
7. Præses Samnii.
8.   ,,   Sardiniæ.
9.   ,,   Corsicæ.
10.   ,,   Valeriæ.

B. *Vicarius Italiæ.*
1. Consularis Venetiæ et Histriæ.
2.   ,,   Æmiliæ.
3.   ,,   Liguriæ.
4.   ,,   Flaminiæ et Piceni Annonarii.
5. Præses Alpium Cottiarum.
6.   ,,   Rhætiæ I.
7.   ,,   Rhætiæ II.

Illyrium Occidentale {
8. Consularis Pannoniæ II.
9. Corrector Saviæ.
10. Præses Pannoniæ I.
11.   ,,   Dalmatiæ.
12.   ,,   Noricum Mediterraneum.
13.   ,,   Noricum Ripense
14. Dux Valeriæ Ripensis.
}

C. *Vicarius Africæ.*
1. Consularis Byzacii.
2.   ,,   Numidiæ.
3. Præses Tripolitanæ.
4.   ,,   Mauritaniæ Sitifensis.
5.   ,,   Mauritaniæ Cæsariensis.
    The Proconsul of Africa was directly under the Emperor, and not under the Præfectus Præt. Ital.
    (Together 30.)

III. Præfectus Prætorio Illyrici.	IV. Præfectus Prætorio Orientis.

III. PRÆFECTUS PRÆTORIO ILLYRICI.

A. *Directly under the Præfect.*
The Diocese of Dacia.
1. Consularis Daciæ Mediterraneæ.
2. Præses Mœsiæ I.
3. ,, Prævalitanæ.
4. ,, Dardaniæ.
5. Dux Daciæ Ripensis.

B. *Under a Proconsul.*
Achaia.

C. *Under the Vicarius Macedoniæ.*
1. Consularis Macedoniæ.
2. ,, Cretæ.
3. Præses Thessaliæ.
4. ,, Epiri Veteris.
5. ,, Epiri Novæ.
6. ,, Macedoniæ Salutaris.
A part of this last belonged to the Diocœsis Dacia.
(Together 12.)

IV. PRÆFECTUS PRÆTORIO ORIENTIS.

A. *Comes Orientis.*
1. Consularis Palæstinæ I.
2. ,, Phœnices.
3. ,, Syriæ I.
4. ,, Ciliciæ.
5. ,, Cypri.
6. Præses Palæstinæ II.
7. ,, Palæstinæ Salutaris.
8. ,, Phœnices Libani.
9. ,, Euphratensis.
10. ,, Syriæ Salutaris.
11. ,, Osrhoënæ.
12. ,, Mesopotamiæ.
13. ,, Ciliciæ II.
14. Comes Rei Militaris Isauriæ.
15. Dux Arabiæ.

B. *Præfectus Augustalis.*
1. Præses Libyæ Sup.
2. ,, Libyæ Inf.
3. ,, Thebaidos.
4. ,, Ægypti.
5. ,, Arcadiæ.
6. Corrector Augustamnicæ.

C. *Vicarius Diocœseos Asianæ.*
1. Consularis Pamphyliæ.
2. ,, Lydiæ.
3. ,, Cariæ.
4. ,, Lyciæ.
5. ,, Lycaoniæ.
6. ,, Pisidiæ.
7. ,, Phrygiæ Pacatianæ.
8. ,, Phrygiæ Salutaris.

D. *Vicarius Ponticæ.*
1. Consularis Bithyniæ.
2. ,, Galatiæ.
3. Corrector Paphlagoniæ.
4. Præses Honoriados.
5. ,, Galatiæ Salutaris.
6. ,, Cappadociæ I.
7. ,, Cappadociæ II.
8. ,, Helenoponti.
9. ,, Ponti Polemoniaci.
10. ,, Armeniæ I.
11. ,, Armeniæ II.

E. *Vicarius Thraciarum.*
1. Consularis Europæ.
2. ,, Thraciæ.
3. Præses Hæmimonti.
4. ,, Rhodopæ.
5. ,, Mœsiæ II.
6. ,, Scythiæ.
Directly under the Emperor, the Proconsul of Asia: under him,
1. Consularis Hellesponti.
2. Præses Insularum.
(Together 49.)   —S.

marriage with a native or an inhabitant;[1] or from purchasing slaves, lands, or houses within the extent of his jurisdiction.[2] Notwithstanding these rigorous precautions, the emperor Constantine, after a reign of twenty-five years, still deplores the venal and oppressive administration of justice, and expresses the warmest indignation that the audience of the judge, his despatch of business, his seasonable delays, and his final sentence, were publicly sold, either by himself or by the officers of his court. The continuance, and perhaps the impunity, of these crimes is attested by the repetition of impotent laws and ineffectual menaces.[3]

All the civil magistrates were drawn from the profession of the law. The celebrated Institutes of Justinian are addressed to the youth of his dominions who had devoted themselves to the study of Roman jurisprudence; and the sovereign condescends to animate their diligence by the assurance that their skill and ability would in time be rewarded by an adequate share in the government of the republic.[4] The rudiments of this lucrative science were taught in all the considerable cities of the East and West; but the most famous school was that of Berytus,[5] on the coast of Phœnicia, which flourished above three centuries from the time of Alexander Severus, the author perhaps of an institution so advantageous to his native country. After a regular course of education, which lasted five years, the students dispersed themselves through the provinces in search of fortune and honours; nor could they want an inexhaustible supply of business in a great empire already corrupted by the multiplicity of laws,

---

[1] Pandect. l. xxiii. tit. ii. n. 38, 57, 63.

[2] In jure continetur, ne quis in administratione constitutus aliquid compararet. Cod. Theod. l. viii. tit. xv. leg. 1. This maxim of common law was enforced by a series of edicts (see the remainder of the title) from Constantine to Justin. From this prohibition, which is extended to the meanest officers of the governor, they except only clothes and provisions. The purchase within five years may be recovered; after which, on information, it devolves to the treasury.

[3] Cessent rapaces jam nunc officialium manus; cessent, inquam; nam si moniti non cessaverint, gladiis præcidentur. etc. Cod. Theod. l. i tit. vii. leg. 1. Zeno enacted that all governors should remain in the province, to answer any accusations, fifty days after the expiration of their power. Cod. Justinian, l. i. tit. xlix. leg. 1.

[4] Summâ igitur ope, et alacri studio has leges nostras accipite; et vosmetipsos sic eruditos ostendite, ut spes vos pulcherrima foveat; toto legitimo opere perfecto, posse etiam nostram rempublicam in partibus ejus vobis credendis gubernari. Justinian. in prœem. Institutionum.

[5] The splendour of the school of Berytus, which preserved in the East the language and jurisprudence of the Romans, may be computed to have lasted from the third to the middle of the sixth century. Heinecc. Jur. Rom. Hist. p. 351-356.

of arts, and of vices. The court of the Prætorian præfect of the East could alone furnish employment for one hundred and fifty advocates, sixty-four of whom were distinguished by peculiar privileges, and two were annually chosen with a salary of sixty pounds of gold to defend the causes of the treasury. The first experiment was made of their judicial talents by appointing them to act occasionally as assessors to the magistrates; from thence they were often raised to preside in the tribunals before which they had pleaded. They obtained the government of a province; and, by the aid of merit, of reputation, or of favour, they ascended, by successive steps, to the *illustrious* dignities of the state.[1] In the practice of the bar these men had considered reason as the instrument of dispute; they interpreted the laws according to the dictates of private interest; and the same pernicious habits might still adhere to their characters in the public administration of the state. The honour of a liberal profession has indeed been vindicated by ancient and modern advocates, who have filled the most important stations with pure integrity and consummate wisdom; but in the decline of Roman jurisprudence the ordinary promotion of lawyers was pregnant with mischief and disgrace. The noble art, which had once been preserved as the sacred inheritance of the patricians, was fallen into the hands of freedmen and plebeians,[2] who, with cunning rather than with skill, exercised a sordid and pernicious trade. Some of them procured admittance into families for the purpose of fomenting differences, of encouraging suits, and of preparing a harvest of gain for themselves or their brethren. Others,

---

[1] As in a former period I have traced the civil and military promotion of Pertinax, I shall here insert the civil honours of Mallius Theodorus. 1. He was distinguished by his eloquence while he pleaded as an advocate in the court of the Prætorian præfect. 2. He governed one of the provinces of Africa, either as president or consular, and deserved, by his administration, the honour of a brass statue. 3. He was appointed vicar, or vice-præfect of Macedonia. 4. Quæstor. 5. Count of the sacred largesses. 6. Prætorian præfect of the Gauls; whilst he might yet be represented as a young man. 7. After a retreat, perhaps a disgrace, of many years, which Mallius (confounded by some critics with the poet Manilius, see Fabricius Bibliothec. Latin edit. Ernest. tom. i. c. 18, p. 501) employed in the study of the Grecian philosophy, he was named Prætorian præfect of Italy, in the year 397. 8. While he still exercised that great office, he was created, in the year 399, consul for the West; and his name, on account of the infamy of his colleague, the eunuch Eutropius, often stands alone in the Fasti. 9. In the year 408 Mallius was appointed a second time Prætorian præfect of Italy. Even in the venal panegyric of Claudian we may discover the merit of Mallius Theodorus, who, by a rare felicity, was the intimate friend both of Symmachus and of St. Augustin. See Tillemont, Hist. des Emp. tom. v. p. 1110-1114.

[2] Mamertinus in Panegyr. Vet. xi. [x.] 20. Asterius apud Photium, p. 1500.

recluse in their chambers, maintained the gravity of legal professors, by furnishing a rich client with subtleties to confound
the plainest truth, and with arguments to colour the most unjustifiable pretensions. The splendid and popular class was
composed of the advocates, who filled the Forum with the sound
of their turgid and loquacious rhetoric. Careless of fame and
of justice, they are described for the most part as ignorant and
rapacious guides, who conducted their clients through a maze
of expense, of delay, and of disappointment; from whence, after
a tedious series of years, they were at length dismissed, when their
patience and fortune were almost exhausted.[1]

III. In the system of policy introduced by Augustus, the
governors, those at least of the Imperial provinces, were invested
with the full powers of the sovereign himself. Ministers of peace
and war, the distribution of rewards and punishments depended
on them alone, and they successively appeared on their tribunal
in the robes of civil magistracy, and in complete armour at the
head of the Roman legions.[2] The influence of the revenue, the
authority of law, and the command of a military force, concurred
to render their power supreme and absolute; and whenever they
were tempted to violate their allegiance, the loyal province which
they involved in their rebellion was scarcely sensible of any
change in its political state. From the time of Commodus to
the reign of Constantine near one hundred governors might be
enumerated, who, with various success, erected the standard
of revolt; and though the innocent were too often sacrificed, the
guilty might be sometimes prevented, by the suspicious cruelty
of their master.[3] To secure his throne and the public tranquillity
from these formidable servants, Constantine resolved to divide
the military from the civil administration, and to establish, as
a permanent and professional distinction, a practice which had
been adopted only as an occasional expedient. The supreme

[1] The curious passage of Ammianus (l. xxx. c. 4), in which he paints the
manners of contemporary lawyers, affords a strange mixture of sound
sense, false rhetoric, and extravagant satire. Godefroy (Prolegom. ad
Cod. Theod. c. i. p. 185) supports the historian by similar complaints and
authentic facts. In the fourth century many camels might have been
laden with law-books. Eunapius in Vit. Ædesii, p. 72.

[2] See a very splendid example in the Life of Agricola, particularly c. 20,
21. The lieutenant of Britain was intrusted with the same powers which
Cicero, proconsul of Cilicia, had exercised in the name of the senate and
people.

[3] The Abbé Dubos, who has examined with accuracy (see Hist. de la
Monarchie Françoise tom. i. p. 41-100, edit. 1742) the institutions of
Augustus and of Constantine, observes that, if Otho had been put to death
the day before he executed his conspiracy, Otho would now appear in
history as innocent as Corbulo.

jurisdiction exercised by the Prætorian præfects over the armies of the empire was transferred to the two *masters general* whom he instituted, the one for the *cavalry*, the other for the *infantry ;* and though each of these *illustrious* officers was more peculiarly responsible for the discipline of those troops which were under his immediate inspection, they both indifferently commanded in the field the several bodies, whether of horse or foot, which were united in the same army.[1]   Their number was soon doubled by the division of the East and West; and as separate generals of the same rank and title were appointed on the four important frontiers of the Rhine, of the Upper and the Lower Danube, and of the Euphrates, the defence of the Roman empire was at length committed to eight masters general of the cavalry and infantry. Under their orders, thirty - five military commanders were stationed in the provinces: three in Britain, six in Gaul, one in Spain, one in Italy, five on the Upper and four on the Lower Danube, in Asia eight, three in Egypt, and four in Africa.   The titles of *counts* and *dukes*,[2] by which they were properly distinguished, have obtained in modern languages so very different a sense that the use of them may occasion some surprise.   But it should be recollected that the second of those appellations is only a corruption of the Latin word which was indiscriminately applied to any military chief.   All these provincial generals were therefore *dukes ;* but no more than ten among them were dignified with the rank of *counts* or companions, a title of honour, or rather of favour, which had been recently invented in the court of Constantine.   A gold belt was the ensign which distinguished the office of the counts and dukes; and, besides their pay, they received a liberal allowance sufficient to maintain one hundred and ninety servants and one hundred and fifty-eight horses.   They were strictly prohibited from interfering in any matter which related to the administration of justice or the revenue; but the command which they exercised over the troops of their department was independent of the authority of the

---

[1] Zosimus, l. ii. [c. 33] p. 110.   Before the end of the reign of Constantius the *magistri militum* were already increased to four.   See Valesius ad Ammian. l. xvi. c. 7.

[2] Though the military counts and dukes are frequently mentioned, both in history and the codes, we must have recourse to the Notitia for the exact knowledge of their number and stations.   For the institution, rank, privileges, etc., of the counts in general, see Cod. Theod. l. vi. tit. xii.-xx. with the commentary of Godefroy.

[The position of a duke or *dux* and a count or *comes*, corresponded to that of the *præses* or civil governor of a province.   The name comes or count was (says Bury) derived from the comiter who attended the princeps when he paid his official visit to the provinces.—O.S.]

magistrates. About the same time that Constantine gave a legal sanction to the ecclesiastical order, he instituted in the Roman empire the nice balance of the civil and the military powers. The emulation, and sometimes the discord, which reigned between two professions of opposite interests and incompatible manners, was productive of beneficial and of pernicious consequences. It was seldom to be expected that the general and the civil governor of a province should either conspire for the disturbance, or should unite for the service, of their country. While the one delayed to offer the assistance which the other disdained to solicit, the troops very frequently remained without orders or without supplies, the public safety was betrayed, and the defenceless subjects were left exposed to the fury of the barbarians. The divided administration, which had been formed by Constantine, relaxed the vigour of the state, while it secured the tranquillity of the monarch.

The memory of Constantine has been deservedly censured for another innovation which corrupted military discipline, and prepared the ruin of the empire. The nineteen years which preceded his final victory over Licinius had been a period of licence and intestine war. The rivals who contended for the possession of the Roman world had withdrawn the greatest part of their forces from the guard of the general frontier; and the principal cities which formed the boundary of their respective dominions were filled with soldiers, who considered their countrymen as their most implacable enemies. After the use of these internal garrisons had ceased with the civil war, the conqueror wanted either wisdom or firmness to revive the severe discipline of Diocletian, and to suppress a fatal indulgence which habit had endeared and almost confirmed to the military order. From the reign of Constantine a popular and even legal distinction was admitted between the *Palatines* [1] and the *Borderers ;* the troops

---

[1] Zosimus, l. ii. [c. 34] p. 111. The distinction between the two classes of Roman troops is very darkly expressed in the historians, the laws, and the Notitia. Consult, however, the copious *paratitlon* or abstract, which Godefroy has drawn up, of the seventh book, de Re Militari, of the Theodosian Code, l. vii. tit. i. leg. 18; l. viii. tit. i. leg. 10.

[With regard to the new military organisation introduced into the empire in the epoch of Diocletian and Constantine, see Mommsen's article in *Hermes* for 1889 (vol. xxiv. p. 129) entitled *Das römische Militärwesen seit Diocletian*, and the masterly summary of it which appears in Appendix No. 12, vol. ii. of Bury's Gibbon. Briefly stated the points are as follow, viz.—that under Diocletian the regular army was divided into two main sections,—(1) the troops that accompanied the emperor as he moved throughout the empire, and (2) the troops that were stationary on the frontiers. The former were called *milites in sacro comitatu*, the latter *limitanei*.

of the court, as they were improperly styled, and the troops of the frontier. The former, elevated by the superiority of their pay and privileges, were permitted, except in the extraordinary emergencies of war, to occupy their tranquil stations in the heart of the provinces. The most flourishing cities were oppressed by the intolerable weight of quarters. The soldiers insensibly forgot the virtues of their profession, and contracted only the vices of civil life. They were either degraded by the industry of mechanic trades, or enervated by the luxury of baths and theatres. They soon became careless of their martial exercises, curious in their diet and apparel, and, while they inspired terror to the subjects of the empire, they trembled at the hostile approach of the barbarians.[1] The chain of fortifications which Diocletian and his colleagues had extended along the banks of the great rivers was no longer maintained with the same care, or defended with the same vigilance. The numbers which still remained under the name of the troops of the frontier might be sufficient for the ordinary defence. But their spirit was degraded by the humiliating reflection that *they*, who were exposed to the hardships and dangers of a perpetual warfare, were rewarded only with about two-thirds of the pay and emoluments which were lavished on the troops of the court. Even the bands or legions that were raised the nearest to the level of those unworthy favourites were in some measure disgraced by the title of honour which they were allowed to assume. It was in vain that Constantine repeated the most dreadful menaces of fire and sword against the Borderers who should dare to desert their colours, to connive at the inroads of the barbarians, or to participate in the spoil.[2] The mischiefs which flow from injudicious counsels are seldom removed by the application of partial severities: and though succeeding princes laboured to restore the strength and numbers of the frontier garrisons, the empire, till the last moment of its dissolution, continued to languish under the mortal wound which had been so rashly or so weakly inflicted by the hand of Constantine.

The same timid policy, of dividing whatever is united, of

Early in Constantine's reign the *milites in sacro comitatu* were broken into two, the *comitatenses* and the *Palatini*. There were, therefore, three classes, *Palatini*, *Comitatenses*, and *limitanei*.—O. S.]

[1] Ferox erat in suos miles et rapax, ignavus vero in hostes et fractus. Ammian. l. xxii. c. 4. He observes that they loved downy beds and houses of marble, and that their cups were heavier than their swords.

[2] Cod. Theod. l. vii. tit. i. leg. 1; tit. xii. leg. 1. See Howell's Hist. of the World, vol. ii. p. 19. That learned historian, who is not sufficiently known, labours to justify the character and policy of Constantine.

reducing whatever is eminent, of dreading every active power, and of expecting that the most feeble will prove the most obedient, seems to pervade the institutions of several princes, and particularly those of Constantine. The martial pride of the legions, whose victorious camps had so often been the scene of rebellion, was nourished by the memory of their past exploits, and the consciousness of their actual strength. As long as they maintained their ancient establishment of six thousand men, they subsisted, under the reign of Diocletian, each of them singly, a visible and important object in the military history of the Roman empire. A few years afterwards these gigantic bodies were shrunk to a very diminutive size; and when *seven* legions, with some auxiliaries, defended the city of Amida against the Persians, the total garrison, with the inhabitants of both sexes, and the peasants of the deserted country, did not exceed the number of twenty thousand persons.[1] From this fact, and from similar examples, there is reason to believe that the constitution of the legionary troops, to which they partly owed their valour and discipline, was dissolved by Constantine; and that the bands of Roman infantry, which still assumed the same names and the same honours, consisted only of one thousand or fifteen hundred men.[2] The conspiracy of so many separate detachments, each of which was awed by the sense of its own weakness, could easily be checked; and the successors of Constantine might indulge their love of ostentation, by issuing their orders to one hundred and thirty-two legions, inscribed on the muster-roll of their numerous armies. The remainder of their troops was distributed into several hundred cohorts of infantry, and squadrons of cavalry. Their arms, and titles, and ensigns were calculated to inspire terror, and to display the variety of nations who marched under the Imperial standard. And not a vestige was left of that severe simplicity which, in the ages of freedom and victory, had distinguished the line of battle of a Roman army from the confused host of an Asiatic monarch.[3] A more particular enumeration, drawn from the *Notitia*, might exercise the

[1] Ammian, l. xix. c. 2. He observes (c. 5) that the desperate sallies of two Gallic legions were like a handful of water thrown on a great conflagration.

[2] Pancirolus ad Notitiam, p. 96. Mémoires de l'Académie des Inscriptions, tom. xxv. p. 491.

[3] Romana acies unius prope formæ erat et hominum et armorum genere. —Regia acies varia magis multis gentibus dissimilitudine armorum auxiliorumque erat. T. Liv. l. xxxvii. c. 39, 40. Flaminius [Flamininus], even before the event, had compared the army of Antiochus to a supper in which the flesh of one vile animal was diversified by the skill of the cooks. See the Life of Flaminius [Flamininus] in Plutarch.

diligence of an antiquary; but the historian will content himself with observing that the number of permanent stations or garrisons established on the frontiers of the empire amounted to five hundred and eighty-three; and that, under the successors of Constantine, the complete force of the military establishment was computed at six hundred and forty-five thousand soldiers.[1] An effort so prodigious surpassed the wants of a more ancient and the faculties of a later period.

In the various states of society armies are recruited from very different motives. Barbarians are urged by the love of war; the citizens of a free republic may be prompted by a principle of duty; the subjects, or at least the nobles, of a monarchy are animated by a sentiment of honour; but the timid and luxurious inhabitants of a declining empire must be allured into the service by the hopes of profit, or compelled by the dread of punishment. The resources of the Roman treasury were exhausted by the increase of pay, by the repetition of donatives, and by the invention of new emoluments and indulgences, which, in the opinion of the provincial youth, might compensate the hardships and dangers of a military life. Yet, although the stature was lowered,[2] although slaves, at least by a tacit connivance, were indiscriminately received into the ranks, the insurmountable difficulty of procuring a regular and adequate supply of volunteers obliged the emperors to adopt more effectual and coercive methods. The lands bestowed on the veterans, as the free reward of their valour, were henceforwards granted under a condition which contains the first rudiments of the feudal tenures—that their sons, who succeeded to the inheritance, should devote themselves to the profession of arms as soon as they attained the age of manhood; and their cowardly refusal was punished by the loss of honour, of fortune, or even of life.[3] But as the annual growth of the sons of the veterans bore a very small proportion to the demands of the service, levies of men were frequently required from the provinces, and every proprietor was obliged either to take up arms, or to procure a substitute, or to purchase his

[1] Agathias, l. v. p. 157, edit. Louvre [c. 13, p. 305, ed. Bonn].

[2] Valentinian (Cod. Theodos. l. vii. tit. xiii. leg. 3) fixes the standard at five feet seven inches, about five feet four inches and a half English measure. It had formerly been five feet ten inches, and in the best corps six Roman feet. Sed tunc erat amplior multitudo, et plures militiam sequebantur armatam. Vegetius de Re Militari, l. i. c. 5.

[3] See the two titles, De Veteranis and De Filiis Veteranorum [tit. xx. xxii.], in the seventh book of the Theodosian Code. The age at which their military service was required varied from twenty-five to sixteen. If the sons of the veterans appeared with a horse, they had a right to serve in the cavalry; two horses gave them some valuable privileges.

exemption by the payment of a heavy fine. The sum of forty-two pieces of gold, to which it was *reduced*, ascertains the exorbitant price of volunteers, and the reluctance with which the government admitted of this alternative.[1] Such was the horror for the profession of a soldier which had affected the minds of the degenerate Romans that many of the youth of Italy and the provinces chose to cut off the fingers of their right hand to escape from being pressed into the service; and this strange expedient was so commonly practised as to deserve the severe animadversion of the laws,[2] and a peculiar name in the Latin language.[3]

The introduction of barbarians into the Roman armies became every day more universal, more necessary, and more fatal. The most daring of the Scythians, of the Goths, and of the Germans, who delighted in war, and who found it more profitable to defend than to ravage the provinces, were enrolled not only in the auxiliaries of their respective nations, but in the legions themselves, and among the most distinguished of the Palatine troops.

[1] Cod. Theod. l. vii. tit. xiii. leg. 7. According to the historian Socrates (see Godefroy ad loc.), the same emperor Valens sometimes required eighty pieces of gold for a recruit. In the following law it is faintly expressed that slaves shall not be admitted inter optimas lectissimorum militum turmas.
[Finlay, in his excellent work, *Greece under the Romans*, says, " The necessity of preventing the possibility of a falling off in the revenue was, in the eyes of the imperial court, of as much consequence as the maintenance of the efficiency of the army. Proprietors of land and citizens of wealth were not allowed to enrol themselves as soldiers, lest they should escape from paying their taxes. Only those plebeians and peasants who were not subject to the land tax were received as warriors. It was the duty of the poor to serve in person, and of the rich to supply the revenues of the state." The effect of this was that the Roman forces were often recruited with slaves, in spite of the laws passed to prevent this; and not long after the time of Constantine, slaves were often admitted to enter the army on receiving their freedom." Cf. Finlay's *Greece*, p. 131, also *History of the Byzantine Empire*, p. 33.—O. S.]
[2] The person and property of a Roman knight, who had mutilated his two sons, were sold at public auction by order of Augustus. (Sueton. in August. c. 24.) The moderation of that artful usurper proves that this example of severity was justified by the spirit of the times. Ammianus makes a distinction between the effeminate Italians and the hardy Gauls (l. xv. c. 12). Yet only fifteen years afterwards, Valentinian, in a law addressed to the præfect of Gaul, is obliged to enact that these cowardly deserters shall be burnt alive. (Cod. Theod. l. vii. tit. xiii. leg. 5.) Their numbers in Illyricum were so considerable that the province complained of a scarcity of recruits. (Id. leg. 10.)
[3] They were called *Murci*. *Murcidus* is found in Plautus and Festus to denote a lazy and cowardly person, who, according to Arnobius and Augustin, was under the immediate protection of the goddess *Murcia*. From this particular instance of cowardice *murcare* is used as synonymous to *mutilare* by the writers of the middle Latinity. See Lindenbrogius and Valesius ad Ammian. Marcellin. l. xv. c. 12.

As they freely mingled with the subjects of the empire, they gradually learned to despise their manners and to imitate their arts. They abjured the implicit reverence which the pride of Rome had exacted from their ignorance, while they acquired the knowledge and possession of those advantages by which alone she supported her declining greatness. The barbarian soldiers who displayed any military talents were advanced, without exception, to the most important commands; and the names of the tribunes, of the counts and dukes, and of the generals themselves, betray a foreign origin, which they no longer condescended to disguise. They were often intrusted with the conduct of a war against their countrymen; and though most of them preferred the ties of allegiance to those of blood, they did not always avoid the guilt, or at least the suspicion, of holding a treasonable correspondence with the enemy, of inviting his invasion, or of sparing his retreat. The camps and the palace of the son of Constantine were governed by the powerful faction of the Franks, who preserved the strictest connection with each other and with their country, and who resented every personal affront as a national indignity.[1] When the tyrant Caligula was suspected of an intention to invest a very extraordinary candidate with the consular robes, the sacrilegious profanation would have scarcely excited less astonishment if, instead of a horse, the noblest chieftain of Germany or Britain had been the object of his choice. The revolution of three centuries had produced so remarkable a change in the prejudices of the people, that, with the public approbation, Constantine showed his successors the example of bestowing the honours of the consulship on the barbarians who, by their merit and services, had deserved to be ranked among the first of the Romans.[2] But as these hardy veterans, who had been educated in the ignorance or contempt of the laws, were incapable of exercising any civil offices, the powers of the human mind were contracted by the irreconcilable separation of talents as well as of professions. The accomplished citizens of the Greek and Roman republics, whose characters

---

[1] Malarichus—adhibitis Francis quorum ea tempestate in palatio multitudo florebat, erectius jam loquebatur tumultuabaturque. Ammian. l. xv. c. 5.

[2] Barbaros omnium primus, ad usque fasces auxerat et trabeas consulares. Ammian. l. xxi. c. 10. Eusebius (in Vit. Constantin. l. iv. c. 7) and Aurelius Victor seem to confirm the truth of this assertion; yet in the thirty-two consular Fasti of the reign of Constantine I cannot discover the name of a single barbarian. I should therefore interpret the liberality of that prince as relative to the ornaments, rather than to the office, of the consulship.

could adapt themselves to the bar, the senate, the camp, or the schools, had learned to write, to speak, and to act with the same spirit, and with equal abilities.

IV. Besides the magistrates and generals, who at a distance from the court diffused their delegated authority over the provinces and armies, the emperor conferred the rank of *Illustrious* on seven of his more immediate servants, to whose fidelity he intrusted his safety, or his counsels, or his treasures. 1. The private apartments of the palace were governed by a favourite eunuch, who, in the language of that age, was styled the *præpositus*, or præfect of the sacred bedchamber. His duty was to attend the emperor in his hours of state or in those of amusement, and to perform about his person all those menial services which can only derive their splendour from the influence of royalty. Under a prince who deserved to reign, the great chamberlain (for such we may call him) was an useful and humble domestic; but an artful domestic, who improves every occasion of unguarded confidence, will insensibly acquire over a feeble mind that ascendant which harsh wisdom and uncomplying virtue can seldom obtain. The degenerate grandsons of Theodosius, who were invisible to their subjects, and contemptible to their enemies, exalted the præfects of their bedchamber above the heads of all the ministers of the palace; [1] and even his deputy, the first of the splendid train of slaves who waited in the presence, was thought worthy to rank before the *respectable* proconsuls of Greece or Asia. The jurisdiction of the chamberlain was acknowledged by the *counts*, or superintendents, who regulated the two important provinces of the magnificence of the wardrobe, and of the luxury of the Imperial table.[2] 2. The principal administration of public affairs was committed to the diligence and abilities of the *master of the offices*.[3] He was the supreme magistrate of the palace, inspected the discipline of the civil and military *schools*, and received appeals from all parts of the

---

[1] Cod. Theod. l. vi. tit. 8.

[2] By a very singular metaphor, borrowed from the military character of the first emperors, the steward of their household was styled the count of their camp (comes castrensis). Cassiodorus very seriously represents to him that his own fame, and that of the empire, must depend on the opinion which foreign ambassadors may conceive of the plenty and magnificence of the royal table. (Variar. l. vi. epistol. 9.)

[3] Gutherius (de Officiis Domûs Augustæ, l. ii. c. 20, l. iii.) has very accurately explained the functions of the master of the offices, and the constitution of the subordinate *scrinia*. But he vainly attempts, on the most doubtful authority, to deduce from the time of the Antonines, or even of Nero, the origin of a magistrate who cannot be found in history before the reign of Constantine.

empire, in the causes which related to that numerous army of
privileged persons who, as the servants of the court, had obtained
for themselves and families a right to decline the authority of
the ordinary judges. The correspondence between the prince
and his subjects was managed by the four *scrinia*, or offices of
this minister of state. The first was appropriated to memorials,
the second to epistles, the third to petitions, and the fourth to
papers and orders of a miscellaneous kind. Each of these was
directed by an inferior *master* of *respectable* dignity, and the whole
business was despatched by an hundred and forty-eight secretaries, chosen for the most part from the profession of the law,
on account of the variety of abstracts of reports and references
which frequently occurred in the exercise of their several
functions. From a condescension which in former ages would
have been esteemed unworthy of the Roman majesty, a particular
secretary was allowed for the Greek language; and interpreters
were appointed to receive the ambassadors of the barbarians;
but the department of foreign affairs, which constitutes so
essential a part of modern policy, seldom diverted the attention
of the master of the offices. His mind was more seriously engaged
by the general direction of the posts and arsenals of the empire.
There were thirty-four cities, fifteen in the East and nineteen
in the West, in which regular companies of workmen were perpetually employed in fabricating defensive armour, offensive
weapons of all sorts, and military engines, which were deposited
in the arsenals, and occasionally delivered for the service of the
troops. 3. In the course of nine centuries the office of *quæstor*
had experienced a very singular revolution. In the infancy of
Rome, two inferior magistrates were annually elected by the
people, to relieve the consuls from the invidious management of
the public treasure;[1] a similar assistant was granted to every
proconsul and to every prætor who exercised a military or provincial command; with the extent of conquest, the two quæstors
were gradually multiplied to the number of four, of eight, of

---

[1] Tacitus (Annal. xi. 22) says that the first quæstors were elected by the
people sixty-four years after the foundation of the republic; but he is of
opinion that they had, long before that period, been annually appointed
by the consuls, and even by the kings. But this obscure point of antiquity
is contested by other writers.
[Niebuhr endeavours to reconcile these conflicting statements by showing that there were in the early days of the republic two different classes of
officers bearing this name: one called *Quæstores parricidii*, who were public
accusers, and the other called *Quæstores classici*, the financial officers. The
former existed at Rome in the kingly period, while the latter did not exist
until the time of the republic. Cf. Smith's Dictionary of Greek and
Roman Antiquities.—O. S.

twenty, and for a short time, perhaps, of forty;[1] and the noblest citizens ambitiously solicited an office which gave them a seat in the senate, and a just hope of obtaining the honours of the republic. Whilst Augustus affected to maintain the freedom of election, he consented to accept the annual privilege of recommending, or rather indeed of nominating, a certain proportion of candidates; and it was his custom to select one of these distinguished youths to read his orations or epistles in the assemblies of the senate.[2] The practice of Augustus was imitated by succeeding princes; the occasional commission was established as a permanent office; and the favoured quæstor, assuming a new and more illustrious character, alone survived the suppression of his ancient and useless colleagues.[3] As the orations which he composed in the name of the emperor[4] acquired the force, and at length the form, of absolute edicts, he was considered as the representative of the legislative power, the oracle of the council, and the original source of the civil jurisprudence. He was sometimes invited to take his seat in the supreme judicature of the Imperial consistory, with the Prætorian præfects and the master of the offices; and he was frequently requested to resolve the doubts of inferior judges: but as he was not oppressed with a variety of subordinate business, his leisure and talents were

---

[1] Tacitus (Annal. xi. 22) seems to consider twenty as the highest number of quæstors; and Dion (l. xliii. [c. 47] p. 374) insinuates that, if the dictator Cæsar once created forty, it was only to facilitate the payment of an immense debt of gratitude. Yet the augmentation which he made of prætors subsisted under the succeeding reigns.

[2] Sueton. in August. c. 65, and Torrent. ad loc. Dion Cas. p. 755.

[3] The youth and inexperience of the quæstors, who entered on that important office in their twenty-fifth year (Lips. Excurs. ad Tacit. l. iii. D.), engaged Augustus to remove them from the management of the treasury; and though they were restored by Claudius, they seem to have been finally dismissed by Nero. (Tacit. Annal. xiii. 29. Sueton. in Aug. c. 36, in Claud. c. 24. Dion, p. 696 [l. liii. c. 2], 961 [l. lx. c. 24], etc. Plin. Epistol. x. 20, et alibi.) In the provinces of the Imperial division, the place of the quæstors was more ably supplied by the *procurators* (Dion Cas. p. 707 [l. liii. c. 15]; Tacit. in Vit. Agricol. c. 15); or, as they were afterwards called, *rationales*. (Hist. August. p. 130 [Lamprid. Alex. Sever. cc. 45, 46].) But in the provinces of the senate we may still discover a series of quæstors till the reign of Marcus Antoninus. (See the Inscriptions of Gruter, the Epistles of Pliny, and a decisive fact in the Augustan History, p. 64 [Spartian. Sever. c. 2].) From Ulpian we may learn (Pandect. l. i. tit. 13) that, under the government of the House of Severus, their provincial administration was abolished; and in the subsequent troubles the annual or triennial elections of quæstors must have naturally ceased.

[4] Cum patris nomine et epistolas ipse dictaret, et edicta conscriberet, orationesque in senatu recitaret, etiam quæstoris vice. Sueton. in Tit. c. 6. The office must have acquired new dignity, which was occasionally executed by the heir apparent of the empire. Trajan intrusted the same care to Hadrian, his quæstor and cousin. See Dodwell, Prælection. Cambden. x. xi. p. 362-394.

employed to cultivate that dignified style of eloquence which, in the corruption of taste and language, still preserves the majesty of the Roman laws.[1]　In some respects the office of the Imperial quæstor may be compared with that of a modern chancellor; but the use of a great seal, which seems to have been adopted by the illiterate barbarians, was never introduced to attest the public acts of the emperors.　4. The extraordinary title of *count of the sacred largesses* was bestowed on the treasurer-general of the revenue, with the intention perhaps of inculcating that every payment flowed from the voluntary bounty of the monarch.　To conceive the almost infinite detail of the annual and daily expense of the civil and military administration in every part of a great empire would exceed the powers of the most vigorous imagination.　The actual account employed several hundred persons, distributed into eleven different offices, which were artfully contrived to examine and control their respective operations.　The multitude of these agents had a natural tendency to increase; and it was more than once thought expedient to dismiss to their native homes the useless super-numeraries, who, deserting their honest labours, had pressed with too much eagerness into the lucrative profession of the finances.[2]　Twenty-nine provincial receivers, of whom eighteen were honoured with the title of count, corresponded with the treasurer; and he extended his jurisdiction over the mines from whence the precious metals were extracted, over the mints in which they were converted into the current coin, and over the public treasuries of the most important cities, where they were deposited for the service of the state.　The foreign trade of the empire was regulated by this minister, who directed likewise all the linen and woollen manufactures, in which the successive operations of spinning, weaving, and dyeing were executed, chiefly by women of a servile condition, for the use of the palace and army.　Twenty-six of these institutions are enumerated in the West, where the arts had been more recently introduced, and a still larger proportion may be allowed for the industrious provinces of the East.[3]　5. Besides the public revenue, which

---

[1]　———— Terris edicta daturus,
Supplicibus responsa, venis.　Oracula regis
Eloquio crevere tuo; nec dignius unquam
Majestas meminit sese Romana locutam.

Claudian in Consulat. Mall. Theodor. 33.　See likewise Symmachus (Epistol. i. 17) and Cassiodorus (Variar. vi. 5).

[2] Cod. Theod. l. vi. tit. 30.　Cod. Justinian. l. xii. tit. 24.

[3] In the departments of the two counts of the treasury the eastern part of the *Notitia* happens to be very defective.　It may be observed that **we**

an absolute monarch might levy and expend according to his pleasure, the emperors, in the capacity of opulent citizens, possessed a very extensive property, which was administered by the *count* or treasurer of *the private estate.* Some part had perhaps been the ancient demesnes of kings and republics; some accessions might be derived from the families which were successively invested with the purple; but the most considerable portion flowed from the impure source of confiscations and forfeitures. The Imperial estates were scattered through the provinces from Mauritania to Britain; but the rich and fertile soil of Cappadocia tempted the monarch to acquire in that country his fairest possessions,[1] and either Constantine or his successors embraced the occasion of justifying avarice by religious zeal. They suppressed the rich temple of Comana, where the high-priest of the goddess of war supported the dignity of a sovereign prince; and they applied to their private use the consecrated lands, which were inhabited by six thousand subjects or slaves of the deity and her ministers.[2] But these were not the valuable inhabitants: the plains that stretch from the foot of Mount Argæus to the banks of the Sarus bred a generous race of horses, renowned above all others in the ancient world for their majestic shape and incomparable swiftness. These *sacred* animals, destined for the service of the palace and the Imperial games, were protected by the laws from the profanation of a vulgar master.[3] The demesnes of Cappadocia were important enough to require the inspection of a *count* ;[4] officers of an inferior rank were stationed in the other parts of the empire; and the deputies of the private, as well as those of the public treasurer, were maintained in the exercise of their independent

had a treasury chest in London, and a gyneceum or manufacture at Winchester. But Britain was not thought worthy either of a mint or of an arsenal. Gaul alone possessed three of the former and eight of the latter.

[1] Cod. Theod. l. vi. tit. xxx. leg. 2; and Godefroy ad loc.

[2] Strabon. Geograph. l. xii. p. 809 [p. 535, edit. Casaub.]. The other temple of Comana, in Pontus, was a colony from that of Cappadocia, l. xii. p. 835 [p. 557, ed. Casaub.]. The president Des Brosses (see his Saluste, tom. ii. p. 21) conjectures that the deity adored in both Comanas was Beltis, the Venus of the East, the goddess of generation; a very different being indeed from the goddess of war.

[3] Cod. Theod. l. x. tit. vi. de Grege Dominico. Godefroy has collected every circumstance of antiquity relative to the Cappadocian horses. One of the finest breeds, the Palmatian, was the forfeiture of a rebel, whose estate lay about sixteen miles from Tyana, near the great road between Constantinople and Antioch.

[4] Justinian (Novell. 30) subjected the province of the count of Cappadocia to the immediate authority of the favourite eunuch, who presided over the sacred bedchamber.

functions, and encouraged to control the authority of the provincial magistrates.[1] 6, 7. The chosen bands of cavalry and infantry, which guarded the person of the emperor, were under the immediate command of the *two counts of the domestics*. The whole number consisted of three thousand five hundred men, divided into seven *schools*, or troops, of five hundred each; and in the East this honourable service was almost entirely appropriated to the Armenians. Whenever, on public ceremonies, they were drawn up in the courts and porticos of the palace, their lofty stature, silent order, and splendid arms of silver and gold, displayed a martial pomp not unworthy of the Roman majesty.[2] From the seven schools two companies of horse and foot were selected, of the *protectors*, whose advantageous station was the hope and reward of the most deserving soldiers. They mounted guard in the interior apartments, and were occasionally despatched into the provinces, to execute with celerity and vigour the orders of their master.[3] The counts of the domestics had succeeded to the office of the Prætorian præfects; like the præfects, they aspired from the service of the palace to the command of armies.

The perpetual intercourse between the court and the provinces was facilitated by the construction of roads and the institution of posts. But these beneficial establishments were accidentally connected with a pernicious and intolerable abuse. Two or three hundred *agents* or messengers were employed, under the jurisdiction of the master of the offices, to announce the names of the annual consuls, and the edicts or victories of the emperors. They insensibly assumed the licence of reporting whatever they could observe of the conduct either of magistrates or of private citizens; and were soon considered as the eyes of the monarch [4] and the scourge of the people. Under the warm influence of a feeble reign they multiplied to the incredible number of ten thousand, disdained the mild though frequent admonitions of the laws, and exercised in the profitable management of the posts a rapacious and insolent oppression. These official spies,

---

[1] Cod. Theod. l. vi. tit. xxx. leg. 4, etc.

[2] Pancirolus, p. 102, 136. The appearance of these military domestics is described in the Latin poem of Corippus, De Laudibus Justin. l. iii. 157-179, p. 419, 420 of the Appendix Hist. Byzantin. Rom. 1777.

[3] Ammianus Marcellinus, who served so many years, obtained only the rank of a protector. The first ten among these honourable soldiers were *Clarissimi*.

[4] Xenophon, Cyropæd. l. viii. [c. 2, §§ 10, 11.] Brisson, de Regno Persico, l. i. N°. 190, p. 264. The emperors adopted with pleasure this Persian metaphor.

who regularly corresponded with the palace, were encouraged, by favour and reward, anxiously to watch the progress of every treasonable design, from the faint and latent symptoms of disaffection, to the actual preparation of an open revolt. Their careless or criminal violation of truth and justice was covered by the consecrated mask of zeal; and they might securely aim their poisoned arrows at the breast either of the guilty or the innocent, who had provoked their resentment, or refused to purchase their silence. A faithful subject, of Syria perhaps, or of Britain, was exposed to the danger, or at least to the dread, of being dragged in chains to the court of Milan or Constantinople, to defend his life and fortune against the malicious charge of these privileged informers. The ordinary administration was conducted by those methods which extreme necessity can alone palliate; and the defects of evidence were diligently supplied by the use of torture.[1]

The deceitful and dangerous experiment of the criminal *quæstion*, as it is emphatically styled, was admitted, rather than approved, in the jurisprudence of the Romans. They applied this sanguinary mode of examination only to servile bodies, whose sufferings were seldom weighed by those haughty republicans in the scale of justice or humanity; but they would never consent to violate the sacred person of a citizen till they possessed the clearest evidence of his guilt.[2] The annals of tyranny, from the reign of Tiberius to that of Domitian, circumstantially relate the executions of many innocent victims; but, as long as the faintest remembrance was kept alive of the national freedom and honour, the last hours of a Roman were secure from the danger of ignominious torture.[3] The conduct of the provincial magistrates was not, however, regulated by the practice of the city, or the strict maxims of the civilians. They found the use of torture established not only among the slaves of oriental despotism, but among the Macedonians, who obeyed a limited

---

[1] For the *Agentes in Rebus*, see Ammian. l. xv. c. 3, l. xvi. c. 5, l. xxii. c. 7, with the curious annotations of Valesius. Cod. Theod. l. vi. tit. xxvii. xxviii. xxix. Among the passages collected in the Commentary of Godefroy, the most remarkable is one from Libanius, in his discourse concerning the death of Julian.

[2] The Pandects (l. xlviii. tit. xviii.) contain the sentiments of the most celebrated civilians on the subject of torture. They strictly confine it to slaves; and Ulpian himself is ready to acknowlege that Res est fragilis, et periculosa, et quæ veritatem fallat. [§ 23.]

[3] In the conspiracy of Piso against Nero, Epicharis (libertina mulier) was the only person tortured; the rest were *intacti tormentis*. It would be superfluous to add a weaker, and it would be difficult to find a stronger, example. Tacit. Annal. xv. 57.

monarch; among the Rhodians, who flourished by the liberty of commerce; and even among the sage Athenians, who had asserted and adorned the dignity of human kind.[1] The acquiescence of the provincials encouraged their governors to acquire, or perhaps to usurp, a discretionary power of employing the rack, to extort from vagrants or plebeian criminals the confession of their guilt, till they insensibly proceeded to confound the distinctions of rank, and to disregard the privileges of Roman citizens. The apprehensions of the subjects urged them to solicit, and the interest of the sovereign engaged him to grant, a variety of special exemptions, which tacitly allowed, and even authorised, the general use of torture. They protected all persons of illustrious or honourable rank, bishops and their presbyters, professors of the liberal arts, soldiers and their families, municipal officers, and their posterity to the third generation, and all children under the age of puberty.[2] But a fatal maxim was introduced into the new jurisprudence of the empire, that in the case of treason, which included every offence that the subtlety of lawyers could derive from an *hostile intention* towards the prince or republic,[3] all privileges were suspended, and all conditions were reduced to the same ignominious level. As the safety of the emperor was avowedly preferred to every consideration of justice or humanity, the dignity of age and the tenderness of youth were alike exposed to the most cruel tortures; and the terrors of a malicious information, which might select them as the accomplices, or even as the witnesses, perhaps, of an imaginary crime, perpetually hung over the heads of the principal citizens of the Roman world.[4]

These evils, however terrible they may appear, were confined to the smaller number of Roman subjects whose dangerous

---

[1] Dicendum . . . de institutis Atheniensium, Rhodiorum, doctissimorum hominum, apud quos etiam (id quod acerbissimum est) liberi, civesque torquentur. Cicero, Partit. Orat. c. 34. We may learn from the trial of Philotas the practice of the Macedonians. (Diodor. Sicul. l. xvii. [c. 80] p. 604. Q. Curt. l. vi. c. 11.)

[2] Heineccius (Element. Jur. Civil. part vii. p. 81) has collected these exemptions into one view.

[3] This definition of the sage Ulpian (Pandect. l. xlviii. tit. iv.) seems to have been adapted to the court of Caracalla, rather than to that of Alexander Severus. See the Codes of Theodosius and Justinian ad leg. Juliam majestatis.

[4] Arcadius Charisius is the oldest lawyer quoted in the Pandects to justify the universal practice of torture in all cases of treason; but this maxim of tyranny, which is admitted by Ammianus (l. xix. c. 12) with the most respectful terror, is enforced by several laws of the successors of Constantine. See Cod. Theod. l. ix. tit. xxxv. In majestatis crimine omnibus æqua est conditio. [leg. 1.]

situation was in some degree compensated by the enjoyment of
those advantages, either of nature or of fortune, which exposed
them to the jealousy of the monarch.   The obscure millions of
a great empire have much less to dread from the cruelty than
from the avarice of their masters; and *their* humble happiness
is principally affected by the grievance of excessive taxes, which,
gently pressing on the wealthy, descend with accelerated weight
on the meaner and more indigent classes of society.   An ingenious philosopher [1] has calculated the universal measure of the
public impositions by the degrees of freedom and servitude; and
ventures to assert that, according to an invariable law of nature,
it must always increase with the former, and diminish in a just
proportion to the latter.   But this reflection, which would tend
to alleviate the miseries of despotism, is contradicted at least by
the history of the Roman empire; which accuses the same
princes of despoiling the senate of its authority, and the provinces of their wealth.   Without abolishing all the various
customs and duties on merchandises, which are imperceptibly
discharged by the apparent choice of the purchaser, the policy of
Constantine and his successors preferred a simple and direct
mode of taxation, more congenial to the spirit of an arbitrary
government.[2]

The name and use of the *indictions*,[3] which serve to ascertain
the chronology of the middle ages, was derived from the regular

[1] Montesquieu, Esprit des Loix, l. xii. c. 13.

[2] Mr. Hume (Essays, vol. i. p. 389) has seen this important truth with
some degree of perplexity.

[3] The cycle of indictions, which may be traced as high as the reign of
Constantius, or perhaps of his father Constantine, is still employed by the
Papal court: but the commencement of the year has been very reasonably
altered to the first of January.   See l'Art de vérifier les Dates, p. xi.; and
Dictionnaire Raison. de la Diplomatique, tom. ii. p. 25; two accurate
treatises, which come from the workshop of the Benedictines.

[The indictions as a chronological era begin September 1, A.D. 312 (cf.
Clinton, Fasti Rom. vol. i. p. 364).   The way in which the indiction was
used as a chronological era in the time of Constantine and long after is
worthy of note.   From September 1, A.D. 312, successive periods of fifteen
years were reckoned.   When an indiction is mentioned, it is quite uncertain which of these periods of fifteen years is meant, and it is only the
number of a particular year occurring in the period that is expressed.
This separate year and not the period of fifteen years is called an indiction.
Thus when the seventh indiction occurs in a document, this document
belongs to the seventh year of one of these periods of fifteen years, but to
which of them is uncertain.   This continued to be the usage of the word
until the twelfth century, when it became the practice to call the period
of fifteen years the indiction, and to reckon from the birth of Christ the
number of indictions, *i.e.*, the periods of fifteen years.   Cf. Savigny *Ueber
die Römische Steuerverfassung*, in *Vermischte Schriften*, vol. ii. p. 130.—O. S.]

practice of the Roman tributes.[1] The emperor subscribed with his own hand, and in purple ink, the solemn edict, or indiction, which was fixed up in the principal city of each diocese during two months previous to the first day of September. And, by a very easy connection of ideas, the word *indiction* was transferred to the measure of tribute which it prescribed, and to the annual term which it allowed for the payment. This general estimate of the supplies was proportioned to the real and imaginary wants of the state; but as often as the expense exceeded the revenue, or the revenue fell short of the computation, an additional tax, under the name of *superindiction,* was imposed on the people, and the most valuable attribute of sovereignty was communicated to the Prætorian præfects, who, on some occasions, were permitted to provide for the unforeseen and extraordinary exigencies of the public service. The execution of these laws (which it would be tedious to pursue in their minute and intricate detail) consisted of two distinct operations: the resolving the general imposition into its constituent parts, which were assessed on the provinces, the cities, and the individuals of the Roman world; and the collecting the separate contributions of the individuals, the cities, and the provinces, till the accumulated sums were poured into the Imperial treasuries. But as the account between the monarch and the subject was perpetually open, and as the renewal of the demand anticipated the perfect discharge of the preceding obligation, the weighty machine of the finances was moved by the same hands round the circle of its yearly revolution. Whatever was honourable or important in the administration of the revenue was committed to the wisdom of the præfects and their provincial representatives; the lucrative functions were claimed by a crowd of subordinate officers, some of whom depended on the treasurer, others on the governor of the province; and who, in the inevitable conflicts of a perplexed jurisdiction, had frequent opportunities of disputing with each other the spoils of the people. The laborious offices, which could be productive only of envy and reproach, of expense and danger, were imposed on the *Decurions,* who formed the corporations of the cities, and whom the severity of the Imperial laws had condemned to sustain the burthens of civil society.[2] The whole landed property of the empire (without

---

[1] The first twenty-eight titles of the eleventh book of the Theodosian Code are filled with the circumstantial regulations on the important subject of tributes; but they suppose a clearer knowledge of fundamental principles than it is at present in our power to attain.

[2] The title concerning the Decurions (l. xii. tit. i.) is the most ample in

excepting the patrimonial estates of the monarch) was the object of ordinary taxation; and every new purchaser contracted the obligations of the former proprietor. An accurate *census*,[1] or survey, was the only equitable mode of ascertaining the proportion which every citizen should be obliged to contribute for the public service; and from the well-known period of the indictions, there is reason to believe that this difficult and expensive operation was repeated at the regular distance of fifteen yeais. The lands were measurèd by surveyors, who were sent into the provinces; their nature, whether arable or pasture, or vineyards or woods, was distinctly reported; and an estimate was made of their common value from the average produce of five years. The numbers of slaves and of cattle constituted an essential part of the report; an oath was administered to the proprietors which bound them to disclose the true state of their affairs; and their attempts to prevaricate, or elude the intention of the legislator, were severely watched, and punished as a capital crime, which included the double guilt of treason and sacrilege.[2] A large portion of the tribute was paid in money; and of the current coin of the empire, gold alone could be legally accepted.[3] The remainder of the taxes, according to the proportions determined by the annual indiction, was furnished in a

the whole Theodosian Code; since it contains not less than one hundred and ninety-two distinct laws to ascertain the duties and privileges of that useful order of citizens.

[The Decuriones (also styled *Curiales*) were the members of the senate in the municipal towns. This senate was called *Ordo Decurionum*. In the times of the republic admission into the Ordo Decurionum was an honour, but under the despotism of the empire, the position of the Decurions was most lamentable. The plebeian carefully avoided this dangerous distinction, and the Decurions themselves sought to escape from it in every way. Many became soldiers and even slaves to conceal themselves. Their miserable condition arose from the oppression of the government. The Decurions had not merely to collect the taxes, but they were responsible for their colleagues; they had to take up the lands abandoned by the proprietors on account of the intolerable weight of the taxes attaching to them, and they had finally to make up all deficiencies out of their private resources. (Cf. Savigny, *Geschichte des Römischen Rechts*, vol. i. p. 40, *sq.*)—O. S.]

[1] Habemus enim et hominum numerum qui delati sunt, et agrorum modum. Eumenius in Panegyr. Vet. viii. [vii.] 6. See Cod. Theod. l. xiii. tit. x. xi. with Godefroy's Commentary.

[2] Siquis sacrilegâ vitem falce succiderit; aut feracium ramorum fœtus hebetaverit, quo declinet fidem Censuum, et mentiatur callide paupertatis ingenium, mox detectus capitale subibit exitium, et bona ejus in Fisci jura migrabunt. Cod. Theod. l. xiii. tit. xi. leg 1. Although this law is not without its studied obscurity, it is, however, clear enough to prove the minuteness of the inquisition, and the disproportion of the penalty.

[3] The astonishment of Pliny would have ceased. Equidem miror P. R. victis gentibus [in tributo] semper argentum imperitasse, non aurum. Hist. Natur. xxxiii. 15.

manner still more direct, and still more oppressive. According to the different nature of lands, their real produce in the various articles of wine or oil, corn or barley, wood or iron, was transported by the labour or at the expense of the provincials to the Imperial magazines, from whence they were occasionally distributed, for the use of the court, of the army, and of the two capitals, Rome and Constantinople. The commissioners of the revenue were so frequently obliged to make considerable purchases, that they were strictly prohibited from allowing any compensation, or from receiving in money the value of those supplies which were exacted in kind. In the primitive simplicity of small communities this method may be well adapted to collect the almost voluntary offerings of the people; but it is at once susceptible of the utmost latitude and of the utmost strictness, which in a corrupt and absolute monarchy must introduce a perpetual contest between the power of oppression and the arts of fraud.[1] The agriculture of the Roman provinces was insensibly ruined, and, in the progress of despotism, which tends to disappoint its own purpose, the emperors were obliged to derive some merit from the forgiveness of debts, or the remission of tributes, which their subjects were utterly incapable of paying. According to the new division of Italy, the fertile and happy province of Campania, the scene of the early victories and of the delicious retirements of the citizens of Rome, extended between the sea and the Apennine from the Tiber to the Silarus. Within sixty years after the death of Constantine, and on the evidence of an actual survey, an exemption was granted in favour of three hundred and thirty thousand English acres of desert and uncultivated land, which amounted to one-eighth of the whole surface of the province. As the footsteps of the barbarians had not yet been seen in Italy, the cause of this amazing desolation, which is recorded in the laws, can be ascribed only to the administration of the Roman emperors.[2]

[1] Some precautions were taken (see Cod. Theod. l. xi. tit. ii. and Cod. Justinian. l. x. tit. xxvii. leg. 1, 2, 3) to restrain the magistrates from the abuse of their authority, either in the exaction or in the purchase of corn: but those who had learning enough to read the orations of Cicero against Verres (iii. de Frumento) might instruct themselves in all the various arts of oppression, with regard to the weight, the price, the quality, and the carriage. The avarice of an unlettered governor would supply the ignorance of precept or precedent.

[2] Cod. Theod. l. xi. tit. xxviii. leg. 2, published the 24th of March, A.D. 395, by the emperor Honorius, only two months after the death of his father Theodosius. He speaks of 528,042 Roman jugera, which I have reduced to the English measure. The jugerum contained 28,800 square Roman feet.

Either from design or from accident, the mode of assessment seemed to unite the substance of a land-tax with the forms of a capitation.[1] The returns which were sent of every province or district expressed the number of tributary subjects, and the amount of the public impositions. The latter of these sums was divided by the former; and the estimate, that such a province contained so many *capita*, or heads of tribute, and that each *head* was rated at such a price, was universally received, not only in the popular, but even in the legal computation. The value of a tributary head must have varied, according to many accidental, or at least fluctuating circumstances: but some knowledge has been preserved of a very curious fact, the more important since it relates to one of the richest provinces of the Roman empire, and which now flourishes as the most splendid of the European kingdoms. The rapacious ministers of Constantius had exhausted the wealth of Gaul, by exacting twenty-five pieces of gold for the annual tribute of every head. The humane policy of his successor reduced the capitation to seven

[1] Godefroy (Cod. Theod. tom. v. p. 116 [l. xiv. tit. x. leg. 2]) argues with weight and learning on the subject of the capitation; but while he explains the *caput* as a share or measure of property, he too absolutely excludes the idea of a personal assessment.

[Gibbon has here fallen into serious error respecting the finances of this period of the empire, by concluding that the word *capitatio* had only one signification. But *capitatio* signified both the " land-tax " and the " poll-tax," which were the two principal taxes of the period. For the purposes of the land-tax, the whole land of the empire was measured and divided into a certain number of pieces, each of which had to pay the same sum of money as a tax. Such a piece of land was called *caput*, sometimes *jugum*, whence the tax was often named *capitatio* and sometimes *jugatio*. Since each *caput* was of the same value and paid the same tax, its size must of course have varied according to the nature of the land composing it. For each financial year which commenced on 1st September, the whole amount of the land-tax was fixed, and was then divided among the *capita*. The payment had to be made in three instalments—1st of January, 1st of May, and 1st of September. The tribute appointed for each year was called the *indictio*, a term which (as has been shown in the note on p. 122) came to be applied to the financial year

The *Poll-Tax*, on the other hand, was called sometimes simply *capitatio*, sometimes *humana capitatio. capitalis illatio*, and *capitatio plebeia*. The amount of this is unknown, the whole question being very obscure. Every person in the empire was liable for it, with the exception of those who paid the land-tax, and all persons above the rank of plebeians. The expression *plebeia capitalis* shows that it was a peculiar burthen of the plebeians, but if the latter possessed land it follows that they did not pay both. Consequently the classes from which the poll-tax was chiefly levied were (1) the free inhabitants of towns who possessed neither rank nor landed property; (2) the Coloni in the country; (3) the slaves. By an edict of Diocletian which, though repealed by Galerius, was renewed by Licinius, the *plebs urbana* and their slaves were exempt, so that the tax ultimately fell on the Coloni and the agricultural slaves. Cf. Savigny and Mommsen's article in *Hermes*, **3**, 429, *sq.*—O. S.]

pieces.[1] A moderate proportion between these opposite extremes of extraordinary oppression and of transient indulgence may therefore be fixed at sixteen pieces of gold, or about nine pounds sterling, the common standard, perhaps, of the impositions of Gaul.[2] But this calculation, or rather indeed the facts from whence it is deduced, cannot fail of suggesting two difficulties to a thinking mind, who will be at once surprised by the *equality* and by the *enormity* of the capitation. An attempt to explain them may perhaps reflect some light on the interesting subject of the finances of the declining empire.

I. It is obvious that, as long as the immutable constitution of human nature produces and maintains so unequal a division of property, the most numerous part of the community would be deprived of their subsistence by the equal assessment of a tax from which the sovereign would derive a very trifling revenue. Such, indeed, might be the theory of the Roman capitation; but, in the practice, this unjust equality was no longer felt, as the tribute was collected on the principle of a *real*, not of a *personal* imposition. Several indigent citizens contributed to compose a single *head*, or share of taxation; while the wealthy provincial, in proportion to his fortune, alone represented several of those imaginary beings. In a poetical request, addressed to one of the last and most deserving of the Roman princes who reigned in Gaul, Sidonius Apollinaris personifies his tribute under the figure of a triple monster, the Geryon of the Grecian

[1] Quid profuerit (*Julianus*) anhelantibus extremâ penuriâ Gallis, hinc maxime claret, quod primitus partes eas ingressus, pro *capitibus* singulis tributi nomine vicenos quinos aureos reperit flagitari: discedens vero septenos tantum, munera universa complentes. Ammian. l. xvi. c. 5.

[2] In the calculation of any sum of money under Constantine and his successors, we need only refer to the excellent discourse of Mr. Greaves on the Denarius for the proof of the following principles: 1. That the ancient and modern Roman pound, containing 5256 grains of Troy weight, is about one-twelfth lighter than the English pound, which is composed of 5760 of the same grains. 2. That the pound of gold, which had once been divided into forty-eight *aurei*, was at this time coined into seventy-two smaller pieces of the same denomination. 3. That five of these aurei were the legal tender for a pound of silver, and that consequently the pound of gold was exchanged for fourteen pounds eight ounces of silver, according to the Roman, or about thirteen pounds according to the English weight. 4. That the English pound of silver is coined into sixty-two shillings. From these elements we may compute the Roman pound of gold, the usual method of reckoning large sums, at forty pounds sterling, and we may fix the currency of the *aureus* at somewhat more than eleven shillings.

[The *aureus* in the time of Constantine was equal to ten shillings English money. The *capita* in Gaul were not "heads of tribute," but pieces of land. Each piece of land had to pay before Julian's administration twenty-five *aurei* or £12 10s., which the latter reduced to seven aurei or £3 10s.—O. S.]

fables, and entreats the new Hercules that he would most
graciously be pleased to save his life by cutting off three of his
heads.[1] The fortune of Sidonius far exceeded the customary
wealth of a poet; but if he had pursued the allusion, he must
have painted many of the Gallic nobles with the hundred heads
of the deadly Hydra, spreading over the face of the country, and
devouring the substance of an hundred families. II. The difficulty of allowing an annual sum of about nine pounds sterling,
even for the average of the capitation of Gaul, may be rendered
more evident by the comparison of the present state of the same
country, as it is now governed by the absolute monarch of
an industrious, wealthy, and affectionate people. The taxes of
France cannot be magnified, either by fear or by flattery, beyond
the annual amount of eighteen millions sterling, which ought,
perhaps, to be shared among four-and-twenty millions of inhabitants.[2] Seven millions of these, in the capacity of fathers, or
brothers, or husbands, may discharge the obligations of the
remaining multitude of women and children; yet the equal proportion of each tributary subject will scarcely rise above fifty
shillings of our money, instead of a proportion almost four times
as considerable, which was regularly imposed on their Gallic
ancestors. The reason of this difference may be found, not so
much in the relative scarcity or plenty of gold and silver, as in
the different state of society in ancient Gaul and in modern
France. In a country where personal freedom is the privilege
of every subject, the whole mass of taxes, whether they are levied

---

[1] Geryones nos esse puta, monstrumque tributum,
  Hîc *capita* ut vivam, tu mihi tolle *tria*.
                    Sidon. Apollinar. Carm. xiii. [v. 19.]
   The reputation of Father Sirmond led me to expect more satisfaction
than I have found in his note (p. 144) on this remarkable passage. The
words, suo vel *suorum* nomine, betray the perplexity of the commentator.

[2] This assertion, however formidable it may seem, is founded on the
original registers of births, deaths, and marriages, collected by public
authority, and now deposited in the *Contrôle Général* at Paris. The
annual average of births throughout the whole kingdom, taken in five
years (from 1770 to 1774, both inclusive), is 479,649 boys and 449,269 girls,
in all 928,918 children. The province of French Hainault alone furnishes
9906 births; and we are assured, by an actual enumeration of the people,
annually repeated from the year 1773 to the year 1776, that, upon an
average, Hainault contains 257,097 inhabitants. By the rules of fair
analogy, we might infer that the ordinary proportion of annual births to
the whole people is about 1 to 26; and that the kingdom of France contains 24,151,868 persons of both sexes and of every age. If we content
ourselves with the more moderate proportion of 1 to 25, the whole population will amount to 23,222,950. From the diligent researches of the
French government (which are not unworthy of our own imitation) we
may hope to obtain a still greater degree of certainty on this important
subject.

on property or on consumption, may be fairly divided among the whole body of the nation. But the far greater part of the lands of ancient Gaul, as well as of the other provinces of the Roman world, were cultivated by slaves, or by peasants, whose dependent condition was a less rigid servitude.[1] In such a state the poor were maintained at the expense of the masters who enjoyed the fruits of their labour; and as the rolls of tribute were filled only with the names of those citizens who possessed the means of an honourable, or at least of a decent subsistence, the comparative smallness of their numbers explains and justifies the high rate of their capitation. The truth of this assertion may be illustrated by the following example:—The Ædui, one of the most powerful and civilised tribes or *cities* of Gaul, occupied an extent of territory which now contains above five hundred thousand inhabitants, in the two ecclesiastical dioceses of Autun and Nevers; [2] and with the probable accession of those of Châlons and Mâçon,[3] the population would amount to eight hundred thousand souls. In the time of Constantine the territory of the Ædui afforded no more than twenty-five thousand *heads* of capitation, of whom seven thousand were discharged by that prince from the intolerable weight of tribute.[4] A just analogy would seem to countenance the opinion of an ingenious historian,[5] that the free and tributary citizens did not surpass the number of

[1] Cod. Theod. l. v. tit. ix. x. xi. Cod. Justinian. l. xi. tit. lxiii. Coloni appellantur qui conditionem debent genitali solo, propter agriculturam sub dominio possessorum. Augustin. de Civitate Dei, l. x. c. i.

[2] The ancient jurisdiction of (*Augustodunum*) Autun in Burgundy, the capital of the Ædui, comprehended the adjacent territory of (*Noviodunum*) Nevers. See d'Anville, Notice de l'Ancienne Gaule, p. 491. The two dioceses of Autun and Nevers are now composed, the former of 610, and the latter of 160 parishes. The registers of births, taken during eleven years, in 476 parishes of the same province of Burgundy, and multiplied by the moderate proportion of 25 (see Messance, Recherches sur la Population, p. 142), may authorise us to assign an average number of 656 persons for each parish, which, being again multiplied by the 770 parishes of the dioceses of Nevers and Autun, will produce the sum of 505,120 persons for the extent of country which was once possessed by the Ædui.

[3] We might derive an additional supply of 301,750 inhabitants from the dioceses of Châlons (*Cabillonum*) and of Mâçon (*Matisco*) ; since they contain, the one 200, and the other 260 parishes. This accession of territory might be justified by very specious reasons. 1. Châlons and Mâçon were undoubtedly within the original jurisdiction of the Ædui. (See d'Anville, Notice, p. 187. 443.) 2. In the Notitia of Gaul they are enumerated not as *Civitates*, but merely as *Castra*. 3. They do not appear to have been episcopal seats before the fifth and sixth centuries. Yet there is a passage in Eumenius (Panegyr. Vet. viii. [vii.] 7) which very forcibly deters me from extending the territory of the Ædui, in the reign of Constantine, along the beautiful banks of the navigable Saône.

[4] Eumenius in Panegyr. Vet. viii. [vii.] 11.

[5] L'Abbé du Bos, Hist. Critique de la M. F. tom. i. p. 121.

half a million; and if, in the ordinary administration of government, their annual payments may be computed at about four millions and a half of our money, it would appear that, although the share of each individual was four times as considerable, a fourth part only of the modern taxes of France was levied on the Imperial province of Gaul. The exactions of Constantius may be calculated at seven millions sterling, which were reduced to two millions by the humanity or the wisdom of Julian.

But this tax or capitation on the proprietors of land would have suffered a rich and numerous class of free citizens to escape. With the view of sharing that species of wealth which is derived from art or labour, and which exists in money or in merchandise, the emperors imposed a distinct and personal tribute on the trading part of their subjects.[1] Some exemptions, very strictly confined both in time and place, were allowed to the proprietors who disposed of the produce of their own estates. Some indulgence was granted to the profession of the liberal arts; but every other branch of commercial industry was affected by the severity of the law. The honourable merchant of Alexandria, who imported the gems and spices of India for the use of the western world; the usurer, who derived from the interest of money a silent and ignominious profit; the ingenious manufacturer, the diligent mechanic, and even the most obscure retailer of a sequestered village, were obliged to admit the officers of the revenue into the partnership of their gain; and the sovereign of the Roman empire, who tolerated the profession, consented to share the infamous salary of public prostitutes. As this general tax upon industry was collected every fourth year, it was styled the *Lustral Contribution :* and the historian Zosimus [2] laments that the approach of the fatal period was announced by the tears and terrors of the citizens, who were often compelled by the impending scourge to embrace the most abhorred and unnatural methods of procuring the sum at which their poverty had been assessed. The testimony of Zosimus cannot indeed be justified from the charge of passion and pre-

---

[1] See Cod. Theod. l. xiii. tit. i. and iv.

[2] Zosimus, l. ii. [c. 38] p. 115. There is probably as much passion and prejudice in the attack of Zosimus as in the elaborate defence of the memory of Constantine by the zealous Dr. Howell. Hist. of the World, vol. ii. p. 20.

[The emperor Theodosius put an end by law to this disgraceful source of revenue. But before depriving himself of it, he made sure of supplying the deficit. A rich patrician, Florentius, indignant at this legalised licentiousness, protested to the emperor, and actually offered his property to make up the deficit. The emperor had the baseness to accept the offer. —O. S.]

judice; but, from the nature of this tribute, it seems reasonable to conclude that it was arbitrary in the distribution, and extremely rigorous in the mode of collecting. The secret wealth of commerce, and the precarious profits of art or labour, are susceptible only of a discretionary valuation, which is seldom disadvantageous to the interest of the treasury; and as the person of the trader supplies the want of a visible and permanent security, the payment of the imposition, which, in the case of a land-tax, may be obtained by the seizure of property, can rarely be extorted by any other means than those of corporal punishments. The cruel treatment of the insolvent debtors of the state is attested, and was perhaps mitigated, by a very humane edict of Constantine, who, disclaiming the use of racks and of scourges, allots a spacious and airy prison for the place of their confinement.[1]

These general taxes were imposed and levied by the absolute authority of the monarch; but the occasional offerings of the *coronary gold* still retained the name and semblance of popular consent. It was an ancient custom that the allies of the republic, who ascribed their safety or deliverance to the success of the Roman arms, and even the cities of Italy, who admired the virtues of their victorious general, adorned the pomp of his triumph by their voluntary gifts of crowns of gold, which, after the ceremony, were consecrated in the temple of Jupiter, to remain a lasting monument of his glory to future ages. The progress of zeal and flattery soon multiplied the number, and increased the size, of these popular donations; and the triumph of Cæsar was enriched with two thousand eight hundred and twenty-two massy crowns, whose weight amounted to twenty thousand four hundred and fourteen pounds of gold. This treasure was immediately melted down by the prudent dictator, who was satisfied that it would be more serviceable to his soldiers than to the gods: his example was imitated by his successors; and the custom was introduced of exchanging these splendid ornaments for the more acceptable present of the current gold coin of the empire.[2] The spontaneous offering was at length exacted as the debt of duty; and, instead of being confined to the occasion of a triumph, it was supposed to be granted by the several cities and provinces of the monarchy as often as the

[1] Cod. Theod. l. xi. tit. vii. leg. 3.
[2] See Lipsius de Magnitud. Romanâ, l. ii. c. 9. The Tarragonese Spain presented the emperor Claudius with a crown of gold of seven, and Gaul with another of nine, *hundred* pounds weight. I have followed the rational emendation of Lipsius.

emperor condescended to announce his accession, his consulship, the birth of a son, the creation of a Cæsar, a victory over the barbarians, or any other real or imaginary event which graced the annals of his reign. The peculiar free gift of the senate of Rome was fixed by custom at sixteen hundred pounds of gold, or about sixty-four thousand pounds sterling. The oppressed subjects celebrated their own felicity that their sovereign should graciously consent to accept this feeble but voluntary testimony of their loyalty and gratitude.[1]

A people elated by pride, or soured by discontent, is seldom qualified to form a just estimate of their actual situation. The subjects of Constantine were incapable of discerning the decline of genius and manly virtue, which so far degraded them below the dignity of their ancestors; but they could feel and lament the rage of tyranny, the relaxation of discipline, and the increase of taxes. The impartial historian, who acknowledges the justice of their complaints, will observe some favourable circumstances which tended to alleviate the misery of their condition. The threatening tempest of barbarians, which so soon subverted the foundations of Roman greatness, was still repelled, or suspended, on the frontiers. The arts of luxury and literature were cultivated, and the elegant pleasures of society were enjoyed, by the inhabitants of a considerable portion of the globe. The forms, the pomp, and the expense of the civil administration contributed to restrain the irregular licence of the soldiers; and although the laws were violated by power, or perverted by subtlety, the sage principles of the Roman jurisprudence preserved a sense of order and equity unknown to the despotic governments of the East. The rights of mankind might derive some protection from religion and philosophy; and the name of freedom, which could no longer alarm, might sometimes admonish, the successors of Augustus, that they did not reign over a nation of Slaves or Barbarians.[2]

---

[1] Cod. Theod. l. xii. tit. xiii. The senators were supposed to be exempt from the *Aurum Coronarium* ; but the *Auri Oblatio*, which was required at their hands, was precisely of the same nature.

[2] The great Theodosius, in his judicious advice to his son (Claudian. in iv. Consulat. Honorii, 214, etc.), distinguishes the station of a Roman prince from that of a Parthian monarch. Virtue was necessary for the one; birth might suffice for the other.

CHAPTER XVIII

Character of Constantine—Gothic War—Death of Constantine—Division
of the Empire among his three Sons—Persian War—Tragic Deaths of
Constantine the Younger and Constans—Usurpation of Magnentius—
Civil War—Victory of Constantius

THE character of the prince who removed the seat of empire,
and introduced such important changes into the civil and
religious constitution of his country, has fixed the attention, and
divided the opinions, of mankind. By the grateful zeal of the
Christians the deliverer of the church has been decorated with
every attribute of a hero, and even of a saint; while the discontent of the vanquished party has compared Constantine to the
most abhorred of those tyrants who, by their vice and weakness,
dishonoured the Imperial purple. The same passions have, in
some degree, been perpetuated to succeeding generations, and
the character of Constantine is considered, even in the present
age, as an object either of satire or of panegyric. By the impartial union of those defects which are confessed by his warmest
admirers, and of those virtues which are acknowledged by his
most implacable enemies, we might hope to delineate a just
portrait of that extraordinary man, which the truth and candour
of history should adopt without a blush.[1] But it would soon
appear that the vain attempt to blend such discordant colours,
and to reconcile such inconsistent qualities, must produce a
figure monstrous rather than human, unless it is viewed in its
proper and distinct lights by a careful separation of the different
periods of the reign of Constantine.

The person, as well as the mind, of Constantine had been
enriched by nature with her choicest endowments. His stature
was lofty, his countenance majestic, his deportment graceful;
his strength and activity were displayed in every manly exercise,
and, from his earliest youth to a very advanced season of life, he
preserved the vigour of his constitution by a strict adherence to
the domestic virtues of chastity and temperance. He delighted
in the social intercourse of familiar conversation; and though
he might sometimes indulge his disposition to raillery with less

---

[1] On ne se trompera point sur Constantin en croyant tout le mal qu'en
dit Eusèbe, et tout le bien qu'en dit Zosime. Fleury, Hist. Ecclésiastique,
tom. iii. p. 233. Eusebius and Zosimus form indeed the two extremes of
flattery and invective. The intermediate shades are expressed by those
writers whose character or situation variously tempered the influence of
their religious zeal.

reserve than was required by the severe dignity of his station, the courtesy and liberality of his manners gained the hearts of all who approached him. The sincerity of his friendship has been suspected; yet he showed, on some occasions, that he was not incapable of a warm and lasting attachment. The disadvantage of an illiterate education had not prevented him from forming a just estimate of the value of learning; and the arts and sciences derived some encouragement from the munificent protection of Constantine. In the despatch of business his diligence was indefatigable; and the active powers of his mind were almost continually exercised in reading, writing, or meditating, in giving audience to ambassadors, and in examining the complaints of his subjects. Even those who censured the propriety of his measures were compelled to acknowledge that he possessed magnanimity to conceive, and patience to execute, the most arduous designs, without being checked either by the prejudices of education or by the clamours of the multitude. In the field he infused his own intrepid spirit into the troops, whom he conducted with the talents of a consummate general; and to his abilities, rather than to his fortune, we may ascribe the signal victories which he obtained over the foreign and domestic foes of the republic. He loved glory as the reward, perhaps as the motive, of his labours. The boundless ambition which, from the moment of his accepting the purple at York, appears as the ruling passion of his soul, may be justified by the dangers of his own situation, by the character of his rivals, by the consciousness of superior merit, and by the prospect that his success would enable him to restore peace and order to the distracted empire. In his civil wars against Maxentius and Licinius he had engaged on his side the inclinations of the people, who compared the undissembled vices of those tyrants with the spirit of wisdom and justice which seemed to direct the general tenor of the administration of Constantine.[1]

Had Constantine fallen on the banks of the Tiber, or even in the plains of Hadrianople, such is the character which, with a few exceptions, he might have transmitted to posterity. But the conclusion of his reign (according to the moderate and indeed tender sentence of a writer of the same age) degraded him from the rank which he had acquired among the most deserving of

---

[1] The virtues of Constantine are collected for the most part from Eutropius and the younger Victor, two sincere pagans, who wrote after the extinction of his family. Even Zosimus and the *Emperor* Julian acknowledge his personal courage and military achievements.

the Roman princes.[1] In the life of Augustus we behold the tyrant of the republic converted almost by imperceptible degrees into the father of his country and of human kind. In that of Constantine we may contemplate a hero, who had so long inspired his subjects with love and his enemies with terror, degenerating into a cruel and dissolute monarch, corrupted by his fortune, or raised by conquest above the necessity of dissimulation. The general peace which he maintained during the last fourteen years of his reign was a period of apparent splendour rather than of real prosperity; and the old age of Constantine was disgraced by the opposite yet reconcilable vices of rapaciousness and prodigality. The accumulated treasures found in the palaces of Maxentius and Licinius were lavishly consumed; the various innovations introduced by the conqueror were attended with an increasing expense; the cost of his buildings, his court, and his festivals required an immediate and plentiful supply; and the oppression of the people was the only fund which could support the magnificence of the sovereign.[2] His unworthy favourites, enriched by the boundless liberality of their master, usurped with impunity the privilege of rapine and corruption.[3] A secret but universal decay was felt in every part of the public administration, and the emperor himself, though he still retained the obedience, gradually lost the esteem, of his subjects. The dress and manners which, towards the decline of life, he chose to effect, served only to degrade him in the eyes of mankind. The Asiatic pomp which had been adopted by the pride of Diocletian assumed an air of softness and effeminacy in the person of Constantine. He is represented with false hair of various colours, laboriously arranged by the skilful artists of the times; a diadem of a new and more expensive fashion; a profusion of gems and pearls, of collars and bracelets; and a varie-

---

[1] See Eutropius, x. 6 [4]. In primo Imperii tempore optimis principibus, ultimo mediis comparandus. From the ancient Greek version of Pœanius (edit. Havercamp. p. 697), I am inclined to suspect that Eutropius had originally written *vix* mediis; and that the offensive monosyllable was dropped by the wilful inadvertency of transcribers. Aurelius Victor expresses the general opinion by a vulgar and indeed obscure proverb. *Trachala* decem annis præstantissimus; duodecim sequentibus *latro;* decem novissimis *pupillus* ob immodicas profusiones. [Epit. c. 41.]

[2] Julian, Orat. i. p. 8, in a flattering discourse pronounced before the son of Constantine; and Cæsares, p. 335. Zosimus [l. ii. c. 38], p. 114, 115. The stately buildings of Constantinople, etc., may be quoted as a lasting and unexceptionable proof of the profuseness of their founder.

[3] The impartial Ammianus deserves all our confidence. Proximorum fauces aperuit primus omnium Constantinus. l. xvi. c. 8. Eusebius himself confesses the abuse (Vit. Constantin. l. iv. c. 29, 54); and some of the Imperial laws feebly point out the remedy. See vol. i. pp. 378, 381.

gated flowing robe of silk, most curiously embroidered with
flowers of gold. In such apparel, scarcely to be excused by the
youth and folly of Elagabalus, we are at a loss to discover the
wisdom of an aged monarch and the simplicity of a Roman
veteran.[1] A mind thus relaxed by prosperity and indulgence
was incapable of rising to that magnanimity which disdains
suspicion and dares to forgive. The deaths of Maximian and
Licinius may perhaps be justified by the maxims of policy as
they are taught in the schools of tyrants; but an impartial narrative of the executions, or rather murders, which sullied the
declining age of Constantine, will suggest to our most candid
thoughts the idea of a prince who could sacrifice, without
reluctance, the laws of justice and the feelings of nature to the
dictates either of his passions or of his interest.

The same fortune which so invariably followed the standard
of Constantine seemed to secure the hopes and comforts of his
domestic life. Those among his predecessors who had enjoyed
the longest and most prosperous reigns, Augustus, Trajan, and
Diocletian, had been disappointed of posterity; and the frequent
revolutions had never allowed sufficient time for any Imperial
family to grow up and multiply under the shade of the purple.
But the royalty of the Flavian line, which had been first
ennobled by the Gothic Claudius, descended through several
generations; and Constantine himself derived from his royal
father the hereditary honours which he transmitted to his
children. The emperor had been twice married. Minervina,
the obscure but lawful object of his youthful attachment,[2] had
left him only one son, who was called Crispus. By Fausta, the
daughter of Maximian, he had three daughters, and three sons
known by the kindred names of Constantine, Constantius, and
Constans. The unambitious brothers of the great Constantine,
Julius Constantius, Dalmatius, and Hannibalianus,[3] were per-

---

[1] Julian, in the Cæsars, attempts to ridicule his uncle. His suspicious
testimony is confirmed, however, by the learned Spanheim, with the
authority of medals (see Commentaire, p. 156, 299, 397, 459). Eusebius
(Orat. c. 5) alleges that Constantine dressed for the public, not for himself.
Were this admitted, the vainest coxcomb could never want an excuse.

[2] Zosimus [l. ii. c. 20] and Zonaras agree in representing Minervina as the
concubine of Constantine; but Ducange has very gallantly rescued her
character, by producing a decisive passage from one of the panegyrics.
" Ab ipso fine pueritiæ te matrimonii legibus dedisti."

[3] Ducange (Familiæ Byzantinæ, p. 44) bestows on him, after Zonaras, the
name of Constantine; a name somewhat unlikely, as it was already occupied
by the elder brother. That of Hannibalianus is mentioned in the Paschal
Chronicle, and is approved by Tillemont, Hist. des Empereurs, tom. iv.
p. 527.

The Following is the Genealogical Table of the Family of Constantine:—

Crispus, brother of the emperor Claudius Gothicus.

Claudia=Eutropius.

Constantius I., Chlorus=Theodora, daughter of Maximianus, Imp. For issue of Constantius Chlorus by Theodora, see below.

Helena=Constantius I., Chlorus, Imp. ob. 306.

Minervina=Constantinus I.=Fausta, daughter of Maximianus. Imp. ob. 337.

Crispus, ob. 326.

Constantinus II. Imp. ob. 340.

Constantinus II. Imp. ob. 361.

Constantia Postuma=Gratianus, Imp. ob. 383.

Constans, Imp. ob. 350.

Constantina, ob. 354. m. 1. Hannibalianus. 2. Gallus Caesar.

Helena, ob. 360. m. Julianus, aft. Imp.

Issue of Constantius I. (Chlorus) by Theodora.

Galla=Constantius=Basilina.

Dalmatius.

Hannibalianus, or Constantinus.

Dalmatius.

Hannibalianus, m. Constantina. See above.

Constantia, m. Licinius, Imp.

Licinius.

Anastasia, m. Bassianus Caesar.

Eutropia, m. Nepotianus.

Nepotianus, ob. 350.

Gallus Caesar, ob. 354. m. Constantina. See above,

Julianus, Imp. ob. 363. m. Helena. See above.

—S.

mitted to enjoy the most honourable rank and the most affluent
fortune that could be consistent with a private station. The
youngest of the three lived without a name and died without
posterity. His two elder brothers obtained in marriage the
daughters of wealthy senators, and propagated new branches of
the Imperial race. Gallus and Julian afterwards became the
most illustrious of the children of Julius Constantius, the *Patrician.* The two sons of Dalmatius, who had been decorated with
the vain title of *Censor,* were named Dalmatius and Hannibalianus. The two sisters of the great Constantine, Anastasia
and Eutropia, were bestowed on Optatus and Nepotianus, two
senators of noble birth and of consular dignity. His third
sister, Constantia, was distinguished by her pre-eminence of
greatness and of misery. She remained the widow of the vanquished Licinius; and it was by her entreaties that an innocent
boy, the offspring of their marriage, preserved, for some time,
his life, the title of Cæsar, and a precarious hope of the succession.
Besides the females and the allies of the Flavian house, ten or
twelve males, to whom the language of modern courts would
apply the title of princes of the blood, seemed, according to the
order of their birth, to be destined either to inherit or to support
the throne of Constantine. But in less than thirty years this
numerous and increasing family was reduced to the persons of
Constantius and Julian, who alone had survived a series of
crimes and calamities such as the tragic poets have deplored in
the devoted lines of Pelops and of Cadmus.

Crispus, the eldest son of Constantine, and the presumptive
heir of the empire, is represented by impartial historians as an
amiable and accomplished youth. The care of his education, or
at least of his studies, was intrusted to Lactantius, the most
eloquent of the Christians; a preceptor admirably qualified to
form the taste and to excite the virtues of his illustrious disciple.[1]
At the age of seventeen Crispus was invested with the title of
Cæsar, and the administration of the Gallic provinces, where the
inroads of the Germans gave him an early occasion of signalising
his military prowess. In the civil war which broke out soon
afterwards, the father and son divided their powers; and this
history has already celebrated the valour as well as conduct displayed by the latter in forcing the straits of the Hellespont, so

[1] Jerom. in Chron. The poverty of Lactantius may be applied either to
the praise of the disinterested philosopher, or to the shame of the unfeeling
patron. See Tillemont, Mém. Ecclésiast. tom. vi. part i. p. 345. Dupin,
Bibliothèque Ecclésiast. tom. i. p. 205. Lardner's Credibility of the
Gospel History, part ii. vol. vii. p. 66.

obstinately defended by the superior fleet of Licinius. This naval victory contributed to determine the event of the war, and the names of Constantine and of Crispus were united in the joyful acclamations of their eastern subjects, who loudly proclaimed that the world had been subdued, and was now governed, by an emperor endowed with every virtue, and by his illustrious son, a prince beloved of Heaven, and the lively image of his father's perfections. The public favour, which seldom accompanies old age, diffused its lustre over the youth of Crispus. He deserved the esteem and he engaged the affections of the court, the army, and the people. The experienced merit of a reigning monarch is acknowledged by his subjects with reluctance, and frequently denied with partial and discontented murmurs; while, from the opening virtues of his successor, they fondly conceive the most unbounded hopes of private as well as public felicity.[1]

This dangerous popularity soon excited the attention of Constantine, who, both as a father and as a king, was impatient of an equal. Instead of attempting to secure the allegiance of his son by the generous ties of confidence and gratitude, he resolved to prevent the mischiefs which might be apprehended from dissatisfied ambition. Crispus soon had reason to complain that, while his infant brother Constantius was sent with the title of Cæsar to reign over his peculiar department of the Gallic provinces,[2] *he*, a prince of mature years, who had performed such recent and signal services, instead of being raised to the superior rank of Augustus, was confined almost a prisoner to his father's court, and exposed, without power or defence, to every calumny which the malice of his enemies could suggest. Under such painful circumstances the royal youth might not always be able to compose his behaviour or suppress his discontent; and we may be assured that he was encompassed by a train of indiscreet or perfidious followers, who assiduously studied to inflame, and who were perhaps instructed to betray, the unguarded warmth of his resentment. An edict of Constantine, published about

---

[1] Euseb. Hist. Ecclesiast. l. x. c. 9. Eutropius (x. 4) styles him " egregium virum; " and Julian (Orat. i.) very plainly alludes to the exploits of Crispus in the civil war. See Spanheim, Comment. p. 92.

[2] Compare Idatius and the Paschal Chronicle with Ammianus (l. xiv. c. 5). The *year* in which Constantius was created Cæsar seems to be more accurately fixed by the two chronologists; but the historian who lived in his court could not be ignorant of the *day* of the anniversary. For the appointment of the new Cæsar to the provinces of Gaul, see Julian, Orat. i. p. 12; Godefroy, Chronol. Legum, p. 26; and Blondel, de la Primauté de l'Eglise, p. 1183.

this time, manifestly indicates his real or affected suspicions that a secret conspiracy had been formed against his person and government. By all the allurements of honours and rewards he invites informers of every degree to accuse, without exception, his magistrates or ministers, his friends or his most intimate favourites, protesting, with a solemn asseveration, that he himself will listen to the charge, that he himself will revenge his injuries; and concluding with a prayer, which discovers some apprehension of danger, that the providence of the Supreme Being may still continue to protect the safety of the emperor and of the empire.[1]

The informers who complied with so liberal an invitation were sufficiently versed in the arts of courts to select the friends and adherents of Crispus as the guilty persons; nor is there any reason to distrust the veracity of the emperor, who had promised an ample measure of revenge and punishment. The policy of Constantine maintained, however, the same appearances of regard and confidence towards a son whom he began to consider as his most irreconcilable enemy. Medals were struck with the customary vows for the long and auspicious reign of the young Cæsar;[2] and as the people, who was not admitted into the secrets of the palace, still loved his virtues and respected his dignity, a poet, who solicits his recall from exile, adores with equal devotion the majesty of the father and that of the son.[3] The time was now arrived for celebrating the august ceremony of the twentieth year of the reign of Constantine, and the emperor, for that purpose, removed his court from Nicomedia to Rome, where the most splendid preparations had been made for his reception. Every eye and every tongue affected to express their sense of the general happiness, and the veil of ceremony and dissimulation was drawn for a while over the darkest designs of revenge and murder.[4] In the midst of the festival the unfortunate Crispus was apprehended by order of the emperor, who laid aside the tenderness of a father without assuming the equity of a judge. The examination was short and private;[5] and as it was thought decent to conceal the fate of the

[1] Cod. Theod. l. ix. tit. iv. [tit. 1, leg. 4.] Godefroy suspected the secret motives of this law. Comment. tom. iii. p. 9.

[2] Ducange, Fam. Byzant. p. 28. Tillemont, tom. iv. p. 610.

[3] His name was Porphyrius Optatianus. The date of his panegyric, written according to the taste of the age in vile acrostics, is settled by Scaliger ad Euseb. p. 250; Tillemont, tom. iv. p. 607; and Fabricius, Biblioth. Latin. l. iv. c. 1.

[4] Zosim. l. ii. [c. 29] p. 103. Godefroy, Chronol. Legum. p. 28.

Ἀκρίτως, *without a trial*, is the strong and most probably the just ex-young prince from the eyes of the Roman people, he was sent under a strong guard to Pola, in Istria, where, soon afterwards, he was put to death, either by the hand of the executioner or by the more gentle operation of poison.[1] The Cæsar Licinius, a youth of amiable manners, was involved in the ruin of Crispus,[2] and the stern jealousy of Constantine was unmoved by the prayers and tears of his favourite sister, pleading for the life of a son whose rank was his only crime, and whose loss she did not long survive. The story of these unhappy princes, the nature and evidence of their guilt, the forms of their trial, and the circumstances of their death, were buried in mysterious obscurity, and the courtly bishop, who has celebrated in an elaborate work the virtues and piety of his hero, observes a prudent silence on the subject of these tragic events.[3] Such haughty contempt for the opinion of mankind, whilst it imprints an indelible stain on the memory of Constantine, must remind us of the very different behaviour of one of the greatest monarchs of the present age. The Czar Peter, in the full possession of despotic power, submitted to the judgment of Russia, of Europe, and of posterity, the reasons which had compelled him to subscribe the condemnation of a criminal, or at least of a degenerate, son.[4]

The innocence of Crispus was so universally acknowledged that the modern Greeks, who adore the memory of their founder, are reduced to palliate the guilt of a parricide which the common feelings of human nature forebade them to justify. They pretend that, as soon as the afflicted father discovered the falsehood of the accusation by which his credulity had been so fatally

pression of Suidas. The elder Victor, who wrote under the next reign, speaks with becoming caution. " Natû grandior, incertum quâ causâ, patris judicio occidisset." [De Cæsar. c. 41.] If we consult the succeeding writers, Eutropius, the younger Victor, Orosius, Jerom, Zosimus, Philostorgius, and Gregory of Tours, their knowledge will appear gradually to increase as their means of information must have diminished, a circumstance which frequently occurs in historical disquisition.

[1] Ammianus (l. xiv. c. 11) uses the general expression of *peremptum.* Codinus (p. 34) [p. 63, ed. Bonn] beheads the young prince; but Sidonius Apollinaris (Epistol. v. 8), for the sake perhaps of an antithesis to Fausta's *warm* bath, chooses to administer a draught of *cold* poison.

[2] Sororis filium, commodæ indolis juvenem. Eutropius, x. 6 [4]. May I not be permitted to conjecture that Crispus had married Helena, the daughter of the emperor Licinius, and that on the happy delivery of the princess, in the year 322, a general pardon was granted by Constantine? See Ducange, Fam. Byzant. p. 47, and the law (l. ix. tit. xxxvii.) of the Theodosian code, which has so much embarrassed the interpreters. Godefroy, tom. iii. p. 267.

[3] See the Life of Constantine, particularly [Euseb.] l. ii. c. 19, 20. Two hundred and fifty years afterwards Evagrius (l. iii. c. 41) deduced from the silence of Eusebius a vain argument against the reality of the fact.

[4] Histoire de Pierre le Grand, par Voltaire, part ii. c. 10.

misled, he published to the world his repentance and remorse;
that he mourned forty days, during which he abstained from
the use of the bath and all the ordinary comforts of life; and
that, for the lasting instruction of posterity, he erected a golden
statue of Crispus, with this memorable inscription,—TO MY SON,
WHOM I UNJUSTLY CONDEMNED.[1] A tale so moral and so
interesting would deserve to be supported by less exceptionable
authority; but if we consult the more ancient and authentic
writers, they will inform us that the repentance of Constantine
was manifested only in acts of blood and revenge, and that he
atoned for the murder of an innocent son by the execution,
perhaps, of a guilty wife. They ascribe the misfortunes of
Crispus to the arts of his stepmother Fausta, whose implacable
hatred or whose disappointed love renewed in the palace of
Constantine the ancient tragedy of Hippolytus and of Phædra.[2]
Like the daughter of Minos, the daughter of Maximian accused
her son-in-law of an incestuous attempt on the chastity of his
father's wife, and easily obtained, from the jealousy of the
emperor, a sentence of death against a young prince whom she
considered with reason as the most formidable rival of her
own children. But Helena, the aged mother of Constantine,
lamented and revenged the untimely fate of her grandson Crispus;
nor was it long before a real or pretended discovery was made
that Fausta herself entertained a criminal connection with a
slave belonging to the Imperial stables.[3] Her condemnation
and punishment were the instant consequences of the charge,
and the adulteress was suffocated by the steam of a bath, which,
for that purpose, had been heated to an extraordinary degree.[4]
By some it will perhaps be thought that the remembrance of a
conjugal union of twenty years, and the honour of their common
offspring, the destined heirs of the throne, might have softened

---

[1] In order to prove that the statue was erected by Constantine, and afterwards concealed by the malice of the Arians, Codinus very readily creates
(p. 34 [p. 63, ed. Bonn]) two witnesses, Hippolytus and the younger Herodotus, to whose imaginary histories he appeals with unblushing confidence.

[2] Zosimus (l. ii. [c. 29] p. 103) may be considered as our original. The
ingenuity of the moderns, assisted by a few hints from the ancients, has
illustrated and improved his obscure and imperfect narrative.

[3] Philostorgius, l. ii. c. 4. Zosimus (l. ii. p. 104 [c. 29], 116 [c. 39]) imputes to Constantine the death of two wives, of the innocent Fausta, and
of an adulteress who was the mother of his three successors. According to
Jerom, three or four years elapsed between the death of Crispus and that
of Fausta. The elder Victor is prudently silent.

[4] If Fausta was put to death, it is reasonable to believe that the private
apartments of the palace were the scene of her execution. The orator
Chrysostom indulges his fancy by exposing the naked empress on a desert
mountain to be devoured by wild beasts.

the obdurate heart of Constantine, and persuaded him to suffer his wife, however guilty she might appear, to expiate her offences in a solitary prison. But it seems a superfluous labour to weigh the propriety, unless we could ascertain the truth, of this singular event, which is attended with some circumstances of doubt and perplexity. Those who have attacked, and those who have defended, the character of Constantine, have alike disregarded two very remarkable passages of two orations pronounced under the succeeding reign. The former celebrates the virtues, the beauty, and the fortune of the empress Fausta, the daughter, wife, sister, and mother of so many princes.[1] The latter asserts, in explicit terms, that the mother of the younger Constantine, who was slain three years after his father's death, survived to weep over the fate of her son.[2] Notwithstanding the positive testimony of several writers of the Pagan as well as of the Christian religion, there may still remain some reason to believe, or at least to suspect, that Fausta escaped the blind and suspicious cruelty of her husband. The deaths of a son and of a nephew, with the execution of a great number of respectable and perhaps innocent friends,[3] who were involved in their fall, may be sufficient, however, to justify the discontent of the Roman people, and to explain the satirical verses affixed to the palace gate, comparing the splendid and bloody reigns of Constantine and Nero.[4]

By the death of Crispus the inheritance of the empire seemed to devolve on the three sons of Fausta, who have been already mentioned under the names of Constantine, of Constantius, and of Constans. These young princes were successively invested with the title of Cæsar, and the dates of their promotion may be

---

[1] Julian. Orat. i. [p. 9]. He seems to call her the mother of Crispus. She might assume that title by adoption. At least, she was not considered as his mortal enemy. Julian compares the fortune of Fausta with that of Parysatis, the Persian queen. A Roman would have more naturally recollected the second Agrippina:—

> Et moi, qui sur le trône ai suivi mes ancêtres:
> Moi, fille, femme, sœur, et mère de vos maîtres.

[2] Monod. in Constantin. Jun. c. 4, ad Calcem Eutrop. edit. Havercamp. The orator styles her the most divine and pious of queens.

[3] Interfecit numerosos amicos. Eutrop. x. 6 [4].

[4] Saturni aurea sæcula quis requirat?
> Sunt hæc gemmea, sed Neroniana.
>
> Sidon. Apollinar. v. 8.

It is somewhat singular that these satirical lines should be attributed, not to an obscure libeller or a disappointed patriot, but to Ablavius, prime minister and favourite of the emperor. We may now perceive that the imprecations of the Roman people were dictated by humanity as well as by superstition. Zosim. l. ii. [c. 30] p. 105.

referred to the tenth, the twentieth, and the thirtieth years of the reign of their father.[1] This conduct, though it tended to multiply the future masters of the Roman world, might be excused by the partiality of paternal affection; but it is not so easy to understand the motives of the emperor, when he endangered the safety both of his family and of his people by the unnecessary elevation of his two nephews, Dalmatius and Hannibalianus. The former was raised, by the title of Cæsar, to an equality with his cousins. In favour of the latter, Constantine invented the new and singular appellation of *Nobilissimus*,[2] to which he annexed the flattering distinction of a robe of purple and gold. But of the whole series of Roman princes in any age of the empire Hannibalianus alone was distinguished by the title of KING, a name which the subjects of Tiberius would have detested as the profane and cruel insult of capricious tyranny. The use of such a title, even as it appears under the reign of Constantine, is a strange and unconnected fact, which can scarcely be admitted on the joint authority of Imperial medals and contemporary writers.[3]

The whole empire was deeply interested in the education of these five youths, the acknowledged successors of Constantine. The exercises of the body prepared them for the fatigues of war and the duties of active life. Those who occasionally mention the education or talents of Constantius allow that he excelled in the gymnastic arts of leaping and running; that he was a dexterous archer, a skilful horseman, and a master of all the different weapons used in the service either of the cavalry or of the infantry.[4] The same assiduous cultivation was bestowed, though not perhaps with equal success, to improve the minds of

---

[1] Euseb. Orat. in Constantin. c. 3. These dates are sufficiently correct to justify the orator.

[The correct dates should certainly be given; they took place in 317, 323, and 333 A.D.—O. S.]

[2] Zosim. l. ii. [c. 39] p. 117. Under the predecessors of Constantine, *Nobilissimus* was a vague epithet rather than a legal and determined title.

[3] Adstruunt nummi veteres ac singulares. Spanheim de Usu Numismat. Dissertat. xii. vol. ii. p. 357. Ammianus speaks of this Roman king (l. xiv. c. 1, and Valesius ad loc.). The Valesian fragment styles him King of kings; and the Paschal Chronicle (p. 286 [p. 228, ed. Ven.; vol. i. p. 532, ed. Bonn]), by employing the word Ρῆγα, acquires the weight of Latin evidence.

[Hannibalianus reigned over the Pontic and Armenian districts, in 335 A.D. There still exist medals struck in his honour on which the same title is found, " FL. Hannibaliano Regi." Armenia, of course, means here the Lesser Armenia.—O. S.]

[4] His dexterity in martial exercises is celebrated by Julian (Orat. i. p. 11, Orat. ii. p 53) and allowed by Ammianus (l. xxi. c. 16).

the sons and nephews of Constantine.[1] The most celebrated professors of the Christian faith, of the Grecian philosophy, and of the Roman jurisprudence, were invited by the liberality of the emperor, who reserved for himself the important task of instructing the royal youths in the science of government and the knowledge of mankind. But the genius of Constantine himself had been formed by adversity and experience. In the free intercourse of private life, and amidst the dangers of the court of Galerius, he had learned to command his own passions, to encounter those of his equals, and to depend for his present safety and future greatness on the prudence and firmness of his personal conduct. His destined successors had the misfortune of being born and educated in the Imperial purple. Incessantly surrounded with a train of flatterers, they passed their youth in the enjoyment of luxury and the expectation of a throne; nor would the dignity of their rank permit them to descend from that elevated station from whence the various characters of human nature appear to wear a smooth and uniform aspect. The indulgence of Constantine admitted them, at a very tender age, to share the administration of the empire; and they studied the art of reigning, at the expense of the people intrusted to their care. The younger Constantine was appointed to hold his court in Gaul; and his brother Constantius exchanged that department, the ancient patrimony of their father, for the more opulent, but less martial, countries of the East. Italy, the Western Illyricum, and Africa, were accustomed to revere Constans, the third of his sons, as the representative of the great Constantine. He fixed Dalmatius on the Gothic frontier, to which he annexed the government of Thrace, Macedonia, and Greece. The city of Cæsarea was chosen for the residence of Hannibalianus; and the provinces of Pontus, Cappadocia, and the Lesser Armenia, were designed to form the extent of his new kingdom. For each of these princes a suitable establishment was provided. A just proportion of guards, of legions, and of auxiliaries, was allotted for their respective dignity and defence. The ministers and generals who were placed about their persons were such as Constantine could trust to assist, and even to control, these youthful sovereigns in the exercise of their delegated power. As they advanced in years and experience, the limits

[1] Euseb. in Vit. Constantin. l. iv. c. 51. Julian, Orat. i. p. 11-16, with Spanheim's elaborate Commentary. Libanius, Orat. iii. p. 109 [ed. Paris 1627]. Constantius studied with laudable diligence; but the dulness of his fancy prevented him from succeeding in the art of poetry, or even of rhetoric.

of their authority were insensibly enlarged: but the emperor always reserved for himself the title of Augustus; and while he showed the *Cæsars* to the armies and provinces, he maintained every part of the empire in equal obedience to its supreme head.[1] The tranquillity of the last fourteen years of his reign was scarcely interrupted by the contemptible insurrection of a camel-driver in the island of Cyprus,[2] or by the active part which the policy of Constantine engaged him to assume in the wars of the Goths and Sarmatians.

Among the different branches of the human race, the Sarmatians form a very remarkable shade; as they seem to unite the manners of the Asiatic barbarians with the figure and complexion of the ancient inhabitants of Europe. According to the various accidents of peace and war, of alliance or conquest, the Sarmatians were sometimes confined to the banks of the Tanais, and they sometimes spread themselves over the immense plains which lie between the Vistula and the Volga.[3] The care of their numerous flocks and herds, the pursuit of game, and the exercise of war, or rather of rapine, directed the vagrant motions of the Sarmatians. The movable camps or cities, the ordinary residence of their wives and children, consisted only of large waggons drawn by oxen, and covered in the form of tents. The military strength of the nation was composed of cavalry; and the custom of their warriors to lead in their hand one or two spare horses enabled them to advance and to retreat with a rapid diligence, which surprised the security, and eluded the pursuit, of a distant enemy.[4] Their poverty of iron prompted their rude industry to invent a sort of cuirass, which was capable of resisting a sword or javelin, though it was formed only of horses' hoofs, cut into thin and polished slices, carefully laid over each other in the manner of scales or feathers, and strongly

[1] Eusebius (l. iv. c. 51, 52), with a design of exalting the authority and glory of Constantine, affirms that he divided the Roman empire as a private citizen might have divided his patrimony. His distribution of the provinces may be collected from Eutropius, the two Victors, and the Valesian fragment.

[2] Calocerus, the obscure leader of this rebellion, or rather tumult, was apprehended and burnt alive in the market-place of Tarsus, by the vigilance of Dalmatius. See the elder Victor, the Chronicle of Jerom, and the doubtful traditions of Theophanes and Cedrenus.

[3] Cellarius has collected the opinions of the ancients concerning the European and Asiatic Sarmatia; and M. d'Anville has applied them to modern geography with the skill and accuracy which always distinguish that excellent writer.

[4] Ammian. l. xvii. c. 12. The Sarmatian horses were castrated to prevent the mischievous accidents which might happen from the noisy and ungovernable passions of the males.

sewed upon an under garment of coarse linen.[1] The offensive
arms of the Sarmatians were short daggers, long lances, and
a weighty bow with a quiver of arrows. They were reduced to
the necessity of employing fish-bones for the points of their
weapons; but the custom of dipping them in a venomous liquor,
that poisoned the wounds which they inflicted, is alone sufficient
to prove the most savage manners; since a people impressed
with a sense of humanity would have abhorred so cruel a practice,
and a nation skilled in the arts of war would have disdained so
impotent a resource.[2] Whenever these barbarians issued from
their deserts in quest of prey, their shaggy beards, uncombed
locks, the furs with which they were covered from head to foot,
and their fierce countenances, which seemed to express the innate
cruelty of their minds, inspired the more civilised provincials
of Rome with horror and dismay.

The tender Ovid, after a youth spent in the enjoyment of
fame and luxury, was condemned to an hopeless exile on the
frozen banks of the Danube, where he was exposed, almost
without defence, to the fury of these monsters of the desert,
with whose stern spirits he feared that his gentle shade might
hereafter be confounded. In his pathetic, but sometimes unmanly lamentations,[3] he describes in the most lively colours the
dress and manners, the arms and inroads, of the Getæ and Sarmatians, who were associated for the purposes of destruction;
and from the accounts of history there is some reason to believe
that these Sarmatians were the Jazygæ, one of the most numerous
and warlike tribes of the nation. The allurements of plenty
engaged them to seek a permanent establishment on the frontiers

---

[1] Pausanias, l. i. [c. 21, § 5] p. 50, edit. Kuhn. That inquisitive traveller
had carefully examined a Sarmatian cuirass which was preserved in the
temple of Æsculapius at Athens.

[2] Aspicis et mitti sub adunco toxica ferro,
Et telum causas mortis habere duas.

Ovid, ex Ponto, l. iv. ep. 7, ver. 11.

See in the Recherches sur les Américains, tom. ii. p. 236-271, a very curious
dissertation on poisoned darts. The venom was commonly extracted from
the vegetable reign; but that employed by the Scythians appears to have
been drawn from the viper and a mixture of human blood. The use of
poisoned arms, which has been spread over both worlds, never preserved a
savage tribe from the arms of a disciplined enemy.

[3] The nine books of Poetical Epistles which Ovid composed during the
seven first years of his melancholy exile, possess, besides the merit of
elegance, a double value. They exhibit a picture of the human mind under
very singular circumstances; and they contain many curious observations,
which no Roman, except Ovid, could have an opportunity of making.
Every circumstance which tends to illustrate the history of the barbarians
has been drawn together by the very accurate Count de Buat, Hist.
Ancienne des Peuples de l'Europe, tom. iv. c. xvi. p. 286-317.

of the empire. Soon after the reign of Augustus they obliged the Dacians, who subsisted by fishing on the banks of the river Theiss or Tibiscus, to retire into the hilly country, and to abandon to the victorious Sarmatians the fertile plains of the Upper Hungary, which are bounded by the course of the Danube and the semicircular enclosure of the Carpathian mountains.[1] In this advantageous position they watched or suspended the moment of attack, as they were provoked by injuries or appeased by presents; they gradually acquired the skill of using more dangerous weapons; and although the Sarmatians did not illustrate their name by any memorable exploits, they occasionally assisted their eastern and western neighbours, the Goths and the Germans, with a formidable body of cavalry. They lived under the irregular aristocracy of their chieftains;[2] but after they had received into their bosom the fugitive Vandals, who yielded to the pressure of the Gothic power, they seem to have chosen a king from that nation, and from the illustrious race of the Astingi, who had formerly dwelt on the shores of the northern ocean.[3]

This motive of enmity must have inflamed the subjects of contention which perpetually arise on the confines of warlike and independent nations. The Vandal princes were stimulated by fear and revenge; the Gothic kings aspired to extend their dominion from the Euxine to the frontiers of Germany; and the waters of the Maros, a small river which falls into the Theiss, were stained with the blood of the contending barbarians. After some experience of the superior strength and numbers of their adversaries, the Sarmatians implored the protection of the

[1] The Sarmatian Jazygæ were settled on the banks of the Pathissus or Tibiscus, when Pliny, in the year 79, published his Natural History. See l. iv. c. 25. In the time of Strabo and Ovid, sixty or seventy years before, they appear to have inhabited beyond the Getæ, along the coast of the Euxine.

[2] Principes Sarmatarum Jazygum penes quos civitatis regimen . . . plebem quoque et vim equitum, quâ solâ valent, offerebant. Tacit. Hist. iii. 5. This offer was made in the civil war between Vitellius and Vespasian.

[3] This hypothesis of a Vandal king reigning over Sarmatian subjects seems necessary to reconcile the Goth Jornandes with the Greek and Latin historians of Constantine. It may be observed that Isidore, who lived in Spain under the dominion of the Goths, gives them for enemies, not the Vandals, but the Sarmatians. See his Chronicle in Grotius, p. 709.

[It is now generally admitted that if the Sarmatians were not of Sclavonic origin, there must have been many Sclavonic settlers amongst them to account for the purely Sclavonic names that occur. On the other hand, Safarik, in his Slawische Alterthümer, attempted to prove that such tribes as the Alani Roxolani, Bastarnæ, Jazyges, were allied to the Persians and Medes, and therefore belonged to an Iranian stock. The question is very obscure to this day. Cf. Niebuhr, Kleine Schriften.—O. S.]

Roman monarch, who beheld with pleasure the discord of the
nations, but who was justly alarmed by the progress of the
Gothic arms. As soon as Constantine had declared himself in
favour of the weaker party, the haughty Araric, king of the
Goths, instead of expecting the attack of the legions, boldly
passed the Danube, and spread terror and devastation through
the province of Mæsia. To oppose the inroad of this destroying
host the aged emperor took the field in person; but on this occasion either his conduct or his fortune betrayed the glory which
he had acquired in so many foreign and domestic wars. He had
the mortification of seeing his troops fly before an inconsiderable
detachment of the barbarians, who pursued them to the edge of
their fortified camp, and obliged him to consult his safety by a
precipitate and ignominious retreat.[1] The event of a second and
more successful action retrieved the honour of the Roman name;
and the powers of art and discipline prevailed, after an obstinate
contest, over the efforts of irregular valour. The broken army
of the Goths abandoned the field of battle, the wasted province,
and the passage of the Danube: and although the eldest of the
sons of Constantine was permitted to supply the place of his
father, the merit of the victory, which diffused universal joy,
was ascribed to the auspicious counsels of the emperor himself.

He contributed at least to improve this advantage by his
negotiations with the free and warlike people of Chersonesus,[2]
whose capital, situate on the western coast of the Tauric or
Crimæan peninsula, still retained some vestiges of a Grecian
colony, and was governed by a perpetual magistrate, assisted by

---

[1] [No other author, ancient or modern, mentions this defeat of Constantine by the Goths. It is one of the few positive errors in historic fact to be
recorded against Gibbon—O. S.]

[2] I may stand in need of some apology for having used, without scruple,
the authority of Constantine Porphyrogenitus, in all that relates to the
wars and negotiations of the Chersonites. I am aware that he was a Greek
of the tenth century, and that his accounts of ancient history are frequently confused and fabulous. But on this occasion his narrative is, for
the most part, consistent and probable; nor is there much difficulty in
conceiving that an emperor might have access to some secret archives
which had escaped the diligence of meaner historians. For the situation
and history of Chersone, see Peyssonel, des Peuples barbares qui ont habité
les Bords du Danube, c. xvi. 84-90.

[Gibbon has here fallen into another peculiar error. He has confounded
the inhabitants of the city of Cherson, the ancient Chersonesus, with the
people of the Chersonesus Taurica. The very author he cites, Constantine
Porphyrogenitus, if read with care, would have kept him right, for he
clearly distinguishes between the republic of Cherson from the rest of the
Tauric peninsula, then possessed by the kings of the Cimmerian Bosphorus,
and that the city of Cherson alone furnished succours to the Romans.—
O. S.]

a council of senators, emphatically styled the Fathers of the City. The Chersonites were animated against the Goths by the memory of the wars which, in the preceding century, they had maintained with unequal forces against the invaders of their country. They were connected with the Romans by the mutual benefits of commerce; as they were supplied from the provinces of Asia with corn and manufactures, which they purchased with their only productions, salt, wax, and hides. Obedient to the requisition of Constantine, they prepared, under the conduct of their magistrate Diogenes, a considerable army, of which the principal strength consisted in cross-bows and military chariots. The speedy march and intrepid attack of the Chersonites, by diverting the attention of the Goths, assisted the operations of the Imperial generals. The Goths, vanquished on every side, were driven into the mountains, where, in the course of a severe campaign, above an hundred thousand were computed to have perished by cold and hunger. Peace was at length granted to their humble supplications; the eldest son of Araric was accepted as the most valuable hostage; and Constantine endeavoured to convince their chiefs, by a liberal distribution of honours and rewards, how far the friendship of the Romans was preferable to their enmity. In the expressions of his gratitude towards the faithful Chersonites, the emperor was still more magnificent. The pride of the nation was gratified by the splendid and almost royal decorations bestowed on their magistrate and his successors. A perpetual exemption from all duties was stipulated for their vessels which traded to the ports of the Black Sea. A regular subsidy was promised, of iron, corn, oil, and of every supply which could be useful either in peace or war. But it was thought that the Sarmatians were sufficiently rewarded by their deliverance from impending ruin; and the emperor, perhaps with too strict an economy, deducted some part of the expenses of the war from the customary gratifications which were allowed to that turbulent nation.[1]

Exasperated by this apparent neglect, the Sarmatians soon forgot, with the levity of barbarians, the services which they had so lately received, and the dangers which still threatened their safety. Their inroads on the territory of the empire provoked the indignation of Constantine to leave them to their fate; and

---

[1] [Not only was there no such deduction made from the customary "gratifications" made to the nation in question, but after his victory, and to punish the Sarmatians for their ravages committed, he withheld the sums that it had been the custom to bestow.—O. S.]

he no longer opposed the ambition of Geberic, a renowned warrior, who had recently ascended the Gothic throne. Wisumar, the Vandal king, whilst, alone and unassisted, he defended his dominions with undaunted courage, was vanquished and slain in a decisive battle which swept away the flower of the Sarmatian youth. The remainder of the nation embraced the desperate expedient of arming their slaves, a hardy race of hunters and herdsmen, by whose tumultuary aid they revenged their defeat, and expelled the invader from their confines. But they soon discovered that they had exchanged a foreign for a domestic enemy, more dangerous and more unplacable. Enraged by their former servitude, elated by their present glory, the slaves, under the name of Limigantes, claimed and usurped the possession of the country which they had saved. Their masters, unable to withstand the ungoverned fury of their populace, preferred the hardships of exile to the tyranny of their servants. Some of the fugitive Sarmatians solicited a less ignominious dependence under the hostile standard of the Goths. A more numerous band retired beyond the Carpathian mountains, among the Quadi, their German allies, and were easily admitted to share a superfluous waste of uncultivated land. But the far greater part of the distressed nation turned their eyes towards the fruitful provinces of Rome. Imploring the protection and forgiveness of the emperor, they solemnly promised, as subjects in peace, and as soldiers in war, the most inviolable fidelity to the empire which should graciously receive them into its bosom. According to the maxims adopted by Probus and his successors, the offers of this barbarian colony were eagerly accepted; and a competent portion of lands in the provinces of Pannonia, Thrace, Macedonia, and Italy, were immediately assigned for the habitation and subsistence of three hundred thousand Sarmatians.[1]

By chastising the pride of the Goths, and by accepting the homage of a suppliant nation, Constantine asserted the majesty of the Roman empire; and the ambassadors of Æthiopia, Persia, and the most remote countries of India, congratulated the peace

---

[1] The Gothic and Sarmatian wars are related in so broken and imperfect a manner, that I have been obliged to compare the following writers, who mutually supply, correct, and illustrate each other. Those who will take the same trouble may acquire a right of criticising my narrative. Ammianus, l. xvii. c. 12. Anonym. Valesian. p. 715. Eutropius, x. 7 [4]. Sextus Rufus de Provinciis, c. 26. Julian, Orat. i. p. 9, and Spanheim, Comment. p. 94. Hieronym. in Chron. Euseb. in Vit. Constantin. l. iv. c. 6. Socrates, l. i. c. 18. Sozomen, l. i. c. 8. Zosimus, l. ii. [c. 21] p. 108. Jornandes de Reb. Geticis, c. 22. Isidorus in Chron. p. 709; in Hist. Gothorum Grotii. Constantin. Porphyrogenitus de Administrat. Imperii. c. 53, p. 208, edit. Meursii [p. 144 *sqq.* ed. Paris; vol. iii. p. 244 *sqq.* ed. Bonn].

and prosperity of his government.[1] If he reckoned among the favours of fortune the death of his eldest son, of his nephew, and perhaps of his wife, he enjoyed an uninterrupted flow of private as well as public felicity till the thirtieth year of his reign; a period which none of his predecessors, since Augustus, had been permitted to celebrate. Constantine survived that solemn festival about ten months; and, at the mature age of sixty-four, after a short illness, he ended his memorable life at the palace of Aquyrion, in the suburbs of Nicomedia, whither he had retired for the benefit of the air, and with the hope of recruiting his exhausted strength by the use of the warm baths. The excessive demonstrations of grief, or at least of mourning, surpassed whatever had been practised on any former occasion. Notwithstanding the claims of the senate and people of ancient Rome, the corpse of the deceased emperor, according to his last request, was transported to the city which was destined to preserve the name and memory of its founder. The body of Constantine, adorned with the vain symbols of greatness, the purple and diadem, was deposited on a golden bed in one of the apartments of the palace, which for that purpose had been splendidly furnished and illuminated. The forms of the court were strictly maintained. Every day, at the appointed hours, the principal officers of the state, the army, and the household, approaching the person of their sovereign with bended knees and a composed countenance, offered their respectful homage as seriously as if he had been still alive. From motives of policy, this theatrical representation was for some time continued; nor could flattery neglect the opportunity of remarking that Constantine alone, by the peculiar indulgence of Heaven, had reigned after his death.[2]

But this reign could subsist only in empty pageantry; and it was soon discovered that the will of the most absolute monarch is seldom obeyed when his subjects have no longer anything to hope from his favour, or to dread from his resentment. The same ministers and generals who bowed with such reverential

---

[1] Eusebius (in Vit. Const. l. iv. c. 50) remarks three circumstances relative to these Indians. 1. They came from the shores of the eastern ocean; a description which might be applied to the coast of China or Coromandel. 2. They presented shining gems and unknown animals. 3. They protested their kings had erected statues to represent the supreme majesty of Constantine.

[2] Funus relatum in urbem sui nominis, quod sane P. R. ægerrime tulit. Aurelius Victor [de Cæsar. c. 41]. Constantine prepared for himself a stately tomb in the church of the Holy Apostles. Euseb. l. iv. c. 60. The best, and indeed almost the only account of the sickness, death, and funeral of Constantine, is contained in the fourth book of his Life by Eusebius.

awe before the inanimate corpse of their deceased sovereign were engaged in secret consultations to exclude his two nephews, Dalmatius and Hannibalianus, from the share which he had assigned them in the succession of the empire. We are too imperfectly acquainted with the court of Constantine to form any judgment of the real motives which influenced the leaders of the conspiracy; unless we should suppose that they were actuated by a spirit of jealousy and revenge against the præfect Ablavius, a proud favourite, who had long directed the counsels and abused the confidence of the late emperor. The arguments by which they solicited the concurrence of the soldiers and people are of a more obvious nature: and they might with decency, as well as truth, insist on the superior rank of the children of Constantine, the danger of multiplying the number of sovereigns, and the impending mischiefs which threatened the republic, from the discord of so many rival princes who were not connected by the tender sympathy of fraternal affection. The intrigue was conducted with zeal and secrecy, till a loud and unanimous declaration was procured from the troops that they would suffer none except the sons of their lamented monarch to reign over the Roman empire.[1] The younger Dalmatius, who was united with his collateral relations by the ties of friendship and interest, is allowed to have inherited a considerable share of the abilities of the great Constantine; but, on this occasion, he does not appear to have concerted any measures for supporting by arms the just claims which himself and his royal brother derived from the liberality of their uncle. Astonished and overwhelmed by the tide of popular fury, they seem to have remained, without the power of flight or of resistance, in the hands of their implacable enemies. Their fate was suspended till the arrival of Constantius, the second,[2] and perhaps the most favoured, of the sons of Constantine.

The voice of the dying emperor had recommended the care of his funeral to the piety of Constantius; and that prince, by the vicinity of his eastern station, could easily prevent the diligence of his brothers, who resided in their distant governments of Italy

---

[1] Eusebius (l. iv. c. 68) terminates his narrative by this loyal declaration of the troops, and avoids all the invidious circumstances of the subsequent massacre.

[2] The character of Dalmatius is advantageously, though concisely, drawn by Eutropius (x. 9 [5]). Dalmatius Cæsar prosperrimâ indole, neque patruo absimilis, *haud multo* post oppressus est factione militari. As both Jerom and the Alexandrian Chronicle mention the third year of the Cæsar, which did not commence till the 18th or 24th of September, A.D. 337, it is certain that these military factions continued above four months

and Gaul. As soon as he had taken possession of the palace of Constantinople, his first care was to remove the apprehensions of his kinsmen, by a solemn oath which he pledged for their security. His next employment was to find some specious pretence which might release his conscience from the obligation of an imprudent promise. The arts of fraud were made subservient to the designs of cruelty; and a manifest forgery was attested by a person of the most sacred character. From the hands of the bishop of Nicomedia, Constantius received a fatal scroll, affirmed to be the genuine testament of his father; in which the emperor expressed his suspicions that he had been poisoned by his brothers; and conjured his sons to revenge his death, and to consult their own safety, by the punishment of the guilty.[1] Whatever reasons might have been alleged by these unfortunate princes to defend their life and honour against so incredible an accusation, they were silenced by the furious clamours of the soldiers, who declared themselves, at once, their enemies, their judges, and their executioners. The spirit, and even the forms, of legal proceedings were repeatedly violated in a promiscuous massacre; which involved the two uncles of Constantius, seven of his cousins, of whom Dalmatius and Hannibalianus were the most illustrious, the Patrician Optatus, who had married a sister of the late emperor, and the præfect Ablavius, whose power and riches had inspired him with some hopes of obtaining the purple. If it were necessary to aggravate the horrors of this bloody scene, we might add that Constantius himself had espoused the daughter of his uncle Julius, and that he had bestowed his sister in marriage on his cousin Hannibalianus. These alliances, which the policy of Constantine, regardless of the public prejudice,[2] had formed between the several branches

---

[1] I have related this singular anecdote on the authority of Philostorgius, l. ii. c. 16. But if such a pretext was ever used by Constantius and his adherents, it was laid aside with contempt as soon as it served their immediate purpose. Athanasius (tom. i. p. 856) mentions the oath which Constantius had taken for the security of his kinsmen.

[2] Conjuga sobrinarum diu ignorata, tempore addito percrebuisse. Tacit. Annal. xii. 6, and Lipsius ad loc. The repeal of the ancient law, and the practice of five hundred years, were insufficient to eradicate the prejudices of the Romans, who still considered the marriages of cousins-german as a species of imperfect incest (Augustin de Civitate Dei, xv. 6); and Julian, whose mind was biassed by superstition and resentment, stigmatises these unnatural alliances between his own cousins with the opprobious epithet of γαμῶν τε οὐ γαμῶν (Orat. vii. p. 228). The jurisprudence of the canons has since revived and enforced this prohibition, without being able to introduce it either into the civil or the common law of Europe. See, on the subject of these marriages, Taylor's Civil Law, p. 331; Brouer, de Jure

of the Imperial house, served only to convince mankind that these princes were as cold to the endearments of conjugal affection, as they were insensible to the ties of consanguinity and the moving entreaties of youth and innocence. Of so numerous a family, Gallus and Julian alone, the two youngest children of Julius Constantius, were saved from the hands of the assassins, till their rage, satiated with slaughter, had in some measure subsided. The emperor Constantius, who, in the absence of his brothers, was the most obnoxious to guilt and reproach, discovered, on some future occasions, a faint and transient remorse for those cruelties which the perfidious counsels of his ministers and the irresistible violence of the troops, had extorted from his in-experienced youth.[1]

The massacre of the Flavian race was succeeded by a new division of the provinces, which was ratified in a personal interview of the three brothers. Constantine, the eldest of the Cæsars, obtained, with a certain pre-eminence of rank, the possession of the new capital, which bore his own name and that of his father. Thrace and the countries of the East were allotted for the patrimony of Constantius; and Constans was acknowledged as the lawful sovereign of Italy, Africa, and the western Illyricum. The armies submitted to their hereditary right, and they condescended, after some delay, to accept from the Roman senate the title of *Augustus*. When they first assumed the reins of government, the eldest of these princes was twenty-one, the second twenty, and the third only seventeen, years of age.[2]

While the martial nations of Europe followed the standards of his brothers, Constantius, at the head of the effeminate troops of Asia, was left to sustain the weight of the Persian war. At the decease of Constantine, the throne of the East was filled by Sapor, son of Hormouz, or Hormisdas, and grandson of Narses, who, after the victory of Galerius, had humbly confessed the superiority

---

Connub. l. ii. c. 12; Hericourt, des Loix Ecclésiastiques, part iii. c. 5; Fleury, Institutions du Droit Canonique, tom. i. p. 331, Paris, 1767; and Fra Paolo, Istoria del Concilio Trident. l. viii.

[1] Julian (ad S. P. Q. Athen. p. 270) charges his cousin Constantius with the whole guilt of a massacre from which he himself so narrowly escaped. His assertion is confirmed by Athanasius, who, for reasons of a very different nature, was not less an enemy of Constantius (tom. i. p. 856). Zosimus [ii. 40] joins in the same accusation. But the three abbreviators, Eutropius and the Victors, use very qualifying expressions:—" sinente potius quam jubente; " " incertum quo suasore; " " vi militum."

[2] Euseb. in Vit. Constantin. l. iv. c. 69. Zosimus, l. ii. [c. 39] p. 117. Idat. in Chron. See two notes of Tillemont, Hist. des Empereurs, tom. iv. p. 1086-1091. The reign of the eldest brother at Constantinople is noticed only in the Alexandrian Chronicle.

of the Roman power. Although Sapor was in the thirtieth year of his long reign, he was still in the vigour of youth, as the date of his accession, by a very strange fatality, had preceded that of his birth. The wife of Hormouz remained pregnant at the time of her husband's death, and the uncertainty of the sex, as well as of the event, excited the ambitious hopes of the princes of the house of Sassan. The apprehensions of civil war were at length removed by the positive assurance of the Magi that the widow of Hormouz had conceived, and would safely produce a son. Obedient to the voice of superstition, the Persians prepared, without delay, the ceremony of his coronation. A royal bed, on which the queen lay in state, was exhibited in the midst of the palace; the diadem was placed on the spot which might be supposed to conceal the future heir of Artaxerxes, and the prostrate satraps adored the majesty of their invisible and insensible sovereign.[1] If any credit can be given to this marvellous tale, which seems, however, to be countenanced by the manners of the people and by the extraordinary duration of his reign, we must admire not only the fortune but the genius of Sapor. In the soft sequestered education of a Persian harem the royal youth could discover the importance of exercising the vigour of his mind and body, and by his personal merit deserved a throne on which he had been seated while he was yet unconscious of the duties and temptations of absolute power. His minority was exposed to the almost inevitable calamities of domestic discord; his capital was surprised and plundered by Thair, a powerful king of Yemen or Arabia, and the majesty of the royal family was degraded by the captivity of a princess, the sister of the deceased king. But as soon as Sapor attained the age of manhood the presumptuous Thair, his nation, and his country, fell beneath the first effort of the young warrior, who used his victory with so judicious a mixture of rigour and clemency that he obtained from the fears and gratitude of the Arabs the title of *Dhoulacnaf*, or protector of the nation.[2]

[1] Agathias, who lived in the sixth century, is the author of this story (l. iv. p. 135, edit. Louvre [c. 25, p. 262, ed. Bonn]). He derived his information from some extracts of the Persian Chronicles, obtained and translated by the interpreter Sergius during his embassy at that court. The coronation of the mother of Sapor is likewise mentioned by Schikard (Tarikh, p. 116) and d'Herbelot (Bibliothèque Orientale, p. 763).

[2] D'Herbelot, Bibliothèque Orientale, p. 764.

[Sir John Malcolm, in his *History of Persia* has stated that Gibbon has made an error in the derivation of the name "Dhoulacnaf." It means Zoolaktaf, or Lord of the Shoulders, from his directing the shoulders of his captives to be pierced and then dislocated by a string passed through them.—O. S.]

The ambition of the Persian, to whom his enemies ascribe the virtues of a soldier and a statesman, was animated by the desire of revenging the disgrace of his fathers, and of wresting from the hands of the Romans the five provinces beyond the Tigris. The military fame of Constantine, and the real or apparent strength of his government, suspended the attack, and, while the hostile conduct of Sapor provoked the resentment, his artful negotiations amused the patience of the Imperial court. The death of Constantine was the signal of war,[1] and the actual condition of the Syrian and Armenian frontier seemed to encourage the Persians by the prospect of a rich spoil and an easy conquest. The example of the massacres of the palace diffused a spirit of licentiousness and sedition among the troops of the East, who were no longer restrained by their habits of obedience to a veteran commander. By the prudence of Constantius, who, from the interview with his brothers in Pannonia, immediately hastened to the banks of the Euphrates, the legions were gradually restored to a sense of duty and discipline; but the season of anarchy had permitted Sapor to form the siege of Nisibis, and to occupy several of the most important fortresses of Mesopotamia.[2] In Armenia the renowned Tiridates had long enjoyed the peace and glory which he deserved by his valour and fidelity to the cause of Rome. The firm alliance which he maintained with Constantine was productive of spiritual as well as of temporal benefits; by the conversion of Tiridates the character of a saint was applied to that of a hero, the Christian faith was preached and established from the Euphrates to the shores of the Caspian, and Armenia was attached to the empire by the double ties of policy and of religion. But as many of the Armenian nobles still refused to abandon the plurality of their gods and of their wives, the public tranquillity was disturbed by a discontented faction, which insulted the feeble age of their sovereign, and impatiently expected the hour of his death. He died at length, after a reign of fifty-six years, and the fortune of the Armenian monarchy expired with Tiridates. His lawful heir was driven into exile, the Christian priests were either murdered or expelled from their churches, the barbarous tribes of Albania were solicited to descend from their mountains, and two of the most

---

[1] Sextus Rufus (c. 26), who on this occasion is no contemptible authority, affirms that the Persians sued in vain for peace, and that Constantine was preparing to march against them: yet the superior weight of the testimony of Eusebius obliges us to admit the preliminaries, if not the ratification, of the treaty. See Tillemont, Hist. des Empereurs, tom. iv. p. 420.

[2] Julian. Orat. i. p. 20.

powerful governors, usurping the ensigns or the powers of
royalty, implored the assistance of Sapor, and opened the gates
of their cities to the Persian garrisons. The Christian party,
under the guidance of the archbishop of Artaxata, the immediate successor of St. Gregory the Illuminator, had recourse
to the piety of Constantius. After the troubles had continued
about three years, Antiochus, one of the officers of the household,
executed with success the Imperial commission of restoring
Chosroes, the son of Tiridates, to the throne of his fathers, of
distributing honours and rewards among the faithful servants
of the house of Arsaces, and of proclaiming a general amnesty,
which was accepted by the greater part of the rebellious satraps.
But the Romans derived more honour than advantage from this
revolution. Chosroes was a prince of a puny stature and a
pusillanimous spirit. Unequal to the fatigues of war, averse to
the society of mankind, he withdrew from his capital to a retired
palace which he built on the banks of the river Eleutherus, and
in the centre of a shady grove, where he consumed his vacant
hours in the rural sports of hunting and hawking. To secure
this inglorious ease, he submitted to the conditions of peace
which Sapor condescended to impose: the payment of an annual
tribute, and the restitution of the fertile province of Atropatene,
which the courage of Tiridates and the victorious arms of Galerius
had annexed to the Armenian monarchy.[1]

[1] Julian. Orat. i. p. 20, 21. Moses of Chorene, l. ii. c. 89, l. iii. c. 1-9,
p. 226-240. The perfect agreement between the vague hints of the contemporary orator and the circumstantial narrative of the national historian,
gives light to the former and weight to the latter. For the credit of Moses
it may be likewise observed that the name of Antiochus is found a few
years before in a civil office of inferior dignity. See Godefroy, Cod. Theod.
tom. vi. p. 350.

[Gibbon has endeavoured in his history (says Milman) to make use of
the information furnished by Moses of Chorene, the only Armenian historian then translated into Latin. Gibbon, however, has not perceived the
chronological difficulties that occur in the narrative of Moses of Chorene,
and he has committed an anachronism of some thirty years, assigning to
the reign of Constantius many events that took place in that of Constantius.
This affects very materially his view of the history of Armenia. It is therefore essential that a short sketch of this period of Armenian history should
be given. Tiridates, the first Christian king of Armenia, died A.D. 314, and
his son Chosroes II. was placed on the throne by a Roman army commanded by Antiochus. This was during the reign of Licinius in the East.
Chosroes was succeeded by his son, Diran, in 322. The latter was a weak
prince, and in the sixteenth year of his reign was betrayed into the power
of Sapor the Persian king by the treachery of his chamberlain. He was
blinded, and his son and wife shared his captivity, but the princes and
nobles of Armenia claimed the protection of the Romans. Constantine
espoused their cause, but almost immediately after he died, and the war
was carried on by his son Constantius. The king of Persia attempted to
make himself master of Armenia, but the resistance, the advance, of Con-

During the long period of the reign of Constantius the provinces of the East were afflicted by the calamities of the Persian war. The irregular incursions of the light troops alternately spread terror and devastation beyond the Tigris and beyond the Euphrates, from the gates of Ctesiphon to those of Antioch; and this active service was performed by the Arabs of the desert, who were divided in their interest and affections, some of their independent chiefs being enlisted in the party of Sapor, whilst others had engaged their doubtful fidelity to the emperor.[1] The more grave and important operations of the war were conducted with equal vigour; and the armies of Rome and Persia encountered each other in nine bloody fields, in two of which Constantius himself commanded in person.[2] The event of the day was most commonly adverse to the Romans, but in the battle of Singara their imprudent valour had almost achieved a signal and decisive victory. The stationary troops of Singara retired on the approach of Sapor, who passed the Tigris over three bridges, and occupied near the village of Hilleh an advantageous camp, which, by the labour of his numerous pioneers, he surrounded in one day with a deep ditch and a lofty rampart. His formidable host, when it was drawn out in order of battle, covered the banks of the river, the adjacent heights, and the whole extent of a plain of above twelve miles which separated the two armies. Both were alike impatient to engage, but the barbarians, after a slight resistance, fled in disorder, unable to

stantius, and a defeat which the Persians sustained at Oskha in Armenia, and the failure before Nisibis, forced Shahpour, the Persian king, to submit to terms of peace. Diran and his son were released from captivity, but Diran refused to reascend the throne, and retired to an obscure religious retreat, his son Arsaces being crowned king. Arsaces pursued a vacillating policy between the influence of Rome and Persia, and the war recommenced in 345.—O. S.]

[1] Ammianus (xiv. 4) gives a lively description of the wandering and predatory life of the Saracens, who stretched from the confines of Assyria to the cataracts of the Nile. It appears from the adventures of Malchus, which Jerom has related in so entertaining a manner, that the high road between Beræa and Edessa was infested by these robbers. See Hieronym. tom. i. p. 256.

[2] We shall take from Eutropius the general idea of the war (x. 10 [6]). A Persis enim multa et gravia perpessus, sæpe captis oppidis, obsessis urbibus, cæsis exercitibus, nullumque ei contra Saporem prosperum prœlium fuit, nisi quod apud Singaram, etc. This honest account is confirmed by the hints of Ammianus, Rufus, and Jerom. The two first orations of Julian, and the third oration of Libanius, exhibit a more flattering picture; but the recantation of both those orators after the death of Constantius, while it restores us to the possession of the truth, degrades their own character and that of the emperor. The commentary of Spanheim on the first oration of Julian is profusely learned. See likewise the judicious observations of Tillemont, Hist. des Empereurs, tom. iv. p. 656.

resist, or desirous to weary, the strength of the heavy legions, who, fainting with heat and thirst, pursued them across the plain, and cut in pieces a line of cavalry clothed in complete armour, which had been posted before the gates of the camp to protect their retreat. Constantius, who was hurried along in the pursuit, attempted, without effect, to restrain the ardour of his troops, by representing to them the dangers of the approaching night, and the certainty of completing their success with the return of day. As they depended much more on their own valour than on the experience or the abilities of their chief, they silenced by their clamours his timid remonstrances, and, rushing with fury to the charge, filled up the ditch, broke down the rampart, and dispersed themselves through the tents to recruit their exhausted strength, and to enjoy the rich harvest of their labours. But the prudent Sapor had watched the moment of victory. His army, of which the greater part, securely posted on the heights, had been spectators of the action, advanced in silence and under the shadow of the night, and his Persian archers, guided by the illumination of the camp, poured a shower of arrows on a disarmed and licentious crowd. The sincerity of history [1] declares that the Romans were vanquished with a dreadful slaughter, and that the flying remnant of the legions was exposed to the most intolerable hardships. Even the tenderness of panegyric, confessing that the glory of the emperor was sullied by the disobedience of his soldiers, chooses to draw a veil over the circumstances of this melancholy retreat. Yet one of those venal orators, so jealous of the fame of Constantius, relates, with amazing coolness, an act of such incredible cruelty, as, in the judgment of posterity, must imprint a far deeper stain on the honour of the Imperial name. The son of Sapor, the heir of his crown, had been made a captive in the Persian camp. The unhappy youth, who might have excited the compassion of the most savage enemy, was scourged, tortured, and publicly executed by the inhuman Romans.[2]

Whatever advantages might attend the arms of Sapor in the field, though nine repeated victories diffused among the nations the fame of his valour and conduct, he could not hope to succeed in the execution of his designs while the fortified towns of Mesopotamia, and, above all, the strong and ancient city of Nisibis,

---

[1] Acerrimâ nocturnâ concertatione pugnatum est, nostrorum copiis ingenti strage confossis. Ammian. xviii. 5. See likewise Eutropius, x. 10 [6], and S. Rufus, c. 27.
[2] Libanius, Orat. iii. p. 133, with Julian. Orat. i. p. 24, and Spanheim's Commentary, p. 179.

remained in the possession of the Romans. In the space of twelve years Nisibis, which, since the time of Lucullus, had been deservedly esteemed the bulwark of the East, sustained three memorable sieges against the power of Sapor; and the disappointed monarch, after urging his attacks above sixty, eighty, and an hundred days, was thrice repulsed with loss and ignominy.[1] This large and populous city was situate about two days' journey from the Tigris, in the midst of a pleasant and fertile plain at the foot of Mount Masius. A treble enclosure of brick walls was defended by a deep ditch;[2] and the intrepid resistance of Count Lucilianus and his garrison was seconded by the desperate courage of the people. The citizens of Nisibis were animated by the exhortations of their bishop,[3] inured to arms by the presence of danger, and convinced of the intentions of Sapor to plant a Persian colony in their room, and to lead them away into distant and barbarous captivity. The event of the two former sieges elated their confidence and exasperated the haughty spirit of the Great King, who advanced a third time towards Nisibis, at the head of the united forces of Persia and India. The ordinary machines, invented to batter or undermine the walls, were rendered ineffectual by the superior skill of the Romans, and many days had vainly elapsed when Sapor embraced a resolution worthy of an eastern monarch who believed that the elements themselves were subject to his power. At the stated season of the melting of the snows in Armenia, the river Mygdonius, which divides the plain and the city of Nisibis, forms, like the Nile,[4] an inundation over the adjacent country. By the labour of the Persians the course of the river was stopped below

---

[1] See Julian. Orat. i. p. 27; Orat. ii. p. 62, etc.; with the Commentary of Spanheim (p. 188-202), who illustrates the circumstances, and ascertains the time of the three sieges of Nisibis. Their dates are likewise examined by Tillemont (Hist. des Empereurs, tom. iv. p. 668, 671, 674). Something is added from Zosimus, l. iii. [c. 8] p. 151, and the Alexandrian Chronicle, p. 290.

[2] Sallust. Fragment. lxxxiv. edit. Brosses, and Plutarch in Lucull. [c. 32] tom. iii. p. 184. Nisibis is now reduced to one hundred and fifty houses; the marshy lands produce rice, and the fertile meadows, as far as Mosul and the Tigris, are covered with the ruins of towns and villages. See Niebuhr, Voyages, tom. ii. p. 300-309.

[3] The miracles which Theodoret (l. ii. c. 30) ascribes to St. James, bishop of Edessa, were at least performed in a worthy cause, the defence of his country. He appeared on the walls under the figure of the Roman emperor, and sent an army of gnats to sting the trunks of the elephants, and to discomfit the host of the new Senacherib.

[4] Julian. Orat. i. p. 27. Though Niebuhr (tom. ii. p. 307) allows a very considerable swell to the Mygdonius, over which he saw a bridge of twelve arches; it is difficult, however, to understand this parallel of a trifling rivulet with a mighty river. There are many circumstances obscure, and almost unintelligible, in the description of these stupendous waterworks.

the town, and the waters were confined on every side by solid mounds of earth. On this artificial lake a fleet of armed vessels, filled with soldiers, and with engines which discharged stones of five hundred pounds weight, advanced in order of battle, and engaged, almost upon a level, the troops which defended the ramparts. The irresistible force of the waters was alternately fatal to the contending parties, till at length a portion of the walls, unable to sustain the accumulated pressure, gave way at once, and exposed an ample breach of one hundred and fifty feet. The Persians were instantly driven to the assault, and the fate of Nisibis depended on the event of the day. The heavy-armed cavalry, who led the van of a deep column, were embarrassed in the mud, and great numbers were drowned in the unseen holes which had been filled by the rushing waters. The elephants, made furious by their wounds, increased the disorder, and trampled down thousands of the Persian archers. The Great King, who, from an exalted throne, beheld the misfortunes of his arms, sounded, with reluctant indignation, the signal of the retreat, and suspended for some hours the prosecution of the attack. But the vigilant citizens improved the opportunity of the night, and the return of day discovered a new wall of six feet in height rising every moment to fill up the interval of the breach. Notwithstanding the disappointment of his hopes and the loss of more than twenty thousand men, Sapor still pressed the reduction of Nisibis with an obstinate firmness which could have yielded only to the necessity of defending the eastern provinces of Persia against a formidable invasion of the Massagetæ.[1] Alarmed by this intelligence, he hastily relinquished the siege, and marched with rapid diligence from the banks of the Tigris to those of the Oxus. The danger and difficulties of the Scythian war engaged him soon afterwards to conclude, or at least to observe, a truce with the Roman emperor, which was equally grateful to both princes, as Constantius himself, after the deaths of his two brothers, was involved, by the revolutions of the West, in a civil contest which required and seemed to exceed the most vigorous exertion of his undivided strength.

After the partition of the empire three years had scarcely elapsed before the sons of Constantine seemed impatient to convince mankind that they were incapable of contenting them-

---

[1] We are obliged to Zonaras (tom. ii. l. xiii. [c. 7] p. 11 [15]) for this invasion of the Massagetæ, which is perfectly consistent with the general series of events, to which we are darkly led by the broken history of Ammianus.

selves with the dominions which they were unqualified to govern. The eldest of those princes soon complained that he was defrauded of his just proportion of the spoils of their murdered kinsmen; and though he might yield to the superior guilt and merit of Constantius, he exacted from Constans the cession of the African provinces, as an equivalent for the rich countries of Macedonia and Greece which his brother had acquired by the death of Dalmatius. The want of sincerity which Constantine experienced in a tedious and fruitless negotiation exasperated the fierceness of his temper, and he eagerly listened to those favourites who suggested to him that his honour, as well as his interest, was concerned in the prosecution of the quarrel. At the head of a tumultuary band, suited for rapine rather than for conquest, he suddenly broke into the dominions of Constans, by the way of the Julian Alps, and the country round Aquileia felt the first effects of his resentment. The measures of Constans, who then resided in Dacia, were directed with more prudence and ability. On the news of his brother's invasion he detached a select and disciplined body of his Illyrian troops, proposing to follow them in person with the remainder of his forces. But the conduct of his lieutenants soon terminated the unnatural contest. By the artful appearances of flight, Constantine was betrayed into an ambuscade, which had been concealed in a wood, where the rash youth, with a few attendants, was surprised, surrounded, and slain. His body, after it had been found in the obscure stream of the Alsa, obtained the honours of an Imperial sepulchre, but his provinces transferred their allegiance to the conqueror, who, refusing to admit his elder brother Constantius to any share in these new acquisitions, maintained the undisputed possession of more than two-thirds of the Roman empire.[1]

The fate of Constans himself was delayed about ten years longer, and the revenge of his brother's death was reserved for the more ignoble hand of a domestic traitor. The pernicious tendency of the system introduced by Constantine was displayed in the feeble administration of his sons, who, by their vices and weakness, soon lost the esteem and affections of their people. The pride assumed by Constans from the unmerited success of his arms was rendered more contemptible by his want of abilities

[1] The causes and the events of this civil war are related with much perplexity and contradiction. I have chiefly followed Zonaras and the younger Victor. The monody (ad calcem Eutrop. edit. Havercamp.) pronounced on the death of Constantine might have been very instructive; but prudence and false taste engaged the orator to involve himself in vague declamation.

and application.   His fond partiality towards some German
captives, distinguished only by the charms of youth, was an
object of scandal to the people; [1] and Magnentius, an ambitious
soldier, who was himself of barbarian extraction, was encouraged
by the public discontent to assert the honour of the Roman
name.[2]   The chosen bands of Jovians and Herculians, who
acknowledged Magnentius as their leader, maintained the most
respectable and important station in the Imperial camp.   The
friendship of Marcellinus, count of the sacred largesses, supplied
with a liberal hand the means of seduction.   The soldiers were
convinced, by the most specious arguments, that the republic
summoned them to break the bonds of hereditary servitude,
and, by the choice of an active and vigilant prince, to reward
the same virtues which had raised the ancestors of the degenerate
Constans from a private condition to the throne of the world.
As soon as the conspiracy was ripe for execution, Marcellinus,
under the pretence of celebrating his son's birthday, gave a
splendid entertainment to the *illustrious* and *honourable* persons
of the court of Gaul, which then resided in the city of Autun.
The intemperance of the feast was artfully protracted till a very
late hour of the night, and the unsuspecting guests were tempted
to indulge themselves in a dangerous and guilty freedom of
conversation.   On a sudden the doors were thrown open, and
Magnentius, who had retired for a few moments, returned into
the apartment, invested with the diadem and purple.   The
conspirators instantly saluted him with the titles of Augustus
and Emperor.   The surprise, the terror, the intoxication, the
ambitious hopes, and the mutual ignorance of the rest of the
assembly prompted them to join their voices to the general
acclamation.   The guards hastened to take the oath of fidelity,
the gates of the town were shut, and before the dawn of day
Magnentius became master of the troops and treasure of the
palace and city of Autun.   By his secrecy and diligence he entertained some hopes of surprising the person of Constans, who

---

[1] Quarum (*gentium*) obsides pretio quæsitos pueros venustiores, quod
cultius habuerat, libidine hujusmodi arsisse *pro certo* habetur.   [De Cæs.
41.]   Had not the depraved taste of Constans been publicly avowed, the
elder Victor, who held a considerable office in his brother's reign, would
not have asserted it in such positive terms.

[2] Julian. Orat. i. and ii.   Zosim. l. ii. [c. 42] p. 134.   Victor in Epitome
[c. 41].   There is reason to believe that Magnentius was born in one of
those barbarian colonies which Constantius Chlorus had established in
Gaul (see this History, vol. i. p. 352).   His behaviour may remind us of the
patriot earl of Leicester, the famous Simon de Montfort, who could persuade the good people of England that he, a Frenchman by birth, had
taken arms to deliver them from foreign favourites.

was pursuing in the adjacent forest his favourite amusement of hunting, or perhaps some pleasures of a more private and criminal nature. The rapid progress of fame allowed him, however, an instant for flight, though the desertion of his soldiers and subjects deprived him of the power of resistance. Before he could reach a seaport in Spain, where he intended to embark, he was over-taken near Helena,[1] at the foot of the Pyrenees, by a party of light cavalry, whose chief, regardless of the sanctity of a temple, executed his commission by the murder of the son of Constantine.[2]

As soon as the death of Constans had decided this easy but important revolution, the example of the court of Autun was imitated by the provinces of the West. The authority of Mag-nentius was acknowledged through the whole extent of the two great præfectures of Gaul and Italy; and the usurper prepared, by every act of oppression, to collect a treasure which might discharge the obligation of an immense donative and supply the expenses of a civil war. The martial countries of Illyricum, from the Danube to the extremity of Greece, had long obeyed the government of Vetranio, an aged general, beloved for the simplicity of his manners, and who had acquired some reputation by his experience and services in war.[3] Attached by habit, by duty, and by gratitude to the house of Constantine, he immedi-ately gave the strongest assurances to the only surviving son of his late master that he would expose, with unshaken fidelity, his person and his troops to inflict a just revenge on the traitors of Gaul. But the legions of Vetranio were seduced, rather than provoked, by the example of rebellion; their leader soon betrayed a want of firmness or a want of sincerity, and his ambition derived a specious pretence from the approbation of the princess Con-stantina. That cruel and aspiring woman, who had obtained from the great Constantine, her father, the rank of *Augusta,* placed the diadem with her own hands on the head of the Illyrian general, and seemed to expect from his victory the

---

[1] This ancient city had once flourished under the name of Illiberis (Pom-ponius Mela, ii. 5). The munificence of Constantine gave it new splendour, and his mother's name. Helena (it is still called Elne) became the seat of a bishop, who long afterwards transferred his residence to Perpignan, the capital of modern Rousillon. See d'Anville, Notice de l'Ancienne Gaule, p. 380; Longuerue, Description de la France, p. 223; and the Marca His-panica, l. i. c. 2.

[2] Zosimus, l. ii. [c. 42] p. 119, 120; Zonaras, tom. ii. l. xiii. [c. 6] p. 13; and the Abbreviators.

[3] Eutropius (x. 10 [6]) describes Vetranio with more temper, and prob-ably with more truth, than either of the two Victors. Vetranio was born of obscure parents in the wildest parts of Mæsia; and so much had his education been neglected, that, after his elevation, he studied the alphabet.

accomplishment of those unbounded hopes of which she had been disappointed by the death of her husband Hannibalianus.   Perhaps it was without the consent of Constantina that the new emperor formed a necessary, though dishonourable, alliance with the usurper of the West, whose purple was so recently stained with her brother's blood.[1]

The intelligence of these important events, which so deeply affected the honour and safety of the Imperial house, recalled the arms of Constantius from the inglorious prosecution of the Persian war. He recommended the care of the East to his lieutenants, and afterwards to his cousin Gallus, whom he raised from a prison to a throne, and marched towards Europe, with a mind agitated by the conflict of hope and fear, of grief and indignation. On his arrival at Heraclea in Thrace, the emperor gave audience to the ambassadors of Magnentius and Vetranio. The first author of the conspiracy, Marcellinus, who in some measure had bestowed the purple on his new master, boldly accepted this dangerous commission; and his three colleagues were selected from the illustrious personages of the state and army.   These deputies were instructed to soothe the resentment, and to alarm the fears, of Constantius. They were empowered to offer him the friendship and alliance of the western princes, to cement their union by a double marriage,—of Constantius with the daughter of Magnentius, and of Magnentius himself with the ambitious Constantina,—and to acknowledge in the treaty the pre-eminence of rank which might justly be claimed by the emperor of the East. Should pride and mistaken piety urge him to refuse these equitable conditions, the ambassadors were ordered to expatiate on the inevitable ruin which must attend his rashness, if he ventured to provoke the sovereigns of the West to exert their superior strength, and to employ against him that valour, those abilities, and those legions, to which the house of Constantine had been indebted for so many triumphs. Such propositions and such arguments appeared to deserve the most serious attention; the answer of Constantius was deferred till the next day; and as he had reflected on the importance of justifying a civil war in the opinion of the people, he thus addressed his council, who listened with real or affected credulity: " Last night," said he, " after I retired to rest, the shade of the great Constantine, embracing the corpse of my murdered brother, rose before my eyes; his well-known voice

[1] The doubtful, fluctuating conduct of Vetranio is described by Julian in his first oration [p. 30, sqq.], and accurately explained by Spanheim, who discusses the situation and behaviour of Constantina.

awakened me to revenge, forbade me to despair of the republic, and assured me of the success and immortal glory which would crown the justice of my arms." The authority of such a vision, or rather of the prince who alleged it, silenced every doubt, and excluded all negotiation. The ignominious terms of peace were rejected with disdain. One of the ambassadors of the tyrant was dismissed with the haughty answer of Constantius; his colleagues, as unworthy of the privileges of the law of nations, were put in irons; and the contending powers prepared to wage an implacable war.[1]

Such was the conduct, and such perhaps was the duty, of the brother of Constans towards the perfidious usurper of Gaul. The situation and character of Vetranio admitted of milder measures; and the policy of the Eastern emperor was directed to disunite his antagonists, and to separate the forces of Illyricum from the cause of rebellion. It was an easy task to deceive the frankness and simplicity of Vetranio, who, fluctuating some time between the opposite views of honour and interest, displayed to the world the insincerity of his temper, and was insensibly engaged in the snares of an artful negotiation. Constantius acknowledged him as a legitimate and equal colleague in the empire, on condition that he would renounce his disgraceful alliance with Magnentius, and appoint a place of interview on the frontiers of their respective provinces, where they might pledge their friendship by mutual vows of fidelity, and regulate by common consent the future operations of the civil war. In consequence of this agreement, Vetranio advanced to the city of Sardica,[2] at the head of twenty thousand horse, and of a more numerous body of infantry; a power so far superior to the forces of Constantius, that the Illyrian emperor appeared to command the life and fortunes of his rival, who, depending on the success of his private negotiations, had seduced the troops and undermined the throne of Vetranio. The chiefs, who had secretly embraced the party of Constantius, prepared in his favour a public spectacle, calculated to discover and inflame the passions of the multitude.[3] The united armies were commanded to

[1] See Peter the Patrician, in the Excerpta Legationum, p. 28 [ed. Paris.; cap. 14, p. 130, ed. Bonn].

[2] Zonaras, tom. ii. l. xiii. [c. 7] p. 15. The position of Sardica, near the modern city of Sophia, appears better suited to this interview than the situation of either Naissus of Sirmium, where it is placed by Jerom, Socrates, and Sozomen.

[3] See the two first orations of Julian, particularly p. 31; and Zosimus, l. ii. [c. 44] p. 122. The distinct narrative of the historian serves to illustrate the diffuse but vague descriptions of the orator.

assemble in a large plain near the city. In the centre, according
to the rules of ancient discipline, a military tribunal, or rather
scaffold, was erected, from whence the emperors were accustomed, on solemn and important occasions, to harangue the
troops. The well-ordered ranks of Romans and barbarians, with
drawn swords, or with erected spears, the squadrons of cavalry,
and the cohorts of infantry, distinguished by the variety of their
arms and ensigns, formed an immense circle round the tribunal;
and the attentive silence which they preserved was sometimes
interrupted by loud bursts of clamour or of applause. In the
presence of this formidable assembly the two emperors were
called upon to explain the situation of public affairs: the precedency of rank was yielded to the royal birth of Constantius;
and though he was indifferently skilled in the arts of rhetoric,
he acquitted himself, under these difficult circumstances, with
firmness, dexterity, and eloquence. The first part of his oration
seemed to be pointed only against the tyrant of Gaul; but
while he tragically lamented the cruel murder of Constans, he
insinuated that none, except a brother, could claim a right to
the succession of his brother. He displayed, with some complacency, the glories of his Imperial race; and recalled to the
memory of the troops the valour, the triumphs, the liberality
of the great Constantine, to whose sons they had engaged their
allegiance by an oath of fidelity, which the ingratitude of his
most favoured servants had tempted them to violate. The
officers, who surrounded the tribunal, and were instructed to
act their parts in this extraordinary scene, confessed the irresistible power of reason and eloquence, by saluting the emperor
Constantius as their lawful sovereign. The contagion of loyalty
and repentance was communicated from rank to rank, till the
plain of Sardica resounded with the universal acclamation of
" Away with these upstart usurpers! Long life and victory to
the son of Constantine! Under his banners alone we will fight
and conquer." The shout of thousands, their menacing gestures,
the fierce clashing of their arms, astonished and subdued the
courage of Vetranio, who stood, amidst the defection of his
followers, in anxious and silent suspense. Instead of embracing
the last refuge of generous despair, he tamely submitted to his
fate, and, taking the diadem from his head, in the view of both
armies fell prostrate at the feet of his conqueror. Constantius
used his victory with prudence and moderation; and raising
from the ground the aged suppliant, whom he affected to style
by the endearing name of Father, he gave him his hand to

descend from the throne. The city of Prusa was assigned for the exile or retirement of the abdicated monarch, who lived six years in the enjoyment of ease and affluence. He often expressed his grateful sense of the goodness of Constantius, and, with a very amiable simplicity, advised his benefactor to resign the sceptre of the world, and to seek for content (where alone it could be found) in the peaceful obscurity of a private condition.[1]

The behaviour of Constantius on this memorable occasion was celebrated with some appearance of justice; and his courtiers compared the studied orations which a Pericles or a Demosthenes addressed to the populace of Athens with the victorious eloquence which had persuaded an armed multitude to desert and depose the object of their partial choice.[2] The approaching contest with Magnentius was of a more serious and bloody kind. The tyrant advanced by rapid marches to encounter Constantius, at the head of a numerous army, composed of Gauls and Spaniards, of Franks and Saxons; of those provincials who supplied the strength of the legions, and of those barbarians who were dreaded as the most formidable enemies of the republic. The fertile plains[3] of the Lower Pannonia, between the Drave, the Save, and the Danube, presented a spacious theatre; and the operations of the civil war were protracted during the summer months by the skill or timidity of the combatants.[4] Constantius had declared his intention of deciding the quarrel in the fields of Cibalis, a name that would animate his troops by the remembrance of the victory which, on the same auspicious ground, had been obtained by the arms of his father Constantine. Yet, by the impregnable fortifications with which the emperor encompassed his camp, he appeared to

[1] The younger Victor assigns to his exile the emphatical appellation of " voluptarium otium." [Epit. c. 41.] Socrates (l. ii. c. 28) is the voucher for the correspondence with the emperor, which would seem to prove that Vetranio was, indeed, prope ad stultitiam simplicissimus.

[2] Eum Constantius . . . facundiæ vi dejectum Imperio in privatum otium removit. Quæ gloria post natum Imperium soli processit eloquio clementiâque, etc. Aurelius Victor [de Cæsar. c. 42]. Julian and Themistius (Orat. iii. and iv.) adorn this exploit with all the artificial and gaudy colouring of their rhetoric.

[3] Busbequius (p. 112) traversed the Lower Hungary and Sclavonia at a time when they were reduced almost to a desert, by the reciprocal hostilities of the Turks and Christians. Yet he mentions with admiration the unconquerable fertility of the soil; and observes that the height of the grass was sufficient to conceal a loaded waggon from his sight. See likewise Browne's Travels, in Harris's Collection, vol. ii. p. 762, etc.

[4] Zosimus gives a very large account of the war and the negotiation (l. ii. [c. 45-54] p. 123-130). But as he neither shows himself a soldier nor a politician, his narrative must be weighed with attention, and received with caution.

decline rather than to invite a general engagement. It was the object of Magnentius to tempt or to compel his adversary to relinquish this advantageous position; and he employed with that view the various marches, evolutions, and stratagems which the knowledge of the art of war could suggest to an experienced officer. He carried by assault the important town of Siscia; made an attack on the city of Sirmium, which lay in the rear of the Imperial camp; attempted to force a passage over the Save into the eastern provinces of Illyricum; and cut in pieces a numerous detachment which he had allured into the narrow passes of Adarne. During the greater part of the summer the tyrant of Gaul showed himself master of the field. The troops of Constantius were harassed and dispirited; his reputation declined in the eye of the world; and his pride condescended to solicit a treaty of peace, which would have resigned to the assassin of Constans the sovereignty of the provinces beyond the Alps. These offers were enforced by the eloquence of Philip the Imperial ambassador; and the council as well as the army of Magnentius were disposed to accept them. But the haughty usurper, careless of the remonstrances of his friends, gave orders that Philip should be detained as a captive, or at least as a hostage; while he despatched an officer to reproach Constantius with the weakness of his reign, and to insult him by the promise of a pardon if he would instantly abdicate the purple. " That he should confide in the justice of his cause, and the protection of an avenging Deity," was the only answer which honour permitted the emperor to return. But he was so sensible of the difficulties of his situation, that he no longer dared to retaliate the indignity which had been offered to his representative. The negotiation of Philip was not, however, ineffectual, since he determined Sylvanus the Frank, a general of merit and reputation, to desert with a considerable body of cavalry a few days before the battle of Mursa.

The city of Mursa, or Essek, celebrated in modern times for a bridge of boats, five miles in length, over the river Drave, and the adjacent morasses,[1] has been always considered as a place of importance in the wars of Hungary. Magnentius, directing his march towards Mursa, set fire to the gates, and, by a sudden assault, had almost scaled the walls of the town. The vigilance

---

[1] This remarkable bridge, which is flanked with towers and supported on large wooden piles, was constructed, A.D. 1566, by Sultan Soliman, to facilitate the march of his armies into Hungary. See Browne's Travels, and Busching's System of Geography, vol. ii. p. 90.

of the garrison extinguished the flames; the approach of Constantius left him no time to continue the operations of the siege; and the emperor soon removed the only obstacle that could embarrass his motions, by forcing a body of troops which had taken post in an adjoining amphitheatre. The field of battle round Mursa was a naked and level plain: on this ground the army of Constantius formed, with the Drave on their right; while their left, either from the nature of their disposition, or from the superiority of their cavalry, extended far beyond the right flank of Magnentius.[1] The troops on both sides remained under arms in anxious expectation during the greatest part of the morning; and the son of Constantine, after animating his soldiers by an eloquent speech, retired into a church at some distance from the field of battle, and committed to his generals the conduct of this decisive day.[2] They deserved his confidence by the valour and military skill which they exerted. They wisely began the action upon the left; and advancing their whole wing of cavalry in an oblique line, they suddenly wheeled it on the right flank of the enemy, which was unprepared to resist the impetuosity of their charge. But the Romans of the West soon rallied by the habits of discipline; and the barbarians of Germany supported the renown of their national bravery. The engagement soon became general; was maintained with various and singular turns of fortune; and scarcely ended with the darkness of the night. The signal victory which Constantius obtained is attributed to the arms of his cavalry. His cuirassiers are described as so many massy statues of steel, glittering with their scaly armour, and breaking with their ponderous lances the firm array of the Gallic legions. As soon as the legions gave way, the lighter and more active squadrons of the second line rode sword in hand into the intervals and completed the disorder. In the meanwhile, the huge bodies of the Germans were exposed almost naked to the dexterity of the Oriental archers; and whole troops of those barbarians were urged by anguish and despair to precipitate themselves into the broad and rapid

---

[1] This position, and the subsequent evolutions, are clearly, though concisely, described by Julian, Orat. i. p. 36.

[2] Sulpicius Severus, l. ii. p. 405 [ed. Lugd. Bat. 1647]. The emperor passed the day in prayer with Valens, the Arian bishop of Mursa, who gained his confidence by announcing the success of the battle. M. de Tillemont (Hist. des Empereurs, tom. iv. p. 1110) very properly remarks the silence of Julian with regard to the personal prowess of Constantius in the battle of Mursa. The silence of flattery is sometimes equal to the most positive and authentic evidence.

stream of the Drave.[1]   The number of the slain was computed
at fifty-four thousand men, and the slaughter of the conquerors
was more considerable than that of the vanquished;[2] a circumstance which proves the obstinacy of the contest, and justifies
the observation of an ancient writer, that the forces of the empire
were consumed in the fatal battle of Mursa, by the loss of a
veteran army, sufficient to defend the frontiers, or to add new
triumphs to the glory of Rome.[3]   Notwithstanding the invectives of a servile orator, there is not the least reason to believe
that the tyrant deserted his own standard in the beginning of the
engagement.   He seems to have displayed the virtues of a
general and of a soldier till the day was irrecoverably lost, and
his camp in the possession of the enemy.   Magnentius then
consulted his safety, and, throwing away the Imperial ornaments,
escaped with some difficulty from the pursuit of the light horse,
who incessantly followed his rapid flight from the banks of the
Drave to the foot of the Julian Alps.[4]

The approach of winter supplied the indolence of Constantius
with specious reasons for deferring the prosecution of the war till
the ensuing spring.   Magnentius had fixed his residence in the
city of Aquileia, and showed a seeming resolution to dispute the
passage of the mountains and morasses which fortified the confines of the Venetian province.   The surprisal of a castle in the
Alps by the secret march of the Imperialists could scarcely have
determined him to relinquish the possession of Italy, if the

---

[1] Julian. Orat. i. p. 36, 37; and Orat. ii. p. 59, 60. Zonaras, tom. ii. l.
xliii. [c. 8] p. 17. Zosimus, l. ii. [c. 49-52] p. 130-133. The last of these
celebrates the dexterity of the archer Menelaus, who could discharge three
arrows at the same time; an advantage which, according to his apprehension of military affairs, materially contributed to the victory of Constantius.

[2] According to Zonaras [l. c.], Constantius, out of 80,000 men, lost
30,000; and Magnentius lost 24,000 out of 36,000. The other articles of
this account seem probable and authentic, but the numbers of the tyrant's
army must have been mistaken, either by the author or his transcribers.
Magnentius had collected the whole force of the West, Romans and barbarians, into one formidable body, which cannot fairly be estimated at less
than 100,000 men. Julian. Orat. i. p. 34, 35.

[3] Ingentes R. I. vires eâ dimicatione consumptæ sunt, ad quælibet bella
externa idoneæ, quæ multum triumphorum possent securitatisque conferre.
Eutropius, x. 13 [6]. The younger Victor expresses himself to the same
effect.

[4] On this occasion we must prefer the unsuspected testimony of Zosimus
and Zonaras to the flattering assertions of Julian. The younger Victor
paints the character of Magnentius in a singular light: "Sermonis acer,
animi tumidi, et immodice timidus; artifex tamen ad occultandam
audaciæ specie formidinem." [Epit. c. 43.] Is it most likely that in the
battle of Mursa his behaviour was governed by nature or by art? I
should incline for the latter.

inclinations of the people had supported the cause of their tyrant.[1] But the memory of the cruelties exercised by his ministers, after the unsuccessful revolt of Nepotian, had left a deep impression of horror and resentment on the minds of the Romans. That rash youth, the son of the princess Eutropia, and the nephew of Constantine, had seen with indignation the sceptre of the West usurped by a perfidious barbarian. Arming a desperate troop of slaves and gladiators, he overpowered the feeble guard of the domestic tranquillity of Rome, received the homage of the senate, and, assuming the title of Augustus, precariously reigned during a tumult of twenty-eight days. The march of some regular forces put an end to his ambitious hopes: the rebellion was extinguished in the blood of Nepotian, of his mother Eutropia, and of his adherents; and the proscription was extended to all who had contracted a fatal alliance with the name and family of Constantine.[2] But as soon as Constantius, after the battle of Mursa, became master of the sea-coast of Dalmatia, a band of noble exiles, who had ventured to equip a fleet in some harbour of the Adriatic, sought protection and revenge in his victorious camp. By their secret intelligence with their countrymen, Rome and the Italian cities were persuaded to display the banners of Constantius on their walls. The grateful veterans, enriched by the liberality of the father, signalised their gratitude and loyalty to the son. The cavalry, the legions, and the auxiliaries of Italy, renewed their oath of allegiance to Constantius; and the usurper, alarmed by the general desertion, was compelled, with the remains of his faithful troops, to retire beyond the Alps into the provinces of Gaul. The detachments, however, which were ordered either to press or to intercept the flight of Magnentius, conducted themselves with the usual imprudence of success; and allowed him, in the plains of Pavia, an opportunity of turning on his pursuers, and of gratifying his despair by the carnage of a useless victory.[3]

---

[1] Julian. Orat. i. p. 38, 39. In that place, however, as well as in Oration ii. p. 97, he insinuates the general disposition of the senate, the people, and the soldiers of Italy, towards the party of the emperor.

[2] The elder Victor describes in a pathetic manner the miserable condition of Rome: " Cujus stolidum ingenium adeo P. R. patribusque exitio fuit, uti passim domus, fora, viæ, templaque, cruore, cadaveribusque opplerentur, bustorum modo." [De Cæsar. c. 42.] Athanasius (tom. i. p. 677) deplores the fate of several illustrious victims, and Julian (Orat. ii. p. 58) execrates the cruelty of Marcellinus, the implacable enemy of the house of Constantine.

[3] Zosim. l. ii. [c. 53] p. 133. Victor in Epitome [c. 42]. The panegyrists of Constantius, with their usual candour, forget to mention this accidental defeat.

The pride of Magnentius was reduced, by repeated misfortunes, to sue, and to sue in vain, for peace. He first despatched a senator, in whose abilities he confided, and afterwards several bishops, whose holy character might obtain a more favourable audience, with the offer of resigning the purple, and the promise of devoting the remainder of his life to the services of the emperor. But Constantius, though he granted fair terms of pardon and reconciliation to all who abandoned the standard of rebellion,[1] avowed his inflexible resolution to inflict a just punishment on the crimes of an assassin whom he prepared to overwhelm on every side by the effort of his victorious arms. An Imperial fleet acquired the easy possession of Africa and Spain, confirmed the wavering faith of the Moorish nations, and landed a considerable force, which passed the Pyrenees, and advanced towards Lyons, the last and fatal station of Magnentius.[2] The temper of the tyrant, which was never inclined to clemency, was urged by distress to exercise every act of oppression which could extort an immediate supply from the cities of Gaul.[3] Their patience was at length exhausted; and Treves, the seat of Praetorian government, gave the signal of revolt, by shutting her gates against Decentius, who had been raised by his brother to the rank either of Caesar or of Augustus.[4] From Treves, Decentius was obliged to retire to Sens, where he was soon surrounded by an army of Germans, whom the pernicious arts of Constantius had introduced into the civil dissensions of Rome.[5] In the meantime the Imperial troops forced the passages of the Cottian Alps, and in the bloody combat of Mount Seleucus irrevocably fixed the title of rebels on the party of Magnentius.[6] He was unable to bring another army into the field; the fidelity of

---

[1] Zonaras, tom. ii. l. xiii. [c. 8] p. 17. Julian, in several places of the two orations, expatiates on the clemency of Constantius to the rebels.

[2] Zosim. l. ii. [c. 53] p. 133. Julian. Orat. i. p. 40, ii. p. 74.

[3] Ammian. xv. 6. Zosim. l. ii. [c. 53] p. 133. Julian, who (Orat. i. p. 40) inveighs against the cruel effects of the tyrant's despair, mentions (Orat. i. p. 34) the oppressive edicts which were dictated by his necessities, or by his avarice. His subjects were compelled to purchase the Imperial demesnes; a doubtful and dangerous species of property, which, in case of a revolution, might be imputed to them as a treasonable usurpation.

[4] The medals of Magnentius celebrate the victories of the *two* Augusti, and of the Caesar. The Caesar was another brother named Desiderius. See Tillemont, Hist. des Empereurs, tom. iv. p. 757.

[5] Julian. Orat. i. p. 40. ii. p. 74; with Spanheim, p. 263. His Commentary illustrates the transactions of this civil war. Mons Seleuci was a small place in the Cottian Alps, a few miles distant from Vapincum, or Gap, an episcopal city of Dauphiné. See d'Anville, Notice de la Gaule, p. 464; and Longuerue, Description de la France, p. 327.

[6] Zosimus, l. ii. [c. 53] p. 134. Liban. Orat. x. p. 268, 269. The latter most vehemently arraigns this cruel and selfish policy of Constantius.

his guards was corrupted; and when he appeared in public to animate them by his exhortations, he was saluted with an unanimous shout of " Long live the emperor Constantius! " The tyrant, who perceived that they were preparing to deserve pardon and rewards by the sacrifice of the most obnoxious criminal, prevented their design by falling on his sword;[1] a death more easy and more honourable than he could hope to obtain from the hands of an enemy whose revenge would have been coloured with the specious pretence of justice and fraternal piety. The example of suicide was imitated by Decentius, who strangled himself on the news of his brother's death. The author of the conspiracy, Marcellinus, had long since disappeared in the battle of Mursa,[2] and the public tranquillity was confirmed by the execution of the surviving leaders of a guilty and unsuccessful faction. A severe inquisition was extended over all who, either from choice or from compulsion, had been involved in the cause of rebellion. Paul, surnamed Catena from his superior skill in the judicial exercise of tyranny, was sent to explore the latent remains of the conspiracy in the remote province of Britain. The honest indignation expressed by Martin, vice-præfect of the island, was interpreted as an evidence of his own guilt; and the governor was urged to the necessity of turning against his breast the sword with which he had been provoked to wound the Imperial minister. The most innocent subjects of the West were exposed to exile and confiscation, to death and torture; and as the timid are always cruel, the mind of Constantius was inaccessible to mercy.[3]

[1] Julian, Orat. i. p. 40. Zosimus, l. ii. [c. 53] p. 134. Socrates, l. ii. c. 32. Sozomen, l. iv. c. 7. The younger Victor describes his death with some horrid circumstances: Transfosso latere, ut erat vasti corporis, vulnere naribusque et ore cruorem effundens, exspiravit. [Epit. c. 42.] If we can give credit to Zonaras, the tyrant, before he expired, had the pleasure of murdering with his own hands his mother and his brother Desiderius.

[2] Julian (Orat. ii. p. 58, 59) seems at a loss to determine whether he inflicted on himself the punishment of his crimes, whether he was drowned in the Drave, or whether he was carried by the avenging dæmons from the field of battle to his destined place of eternal tortures.

[3] Ammian. xiv. 5, xxi. 16.

CHAPTER XIX

Constantius sole Emperor—Elevation and Death of Gallus—Danger and Elevation of Julian—Sarmatian and Persian Wars—Victories of Julian in Gaul

THE divided provinces of the empire were again united by the victory of Constantius; but as that feeble prince was destitute of personal merit either in peace or war; as he feared his generals, and distrusted his ministers; the triumph of his arms served only to establish the reign of the *eunuchs* over the Roman world. Those unhappy beings, the ancient production of Oriental jealousy and despotism,[1] were introduced into Greece and Rome by the contagion of Asiatic luxury.[2] Their progress was rapid; and the eunuchs, who, in the time of Augustus, had been abhorred, as the monstrous retinue of an Egyptian queen,[3] were gradually admitted into the families of matrons, of senators, and of the emperors themselves.[4] Restrained by the severe edicts of Domitian and Nerva,[5] cherished by the pride of Diocletian, reduced to an humble station by the prudence of Constantine,[6] they multiplied in the palaces of his degenerate sons,

[1] Ammianus (l. xiv. c. 6) imputes the first practice of castration to the cruel ingenuity of Semiramis, who is supposed to have reigned above nineteen hundred years before Christ. The use of eunuchs is of high antiquity, both in Asia and Egypt. They are mentioned in the law of Moses, Deuteron. xxiii. 1. See Goguet, Origines des Loix, etc., Part. i. l. i. c. 3.

[2]   Eunuchum dixti velle te;
     Quia solæ utuntur his reginæ——
                    Terent. Eunuch. act i. scene 2.

This play is translated from Menander, and the original must have appeared soon after the eastern conquests of Alexander.

[3]   Miles . . . spadonibus
     Servire rugosis potest.
     Horat. Carm. v. 9 [Epod. ix. 13], and Dacier ad loc.

By the word *spado* the Romans very forcibly expressed their abhorrence of this mutilated condition. The Greek appellation of eunuchs, which insensibly prevailed, had a milder sound and a more ambiguous sense.

[4] We need only mention Posides, a freedman and eunuch of Claudius, in whose favour the emperor prostituted some of the most honourable rewards of military valour. See Sueton. in Claudio, c. 28. Posides employed a great part of his wealth in building.

     Ut *spado* vincebat Capitolia nostra Posides.
                    Juvenal. Sat. xiv. [91.]

[5] Castrari mares vetuit. Sueton. in Domitian. c. 7. See Dion Cassius, l. lxvii. [c. 2] p. 1101; l. lxviii. [c. 2] p. 1119.

[6] There is a passage in the Augustan History, p. 137, in which Lampridius, whilst he praises Alexander Severus and Constantine for restraining the tyranny of the eunuchs, deplores the mischiefs which they occasioned in other reigns. Huc accedit, quod eunuchos nec in consiliis nec in ministeriis

and insensibly acquired the knowledge, and at length the direction, of the secret councils of Constantius. The aversion and
contempt which mankind has so uniformly entertained for that
imperfect species appears to have degraded their character, and
to have rendered them almost as incapable as they were supposed
to be of conceiving any generous sentiment, or of performing any
worthy action.[1]　But the eunuchs were skilled in the arts of
flattery and intrigue; and they alternately governed the mind
of Constantius by his fears, his indolence, and his vanity.[2]
Whilst he viewed in a deceitful mirror the fair appearance of
public prosperity, he supinely permitted them to intercept the
complaints of the injured provinces; to accumulate immense
treasures by the sale of justice and of honours; to disgrace the
most important dignities by the promotion of those who had
purchased at their hands the powers of oppression;[3] and to
gratify their resentment against the few independent spirits who
arrogantly refused to solicit the protection of slaves. Of these
slaves the most distinguished was the chamberlain Eusebius, who
ruled the monarch and the palace with such absolute sway, that
Constantius, according to the sarcasm of an impartial historian,
possessed some credit with this haughty favourite.[4]　By his
artful suggestions, the emperor was persuaded to subscribe the

habuit; qui soli principes perdunt, dum eos more gentium aut regum
Persarum volunt vivere; qui a populo etiam amicissimum semovent; qui
internuntii sunt, aliud quàm respondetur [sæpe], referentes; claudentes
principem suum, et agentes ante omnia ne quid sciat. [Lampr. Alex. Sev.
c. 66.]

[1] Xenophon (Cyropædia, l. vii. [5 § 60] p. 540) has stated the specious
reasons which engaged Cyrus to intrust his person to the guard of eunuchs.
He had observed in animals, that, although the practice of castration might
tame their ungovernable fierceness, it did not diminish their strength or
spirit; and he persuaded himself that those who were separated from the
rest of human kind would be more firmly attached to the person of their
benefactor. But a long experience has contradicted the judgment of
Cyrus. Some particular instances may occur of eunuchs distinguished
by their fidelity, their valour, and their abilities; but if we examine the
general history of Persia, India, and China, we shall find that the power of
the eunuchs has uniformly marked the decline and fall of every dynasty.

[2] See Ammianus Marcellinus, l. xxi. c. 16; l. xxii. c. 4. The whole tenor
of his impartial history serves to justify the invectives of Mamertinus, of
Libanius, and of Julian himself, who have insulted the vices of the court
of Constantius.

[3] Aurelius Victor censures the negligence of his sovereign in choosing the
governors of the provinces and the generals of the army, and concludes his
history with a very bold observation, as it is much more dangerous under a
feeble reign to attack the ministers than the master himself. " Uti verum
absolvam brevi, ut Imperatore ipso clarius, ita apparitorum plerisque
magis atrox nihil." [De Cæsar. c. 42.]

[4] Apud quem (si vere dici debeat) multum Constantius potuit. Ammian.
l. xviii. c. 4.

condemnation of the unfortunate Gallus, and to add a new crime to the long list of unnatural murders which pollute the honour of the house of Constantine.

When the two nephews of Constantine, Gallus and Julian, were saved from the fury of the soldiers, the former was about twelve, and the latter about six, years of age; and, as the eldest was thought to be of a sickly constitution, they obtained with the less difficulty a precarious and dependent life from the affected pity of Constantius, who was sensible that the execution of these helpless orphans would have been esteemed, by all mankind, an act of the most deliberate cruelty.[1] Different cities of Ionia and Bithynia were assigned for the places of their exile and education; but as soon as their growing years excited the jealousy of the emperor, he judged it more prudent to secure those unhappy youths in the strong castle of Macellum, near Cæsarea. The treatment which they experienced during a six years' confinement was partly such as they could hope from a careful guardian, and partly such as they might dread from a suspicious tyrant.[2] Their prison was an ancient palace, the residence of the kings of Cappadocia; the situation was pleasant, the building stately, the enclosure spacious. They pursued their studies, and practised their exercises, under the tuition of the most skilful masters; and the numerous household appointed to attend, or rather to guard, the nephews of Constantine, was not unworthy of the dignity of their birth. But they could not disguise to themselves that they were deprived of fortune, of freedom, and of safety; secluded from the society of all whom they could trust or esteem, and condemned to pass their melancholy hours in the company of slaves devoted to the commands of a tyrant who had already injured them beyond the hope of reconciliation. At length, however, the emergencies of the state compelled the emperor, or rather his eunuchs, to invest Gallus, in the twenty-fifth year of his age, with the title of Cæsar, and to

---

[1] Gregory Nazianzen (Orat. iii. p. 90) reproaches the apostate with his ingratitude towards Mark, bishop of Arethusa, who had contributed to save his life; and we learn, though from a less respectable authority (Tillemont, Hist. des Empereurs, tom. iv. p. 916), that Julian was concealed in the sanctuary of a church.

[Gallus and Julian were not sons of the same mother; their father, Julius Constantius, had had Gallus by his first wife, named Galla; Julian was the son of Basilina, whom he had espoused in a second marriage.—O. S.]

[2] The most authentic account of the education and adventures of Julian is contained in the epistle or manifesto which he himself addressed to the senate and people of Athens. Libanius (Orat. Parentalis), on the side of the Pagans, and Socrates (l. iii. c. 1), on that of the Christians, have preserved several interesting circumstances.

cement this political connection by his marriage with the princess Constantina. After a formal interview, in which the two princes mutually engaged their faith never to undertake anything to the prejudice of each other, they repaired without delay to their respective stations. Constantius continued his march towards the West, and Gallus fixed his residence at Antioch; from whence, with a delegated authority, he administered the five great dioceses of the eastern præfecture.[1] In this fortunate change, the new Cæsar was not unmindful of his brother Julian, who obtained the honours of his rank, the appearances of liberty, and the restitution of an ample patrimony.[2]

The writers the most indulgent to the memory of Gallus, and even Julian himself, though he wished to cast a veil over the frailties of his brother, are obliged to confess that the Cæsar was incapable of reigning. Transported from a prison to a throne, he possessed neither genius nor application, nor docility to compensate for the want of knowledge and experience. A temper naturally morose and violent, instead of being corrected, was soured by solitude and adversity; the remembrance of what he had endured disposed him to retaliation rather than to sympathy; and the ungoverned sallies of his rage were often fatal to those who approached his person, or were subject to his power.[3] Constantina, his wife, is described, not as a woman, but as one of the infernal furies tormented with an insatiate thirst of human blood.[4] Instead of employing her influence to insinuate the mild counsels of prudence and humanity, she exasperated the fierce passions of her husband; and as she retained

---

[1] For the promotion of Gallus see Idatius, Zosimus, and the two Victors. According to Philostorgius (l. iv. c. 1), Theophilus, an Arian bishop, was the witness, and, as it were, the guarantee of this solemn engagement. He supported that character with generous firmness; but M. de Tillemont (Hist. des Empereurs, tom. iv. p. 1120) thinks it very improbable that a heretic should have possessed such virtue.

[2] Julian was at first permitted to pursue his studies at Constantinople, but the reputation which he acquired soon excited the jealousy of Constantius; and the young prince was advised to withdraw himself to the less conspicuous scenes of Bithynia and Ionia.

[3] See Julian ad S. P. Q. A. p. 271. Jerom. in Chron. Aurelius Victor. Eutropius, x. 14 [7]. I shall copy the words of Eutropius, who wrote his abridgment about fifteen years after the death of Gallus, when there was no longer any motive either to flatter or to depreciate his character. " Multis incivilibus gestis Gallus Cæsar . . . vir naturâ ferus et ad tyrannidem pronior, si suo jure imperare licuisset."

[4] Megæra quædam mortalis, inflammatrix sævientis assidua, humani cruoris avida, etc. Ammian. Marcellin. l. xiv. c. 1. The sincerity of Ammianus would not suffer him to misrepresent facts or characters, but his love of *ambitious* ornaments frequently betrayed him into an unnatural vehemence of expression.

the vanity, though she had renounced the gentleness of her sex,
a pearl necklace was esteemed an equivalent price for the murder
of an innocent and virtuous nobleman.[1]   The cruelty of Gallus
was sometimes displayed in the undissembled violence of popular
or military executions: and was sometimes disguised by the
abuse of law and the forms of judicial proceedings.   The private
houses of Antioch, and the palaces of public resort, were besieged
by spies and informers; and the Cæsar himself, concealed in a
plebeian habit, very frequently condescended to assume that
odious character.   Every apartment of the palace was adorned
with the instruments of death and torture, and a general consternation was diffused through the capital of Syria.   The prince
of the East, as if he had been conscious how much he had to
fear, and how little he deserved to reign, selected for the objects
of his resentment the provincials accused of some imaginary
treason, and his own courtiers, whom with more reason he suspected of incensing, by their secret correspondence, the timid
and suspicious mind of Constantius.   But he forgot that he
was depriving himself of his only support, the affection of the
people; whilst he furnished the malice of his enemies with the
arms of truth, and afforded the emperor the fairest pretence
of exacting the forfeit of his purple and of his life.[2]

As long as the civil war suspended the fate of the Roman world,
Constantius dissembled his knowledge of the weak and cruel
administration to which his choice had subjected the East; and
the discovery of some assassins, secretly despatched to Antioch
by the tyrant of Gaul, was employed to convince the public that
the emperor and the Cæsar were united by the same interest, and
pursued by the same enemies.[3]   But when the victory was
decided in favour of Constantius, his dependent colleague became
less useful and less formidable.   Every circumstance of his conduct was severely and suspiciously examined, and it was privately
resolved either to deprive Gallus of the purple, or at least to
remove him from the indolent luxury of Asia to the hardships

[1] His name was Clematius of Alexandria, and his only crime was a refusal
to gratify the desires of his mother-in-law; who solicited his death, because
she had been disappointed of his love. Ammian. l. xiv. c. 1.

[2] See in Ammianus (l. xiv. c. 1, 7) a very ample detail of the cruelties of
Gallus.   His brother Julian (p. 272) insinuates that a secret conspiracy had
been formed against him; and Zosimus names (l. ii. [c. 55] p. 135) the
persons engaged in it; a minister of considerable rank, and two obscure
agents, who were resolved to make their fortune.

[3] Zonaras, l. xiii. [c. 8] tom. ii. p. 17, 18.   The assassins had seduced a
great number of legionaries; but their designs were discovered and revealed by an old woman in whose cottage they lodged.

and dangers of a German war. The death of Theophilus, consular of the province of Syria, who in a time of scarcity had been massacred by the people of Antioch, with the connivance and almost at the instigation of Gallus, was justly resented, not only as an act of wanton cruelty, but as a dangerous insult on the supreme majesty of Constantius. Two ministers of illustrious rank, Domitian the Oriental præfect, and Montius, quæstor of the palace, were empowered by a special commission to visit and reform the state of the East. They were instructed to behave towards Gallus with moderation and respect, and, by the gentlest arts of persuasion, to engage him to comply with the invitation of his brother and colleague. The rashness of the præfect disappointed these prudent measures, and hastened his own ruin as well as that of his enemy. On his arrival at Antioch, Domitian passed disdainfully before the gates of the palace; and, alleging a slight pretence of indisposition, continued several days in sullen retirement, to prepare an inflammatory memorial, which he transmitted to the Imperial court. Yielding at length to the pressing solicitations of Gallus, the præfect condescended to take his seat in council; but his first step was to signify a concise and haughty mandate, importing that the Cæsar should immediately repair to Italy, and threatening that he himself would punish his delay or hesitation by suspending the usual allowance of his household. The nephew and daughter of Constantine, who could ill brook the insolence of a subject, expressed their resentment by instantly delivering Domitian to the custody of a guard. The quarrel still admitted of some terms of accommodation. They were rendered impracticable by the imprudent behaviour of Montius, a statesman whose art and experience were frequently betrayed by the levity of his disposition.[1] The quæstor reproached Gallus, in haughty language, that a prince who was scarcely authorised to remove a municipal magistrate should presume to imprison a Prætorian præfect; convoked a meeting of the civil and military officers, and required them, in the name of their sovereign, to defend the person and dignity of his representatives. By this rash declaration of war the impatient temper of Gallus was provoked to embrace the most desperate counsels. He ordered his guards to stand to their

---

[1] In the present text of Ammianus [xiv. 7] we read *Asper, quidem, sed ad lenitatem* propensior; which forms a sentence of contradictory nonsense. With the aid of an old manuscript, Valesius has rectified the first of these corruptions, and we perceive a ray of light in the substitution of the word *vafer*. If we venture to change *lenitatem* into *levitatem*, this alteration of a single letter will render the whole passage clear and consistent.

arms, assembled the populace of Antioch, and recommended to their zeal the care of his safety and revenge. His commands were too fatally obeyed. They rudely seized the præfect and the quæstor, and, tying their legs together with ropes, they dragged them through the streets of the city, inflicted a thousand insults and a thousand wounds on these unhappy victims, and at last precipitated their mangled and lifeless bodies into the stream of the Orontes.[1]

After such a deed, whatever might have been the designs of Gallus, it was only in a field of battle that he could assert his innocence with any hope of success. But the mind of that prince was formed of an equal mixture of violence and weakness. Instead of assuming the title of Augustus, instead of employing in his defence the troops and treasures of the East, he suffered himself to be deceived by the affected tranquillity of Constantius, who, leaving him the vain pageantry of a court, imperceptibly recalled the veteran legions from the provinces of Asia. But as it still appeared dangerous to arrest Gallus in his capital, the slow and safer arts of dissimulation were practised with success. The frequent and pressing epistles of Constantius were filled with professions of confidence and friendship, exhorting the Cæsar to discharge the duties of his high station, to relieve his colleague from a part of the public cares, and to assist the West by his presence, his counsels, and his arms. After so many reciprocal injuries, Gallus had reason to fear and to distrust. But he had neglected the opportunities of flight and of resistance; he was seduced by the flattering assurances of the tribune Scudilo, who, under the semblance of a rough soldier, disguised the most artful insinuation; and he depended on the credit of his wife Constantina till the unseasonable death of that princess completed the ruin in which he had been involved by her impetuous passions.[2]

After a long delay the reluctant Cæsar set forwards on his journey to the Imperial court. From Antioch to Hadrianople he traversed the wide extent of his dominions with a numerous and stately train; and, as he laboured to conceal his apprehensions from the world, and perhaps from himself, he entertained

---

[1] Instead of being obliged to collect scattered and imperfect hints from various sources, we now enter into the full stream of the history of Ammianus, and need only refer to the seventh and ninth chapters of his fourteenth book. Philostorgius, however (l. iii. c. 28), though partial to Gallus, should not be entirely overlooked.

[2] She had preceded her husband, but died of a fever on the road, at a little place in Bithynia called Cœnum Gallicanum.

the people of Constantinople with an exhibition of the games of the circus. The progress of the journey might, however, have warned him of the impending danger. In all the principal cities he was met by ministers of confidence, commissioned to seize the offices of government, to observe his motions, and to prevent the hasty sallies of his despair. The persons despatched to secure the provinces which he left behind passed him with cold salutations or affected disdain; and the troops whose station lay along the public road were studiously removed on his approach, lest they might be tempted to offer their swords for the service of a civil war.[1] After Gallus had been permitted to repose himself a few days at Hadrianople he received a mandate, expressed in the most haughty and absolute style, that his splendid retinue should halt in that city, while the Cæsar himself, with only ten post-carriages, should hasten to the Imperial residence at Milan. In this rapid journey the profound respect which was due to the brother and colleague of Constantius was insensibly changed into rude familiarity; and Gallus, who discovered in the countenances of the attendants that they already considered themselves as his guards, and might soon be employed as his executioners, began to accuse his fatal rashness, and to recollect with terror and remorse the conduct by which he had provoked his fate. The dissimulation which had hitherto been preserved was laid aside at Petovio in Pannonia. He was conducted to a palace in the suburbs, where the general Barbatio, with a select band of soldiers, who could neither be moved by pity nor corrupted by rewards, expected the arrival of his illustrious victim. In the close of the evening he was arrested, ignominiously stripped of the ensigns of Cæsar, and hurried away to Pola, in Istria, a sequestered prison, which had been so recently polluted with royal blood. The horror which he felt was soon increased by the appearance of his implacable enemy the eunuch Eusebius, who, with the assistance of a notary and a tribune, proceeded to interrogate him concerning the administration of the East. The Cæsar sunk under the weight of shame and guilt, confessed all the criminal actions and all the treasonable designs with which he was charged; and, by imputing them

---

[1] The Thebæan legions, which were then quartered at Hadrianople, sent a deputation to Gallus, with a tender of their services. Ammian. l. xiv. c. 11. The Notitia (s. 6, 20, 38, edit. Labb.) mentions three several legions which bore the name of Thebæan. The zeal of M. de Voltaire to destroy a despicable though celebrated legend has tempted him on the slightest grounds to deny the existence of a Thebæan legion in the Roman armies. See Œuvres de Voltaire, tom. xv. p. 414, quarto edition.

to the advice of his wife, exasperated the indignation of Constantius, who reviewed with partial prejudice the minutes of the examination. The emperor was easily convinced that his own safety was incompatible with the life of his cousin: the sentence of death was signed, despatched, and executed; and the nephew of Constantine, with his hands tied behind his back, was beheaded in prison, like the vilest malefactor.[1] Those who are inclined to palliate the cruelties of Constantius assert that he soon relented, and endeavoured to recall the bloody mandate; but that the second messenger, intrusted with the reprieve, was detained by the eunuchs, who dreaded the unforgiving temper of Gallus, and were desirous of reuniting to *their* empire the wealthy provinces of the East.[2]

Besides the reigning emperor, Julian alone survived of all the numerous posterity of Constantius Chlorus. The misfortune of his royal birth involved him in the disgrace of Gallus. From his retirement in the happy country of Ionia he was conveyed, under a strong guard, to the court of Milan, where he languished above seven months in the continual apprehension of suffering the same ignominious death which was daily inflicted, almost before his eyes, on the friends and adherents of his persecuted family. His looks, his gestures, his silence, were scrutinised with malignant curiosity, and he was perpetually assaulted by enemies whom he had never offended, and by arts to which he was a stranger.[3] But in the school of adversity Julian insensibly acquired the virtues of firmness and discretion. He defended his honour, as well as his life, against the ensnaring subtleties of the eunuchs, who endeavoured to extort some declaration of his sentiments; and whilst he cautiously suppressed his grief and resentment, he nobly disdained to flatter the tyrant by any seeming approbation of his brother's murder. Julian most devoutly ascribes his miraculous deliverance to the protection of

[1] See the complete narrative of the journey and death of Gallus in Ammianus, l. xiv. c. 11. Julian complains that his brother was put to death without a trial; attempts to justify, or at least to excuse, the cruel revenge which he had inflicted on his enemies; but seems at last to acknowledge that he might justly have been deprived of the purple.

[2] Philostorgius, l. iv. c. 1. Zonaras, l. xiii. [c. 9] tom. ii. p. 19. But the former was partial towards an Arian monarch, and the latter transcribed, without choice or criticism, whatever he found in the writings of the ancients.

[3] See Ammianus Marcellin. l. xv. c. 1. 3, 8. Julian himself, in his epistle to the Athenians, draws a very lively and just picture of his own danger and of his sentiments. He shows, however, a tendency to exaggerate his sufferings, by insinuating, though in obscure terms, that they lasted above a year; a period which cannot be reconciled with the truth of chronology.

the gods, who had exempted his innocence from the sentence of destruction pronounced by their justice against the impious house of Constantine.[1]   As the most effectual instrument of their providence, he gratefully acknowledges the steady and generous friendship of the empress Eusebia,[2] a woman of beauty and merit, who, by the ascendant which she had gained over the mind of her husband, counterbalanced in some measure the powerful conspiracy of the eunuchs.   By the intercession of his patroness Julian was admitted into the Imperial presence: he pleaded his cause with a decent freedom; he was heard with favour; and, notwithstanding the efforts of his enemies, who urged the danger of sparing an avenger of the blood of Gallus, the milder sentiment of Eusebia prevailed in the council.   But the effects of a second interview were dreaded by the eunuchs; and Julian was advised to withdraw for a while into the neighbourhood of Milan, till the emperor thought proper to assign the city of Athens for the place of his honourable exile.   As he had discovered from his earliest youth a propensity, or rather passion, for the language, the manners, the learning, and the religion of the Greeks, he obeyed with pleasure an order so agreeable to his wishes. Far from the tumult of arms and the treachery of courts, he spent six months amidst the groves of the Academy, in a free intercourse with the philosophers of the age, who studied to cultivate the genius, to encourage the vanity, and to inflame the devotion of their royal pupil.   Their labours were not unsuccessful; and Julian inviolably preserved for Athens that tender regard which seldom fails to arise in a liberal mind from the recollection of the place where it has discovered and exercised its growing powers.   The gentleness and affability of manners which his temper suggested and his situation imposed, insensibly engaged the affections of the strangers, as well as citizens, with whom he conversed.   Some of his fellow-students might perhaps examine his behaviour with an eye of prejudice and aversion; but Julian established in the schools of Athens a general prepos-

---

[1] Julian has worked the crimes and misfortunes of the family of Constantine into an allegorical fable, which is happily conceived and agreeably related.   It forms the conclusion of the seventh Oration, from whence it has been detached and translated by the Abbé de la Bléterie, Vie de Jovien, tom. ii. p. 385-408.

[2] She was a native of Thessalonica in Macedonia, of a noble family, and the daughter as well as sister of consuls.   Her marriage with the emperor may be placed in the year 352.   In a divided age the historians of all parties agree in her praises.   See their testimonies collected by Tillemont, Hist. des Empereurs, tom. iv. p. 750-754.

session in favour of his virtues and talents, which was soon diffused over the Roman world.[1]

Whilst his hours were passed in studious retirement, the empress, resolute to achieve the generous design which she had undertaken, was not unmindful of the care of his fortune. The death of the late Cæsar had left Constantius invested with the sole command, and oppressed by the accumulated weight, of a mighty empire. Before the wounds of civil discord could be healed, the provinces of Gaul were overwhelmed by a deluge of barbarians. The Sarmatians no longer respected the barrier of the Danube. The impunity of rapine had increased the boldness and numbers of the wild Isaurians; those robbers descended from their craggy mountains to ravage the adjacent country, and had even presumed, though without success, to besiege the important city of Seleucia, which was defended by a garrison of three Roman legions. Above all, the Persian monarch, elated by victory, again threatened the peace of Asia; and the presence of the emperor was indispensably required both in the West and in the East. For the first time Constantius sincerely acknowledged that his single strength was unequal to such an extent of care and of dominion.[2] Insensible to the voice of flattery, which assured him that his all-powerful virtue and celestial fortune would still continue to triumph over every obstacle, he listened with complacency to the advice of Eusebia, which gratified his indolence, without offending his suspicious pride. As she perceived that the remembrance of Gallus dwelt on the emperor's mind, she artfully turned his attention to the opposite characters of the two brothers, which from their infancy had been compared to those of Domitian and of Titus.[3] She accustomed her husband to consider Julian as a youth of a mild, unambitious disposition, whose allegiance and gratitude might be

---

[1] Libanius and Gregory Nazianzen have exhausted the arts as well as the powers of their eloquence to represent Julian as the first of heroes, or the worst of tyrants. Gregory was his fellow-student at Athens; and the symptoms, which he so tragically describes, of the future wickedness of the apostate, amount only to some bodily imperfections, and to some peculiarities in his speech and manner. He protests, however, that he *then* foresaw and foretold the calamities of the church and state (Greg. Nazianzen, Orat. iv. p. 121, 122).

[2] Succumbere tot necessitatibus tamque crebris unum se, quod nunquam fecerat, aperte demonstrans. Ammian. l. xv. c. 8. He then expresses, in their own words, the flattering assurances of the courtiers.

[3] Tantum a temperatis moribus Juliani differens fratris quantum inter Vespasiani filios fuit, Domitianum et Titum. Ammian. l. xiv. c. 11. The circumstances and education of the two brothers were so nearly the same as to afford a strong example of the innate difference of characters.

secured by the gift of the purple, and who was qualified to fill with honour a subordinate station, without aspiring to dispute the commands or to shade the glories of his sovereign and benefactor. After an obstinate though secret struggle, the opposition of the favourite eunuchs submitted to the ascendancy of the empress; and it was resolved that Julian, after celebrating his nuptials with Helena, sister of Constantius, should be appointed, with the title of Cæsar, to reign over the countries beyond the Alps.[1]

Although the order which recalled him to court was probably accompanied by some intimation of his approaching greatness, he appeals to the people of Athens to witness his tears of undissembled sorrow, when he was reluctantly torn away from his beloved retirement.[2] He trembled for his life, for his fame, and even for his virtue; and his sole confidence was derived from the persuasion that Minerva inspired all his actions, and that he was protected by an invisible guard of angels, whom for that purpose she had borrowed from the Sun and Moon. He approached with horror the palace of Milan; nor could the ingenuous youth conceal his indignation when he found himself accosted with false and servile respect by the assassins of his family. Eusebia, rejoicing in the success of her benevolent schemes, embraced him with the tenderness of a sister, and endeavoured, by the most soothing caresses, to dispel his terrors and reconcile him to his fortune. But the ceremony of shaving his beard, and his awkward demeanour when he first exchanged the cloak of a Greek philosopher for the military habit of a Roman prince, amused during a few days the levity of the Imperial court.[3]

The emperors of the age of Constantine no longer deigned to consult with the senate in the choice of a colleague; but they were anxious that their nomination should be ratified by the consent of the army. On this solemn occasion the guards, with the other troops whose stations were in the neighbourhood of Milan, appeared under arms; and Constantius ascended his lofty tribunal, holding by the hand his cousin Julian, who

[1] Ammianus, l. xv. c. 8. Zosimus, l. iii. [c. 2] p. 137, 138.

[2] Julian. ad S. P. Q. A. p. 275, 276. Libanius, Orat. x. p. 268. Julian did not yield till the gods had signified their will by repeated visions and omens. His piety then forbade him to resist.

[3] Julian himself relates (p. 274), with some humour, the circumstances of his own metamorphosis, his downcast looks, and his perplexity at being thus suddenly transported into a new world, where every object appeared strange and hostile.

entered the same day into the twenty-fifth year of his age.[1]   In a studied speech, conceived and delivered with dignity, the emperor represented the various dangers which threatened the prosperity of the republic, the necessity of naming a Cæsar for the administration of the West, and his own intention, if it was agreeable to their wishes, of rewarding with the honours of the purple the promising virtues of the nephew of Constantine.   The approbation of the soldiers was testified by a respectful murmur: they gazed on the manly countenance of Julian, and observed with pleasure that the fire which sparkled in his eyes was tempered by a modest blush on being thus exposed for the first time to the public view of mankind.   As soon as the ceremony of his investiture had been performed, Constantius addressed him with the tone of authority which his superior age and station permitted him to assume; and, exhorting the new Cæsar to deserve, by heroic deeds, that sacred and immortal name, the emperor gave his colleague the strongest assurances of a friendship which should never be impaired by time, nor interrupted by their separation into the most distant climates. As soon as the speech was ended, the troops, as a token of applause, clashed their shields against their knees;[2] while the officers who surrounded the tribunal expressed, with decent reserve, their sense of the merits of the representative of Constantius.

The two princes returned to the palace in the same chariot; and, during the slow procession, Julian repeated to himself a verse of his favourite Homer, which he might equally apply to his fortune and to his fears.[3]   The four-and-twenty days which the Cæsar spent at Milan after his investiture, and the first months of his Gallic reign, were devoted to a splendid but severe captivity; nor could the acquisition of honour compensate for the loss of freedom.[4]   His steps were watched, his correspond-

---

[1] See Ammian. Marcellin. l. xv. c. 8. Zosimus, l. iii. [c. 2] p. 139. Aurelius Victor.   Victor Junior in Epitom. [c. 42.]   Eutrop. x. 14 [7].

[2] Militares omnes horrendo fragore scuta genibus illidentes; quod est prosperitatis indicium plenum; nam contra cum hastis clypei feriuntur, iræ documentum est et doloris. . . .   Ammianus adds, with a nice distinction, Eumque ut potiori reverentia servaretur, nec supra modum laudabant nec infra quam decebat [xv. 8].

[3] Ἕλλαβε πορφύρεος θάνατος, καὶ μοῖρα κραταιή.   The word *purple*, which Homer had used as a vague but common epithet for death, was applied by Julian to express, very aptly, the nature and object of his own apprehensions.

[4] He represents, in the most pathetic terms (p. 277), the distress of his new situation.   The provision for his table was however so elegant and sumptuous, that the young philosopher rejected it with disdain.   Quum

ence was intercepted; and he was obliged, by prudence, to decline the visits of his most intimate friends. Of his former domestics four only were permitted to attend him—two pages, his physician, and his librarian; the last of whom was employed in the care of a valuable collection of books, the gift of the empress, who studied the inclinations as well as the interest of her friend. In the room of these faithful servants an household was formed, such, indeed, as became the dignity of a Cæsar; but it was filled with a crowd of slaves, destitute, and perhaps incapable, of any attachment for their new master, to whom, for the most part, they were either unknown or suspected. His want of experience might require the assistance of a wise council; but the minute instructions which regulated the service of his table, and the distribution of his hours, were adapted to a youth still under the discipline of his preceptors rather than to the situation of a prince intrusted with the conduct of an important war. If he aspired to deserve the esteem of his subjects, he was checked by the fear of displeasing his sovereign; and even the fruits of his marriage-bed were blasted by the jealous artifices of Eusebia [1] herself, who, on this occasion alone, seems to have been unmindful of the tenderness of her sex and the generosity of her character. The memory of his father and of his brothers reminded Julian of his own danger, and his apprehensions were increased by the recent and unworthy fate of Sylvanus. In the summer which preceded his own elevation that general had been chosen to deliver Gaul from the tyranny of the barbarians; but Sylvanus soon discovered that he had left his most dangerous enemies in the Imperial court. A dexterous informer, countenanced by several of the principal ministers, procured from him some recommendatory letters; and, erasing the whole of the contents, except the signature, filled up the vacant parchment with matters of high and treasonable import. By the

legeret libellum assidue, quem Constantius ut privignum ad studia mittens manû suâ conscripserat, prælicenter disponens quid in convivio Cæsaris impendi deberet, Phasianum, et vulvam et sumen exigi petuit et inferri. Ammian. Marcellin. l. xvi. c. 5.

[1] If we recollect that Constantine, the father of Helena, died above eighteen years before in a mature old age, it will appear probable that the daughter, though a virgin, could not be very young at the time of her marriage. She was soon afterwards delivered of a son, who died immediately, quòd obstetrix corrupta mercede, mox natum præsecto plusquam convenerat umbilico necavit. She accompanied the emperor and empress in their journey to Rome, and the latter, quæsitum venenum bibere per fraudem illexit, ut quotiescunque concepisset, immaturum abjiceret partum. Ammian. l. xvi. c. 10. Our physicians will determine whether there exists such a poison. For my own part, I am inclined to hope that the public malignity imputed the effects of accident as the guilt of Eusebia.

industry and courage of his friends the fraud was, however, detected, and in a great council of the civil and military officers, held in the presence of the emperor himself, the innocence of Sylvanus was publicly acknowledged. But the discovery came too late; the report of the calumny, and the hasty seizure of his estate, had already provoked the indignant chief to the rebellion of which he was so unjustly accused. He assumed the purple at his head-quarters of Cologne, and his active powers appeared to menace Italy with an invasion and Milan with a siege. In this emergency Ursicinus, a general of equal rank, regained, by an act of treachery, the favour which he had lost by his eminent services in the East. Exasperated, as he might speciously allege, by injuries of a similar nature, he hastened with a few followers to join the standard, and to betray the confidence, of his too credulous friend. After a reign of only twenty-eight days Sylvanus was assassinated: the soldiers who, without any criminal intention, had blindly followed the example of their leader, immediately returned to their allegiance; and the flatterers of Constantius celebrated the wisdom and felicity of the monarch who had extinguished a civil war without the hazard of a battle.[1]

The protection of the Rhætian frontier, and the persecution of the Catholic church, detained Constantius in Italy above eighteen months after the departure of Julian. Before the emperor returned into the East he indulged his pride and curiosity in a visit to the ancient capital.[2] He proceeded from Milan to Rome along the Æmilian and Flaminian ways; and as soon as he approached within forty miles of the city, the march of a prince who had never vanquished a foreign enemy assumed the appearance of a triumphal procession. His splendid train was composed of all the ministers of luxury; but in a time of profound peace he was encompassed by the glittering arms of the numerous squadrons of his guards and cuirassiers. Their streaming banners of silk, embossed with gold, and shaped in the form of dragons, waved round the person of the emperor. Constantius sat alone in a lofty car resplendent with gold and precious gems; and, except when he bowed his head to pass under the gates of

---

[1] Ammianus (xv 5) was perfectly well informed of the conduct and fate of Sylvanus. He himself was one of the few followers who attended Ursicinus in his dangerous enterprise.

[2] For the particulars of the visit of Constantius to Rome, see Ammianus, l. xvi. c. 10. We have only to add that Themistius was appointed deputy from Constantinople, and that he composed his fourth oration for this ceremony.

the cities, he affected a stately demeanour of inflexible, and, as it might seem, of insensible gravity. The severe discipline of the Persian youth had been introduced by the eunuchs into the Imperial palace; and such were the habits of patience which they had inculcated, that, during a slow and sultry march, he was never seen to move his hand towards his face, or to turn his eyes either to the right or to the left. He was received by the magistrates and senate of Rome; and the emperor surveyed, with attention, the civil honours of the republic and the consular images of the noble families. The streets were lined with an innumerable multitude. Their repeated acclamations expressed their joy at beholding, after an absence of thirty-two years, the sacred person of their sovereign; and Constantius himself expressed, with some pleasantry, his affected surprise that the human race should thus suddenly be collected on the same spot. The son of Constantine was lodged in the ancient palace of Augustus: he presided in the senate, harangued the people from the tribunal which Cicero had so often ascended, assisted with unusual courtesy at the games of the circus, and accepted the crowns of gold, as well as the panegyrics, which had been prepared for this ceremony by the deputies of the principal cities. His short visit of thirty days was employed in viewing the monuments of art and power which were scattered over the seven hills and the interjacent valleys. He admired the awful majesty of the Capitol, the vast extent of the baths of Caracalla and Diocletian, the severe simplicity of the Pantheon, the massy greatness of the amphitheatre of Titus, the elegant architecture of the theatre of Pompey and the Temple of Peace, and, above all, the stately structure of the Forum and column of Trajan; acknowledging that the voice of fame, so prone to invent and to magnify, had made an inadequate report of the metropolis of the world. The traveller who has contemplated the ruins of ancient Rome may conceive some imperfect idea of the sentiments which they must have inspired when they reared their heads in the splendour of unsullied beauty.

The satisfaction which Constantius had received from this journey excited him to the generous emulation of bestowing on the Romans some memorial of his own gratitude and munificence. His first idea was to imitate the equestrian and colossal statue which he had seen in the Forum of Trajan; but, when he had maturely weighed the difficulties of the execution,[1] he chose

---

[1] Hormisdas, a fugitive prince of Persia, observed to the emperor, that, if he made such a horse, he must think of preparing a similar stable (the

rather to embellish the capital by the gift of an Egyptian obelisk. In a remote but polished age, which seems to have preceded the invention of alphabetical writing, a great number of these obelisks had been erected, in the cities of Thebes and Heliopolis, by the ancient sovereigns of Egypt, in a just confidence that the simplicity of their form, and the hardness of their substance, would resist the injuries of time and violence.[1] Several of these extraordinary columns had been transported to Rome by Augustus and his successors as the most durable monuments of their power and victory;[2] but there remained one obelisk which, from its size or sanctity, escaped for a long time the rapacious vanity of the conquerors. It was designed by Constantine to adorn his new city;[3] and, after being removed by his order from the pedestal where it stood before the Temple of the Sun at Heliopolis, was floated down the Nile to Alexandria. The death of Constantine suspended the execution of his purpose, and this obelisk was destined by his son to the ancient capital of the empire. A vessel of uncommon strength and capaciousness was provided to convey this enormous weight of granite, at least an hundred and fifteen feet in length, from the banks of the Nile to those of the Tiber. The obelisk of Constantius was landed about three miles from the city, and elevated, by the efforts of art and labour, in the great circus of Rome.[4]

Forum of Trajan). Another saying of Hormisdas is recorded, " that one thing only had *displeased* him, to find that men died at Rome as well as elsewhere." If we adopt this reading of the text of Ammianus (*displicuisse* instead of *placuisse*), we may consider it as a reproof of Roman vanity. The contrary sense would be that of a misanthrope.

[1] When Germanicus visited the ancient monuments of Thebes, the eldest of the priests explained to him the meaning of these hieroglyphics. Tacit. Annal. ii. c. 60. But it seems probable that before the useful invention of an alphabet these natural or arbitrary signs were the common characters of the Egyptian nation. See Warburton's Divine Legation of Moses, vol. iii. p. 69-243.

[2] See Plin. Hist. Natur. l. xxxvi. c. 14, 15.

[3] Ammian. Marcellin. l. xvii. c. 4. He gives us a Greek interpretation of the hieroglyphics, and his commentator Lindenbrogius adds a Latin inscription, which, in twenty verses of the age of Constantius, contain a short history of the obelisk.

[4] See Donat. Roma Antiqua, l. iii. c. 14, l. iv. c. 12; and the learned, though confused, Dissertation of Bargæus on Obelisks, inserted in the fourth volume of Grævius's Roman Antiquities, p. 1897-1936. This dissertation is dedicated to Pope Sixtus V., who erected the obelisk of Constantius in the square before the patriarchal church of St. John Lateran.

[It is extremely improbable that the obelisk transported by Constantius to Rome now exists. Prof. Bury, expanding Milman's suggestion, thinks that the reference of Ammianus Marcellinus refers to the obelisk of Augustus, and considers that the Greek interpretation by Hermapion of the hierogyphics is concerned with the obelisk of Augustus, and not with that of Constantius.—O. S.]

The departure of Constantius from Rome was hastened by the alarming intelligence of the distress and danger of the Illyrian provinces. The distractions of civil war, and the irreparable loss which the Roman legions had sustained in the battle of Mursa, exposed those countries, almost without defence, to the light cavalry of the barbarians; and particularly to the inroads of the Quadi, a fierce and powerful nation, who seem to have exchanged the institutions of Germany for the arms and military arts of their Sarmatian allies.[1] The garrisons of the frontier were insufficient to check their progress; and the indolent monarch was at length compelled to assemble, from the extremities of his dominions, the flower of the Palatine troops, to take the field in person, and to employ a whole campaign, with the preceding autumn and the ensuing spring, in the serious prosecution of the war. The emperor passed the Danube on a bridge of boats, cut in pieces all that encountered his march, penetrated into the heart of the country of the Quadi, and severely retaliated the calamities which they had inflicted on the Roman province. The dismayed barbarians were soon reduced to sue for peace: they offered the restitution of his captive subjects as an atonement for the past, and the noblest hostages as a pledge of their future conduct. The generous courtesy which was shown to the first among their chieftains who implored the clemency of Constantius encouraged the more timid, or the more obstinate, to imitate their example; and the Imperial camp was crowded with the princes and ambassadors of the most distant tribes, who occupied the plains of the Lesser Poland, and who might have deemed themselves secure behind the lofty ridge of the Carpathian mountains. While Constantius gave laws to the barbarians beyond the Danube, he distinguished, with specious compassion, the Sarmatian exiles, who had been expelled from their native country by the rebellion of their slaves, and who formed a very considerable accession to the power of the Quadi. The emperor, embracing a generous but artful system of policy, released the Sarmatians from the bands of this humiliating dependence, and restored them, by a separate treaty, to the dignity of a nation united under the government of a king, the friend and ally of the republic. He declared his resolution of asserting the justice of their cause, and of securing the peace of the provinces by the extirpation, or at least the banishment, of the Limigantes, whose manners were still infected

[1] The events of this Quadian and Sarmatian war are related by Ammianus, xvi. 10, xvii. 12, 13, xix. 11.

with the vices of their servile origin. The execution of this design was attended with more difficulty than glory. The territory of the Limigantes was protected against the Romans by the Danube, against the hostile barbarians by the Theiss. The marshy lands which lay between those rivers, and were often covered by their inundations, formed an intricate wilderness, pervious only to the inhabitants, who were acquainted with its secret paths and inaccessible fortresses. On the approach of Constantius the Limigantes tried the efficacy of prayers, of fraud, and of arms; but he sternly rejected their supplications, defeated their rude stratagems, and repelled with skill and firmness the efforts of their irregular valour. One of their most warlike tribes, established in a small island towards the conflux of the Theiss and the Danube, consented to pass the river with the intention of surprising the emperor during the security of an amicable conference. They soon became the victims of the perfidy which they meditated. Encompassed on every side, trampled down by the cavalry, slaughtered by the swords of the legions, they disdained to ask for mercy; and, with an undaunted countenance, still grasped their weapons in the agonies of death. After this victory a considerable body of Romans was landed on the opposite banks of the Danube; the Taifalæ, a Gothic tribe engaged in the service of the empire, invaded the Limigantes on the side of the Theiss; and their former masters, the free Sarmatians, animated by hope and revenge, penetrated through the hilly country into the heart of their ancient possessions. A general conflagration revealed the huts of the barbarians, which were seated in the depth of the wilderness; and the soldier fought with confidence on marshy ground, which it was dangerous for him to tread. In this extremity the bravest of the Limigantes were resolved to die in arms rather than to yield: but the milder sentiment, enforced by the authority of their elders, at length prevailed; and the suppliant crowd, followed by their wives and children, repaired to the Imperial camp to learn their fate from the mouth of the conqueror. After celebrating his own clemency, which was still inclined to pardon their repeated crimes, and to spare the remnant of a guilty nation, Constantius assigned for the place of their exile a remote country, where they might enjoy a safe and honourable repose. The Limigantes obeyed with reluctance; but before they could reach, at least before they could occupy, their destined habitations, they returned to the banks of the Danube, exaggerating the hardships of their situation, and requesting, with fervent professions of fidelity, that the emperor would grant them an undisturbed settlement within the limits of the Roman provinces. Instead of consulting his own experience of their incurable perfidy, Constantius listened to his flatterers, who were ready to represent the honour and advantage of accepting a colony of soldiers, at a time when it was much easier to obtain the pecuniary contributions than the military service of the subjects of the empire. The Limigantes were permitted to pass the Danube; and the emperor gave audience to the multitude in a large plain near the modern city of Buda. They surrounded the tribunal, and seemed to hear with respect an oration full of mildness and dignity; when one of the barbarians, casting his shoe into the air, exclaimed with a loud voice, *Marha ! Marha !* a word of defiance, which was received as the signal of the tumult. They rushed with fury to seize the person of the emperor; his royal throne and golden couch were pillaged by these rude hands; but the faithful defence of his guards, who died at his feet, allowed him a moment to mount a fleet horse, and to escape from the confusion. The disgrace which had been incurred by a treacherous surprise was soon retrieved by the numbers and discipline of the Romans; and the combat was only terminated by the extinction of the name and nation of the Limigantes. The free Sarmatians were reinstated in the possession of their ancient seats; and although Constantius distrusted the levity of their character, he entertained some hopes that a sense of gratitude might influence their future conduct. He had remarked the lofty stature and obsequious demeanour of Zizais, one of the noblest of their chiefs. He conferred on him the title of King; and Zizais proved that he was not unworthy to reign, by a sincere and lasting attachment to the interest of his benefactor, who, after this splendid success, received the name of *Sarmaticus* from the acclamations of his victorious army.[1]

While the Roman emperor and the Persian monarch, at the distance of three thousand miles, defended their extreme limits against the barbarians of the Danube and of the Oxus, their intermediate frontier experienced the vicissitudes of a languid war and a precarious truce. Two of the eastern ministers of Constantius, the Prætorian præfect Musonian, whose abilities were disgraced by the want of truth and integrity, and Cassian

---

[1] Genti Sarmatarum, magno decore considens apud eos, regem dedit. Aurelius Victor [Cæsar. 42]. In a pompous oration pronounced by Constantius himself, he expatiates on his own exploits with much vanity and some truth.

duke of Mesopotamia, a hardy and veteran soldier, opened a secret negotiation with the satrap Tamsapor.[1] These overtures of peace, translated into the servile and flattering language of Asia, were transmitted to the camp of the Great King, who resolved to signify, by an ambassador, the terms which he was inclined to grant to the suppliant Romans. Narses, whom he invested with that character, was honourably received in his passage through Antioch and Constantinople: he reached Sirmium after a long journey, and, at his first audience, respectfully unfolded the silken veil which covered the haughty epistle of his sovereign. Sapor, King of Kings, and Brother of the Sun and Moon (such were the lofty titles affected by oriental vanity), expressed his satisfaction that his brother, Constantius Cæsar, had been taught wisdom by adversity. As the lawful successor of Darius Hystaspes, Sapor asserted that the river Strymon, in Macedonia, was the true and ancient boundary of his empire; declaring, however, that, as an evidence of his moderation, he would content himself with the provinces of Armenia and Mesopotamia, which had been fraudulently extorted from his ancestors. He alleged that, without the restitution of these disputed countries, it was impossible to establish any treaty on a solid and permanent basis; and he arrogantly threatened that, if his ambassador returned in vain, he was prepared to take the field in the spring, and to support the justice of his cause by the strength of his invincible arms. Narses, who was endowed with the most polite and amiable manners, endeavoured, as far as was consistent with his duty, to soften the harshness of the message.[2] Both the style and substance were maturely weighed in the Imperial council, and he was dismissed with the following answer: " Constantius had a right to disclaim the officiousness of his ministers, who had acted without any specific orders from the throne: he was not, however, averse to an equal and honourable treaty; but it was highly indecent, as well as absurd, to propose to the sole and victorious emperor of the Roman world the same conditions of peace which he had indignantly rejected at the time when his power was contracted within the narrow limits of the East: the chance of arms was uncertain; and Sapor should recollect that, if the Romans had sometimes been vanquished

---

[1] Ammian. xvi. 9.

[2] Ammianus (xvii. 5) transcribes the haughty letter. Themistius (Orat. iv. p. 57, edit. Petav.) takes notice of the silk covering. Idatius and Zonaras mention the journey of the ambassador; and Peter the Patrician (in Excerpt. Legat. p. 28 [ed. Paris; c. 15, p. 131, ed. Bonn]) has informed us of his conciliating behaviour.

in battle, they had almost always been successful in the event of the war." A few days after the departure of Narses, three ambassadors were sent to the court of Sapor, who was already returned from the Scythian expedition to his ordinary residence of Ctesiphon. A count, a notary, and a sophist, had been selected for this important commission; and Constantius, who was secretly anxious for the conclusion of the peace, entertained some hopes that the dignity of the first of these ministers, the dexterity of the second, and the rhetoric of the third,[1] would persuade the Persian monarch to abate the rigour of his demands. But the progress of their negotiation was opposed and defeated by the hostile arts of Antoninus,[2] a Roman subject of Syria, who had fled from oppression, and was admitted into the councils of Sapor, and even to the royal table, where, according to the custom of the Persians, the most important business was frequently discussed.[3] The dexterous fugitive promoted his interest by the same conduct which gratified his revenge. He incessantly urged the ambition of his new master to embrace the favourable opportunity when the bravest of the Palatine troops were employed with the emperor in a distant war on the Danube. He pressed Sapor to invade the exhausted and defenceless provinces of the East, with the numerous armies of Persia, now fortified by the alliance and accession of the fiercest barbarians. The ambassadors of Rome retired without success, and a second embassy, of a still more honourable rank, was detained in strict confinement, and threatened either with death or exile.

The military historian,[4] who was himself despatched to observe the army of the Persians, as they were preparing to construct a bridge of boats over the Tigris, beheld from an eminence the

---

[1] Ammianus, xvii. 5, and Valesius ad loc. The sophist, or philosopher (in that age these words were almost synonymous), was Eustathius the Cappadocian, the disciple of Jamblichus, and the friend of St. Basil. Eunapius (in Vit. Ædesii, p. 44-47) fondly attributes to this philosophic ambassador the glory of enchanting the barbarian king by the persuasive charms of reason and eloquence. See Tillemont, Hist. des Empereurs, tom. iv. p. 828, 1132.

[2] Ammian. xviii. 5, 6, 8. The decent and respectful behaviour of Antoninus towards the Roman general sets him in a very interesting light; and Ammianus himself speaks of the traitor with some compassion and esteem.

[3] This circumstance, as it is noticed by Ammianus, serves to prove the veracity of Herodotus (l. i. c. 133), and the permanency of the Persian manners. In every age the Persians have been addicted to intemperance, and the wines of Shiraz have triumphed over the law of Mahomet. Brisson de Regno Pers. l. ii. p. 462-472, and Chardin, Voyages en Perse, tom. iii. p. 90.

[4] Ammian. l. xviii. 6, 7, 8, 10.

plain of Assyria, as far as the edge of the horizon, covered with
men, with horses, and with arms. Sapor appeared in the front,
conspicuous by the splendour of his purple. On his left hand,
the place of honour among the Orientals, Grumbates, king of the
Chionites, displayed the stern countenance of an aged and
renowned warrior. The monarch had reserved a similar place
on his right hand for the king of the Albanians, who led his independent tribes from the shores of the Caspian. The satraps and
generals were distributed according to their several ranks, and
the whole army, besides the numerous train of oriental luxury,
consisted of more than one hundred thousand effective men,
inured to fatigue, and selected from the bravest nations of Asia.
The Roman deserter, who in some measure guided the councils
of Sapor, had prudently advised, that, instead of wasting the
summer in tedious and difficult sieges, he should march directly
to the Euphrates, and press forwards without delay to seize the
feeble and wealthy metropolis of Syria. But the Persians were
no sooner advanced into the plains of Mesopotamia than they
discovered that every precaution had been used which could
retard their progress or defeat their design. The inhabitants
with their cattle were secured in places of strength, the green
forage throughout the country was set on fire, the fords of the
river were fortified by sharp stakes, military engines were planted
on the opposite banks, and a seasonable swell of the waters of
the Euphrates deterred the barbarians from attempting the
ordinary passage of the bridge of Thapsacus. Their skilful
guide, changing his plan of operations, then conducted the army
by a longer circuit, but through a fertile territory, towards the
head of the Euphrates, where the infant river is reduced to a
shallow and accessible stream. Sapor overlooked, with prudent
disdain, the strength of Nisibis; but as he passed under the
walls of Amida, he resolved to try whether the majesty of his
presence would not awe the garrison into immediate submission.
The sacrilegious insult of a random dart, which glanced against
the royal tiara, convinced him of his error; and the indignant
monarch listened with impatience to the advice of his ministers,
who conjured him not to sacrifice the success of his ambition to
the gratification of his resentment. The following day Grumbates
advanced towards the gates with a select body of troops, and required the instant surrender of the city, as the only atonement
which could be accepted for such an act of rashness and insolence.
His proposals were answered by a general discharge, and his only
son, a beautiful and valiant youth, was pierced through the heart

by a javelin, shot from one of the balistæ. The funeral of the prince of the Chionites was celebrated according to the rites of his country; and the grief of his aged father was alleviated by the solemn promise of Sapor, that the guilty city of Amida should serve as a funeral pile to expiate the death, and to perpetuate the memory, of his son.

The ancient city of Amid or Amida,[1] which sometimes assumes the provincial appellation of Diarbekir,[2] is advantageously situate in a fertile plain, watered by the natural and artificial channels of the Tigris, of which the least inconsiderable stream bends in a semicircular form round the eastern part of the city. The emperor Constantius had recently conferred on Amida the honour of his own name, and the additional fortifications of strong walls and lofty towers. It was provided with an arsenal of military engines, and the ordinary garrison had been reinforced to the amount of seven legions, when the place was invested by the arms of Sapor.[3] His first and most sanguine hopes depended on the success of a general assault. To the several nations which followed his standard their respective posts were assigned; the south to the Vertæ; the north to the Albanians; the east to the Chionites, inflamed with grief and indignation; the west to the Segestans, the bravest of his warriors, who covered their front with a formidable line of Indian elephants.[4] The Persians, on

[1] For the description of Amida, see d'Herbelot, Bibliothèque Orientale, p. 108; Histoire de Timur Bec, par Cherefeddin Ali, l. iii. c. 41. Ahmed Arabsiades, tom. i. p. 331, c. 43; Voyages de Tavernier, tom. i. p. 301; Voyages d'Otter, tom. ii. p. 273; and Voyages de Niebuhr, tom. ii. p. 324-328. The last of these travellers, a learned and accurate Dane, has given a plan of Amida, which illustrates the operations of the siege.

[2] Diarbekir, which is styled Amid, or Kara-Amid, in the public writings of the Turks, contains above 16,000 houses, and is the residence of a pasha with three tails. The epithet of *Kara* is derived from the *blackness* of the stone which composes the strong and ancient wall of Amida.

[The city of Diarbekir (still called by the Armenians Dikranagerd, the city of Tigranes) is thought to be the same with the famous Tigranocerta, of which the situation was long more than doubtful. Faustus of Byzantium, an Armenian, and nearly contemporary, states that the Persians on becoming masters of it destroyed upwards of 40,000 houses.—O. S.]

[3] The operations of the siege of Amida are very minutely described by Ammianus (xix. 1-9), who acted an honourable part in the defence, and escaped with difficulty when the city was stormed by the Persians.

[4] Of these four nations the Albanians are too well known to require any description. The Segestans [*Sacastenè, St. Martin*] inhabited a large and level country, which still preserves their name, to the south of Khorasan and the west of Hindostan. (See Geographia Nubiensis, p. 133; and d'Herbelot, Bibliothèque Orientale, p. 797.) Notwithstanding the boasted victory of Bahram (vol. i. p. 410), the Segestans, above fourscore years afterwards, appear as an independent nation, the ally of Persia. We are ignorant of the situation of the Vertæ and Chionites, but I am inclined to place them (at least the latter) towards the confines of India and Scythia. See Ammian. xvi. 9.

every side, supported their efforts, and animated their courage; and the monarch himself, careless of his rank and safety, displayed, in the prosecution of the siege, the ardour of a youthful soldier. After an obstinate combat the barbarians were repulsed; they incessantly returned to the charge; they were again driven back with a dreadful slaughter, and two rebel legions of Gauls, who had been banished into the East, signalised their undisciplined courage by a nocturnal sally into the heart of the Persian camp. In one of the fiercest of these repeated assaults, Amida was betrayed by the treachery of a deserter, who indicated to the barbarians a secret and neglected staircase, scooped out of the rock that hangs over the stream of the Tigris. Seventy chosen archers of the royal guard ascended in silence to the third story of a lofty tower, which commanded the precipice; they elevated on high the Persian banner, the signal of confidence to the assailants, and of dismay to the besieged; and if this devoted band could have maintained their post a few minutes longer, the reduction of the place might have been purchased by the sacrifice of their lives. After Sapor had tried, without success, the efficacy of force and of stratagem, he had recourse to the slower but more certain operations of a regular siege, in the conduct of which he was instructed by the skill of the Roman deserters. The trenches were opened at a convenient distance, and the troops destined for that service advanced, under the portable cover of strong hurdles, to fill up the ditch, and undermine the foundations of the walls. Wooden towers were at the same time constructed, and moved forwards on wheels, till the soldiers, who were provided with every species of missile weapons, could engage almost on level ground with the troops who defended the rampart. Every mode of resistance which art could suggest, or courage could execute, was employed in the defence of Amida, and the works of Sapor were more than once destroyed by the fire of the Romans. But the resources of a besieged city may be exhausted. The Persians repaired their losses and pushed their approaches; a large breach was made by the batteringram, and the strength of the garrison, wasted by the sword and by disease, yielded to the fury of the assault. The soldiers, the citizens, their wives, their children, all who had not time to escape through the opposite gate, were involved by the conquerors in a promiscuous massacre.

But the ruin of Amida was the safety of the Roman provinces. As soon as the first transports of victory had subsided, Sapor was at leisure to reflect that to chastise a disobedient city he had lost the flower of his troops and the most favourable season for conquest.[1] Thirty thousand of his veterans had fallen under the walls of Amida during the continuance of a siege which lasted seventy-three days; and the disappointed monarch returned to his capital with affected triumph and secret mortification. It is more than probable that the inconstancy of his barbarian allies was tempted to relinquish a war in which they had encountered such unexpected difficulties; and that the aged king of the Chionites, satiated with revenge, turned away with horror from a scene of action where he had been deprived of the hope of his family and nation. The strength as well as spirit of the army with which Sapor took the field in the ensuing spring was no longer equal to the unbounded views of his ambition. Instead of aspiring to the conquest of the East, he was obliged to content himself with the reduction of two fortified cities of Mesopotamia, Singara and Bezabde;[2] the one situate in the midst of a sandy desert, the other in a small peninsula, surrounded almost on every side by the deep and rapid stream of the Tigris. Five Roman legions, of the diminutive size to which they had been reduced in the age of Constantine, were made prisoners, and sent into remote captivity on the extreme confines of Persia. After dismantling the walls of Singara, the conqueror abandoned that solitary and sequestered place; but he carefully restored the fortifications of Bezabde, and fixed in that important post a garrison or colony of veterans, amply supplied with every means of defence, and animated by high sentiments of honour and fidelity. Towards the close of the campaign the arms of Sapor

---

[1] Ammianus has marked the chronology of this year by three signs, which do not perfectly coincide with each other, or with the series of the history. 1. The corn was ripe when Sapor invaded Mesopotamia: " Cum jam stipulâ flavente turgerent; " a circumstance which, in the latitude of Aleppo, would naturally refer us to the month of April or May. See Harmer's Observations on Scripture, vol. i. p. 41. Shaw's Travels, p. 335, edit. 4to. 2. The progress of Sapor was checked by the overflowing of the Euphrates, which generally happens in July and August. Plin. Hist. Nat. v. 21. Viaggi di Pietro della Valle, tom. i. p. 696. 3. When Sapor had taken Amida, after a siege of seventy-three days, the autumn was far advanced: " Autumno præcipiti hædorumque improbo sidere exorto." To reconcile these apparent contradictions, we must allow for some delay in the Persian king, some inaccuracy in the historian, and some disorder in the seasons.

[Clinton, in his Fasti Romani, says there is no such difficulty as Gibbon advances. Amida was taken about October 7 (hædorum improbo sidere exorto, viz., October 6), and consequently the siege began about July 27. Before the siege the army of Sapor had approached the Euphrates (nivibus tabefactis inflatum) and it began to rise sole obtinente vicesimam partem Cancri, about July 8. Sapor might have consumed two months in Mesopotamia after he had crossed the Tigris in the beginning of May.—O. S.]

[2] The account of these sieges is given by Ammianus, xx. 6, 7.

incurred some disgrace by an unsuccessful enterprise against Virtha, or Tecrit, a strong, or, as it was universally esteemed till the age of Tamerlane, an impregnable fortress of the independent Arabs.[1]

The defence of the East against the arms of Sapor required, and would have exercised, the abilities of the most consummate general; and it seemed fortunate for the state that it was the actual province of the brave Ursicinus, who alone deserved the confidence of the soldiers and people. In the hour of danger Ursicinus[2] was removed from his station by the intrigues of the eunuchs; and the military command of the East was bestowed, by the same influence, on Sabinian, a wealthy and subtle veteran, who had attained the infirmities, without acquiring the experience, of age. By a second order, which issued from the same jealous and inconstant counsels, Ursicinus was again despatched to the frontier of Mesopotamia, and condemned to sustain the labours of a war, the honours of which had been transferred to his unworthy rival. Sabinian fixed his indolent station under the walls of Edessa; and while he amused himself with the idle parade of military exercise, and moved to the sound of flutes in the Pyrrhic dance, the public defence was abandoned to the boldness and diligence of the former general of the East. But whenever Ursicinus recommended any vigorous plan of operations; when he proposed, at the head of a light and active army, to wheel round the foot of the mountains, to intercept the convoys of the enemy, to harass the wide extent of the Persian lines, and to relieve the distress of Amida; the timid and envious commander alleged that he was restrained by his positive orders from endangering the safety of the troops. Amida was at length taken; its bravest defenders, who had escaped the sword of the barbarians, died in the Roman camp by the hand of the executioner; and Ursicinus himself, after supporting the disgrace of a partial inquiry, was punished for the misconduct of Sabinian by the loss of his military rank. But Constantius soon experienced the truth of the prediction which honest indignation had extorted from his injured lieutenant, that, as long

---

[1] For the identity of Virtha and Tecrit, see d'Anville, Géographie Ancienne, tom. ii. p. 201. For the siege of that castle by Timur Bec, or Tamerlane, see Cherefeddin, l. iii. c. 33. The Persian biographer exaggerates the merit and difficulty of this exploit, which delivered the caravans of Bagdad from a formidable gang of robbers.

[2] Ammianus (xviii. 5, 6, xix. 3, xx. 2) represents the merit and disgrace of Ursicinus with that faithful attention which a soldier owed to his general. Some partiality may be suspected, yet the whole account is consistent and probable.

as such maxims of government were suffered to prevail, the emperor himself would find it no easy task to defend his eastern dominions from the invasion of a foreign enemy. When he had subdued or pacified the barbarians of the Danube, Constantius proceeded by slow marches into the East; and after he had wept over the smoking ruins of Amida, he formed, with a powerful army, the siege of Bezabde. The walls were shaken by the reiterated efforts of the most enormous of the battering-rams; the town was reduced to the last extremity; but it was still defended by the patient and intrepid valour of the garrison, till the approach of the rainy season obliged the emperor to raise the siege, and ingloriously to retreat into his winter-quarters at Antioch.[1] The pride of Constantius, and the ingenuity of his courtiers, were at a loss to discover any materials for panegyric in the events of the Persian war; while the glory of his cousin Julian, to whose military command he had intrusted the provinces of Gaul, was proclaimed to the world in the simple and concise narrative of his exploits.

In the blind fury of civil discord, Constantius had abandoned to the barbarians of Germany the countries of Gaul, which still acknowledged the authority of his rival. A numerous swarm of Franks and Alemanni were invited to cross the Rhine by presents and promises, by the hopes of spoil, and by a perpetual grant of all the territories which they should be able to subdue.[2] But the emperor, who for a temporary service had thus imprudently provoked the rapacious spirit of the barbarians, soon discovered and lamented the difficulty of dismissing these formidable allies, after they had tasted the richness of the Roman soil. Regardless of the nice distinction of loyalty and rebellion, these undisciplined robbers treated as their natural enemies all the subjects of the empire who possessed any property which they were desirous of acquiring. Forty-five flourishing cities, Tongres, Cologne, Treves, Worms, Spires, Strasburg, etc., besides a far greater number of towns and villages, were pillaged, and for the

---

[1] Ammian. xx. 11. Omisso vano incepto, hiematurus Antiochiæ redit in Syriam ærumnosam, perpessus et ulcerum sed et atrocia, diuque deflenda. It is *thus* that James Gronovius has restored an obscure passage; and he thinks that this correction alone would have deserved a new edition of his author; whose sense may now be darkly perceived. I expected some additional light from the recent labours of the learned Ernestus. (Lipsiæ, 1773.)

[2] The ravages of the Germans, and the distress of Gaul, may be collected from Julian himself. Orat. ad S. P. Q. Athen. p. 277. Ammian. xv. 11 [8?] Libanius, Orat. x. Zosimus, l. iii. [c. 3] p. 140. Sozomen, l. iii. c. 1. [Mamertin. Grat. Act. c. iv.]

most part reduced to ashes. The barbarians of Germany, still
faithful to the maxims of their ancestors, abhorred the confinement of walls, to which they applied the odious names of prisons
and sepulchres; and, fixing their independent habitations on the
banks of rivers, the Rhine, the Moselle, and the Meuse, they
secured themselves against the danger of a surprise, by a rude
and hasty fortification of large trees, which were felled and
thrown across the roads. The Alemanni were established in the
modern countries of Alsace and Lorraine; the Franks occupied
the island of the Batavians, together with an extensive district
of Brabant, which was then known by the appellation of Toxandria,[1] and may deserve to be considered as the original seat
of their Gallic monarchy.[2] From the sources to the mouth of the
Rhine, the conquests of the Germans extended above forty miles
to the west of that river, over a country peopled by colonies of
their own name and nation; and the scene of their devastations
was three times more extensive than that of their conquests.
At a still greater distance the open towns of Gaul were deserted,
and the inhabitants of the fortified cities, who trusted to their
strength and vigilance, were obliged to content themselves with
such supplies of corn as they could raise on the vacant land within
the enclosure of their walls. The diminished legions, destitute
of pay and provisions, of arms and discipline, trembled at the
approach, and even at the name, of the barbarians.

Under these melancholy circumstances, an inexperienced
youth was appointed to save and to govern the provinces of
Gaul, or rather, as he expresses it himself, to exhibit the vain
image of Imperial greatness. The retired scholastic education
of Julian, in which he had been more conversant with books
than with arms, with the dead than with the living, left him in
profound ignorance of the practical arts of war and government;
and when he awkwardly repeated some military exercise which

[1] Ammianus (xvii. 8). This name seems to be derived from the Toxandri
of Pliny, and very frequently occurs in the histories of the middle age.
Toxandria was a country of woods and morasses, which extended from the
neighbourhood of Tongres to the conflux of the Vahal and the Rhine. See
Valesius, Notit. Galliar. p. 558.

[2] The paradox of P. Daniel, that the Franks never obtained any permanent settlement on this side of the Rhine before the time of Clovis, is
refuted with much learning and good sense by Mr. Biet, who has proved,
by a chain of evidence, their uninterrupted possession of Toxandria one
hundred and thirty years before the accession of Clovis. The Dissertation
of M. Biet was crowned by the Academy of Soissons in the year 1736, and
seems to have been justly preferred to the discourse of his more celebrated
competitor, the Abbé le Bœuf, an antiquarian whose name was happily
expressive of his talents.

it was necessary for him to learn, he exclaimed with a sigh, " O
Plato, Plato, what a task for a philosopher! " Yet even this
speculative philosophy, which men of business are too apt to
despise, had filled the mind of Julian with the noblest precepts
and the most shining examples; had animated him with the love
of virtue, the desire of fame, and the contempt of death.   The
habits of temperance recommended in the schools are still more
essential in the severe discipline of a camp.   The simple wants
of nature regulated the measure of his food and sleep.   Rejecting
with disdain the delicacies provided for his table, he satisfied his
appetite with the coarse and common fare which was allotted to
the meanest soldiers.   During the rigour of a Gallic winter he
never suffered a fire in his bedchamber; and after a short and
interrupted slumber, he frequently rose in the middle of the night
from a carpet spread on the floor, to despatch any urgent business,
to visit his rounds, or to steal a few moments for the prosecution
of his favourite studies.[1]   The precepts of eloquence, which he
had hitherto practised on fancied topics of declamation, were
more usefully applied to excite or to assuage the passions of an
armed multitude: and although Julian, from his early habits of
conversation and literature, was more familiarly acquainted with
the beauties of the Greek language, he had attained a competent
knowledge of the Latin tongue.[2]   Since Julian was not originally
designed for the character of a legislator or a judge, it is probable
that the civil jurisprudence of the Romans had not engaged any
considerable share of his attention: but he derived from his
philosophic studies an inflexible regard for justice, tempered by a
disposition to clemency, the knowledge of the general principles
of equity and evidence, and the faculty of patiently investigating
the most intricate and tedious questions which could be proposed
for his discussion.   The measures of policy, and the operations
of war, must submit to the various accidents of circumstance and
character, and the unpractised student will often be perplexed in
the application of the most perfect theory.   But in the acquisition of this important science Julian was assisted by the active
vigour of his own genius, as well as by the wisdom and experience

---

[1] The private life of Julian in Gaul, and the severe discipline which he
embraced, are displayed by Ammianus (xvi. 5), who professes to praise, and
by Julian himself, who affects to ridicule (Misopogon, p. 340) a conduct
which, in a prince of the house of Constantine, might justly excite the
surprise of mankind.

[2] Aderat Latine quoque disserendi sufficiens sermo.   Ammianus, xvi. 5.
But Julian, educated in the schools of Greece, always considered the
language of the Romans as a foreign and popular dialect, which he might
use on necessary occasions.

of Sallust, an officer of rank, who soon conceived a sincere attachment for a prince so worthy of his friendship; and whose incorruptible integrity was adorned by the talent of insinuating the harshest truths without wounding the delicacy of a royal ear.[1]

Immediately after Julian had received the purple at Milan he was sent into Gaul with a feeble retinue of three hundred and sixty soldiers. At Vienna, where he passed a painful and anxious winter, in the hands of those ministers to whom Constantius had intrusted the direction of his conduct, the Cæsar was informed of the siege and deliverance of Autun. That large and ancient city, protected only by a ruined wall and pusillanimous garrison, was saved by the generous resolution of a few veterans, who resumed their arms for the defence of their country. In his march from Autun, through the heart of the Gallic provinces, Julian embraced with ardour the earliest opportunity of signalising his courage. At the head of a small body of archers and heavy cavalry, he preferred the shorter but the more dangerous of two roads; and sometimes eluding and sometimes resisting the attacks of the barbarians, who were masters of the field, he arrived with honour and safety at the camp near Rheims, where the Roman troops had been ordered to assemble. The aspect of their young prince revived the drooping spirit of the soldiers, and they marched from Rheims in search of the enemy with a confidence which had almost proved fatal to them. The Alemanni, familiarised to the knowledge of the country, secretly collected their scattered forces, and, seizing the opportunity of a dark and rainy day, poured with unexpected fury on the rear-guard of the Romans. Before the inevitable disorder could be remedied, two legions were destroyed; and Julian was taught by experience that caution and vigilance are the most important lessons of the art of war. In a second and more successful action he recovered and established his military fame; but as the agility of the barbarians saved them from the pursuit, his victory was neither bloody nor decisive. He advanced, however, to the banks of the Rhine, surveyed the ruins of Cologne, convinced himself of the difficulties of the war, and retreated on the approach of winter, discontented with the court, with his army, and with his own success.[2]   The power of

[1] We are ignorant of the actual office of this excellent minister, whom Julian afterwards created præfect of Gaul. Sallust was speedily recalled by the jealousy of the emperor; and we may still read a sensible but pedantic discourse (p. 240-252), in which Julian deplores the loss of so valuable a friend, to whom he acknowledges himself indebted for his reputation. See La Blèterie, Préface à la Vie de Jovien, p. 20.

[2] Ammianus (xvi. 2, 3) appears much better satisfied with the success of

the enemy was yet unbroken; and the Cæsar had no sooner separated his troops, and fixed his own quarters at Sens, in the centre of Gaul, than he was surrounded and besieged by a numerous host of Germans. Reduced in this extremity to the resources of his own mind, he displayed a prudent intrepidity which compensated for all the deficiencies of the place and garrison; and the barbarians, at the end of thirty days, were obliged to retire with disappointed rage.

The conscious pride of Julian, who was indebted only to his sword for this signal deliverance, was embittered by the reflection that he was abandoned, betrayed, and perhaps devoted to destruction, by those who were bound to assist him by every tie of honour and fidelity. Marcellus, master-general of the cavalry in Gaul, interpreting too strictly the jealous orders of the court, beheld with supine indifference the distress of Julian, and had restrained the troops under his command from marching to the relief of Sens. If the Cæsar had dissembled in silence so dangerous an insult, his person and authority would have been exposed to the contempt of the world; and if an action so criminal had been suffered to pass with impunity, the emperor would have confirmed the suspicions which received a very specious colour from his past conduct towards the princes of the Flavian family. Marcellus was recalled, and gently dismissed from his office.[1] In his room Severus was appointed general of the cavalry; an experienced soldier, of approved courage and fidelity, who could advise with respect, and execute with zeal; and who submitted, without reluctance, to the supreme command which Julian, by the interest of his patroness Eusebia, at length obtained over the armies of Gaul.[2] A very judicious plan of operations was adopted for the approaching campaign. Julian himself, at the head of the remains of the veteran bands, and of some new levies which he had been permitted to form, boldly penetrated into the centre of the German cantonments, and carefully re-established the fortifications of Saverne, in an advantageous post which would either check the incursions or intercept the retreat of the enemy. At the same time Barbatio, general of

this first campaign than Julian himself; who very fairly owns that he did nothing of consequence, and that he fled before the enemy.

[1] Ammian. xvi. 7. Libanius speaks rather more advantageously of the military talents of Marcellus, Orat. x. p. 272. And Julian insinuates that he would not have been so easily recalled, unless he had given other reasons of offence to the court, p. 278.

[2] Severus, non discors, non arrogans, sed longa militiæ frugalitate compertus; et eum recta præeuntem secuturus, ut ductorem morigerus miles, Ammian. xvi. 11. Zosimus, l. iii. [c. 2] p. 140.

the infantry, advanced from Milan with an army of thirty thousand men, and, passing the mountains, prepared to throw a bridge over the Rhine, in the neighbourhood of Basil. It was reasonable to expect that the Alemanni, pressed on either side by the Roman arms, would soon be forced to evacuate the provinces of Gaul, and to hasten to the defence of their native country. But the hopes of the campaign were defeated by the incapacity, or the envy, or the secret instructions of Barbatio, who acted as if he had been the enemy of the Cæsar, and the secret ally of the barbarians. The negligence with which he permitted a troop of pillagers freely to pass, and to return, almost before the gates of his camp, may be imputed to his want of abilities; but the treasonable act of burning a number of boats, and a superfluous stock of provisions, which would have been of the most essential service to the army of Gaul, was an evidence of his hostile and criminal intentions. The Germans despised an enemy who appeared destitute either of power or of inclination to offend them; and the ignominious retreat of Barbatio deprived Julian of the expected support, and left him to extricate himself from a hazardous situation, where he could neither remain with safety, nor retire with honour.[1]

As soon as they were delivered from the fears of invasion, the Alemanni prepared to chastise the Roman youth who presumed to dispute the possession of that country which they claimed as their own by the right of conquest and of treaties. They employed three days, and as many nights, in transporting over the Rhine their military powers. The fierce Chnodomar, shaking the ponderous javelin which he had victoriously wielded against the brother of Magnentius, led the van of the barbarians, and moderated by his experience the martial ardour which his example inspired.[2] He was followed by six other kings, by ten princes of regal extraction, by a long train of high-spirited nobles, and by thirty-five thousand of the bravest warriors of the tribes of Germany. The confidence derived from the view of their own strength was increased by the intelligence which they received from a deserter, that the Cæsar, with a feeble army of thirteen thousand men, occupied a post about one-and-twenty miles

[1] On the design and failure of the co-operation between Julian and Barbatio, see Ammianus (xvi. 11), and Libanius, Orat. x. p. 273.

[2] Ammianus (xvi. 12) describes with his inflated eloquence the figure and character of Chnodomar. Audax et fidens ingenti robore lacertorum, ubi ardor prœlii sperabatur immanis, equo spumante, sublimior, erectus in jaculum formidandæ vastitatis, armorumque nitore conspicuus: antea strenuus et miles, et utilis præter cæteros ductor . . . Decentium Cæsarem superavit æquo Marte congressus.

from their camp of Strasburg. With this inadequate force Julian resolved to seek and to encounter the barbarian host; and the chance of a general action was preferred to the tedious and uncertain operation of separately engaging the dispersed parties of the Alemanni. The Romans marched in close order, and in two columns; the cavalry on the right, the infantry on the left; and the day was so far spent when they appeared in sight of the enemy, that Julian was desirous of deferring the battle till the next morning, and of allowing his troops to recruit their exhausted strength by the necessary refreshments of sleep and food. Yielding, however, with some reluctance, to the clamours of the soldiers, and even to the opinion of his council, he exhorted them to justify by their valour the eager impatience which, in case of a defeat, would be universally branded with the epithets of rashness and presumption. The trumpets sounded, the military shout was heard through the field, and the two armies rushed with equal fury to the charge. The Cæsar, who conducted in person his right wing, depended on the dexterity of his archers and the weight of his cuirassiers. But his ranks were instantly broken by an irregular mixture of light-horse and of light-infantry, and he had the mortification of beholding the flight of six hundred of his most renowned cuirassiers.[1] The fugitives were stopped and rallied by the presence and authority of Julian, who, careless of his own safety, threw himself before them, and, urging every motive of shame and honour, led them back against the victorious enemy. The conflict between the two lines of infantry was obstinate and bloody. The Germans possessed the superiority of strength and stature, the Romans that of discipline and temper; and as the barbarians who served under the standard of the empire united the respective advantages of both parties, their strenuous efforts, guided by a skilful leader, at length determined the event of the day. The Romans lost four tribunes, and two hundred and forty-three soldiers, in this memorable battle of Strasburg, so glorious to the Cæsar,[2] and so salutary to the afflicted provinces of Gaul. Six thousand

---

[1] After the battle Julian ventured to revive the rigour of ancient discipline by exposing these fugitives in female apparel to the derision of the whole camp. In the next campaign these troops nobly retrieved their honour. Zosimus, l. iii. [c. 3] p. 142.

[2] Julian himself (ad S. P. Q. Athen. p. 279) speaks of the battle of Strasburg with the modesty of conscious merit; ἐμαχεσάμην οὐκ ἀκλεῶς, ἴσως καὶ εἰς ὑμᾶς ἀφίκετο ἡ τοιαύτη μάχη. Zosimus compares it with the victory of Alexander over Darius; and yet we are at a loss to discover any of those strokes of military genius which fix the attention of ages on the conduct and success of a single day.

of the Alemanni were slain in the field, without including those who were drowned in the Rhine, or transfixed with darts whilst they attempted to swim across the river.[1] Chnodomar himself was surrounded and taken prisoner, with three of his brave companions, who had devoted themselves to follow in life or death the fate of their chieftain. Julian received him with military pomp in the council of his officers; and expressing a generous pity for the fallen state, dissembled his inward contempt for the abject humiliation of his captive. Instead of exhibiting the vanquished king of the Alemanni as a grateful spectacle to the cities of Gaul, he respectfully laid at the feet of the emperor this splendid trophy of his victory. Chnodomar experienced an honourable treatment: but the impatient barbarian could not long survive his defeat, his confinement, and his exile.[2]

After Julian had repulsed the Alemanni from the provinces of the Upper Rhine, he turned his arms against the Franks, who were seated nearer to the ocean, on the confines of Gaul and Germany; and who, from their numbers, and still more from their intrepid valour, had ever been esteemed the most formidable of the barbarians.[3] Although they were strongly actuated by the allurements of rapine, they professed a disinterested love of war, which they considered as the supreme honour and felicity of human nature; and their minds and bodies were so completely hardened by perpetual action, that, according to the lively expression of an orator, the snows of winter were as pleasant to them as the flowers of spring. In the month of December which followed the battle of Strasburg, Julian attacked a body of six hundred Franks who had thrown themselves into two castles on the Meuse.[4] In the midst of that severe season they sustained, with inflexible constancy, a siege of fifty-four days, till at length, exhausted by hunger, and satisfied that the vigil-

[1] Ammianus, xvi. 12. Libanius adds 2000 more to the number of the slain (Orat. x. p. 274). But these trifling differences disappear before the 60,000 barbarians whom Zosimus has sacrificed to the glory of his hero (l. iii. [c. 3] p. 141). We might attribute this extravagant number to the carelessnesss of transcribers, if this credulous or partial historian had not swelled the army of 35,000 Alemanni to an innumerable multitude of barbarians, πλῆθος ἄπειρον βαρβάρων. It is our own fault if this detection does not inspire us with proper distrust on similar occasions.

[2] Ammian. xvi. 12. Libanius. Orat. x. p. 276.

[3] Libanius (Orat. iii. p. 137) draws a very lively picture of the manners of the Franks.

[4] Ammianus, xvii. 2. Libanius, Orat. x. p. 278. The Greek orator, by misapprehending a passage of Julian, has been induced to represent the Franks as consisting of a thousand men; and, as his head was always full of the Peloponnesian war, he compares them to the Lacedæmonians, who were besieged and taken in the island of Sphacteria.

ance of the enemy in breaking the ice of the river left them no
hopes of escape, the Franks consented, for the first time, to
dispense with the ancient law which commanded them to conquer
or to die. The Cæsar immediately sent his captives to the court
of Constantius, who, accepting them as a valuable present,[1] rejoiced in the opportunity of adding so many heroes to the choicest
troops of his domestic guards. The obstinate resistance of this
handful of Franks apprised Julian of the difficulties of the
expedition which he meditated for the ensuing spring against
the whole body of the nation. His rapid diligence surprised
and astonished the active barbarians. Ordering his soldiers to
provide themselves with biscuit for twenty days, he suddenly
pitched his camp near Tongres, while the enemy still supposed
him in his winter-quarters of Paris, expecting the slow arrival
of his convoys from Aquitain. Without allowing the Franks
to unite or to deliberate, he skilfully spread his legions from
Cologne to the ocean; and by the terror, as well as by the success
of his arms, soon reduced the suppliant tribes to implore the
clemency and to obey the commands of their conqueror. The
Chamavians submissively retired to their former habitations
beyond the Rhine; but the Salians were permitted to possess
their new establishment of Toxandria, as the subjects and
auxiliaries of the Roman empire.[2] The treaty was ratified by
solemn oaths; and perpetual inspectors were appointed to reside
among the Franks, with the authority of enforcing the strict
observance of the conditions. An incident is related, interesting
enough in itself, and by no means repugnant to the character
of Julian, who ingeniously contrived both the plot and the
catastrophe of the tragedy. When the Chamavians sued for
peace, he required the son of their king, as the only hostage on
whom he could rely. A mournful silence, interrupted by tears
and groans, declared the sad perplexity of the barbarians; and
their aged chief lamented, in pathetic language, that his private

---

[1] Julian. ad S. P. Q. Athen. p. 280. Libanius, Orat. x. p. 278. According to the expression of Libanius, the emperor δῶρα ὠνόμαζε, which La
Bléterie understands (Vie de Julien, p. 118) as an honest confession, and
Valesius (ad Ammian. xvii. 2) as a mean evasion, of the truth. Dom
Bouquet (Historiens de France, tom. i. p. 733), by substituting another
word, ἐνόμισε, would suppress both the difficulty and the spirit of this
passage.

[2] Ammian. xvii. 8; Zosimus, l. iii. [c. 4, sq.] p. 146-150 (his narrative is
darkened by a mixture of fable); and Julian. ad S. P. Q. Athen. p. 280.
His expression, ὑπεδεξάμην μὲν μοῖραν τοῦ Σαλίων ἔθνους, Χαμάβους δὲ
ἐξήλασα. This difference of treatment confirms the opinion that the
Salian Franks were permitted to retain the settlements in Toxandria.

loss was now embittered by a sense of the public calamity. While the Chamavians lay prostrate at the foot of his throne, the royal captive, whom they believed to have been slain, unexpectedly appeared before their eyes; and as soon as the tumult of joy was hushed into attention, the Cæsar addressed the assembly in the following terms:—" Behold the son, the prince, whom you wept. You had lost him by your fault. God and the Romans have restored him to you. I shall still preserve and educate the youth, rather as a monument of my own virtue than as a pledge of your sincerity. Should you presume to violate the faith which you have sworn, the arms of the republic will avenge the perfidy, not on the innocent, but on the guilty." The barbarians withdrew from his presence, impressed with the warmest sentiments of gratitude and admiration.[1]

It was not enough for Julian to have delivered the provinces of Gaul from the barbarians of Germany. He aspired to emulate the glory of the first and most illustrious of the emperors; after whose example he composed his own commentaries of the Gallic war.[2] Cæsar has related, with conscious pride, the manner in which he *twice* passed the Rhine. Julian could boast that, before he assumed the title of Augustus, he had carried the Roman eagles beyond that great river in *three* successful expeditions.[3] The consternation of the Germans after the battle of Strasburg encouraged him to the first attempt; and the reluctance of the troops soon yielded to the persuasive eloquence of a leader who shared the fatigues and dangers which he imposed on the meanest of the soldiers. The villages on either side of the Main, which were plentifully stored with corn and cattle, felt the ravages of an invading army. The principal houses, constructed with some imitation of Roman elegance, were consumed by the flames; and the Cæsar boldly advanced about ten miles, till his progress was stopped by a dark and impenetrable forest, undermined by subterraneous passages, which threatened with secret snares

---

[1] This interesting story, which Zosimus has abridged, is related by Euna-pius (in Excerpt. Legationum, p. 15, 16, 17 [ed. Paris; p. 11 *sq.* ed. Ven.; cap. i. p. 41 *sqq.* ed. Bonn]), with all the amplifications of Grecian rhetoric: but the silence of Libanius, of Ammianus, and of Julian himself, renders the truth of it extremely suspicious.

[2] Libanius, the friend of Julian, clearly insinuates (Orat. iv. p. 178) that his hero had composed the history of his Gallic campaigns. But Zosimus (l. iii. [c. 2] p. 140) seems to have derived his information only from the Orations (λόγοι) and the Epistles of Julian. The discourse which is ad-dressed to the Athenians contains an accurate, though general, account of the war against the Germans.

[3] See Ammian. xvii. 1, 10, xviii. 2; and Zosim. l. iii. p. 144. Julian. ad S. P. Q. Athen. p. 280.

and ambush every step of the assailant. The ground was already covered with snow; and Julian, after repairing an ancient castle which had been erected by Trajan, granted a truce of ten months to the submissive barbarians. At the expiration of the truce Julian undertook a second expedition beyond the Rhine, to humble the pride of Surmar and Hortaire, two of the kings of the Alemanni, who had been present at the battle of Strasburg. They promised to restore all the Roman captives who yet remained alive; and as the Cæsar had procured an exact account from the cities and villages of Gaul of the inhabitants whom they had lost, he detected every attempt to deceive him with a degree of readiness and accuracy which almost established the belief of his supernatural knowledge. His third expedition was still more splendid and important than the two former. The Germans had collected their military powers, and moved along the opposite banks of the river, with a design of destroying the bridge, and of preventing the passage of the Romans. But this judicious plan of defence was disconcerted by a skilful diversion. Three hundred light-armed and active soldiers were detached in forty small boats, to fall down the stream in silence, and to land at some distance from the posts of the enemy. They executed their orders with so much boldness and celerity, that they had almost surprised the barbarian chiefs, who returned in the fearless confidence of intoxication from one of their nocturnal festivals. Without repeating the uniform and disgusting tale of slaughter and devastation, it is sufficient to observe that Julian dictated his own conditions of peace to six of the haughtiest kings of the Alemanni, three of whom were permitted to view the severe discipline and martial pomp of a Roman camp. Followed by twenty thousand captives, whom he had rescued from the chains of the barbarians, the Cæsar repassed the Rhine, after terminating a war the success of which has been compared to the ancient glories of the Punic and Cimbric victories.

As soon as the valour and conduct of Julian had secured an interval of peace, he applied himself to a work more congenial to his humane and philosophic temper. The cities of Gaul, which had suffered from the inroads of the barbarians, he diligently repaired; and seven important posts, between Mentz and the mouth of the Rhine, are particularly mentioned as having been rebuilt and fortified by the order of Julian.[1] The

---

[1] Ammian. xviii. 2. Libanius, Orat. x. p. 279, 280. Of these seven posts, four are at present towns of some consequence—Bingen, Andernach, Bonn, and Nuyss. The other three, Tricesimæ, Quadriburgium, and

vanquished Germans had submitted to the just but humiliating condition of preparing and conveying the necessary materials. The active zeal of Julian urged the prosecution of the work; and such was the spirit which he had diffused among the troops, that the auxiliaries themselves, waiving their exemption from any duties of fatigue, contended in the most servile labours with the diligence of the Roman soldiers. It was incumbent on the Cæsar to provide for the subsistence as well as for the safety of the inhabitants and of the garrisons. The desertion of the former, and the mutiny of the latter, must have been the fatal and inevitable consequences of famine. The tillage of the provinces of Gaul had been interrupted by the calamities of war; but the scanty harvests of the continent were supplied, by his paternal care, from the plenty of the adjacent island. Six hundred large barques, framed in the forest of the Ardennes, made several voyages to the coast of Britain; and returning from thence, laden with corn, sailed up the Rhine, and distributed their cargoes to the several towns and fortresses along the banks of the river.[1] The arms of Julian had restored a free and secure navigation, which Constantius had offered to purchase at the expense of his dignity, and of a tributary present of two thousand pounds of silver. The emperor parsimoniously refused to his soldiers the sums which he granted with a lavish and trembling hand to the barbarians. The dexterity, as well as the firmness of Julian, was put to a severe trial, when he took the field with a discontented army, which had already served two campaigns without receiving any regular pay or any extraordinary donative.[2]

A tender regard for the peace and happiness of his subjects was the ruling principle which directed, or seemed to direct, the administration of Julian.[3] He devoted the leisure of his winter-quarters to the offices of civil government; and affected to assume with more pleasure the character of a magistrate than

Castra Herculis, or Heraclea, no longer subsist; but there is room to believe that, on the ground of Quadriburgium, the Dutch have constructed the fort of Schenk, a name so offensive to the fastidious delicacy of Boileau. See d'Anville, Notice de l'Ancienne Gaule, p. 183; Boileau, Epître iv. and the notes.

[1] We may credit Julian himself, Orat. ad S. P. Q. Atheniensem, p. 279, *sq.*, who gives a very particular account of the transaction. Zosimus adds two hundred vessels more, l. iii. [c. 5] p. 145. If we computed the 600 corn ships of Julian at only seventy tons each, they were capable of exporting 120,000 quarters (see Arbuthnot's Weights and Measures, p. 237); and the country which could bear so large an exportation must already have attained an improved state of agriculture.

[2] The troops once broke out into a mutiny, immediately before the second passage of the Rhine. Ammian. xvii. 9.

[3] Ammian. xvi. 5, xviii. 1. Mamertinus in Panegyr. Vet. xi. 4.

that of a general. Before he took the field he devolved on the provincial governors most of the public and private causes which had been referred to his tribunal; but, on his return, he carefully revised their proceedings, mitigated the rigour of the law, and pronounced a second judgment on the judges themselves. Superior to the last temptation of virtuous minds, an indiscreet and intemperate zeal for justice, he restrained, with calmness and dignity, the warmth of an advocate who prosecuted, for extortion, the president of the Narbonnese province. " Who will ever be found guilty," exclaimed the vehement Delphidius, " if it be enough to deny? " " And who," replied Julian, " will ever be innocent, if it is sufficient to affirm? " In the general administration of peace and war, the interest of the sovereign is commonly the same as that of his people; but Constantius would have thought himself deeply injured, if the virtues of Julian had defrauded him of any part of the tribute which he extorted from an oppressed and exhausted country. The prince who was invested with the ensigns of royalty might some-times presume to correct the rapacious insolence of the inferior agents, to expose their corrupt arts, and to introduce an equal and easier mode of collection. But the management of the finances was more safely intrusted to Florentius, Prætorian præfect of Gaul, an effeminate tyrant, incapable of pity or remorse: and the haughty minister complained of the most decent and gentle opposition, while Julian himself was rather inclined to censure the weakness of his own behaviour. The Cæsar had rejected with abhorrence a mandate for the levy of an extraordinary tax; a new superindiction, which the præfect had offered for his signature; and the faithful picture of the public misery, by which he had been obliged to justify his refusal, offended the court of Constantius. We may enjoy the pleasure of reading the sentiments of Julian, as he expresses them with warmth and freedom in a letter to one of his most intimate friends. After stating his own conduct, he proceeds in the following terms:—" Was it possible for the disciple of Plato and Aristotle to act otherwise than I have done? Could I abandon the un-happy subjects intrusted to my care? Was I not called upon to defend them from the repeated injuries of these unfeeling robbers? A tribune who deserts his post is punished with death, and deprived of the honours of burial. With what justice could I pronounce *his* sentence, if, in the hour of danger, I myself neglected a duty far more sacred and far more important? God has placed me in this elevated post; his providence will guard and support me. Should I be condemned to suffer, I shall derive comfort from the testimony of a pure and upright conscience. Would to Heaven that I still possessed a counsellor like Sallust! If they think proper to send me a successor, I shall submit without reluctance; and had much rather improve the short opportunity of doing good, than enjoy a long and lasting impunity of evil." [1] The precarious and dependent situation of Julian displayed his virtues and concealed his defects. The young hero who supported, in Gaul, the throne of Constantius, was not permitted to reform the vices of the government; but he had courage to alleviate or to pity the distress of the people. Unless he had been able to revive the martial spirit of the Romans, or to introduce the arts of industry and refinement among their savage enemies, he could not entertain any rational hopes of securing the public tranquillity, either by the peace or conquest of Germany. Yet the victories of Julian suspended for a short time the inroads of the barbarians, and delayed the ruin of the Western Empire.

His salutary influence restored the cities of Gaul, which had been so long exposed to the evils of civil discord, barbarian war, and domestic tyranny; and the spirit of industry was revived with the hopes of enjoyment. Agriculture, manufactures, and commerce again flourished under the protection of the laws; and the *curiæ*, or civil corporations, were again filled with useful and respectable members: the youth were no longer apprehensive of marriage; and married persons were no longer apprehensive of posterity: the public and private festivals were celebrated with customary pomp; and the frequent and secure intercourse of the provinces displayed the image of national prosperity.[2] A mind like that of Julian must have felt the general happiness of which he was the author; but he viewed with peculiar satisfaction and complacency the city of Paris, the seat of his winter residence, and the object even of his partial affection.[3] That splendid capital, which now embraces an ample territory on

[1] Ammian. xvii. 3. Julian. Epistol. xvii. edit. Spanheim. Such a conduct almost justifies the encomium of Mamertinus. Ita illi anni spatia divisa sunt, ut aut Barbaros domitet, aut civibus jura restituat; perpetuum professus, aut contra hostem, aut contra vitia, certamen.

[2] Libanius, Orat. Parental. in Imp. Julian. c. 38, in Fabricius Bibliothec. Græc. tom. vii. p. 263, 264.

[3] See Julian. in Misopogon. p. 340, 341. The primitive state of Paris is illustrated by Henry Valesius (ad Ammian. xx. 4), his brother Hadrian Valesius, or de Valois, and M. d'Anville (in their respective Notitias of ancient Gaul), the Abbé de Longuerue (Description de la France, tom. i. p. 12, 13), and M. Bonamy (in the Mém. de l'Académie des Inscriptions, tom. xv. p. 656-691).

either side of the Seine, was originally confined to the small island in the midst of the river, from whence the inhabitants derived a supply of pure and salubrious water. The river bathed the foot of the walls; and the town was accessible only by two wooden bridges. A forest overspread the northern side of the Seine, but on the south, the ground which now bears the name of the University was insensibly covered with houses, and adorned with a palace and amphitheatre, baths, an aqueduct, and a field of Mars for the exercise of the Roman troops. The severity of the climate was tempered by the neighbourhood of the ocean; and with some precautions, which experience had taught, the vine and fig-tree were successfully cultivated. But in remarkable winters the Seine was deeply frozen; and the huge pieces of ice that floated down the stream might be compared, by an Asiatic, to the blocks of white marble which were extracted from the quarries of Phrygia. The licentiousness and corruption of Antioch recalled to the memory of Julian the severe and simple manners of his beloved Lutetia,[1] where the amusements of the theatre were unknown or despised. He indignantly contrasted the effeminate Syrians with the brave and honest simplicity of the Gauls, and almost forgave the intemperance which was the only stain of the Celtic character.[2] If Julian could now revisit the capital of France, he might converse with men of science and genius, capable of understanding and of instructing a disciple of the Greeks; he might excuse the lively and graceful follies of a nation whose martial spirit has never been enervated by the indulgence of luxury; and he must applaud the perfection of that inestimable art which softens and refines and embellishes the intercourse of social life.

---

[1] Τὴν φίλην Λευκετίαν. Julian. in Misopogon. p. 340. Leucetia, or Lutetia, was the ancient name of the city which, according to the fashion of the fourth century, assumed the territorial appellation of *Parisii*.

[2] Julian. in Misopogon. p. 359, 360.

CHAPTER XX

The Motives, Progress, and Effects of the Conversion of Constantine—
    Legal Establishment and Constitution of the Christian or Catholic
    Church

THE public establishment of Christianity may be considered as
one of the most important and domestic revolutions which
excite the most lively curiosity, and afford the most valuable
instruction. The victories and the civil policy of Constantine
no longer influence the state of Europe; but a considerable
portion of the globe still retains the impression which it received
from the conversion of that monarch;. and the ecclesiastical
institutions of his reign are still connected, by an indissoluble
chain, with the opinions, the passions, and the interests of the
present generation.

In the consideration of a subject which may be examined with
impartiality, but cannot be viewed with indifference, a difficulty immediately arises of a very unexpected nature—that of
ascertaining the real and precise date of the conversion of Constantine. The eloquent Lactantius, in the midst of his court,
seems impatient[1] to proclaim to the world the glorious example
of the sovereign of Gaul; who, in the first moments of his reign,
acknowledged and adored the majesty of the true and only God.[2]
The learned Eusebius has ascribed the faith of Constantine to the
miraculous sign which was displayed in the heavens whilst he
meditated and prepared the Italian expedition.[3] The historian
Zosimus maliciously asserts that the emperor had imbrued his

---

[1] The date of the Divine Institutions of Lactantius has been accurately
discussed, difficulties have been started, solutions proposed, and an expedient imagined of two *original* editions—the former published during
the persecutions of Diocletian, the latter under that of Licinius. See
Dufresnoy, Præfat. p. v. Tillemont, Mém. Ecclésiast. tom. vi. p. 465-470.
Lardner's Credibility, part ii. vol. vii. p. 78-86. For my own part, I am
almost convinced that Lactantius dedicated his Institutions to the sovereign of Gaul, at a time when Galerius, Maximin, and even Licinius, persecuted the Christians; that is, between the years 306 and 311.

[2] Lactant. Divin. Institut. i. 1, vii. 26. The first and most important of
these passages is indeed wanting in twenty-eight manuscripts, but it is
found in nineteen. If we weigh the comparative value of those manuscripts, one of 900 years old, in the king of France's library, may be alleged
in its favour; but the passage is omitted in the correct manuscript of
Bologna, which the P. de Montfaucon ascribes to the sixth or seventh
century (Diarium Italic. p. 409). The taste of most of the editors (except
Isæus, see Lactant. edit. Dufresnoy, tom. i. p. 596) has felt the genuine
style of Lactantius.

[3] Euseb. in Vit. Constant. l. i. c. 27-32.

hands in the blood of his eldest son before he publicly renounced the gods of Rome and of his ancestors.[1] The perplexity produced by these discordant authorities is derived from the behaviour of Constantine himself. According to the strictness of ecclesiastical language, the first of the *Christian* emperors was unworthy of that name till the moment of his death; since it was only during his last illness that he received, as a catechumen, the imposition of hands,[2] and was afterwards admitted, by the initiatory rites of baptism, into the number of the faithful.[3] The Christianity of Constantine must be allowed in a much more vague and qualified sense; and the nicest accuracy is required in tracing the slow and almost imperceptible gradations by which the monarch declared himself the protector, and at length the proselyte, of the church. It was an arduous task to eradicate the habits and prejudices of his education, to acknowledge the divine power of Christ, and to understand that the truth of *his* revelation was incompatible with the worship of the gods. The obstacles which he had probably experienced in his own mind instructed him to proceed with caution in the momentous change of a national religion; and he insensibly discovered his new opinions, as far as he could enforce them with safety and with effect. During the whole course of his reign, the stream of Christianity flowed with a gentle, though accelerated, motion: but its general direction was sometimes checked, and sometimes diverted, by the accidental circumstances of the times, and by the prudence, or possibly by the caprice, of the monarch. His ministers were permitted to signify the intentions of their master in the various language which was best adapted to their respective principles;[4] and he artfully balanced the hopes and

[1] Zosimus, l. ii. [c. 29] p. 104.

[2] That rite was *always* used in making a catechumen (see Bingham's Antiquities, l. x. c. i. p. 419; Dom Chardon, Hist. des Sacremens, tom. i. p. 62), and Constantine received it for the *first* time (Euseb. in Vit. Constant. l. iv. c. 61) immediately before his baptism and death. From the connection of these two facts, Valesius (ad loc. Euseb.) has drawn the conclusion which is reluctantly admitted by Tillemont (Hist. des Empereurs, tom. iv. p. 628), and opposed with feeble arguments by Mosheim (p. 968).

[3] Euseb. in Vit. Constant. l. iv. c. 61, 62, 63. The legend of Constantine's baptism at Rome, thirteen years before his death, was invented in the eighth century, as a proper motive for his *donation*. Such has been the gradual progress of knowledge, that a story, of which Cardinal Baronius (Annal. Ecclesiast. A.D. 324, No. 43-49) declared himself the unblushing advocate, is now feebly supported, even within the verge of the Vatican. See the Antiquitates Christianæ, tom. ii. p. 232—a work published with six approbations at Rome, in the year 1751, by Father Mamachi, a learned Dominican.

[4] The quæstor, or secretary, who composed the law of the Theodosian Code, makes his master say with indifference, " hominibus supra dictæ

fears of his subjects, by publishing in the same year two edicts; the first of which enjoined the solemn observance of Sunday,[1] and the second directed the regular consultation of the Arus- pices.[2] While this important revolution yet remained in suspense, the Christians and the Pagans watched the conduct of their sovereign with the same anxiety, but with very opposite sentiments. The former were prompted by every motive of zeal, as well as vanity, to exaggerate the marks of his favour and the evidences of his faith. The latter, till their just apprehensions were changed into despair and resentment, attempted to con- ceal from the world, and from themselves, that the gods of Rome could no longer reckon the emperor in the number of their votaries. The same passions and prejudices have engaged the partial writers of the times to connect the public profession of Christianity with the most glorious or the most ignominious era of the reign of Constantine.

Whatever symptoms of Christian piety might transpire in the discourses or actions of Constantine, he persevered till he was near forty years of age in the practice of the established religion; [3] and the same conduct which in the court of Nicomedia might be imputed to his fear, could be ascribed only to the inclination or policy of the sovereign of Gaul. His liberality restored and enriched the temples of the gods; the medals which issued from his Imperial mint are impressed with the figures and attributes of Jupiter and Apollo, of Mars and Hercules; and his filial piety increased the council of Olympus by the solemn apotheosis of his father Constantius.[4] But the devotion of Constantine was more peculiarly directed to the genius of the Sun, the Apollo of Greek and Roman mythology; and he was pleased to be repre-

---

religionis " (l. xvi. tit. ii. leg. 1). The minister of ecclesiastical affairs was allowed a more devout and respectful style, τῆς ἐνθέσμου καὶ ἁγιωτάτης καθολικῆς θρησκείας; the legal, most holy, and catholic worship. See Euseb. Hist. Eccles. l. x. c. 6.

[1] Cod. Theodos. l. ii. tit. viii. leg. 1. Cod. Justinian. l. iii. tit. xii. leg. 3. Constantine styles the Lord's day *dies solis*, a name which could not offend the ears of his Pagan subjects.

[2] Cod. Theodos. l. xvi. tit. x. leg. 1. Godefroy, in the character of a commentator, endeavours (tom. vi. p. 257) to excuse Constantine; but the more zealous Baronius (Annal. Eccles. A.D. 321, No. 18) censures his pro- fane conduct with truth and asperity.

[3] Theodoret (l. i. c. 18) seems to insinuate that Helena gave her son a Christian education; but we may be assured, from the superior authority of Eusebius (in Vit. Constant. l. iii. c. 47), that she herself was indebted to Constantine for the knowledge of Christianity.

[4] See the medals of Constantine in Ducange and Banduri. As few cities had retained the privilege of coining, almost all the medals of that age issued from the mint under the sanction of the Imperial authority.

sented with the symbols of the God of Light and Poetry. The unerring shafts of that deity, the brightness of his eyes, his laurel wreath, immortal beauty, and elegant accomplishments, seem to point him out as the patron of a young hero. The altars of Apollo were crowned with the votive offerings of Constantine; and the credulous multitude were taught to believe that the emperor was permitted to behold with mortal eyes the visible majesty of their tutelar deity; and that, either waking or in a vision, he was blessed with the auspicious omens of a long and victorious reign. The Sun was universally celebrated as the invincible guide and protector of Constantine; and the Pagans might reasonably expect that the insulted god would pursue with unrelenting vengeance the impiety of his ungrateful favourite.[1]

As long as Constantine exercised a limited sovereignty over the provinces of Gaul, his Christian subjects were protected by the authority, and perhaps by the laws, of a prince who wisely left to the gods the care of vindicating their own honour. If we may credit the assertion of Constantine himself, he had been an indignant spectator of the savage cruelties which were inflicted, by the hands of Roman soldiers, on those citizens whose religion was their only crime.[2] In the East and in the West he had seen the different effects of severity and indulgence; and as the former was rendered still more odious by the example of Galerius, his implacable enemy, the latter was recommended to his imitation by the authority and advice of a dying father. The son of Constantius immediately suspended or repealed the edicts of persecution, and granted the free exercise of their religious ceremonies to all those who had already professed themselves members of the church. They were soon encouraged to depend on the favour as well as on the justice of their sovereign, who had imbibed a secret and sincere reverence for the name of Christ, and for the God of the Christians.[3]

About five months after the conquest of Italy, the emperor

[1] The panegyric of Eumenius (vii. [vi.] inter Panegyr. Vet.), which was pronounced a few months before the Italian war, abounds with the most unexceptionable evidence of the Pagan superstition of Constantine, and of his particular veneration for Apollo, or the Sun; to which Julian alludes (Orat. vii. p. 228, ἀπολείπων σέ). See Commentaire de Spanheim sur les Césars, p. 317.

[2] Constantin. Orat. ad Sanctos, c. 25. But it might easily be shown that the Greek translator has improved the sense of the Latin original; and the aged emperor might recollect the persecution of Diocletian with a more lively abhorrence than he had actually felt in the days of his youth and Paganism.

[3] See Euseb. Hist. Eccles. l. viii. 13, l. ix. 9; and in Vit. Const. l. i. c. 16, 17. Lactant. Divin. Institut. i. 1. Cæcilius de Mort. Persecut. c. 25.

made a solemn and authentic declaration of his sentiments by the celebrated edict of Milan, which restored peace to the catholic church. In the personal interview of the two western princes, Constantine, by the ascendant of genius and power, obtained the ready concurrence of his colleague, Licinius; the union of their names and authority disarmed the fury of Maximin; and, after the death of the tyrant of the East, the edict of Milan was received as a general and fundamental law of the Roman world.[1]

The wisdom of the emperors provided for the restitution of all the civil and religious rights of which the Christians had been so unjustly deprived. It was enacted that the places of worship, and public lands, which had been confiscated, should be restored to the church, without dispute, without delay, and without expense: and this severe injunction was accompanied with a gracious promise, that, if any of the purchasers had paid a fair and adequate price, they should be indemnified from the Imperial treasury. The salutary regulations which guard the future tranquillity of the faithful are framed on the principles of enlarged and equal toleration; and such an equality must have been interpreted by a recent sect as an advantageous and honourable distinction. The two emperors proclaim to the world that they have granted a free and absolute power to the Christians, and to all others, of following the religion which each individual thinks proper to prefer, to which he has addicted his mind, and which he may deem the best adapted to his own use. They carefully explain every ambiguous word, remove every exception, and exact from the governors of the provinces a strict obedience to the true and simple meaning of an edict which was designed to establish and secure, without any limitation, the claims of religious liberty. They condescend to assign two weighty reasons which have induced them to allow this universal toleration: the humane intention of consulting the peace and happiness of their people; and the pious hope that by such a conduct they shall appease and propitiate *the Deity*, whose seat is in heaven. They gratefully acknowledge the many signal proofs which they have received of the divine favour; and they trust that the same Providence will for ever continue to protect the prosperity of the prince and people. From these vague and indefinite expressions

---

[1] Cæcilius (de Mort. Persecut. c. 48) has preserved the Latin original; and Eusebius (Hist. Eccles. l. x. c. 5) has given a Greek translation of this perpetual edict, which refers to some provisional regulations.

[The issue of the edict of Milan is now regarded as, to say the least of it, a very improbable occurrence. Cf. Seeck, *Zeitschrift für Kirchengeschichte*, 12, p. 181.—O. S.]

of piety three suppositions may be deduced, of a different, but not of an incompatible nature. The mind of Constantine might fluctuate between the Pagan and the Christian religions. According to the loose and complying notions of Polytheism, he might acknowledge the God of the Christians as *one* of the *many* deities who compose the hierarchy of heaven. Or perhaps he might embrace the philosophic and pleasing idea that, notwithstanding the variety of names, of rites, and of opinions, all the sects and all the nations of mankind are united in the worship of the common Father and Creator of the universe.[1]

But the counsels of princes are more frequently influenced by views of temporal advantage than by considerations of abstract and speculative truth. The partial and increasing favour of Constantine may naturally be referred to the esteem which he entertained for the moral character of the Christians, and to a persuasion that the propagation of the Gospel would inculcate the practice of private and public virtue. Whatever latitude an absolute monarch may assume in his own conduct, whatever indulgence he may claim for his own passions, it is undoubtedly his interest that all his subjects should respect the natural and civil obligations of society. But the operation of the wisest laws is imperfect and precarious. They seldom inspire virtue, they cannot always restrain vice. Their power is insufficient to prohibit all that they condemn, nor can they always punish the actions which they prohibit. The legislators of antiquity had summoned to their aid the powers of education and of opinion. But every principle which had once maintained the vigour and purity of Rome and Sparta was long since extinguished in a declining and despotic empire. Philosophy still exercised her temperate sway over the human mind, but the cause of virtue derived very feeble support from the influence of the Pagan superstition. Under these discouraging circumstances a prudent magistrate might observe with pleasure the progress of a religion which diffused among the people a pure, benevolent, and universal system of ethics, adapted to every duty and every condition of life, recommended as the will and reason of the supreme Deity, and enforced by the sanction of eternal rewards or punish-

---

[1] A panegyric of Constantine, pronounced seven or eight months after the edict of Milan (see Gothofred. Chronolog. Legum, p. 7; and Tillemont, Hist. des Empereurs, tom. iv. p. 246), uses the following remarkable expression:—" Summe rerum sator, cujus tot nomina sunt, quot linguas gentium esse voluisti, quem enim te ipse dici velis, scire non possumus." (Panegyr. Vet. ix. [viii.] 26.) In explaining Constantine's progress in the faith, Mosheim (p. 971, etc.) is ingenious, subtle, prolix.

ments. The experience of Greek and Roman history could not inform the world how far the system of national manners might be reformed and improved by the precepts of a divine revelation; and Constantine might listen with some confidence to the flattering, and indeed reasonable, assurances of Lactantius. The eloquent apologist seemed firmly to expect, and almost ventured to promise, *that* the establishment of Christianity would restore the innocence and felicity of the primitive age; *that* the worship of the true God would extinguish war and dissension among those who mutually considered themselves as the children of a common parent; *that* every impure desire, every angry or selfish passion, would be restrained by the knowledge of the Gospel; and *that* the magistrates might sheath the sword of justice among a people who should be universally actuated by the sentiments of truth and piety, of equity and moderation, of harmony and universal love.[1]

The passive and unresisting obedience which bows under the yoke of authority, or even of oppression, must have appeared in the eyes of an absolute monarch the most conspicuous and useful of the evangelic virtues.[2] The primitive Christians derived the institution of civil government, not from the consent of the people, but from the decrees of Heaven. The reigning emperor, though he had usurped the sceptre by treason and murder, immediately assumed the sacred character of vicegerent of the Deity. To the Deity alone he was accountable for the abuse of his power; and his subjects were indissolubly bound by their oath of fidelity to a tyrant who had violated every law of nature and society. The humble Christians were sent into the world as sheep among wolves; and since they were not permitted to employ force even in the defence of their religion, they should be still more criminal if they were tempted to shed the blood of their fellow-creatures in disputing the vain privileges or the sordid possessions of this transitory life. Faithful to the doctrine of the apostle, who in the reign of Nero had preached the duty of unconditional submission, the Christians of the three first centuries preserved their conscience pure and innocent of the guilt of secret conspiracy or open rebellion. While they experienced the rigour of persecution, they were never provoked either to meet their tyrants in the field, or indignantly to with-

[1] See the elegant description of Lactantius (Divin. Institut. v. 8), who is much more perspicuous and positive than becomes a discreet prophet.
[2] The political system of the Christians is explained by Grotius, de Jure Belli et Pacis, l. i. c. 3, 4. Grotius was a republican and an exile, but the mildness of his temper inclined him to support the established powers.

draw themselves into some remote and sequestered corner of the globe.[1] The protestants of France, of Germany, and of Britain, who asserted with such intrepid courage their civil and religious freedom, have been insulted by the invidious comparison between the conduct of the primitive and of the reformed Christians.[2] Perhaps, instead of censure, some applause may be due to the superior sense and spirit of our ancestors, who had convinced themselves that religion cannot abolish the unalienable rights of human nature.[3] Perhaps the patience of the primitive church may be ascribed to its weakness as well as to its virtue. A sect of unwarlike plebeians, without leaders, without arms, without fortifications, must have encountered inevitable destruction in a rash and fruitless resistance to the master of the Roman legions. But the Christians, when they deprecated the wrath of Diocletian, or solicited the favour of Constantine, could allege, with truth and confidence, that they held the principle of passive obedience, and that, in the space of three centuries, their conduct had always been conformable to their principles. They might add that the throne of the emperors would be established on a fixed and permanent basis if all their subjects, embracing the Christian doctrine, should learn to suffer and to obey.

In the general order of Providence princes and tyrants are considered as the ministers of Heaven, appointed to rule or to chastise the nations of the earth. But sacred history affords many illustrious examples of the more immediate interposition of the Deity in the government of his chosen people. The sceptre and the sword were committed to the hands of Moses, of Joshua, of Gideon, of David, of the Maccabees; the virtues of those heroes were the motive or the effect of the divine favour, the success of their arms was destined to achieve the deliverance or the triumph of the church. If the judges of Israel were occasional and temporary magistrates, the kings of Judah derived from the royal unction of their great ancestor an heredi-

---

[1] Tertullian, Apolog. c. 32, 34, 35, 36. Tamen nunquam Albiniani, nec Nigriani vel Cassiani inveniri potuerunt Christiani. Ad Scapulam, c. 2. If this assertion be strictly true, it excludes the Christians of that age from all civil and military employments, which would have compelled them to take an active part in the service of their respective governors. See Moyle's Works, vol. ii. p. 349.

[2] See the artful Bossuet (Hist. des Variations des Eglises Protestantes, tom. iii. p. 210-258), and the malicious Bayle (tom. ii. p. 620). I *name* Bayle, for he was certainly the author of the Avis aux Réfugiés; consult the Dictionnaire Critique de Chauffepié, tom. i. part ii. p. 145.

[3] Buchanan is the earliest, or at least the most celebrated, of the reformers, who has justified the theory of resistance. See his Dialogue de Jure Regni apud Scotos, tom. ii. p. 28, 30, edit. fol. Ruddiman.

tary and indefeasible right, which could not be forfeited by their
own vices, nor recalled by the caprice of their subjects. The
same extraordinary providence, which was no longer confined
to the Jewish people, might elect Constantine and his family
as the protectors of the Christian world; and the devout
Lactantius announces, in a prophetic tone, the future glories of
his long and universal reign.[1]   Galerius and Maximin, Maxentius
and Licinius, were the rivals who shared with the favourite of
Heaven the provinces of the empire. The tragic deaths of
Galerius and Maximin soon gratified the resentment, and fulfilled the sanguine expectations, of the Christians. The success
of Constantine against Maxentius and Licinius removed the two
formidable competitors who still opposed the triumph of the
second David, and his cause might seem to claim the peculiar
interposition of Providence. The character of the Roman
tyrant disgraced the purple and human nature; and though the
Christians might enjoy his precarious favour, they were exposed,
with the rest of his subjects, to the effects of his wanton and
capricious cruelty. The conduct of Licinius soon betrayed the
reluctance with which he had consented to the wise and humane
regulations of the edict of Milan. The convocation of provincial
synods was prohibited in his dominions; his Christian officers
were ignominiously dismissed; and if he avoided the guilt, or
rather danger, of a general persecution, his partial oppressions
were rendered still more odious by the violation of a solemn and
voluntary engagement.[2]   While the East, according to the lively
expression of Eusebius, was involved in the shades of infernal
darkness, the auspicious rays of celestial light warmed and illuminated the provinces of the West. The piety of Constantine
was admitted as an unexceptionable proof of the justice of his
arms; and his use of victory confirmed the opinion of the
Christians, that their hero was inspired and conducted by the
Lord of Hosts. The conquest of Italy produced a general edict
of toleration; and as soon as the defeat of Licinius had invested
Constantine with the sole dominion of the Roman world, he
immediately, by circular letters, exhorted all his subjects to

---

[1] Lactant. Divin. Institut. i. 1. Eusebius, in the course of his History,
his Life, and his Oration, repeatedly inculcates the divine right of Constantine to the empire.

[2] Our imperfect knowledge of the persecution of Licinius is derived from
Eusebius (Hist. Eccles. l. x. c. 8; Vit. Constantin. l. i. c. 49-56, l. ii. c. 1, 2),
Aurelius Victor mentions his cruelty in general terms.

[The persecution of Licinius was not by any means severe. Certain
bishops were killed, but few if any of the rank and file of Christian adherents.
(Cf. Görres, *Die Licinianische Christenverfolgung*, pp. 32-40.—O. S.]

imitate, without delay, the example of their sovereign, and to embrace the divine truth of Christianity.[1]

The assurance that the elevation of Constantine was intimately connected with the designs of Providence instilled into the minds of the Christians two opinions, which, by very different means, assisted the accomplishment of the prophecy. Their warm and active loyalty exhausted in his favour every resource of human industry; and they confidently expected that their strenuous efforts would be seconded by some divine and miraculous aid. The enemies of Constantine have imputed to interested motives the alliance which he insensibly contracted with the catholic church, and which apparently contributed to the success of his ambition. In the beginning of the fourth century the Christians still bore a very inadequate proportion to the inhabitants of the empire; but among a degenerate people, who viewed the change of masters with the indifference of slaves, the spirit and union of a religious party might assist the popular leader, to whose service, from a principle of conscience, they had devoted their lives and fortunes.[2] The example of his father had instructed Constantine to esteem and to reward the merit of the Christians; and in the distribution of public offices he had the advantage of strengthening his government by the choice of ministers or generals in whose fidelity he could repose a just and unreserved confidence. By the influence of these dignified missionaries the proselytes of the new faith must have multiplied in the court and army; the barbarians of Germany, who filled the ranks of the legions, were of a careless temper, which acquiesced without resistance in the religion of their commander; and when they passed the Alps it may fairly be presumed that a great number of the soldiers had already consecrated their swords to the service of Christ and of Constantine.[3] The habits of mankind and the interest of religion gradually abated the horror of war and bloodshed which had so long prevailed among the Christians; and in

[1] Euseb. in Vit. Constant. l. ii. c. 24-42, 48-60.

[2] In the beginning of the last century the papists of England were only a *thirtieth*, and the protestants of France only a *fifteenth*, part of the respective nations to whom their spirit and power were a constant object of apprehension. See the relations which Bentivoglio (who was then nuncio at Brussels, and afterwards cardinal) transmitted to the court of Rome (Relazione, tom. ii. p. 211, 241). Bentivoglio was curious, well-informed, but somewhat partial.

[3] This careless temper of the Germans appears almost uniformly in the history of the conversion of each of the tribes. The legions of Constantine were recruited with Germans (Zosimus, l. ii. [c. 15] p. 86); and the court even of his father had been filled with Christians. See the first book of the Life of Constantine, by Eusebius.

the councils which were assembled under the gracious protection of Constantine the authority of the bishops was seasonably employed to ratify the obligation of the military oath, and to inflict the penalty of excommunication on those soldiers who threw away their arms during the peace of the church.[1] While Constantine in his own dominions increased the number and zeal of his faithful adherents, he could depend on the support of a powerful faction in those provinces which were still possessed or usurped by his rivals. A secret disaffection was diffused among the Christian subjects of Maxentius and Licinius; and the resentment which the latter did not attempt to conceal served only to engage them still more deeply in the interest of his competitor. The regular correspondence which connected the bishops of the most distant provinces enabled them freely to communicate their wishes and their designs, and to transmit without danger any useful intelligence, or any pious contributions, which might promote the service of Constantine, who publicly declared that he had taken up arms for the deliverance of the church.[2]

The enthusiasm which inspired the troops, and perhaps the emperor himself, had sharpened their swords while it satisfied their conscience. They marched to battle with the full assurance that the same God who had formerly opened a passage to the Israelites through the waters of Jordan, and had thrown down the walls of Jericho at the sound of the trumpets of Joshua, would display his visible majesty and power in the victory of Constantine. The evidence of ecclesiastical history is prepared to affirm that their expectations were justified by the conspicuous miracle to which the conversion of the first Christian emperor has been almost unanimously ascribed. The real or imaginary cause of so important an event deserves and demands the attention of posterity; and I shall endeavour to form a just estimate of the famous vision of Constantine, by a distinct consideration of the *standard*, the *dream*, and the *celestial sign ;* by separating the historical, the natural, and the marvellous parts

---

[1] De his qui arma projiciunt in *pace*, placuit eos abstinere a communione. Concil. Arelat. Canon iii.   The best critics apply these words to the *peace of the church.*

[2] Eusebius always considers the second civil war against Licinius as a sort of religious crusade.   At the invitation of the tyrant, some Christian officers had resumed their *zones ;* or, in other words, had returned to the military service.   Their conduct was afterwards censured by the twelfth canon of the Council of Nice; if this particular application may be received, instead of the loose and general sense of the Greek interpreters, Balsamon, Zonaras, and Alexis Aristenus.   See Beveridge, Pandect. Eccles. Græc. tom. i. p. 72, tom. ii. p. 78.   Annotation.

of this extraordinary story, which, in the composition of a specious argument, have been artfully confounded in one splendid and brittle mass.

I. An instrument of the tortures which were inflicted only on slaves and strangers became an object of horror in the eyes of a Roman citizen; and the ideas of guilt, of pain, and of ignominy, were closely united with the idea of the cross.[1] The piety, rather than the humanity, of Constantine soon abolished in his dominions the punishment which the Saviour of mankind had condescended to suffer;[2] but the emperor had already learned to despise the prejudices of his education and of his people, before he could erect in the midst of Rome his own statue, bearing a cross in its right hand, with an inscription which referred the victory of his arms, and the deliverance of Rome, to the virtue of that salutary sign, the true symbol of force and courage.[3] The same symbol sanctified the arms of the soldiers of Constantine; the cross glittered on their helmet, was engraved on their shields, was interwoven into their banners; and the consecrated emblems which adorned the person of the emperor himself were distinguished only by richer materials and more exquisite workmanship.[4] But the principal standard which displayed the

---

[1] Nomen ipsum *crucis* absit non modo a corpore civium Romanorum, sed etiam a cogitatione, oculis, auribus. Cicero pro Rabirio, c. 5. The Christian writers, Justin, Minucius Felix, Tertullian, Jerom, and Maximus of Turin, have investigated with tolerable success the figure or likeness of a cross in almost every object of nature or art; in the intersection of the meridian and equator, the human face, a bird flying, a man swimming, a mast and yard, a plough, a *standard*, etc., etc., etc. See Lipsius de Cruce, l. i. c. 9.

[2] See Aurelius Victor [de Cæsar. c. 41], who considers this law as one of the examples of Constantine's piety. An edict so honourable to Christianity deserved a place in the Theodosian Code, instead of the indirect mention of it which seems to result from the comparison of the fifth and eighteenth titles of the ninth book.

[3] Eusebius, in Vit. Constantin. l. i. c. 40. This statue, or at least the cross and inscription, may be ascribed with more probability to the second, or even the third, visit of Constantine to Rome. Immediately after the defeat of Maxentius, the minds of the senate and people were scarcely ripe for this public monument.

[4] Agnoscas, regina, libens mea signa necesse est;
  In quibus effigies *crucis* aut gemmata refulget
  Aut longis solido ex auro præfertur in hastis.
  Hoc signo invictus, transmissis Alpibus ultor
  Servitium solvit miserabile Constantinus.
  .   .   .   .
  Christus *purpureum* gemmanti textus in auro
  Signabat *Labarum*, clipeorum insignia Christus
  Scripserat; ardebat summis *crux* addita cristis.
  Prudent. in Symmachum, l. i. 464, 486.

triumph of the cross was styled the *Labarum*,[1] an obscure, though celebrated, name, which has been vainly derived from almost all the languages of the world. It is described [2] as a long pike intersected by a transversal beam. The silken veil which hung down from the beam was curiously inwrought with the images of the reigning monarch and his children. The summit of the pike supported a crown of gold, which enclosed the mysterious monogram, at once expressive of the figure of the cross and the initial letters of the name of Christ.[3] The safety of the labarum was intrusted to fifty guards of approved valour and fidelity; their station was marked by honours and emoluments; and some fortunate accidents soon introduced an opinion that as long as the guards of the labarum were engaged in the execution of their office they were secure and invulnerable amidst the darts of the enemy. In the second civil war Licinius felt and dreaded the power of this consecrated banner, the sight of which in the distress of battle animated the soldiers of Constantine with an invincible enthusiasm, and scattered terror and dismay through the ranks of the adverse legions.[4] The Christian emperors, who respected the example of Constantine, displayed in all their military expeditions the standard of the cross; but when the degenerate successors of Theodosius had ceased to appear in person at the head of their armies, the labarum was deposited as a venerable but useless relic in the palace of Constantinople.[5] Its honours are still preserved on the medals of

[1] The derivation and meaning of the word *Labarum* or *Laborum*, which is employed by Gregory Nazianzen, Ambrose, Prudentius, etc., still remain totally unknown, in spite of the efforts of the critics, who have ineffectually tortured the Latin, Greek, Spanish, Celtic, Teutonic, Illyric, Armenian, etc., in search of an etymology. See Ducange, in Gloss. Med. and infim. Latinitat. sub voce *Labarum*, and Godefroy, ad Cod. Theodos. tom ii. p. 143.

[2] Euseb. in Vit. Constantin. l. i. c. 30, 31. Baronius (Annal. Eccles. A.D. 312, No. 26) has engraved a representation of the Labarum.

[3] Transversâ X literâ, summo capite circumflexo, Christum in scutis notat. Cæcilius de M. P. c. 44. Cuper (ad M. P. in edit. Lactant. tom. ii. p. 500) and Baronius (A.D. 312, No. 25) have engraved from ancient monuments several specimens—as thus, ☧ or ☧ —of these monograms, which became extremely fashionable in the Christian world.

[4] Euseb. in Vit. Constantin. l. ii. c. 7, 8, 9. He introduces the Labarum before the Italian expedition; but his narrative seems to indicate that it was never shown at the head of an army, till Constantine, above ten years afterwards, declared himself the enemy of Licinius and the deliverer of the church.

[5] See Cod. Theod. l. vi. tit. xxv. Sozomen, l. i. c. 2 [c. 4]. Theophan. Chronograph. p. 11. Theophanes lived towards the end of the eighth century, almost five hundred years after Constantine. The modern Greeks were not inclined to display in the field the standard of the empire

the Flavian family. Their grateful devotion has placed the monogram of Christ in the midst of the ensigns of Rome. The solemn epithets of safety of the republic, glory of the army, restoration of public happiness, are equally applied to the religious and military trophies; and there is still extant a medal of the emperor Constantius, where the standard of the labarum is accompanied with these memorable words, BY THIS SIGN THOU SHALT CONQUER.[1]

II. In all occasions of danger or distress it was the practice of the primitive Christians to fortify their minds and bodies by the sign of the cross, which they used in all their ecclesiastical rites, in all the daily occurrences of life, as an infallible preservative against every species of spiritual or temporal evil.[2] The authority of the church might alone have had sufficient weight to justify the devotion of Constantine, who, in the same prudent and gradual progress, acknowledged the truth and assumed the symbol of Christianity. But the testimony of a contemporary writer, who in a formal treatise has avenged the cause of religion, bestows on the piety of the emperor a more awful and sublime character. He affirms, with the most perfect confidence, that, in the night which preceded the last battle against Maxentius, Constantine was admonished in a dream to inscribe the shields of his soldiers with the *celestial sign of God*, the sacred monogram of the name of Christ; that he executed the commands of Heaven, and that his valour and obedience were rewarded by the decisive victory of the Milvian Bridge. Some considerations might perhaps incline a sceptical mind to suspect the judgment or the veracity of the rhetorician, whose pen, either from zeal or interest, was devoted to the cause of the prevailing faction.[3]

and of Christianity; and though they depended on every superstitious hope of *defence*, the promise of *victory* would have appeared too bold a fiction.

[1] The Abbé du Voisin, p. 103, etc., alleges several of these medals, and quotes a particular dissertation of a Jesuit, the Père de Grainville, on this subject.

[2] Tertullian, de Coronâ, c. 3. Athanasius, tom. i. p. 101 [p. 89, ed. Bened. 1698; de Incarn. Verbi Dei, c. 48]. The learned Jesuit Petavius (Dogmata Theolog. l. xv. c. 9, 10) has collected many similar passages on the virtues of the cross, which in the last age embarrassed our protestant disputants.

[3] Cæcilius, de M. P. c. 44. It is certain that this historical declamation was composed and published while Licinius, sovereign of the East, still preserved the friendship of Constantine and of the Christians. Every reader of taste must perceive that the style is of a very different and inferior character to that of Lactantius; and such indeed is the judgment of Le Clerc and Lardner (Bibliothèque Ancienne et Moderne, tom. iii. p. 438; Credibility of the Gospel, etc., part ii. vol. vii. p. 94). Three arguments from the title of the book, and from the names of Donatus and

He appears to have published his Deaths of the Persecutors at Nicomedia about three years after the Roman victory; but the interval of a thousand miles, and a thousand days, will allow an ample latitude for the invention of declaimers, the credulity of party, and the tacit approbation of the emperor himself; who might listen without indignation to a marvellous tale which exalted his fame and promoted his designs. In favour of Licinius, who still dissembled his animosity to the Christians, the same author has provided a similar vision, of a form of prayer, which was communicated by an angel, and repeated by the whole army before they engaged the legions of the tyrant Maximin.[1] The frequent repetition of miracles serves to provoke, where it does not subdue, the reason of mankind; but if the dream of Constantine is separately considered, it may be naturally explained either by the policy or the enthusiasm of the emperor. Whilst his anxiety for the approaching day, which must decide the fate of the empire, was suspended by a short and interrupted slumber, the venerable form of Christ, and the well-known symbol of his religion, might forcibly offer themselves to the active fancy of a prince who reverenced the name, and had perhaps secretly implored the power, of the God of the Christians. As readily might a consummate statesman indulge himself in the use of one of those military stratagems, one of those pious frauds, which Philip and Sertorius had employed with such art and effect.[2] The præternatural origin of dreams was universally admitted by the nations of antiquity, and a considerable part of the Gallic army was already prepared to place their confidence in the salutary sign of the Christian religion. The secret vision

Cæcilius, are produced by the advocates for Lactantius (see the P. Lestocq, tom. ii. p. 46-60). Each of these proofs is singly weak and defective; but their concurrence has great weight. I have often fluctuated, and shall *tamely* follow the Colbert MS. in calling the author (whoever he was) Cæcilius.

[1] Cæcilius, de M. P. c. 46. There seems to be some reason in the observation of M. de Voltaire (Œuvres, tom. xiv. p. 307), who ascribes to the success of Constantine the superior fame of his Labarum above the angel of Licinius. Yet even this angel is favourably entertained by Pagi, Tillemont, Fleury, etc., who are fond of increasing their stock of miracles.

[2] Besides these well-known examples, Tollius (Preface to Boileau's translation of Longinus) has discovered a vision of Antigonus, who assured his troops that he had seen a pentagon (the symbol of safety) with these words, " In this conquer." But Tollius has most inexcusably omitted to produce his authority; and his own character, literary as well as moral, is not free from reproach (see Chauffepié, Dictionnaire Critique, tom. iv. p. 460). Without insisting on the silence of Diodorus, Plutarch, Justin, etc., it may be observed that Polyænus, who in a separate chapter (l. iv. c. 6) has collected nineteen military stratagems of Antigonus, is totally ignorant of this remarkable vision.

of Constantine could be disproved only by the event; and the intrepid hero who had passed the Alps and the Apennine might view with careless despair the consequences of a defeat under the walls of Rome. The senate and people, exulting in their own deliverance from an odious tyrant, acknowledged that the victory of Constantine surpassed the powers of man, without daring to insinuate that it had been obtained by the protection of the *gods*. The triumphal arch, which was erected about three years after the event, proclaims, in ambiguous language, that, by the greatness of his own mind, and by an *instinct* or impulse of the Divinity, he had saved and avenged the Roman republic.[1] The Pagan orator, who had seized an earlier opportunity of celebrating the virtues of the conqueror, supposes that he alone enjoyed a secret and intimate commerce with the Supreme Being, who delegated the care of mortals to his subordinate deities; and thus assigns a very plausible reason why the subjects of Constantine should not presume to embrace the new religion of their sovereign.[2]

III. The philosopher, who with calm suspicion examines the dreams and omens, the miracles and prodigies, of profane or even of ecclesiastical history, will probably conclude that, if the eyes of the spectators have sometimes been deceived by fraud, the understanding of the readers has much more frequently been insulted by fiction. Every event, or appearance, or accident, which seems to deviate from the ordinary course of nature, has been rashly ascribed to the immediate action of the Deity; and the astonished fancy of the multitude has sometimes given shape and colour, language and motion, to the fleeting but uncommon meteors of the air.[3] Nazarius and Eusebius are the two most celebrated orators who, in studied panegyrics, have laboured to exalt the glory of Constantine. Nine years after the Roman victory Nazarius [4] describes an army of divine warriors,

---

[1] Instinctu Divinitatis, mentis magnitudine. The inscription on the triumphal arch of Constantine, which has been copied by Baronius, Gruter, etc., may still be perused by every curious traveller.

[2] Habes profecto aliquid cum illâ mente Divinâ secretum; quæ delegatâ nostrâ Diis Minoribus curâ uni se tibi dignatur ostendere. Panegyr. Vet. ix. [viii.] 2.

[3] M. Freret (Mémoires de l'Académie des Inscriptions, tom. iv. p. 411-437) explains, by physical causes, many of the prodigies of antiquity; and Fabricius, who is abused by both parties, vainly tries to introduce the celestial cross of Constantine among the solar halos. Bibliothec. Græc. tom. vi. p. 8-29.

[4] Nazarius inter Panegyr. Vet. x. [ix.] 14, 15. It is unnecessary to name the moderns, whose undistinguishing and ravenous appetite has swallowed even the Pagan bait of Nazarius.

who seemed to fall from the sky; he marks their beauty, their spirit, their gigantic forms, the stream of light which beamed from their celestial armour, their patience in suffering themselves to be heard, as well as seen, by mortals; and their declaration that they were sent, that they flew, to the assistance of the great Constantine. For the truth of this prodigy the Pagan orator appeals to the whole Gallic nation, in whose presence he was then speaking; and seems to hope that the ancient apparitions[1] would now obtain credit from this recent and public event. The Christian fable of Eusebius, which, in the space of twenty-six years, might arise from the original dream, is cast in a much more correct and elegant mould. In one of the marches of Constantine he is reported to have seen with his own eyes the luminous trophy of the cross, placed above the meridian sun, and inscribed with the following words: BY THIS CONQUER. This amazing object in the sky astonished the whole army, as well as the emperor himself, who was yet undetermined in the choice of a religion: but his astonishment was converted into faith by the vision of the ensuing night. Christ appeared before his eyes; and displaying the same celestial sign of the cross, he directed Constantine to frame a similar standard, and to march, with an assurance of victory, against Maxentius and all his enemies.[2] The learned bishop of Cæsarea appears to be sensible that the recent discovery of this marvellous anecdote would excite some surprise and distrust among the most pious of his readers. Yet, instead of ascertaining the precise circumstances of time and place, which always serve to detect falsehood or establish truth;[3] instead of collecting and recording the evidence of so many living witnesses, who must have been spectators of this stupendous miracle,[4] Eusebius contents himself with alleging a very singular testimony, that of the deceased Constantine, who, many years after the event, in the freedom of conversation, had

[1] The apparitions of Castor and Pollux, particularly to announce the Macedonian victory, are attested by historians and public monuments. See Cicero de Naturâ Deorum, ii. 2, iii. 5, 6. Florus, ii. 12. Valerius Maximus, l. i. c. 8, No. 1. Yet the most recent of these miracles is omitted, and indirectly denied, by Livy (xlv. 1).

[2] Eusebius [Vit. Constant.], l. i. c. 28, 29, 30. The silence of the same Eusebius, in his Ecclesiastical History, is deeply felt by those advocates for the miracle who are not absolutely callous.

[3] The narrative of Constantine seems to indicate that he saw the cross in the sky before he passed the Alps against Maxentius. The scene has been fixed by provincial vanity at Treves, Besançon, etc. See Tillemont, Hist. des Empereurs, tom. iv. p. 573.

[4] The pious Tillemont (Mém. Ecclés. tom. vii. p. 1317) rejects with a sigh the useful Acts of Artemius, a veteran and a martyr, who attests as an eye-witness the vision of Constantine.

related to him this extraordinary incident of his own life, and had attested the truth of it by a solemn oath. The prudence and gratitude of the learned prelate forbade him to suspect the veracity of his victorious master; but he plainly intimates that, in a fact of such a nature, he should have refused his assent to any meaner authority. This motive of credibility could not survive the power of the Flavian family; and the celestial sign, which the Infidels might afterwards deride,[1] was disregarded by the Christians of the age which immediately followed the conversion of Constantine.[2] But the catholic church, both of the East and of the West, has adopted a prodigy which favours, or seems to favour, the popular worship of the cross. The vision of Constantine maintained an honourable place in the legend of superstition till the bold and sagacious spirit of criticism presumed to depreciate the triumph, and to arraign the truth, of the first Christian emperor.[3]

The protestant and philosophic readers of the present age will incline to believe that, in the account of his own conversion, Constantine attested a wilful falsehood by a solemn and deliberate perjury. They may not hesitate to pronounce that, in the choice of a religion, his mind was determined only by a sense of interest; and that (according to the expression of a profane poet [4]) he used the altars of the church as a convenient footstool

[1] Gelasius Cyzic. in Act. Concil. Nicen. l. i. c. 4.

[2] The advocates for the vision are unable to produce a single testimony from the Fathers of the fourth and fifth centuries, who in their voluminous writings repeatedly celebrate the triumph of the church and of Constantine. As these venerable men had not any dislike to a miracle, we may suspect (and the suspicion is confirmed by the ignorance of Jerom) that they were all unacquainted with the Life of Constantine by Eusebius. This tract was recovered by the diligence of those who translated or continued his Ecclesiastical History, and who have represented in various colours the vision of the cross.

[3] Godefroy was the first who, in the year 1643 (Not. ad Philostorgium, l. i. c. 6, p. 16), expressed any doubt of a miracle which had been supported with equal zeal by Cardinal Baronius and the Centuriators of Magdeburg. Since that time many of the protestant critics have inclined towards doubt and disbelief. The objections are urged with great force by M. Chauffepié (Dictionnaire Critique, tom. iv. p. 6-11); and in the year 1774 a doctor of Sorbonne, the Abbé du Voisin, published an apology, which deserves the praise of learning and moderation.

[4] Lors Constantin dit ces propres paroles:
J'ai renversé le culte des idoles:
Sur les débris de leurs temples fumans
Au Dieu du Ciel j'ai prodigué l'encens.
Mais tous mes soins pour sa grandeur suprême
N'eurent jamais d'autre objet que moi-même;
Les saints autels n'étoient à mes regards
Qu'un marchepié du trône des Césars.
L'ambition, la fureur, les délices

to the throne of the empire. A conclusion so harsh and so absolute is not, however, warranted by our knowledge of human nature, of Constantine, or of Christianity. In an age of religious fervour the most artful statesmen are observed to feel some part of the enthusiasm which they inspire; and the most orthodox saints assume the dangerous privilege of defending the cause of truth by the arms of deceit and falsehood. Personal interest is often the standard of our belief, as well as of our practice; and the same motives of temporal advantage which might influence the public conduct and professions of Constantine would insensibly dispose his mind to embrace a religion so propitious to his fame and fortunes. His vanity was gratified by the flattering assurance that *he* had been chosen by Heaven to reign over the earth: success had justified his divine title to the throne, and that title was founded on the truth of the Christian revelation. As real virtue is sometimes excited by undeserved applause, the specious piety of Constantine, if at first it was only specious, might gradually, by the influence of praise, of habit, and of example, be matured into serious faith and fervent devotion. The bishops and teachers of the new sect, whose dress and manners had not qualified them for the residence of a court, were admitted to the Imperial table; they accompanied the monarch in his expeditions; and the ascendant which one of them, an Egyptian or a Spaniard,[1] acquired over his mind was imputed by the Pagans to the effect of magic.[2] Lactantius, who has adorned the precepts of the Gospel with the eloquence of Cicero,[3] and Eusebius, who has consecrated the learning and philosophy of the Greeks to the service of religion,[4] were both

---

> Etoient mes dieux, avoient mes sacrifices.
> L'or des Chrétiens, leurs intrigues, leur sang
> Ont cimenté ma fortune et mon rang.

The poem which contains these lines may be read with pleasure, but cannot be named with decency.

[1] This favourite was probably the great Osius, bishop of Cordova, who preferred the pastoral care of the whole church to the government of a particular diocese. His character is magnificently though concisely expressed by Athanasius (tom. i. p. 703 [tom. ii. p. 535, ed. Bened. 1777]). See Tillemont, Mém. Ecclés. tom. vii. p. 524-561. Osius was accused, perhaps unjustly, of retiring from court with a very ample fortune.

[2] See Eusebius (in Vit. Constant. passim), and Zosimus, l. ii. [c. 29] p. 104.

[3] The Christianity of Lactantius was of a moral rather than of a mysterious cast. "Erat pæne rudis (says the orthodox Bull) disciplinæ Christianæ, et in rhetoricâ melius quam in theologiâ versatus." Defensio Fidei Nicenæ, sect. ii. c. 14.

[4] Fabricius, with his usual diligence, has collected a list of between three and four hundred authors quoted in the Evangelical Preparation of Eusebius. See Bibl. Græc. l. v. c. 4, tom. vi. p. 37-56.

received into the friendship and familiarity of their sovereign; and those able masters of controversy could patiently watch the soft and yielding moments of persuasion, and dexterously apply the arguments which were the best adapted to his character and understanding. Whatever advantages might be derived from the acquisition of an Imperial proselyte, he was distinguished by the splendour of his purple, rather than by the superiority of wisdom or virtue, from the many thousands of his subjects who had embraced the doctrines of Christianity. Nor can it be deemed incredible that the mind of an unlettered soldier should have yielded to the weight of evidence which, in a more enlightened age, has satisfied or subdued the reason of a Grotius, a Pascal, or a Locke. In the midst of the incessant labours of his great office this soldier employed, or affected to employ, the hours of the night in the diligent study of the Scriptures, and the composition of theological discourses, which he afterwards pronounced in the presence of a numerous and applauding audience. In a very long discourse, which is still extant, the royal preacher expatiates on the various proofs of religion; but he dwells with peculiar complacency on the Sibylline verses,[1] and the fourth eclogue of Virgil.[2] Forty years before the birth of Christ, the Mantuan bard, as if inspired by the celestial muse of Isaiah, had celebrated, with all the pomp of oriental metaphor, the return of the Virgin, the fall of the serpent, the approaching birth of a godlike child, the offspring of the great Jupiter, who should expiate the guilt of human kind and govern the peaceful universe with the virtues of his father; the rise and appearance of an heavenly race, a primitive nation throughout the world; and the gradual restoration of the innocence and felicity of the golden age. The poet was perhaps unconscious of the secret sense and object of these sublime predictions, which have been so unworthily applied to the infant son of a consul, or a triumvir:[3] but if a more splendid, and indeed specious, interpretation of the fourth eclogue contributed to the conversion

---

[1] See Constantin. Orat. ad Sanctos, c. 19, 20. He chiefly depends on a mysterious acrostic, composed in the sixth age after the Deluge by the Erythræan Sibyl, and translated by Cicero into Latin. The initial letters of the thirty-four Greek verses form this prophetic sentence:—JESUS CHRIST, SON OF GOD, SAVIOUR OF THE WORLD.

[2] In his paraphrase of Virgil the emperor has frequently assisted and improved the literal sense of the Latin text. See Blondel, des Sibylles, l. i. c. 14, 15, 16.

[3] The different claims of an elder and younger son of Pollio, of Julia, of Drusus, of Marcellus, are found to be incompatible with chronology, history, and the good sense of Virgil.

of the first Christian emperor, Virgil may deserve to be ranked among the most successful missionaries of the Gospel.[1]

The awful mysteries of the Christian faith and worship were concealed from the eyes of strangers, and even of catechumens, with an affected secrecy, which served to excite their wonder and curiosity.[2] But the severe rules of discipline which the prudence of the bishops had instituted were relaxed by the same prudence in favour of an Imperial proselyte, whom it was so important to allure, by every gentle condescension, into the pale of the church; and Constantine was permitted, at least by a tacit dispensation, to enjoy *most* of the privileges, before he had contracted *any* of the obligations, of a Christian. Instead of retiring from the congregation when the voice of the deacon dismissed the profane multitude, he prayed with the faithful, disputed with the bishops, preached on the most sublime and intricate subjects of theology, celebrated with sacred rites the vigil of Easter, and publicly declared himself, not only a partaker, but, in some measure, a priest and hierophant of the Christian mysteries.[3] The pride of Constantine might assume, and his services had deserved, some extraordinary distinction; an ill-timed rigour might have blasted the unripened fruits of his conversion; and if the doors of the church had been strictly closed against a prince who had deserted the altars of the gods, the master of the empire would have been left destitute of any form of religious worship. In his last visit to Rome he piously disclaimed and insulted the superstition of his ancestors, by refusing to lead the military procession of the equestrian order, and to offer the public vows to the Jupiter of the Capitoline Hill.[4] Many years before his baptism and death Constantine had proclaimed to the world that neither his person nor his image should evermore be seen within the walls of an idolatrous temple; while he distributed through the provinces a variety of medals

[1] See Lowth, de Sacrâ Poesi Hebræorum Prælect. xxi. p. 289-293. In the examination of the fourth eclogue, the respectable bishop of London has displayed learning, taste, ingenuity, and a temperate enthusiasm, which exalts his fancy without degrading his judgment.

[2] The distinction between the public and the secret parts of divine service, the *missa catechumenorum* and the *missa fidelium*, and the mysterious veil which piety or policy had cast over the latter, are very judiciously explained by Thiers, Exposition du Saint Sacrement, l. i. c. 8-12, p. 59-91; but as on this subject the papists may reasonably be suspected, a Protestant reader will depend with more confidence on the learned Bingham, Antiquities, l. x. c. 5.

[3] See Eusebius in Vit. Const. l. iv. c. 15-32, and the whole tenor of Constantine's sermon. The faith and devotion of the emperor has furnished Baronius with a specious argument in favour of his early baptism.

[4] Zosimus, l. ii. [c. 29] p. 105.

and pictures which represented the emperor in an humble and suppliant posture of Christian devotion.[1]

The pride of Constantine, who refused the privileges of a catechumen, cannot easily be explained or excused; but the delay of his baptism may be justified by the maxims and the practice of ecclesiastical antiquity. The sacrament of baptism [2] was regularly administered by the bishop himself, with his assistant clergy, in the cathedral church of the diocese, during the fifty days between the solemn festivals of Easter and Pentecost; and this holy term admitted a numerous band of infants and adult persons into the bosom of the church. The discretion of parents often suspended the baptism of their children till they could understand the obligations which they contracted: the severity of ancient bishops exacted from the new converts a novitiate of two or three years; and the catechumens themselves, from different motives of a temporal or a spiritual nature, were seldom impatient to assume the character of perfect and initiated Christians. The sacrament of baptism was supposed to contain a full and absolute expiation of sin; and the soul was instantly restored to its original purity, and entitled to the promise of eternal salvation. Among the proselytes of Christianity there were many who judged it imprudent to precipitate a salutary rite which could not be repeated; to throw away an inestimable privilege which could never be recovered. By the delay of their baptism they could venture freely to indulge their passions in the enjoyment of this world, while they still retained in their own hands the means of a sure and easy absolution.[3]

[1] Eusebius in Vit. Constant. l. iv. c. 15, 16.

[2] The theory and practice of antiquity, with regard to the sacrament of baptism, have been copiously explained by Dom Chardon, Hist. des Sacremens, tom. i. p. 3-405; Dom Martenne, de Ritibus Ecclesiæ Antiquis, tom. i.; and by Bingham, in the tenth and eleventh books of his Christian Antiquities. One circumstance may be observed in which the modern churches have materially departed from the ancient custom. The sacrament of baptism (even when it was administered to infants) was immediately followed by confirmation and the holy communion.

[3] The Fathers, who censured this criminal delay, could not deny the certain and victorious efficacy even of a death-bed baptism. The ingenious rhetoric of the Chrysostom could find only three arguments against these prudent Christians. 1. That we should love and pursue virtue for her own sake, and not merely for the reward. 2. That we may be surprised by death without an opportunity of baptism. 3. That, although we shall be placed in heaven, we shall only twinkle like little stars, when compared to the suns of righteousness who have run their appointed course with labour, with success, and with glory. Chrysostom, in Epist. ad Hebræos, Homil. xiii. apud Chardon, Hist. des Sacremens, tom. i. p. 49. I believe that this delay of baptism, though attended with the most pernicious consequences, was never condemned by any general or provincial council, or by any public act or declaration of the church. The zeal of the bishops was easily kindled on much slighter occasions.

The sublime theory of the Gospel had made a much fainter impression on the heart than on the understanding of Constantine himself. He pursued the great object of his ambition through the dark and bloody paths of war and policy; and, after the victory, he abandoned himself, without moderation, to the abuse of his fortune. Instead of asserting his just superiority above the imperfect heroism and profane philosophy of Trajan and the Antonines, the mature age of Constantine forfeited the reputation which he had acquired in his youth. As he gradually advanced in the knowledge of truth, he proportionably declined in the practice of virtue; and the same year of his reign in which he convened the council of Nice was polluted by the execution, or rather murder, of his eldest son. This date is alone sufficient to refute the ignorant and malicious suggestions of Zosimus,[1] who affirms that, after the death of Crispus, the remorse of his father accepted from the ministers of Christianity the expiation which he had vainly solicited from the Pagan pontiffs. At the time of the death of Crispus the emperor could no longer hesitate in the choice of a religion; he could no longer be ignorant that the church was possessed of an infallible remedy, though he chose to defer the application of it till the approach of death had removed the temptation and danger of a relapse. The bishops whom he summoned in his last illness to the palace of Nicomedia were edified by the fervour with which he requested and received the sacrament of baptism, by the solemn protestation that the remainder of his life should be worthy of a disciple of Christ, and by his humble refusal to wear the Imperial purple after he had been clothed in the white garment of a Neophyte. The example and reputation of Constantine seemed to countenance the delay of baptism.[2] Future tyrants were encouraged to believe that the innocent blood which they might shed in a long reign would instantly be washed away in the waters of regeneration; and the abuse of religion dangerously undermined the foundations of moral virtue.

The gratitude of the church has exalted the virtues and excused the failings of a generous patron, who seated Christianity on the throne of the Roman world; and the Greeks, who celebrate the festival of the Imperial saint, seldom mention the

---

[1] Zosimus, l. ii. [c. 29] p. 104. For this disingenuous falsehood he has deserved and experienced the harshest treatment from all the ecclesiastical writers, except Cardinal Baronius (A.D. 324, No. 15-28), who had occasion to employ the infidel on a particular service against the Arian Eusebius.

[2] Eusebius [Vit. Constant.], l. iv. c. 61, 62, 63. The bishop of Cæsarea supposes the salvation of Constantine with the most perfect confidence.

name of Constantine without adding the title of *equal to the Apostles*.[1] Such a comparison, if it alludes to the character of those divine missionaries, must be imputed to the extravagance of impious flattery. But if the parallel is confined to the extent and number of their evangelic victories, the success of Constantine might perhaps equal that of the Apostles themselves. By the edicts of toleration he removed the temporal disadvantages which had hitherto retarded the progress of Christianity; and its active and numerous ministers received a free permission, a liberal encouragement, to recommend the salutary truths of revelation by every argument which could affect the reason or piety of mankind. The exact balance of the two religions continued but a moment; and the piercing eye of ambition and avarice soon discovered that the profession of Christianity might contribute to the interest of the present, as well as of a future life.[2] The hopes of wealth and honours, the example of an emperor, his exhortations, his irresistible smiles, diffused conviction among the venal and obsequious crowds which usually fill the apartments of a palace. The cities which signalised a forward zeal by the voluntary destruction of their temples were distinguished by municipal privileges and rewarded with popular donatives; and the new capital of the East gloried in the singular advantage that Constantinople was never profaned by the worship of idols.[3] As the lower ranks of society are governed by imitation, the conversion of those who possessed any eminence of birth, of power, or of riches, was soon followed by dependent multitudes.[4] The salvation of the common people was pur-

---

[1] See Tillemont, Hist. des Empereurs, tom. iv. p. 429. The Greeks, the Russians, and, in the darker ages, the Latins themselves, have been desirous of placing Constantine in the catalogue of saints.

[2] See the third and fourth books of his Life. He was accustomed to say that, whether Christ was preached in pretence or in truth, he should still rejoice (l. iii. c. 58).

[3] M. de Tillemont (Hist. des Empereurs, tom. iv. p. 374, 616) has defended with strength and spirit the virgin purity of Constantinople against some malevolent insinuations of the Pagan Zosimus.

[4] The author of the Histoire Politique et Philosophique des deux Indes (tom. i. p. 9) condemns a law of Constantine which gave freedom to all the slaves who should embrace Christianity. The emperor did indeed publish a law which restrained the Jews from circumcising, perhaps from keeping, any Christian slaves (see Euseb. in Vit. Constant. l. iv. c. 27, and Cod. Theod. l. xvi. tit. ix., with Godefroy's Commentary, tom. vi. p. 247). But this imperfect exception related only to the Jews; and the great body of slaves, who were the property of Christian or Pagan masters, could not improve their temporal condition by changing their religion. I am ignorant by what guides the Abbé Raynal was deceived, as the total absence of quotations is the unpardonable blemish of his entertaining history.

chased at an easy rate, if it be true that, in one year, twelve thousand men were baptised at Rome, besides a proportionable number of women and children, and that a white garment, with twenty pieces of gold, had been promised by the emperor to every convert.[1] The powerful influence of Constantine was not circumscribed by the narrow limits of his life or of his dominions. The education which he bestowed on his sons and nephews secured to the empire a race of princes whose faith was still more lively and sincere, as they imbibed, in their earliest infancy, the spirit, or at least the doctrine, of Christianity. War and commerce had spread the knowledge of the Gospel beyond the confines of the Roman provinces; and the barbarians, who had disdained an humble and proscribed sect, soon learned to esteem a religion which had been so lately embraced by the greatest monarch and the most civilised nation of the globe.[2] The Goths and Germans, who enlisted under the standard of Rome, revered the cross which glittered at the head of the legions, and their fierce countrymen received at the same time the lessons of faith and of humanity. The kings of Iberia and Armenia worshipped the God of their protector;[3] and their subjects, who have invariably preserved the name of Christians, soon formed a sacred and perpetual connection with their Roman brethren. The

[1] See Acta Sti. Silvestri, and Hist. Eccles. Nicephor. Callist. l. vii. c. 34, ap. Baronium Annal. Eccles. A.D. 324, No. 67, 74. Such evidence is contemptible enough; but these circumstances are in themselves so probable, that the learned Dr. Howell (History of the World, vol. iii. p. 14) has not scrupled to adopt them.

[2] The conversion of the barbarians under the reign of Constantine is celebrated by the ecclesiastical historians (see Sozomen, l. ii. c. 6, and Theodoret, l. i. c. 23, 24). But Rufinus, the Latin translator of Eusebius, deserves to be considered as an original authority. His information was curiously collected from one of the companions of the Apostle of Æthiopia, and from Bacurius, an Iberian prince, who was count of the domestics. Father Mamachi has given an ample compilation on the progress of Christianity, in the first and second volumes of his great but imperfect work.

[3] [According to the Georgian Chronicles, Iberia (Georgia) was converted by the virgin Nino, who effected an extraordinary cure on the wife of the king, Mihran. The temple of the god Aramazt or Armaz, not far from the capital Mtskhitha, was destroyed, and the cross erected in its place. St. Martin has also shown that Armenia was the first nation which embraced Christianity. Gibbon himself came to entertain this view, for in his " Vindication, Miscell. Works, iv. 577, he says, " Instead of maintaining that the conversion of Armenia was not attempted with any degree of success until the sceptre was in the hands of an orthodox emperor, I ought to have said that the seeds of the faith were deeply sown during the season of the last and greatest persecution, that many Roman exiles might assist the labours of Gregory, and that the renowned Tiridates, the hero of the East, may dispute with Constantine the honour of being the first sovereign who embraced the Christian religion."—O. S.]

Christians of Persia were suspected, in time of war, of preferring their religion to their country; but as long as peace subsisted between the two empires, the persecuting spirit of the Magi was effectually restrained by the interposition of Constantine.[1] The rays of the Gospel illuminated the coast of India. The colonies of Jews who had penetrated into Arabia and Æthiopia [2] opposed the progress of Christianity; but the labour of the missionaries was in some measure facilitated by a previous knowledge of the Mosaic revelation; and Abyssinia still reveres the memory of Frumentius, who, in the time of Constantine, devoted his life to the conversion of those sequestered regions. Under the reign of his son Constantius, Theophilus,[3] who was himself of Indian extraction, was invested with the double character of ambassador and bishop. He embarked on the Red Sea with two hundred horses of the purest breed of Cappadocia, which were sent by the emperor to the prince of the Sabæans, or Homerites. Theophilus was intrusted with many other useful or curious presents, which might raise the admiration and conciliate the friendship of the barbarians; and he successfully employed several years in a pastoral visit to the churches of the torrid zone.[4]

The irresistible power of the Roman emperors was displayed in the important and dangerous change of the national religion. The terrors of a military force silenced the faint and unsupported murmurs of the Pagans, and there was reason to expect that the cheerful submission of the Christian clergy, as well as people, would be the result of conscience and gratitude. It was long since established as a fundamental maxim of the Roman constitution, that every rank of citizens was alike subject to the laws, and that the care of religion was the right as well as duty of the civil magistrate. Constantine and his successors could

---

[1] See in Eusebius (in Vit. Constant. l. iv. c. 9, sqq.) the pressing and pathetic epistle of Constantine in favour of his Christian brethren of Persia.

[2] See Basnage, Hist. des Juifs, tom. vii. p. 182, tom. viii. p. 333, tom. ix. p. 810. The curious diligence of this writer pursues the Jewish exiles to the extremities of the globe.

[3] Theophilus had been given in his infancy as a hostage by his countrymen of the isle of Diva, and was educated by the Romans in learning and piety. The Maldives, of which Male, or *Diva*, may be the capital, are a cluster of 1900 or 2000 minute islands in the Indian Ocean. The ancients were imperfectly acquainted with the Maldives, but they are described in the two Mahometan travellers of the ninth century, published by Renaudot, Geograph. Nubiensis, p. 30, 31. D'Herbelot, Bibliothèque Orientale, p. 704. Hist. Générale des Voyages, tom. viii.

[4] Philostorgius, l. iii. c. 4, 5, 6, with Godefroy's learned observations. The historical narrative is soon lost in an inquiry concerning the seat of Paradise, strange monsters, etc.

not easily persuade themselves that they had forfeited, by their conversion, any branch of the Imperial prerogatives, or that they were incapable of giving laws to a religion which they had protected and embraced. The emperors still continued to exercise a supreme jurisdiction over the ecclesiastical order; and the sixteenth book of the Theodosian code represents, under a variety of titles, the authority which they assumed in the government of the catholic church.

But the distinction of the spiritual and temporal powers,[1] which had never been imposed on the free spirit of Greece and Rome, was introduced and confirmed by the legal establishment of Christianity. The office of supreme pontiff, which, from the time of Numa to that of Augustus, had always been exercised by one of the most eminent of the senators, was at length united to the Imperial dignity. The first magistrate of the state, as often as he was prompted by superstition or policy, performed with his own hands the sacerdotal functions;[2] nor was there any order of priests, either at Rome or in the provinces, who claimed a more sacred character among men, or a more intimate communication with the gods. But in the Christian church, which intrusts the service of the altar to a perpetual succession of consecrated ministers, the monarch, whose spiritual rank is less honourable than that of the meanest deacon, was seated below the rails of the sanctuary, and confounded with the rest of the faithful multitude.[3] The emperor might be saluted as the father of his people, but he owed a filial duty and reverence to the fathers of the church; and the same marks of respect which Constantine had paid to the persons of saints and confessors were soon exacted by the pride of the episcopal order.[4] A secret

[1] See the epistle of Osius, ap. Athanasium, vol. i. p. 840. The public remonstrance which Osius was forced to address to the son contained the same principles of ecclesiastical and civil government which he had secretly instilled into the mind of the father.

[2] M. de la Bastie (Mémoires de l'Académie des Inscriptions, tom. xv. p. 38-61) has evidently proved that Augustus and his successors exercised in person all the sacred functions of pontifex maximus, or high priest, of the Roman empire.

[3] Something of a contrary practice had insensibly prevailed in the church of Constantinople; but the rigid Ambrose commanded Theodosius to retire below the rails, and taught him to know the difference between a king and a priest. See Theodoret, l. v. c. 18.

[4] At the table of the emperor Maximus, Martin, bishop of Tours, received the cup from an attendant, and gave it to the presbyter his companion, before he allowed the emperor to drink; the empress waited on Martin at table. Sulpicius Severus, in Vit. Sti. Martin. c. 23, and Dialogue ii. 7. Yet it may be doubted whether these extraordinary compliments were paid to the bishop or the saint. The honours usually granted to the former character may be seen in Bingham's Antiquities, l. ii. c. 9, and

conflict between the civil and ecclesiastical jurisdictions embarrassed the operations of the Roman government; and a pious emperor was alarmed by the guilt and danger of touching with a profane hand the ark of the covenant. The separation of men into the two orders of the clergy and of the laity was, indeed, familiar to many nations of antiquity; and the priests of India, of Persia, of Assyria, of Judea, of Æthiopia, of Egypt, and of Gaul, derived from a celestial origin the temporal power and possessions which they had acquired. These venerable institutions had gradually assimilated themselves to the manners and government of their respective countries; [1] but the opposition or contempt of the civil power served to cement the discipline of the primitive church. The Christians had been obliged to elect their own magistrates, to raise and distribute a peculiar revenue, and to regulate the internal policy of their republic by a code of laws, which were ratified by the consent of the people and the practice of three hundred years. When Constantine embraced the faith of the Christians, he seemed to contract a perpetual alliance with a distinct and independent society; and the privileges granted or confirmed by that emperor, or by his successors, were accepted, not as the precarious favours of the court, but as the just and inalienable rights of the ecclesiastical order.

The catholic church was administered by the spiritual and legal jurisdiction of eighteen hundred bishops; [2] of whom one thousand were seated in the Greek, and eight hundred in the Latin, provinces of the empire. The extent and boundaries of their respective dioceses had been variously and accidentally decided by the zeal and success of the first missionaries, by the wishes of the people, and by the propagation of the Gospel. Episcopal churches were closely planted along the banks of the Nile, on the sea-coast of Africa, in the proconsular Asia, and through the southern provinces of Italy. The bishops of Gaul

Vales. ad Theodoret, l. iv. c. 6. See the haughty ceremonial which Leontius, bishop of Tripoli, imposed on the empress. Tillemont, Hist. des Empereurs, tom. iv. p. 754. (Patres Apostol. tom. ii. p. 179.)

[1] Plutarch, in his treatise of Isis and Osiris, informs us that the kings of Egypt, who were not already priests, were initiated, after their election, into the sacerdotal order.

[2] The numbers are not ascertained by any ancient writer or original catalogue; for the partial lists of the eastern churches are comparatively modern. The patient diligence of Charles a Sto. Paolo, of Luke Holstenius, and of Bingham, has laboriously investigated all the episcopal sees of the catholic church, which was almost commensurate with the Roman empire. The ninth book of the Christian Antiquities is a very accurate map of ecclesiastical geography.

and Spain, of Thrace and Pontus, reigned over an ample territory, and delegated their rural suffragans to execute the subordinate duties of the pastoral office.[1] A Christian diocese might be spread over a province, or reduced to a village; but all the bishops possessed an equal and indelible character; they all derived the same powers and privileges from the apostles, from the people, and from the laws. While the *civil* and *military* professions were separated by the policy of Constantine, a new and perpetual order of *ecclesiastical* ministers, always respectable, sometimes dangerous, was established in the church and state. The important review of their station and attributes may be distributed under the following heads: I. Popular election. II. Ordination of the clergy. III. Property. IV. Civil jurisdiction. V. Spiritual censures. VI. Exercise of public oratory. VII. Privilege of legislative assemblies.

I. The freedom of elections subsisted long after the legal establishment of Christianity,[2] and the subjects of Rome enjoyed in the church the privilege which they had lost in the republic, of choosing the magistrates whom they were bound to obey. As soon as a bishop had closed his eyes, the metropolitan issued a commission to one of his suffragans to administer the vacant see, and prepare, within a limited time, the future election. The right of voting was vested in the inferior clergy, who were best qualified to judge of the merit of the candidates; in the senators or nobles of the city, all those who were distinguished by their rank or property; and finally in the whole body of the people,

---

[1] On the subject of the rural bishops, or *Chorepiscopi*, who voted in synods, and conferred the minor orders, see Thomassin, Discipline de l'Eglise, tom. i. p. 447, etc., and Chardon, Hist. des Sacramens, tom. v. p. 395, etc. They do not appear till the fourth century; and this equivocal character, which had excited the jealousy of the prelates, was abolished before the end of the tenth, both in the East and the West.

[2] Thomassin (Discipline de l'Eglise, tom. ii. l. ii. c. 1-8, p. 673-721) has copiously treated of the election of bishops during the five first centuries, both in the East and in the West; but he shows a very partial bias in favour of the episcopal aristocracy. Bingham (l. iv. c. 2) is moderate; and Chardon (Hist. des Sacremens, tom. v. p. 106-128) is very clear and concise.

[The freedom of election of bishops and other clergy by the community was, however, very limited, and, as Guizot says, was soon annihilated. Already by the third century the deacons were no longer nominated by the community, but by the bishops. Although it appears from the letters of Cyprian that even in his time no priest could be elected without the consent of the community (cf. Epistle 68), that election was far from being altogether free. The bishop proposed to the parishioners the candidate he had chosen, and they were permitted to make such objections as might be suggested by his conduct and morals (St. Cyprian, Epistle 33). They lost this last right about the middle of the fourth century.—O. S.]

who on the appointed day flocked in multitudes from the most remote parts of the diocese,[1] and sometimes silenced, by their tumultuous acclamations, the voice of reason and the laws of discipline. These acclamations might accidentally fix on the head of the most deserving competitor, of some ancient presbyter, some holy monk, or some layman conspicuous for his zeal and piety. But the episcopal chair was solicited, especially in the great and opulent cities of the empire, as a temporal rather than as a spiritual dignity. The interested views, the selfish and angry passions, the arts of perfidy and dissimulation, the secret corruption, the open and even bloody violence which had formerly disgraced the freedom of election in the commonwealths of Greece and Rome, too often influenced the choice of the successors of the apostles. While one of the candidates boasted the honours of his family, a second allured his judges by the delicacies of a plentiful table, and a third, more guilty than his rivals, offered to share the plunder of the church among the accomplices of his sacrilegious hopes.[2] The civil as well as ecclesiastical laws attempted to exclude the populace from this solemn and important transaction. The canons of ancient discipline, by requiring several episcopal qualifications of age, station, etc., restrained in some measure the indiscriminate caprice of the electors. The authority of the provincial bishops, who were assembled in the vacant church to consecrate the choice of the people, was interposed to moderate their passions and to correct their mistakes. The bishops could refuse to ordain an unworthy candidate, and the rage of contending factions sometimes accepted their impartial mediation. The submission or the resistance of the clergy and people, on various occasions, afforded different precedents, which were insensibly converted into positive laws and provincial customs:[3] but it was everywhere admitted, as a fundamental maxim of religious policy, that no bishop could be imposed on an orthodox church without the consent of its members. The emperors, as the guardians of the public peace,

[1] Incredibilis multitudo, non solum ex eo oppido (*Tours*), sed etiam ex vicinis urbibus ad suffragia ferenda convenerat, etc. Sulpicius Severus, in Vit. Martin. c. 7. The council of Laodicea (canon xiii.) prohibits mobs and tumults; and Justinian confines the right of election to the nobility. Novell. cxxiii. 1.

[2] The epistles of Sidonius Apollinaris (iv. 25, vii. 5, 9) exhibit some of the scandals of the Gallican church; and Gaul was less polished and less corrupt than the East.

[3] A compromise was sometimes introduced by law or by consent; either the bishops or the people chose one of the three candidates who had been named by the other party.

and as the first citizens of Rome and Constantinople, might effectually declare their wishes in the choice of a primate; but those absolute monarchs respected the freedom of ecclesiastical elections, and, while they distributed and resumed the honours of the state and army, they allowed eighteen hundred perpetual magistrates to receive their important offices from the free suffrages of the people.[1] It was agreeable to the dictates of justice that these magistrates should not desert an honourable station from which they could not be removed; but the wisdom of councils endeavoured, without much success, to enforce the residence, and to prevent the translation, of bishops. The discipline of the West was indeed less relaxed than that of the East; but the same passions which made those regulations necessary rendered them ineffectual. The reproaches which angry prelates have so vehemently urged against each other serve only to expose their common guilt and their mutual indiscretion.

II. The bishops alone possessed the faculty of *spiritual* generation, and this extraordinary privilege might compensate, in some degree, for the painful celibacy [2] which was imposed as a virtue, as a duty, and at length as a positive obligation. The religions of antiquity, which established a separate order of priests, dedicated a holy race, a tribe or family, to the perpetual service of the gods.[3] Such institutions were founded for possession rather than conquest. The children of the priests enjoyed, with

---

[1] All the examples quoted by Thomassin (Discipline de l'Eglise, tom. ii. l. ii. c. vi. p. 704-714) appear to be extraordinary acts of power, and even of oppression. The confirmation of the bishop of Alexandria is mentioned by Philostorgius as a more regular proceeding (Hist. Eccles. l. ii. 11).
[On this point Planck in his *Geschichte der Christlich-kirchlichen Gesellschafts-verfassung* (vol. i. p. 263) says, " From the middle of the fourth century the bishops of some of the larger churches, particularly those of the Imperial residence, were almost always chosen under the influence of the court, and were often directly and immediately nominated by the emperor."—O. S.]

[2] The celibacy of the clergy during the first five or six centuries is a subject of discipline, and indeed of controversy, which has been very diligently examined. See in particular Thomassin, Discipline de l'Eglise, tom. i. l. ii. c. lx. lxi. p. 886-902; and Bingham's Antiquities, l. iv. c. 5. By each of these learned but partial critics one half of the truth is produced, and the other is concealed.

[3] Diodorus Siculus attests and approves the hereditary succession of the priesthood among the Egyptians, the Chaldeans, and the Indians (l. i. [c. 73] p. 84, l. ii. [c. 29 and 40] p. 142, 153, edit. Wesseling). The Magi are described by Ammianus as a very numerous family: " Per sæcula multa ad præsens unâ eâdemque prosapiâ multitudo creata, Deorum cultibus dedicatur " (xxiii. 6). Ausonius celebrates the *Stirps Druidarum* (De Professorib. Burdigal. iv. [7]); but we may infer from the remark of Cæsar (Bell. Gall. vi.13), that in the Celtic hierarchy some room was left for choice and emulation.

proud and indolent security, their sacred inheritance; and the
fiery spirit of enthusiasm was abated by the cares, the pleasures,
and the endearments of domestic life. But the Christian
sanctuary was open to every ambitious candidate who aspired
to its heavenly promises or temporal possessions. The office of
priests, like that of soldiers or magistrates, was strenuously
exercised by those men whose temper and abilities had prompted
them to embrace the ecclesiastical profession, or who had been
selected by a discerning bishop as the best qualified to promote
the glory and interest of the church. The bishops [1] (till the
abuse was restrained by the prudence of the laws) might con-
strain the reluctant and protect the distressed, and the imposition of hands for ever bestowed some of the most valuable
privileges of civil society. The whole body of the catholic
clergy, more numerous, perhaps, than the legions, was exempted
by the emperors from all service, private or public, all municipal
offices, and all personal taxes and contributions, which pressed
on their fellow-citizens with intolerable weight; and the duties
of their holy profession were accepted as a full discharge of their
obligations to the republic.[2] Each bishop acquired an absolute
and indefeasible right to the perpetual obedience of the clerk
whom he ordained; the clergy of each episcopal church, with
its dependent parishes, formed a regular and permanent society;

---

[1] The subject of the vocation, ordination, obedience, etc., of the clergy,
is laboriously discussed by Thomassin (Discipline de l'Eglise, tom. ii. p. 1-
83) and Bingham (in the 4th book of his Antiquities, more especially the
4th, 6th, and 7th chapters). When the brother of St. Jerom was ordained
in Cyprus, the deacons forcibly stopped his mouth, lest he should make a
solemn protestation which might invalidate the holy rites.

[2] The charter of immunities, which the clergy obtained from the Christian
emperors, is contained in the 16th book of the Theodosian code; and is
illustrated with tolerable candour by the learned Godefroy, whose mind
was balanced by the opposite prejudices of a civilian and a Protestant.

[This exemption from service was very much limited, according to
Guizot. The municipal offices were of two kinds, the one attached to the
individual in his character of *inhabitant*, and the other in that of *proprietor*. Constantine had exempted ecclesiastics from offices of the first
description. (Eusebius, Eccles. His. lib. x. c. 7). They sought also to be
exempted from the second (*munera patrimoniorum*). The rich, to obtain
this privilege, secured subordinate situations among the clergy. Constantine in 320 A.D. published an edict by which he prohibited the more opulent
citizens (decuriones and curiales) from embracing the ecclesiastical profession, and the bishops from admitting new ecclesiastics, before a place
should be vacant by the death of the occupant. Valentinian I., by a
rescript more general, forbade any rich citizen to obtain a situation in the
church, and also enacted that ecclesiastics who wished to be exempt from
services which they were bound to discharge as proprietors, should be
obliged to give up their property to their relatives.—O. S.]

and the cathedrals of Constantinople [1] and Carthage [2] maintained their peculiar establishment of five hundred ecclesiastical ministers. Their ranks [3] and numbers were insensibly multiplied by the superstition of the times, which introduced into the church the splendid ceremonies of a Jewish or Pagan temple; and a long train of priests, deacons, sub-deacons, acolytes, exorcists, readers, singers, and doorkeepers contributed, in their respective stations, to swell the pomp and harmony of religious worship. The clerical name and privilege were extended to many pious fraternities, who devoutly supported the ecclesiastical throne. [4] Six hundred *parabolani*, or adventurers, visited the sick at Alexandria; eleven hundred *copiatæ*, or gravediggers, buried the dead at Constantinople; and the swarms of monks, who arose from the Nile, overspread and darkened the face of the Christian world.

III. The edict of Milan secured the revenue as well as the peace of the church. [5] The Christians not only recovered the lands and houses of which they had been stripped by the persecuting laws of Diocletian, but they acquired a perfect title to all the possessions which they had hitherto enjoyed by the connivance of the magistrate. As soon as Christianity became the religion of the emperor and the empire, the national clergy might claim a decent and honourable maintenance: and the payment of an annual tax might have delivered the people from the more oppressive tribute which superstition imposes on her votaries. But as the wants and expenses of the church increased with her prosperity,

---

[1] Justinian. Novell. ciii. Sixty presbyters or priests, one hundred deacons, forty deaconesses, ninety sub-deacons, one hundred and ten readers, twenty-five chanters, and one hundred doorkeepers; in all, five hundred and twenty-five. This moderate number was fixed by the emperor to relieve the distress of the church, which had been involved in debt and usury by the expense of a much higher establishment.

[2] Universus clerus ecclesiæ Carthaginiensis . . . fere *quingenti* vel amplius; inter quos quamplurimi erant lectores infantuli. Victor Vitensis, de Persecut. Vandal. v. 9, p. 78, edit. Ruinart. This remnant of a more prosperous state still subsisted under the oppression of the Vandals.

[3] The number of *seven* orders has been fixed in the Latin church, exclusive of the episcopal character. But the four inferior ranks, the minor orders, are now reduced to empty and useless titles.

[4] See Cod. Theodos. l. xvi. tit. ii. leg. 42, 43. Godefroy's Commentary, and the Ecclesiastical History of Alexandria, show the danger of these pious institutions, which often disturbed the peace of that turbulent capital.

[5] The edict of Milan (de M. P. c. 48) acknowledges, by reciting, that there existed a species of landed property, ad jus corporis eorum, id est, ecclesiarum non hominum singulorum pertinentia. Such a solemn declaration of the supreme magistrate must have been received in all the tribunals as a maxim of civil law.

the ecclesiastical order was still supported and enriched by the voluntary oblations of the faithful. Eight years after the edict of Milan, Constantine granted to all his subjects the free and universal permission of bequeathing their fortunes to the holy catholic church; [1] and their devout liberality, which during their lives was checked by luxury or avarice, flowed with a profuse stream at the hour of their death. The wealthy Christians were encouraged by the example of their sovereign. An absolute monarch, who is rich without patrimony, may be charitable without merit; and Constantine too easily believed that he should purchase the favour of Heaven if he maintained the idle at the expense of the industrious, and distributed among the saints the wealth of the republic. The same messenger who carried over to Africa the head of Maxentius might be intrusted with an epistle to Cæcilian, bishop of Carthage. The emperor acquaints him that the treasurers of the province are directed to pay into his hands the sum of three thousand *folles*, or eighteen thousand pounds sterling, and to obey his farther requisitions for the relief of the churches of Africa, Numidia, and Mauritania.[2] The liberality of Constantine increased in a just proportion to his faith and to his vices. He assigned in each city a regular allowance of corn to supply the fund of ecclesiastical charity, and the persons of both sexes who embraced the monastic life became the peculiar favourites of their sovereign. The Christian temples of Antioch, Alexandria, Jerusalem, Constantinople, etc., displayed the ostentatious piety of a prince ambitious in a declining age to equal the perfect labours of antiquity.[3] The form of these religious edifices was simple and oblong, though they might sometimes swell into the shape of a dome, and sometimes branch into the figure of a cross. The timbers were framed for the most part of cedars of Libanus; the roof was covered with tiles, perhaps of gilt brass; and the walls, the columns, the pave-

---

[1] Habeat unusquisque licentiam sanctissimo Catholicæ (*ecclesiæ*) venerabilique concilio, decedens bonorum quod optavit relinquere. Cod. Theodos. l. xvi. tit. ii. leg. 4. This law was published at Rome, A.D. 321, at a time when Constantine might foresee the probability of a rupture with the emperor of the East.

[2] Eusebius, Hist. Eccles. l. x. 6, in Vit. Constantin. l. iv. c. 28. He repeatedly expatiates on the liberality of the Christian hero, which the bishop himself had an opportunity of knowing, and even of tasting.

[3] Eusebius, Hist. Eccles. l. x. c. 2, 3, 4. The bishop of Cæsarea, who studied and gratified the taste of his master, pronounced in public an elaborate description of the church of Jerusalem (in Vit. Const. l. iv. c. 46). It no longer exists, but he has inserted in the Life of Constantine (l. iii. c. 36) a short account of the architecture and ornaments. He likewise mentions the church of the Holy Apostles at Constantinople (l. iv. c. 58).

ment, were incrusted with variegated marbles. The most
precious ornaments of gold and silver, of silk and gems, were
profusely dedicated to the service of the altar, and this specious
magnificence was supported on the solid and perpetual basis of
landed property. In the space of two centuries, from the reign
of Constantine to that of Justinian, the eighteen hundred
churches of the empire were enriched by the frequent and unalienable gifts of the prince and people. An annual income of
six hundred pounds sterling may be reasonably assigned to the
bishops, who were placed at an equal distance between riches
and poverty,[1] but the standard of their wealth insensibly rose
with the dignity and opulence of the cities which they governed.
An authentic but imperfect[2] rent-roll specifies some houses,
shops, gardens, and farms, which belonged to the three *Basilicæ*
of Rome—St. Peter, St. Paul, and St. John Lateran—in the
provinces of Italy, Africa, and the East. They produce, besides
a reserved rent of oil, linen, paper, aromatics, etc., a clear annual
revenue of twenty-two thousand pieces of gold, or twelve thousand pounds sterling. In the age of Constantine and Justinian
the bishops no longer possessed, perhaps they no longer deserved,
the unsuspecting confidence of their clergy and people. The
ecclesiastical revenues of each diocese were divided into four
parts, for the respective uses of the bishop himself, of his inferior
clergy, of the poor, and of the public worship; and the abuse of
this sacred trust was strictly and repeatedly checked.[3] The
patrimony of the church was still subject to all the public impositions of the state.[4] The clergy of Rome, Alexandria, Thessa-

---

[1] See Justinian, Novell. cxxiii. 3. The revenue of the patriarchs, and
the most wealthy bishops, is not expressed: the highest annual valuation
of a bishopric is stated at *thirty*, and the lowest at *two*, pounds of gold; the
medium might be taken at *sixteen*, but these valuations are much below
the real value.

[2] See Baronius (Annal. Eccles. A.D. 324, No. 58, 65, 70, 71). Every
record which comes from the Vatican is justly suspected; yet these rent-
rolls have an ancient and authentic colour; and it is at least evident that,
if forged, they were forged in a period when *farms*, not *kingdoms*, were the
objects of papal avarice.

[3] See Thomassin, Discipline de l'Eglise, tom. iii. l. ii. c. 13, 14, 15, p. 689-
706. The legal division of the ecclesiastical revenue does not appear to
have been established in the time of Ambrose and Chrysostom. Simplicius
and Gelasius, who were bishops of Rome in the latter part of the fifth
century, mention it in their pastoral letters as a general law, which was
already confirmed by the custom of Italy.

[4] Ambrose, the most strenuous asserter of ecclesiastical privileges,
submits without a murmur to the payment of the land-tax. " Si tributum
petit Imperator, non negamus; agri ecclesiæ solvunt tributum; solvimus
quæ sunt Cæsaris Cæsari, et quæ sunt Dei Deo; tributum Cæsaris est;
non negatur." Baronius labours to interpret this tribute as an act of

lonica, etc., might solicit and obtain some partial exemptions; but the premature attempt of the great council of Rimini, which aspired to universal freedom, was successfully resisted by the son of Constantine.[1]

IV. The Latin clergy, who erected their tribunal on the ruins of the civil and common law, have modestly accepted, as the gift of Constantine,[2] the independent jurisdiction which was the fruit of time, of accident, and of their own industry. But the liberality of the Christian emperors had actually endowed them with some legal prerogatives which secured and dignified the sacerdotal character.[3] 1. Under a despotic government, the bishops alone enjoyed and asserted the inestimable privilege of being tried only by their *peers ;* and even in a capital accusation, a synod of their brethren were the sole judges of their guilt or innocence. Such a tribunal, unless it was inflamed by personal resentment or religious discord, might be favourable, or even partial, to the sacerdotal order: but Constantine was satisfied [4] that secret impunity would be less pernicious than public scandal, and the Nicene council was edified by his public declaration, that, if he surprised a bishop in the act of adultery, he should cast his Imperial mantle over the episcopal sinner. 2. The

charity rather than of duty (Annal. Eccles. A.D. 387); but the words, if not the intentions of Ambrose, are more candidly explained by Thomassin, Discipline de l'Eglise, tom. iii. l. i. c. 34, p. 268.

[1] In Ariminensi synodo super ecclesiarum et clericorum privilegiis tractatû habito, usque eo dispositio progressa est, ut juga quæ viderentur ad ecclesiam pertinere. a publicâ functione cessarent inquietudine desistente; quod nostra videtur dudum sanctio repulsisse. Cod. Theod. l. xvi. tit. ii. leg. 15. Had the synod of Rimini carried this point, such practical merit might have atoned for some speculative heresies.

[2] From Eusebius (in Vit. Constant. l. iv. c. 27) and Sozomen (l. i. c. 9) we are assured that the episcopal jurisdiction was extended and confirmed by Constantine; but the forgery of a famous edict, which was never fairly inserted in the Theodosian Code (see at the end. tom. vi. p. 303), is demonstrated by Godefroy in the most satisfactory manner. It is strange that M. de Montesquieu, who was a lawyer as well as a philosopher, should allege this edict of Constantine (Esprit des Loix, l. xxix. c. 16) without intimating any suspicion.

[3] The subject of ecclesiastical jurisdiction has been involved in a mist of passion, of prejudice, and of interest. Two of the fairest books which have fallen into my hands are the Institutes of Canon Law, by the Abbé de Fleury, and the Civil History of Naples, by Giannone. Their moderation was the effect of situation as well as of temper. Fleury was a French ecclesiastic, who respected the authority of the parliaments; Giannone was an Italian lawyer, who dreaded the power of the church. And here let me observe that, as the general propositions which I advance are the result of *many* particular and imperfect facts, I must either refer the reader to those modern authors who have expressly treated the subject, or swell these notes to a disagreeable and disproportioned size.

[4] Tillemont has collected from Rufinus, Theodoret, etc., the sentiments and language of Constantine. Mém. Ecclés. tom. iii. p. 749, 750.

domestic jurisdiction of the bishops was at once a privilege and a restraint of the ecclesiastical order, whose civil causes were decently withdrawn from the cognisance of a secular judge. Their venial offences were not exposed to the shame of a public trial or punishment; and the gentle correction which the tenderness of youth may endure from its parents or instructors was inflicted by the temperate severity of the bishops. But if the clergy were guilty of any crime which could not be sufficiently expiated by their degradation from an honourable and beneficial profession, the Roman magistrate drew the sword of justice, without any regard to ecclesiastical immunities. 3. The arbitration of the bishops was ratified by a positive law; and the judges were instructed to execute, without appeal or delay, the episcopal decrees, whose validity had hitherto depended on the consent of the parties. The conversion of the magistrates themselves, and of the whole empire, might gradually remove the fears and scruples of the Christians. But they still resorted to the tribunal of the bishops, whose abilities and integrity they esteemed; and the venerable Austin enjoyed the satisfaction of complaining that his spiritual functions were perpetually interrupted by the invidious labour of deciding the claim or the possession of silver and gold, of lands and cattle. 4. The ancient privilege of sanctuary was transferred to the Christian temples, and extended, by the liberal piety of the younger Theodosius, to the precincts of consecrated ground.[1] The fugitive, and even guilty, suppliants were permitted to implore either the justice or the mercy of the Deity and his ministers. The rash violence of despotism was suspended by the mild interposition of the church, and the lives or fortunes of the most eminent subjects might be protected by the mediation of the bishop.

V. The bishop was the perpetual censor of the morals of his people. The discipline of penance was digested into a system of canonical jurisprudence,[2] which accurately defined the duty

---

[1] See Cod. Theod. l. ix. tit. xlv. leg. 4. In the works of Fra Paolo (tom. iv. p. 192, etc.) there is an excellent discourse on the origin, claims, abuses, and limits of sanctuaries. He justly observes that ancient Greece might perhaps contain fifteen or twenty *asyla* or sanctuaries; a number which at present may be found in Italy within the walls of a single city.

[2] The penitential jurisprudence was continually improved by the canons of the councils. But as many cases were still left to the discretion of the bishops, they occasionally published, after the example of the Roman prætor, the rules of discipline which they proposed to observe. Among the canonical epistles of the fourth century, those of Basil the Great were the most celebrated. They are inserted in the Pandects of Beveridge (tom. ii. p. 47-151), and are translated by Chardon, Hist. des Sacremens, tom. iv. p. 219-277.

of private or public confession, the rules of evidence, the degrees of guilt, and the measure of punishment. It was impossible to execute this spiritual censure, if the Christian pontiff, who punished the obscure sins of the multitude, respected the conspicuous vices and destructive crimes of the magistrate: but it was impossible to arraign the conduct of the magistrate without controlling the administration of civil government. Some considerations of religion, or loyalty, or fear, protected the sacred persons of the emperors from the zeal or resentment of the bishops; but they boldly censured and excommunicated the subordinate tyrants who were not invested with the majesty of the purple. St. Athanasius excommunicated one of the ministers of Egypt, and the interdict which he pronounced of fire and water was solemnly transmitted to the churches of Cappodocia.[1] Under the reign of the younger Theodosius, the polite and eloquent Synesius, one of the descendants of Hercules,[2] filled the episcopal seat of Ptolemais, near the ruins of ancient Cyrene,[3] and the philosophic bishop supported with dignity the character which he had assumed with reluctance.[4] He vanquished the monster of Libya, the president Andronicus, who abused the authority of a venal office, invented new modes of rapine and torture,

---

[1] Basil. Epistol. xlvii. in Baronius (Annal. Eccles. A.D. 370, No. 91), who declares that he purposely relates it to convince governors that they were not exempt from a sentence of excommunication. In his opinion, even a royal head is not safe from the thunders of the Vatican; and the cardinal shows himself much more consistent than the lawyers and theologians of the Gallican church.

[2] The long series of his ancestors, as high as Eurysthenes, the first Doric king of Sparta, and the fifth in lineal descent from Hercules, was inscribed in the public registers of Cyrene, a Lacedæmonian colony. (Synes. Epist. lvii. p. 197, edit. Petav.) Such a pure and illustrious pedigree of seventeen hundred years, without adding the royal ancestors of Hercules, cannot be equalled in the history of mankind.

[3] Synesius (de Regno, p. 2 [ed. Par. 1612]) pathetically deplores the fallen and ruined state of Cyrene, πόλις Ἑλληνίς, παλαιὸν ὄνομα καὶ σεμνὸν, καὶ ἐν ᾠδῇ μυρίᾳ τῶν πάλαι σοφῶν, νῦν πένης καὶ κατηφὴς, καὶ μέγα ἐρείπιον. Ptolemais, a new city, 82 miles to the westward of Cyrene, assumed the metropolitan honours of the Pentapolis, or Upper Libya, which were afterwards transferred to Sozusa. See Wesseling, Itinerar. p. 67, 68, 732. Cellarius Geograph. tom. ii. part ii. p. 72, 74. Carolus a Sto. Paulo, Geograph. Sacra, p. 273. D'Anville, Géographie Ancienne, tom. iii. p. 43, 44. Mémoires de l'Acad. des Inscriptions, tom. xxxvii. p. 363-391.

[4] Synesius had previously represented his own disqualifications (Epist. cv. p. 246-250). He loved profane studies and profane sports; he was incapable of supporting a life of celibacy; he disbelieved the resurrection; and he refused to preach *fables* to the people, unless he might be permitted to *philosophise* at home. Theophilus, primate of Egypt, who knew his merit, accepted this extraordinary compromise. See the Life of Synesius in Tillemont, Mém. Ecclés. tom. xii. p. 499-554.

and aggravated the guilt of oppression by that of sacrilege.[1]
After a fruitless attempt to reclaim the haughty magistrate by
mild and religious admonition, Synesius proceeds to inflict the
last sentence of ecclesiastical justice,[2] which devotes Andronicus,
with his associates and their *families*, to the abhorrence of earth
and heaven. The impenitent sinners, more cruel than Phalaris
or Sennacherib, more destructive than war, pestilence, or a cloud
of locusts, are deprived of the name and privileges of Christians,
of the participation of the sacraments, and of the hope of Paradise. The bishop exhorts the clergy, the magistrates, and the
people to renounce all society with the enemies of Christ, to
exclude them from their houses and tables, and to refuse them the
common offices of life, and the decent rites of burial. The church
of Ptolemais, obscure and contemptible as she may appear, addresses this declaration to all her sister churches of the world;
and the profane who reject her decrees will be involved in the
guilt and punishment of Andronicus and his impious followers.
These spiritual terrors were enforced by a dexterous application
to the Byzantine court; the trembling president implored the
mercy of the church, and the descendant of Hercules enjoyed
the satisfaction of raising a prostrate tyrant from the ground.[3]
Such principles and such examples insensibly prepared the
triumph of the Roman pontiffs, who have trampled on the necks
of kings.

VI. Every popular government has experienced the effects of
rude or artificial eloquence. The coldest nature is animated, the
firmest reason is moved, by the rapid communication of the prevailing impulse; and each hearer is affected by his own passions
and by those of the surrounding multitude. The ruin of civil
liberty had silenced the demagogues of Athens and the tribunes
of Rome; the custom of preaching, which seems to constitute
a considerable part of Christian devotion, had not been introduced into the temples of antiquity; and the ears of monarchs
were never invaded by the harsh sound of popular eloquence till
the pulpits of the empire were filled with sacred orators, who

---

[1] See the invective of Synesius, Epist. lvii. p. 191-201. The promotion
of Andronicus was illegal, since he was a native of Berenice, in the same
province. The instruments of tortures are curiously specified—the πιε-
στήριον, or press, the δακτυλήθρα, the ποδοστράβη, the ῥινολάβις, the
ὠτάγρα, and the χειλοστρόφιον, that variously pressed or distended the
fingers, the feet, the nose, the ears, and the lips of the victims.
[2] The sentence of excommunication is expressed in a rhetorical style.
(Synesius, Epist. lviii. p. 201-203.) The method of involving whole
families, though somewhat unjust, was improved into national interdicts.
[3] See Synesius, Epist. xlvii. p. 186, 187; Epist. lxxii. p. 218, 219; Epist.
lxxxix, p. 230, 231.

possessed some advantages unknown to their profane predecessors.[1]   The arguments and rhetoric of the tribune were
instantly opposed, with equal arms, by skilful and resolute
antagonists; and the cause of truth and reason might derive an
accidental support from the conflict of hostile passions.   The
bishop, or some distinguished presbyter to whom he cautiously
delegated the powers of preaching, harangued, without the danger
of interruption or reply, a submissive multitude, whose minds
had been prepared and subdued by the awful ceremonies of
religion.   Such was the strict subordination of the catholic
church, that the same concerted sounds might issue at once from
an hundred pulpits of Italy or Egypt, if they were *tuned* [2] by the
master-hand of the Roman or Alexandrian primate.   The design
of this institution was laudable, but the fruits were not always
salutary.   The preachers recommended the practice of the social
duties; but they exalted the perfection of monastic virtue, which
is painful to the individual, and useless to mankind.   Their
charitable exhortations betrayed a secret wish that the clergy
might be permitted to manage the wealth of the faithful for the
benefit of the poor.   The most sublime representations of the
attributes and laws of the Deity were sullied by an idle mixture
of metaphysical subtleties, puerile rites, and fictitious miracles:
and they expatiated, with the most fervent zeal, on the religious
merit of hating the adversaries and obeying the ministers of the
church.   When the public peace was distracted by heresy and
schism, the sacred orators sounded the trumpet of discord, and
perhaps of sedition.   The understandings of their congregations
were perplexed by mystery, their passions were inflamed by
invectives; and they rushed from the Christian temples of
Antioch or Alexandria, prepared either to suffer or to inflict
martyrdom.   The corruption of taste and language is strongly
marked in the vehement declamations of the Latin bishops; but
the compositions of Gregory and Chrysostom have been compared
with the most splendid models of Attic, or at least of Asiatic,
eloquence.[3]

[1] See Thomassin (Discipline de l'Eglise, tom. ii. l. iii. c. 83, p. 1761-1770)
and Bingham (Antiquities, vol. i. l. xiv. c. 4, p. 688-717).   Preaching was
considered as the most important office of the bishop; but this function
was sometimes intrusted to such presbyters as Chrysostom and Augustin.

[2] Queen Elizabeth used this expression and practised this art whenever
she wished to prepossess the minds of her people in favour of any extraordinary measure of government.   The hostile effects of this *music* were
apprehended by her successor, and severely felt by his son.   " When pulpit
drum ecclesiastic," etc.   See Heylin's Life of Archbishop Laud, p. 153.

[3] Those modest orators acknowledged that, as they were destitute of
the gift of miracles, they endeavoured to acquire the arts of eloquence.

VII. The representatives of the Christian republic were regularly assembled in the spring and autumn of each year; and these synods diffused the spirit of ecclesiastical discipline and legislation through the hundred and twenty provinces of the Roman world.[1] The archbishop or metropolitan was empowered by the laws to summon the suffragan bishops of his province; to revise their conduct, to vindicate their rights, to declare their faith, and to examine the merit of the candidates who were elected by the clergy and people to supply the vacancies of the episcopal college. The primates of Rome, Alexandria, Antioch, Carthage, and afterwards Constantinople, who exercised a more ample jurisdiction, convened the numerous assembly of their dependent bishops. But the convocation of great and extraordinary synods was the prerogative of the emperor alone. Whenever the emergencies of the church required this decisive measure, he despatched a peremptory summons to the bishops or the deputies of each province, with an order for the use of post-horses and a competent allowance for the expenses of their journey. At an early period, when Constantine was the protector rather than the proselyte of Christianity, he referred the African controversy to the council of Arles; in which the bishops of York, of Treves, of Milan, and of Carthage, met as friends and brethren, to debate in their native tongue on the common interest of the Latin or Western church.[2] Eleven years afterwards, a more numerous and celebrated assembly was convened at Nice in Bithynia, to extinguish, by their final sentence, the subtle disputes which had arisen in Egypt on the subject of the Trinity. Three hundred and eighteen bishops obeyed the summons of their indulgent master; the ecclesiastics of every rank and sect and denomination have been computed at two thousand and forty-eight persons;[3] the Greeks appeared in person; and the consent of the Latins was expressed by the legates of the Roman pontiff.

---

[1] The council of Nice, in the fourth, fifth, sixth, and seventh canons, has made some fundamental regulations concerning synods, metropolitans, and primates. The Nicene canons have been variously tortured, abused, interpolated, or forged, according to the interest of the clergy. The *Suburbicarian* churches, assigned (by Rufinus) to the bishop of Rome, have been made the subject of vehement controversy. (See Sirmond, Opera, tom. iv. p. 1-238.)

[2] We have only thirty-three or forty-seven episcopal subscriptions; but Ado, a writer indeed of small account, reckons six hundred bishops in the council of Arles. Tillemont, Mém. Ecclés. tom. vi. p. 422.

[3] See Tillemont, tom. vi. p. 915, and Beausobre, Hist. du Manichéisme, tom. i. p. 529. The name of *bishop*, which is given by Eutychius to the 2048 ecclesiastics (Annal. tom. i. p. 440, vers. Pocock), must be extended far beyond the limits of an orthodox or even episcopal ordination.

The session, which lasted about two months, was frequently honoured by the presence of the emperor. Leaving his guards at the door, he seated himself (with the permission of the council) on a low stool in the midst of the hall. Constantine listened with patience and spoke with modesty; and while he influenced the debates, he humbly professed that he was the minister, not the judge, of the successors of the apostles, who had been established as priests and as gods upon earth.[1] Such profound reverence of an absolute monarch towards a feeble and unarmed assembly of his own subjects can only be compared to the respect with which the senate had been treated by the Roman princes who adopted the policy of Augustus. Within the space of fifty years, a philosophic spectator of the vicissitudes of human affairs might have contemplated Tacitus in the senate of Rome, and Constantine in the council of Nice. The fathers of the Capitol and those of the church had alike degenerated from the virtues of their founders; but as the bishops were more deeply rooted in the public opinion, they sustained their dignity with more decent pride, and sometimes opposed with a manly spirit the wishes of their sovereign. The progress of time and superstition erased the memory of the weakness, the passion, the ignorance, which disgraced these ecclesiastical synods; and the catholic world has unanimously submitted [2] to the *infallible* decrees of the general councils.[3]

[1] See Euseb. in Vit. Constantin. l. iii. c. 6-21. Tillemont. Mém. Ecclésiastiques, tom. vi. p. 669-759.

[2] Sancimus igitur vicem legum obtinere, quæ a quatuor Sanctis Conciliis . . . expositæ sunt aut firmatæ. Prædictarum enim quatuor synodorum dogmata sicut sanctas Scripturas et regulas sicut leges observamus. Justinian, Novell. cxxxi. Beveridge (ad Pandect. proleg. p. 2) remarks that the emperors never made new laws in ecclesiastical matters; and Giannone observes, in a very different spirit, that they gave a legal sanction to the canons of councils. Istoria Civile di Napoli, tom. i. p. 136.

[3] See the article CONCILE in the Encyclopédie, tom. iii. p. 668-679, édition de Lucques. The author, M. le docteur Bouchaud, has discussed, according to the principles of the Gallican church, the principal questions which relate to the form and constitution of general, national, and provincial councils. The editors (see Preface, p. xvi.) have reason to be proud of *this* article. Those who consult their immense compilation seldom depart so well satisfied.

CHAPTER XXI

Persecution of Heresy—The Schism of the Donatists—The Arian Controversy—Athanasius—Distracted State of the Church and Empire under Constantine and his Sons—Toleration of Paganism

THE grateful applause of the clergy has consecrated the memory of a prince who indulged their passions and promoted their interest. Constantine gave them security, wealth, honours, and revenge; and the support of the orthodox faith was considered as the most sacred and important duty of the civil magistrate. The edict of Milan, the great charter of toleration, had confirmed to each individual of the Roman world the privilege of choosing and professing his own religion. But this inestimable privilege was soon violated: with the knowledge of truth the emperor imbibed the maxims of persecution; and the sects which dissented from the catholic church were afflicted and oppressed by the triumph of Christianity. Constantine easily believed that the heretics, who presumed to dispute *his* opinions or to oppose *his* commands, were guilty of the most absurd and criminal obstinacy; and that a seasonable application of moderate severities might save those unhappy men from the danger of an everlasting condemnation. Not a moment was lost in excluding the ministers and teachers of the separated congregations from any share of the rewards and immunities which the emperor had so liberally bestowed on the orthodox clergy. But as the sectaries might still exist under the cloud of royal disgrace, the conquest of the East was immediately followed by an edict which announced their total destruction.[1] After a preamble filled with passion and reproach, Constantine absolutely prohibits the assemblies of the heretics, and confiscates their public property to the use either of the revenue or of the catholic church. The sects against whom the Imperial severity was directed appear to have been the ad_erents of Paul of Samosata; the Montanists of Phrygia, who maintained an enthusiastic succession of prophecy; the Novatians, who sternly rejected the temporal efficacy of repentance; the Marcionites and Valentinians, under whose leading banners the various Gnostics of Asia and Egypt had insensibly rallied; and perhaps the Manichæans, who had recently imported from Persia a more artful composition of Oriental and

[1] Eusebius in Vit. Constantin. l. iii. c. 63, 64, 65, 66.

Christian theology.[1] The design of extirpating the name, or at least of restraining the progress, of these odious heretics, was prosecuted with vigour and effect. Some of the penal regulations were copied from the edicts of Diocletian; and this method of conversion was applauded by the same bishops who had felt the hand of oppression, and had pleaded for the rights of humanity. Two immaterial circumstances may serve, however, to prove that the mind of Constantine was not entirely corrupted by the spirit of zeal and bigotry. Before he condemned the Manichæans and their kindred sects, he resolved to make an accurate inquiry into the nature of their religious principles. As if he distrusted the impartiality of his ecclesiastical counsellors, this delicate commission was intrusted to a civil magistrate, whose learning and moderation he justly esteemed, and of whose venal character he was probably ignorant.[2] The emperor was soon convinced that he had too hastily proscribed the orthodox faith and the exemplary morals of the Novatians, who had dissented from the church in some articles of discipline which were not perhaps essential to salvation. By a particular edict he exempted them from the general penalties of the law;[3] allowed them to build a church at Constantinople ; respected the miracles of their saints; invited their bishop, Acesius, to the council of Nice; and gently ridiculed the narrow tenets of his sect by a familiar jest, which from the mouth of a sovereign must have been received with applause and gratitude.[4]

The complaints and mutual accusations which assailed the throne of Constantine, as soon as the death of Maxentius had submitted Africa to his victorious arms, were ill adapted to edify an imperfect proselyte. He learned with surprise that the

---

[1] After some examination of the various opinions of Tillemont, Beausobre, Lardner, etc., I am convinced that Manes did not propagate his sect, even in Persia, before the year 270. It is strange that a philosophic and foreign heresy should have penetrated so rapidly into the African provinces; yet I cannot easily reject the edict of Diocletian against the Manichæans, which may be found in Baronius. (Annal. Eccl. A.D. 287.)

[2] Constantinus enim, cum limatius superstitionum quæreret sectas, Manichæorum et similium, etc., Ammian. xv. 13. Strategius, who from this commission obtained the surname of *Musonianus*, was a Christian of the Arian sect. He acted as one of the counts at the council of Sardica. Libanius praises his mildness and prudence. Vales. ad locum Ammian.

[3] Cod. Theod. l. xvi. tit. v. leg. 2. As the general law is not inserted in the Theodosian Code, it is probable that, in the year 438, the sects which it had condemned were already extinct.

[4] Sozomen, l. i. c. 22. Socrates, l. i. c. 10. These historians have been suspected, but I think without reason, of an attachment to the Novatian doctrine. The emperor said to the bishop, " Acesius, take a ladder, and get up to heaven by yourself." Most of the Christian sects have, by turns, borrowed the ladder of Acesius.

provinces of that great country, from the confines of Cyrene to the Columns of Hercules, were distracted with religious discord.[1] The source of the division was derived from a double election in the church of Carthage, the second in rank and opulence of the ecclesiastical thrones of the West. Cæcilian and Majorinus were the two rival primates of Africa; and the death of the latter soon made room for Donatus, who, by his superior abilities and apparent virtues, was the firmest support of his party. The advantage which Cæcilian might claim from the priority of his ordination was destroyed by the illegal, or at least indecent, haste with which it had been performed, without expecting the arrival of the bishops of Numidia. The authority of these bishops, who, to the number of seventy, condemned Cæcilian, and consecrated Majorinus, is again weakened by the infamy of some of their personal characters; and by the female intrigues, sacrilegious bargains, and tumultuous proceedings, which are imputed to this Numidian council.[2] The bishops of the contending factions maintained, with equal ardour and obstinacy, that their adversaries were degraded, or at least dishonoured, by the odious crime of delivering the Holy Scriptures to the officers of Diocletian. From their mutual reproaches, as well as from the story of this dark transaction, it may justly be inferred that the late persecution had embittered the zeal, without reforming the manners, of the African Christians. That divided church was incapable of affording an impartial judicature; the controversy was solemnly tried in five successive tribunals, which were appointed by the emperor; and the whole proceeding, from the first appeal to the final sentence, lasted above three years. A severe inquisition, which was taken by the Prætorian vicar and the proconsul of Africa, the report of two episcopal visitors who had been sent to Carthage, the decrees of the councils

[1] The best materials for this part of ecclesiastical history may be found in the edition of Optatus Milevitanus, published (Paris, 1700) by M. Dupin, who has enriched it with critical notes, geographical discussions, original records, and an accurate abridgment of the whole controversy. M. de Tillemont has bestowed on the Donatists the greatest part of a volume (tom. vi. part i.): and I am indebted to him for an ample collection of all the passages of his favourite St. Augustin which relate to those heretics.

[2] Schisma igitur illo tempore confusæ mulieris iracundia peperit; ambitus nutrivit; avaritia roboravit. Optatus, l. i. c. 19. The language of Purpurius is that of a furious madman. Dicitur te necasse filios sororis tuæ duos. Purpurius respondit: Putas me terreri à te . . . occidi; et occido eos qui contra me faciunt. Acta Concil. Cirtensis, ad calc. Optat. p. 274. When Cæcilian was invited to an assembly of bishops, Purpurius said to his brethren, or rather to his accomplices, " Let him come hither to receive our imposition of hands, and we will break his head by way of penance." Optat. l. i. c. 19.

of Rome and of Arles, and the supreme judgment of Constantine himself in his sacred consistory, were all favourable to the cause of Cæcilian; and he was unanimously acknowledged by the civil and ecclesiastical powers as the true and lawful primate of Africa. The honours and estates of the church were attributed to *his* suffragan bishops, and it was not without difficulty that Constantine was satisfied with inflicting the punishment of exile on the principal leaders of the Donatist faction. As their cause was examined with attention, perhaps it was determined with justice. Perhaps their complaint was not without foundation, that the credulity of the emperor had been abused by the insidious arts of his favourite Osius. The influence of falsehood and corruption might procure the condemnation of the innocent, or aggravate the sentence of the guilty. Such an act, however, of injustice, if it concluded an importunate dispute, might be numbered among the transient evils of a despotic administration, which are neither felt nor remembered by posterity.

But this incident, so inconsiderable that it scarcely deserves a place in history, was productive of a memorable schism, which afflicted the provinces of Africa above three hundred years, and was extinguished only with Christianity itself. The inflexible zeal of freedom and fanaticism animated the Donatists to refuse obedience to the usurpers, whose election they disputed, and whose spiritual powers they denied. Excluded from the civil and religious communion of mankind, they boldly excommunicated the rest of mankind who had embraced the impious party of Cæcilian, and of the Traditors, from whom he derived his pretended ordination. They asserted with confidence, and almost with exultation, that the Apostolical succession was interrupted; that *all* the bishops of Europe and Asia were infected by the contagion of guilt and schism; and that the prerogatives of the catholic church were confined to the chosen portion of the African believers, who alone had preserved inviolate the integrity of their faith and discipline. This rigid theory was supported by the most uncharitable conduct. Whenever they acquired a proselyte, even from the distant provinces of the East, they carefully repeated the sacred rites of baptism [1] and ordination;

---

[1] The councils of Arles, of Nice, and of Trent, confirmed the wise and moderate practice of the church of Rome. The Donatists, however, had the advantage of maintaining the sentiment of Cyprian, and of a considerable part of the primitive church. Vincentius Lirinensis (p. 332, ap. Tillemont, Mém. Ecclés. tom. vi. p. 138) has explained why the Donatists are eternally burning with the Devil, while St. Cyprian reigns in heaven with Jesus Christ.

as they rejected the validity of those which he had already received from the hands of heretics or schismatics. Bishops, virgins, and even spotless infants, were subjected to the disgrace of a public penance before they could be admitted to the communion of the Donatists. If they obtained possession of a church which had been used by their Catholic adversaries, they purified the unhallowed building with the same jealous care which a temple of idols might have required. They washed the pavement, scraped the walls, burnt the altar (which was commonly of wood), melted the consecrated plate, and cast the Holy Eucharist to the dogs, with every circumstance of ignominy which could provoke and perpetuate the animosity of religious factions.[1] Notwithstanding this irreconcilable aversion, the two parties, who were mixed and separated in all the cities of Africa, had the same language and manners, the same zeal and learning, the same faith and worship. Proscribed by the civil and ecclesiastical powers of the empire, the Donatists still maintained in some provinces, particularly in Numidia, their superior numbers; and four hundred bishops acknowledged the jurisdiction of their primate. But the invincible spirit of the sect sometimes preyed on its own vitals: and the bosom of their schismatical church was torn by intestine divisions. A fourth part of the Donatist bishops followed the independent standard of the Maximianists. The narrow and solitary path which their first leaders had marked out continued to deviate from the great society of mankind. Even the imperceptible sect of the Rogatians could affirm, without a blush, that when Christ should descend to judge the earth, he would find his true religion preserved only in a few nameless villages of the Cæsarean Mauritania.[2]

The schism of the Donatists was confined to Africa; the more diffusive mischief of the Trinitarian controversy successively penetrated into every part of the Christian world. The former was an accidental quarrel, occasioned by the abuse of freedom; the latter was a high and mysterious argument, derived from the abuse of philosophy. From the age of Constantine to that of Clovis and Theodoric, the temporal interests both of the Romans and barbarians were deeply involved in the theological disputes of Arianism. The historian may therefore be permitted respect-

---

[1] See the sixth book of Optatus Milevitanus, p. 91-100.

[2] Tillemont, Mém. Ecclésiastiques, tom. vi. part i. p. 253. He laughs at their partial credulity. He revered Augustin, the great doctor of the system of predestination.

fully to withdraw the veil of the sanctuary, and to deduce the progress of reason and faith, of error and passion, from the school of Plato to the decline and fall of the empire.

The genius of Plato, informed by his own meditation or by the traditional knowledge of the priests of Egypt,[1] had ventured to explore the mysterious nature of the Deity. When he had elevated his mind to the sublime contemplation of the first self-existent, necessary cause of the universe, the Athenian sage was incapable of conceiving *how* the simple unity of his essence could admit the infinite variety of distinct and successive ideas which compose the model of the intellectual world; *how* a Being purely incorporeal could execute that perfect model, and mould with a plastic hand the rude and independent chaos. The vain hope of extricating himself from these difficulties, which must ever oppress the feeble powers of the human mind, might induce Plato to consider the divine nature under the threefold modification—of the first cause, the reason, or *Logos*, and the soul or spirit of the universe. His poetical imagination sometimes fixed and animated these metaphysical abstractions; the three *archical* or original principles were represented in the Platonic system as three Gods, united with each other by a mysterious and ineffable generation; and the Logos was particularly considered under the more accessible character of the Son of an Eternal Father, and the Creator and Governor of the world. Such appear to have been the secret doctrines which were cautiously whispered in the gardens of the Academy; and which, according to the more recent disciples of Plato, could not be perfectly understood till after an assiduous study of thirty years.[2]

The arms of the Macedonians diffused over Asia and Egypt the language and learning of Greece; and the theological system of

---

[1] Plato Ægyptum peragravit ut a sacerdotibus barbaris numeros et *cælestia* acciperet. Cicero de Finibus, v. 29. The Egyptians might still preserve the traditional creed of the patriarchs. Josephus has persuaded many of the Christian fathers that Plato derived a part of his knowledge from the Jews; but this vain opinion cannot be reconciled with the obscure state and unsocial manners of the Jewish people, whose scriptures were not accessible to Greek curiosity till more than one hundred years after the death of Plato. See Marsham, Canon. Chron. p. 144. Le Clerc, Epistol. Critic. vii. p. 177-194.

[2] The modern guides who lead me to the knowledge of the Platonic system are Cudworth (Intellectual System, p. 568-620), Basnage (Hist. des Juifs, l. iv. c. 4, p. 53-86), Le Clerc (Epist. Crit. vii. p. 194-209), and Brucker (Hist. Philosoph. tom. i. p. 675-706). As the learning of these writers was equal, and their intention different, an inquisitive observer may derive instruction from their disputes, and certainty from their agreement.

Plato was taught, with less reserve, and perhaps with some
improvements, in the celebrated school of Alexandria.[1] A
numerous colony of Jews had been invited, by the favour of the
Ptolemies, to settle in their new capital.[2] While the bulk of the
nation practised the legal ceremonies, and pursued the lucrative
occupations of commerce, a few Hebrews of a more liberal spirit
devoted their lives to religious and philosophical contemplation.[3]
They cultivated with diligence, and embraced with ardour, the
theological system of the Athenian sage. But their national pride
would have been mortified by a fair confession of their former
poverty: and they boldly marked, as the sacred inheritance of
their ancestors, the gold and jewels which they had so lately
stolen from their Egyptian masters. One hundred years before
the birth of Christ, a philosophical treatise, which manifestly
betrays the style and sentiments of the school of Plato, was produced by the Alexandrian Jews, and unanimously received as a
genuine and valuable relic of the inspired Wisdom of Solomon.[4]
A similar union of the Mosaic faith and the Grecian philosophy
distinguishes the works of Philo, which were composed, for the
most part, under the reign of Augustus.[5] The material soul of
the universe [6] might offend the piety of the Hebrews; but they
applied the character of the Logos to the Jehovah of Moses and
the patriarchs; and the Son of God was introduced upon earth,
under a visible and even human appearance, to perform those

---

[1] Brucker, Hist. Philosoph. tom. i. p. 1349-1357. The Alexandrian
school is celebrated by Strabo (l. xvii. [p. 794, ed. Casaub.]) and Ammianus
(xxii. 16).

[2] Joseph. Antiquitat. l. xii. c. 1, 3. Basnage, Hist. des Juifs, l. vii. c. 7.

[3] For the origin of the Jewish philosophy, see Eusebius, Præparat.
Evangel. viii. 9, 10. According to Philo, the Therapeutæ studied philosophy; and Brucker has proved (Hist. Philosoph. tom. ii. p. 787) that they
gave the preference to that of Plato.

[4] See Calmet, Dissertations sur la Bible, tom. ii. p. 277. The book of the
Wisdom of Solomon was received by many of the fathers as the work of
that monarch; and although rejected by the Protestants for want of a
Hebrew original, it has obtained, with the rest of the Vulgate, the sanction
of the council of Trent.

[5] The Platonism of Philo, which was famous to a proverb, is proved
beyond a doubt by Le Clerc (Epist. Crit. viii. p. 211-228). Basnage (Hist.
des Juifs, l. iv. c. 5) has clearly ascertained that the theological works of
Philo were composed before the death, and most probably before the birth,
of Christ. In such a time of darkness the knowledge of Philo is more
astonishing than his errors. Bull, Defens. Fid. Nicen. s. i. c. i. p. 12

[6] Mens agitat molem, et magno se corpore *miscet.*

Besides this material soul, Cudworth has discovered (p. 562) in Amelius,
Porphyry, Plotinus, and, as he thinks, in Plato himself, a superior spiritual
hypercosmian soul of the universe. But this double soul is exploded by
Brucker, Basnage, and Le Clerc, as an idle fancy of the latter Platonists.

familiar offices which seem incompatible with the nature and attributes of the Universal Cause.[1]

The eloquence of Plato, the name of Solomon, the authority of the school of Alexandria, and the consent of the Jews and Greeks, were insufficient to establish the truth of a mysterious doctrine, which might please, but could not satisfy, a rational mind. A prophet, or apostle, inspired by the Deity, can alone exercise a lawful dominion over the faith of mankind: and the theology of Plato might have been for ever confounded with the philosophical visions of the Academy, the Porch, and the Lyceum, if the name and divine attributes of the *Logos* had not been confirmed by the celestial pen of the last and most sublime of the Evangelists.[2] The Christian Revelation, which was consummated under the reign of Nerva, disclosed to the world the amazing secret, that the LOGOS, who was with God from the beginning, and was God, who had made all things, and for whom all things had been made, was incarnate in the person of Jesus of Nazareth; who had been born of a virgin, and suffered death on the cross. Besides the general design of fixing on a perpetual basis the divine honours of Christ, the most ancient and respectable of the ecclesiastical writers have ascribed to the evangelic theologian a particular intention to confute two opposite heresies, which disturbed the peace of the primitive church.[3] I. The faith of the Ebionites,[4] perhaps of the Nazarenes,[5] was gross and imperfect. They revered Jesus as the greatest of the prophets, endowed with supernatural virtue and power. They ascribed to his person and to his future reign all the predictions of the

[1] Petav. Dogmata Theologica, tom. ii. l. viii. c. 2, p. 791. Bull, Defens. Fid. Nicen. s. i. c. 1, p. 8, 13. This notion, till it was abused by the Arians, was freely adopted in the Christian theology. Tertullian (adv. Praxeam, c. 16) has a remarkable and dangerous passage. After contrasting, with indiscreet wit, the nature of God and the actions of Jehovah, he concludes: Scilicet ut hæc de filio Dei non credenda fuisse, si non scripta essent; fortasse non credenda de Patre licet scripta.

[2] The Platonists admired the beginning of the Gospel of St. John, as containing an exact transcript of their own principles. Augustin. de Civitat. Dei, x. 29. Amelius apud Cyril. advers Julian. l. viii. p. 283. But in the third and fourth centuries the Platonists of Alexandria might improve their Trinity by the secret study of the Christian theology.

[3] See Beausobre, Hist. Critique du Manichéisme, tom. i. p. 377. The Gospel according to St. John is supposed to have been published about seventy years after the death of Christ.

[4] The sentiments of the Ebionites are fairly stated by Mosheim (p. 331) and Le Clerc (Hist. Ecclés. p. 535). The Clementines, published among the apostolical Fathers, are attributed by the critics to one of these sectaries.

[5] Staunch polemics, like Bull (Judicium Eccles. Cathol. c. 2), insist on the orthodoxy of the Nazarenes; which appears less pure and certain in the eyes of Mosheim (p. 330).

Hebrew oracles which relate to the spiritual and everlasting kingdom of the promised Messiah.[1] Some of them might confess that he was born of a virgin; but they obstinately rejected the preceding existence and divine perfections of the *Logos*, or Son of God, which are so clearly defined in the Gospel of St. John. About fifty years afterwards, the Ebionites, whose errors are mentioned by Justin Martyr with less severity than they seem to deserve,[2] formed a very inconsiderable portion of the Christian name. II. The Gnostics, who were distinguished by the epithet of *Docetes*, deviated into the contrary extreme; and betrayed the human, while they asserted the divine nature of Christ. Educated in the school of Plato, accustomed to the sublime idea of the *Logos*, they readily conceived that the brightest *Æon*, or *Emanation* of the Deity, might assume the outward shape and visible appearances of a mortal;[3] but they vainly pretended that the imperfections of matter are incompatible with the purity of a celestial substance. While the blood of Christ yet smoked on Mount Calvary, the Docetes invented the impious and extravagant hypothesis, that, instead of issuing from the womb of the Virgin,[4] he had descended on the banks of the Jordan in the form of perfect manhood; that he had imposed on the senses of his enemies and of his disciples; and that the ministers of Pilate had wasted their impotent rage on an airy phantom, who *seemed* to expire on the cross, and, after three days, to rise from the dead.[5]

[1] The humble condition and sufferings of Jesus have always been a stumbling-block to the Jews. " Deus . . . contrariis coloribus Messiam depinxerat; futurus erat Rex, Judex, Pastor," etc. See Limborch et Orobio Amica Collat. p. 8, 19, 53-76, 192-234. But this objection has obliged the believing Christians to lift up their eyes to a spiritual and everlasting kingdom.

[2] Justin Martyr. Dialog. cum Tryphonte, p. 143, 144. See Le Clerc, Hist. Ecclés. p. 615. Bull, and his editor Grabe (Judicium Eccles. Cathol. c. 7, and Appendix), attempt to distort either the sentiments or the words of Justin; but their violent correction of the text is rejected even by the Benedictine editors.

[3] The Arians reproached the orthodox party with borrowing their Trinity from the Valentinians and Marcionites. See Beausobre, Hist. du Manichéisme, l. iii. c. 5, 7.

[4] Non dignum est ex utero credere Deum, et Deum Christum . . . non dignum est ut tanta majestas per sordes et squalores mulieris transire credatur. The Gnostics asserted the impurity of matter and of marriage; and they were scandalised by the gross interpretations of the fathers, and even of Augustin himself. See Beausobre, tom. ii. p. 523.

[Gibbon confounds here the Marcionites and the Docetæ. The latter accepted Christ's incarnation in the womb of the Virgin.—O. S.]

[5] Apostolis adhuc in sæculo superstitibus apud Judæam Christi sanguine recente, et *phantasma* corpus Domini asserebatur. Cotelerius thinks (Patres Apostol. tom. ii. p. 24) that those who will not allow the *Docetes* to

The divine sanction which the Apostle had bestowed on the fundamental principle of the theology of Plato encouraged the learned proselytes of the second and third centuries to admire and study the writings of the Athenian sage, who had thus marvellously anticipated one of the most surprising discoveries of the Christian revelation. The respectable name of Plato was used by the orthodox,[1] and abused by the heretics,[2] as the common support of truth and error: the authority of his skilful commentators and the science of dialectics were employed to justify the remote consequences of his opinions, and to supply the discreet silence of the inspired writers. The same subtle and profound questions concerning the nature, the generation, the distinction, and the equality of the three divine persons of the mysterious *Triad*, or *Trinity*,[3] were agitated in the philosophical and in the Christian schools of Alexandria. An eager spirit of curiosity urged them to explore the secrets of the abyss; and the pride of the professors and of their disciples was satisfied with the science of words. But the most sagacious of the Christian theologians, the great Athanasius himself, has candidly confessed[4] that, whenever he forced his understanding to meditate on the divinity of the *Logos*, his toilsome and unavailing efforts recoiled on themselves; that the more he thought, the less he comprehended; and the more he wrote, the less capable was he of expressing his thoughts. In every step of the inquiry we are compelled to feel and acknowledge the immeasurable dispropor-

have arisen in the time of the Apostles may with equal reason deny that the sun shines at noonday. These *Docetes*, who formed the most considerable party among the Gnostics, were so called, because they granted only a *seeming* body to Christ.

[1] Some proofs of the respect which the Christians entertained for the person and doctrine of Plato may be found in De la Mothe le Vayer, tom. v. p. 135, etc., edit. 1757; and Basnage, Hist. des Juifs, tom. iv. p. 29, 79, etc.

[2] Doleo bona fide, Platonem omnium hæreticorum condimentarium factum. Tertullian. de Anima, c. 23. Petavius (Dogm. Theolog. tom. iii. proleg. 2) shows that this was a general complaint. Beausobre (tom. i. l. iii. c. 9, 10) has deduced the Gnostic errors from Platonic principles; and as, in the school of Alexandria, those principles were blended with the Oriental philosophy (Brucker, tom. i. p. 1356), the sentiment of Beausobre may be reconciled with the opinion of Mosheim (General History of the Church, vol. i. p. 37).

[3] If Theophilus, bishop of Antioch (see Dupin, Bibliothèque Ecclésiastique, tom. i. p. 66), was the first who employed the word *Triad, Trinity*, that abstract term, which was already familiar to the schools of philosophy, must have been introduced into the theology of the Christians after the middle of the second century.

[4] Athanasius, tom. i. p. 808. His expressions have an uncommon energy; and as he was writing to monks, there could not be any occasion him to *affect* a rational language.

tion between the size of the object and the capacity of the human mind. We may strive to abstract the notions of time, of space, and of matter, which so closely adhere to all the perceptions of our experimental knowledge. But as soon as we presume to reason of infinite substance, of spiritual generation, as often as we deduce any positive conclusions from a negative idea, we are involved in darkness, perplexity, and inevitable contradiction. As these difficulties arise from the nature of the subject, they oppress, with the same insuperable weight, the philosophic and the theological disputant; but we may observe two essential and peculiar circumstances which discriminated the doctrines of the catholic church from the opinions of the Platonic school.

I. A chosen society of philosophers, men of a liberal education and curious disposition, might silently meditate, and temperately discuss in the gardens of Athens or the library of Alexandria, the abstruse questions of metaphysical science. The lofty speculations, which neither convinced the understanding nor agitated the passions of the Platonists themselves, were carelessly overlooked by the idle, the busy, and even the studious part of mankind.[1] But after the *Logos* had been revealed as the sacred object of the faith, the hope, and the religious worship of the Christians, the mysterious system was embraced by a numerous and increasing multitude in every province of the Roman world. Those persons who, from their age, or sex, or occupations, were the least qualified to judge, who were the least exercised in the habits of abstract reasoning, aspired to contemplate the economy of the Divine Nature: and it is the boast of Tertullian [2] that a Christian mechanic could readily answer such questions as had perplexed the wisest of the Grecian sages. Where the subject lies so far beyond our reach, the difference between the highest and the lowest of human understandings may indeed be calculated as infinitely small; yet the degree of weakness may perhaps be measured by the degree of obstinacy and dogmatic confidence. These speculations, instead of being treated as the amusement of a vacant hour, became the most serious business of the present, and the most useful preparation for a future, life. A theology which it was incumbent to believe, which it was

[1] In a treatise which professed to explain the opinions of the ancient philosophers concerning the nature of the gods, we might expect to discover the theological Trinity of Plato. But Cicero very honestly confessed that, though he had translated the Timæus, he could never understand that mysterious dialogue. See Hieronym. præf. ad l. xii. in Isaiam, tom. v. p. 154 [tom. iv. p. 494, ed. Vallars.].

[2] Tertullian. in Apolog. c. 46. See Bayle, Dictionnaire, au mot *Simonide*. His remarks on the presumption of Tertullian are profound and interesting.

impious to doubt, and which it might be dangerous, and even fatal, to mistake, became the familiar topic of private meditation and popular discourse. The cold indifference of philosophy was inflamed by the fervent spirit of devotion; and even the metaphors of common language suggested the fallacious prejudices of sense and experience. The Christians, who abhorred the gross and impure generation of the Greek mythology,[1] were tempted to argue from the familiar analogy of the filial and paternal relations. The character of *Son* seemed to imply a perpetual subordination to the voluntary author of his existence;[2] but as the act of generation, in the most spiritual and abstracted sense, must be supposed to transmit the properties of a common nature,[3] they durst not presume to circumscribe the powers or the duration of the Son of an eternal and omnipotent Father. Fourscore years after the death of Christ, the Christians of Bithynia declared before the tribunal of Pliny that they invoked him as a god: and his divine honours have been perpetuated in every age and country, by the various sects who assume the name of his disciples.[4] Their tender reverence for the memory of Christ, and their horror for the profane worship of any created being, would have engaged them to assert the equal and absolute divinity of the *Logos*, if their rapid ascent towards the throne of heaven had not been imperceptibly checked by the apprehension of violating the unity and sole supremacy of the great Father of Christ, and of the Universe. The suspense and fluctuation produced in the minds of the Christians by these opposite tendencies may be observed in the writings of the theologians who flourished after the end of the apostolic age and before the origin of the Arian controversy. Their suffrage is claimed, with equal confidence, by the orthodox

[1] Lactantius, iv. 8. Yet the *Probole*, or *Prolatio*, which the most orthodox divines borrowed without scruple from the Valentinians, and illustrated by the comparisons of a fountain and stream, the sun and its rays, etc., either meant nothing, or favoured a material idea of the divine generation. See Beausobre, tom. i. l. iii. c. 7, p. 548.

[2] Many of the primitive writers have frankly confessed that the Son owed his being to the *will* of the Father. See Clarke's Scripture Trinity, p. 280-287. On the other hand, Athanasius and his followers seem unwilling to grant what they are afraid to deny. The schoolmen extricate themselves from this difficulty by the distinction of a *preceding* and a *concomitant* will. Petav. Dogm. Theolog. tom. ii. l. vi. c. 8, p. 587-603.

[3] See Petav. Dogm. Theolog. tom. ii. l. ii. c. 10, p. 159.

[4] Carmenque Christo quasi Deo dicere secum invicem. Plin. Epist. x. 97. The sense of *Deus*, Θεός, *Elohim*, in the ancient languages, is critically examined by Le Clerc (Ars Critica, p. 150-156), and the propriety of worshipping a very excellent creature is ably defended by the Socinian Emlyn (Tracts, p. 29-36, 51-145).

and by the heretical parties; and the most inquisitive critics have fairly allowed that, if they had the good fortune of possessing the catholic verity, they have delivered their conceptions in loose, inaccurate, and sometimes contradictory language.[1]

II. The devotion of individuals was the first circumstance which distinguished the Christians from the Platonists: the second was the authority of the church. The disciples of philosophy asserted the rights of intellectual freedom, and their respect for the sentiments of their teachers was a liberal and voluntary tribute which they offered to superior reason. But the Christians formed a numerous and disciplined society; and the jurisdiction of their laws and magistrates was strictly exercised over the minds of the faithful. The loose wanderings of the imagination were gradually confined by creeds and confessions;[2] the freedom of private judgment submitted to the public wisdom of synods; the authority of a theologian was determined by his ecclesiastical rank; and the episcopal successors of the apostles inflicted the censures of the church on those who deviated from the orthodox belief. But in an age of religious controversy every act of oppression adds new force to the elastic vigour of the mind; and the zeal or obstinacy of a spiritual rebel was sometimes stimulated by secret motives of ambition or avarice. A metaphysical argument became the cause or pretence of political contests; the subtleties of the Platonic school were used as the badges of popular factions, and the distance which separated their respective tenets was enlarged or magnified by the acrimony of dispute. As long as the dark heresies of Praxeas and Sabellius laboured to confound the *Father* with the *Son*,[3] the orthodox party might be excused if they adhered more strictly and more earnestly to the *distinction* than to the *equality* of the divine persons. But as soon as the heat of controversy

---

[1] See Daillé, de Usu Patrum, and Le Clerc, Bibliothèque Universelle, tom. x. p. 409. To arraign the faith of the Ante-Nicene fathers was the object, or at least has been the effect, of the stupendous work of Petavius on the Trinity (Dogm. Theolog. tom. ii.); nor has the deep impression been erased by the learned defence of Bishop Bull.

[2] The most ancient creeds were drawn up with the greatest latitude. See Bull (Judicium Eccles. Cathol.), who tries to prevent Episcopius from deriving any advantage from this observation.

[As regards creeds, it is a well-known fact that prior to the Council of Nicæa, no creed had ever been formulated which was to be regarded as a test of orthodoxy. There had been formal expression of Christian belief for the use of catechumens, as has been shown by Prof. Gwatkin, but that was all.—O. S.]

[3] The heresies of Praxeas, Sabellius, etc., are accurately explained by Mosheim (p. 425, 680-714). Praxeas, who came to Rome about the end of the second century, deceived, for some time, the simplicity of the bishop, and was confuted by the pen of the angry Tertullian.

had subsided, and the progress of the Sabellians was no longer an object of terror to the churches of Rome, of Africa, or of Egypt, the tide of theological opinion began to flow with a gentle but steady motion toward the contrary extreme; and the most orthodox doctors allowed themselves the use of the terms and definitions which had been censured in the mouth of the sectaries.[1]   After the edict of toleration had restored peace and leisure to the Christians, the Trinitarian controversy was revived in the ancient seat of Platonism, the learned, the opulent, the tumultuous city of Alexandria; and the flame of religious discord was rapidly communicated from the schools to the clergy, the people, the provinces, and the East.   The abstruse question of the eternity of the *Logos* was agitated in ecclesiastic conferences and popular sermons; and the heterodox opinions of Arius [2] were soon made public by his own zeal and by that of his adversaries.   His most implacable adversaries have acknowledged the learning and blameless life of the eminent presbyter, who, in a former election, had declined, and perhaps generously declined, his pretensions to the episcopal throne.[3]   His competitor Alexander assumed the office of his judge.   The important cause was argued before him; and if at first he seemed to hesitate, he at length pronounced his final sentence as an absolute rule of faith.[4]   The undaunted presbyter, who presumed to resist the authority of his angry bishop, was separated from the communion of the church.   But the pride of Arius was supported by the applause of a numerous party.   He reckoned among his immediate followers two bishops of Egypt, seven presbyters, twelve deacons, and (what may appear almost incredible) seven hundred virgins.   A large majority of the bishops of Asia appeared to support or favour his cause; and their

[1] Socrates acknowledges that the heresy of Arius proceeded from his strong desire to embrace an opinion the most diametrically opposite to that of Sabellius.

[2] The figure and manners of Arius, the character and numbers of his first proselytes, are painted in very lively colours by Epiphanius (tom. i. Hæres. lxix. 3, p. 729 [ed. Paris, 1622]), and we cannot but regret that he should soon forget the historian, to assume the task of controversy.

[3] See Philostorgius (l. i. c. 3), and Godefroy's ample Commentary.   Yet the credibility of Philostorgius is lessened, in the eyes of the orthodox, by his Arianism; and in those of rational critics, by his passion, his prejudice, and his ignorance.

[4] Sozomen (l. i. c. 15) represents Alexander as indifferent, and even ignorant, in the beginning of the controversy; while Socrates (l. i. c. 5) ascribes the origin of the dispute to the vain curiosity of his theological speculations.   Dr. Jortin (Remarks on Ecclesiastical History, vol. ii. p. 178) has censured, with his usual freedom, the conduct of Alexander; πρὸς ὀργὴν ἐξαπτέται . . . ὁμοίως φρόνειν ἐκέλευσε.

measures were conducted by Eusebius of Cæsarea, the most learned of the Christian prelates; and by Eusebius of Nicomedia, who had acquired the reputation of a statesman without forfeiting that of a saint. Synods in Palestine and Bithynia were opposed to the synods of Egypt. The attention of the prince and people was attracted by this theological dispute; and the decision, at the end of six years,[1] was referred to the supreme authority of the general council of Nice.

When the mysteries of the Christian faith were dangerously exposed to public debate, it might be observed that the human understanding was capable of forming three distinct, though imperfect, systems concerning the nature of the Divine Trinity, and it was pronounced that none of these systems, in a pure and absolute sense, were exempt from heresy and error.[2] I. According to the first hypothesis, which was maintained by Arius and his disciples, the *Logos* was a dependent and spontaneous production, created from nothing by the will of the Father. The Son, by whom all things were made,[3] had been begotten before all worlds, and the longest of the astronomical periods could be compared only as a fleeting moment to the extent of his duration; yet this duration was not infinite,[4] and there *had* been a time which preceded the ineffable generation of the *Logos*. On this only-begotten Son the Almighty Father had transfused his ample spirit, and impressed the effulgence of his glory. Visible image of invisible perfection, he saw, at an immeasurable distance beneath his feet, the thrones of the brightest archangels; yet he shone only with a reflected light, and, like the sons of the Roman emperors, who were invested with the titles of Cæsar or Augustus,[5] he governed the universe in obedience to the will

[1] The flames of Arianism might burn for some time in secret; but there is reason to believe that they burst out with violence as early as the year 319. Tillemont, Mém. Ecclés. tom. vi. p. 774-780.

[2] Quid credidit? Certe, *aut* tria nomina audiens tres Deos esse credidit, et idololatra effectus est; *aut* in tribus vocabulis trinominem credens Deum, in Sabellii hæresim incurrit; *aut* edoctus ab Arianis unum esse verum Deum Patrem, filium et spiritum sanctum credidit creaturas. Aut extra hæc quid credere potuerit nescio. Hieronym. adv. Luciferianos [tom. ii. p. 184, ed. Vallars.]. Jerom reserves for the last the orthodox system, which is more complicated and difficult.

[3] As the doctrine of absolute creation from nothing was gradually introduced among the Christians (Beausobre, tom. ii. p. 165-215), the dignity of the *workman* very naturally rose with that of the *work*.

[4] The metaphysics of Dr. Clarke (Scripture Trinity, p. 276-280) could digest an eternal generation from an infinite cause.

[5] This profane and absurd simile is employed by several of the primitive fathers, particularly by Athenagoras, in his Apology to the emperor Marcus and his son; and it is alleged, without censure, by Bull himself. See Defens. Fid. Nicen. sect. iii. c. 5, No. 4.

of his Father and Monarch. II. In the second hypothesis, the *Logos* possessed all the inherent, incommunicable perfections which religion and philosophy appropriate to the Supreme God. Three distinct and infinite minds or substances, three co-equal and co-eternal beings, composed the Divine Essence;[1] and it would have implied contradiction that any of them should not have existed, or that they should ever cease to exist.[2] The advocates of a system which seemed to establish three independent Deities attempted to preserve the unity of the First Cause, so conspicuous in the design and order of the world, by the perpetual concord of their administration and the essential agreement of their will. A faint resemblance of this unity of action may be discovered in the societies of men, and even of animals. The causes which disturb their harmony proceed only from the imperfection and inequality of their faculties; but the omnipotence which is guided by infinite wisdom and goodness cannot fail of choosing the same means for the accomplishment of the same ends. III. Three beings, who, by the self-derived necessity of their existence, possess all the divine attributes in the most perfect degree, who are eternal in duration, infinite in space, and intimately present to each other and to the whole universe, irresistibly force themselves on the astonished mind as one and the same Being,[3] who, in the economy of grace, as well as in that of nature, may manifest himself under different forms, and be considered under different aspects. By this hypothesis a real substantial trinity is refined into a trinity of names and abstract modifications that subsist only in the mind which conceives them. The *Logos* is no longer a person, but an attribute; and it is only in a figurative sense that the epithet of Son can be applied to the eternal reason which was with God from the beginning, and by *which*, not by *whom*, all things were made. The incarnation of the *Logos* is reduced to a mere inspiration of the Divine Wisdom, which filled the soul and directed all the actions of the man Jesus. Thus, after revolving round the

---

[1] See Cudworth's Intellectual System, p. 559, 579. This dangerous hypothesis was countenanced by the two Gregories, of Nyssa and Nazianzen, by Cyril of Alexandria, John of Damascus, etc. See Cudworth, p. 603. Le Clerc, Bibliothèque Universelle, tom. xviii. p. 97-105.

[2] Augustin seems to envy the freedom of the philosophers. Liberis verbis loquuntur philosophi . . . Nos autem non dicimus duo vel tria principia, duos vel tres Deos. De Civitat. Dei, x. 23.

[3] Boethius, who was deeply versed in the philosophy of Plato and Aristotle, explains the unity of the Trinity by the *indifference* of the three persons. See the judicious remarks of Le Clerc, Bibliothèque Choisie, tom. xvi. p. 225, etc.

theological circle, we are surprised to find that the Sabellian ends where the Ebionite had begun, and that the incomprehensible mystery which excites our adoration eludes our inquiry.[1]

If the bishops of the council of Nice [2] had been permitted to follow the unbiassed dictates of their conscience, Arius and his associates could scarcely have flattered themselves with the hopes of obtaining a majority of votes in favour of an hypothesis so directly adverse to the two most popular opinions of the catholic world. The Arians soon perceived the danger of their situation, and prudently assumed those modest virtues which, in the fury of civil and religious dissensions, are seldom practised, or even praised, except by the weaker party. They recommended the exercise of Christian charity and moderation, urged the incomprehensible nature of the controversy, disclaimed the use of any terms or definitions which could not be found in the Scriptures, and offered, by very liberal concessions, to satisfy their adversaries without renouncing the integrity of their own principles. The victorious faction received all their proposals with haughty suspicion, and anxiously sought for some irreconcilable mark of distinction, the rejection of which might involve the Arians in the guilt and consequences of heresy. A letter was publicly read and ignominiously torn, in which their patron, Eusebius of Nicomedia, ingenuously confessed that the admission of the HOMOOUSION, or Consubstantial, a word already familiar to the Platonists, was incompatible with the principles of their theological system. The fortunate opportunity was eagerly embraced by the bishops, who governed the resolutions of the synod, and, according to the lively expressions of Ambrose,[3] they used the sword, which heresy itself had drawn from the scabbard, to cut off the head of the hated monster. The con-

---

[1] If the Sabellians were startled at this conclusion, they were driven down another precipice into the confession that the Father was born of a virgin, that *he* had suffered on the cross; and thus deserved the odious epithet of *Patri-passians*, with which they were branded by their adversaries. See the invectives of Tertullian against Praxeas, and the temperate reflections of Mosheim (p. 423, 681); and Beausobre, tom. i. l. iii. c. 6, p. 533.

[2] The transactions of the council of Nice are related by the ancients, not only in a partial, but in a very imperfect manner. Such a picture as Fra Paolo would have drawn can never be recovered; but such rude sketches as have been traced by the pencil of bigotry, and that of reason, may be seen in Tillemont (Mém. Ecclés. tom. vi. p. 669-759), and in Le Clerc (Bibliothèque Universelle, tom. x. p. 435-454).

[3] We are indebted to Ambrose (De Fide, l. iii. cap. ult.) for the knowledge of this curious anecdote. Hoc verbum posuerunt Patres, quod viderunt adversariis esse formidini; ut tanquam evaginato ab ipsis gladio, ipsum nefandæ caput hæreseos amputarent.

substantiality of the Father and the Son was established by the council of Nice, and has been unanimously received as a fundamental article of the Christian faith by the consent of the Greek, the Latin, the Oriental, and the Protestant churches. But if the same word had not served to stigmatise the heretics and to unite the catholics, it would have been inadequate to the purpose of the majority by whom it was introduced into the orthodox creed. This majority was divided into two parties, distinguished by a contrary tendency to the sentiments of the Tritheists and of the Sabellians. But as those opposite extremes seemed to overthrow the foundations either of natural or revealed religion, they mutually agreed to qualify the rigour of their principles, and to disavow the just, but invidious, consequences which might be urged by their antagonists. The interest of the common cause inclined them to join their numbers and to conceal their differences; their animosity was softened by the healing counsels of toleration, and their disputes were suspended by the use of the mysterious *Homoousion*, which either party was free to interpret according to their peculiar tenets. The Sabellian sense, which, about fifty years before, had obliged the council of Antioch [1] to prohibit this celebrated term, had endeared it to those theologians who entertained a secret but partial affection for a nominal Trinity. But the more fashionable saints of the Arian times, the intrepid Athanasius, the learned Gregory Nazianzen, and the other pillars of the church, who supported with ability and success the Nicene doctrine, appeared to consider the expression of *substance* as if it had been synonymous with that of *nature ;* and they ventured to illustrate their meaning by affirming that three men, as they belong to the same common species, are consubstantial or homoousian to each other.[2] This pure and distinct equality was tempered, on the one hand, by the internal connection and spiritual penetration which indissolubly unites the divine persons;[3] and, on the other, by the pre-eminence of the Father, which was acknowledged as far as

[1] See Bull, Defens. Fid. Nicen. sect. ii. c. i. p. 25-36. He thinks it his duty to reconcile two orthodox synods.

[2] According to Aristotle, the stars were homoousian to each other. " That *Homoousius* means of one substance in *kind*, hath been shown by Petavius, Curcellæus, Cudworth, Le Clerc, etc., and to prove it would be *actum agere*." This is the just remark of Dr. Jortin (vol. ii. p. 212), who examines the Arian controversy with learning, candour, and ingenuity.

[3] See Petavius (Dogm. Theolog. tom. ii. l. iv. c. 16, p. 453, etc.), Cudworth (p. 559), Bull (sect. iv. p. 285-290, edit. Grab.). The περιχώρησις, or *circumincessio*, is perhaps the deepest and darkest corner of the whole theological abyss.

it is compatible with the independence of the Son.[1] Within
these limits the almost invisible and tremulous ball of orthodoxy
was allowed securely to vibrate. On either side, beyond this
consecrated ground, the heretics and the dæmons lurked in
ambush to surprise and devour the unhappy wanderer. But
as the degrees of theological hatred depend on the spirit of the
war rather than on the importance of the controversy, the
heretics who degraded were treated with more severity than those
who annihilated the person of the Son. The life of Athanasius
was consumed in irreconcilable opposition to the impious *madness* of the Arians,[2] but he defended above twenty years the
Sabellianism of Marcellus of Ancyra; and when at last he was
compelled to withdraw himself from his communion, he continued to mention with an ambiguous smile the venial errors of
his respectable friend.[3]

The authority of a general council, to which the Arians themselves had been compelled to submit, inscribed on the banners
of the orthodox party the mysterious characters of the word
Homoousion, which essentially contributed, notwithstanding
some obscure disputes, some nocturnal combats, to maintain and
perpetuate the uniformity of faith, or at least of language. The
Consubstantialists, who by their success have deserved and
obtained the title of Catholics, gloried in the simplicity and
steadiness of their own creed, and insulted the repeated variations
of their adversaries, who were destitute of any certain rule of
faith. The sincerity or the cunning of the Arian chiefs, the fear
of the laws or of the people, their reverence for Christ, their
hatred of Athanasius, all the causes, human and divine, that
influence and disturb the counsels of a theological faction, introduced among the sectaries a spirit of discord and inconstancy, which in the course of a few years erected eighteen
different models of religion,[4] and avenged the violated dignity

---

[1] The third section of Bull's Defence of the Nicene Faith, which some of
his antagonists have called nonsense, and others heresy, is consecrated to
the supremacy of the Father.

[2] The ordinary appellation with which Athanasius and his followers
chose to compliment the Arians was that of *Ariomanites*.

[3] Epiphanius, tom. i. Hæres. lxxii. 4, p. 837. See the adventures of Marcellus, in Tillemont (Mém. Ecclés. tom. vii. p. 880-899). His work, in *one*
book, of the Unity of God, was answered in the *three* books, which are still
extant, of Eusebius. After a long and careful examination, Petavius (tom.
ii. l. i. c. 14, p. 78) has reluctantly pronounced the condemnation of Marcellus.

[4] Athanasius, in his epistle concerning the synods of Seleucia and
Rimini (tom. i. p. 886-905 [p. 735 *seqq.*, ed. Bened.]), has given an ample
list of Arian creeds, which has been enlarged and improved by the labours
of the indefatigable Tillemont (Mém. Ecclés. tom. vi. p. 477).

of the church. The zealous Hilary,[1] who, from the peculiar hardships of his situation, was inclined to extenuate rather than to aggravate the errors of the Oriental clergy, declares that, in the wide extent of the ten provinces of Asia to which he had been banished, there could be found very few prelates who had preserved the knowledge of the true God.[2] The oppression which he had felt, the disorders of which he was the spectator and the victim, appeased, during a short interval, the angry passions of his soul; and in the following passage, of which I shall transcribe a few lines, the bishop of Poitiers unwarily deviates into the style of a Christian philosopher. " It is a thing," says Hilary, " equally deplorable and dangerous, that there are as many creeds as opinions among men, as many doctrines as inclinations, and as many sources of blasphemy as there are faults among us; because we make creeds arbitrarily, and explain them as arbitrarily. The Homoousion is rejected, and received, and explained away by successive synods. The partial or total resemblance of the Father and of the Son is a subject of dispute for these unhappy times. Every year, nay, every moon, we make new creeds to describe invisible mysteries. We repent of what we have done, we defend those who repent, we anathematise those whom we defended. We condemn either the doctrine of others in ourselves, or our own in that of others; and, reciprocally tearing one another to pieces, we have been the cause of each other's ruin." [3]

It will not be expected, it would not perhaps be endured, that I should swell this theological digression by a minute examination of the eighteen creeds, the authors of which, for the most part, disclaimed the odious name of their parent Arius. It is amusing enough to delineate the form, and to trace the vegetation, of a singular plant; but the tedious detail of leaves without flowers, and of branches without fruit, would soon exhaust the

---

[1] Erasmus, with admirable sense and freedom, has delineated the just character of Hilary. To revise his text, to compose the annals of his life, and to justify his sentiments and conduct, is the province of the Benedictine editors.

[2] Absque episcopo Eleusio et paucis cum eo, ex majore parte Asianæ decem provinciæ, inter quas consisto, vere Deum nesciunt. Atque utinam penitus nescirent! cum procliviore enim veniâ ignorarent quam obtrectarent. Hilar. de Synodis, sive de Fide Orientalium, c. 63, p. 1186, edit. Benedict. In the celebrated parallel between atheism and superstition, the bishop of Poitiers would have been surprised in the philosophic society of Bayle and Plutarch.

[3] Hilarius ad Constantium, l. i. c. 4, 5, p. 1227, 1228. This remarkable passage deserved the attention of Mr. Locke, who has transcribed it (vol. iii. p. 470) into the model of his new commonplace book.

patience and disappoint the curiosity of the laborious student. One question, which gradually arose from the Arian controversy, may, however, be noticed, as it served to produce and discriminate the three sects who were united only by their common aversion to the Homoousion of the Nicene synod. 1. If they were asked whether the Son was *like* unto the Father, the question was resolutely answered in the negative by the heretics who adhered to the principles of Arius, or indeed to those of philosophy, which seem to establish an infinite difference between the Creator and the most excellent of his creatures. This obvious consequence was maintained by Aëtius,[1] on whom the zeal of his adversaries bestowed the surname of the Atheist. His restless and aspiring spirit urged him to try almost every profession of human life. He was successively a slave, or at least a husband-man, a travelling tinker, a goldsmith, a physician, a school-master, a theologian, and at last the apostle of a new church, which was propagated by the abilities of his disciple Eunomius.[2] Armed with texts of Scripture, and with captious syllogisms from the logic of Aristotle, the subtle Aëtius had acquired the fame of an invincible disputant, whom it was impossible either to silence or to convince. Such talents engaged the friendship of the Arian bishops, till they were forced to renounce and even to persecute a dangerous ally, who, by the accuracy of his reasoning, had prejudiced their cause in the popular opinion, and offended the piety of their most devoted followers. 2. The omnipotence of the Creator suggested a specious and respectful solution of the *likeness* of the Father and the Son; and faith might humbly receive what reason could not presume to deny, that the Supreme God might communicate his infinite perfections, and create a being similar only to himself.[3] These Arians were powerfully supported by the weight and abilities of their leaders, who had succeeded to the management of the Eusebian

[1] In Philostorgius (l. iii. c. 15) the character and adventures of Aëtius appear singular enough, though they are carefully softened by the hand of a friend. The editor Godefroy (p. 153), who was more attached to his principles than to his author, has collected the odious circumstances which his various adversaries have preserved or invented.

[2] According to the judgment of a man who respected both those sectaries, Aëtius had been endowed with a stronger understanding, and Eunomius had acquired more art and learning (Philostorgius, l. viii. c. 18). The confession and apology of Eunomius (Fabricius, Bibliot. Græc. tom. viii. p. 258-305) is one of the few heretical pieces which have escaped.

[3] Yet, according to the opinion of Estius and Bull (p. 297), there is one power, that of creation, which God *cannot* communicate to a creature. Estius, who so accurately defined the limits of Omnipotence, was a Dutch-man by birth, and by trade a scholastic divine. Dupin, Bibliot. Ecclés. tom. xvii. p. 45.

interest, and who occupied the principal thrones of the East. They detested, perhaps with some affectation, the impiety of Aëtius; they professed to believe, either without reserve or according to the Scriptures, that the Son was different from all *other* creatures, and similar only to the Father. But they denied that he was either of the same or of a similar substance; sometimes boldly justifying their dissent, and sometimes objecting to the use of the word substance, which seems to imply an adequate, or at least a distinct, notion of the nature of the Deity. 3. The sect which asserted the doctrine of a similar substance was the most numerous, at least in the provinces of Asia; and when the leaders of both parties were assembled in the council of Seleucia,[1] *their* opinion would have prevailed by a majority of one hundred and five to forty-three bishops. The Greek word which was chosen to express this mysterious resemblance bears so close an affinity to the orthodox symbol, that the profane of every age have derided the furious contests which the difference of a single diphthong excited between the Homoousians and the Homoiousians. As it frequently happens that the sounds and characters which approach the nearest to each other accidentally represent the most opposite ideas, the observation would be itself ridiculous, if it were possible to mark any real and sensible distinction between the doctrine of the Semi-Arians, as they were improperly styled, and that of the Catholics themselves. The bishop of Poitiers, who in his Phrygian exile very wisely aimed at a coalition of parties, endeavours to prove that, by a pious and faithful interpretation,[2] the *Homoiousion* may be reduced to a consubstantial sense. Yet he confesses that the word has a dark and suspicious aspect; and, as if darkness were congenial to theological disputes, the Semi-Arians, who advanced to the doors of the church, assailed them with the most unrelenting fury.

The provinces of Egypt and Asia, which cultivated the language and manners of the Greeks, had deeply imbibed the venom of the Arian controversy. The familiar study of the Platonic

---

[1] Sabinus (ap. Socrat. l. ii. c. 39) had copied the acts; Athanasius and Hilary have explained the divisions of this Arian synod; the other circumstances which are relative to it are carefully collected by Baronius and Tillemont.

[2] Fideli et piâ intelligentiâ . . . De Synod. c. 77, p. 1193. In his short apologetical notes (first published by the Benedictines from a MS. of Chartres) he observes that he used this cautious expression, quia intelligerem et impiam, p. 1206. See p. 1146. Philostorgius, who saw those objects through a different medium, is inclined to forget the difference of the important diphthong. See in particular viii. 17, and Godefroy, p. 352.

system, a vain and argumentative disposition, a copious and flexible idiom, supplied the clergy and people of the East with an inexhaustible flow of words and distinctions; and, in the midst of their fierce contentions, they easily forgot the doubt which is recommended by philosophy, and the submission which is enjoined by religion. The inhabitants of the West were of a less inquisitive spirit; their passions were not so forcibly moved by invisible objects, their minds were less frequently exercised by the habits of dispute; and such was the happy ignorance of the Gallican church, that Hilary himself, above thirty years after the first general council, was still a stranger to the Nicene creed.[1] The Latins had received the rays of divine knowledge through the dark and doubtful medium of a translation. The poverty and stubbornness of their native tongue was not always capable of affording just equivalents for the Greek terms, for the technical words of the Platonic philosophy,[2] which had been consecrated, by the Gospel or by the church, to express the mysteries of the Christian faith, and a verbal defect might introduce into the Latin theology a long train of error or perplexity.[3] But as the western provincials had the good fortune of deriving their religion from an orthodox source, they preserved with steadiness the doctrine which they had accepted with docility; and when the Arian pestilence approached their frontiers, they were supplied with the seasonable preservative of the Homoousion by the paternal care of the Roman pontiff. Their sentiments and their temper were displayed in the memorable synod of Rimini, which surpassed in numbers the council of Nice, since it was composed of above four hundred bishops of Italy, Africa, Spain, Gaul, Britain, and Illyricum. From the first debates it appeared that only fourscore prelates adhered to the party, though *they* affected to anathematise the name and memory of Arius. But this inferiority was compensated by the advantages of skill, of experience, and of discipline; and the minority was conducted by Valens and Ursacius, two bishops of Illyricum, who had spent

[1] Testor Deum cœli atque terræ me cum neutrum audissem, semper tamen utrumque sensisse. . . . Regeneratus pridem et in episcopatu aliquantisper manens fidem Nicenam nunquam nisi exsulaturus audivi. Hilar. de Synodis, c. xci. p. 1205. The Benedictines are persuaded that he governed the diocese of Poitiers several years before his exile.

[2] Seneca (Epist. lviii.) complains that even the τὸ ὄν of the Platonists (the *ens* of the bolder schoolmen) could not be expressed by a Latin noun.

[3] The preference which the fourth council of the Lateran at length gave to a *numerical* rather than a *generical* unity (see Petav. tom. ii. l. iv. c. 13, p. 424) was favoured by the Latin language: τριάς seems to excite the idea of substance, *trinitas* of qualities.

their lives in the intrigues of courts and councils, and who had been trained under the Eusebian banner in the religious wars of the East. By their arguments and negotiations they embarrassed, they confounded, they at last deceived the honest simplicity of the Latin bishops, who suffered the palladium of the faith to be extorted from their hands by fraud and importunity, rather than by open violence. The council of Rimini was not allowed to separate till the members had imprudently subscribed a captious creed, in which some expressions, susceptible of an heretical sense, were inserted in the room of the Homoousion. It was on this occasion that, according to Jerom, the world was surprised to find itself Arian.[1] But the bishops of the Latin provinces had no sooner reached their respective dioceses than they discovered their mistake, and repented of their weakness. The ignominious capitulation was rejected with disdain and abhorrence, and the Homoousian standard, which had been shaken but not overthrown, was more firmly replanted in all the churches of the West.[2]

Such was the rise and progress, and such were the natural revolutions, of those theological disputes which disturbed the peace of Christianity under the reigns of Constantine and of his sons. But as those princes presumed to extend their despotism over the faith, as well as over the lives and fortunes of their subjects, the weight of their suffrage sometimes inclined the ecclesiastical balance: and the prerogatives of the King of Heaven were settled, or changed, or modified, in the cabinet of an earthly monarch.

The unhappy spirit of discord which pervaded the provinces of the East interrupted the triumph of Constantine; but the emperor continued for some time to view with cool and careless indifference the object of the dispute. As he was yet ignorant of the difficulty of appeasing the quarrels of theologians, he addressed to the contending parties, to Alexander and to Arius, a moderating epistle;[3] which may be ascribed with far greater

[1] Ingemuit totus orbis, et Arianum se esse miratus est. Hieronym. adv. Lucifer. tom. i. p. 145. [Tom. ii. p. 191, ed. Vallars.]

[2] The story of the council of Rimini is very elegantly told by Sulpicius Severus (Hist. Sacra, l. ii. p. 419-430, edit. Lugd. Bat. 1647), and by Jerom, in his dialogue against the Luciferians. The design of the latter is to apologise for the conduct of the Latin bishops, who were deceived, and who repented.

[3] Eusebius, in Vit. Constant. l. ii. c. 64-72. The principles of toleration and religious indifference contained in this epistle have given great offence to Baronius, Tillemont, etc., who suppose that the emperor had some evil counsellor, either Satan or Eusebius, at his elbow. See Jortin's Remarks, tom. ii. p. 183.

reason to the untutored sense of a soldier and statesman than to the dictates of any of his episcopal counsellors. He attributes the origin of the whole controversy to a trifling and subtle question concerning an incomprehensible point of the law, which was foolishly asked by the bishop, and imprudently resolved by the presbyter. He laments that the Christian people, who had the same God, the same religion, and the same worship, should be divided by such inconsiderable distinctions; and he seriously recommends to the clergy of Alexandria the example of the Greek philosophers, who could maintain their arguments without losing their temper, and assert their freedom without violating their friendship. The indifference and contempt of the sovereign would have been, perhaps, the most effectual method of silencing the dispute, if the popular current had been less rapid and impetuous, and if Constantine himself, in the midst of faction and fanaticism, could have preserved the calm possession of his own mind. But his ecclesiastical ministers soon contrived to seduce the impartiality of the magistrate, and to awaken the zeal of the proselyte. He was provoked by the insults which had been offered to his statues; he was alarmed by the real as well as the imaginary magnitude of the spreading mischief; and he extinguished the hope of peace and toleration, from the moment that he assembled three hundred bishops within the walls of the same palace. The presence of the monarch swelled the importance of the debate; his attention multiplied the arguments; and he exposed his person with a patient intrepidity which animated the valour of the combatants. Notwithstanding the applause which has been bestowed on the eloquence and sagacity of Constantine,[1] a Roman general, whose religion might be still a subject of doubt, and whose mind had not been enlightened either by study or by inspiration, was indifferently qualified to discuss, in the Greek language, a metaphysical question, or an article of faith. But the credit of his favourite Osius, who appears to have presided in the council of Nice, might dispose the emperor in favour of the orthodox party; and a well-timed insinuation, that the same Eusebius of Nicomedia, who now protected the heretic, had lately assisted the tyrant,[2] might exasperate him against their adversaries. The Nicene creed was ratified by Constantine; and his firm declaration, that

[1] Eusebius in Vit. Constantin. l. iii. c. 13.

[2] Theodoret has preserved (l. i. c. 20) an epistle from Constantine to the people of Nicomedia, in which the monarch declares himself the public accuser of one of his subjects; he styles Eusebius ὁ τῆς τυραννικῆς ὠμότητος συμμύστης; and complains of his hostile behaviour during the civil war.

those who resisted the divine judgment of the synod must prepare themselves for an immediate exile, annihilated the murmurs
of a feeble opposition; which, from seventeen, was almost
instantly reduced to two, protesting bishops. Eusebius of
Cæsarea yielded a reluctant and ambiguous consent to the
Homoousion;[1] and the wavering conduct of the Nicomedian
Eusebius served only to delay about three months his disgrace
and exile.[2] The impious Arius was banished into one of the
remote provinces of Illyricum; his person and disciples were
branded, by law, with the odious name of Porphyrians; his
writings were condemned to the flames, and a capital punishment was denounced against those in whose possession they
should be found. The emperor had now imbibed the spirit of
controversy, and the angry sarcastic style of his edicts was
designed to inspire his subjects with the hatred which he had
conceived against the enemies of Christ.[3]

But, as if the conduct of the emperor had been guided by
passion instead of principle, three years from the council of Nice
were scarcely elapsed before he discovered some symptoms of
mercy, and even of indulgence, towards the proscribed sect,
which was secretly protected by his favourite sister. The
exiles were recalled; and Eusebius, who gradually resumed his
influence over the mind of Constantine, was restored to the
episcopal throne, from which he had been ignominiously degraded. Arius himself was treated by the whole court with the
respect which would have been due to an innocent and oppressed
man. His faith was approved by the synod of Jerusalem; and
the emperor seemed impatient to repair his injustice, by issuing
an absolute command that he should be solemnly admitted to the
communion in the cathedral of Constantinople. On the same
day which had been fixed for the triumph of Arius, he expired;
and the strange and horrid circumstances of his death might
excite a suspicion that the orthodox saints had contributed
more efficaciously than by their prayers to deliver the church

---

[1] See in Socrates (l. i. c. 8), or rather in Theodoret (l. i. c. 12), an original
letter of Eusebius of Cæsarea, in which he attempts to justify his subscribing the Homoousion. The character of Eusebius has always been a
problem; but those who have read the second critical epistle of Le Clerc
(Ars Critica, tom. iii. p. 30-69) must entertain a very unfavourable opinion
of the orthodoxy and sincerity of the bishop of Cæsarea.

[2] Athanasius, tom. i. p. 727 [tom. i. p. 247, ed. Bened.]; Philostorgius,
l. i. c. 10; and Godefroy's Commentary, p. 41.

[3] Socrates, l. i. c. 9. In his circular letters, which were addressed to the
several cities, Constantine employed against the heretics the arms of ridicule
and *comic* raillery.

from the most formidable of her enemies.[1] The three principal leaders of the catholics, Athanasius of Alexandria, Eustathius of Antioch, and Paul of Constantinople, were deposed on various accusations, by the sentence of numerous councils; and were afterwards banished into distant provinces by the first of the Christian emperors, who, in the last moments of his life received the rites of baptism from the Arian bishop of Nicomedia. The ecclesiastical government of Constantine cannot be justified from the reproach of levity and weakness. But the credulous monarch, unskilled in the stratagems of theological warfare, might be deceived by the modest and specious professions of the heretics, whose sentiments he never perfectly understood; and while he protected Arius, and persecuted Athanasius, he still considered the council of Nice as the bulwark of the Christian faith, and the peculiar glory of his own reign.[2]

The sons of Constantine must have been admitted from their childhood into the rank of catechumens, but they imitated, in the delay of their baptism, the example of their father. Like him, they presumed to pronounce their judgment on mysteries into which they had never been regularly initiated:[3] and the fate of the Trinitarian controversy depended, in a great measure, on the sentiments of Constantius, who inherited the provinces of the East, and acquired the possession of the whole empire. The Arian presbyter or bishop, who had secreted for his use the testament of the deceased emperor, improved the fortunate occasion which had introduced him to the familiarity of a prince whose public counsels were always swayed by his domestic favourites. The eunuchs and slaves diffused the spiritual poison through the palace, and the dangerous infection was communicated by the female attendants to the guards, and

---

[1] We derive the original story from Athanasius (tom. i. p. 670), who expresses some reluctance to stigmatise the memory of the dead. He might exaggerate; but the perpetual commerce of Alexandria and Constantinople would have rendered it dangerous to invent. Those who press the literal narrative of the death of Arius (his bowels suddenly burst out in a privy) must make their option between *poison* and *miracle*.

[2] The change in the sentiments, or at least in the conduct of Constantine, may be traced in Eusebius (in Vit. Constant. l. iii. c. 23, l. iv. c. 41), Socrates (l. i. c. 23-39), Sozomen (l. ii. c. 16-34), Theodoret (l. i. c. 14-34), and Philostorgius (l. ii. c. 1-17). But the first of these writers was too near the scene of action, and the others were too remote from it. It is singular enough that the important task of continuing the history of the church should have been left for two laymen and a heretic.

[3] Quia etiam tum catechumenus sacramentum fidei merito videretur potuisse nescire. Sulp. Sever. Hist. Sacra, l. ii. p. 410.

by the empress to her unsuspicious husband.[1] The partiality
which Constantius always expressed towards the Eusebian
faction was insensibly fortified by the dexterous management of
their leaders; and his victory over the tyrant Magnentius
increased his inclination, as well as ability, to employ the arms
of power in the cause of Arianism. While the two armies were
engaged in the plains of Mursa, and the fate of the two rivals
depended on the chance of war, the son of Constantine passed
the anxious moments in a church of the martyrs, under the walls
of the city. His spiritual comforter, Valens, the Arian bishop
of the diocese, employed the most artful precautions to obtain
such early intelligence as might secure either his favour or his
escape. A secret chain of swift and trusty messengers informed
him of the vicissitudes of the battle; and while the courtiers
stood trembling round their affrighted master, Valens assured
him that the Gallic legions gave way; and insinuated, with some
presence of mind, that the glorious event had been revealed to
him by an angel. The grateful emperor ascribed his success to
the merits and intercession of the bishop of Mursa, whose faith
had deserved the public and miraculous approbation of Heaven.[2]
The Arians, who considered as their own the victory of Constantius, preferred his glory to that of his father.[3] Cyril, bishop of
Jerusalem, immediately composed the description of a celestial
cross, encircled with a splendid rainbow, which, during the
festival of Pentecost, about the third hour of the day, had
appeared over the Mount of Olives, to the edification of the
devout pilgrims and the people of the holy city.[4] The size of
the meteor was gradually magnified; and the Arian historian
has ventured to affirm that it was conspicuous to the two armies
in the plains of Pannonia; and that the tyrant, who is purposely

---

[1] Socrates, l. ii. c. 2.   Sozomen, l. iii. c. 18.   Athanas. tom. i. p. 813, 834
[tom. i. p. 289, ed. Bened. Patav. 1777].   He observes that the eunuchs are
the natural enemies of the *Son.*   Compare Dr. Jortin's Remarks on Ecclesiastical History, vol. iv. p. 3, with a certain genealogy in *Candide* (ch. iv.),
which ends with one of the first companions of Christopher Columbus.
[2] Sulpicius Severus in Hist. Sacra, l. ii. p. 405, 406.
[3] Cyril (apud Baron. A.D. 353, No. 26) expressly observes that in the reign
of Constantine the cross had been found in the bowels of the earth; but
that it had appeared, in the reign of Constantius, in the midst of the
heavens.   This opposition evidently proves that Cyril was ignorant of the
stupendous miracle to which the conversion of Constantine is attributed;
and this ignorance is the more surprising, since it was no more than twelve
years after his death that Cyril was consecrated bishop of Jerusalem by
the immediate successor of Eusebius of Cæsarea.   See Tillemont, Mém.
Ecclés. tom. viii. p. 715.
[4] It is not easy to determine how far the ingenuity of Cyril might be
assisted by some natural appearances of a solar halo.

represented as an idolater, fled before the auspicious sign of
orthodox Christianity.[1]

The sentiments of a judicious stranger, who has impartially
considered the progress of civil or ecclesiastical discord, are
always entitled to our notice: and a short passage of Ammianus,
who served in the armies, and studied the character, of Constantius, is perhaps of more value than many pages of theological
invectives. " The Christian religion, which, in itself," says that
moderate historian, " is plain and simple, *he* confounded by the
dotage of superstition. Instead of reconciling the parties by
the weight of his authority, he cherished and propagated, by
verbal disputes, the differences which his vain curiosity had
excited. The highways were covered with troops of bishops
galloping from every side to the assemblies, which they call
synods; and while they laboured to reduce the whole sect to
their own particular opinions, the public establishment of the
posts was almost ruined by their hasty and repeated journeys." [2]
Our more intimate knowledge of the ecclesiastical transactions
of the reign of Constantius would furnish an ample commentary
on this remarkable passage; which justifies the rational apprehensions of Athanasius, that the restless activity of the clergy,
who wandered round the empire in search of the true faith, would
excite the contempt and laughter of the unbelieving world.[3] As
soon as the emperor was relieved from the terrors of the civil
war, he devoted the leisure of his winter quarters at Arles, Milan,
Sirmium, and Constantinople, to the amusement or toils of controversy: the sword of the magistrate, and even of the tyrant,
was unsheathed, to enforce the reasons of the theologian; and
as he opposed the orthodox faith of Nice, it is readily confessed
that his incapacity and ignorance were equal to his presumption.[4]
The eunuchs, the women, and the bishops, who governed the
vain and feeble mind of the emperor, had inspired him with an

[1] Philostorgius, l. iii. c. 26. He is followed by the author of the Alexandrian Chronicle, by Cedrenus, and by Nicephorus (see Gothofred. Dissert.
p. 188). They could not refuse a miracle, even from the hand of an
enemy.

[2] So curious a passage well deserves to be transcribed. Christianam
religionem absolutam et simplicem, anili superstitione confundens; in quâ
scrutandâ perplexius, quam componendâ gravius excitaret discidia plurima;
quæ progressa fusius aluit concertatione verborum, ut catervis antistitum
jumentis publicis ultro citroque discurrentibus, per synodos (quas appellant)
dum ritum omnem ad suum trahere conantur (Valesius reads *conatur*) rei
vehiculariæ concideret nervos. Ammianus, xxi. 16.

[3] Athanas. tom. i. p. 870.

[4] Socrates, l. ii. c. 35-47. Sozomen, l. iv. c. 12-30. Theodoret, l. ii. c.
18-32. Philostorg. l. iv. c. 4-12, l. v. c. 1-4, l. vi. c. 1-5.

insuperable dislike to the Homoousion; but his timid conscience was alarmed by the impiety of Aëtius. The guilt of that atheist was aggravated by the suspicious favour of the unfortunate Gallus; and even the deaths of the Imperial ministers who had been massacred at Antioch were imputed to the suggestions of that dangerous sophist. The mind of Constantius, which could neither be moderated by reason nor fixed by faith, was blindly impelled to either side of the dark and empty abyss, by his horror of the opposite extreme; he alternately embraced and condemned the sentiments, he successively banished and recalled the leaders, of the Arian and Semi-Arian factions.[1] During the season of public business or festivity, he employed whole days, and even nights, in selecting the words, and weighing the syllables, which composed his fluctuating creeds. The subject of his meditations still pursued and occupied his slumbers: the incoherent dreams of the emperor were received as celestial visions, and he accepted with complacency the lofty title of bishop of bishops, from those ecclesiastics who forgot the interest of their order for the gratification of their passions. The design of establishing an uniformity of doctrine, which had engaged him to convene so many synods in Gaul, Italy, Illyricum, and Asia, was repeatedly baffled by his own levity, by the divisions of the Arians, and by the resistance of the catholics; and he resolved, as the last and decisive effort, imperiously to dictate the decrees of a general council. The destructive earthquake of Nicomedia, the difficulty of finding a convenient place, and perhaps some secret motives of policy, produced an alteration in the summons. The bishops of the East were directed to meet at Seleucia, in Isauria; while those of the West held their deliberations at Rimini, on the coast of the Hadriatic; and instead of two or three deputies from each province, the whole episcopal body was ordered to march. The Eastern council, after consuming four days in fierce and unavailing debate, separated without any definitive conclusion. The council of the West was protracted till the seventh month. Taurus, the Prætorian præfect, was instructed not to dismiss the prelates till they should all be united in the same opinion; and his efforts

---

[1] Sozomen, l. iv. c. 23. Athanas. tom. i. p. 831 [tom. i. p. 281, ed. Ben.]. Tillemont (Mém. Ecclés. tom. vii. p. 947) has collected several instances of the haughty fanaticism of Constantius from the detached treatises of Lucifer of Cagliari. The very titles of these treatises inspire zeal and terror:—" Moriendum pro Dei Filio." " De Regibus Apostaticis." " De non conveniendo cum Hæretico." " De non parcendo in Deum delinquentibus."

were supported by a power of banishing fifteen of the most refractory, and a promise of the consulship if he achieved so difficult an adventure. His prayers and threats, the authority of
the sovereign, the sophistry of Valens and Ursacius, the distress
of cold and hunger, and the tedious melancholy of a hopeless
exile, at length extorted the reluctant consent of the bishops of
Rimini. The deputies of the East and of the West attended the
emperor in the palace of Constantinople, and he enjoyed the
satisfaction of imposing on the world a profession of faith which
established the *likeness*, without expressing the *consubstantiality*,
of the Son of God.[1] But the triumph of Arianism had been
preceded by the removal of the orthodox clergy, whom it was
impossible either to intimidate or to corrupt; and the reign of
Constantius was disgraced by the unjust and ineffectual persecution of the great Athanasius.

We have seldom an opportunity of observing, either in active
or speculative life, what effect may be produced, or what
obstacles may be surmounted, by the force of a single mind,
when it is inflexibly applied to the pursuit of a single object.
The immortal name of Athanasius [2] will never be separated from
the catholic doctrine of the Trinity, to whose defence he consecrated every moment and every faculty of his being. Educated
in the family of Alexander, he had vigorously opposed the early
progress of the Arian heresy: he exercised the important functions of secretary under the aged prelate; and the fathers of the
Nicene council beheld with surprise and respect the rising virtues
of the young deacon. In a time of public danger the dull claims
of age and of rank are sometimes superseded; and within five
months after his return from Nice the deacon Athanasius was
seated on the archiepiscopal throne of Egypt. He filled that
eminent station above forty-six years, and his long administration was spent in a perpetual combat against the powers of
Arianism. Five times was Athanasius expelled from his throne;
twenty years he passed as an exile or a fugitive; and almost

---

[1] Sulp. Sever. Hist. Sacra, l. ii. p. 418-430. The Greek historians were
very ignorant of the affairs of the West.

[2] We may regret that Gregory Nazianzen composed a panegyric instead
of a life of Athanasius, but we should enjoy and improve the advantage of
drawing our most authentic materials from the rich fund of his own
epistles and apologies (tom. i. p. 670-951). I shall not imitate the example
of Socrates (l. ii. c. 1), who published the first edition of his history without
giving himself the trouble to consult the writings of Athanasius. Yet even
Socrates, the more curious Sozomen, and the learned Theodoret, connect
the life of Athanasius with the series of ecclesiastical history. The diligence of Tillemont (tom. viii.) and of the Benedictine editors has collected
every fact and examined every difficulty.

every province of the Roman empire was successively witness to his merit, and his sufferings in the cause of the Homoousion, which he considered as the sole pleasure and business, as the duty and as the glory of his life. Amidst the storms of persecution, the archbishop of Alexandria was patient of labour, jealous of fame, careless of safety; and although his mind was tainted by the contagion of fanaticism, Athanasius displayed a superiority of character and abilities which would have qualified him, far better than the degenerate sons of Constantine, for the government of a great monarchy. His learning was much less profound and extensive than that of Eusebius of Cæsarea, and his rude eloquence could not be compared with the polished oratory of Gregory or Basil; but whenever the primate of Egypt was called upon to justify his sentiments or his conduct, his unpremeditated style, either of speaking or writing, was clear, forcible, and persuasive. He has always been revered in the orthodox school as one of the most accurate masters of the Christian theology; and he was supposed to possess two profane sciences, less adapted to the episcopal character—the knowledge of jurisprudence,[1] and that of divination.[2] Some fortunate conjectures of future events, which impartial reasoners might ascribe to the experience and judgment of Athanasius, were attributed by his friends to heavenly inspiration, and imputed by his enemies to infernal magic.

But as Athanasius was continually engaged with the prejudices and passions of every order of men, from the monk to the emperor, the knowledge of human nature was his first and most important science. He preserved a distinct and unbroken view of a scene which was incessantly shifting; and never failed to improve those decisive moments which are irrecoverably past before they are perceived by a common eye. The archbishop of Alexandria was capable of distinguishing how far he might boldly command, and where he must dexterously insinuate; how long he might contend with power, and when he must withdraw from persecution; and while he directed the thunders of the church against heresy and rebellion, he could assume, in the bosom of his own party, the flexible and indulgent temper of a

---

[1] Sulpicius Severus (Hist. Sacra, l. ii. p. 396) calls him a lawyer, a jurisconsult. This character cannot now be discovered either in the life or writings of Athanasius.

[2] Dicebatur enim fatidicarum sortium fidem, quæve augurales portenderent alites scientissime callens aliquoties prædixisse futura. Ammianus, xv. 7. A prophecy, or rather a joke, is related by Sozomen (l. iv. c. 10), which evidently proves (if the crows speak Latin) that Athanasius understood the language of the crows.

prudent leader.   The election of Athanasius has not escaped the
reproach of irregularity and precipitation;[1] but the propriety of
his behaviour conciliated the affections both of the clergy and of
the people.   The Alexandrians were impatient to rise in arms for
the defence of an eloquent and liberal pastor.   In his distress
he always derived support, or at least consolation, from the
faithful attachment of his parochial clergy; and the hundred
bishops of Egypt adhered, with unshaken zeal, to the cause of
Athanasius.   In the modest equipage which pride and policy
would affect, he frequently performed the episcopal visitation
of his provinces, from the mouth of the Nile to the confines of
Æthiopia; familiarly conversing with the meanest of the populace, and humbly saluting the saints and hermits of the desert.[2]
Nor was it only in ecclesiastical assemblies, among men whose
education and manners were similar to his own, that Athanasius
displayed the ascendancy of his genius.   He appeared with easy
and respectful firmness in the courts of princes; and in the
various turns of his prosperous and adverse fortune he never
lost the confidence of his friends, or the esteem of his enemies.

In his youth the primate of Egypt resisted the great Constantine, who had repeatedly signified his will that Arius should be
restored to the catholic communion.[3]   The emperor respected,
and might forgive, this inflexible resolution; and the faction who
considered Athanasius as their most formidable enemy were constrained to dissemble their hatred, and silently to prepare an
indirect and distant assault.   They scattered rumours and suspicions, represented the archbishop as a proud and oppressive
tyrant, and boldly accused him of violating the treaty which had
been ratified in the Nicene council with the schismatic followers

---

[1] The irregular ordination of Athanasius was slightly mentioned in the
councils which were held against him (see Philostorg. l. ii. c. 11, and Godefroy, p. 71); but it can scarcely be supposed that the assembly of the
bishops of Egypt would solemnly attest a *public* falsehood.   Athanas. tom.
i. p. 726.

[2] See the History of the Fathers of the Desert, published by Rosweide;
and Tillemont, Mém. Ecclés. tom. vii., in the Lives of Antony, Pachomius,
etc.   Athanasius himself, who did not disdain to compose the life of his
friend Antony, has carefully observed how often the holy monk deplored
and prophesied the mischiefs of the Arian heresy.   Athanas. tom. ii. p. 492,
498, etc. [tom. i. p. 677, ed. Bened.]

[3] At first Constantine threatened in *speaking*, but requested in *writing*,
καὶ ἀγράφως μὲν ἠπείλει, γράφων δὲ ἤξίου.   His letters gradually assumed
a menacing tone; but while he required that the entrance of the church
should be open to *all*, he avoided the odious name of Arius.   Athanasius,
like a skilful politician, has accurately marked these distinctions (tom. i.
p. 788 [tom. i. p. 140, ed. Bened.]), which allowed him some scope for
excuse and delay.

of Meletius.[1] Athanasius had openly disapproved that ignominious peace, and the emperor was disposed to believe that he
had abused his ecclesiastical and civil power to persecute those
odious sectaries; that he had sacrilegiously broken a chalice in
one of their churches of Maræotis; that he had whipped or imprisoned six of their bishops; and that Arsenius, a seventh
bishop of the same party, had been murdered, or at least mutilated, by the cruel hand of the primate.[2] These charges, which
affected his honour and his life, were referred by Constantine to
his brother Dalmatius, the censor, who resided at Antioch; the
synods of Cæsarea and Tyre were successively convened; and
the bishops of the East were instructed to judge the cause of
Athanasius before they proceeded to consecrate the new church
of the Resurrection at Jerusalem. The primate might be conscious of his innocence; but he was sensible that the same
implacable spirit which had dictated the accusation would direct
the proceeding and pronounce the sentence. He prudently
declined the tribunal of his enemies, despised the summons of the
synod of Cæsarea; and, after a long and artful delay, submitted
to the peremptory commands of the emperor, who threatened
to punish his criminal disobedience if he refused to appear in the
council of Tyre.[3] Before Athanasius, at the head of fifty Egyptian prelates, sailed from Alexandria, he had wisely secured the
alliance of the Meletians; and Arsenius himself, his imaginary
victim, and his secret friend, was privately concealed in his train.
The synod of Tyre was conducted by Eusebius of Cæsarea, with
more passion, and with less art, than his learning and experience
might promise; his numerous faction repeated the names of
homicide and tyrant; and their clamours were encouraged by

---

[1] The Meletians in Egypt, like the Donatists in Africa, were produced by
an episcopal quarrel which arose from the persecution. I have not leisure
to pursue the obscure controversy, which seems to have been misrepresented by the partiality of Athanasius and the ignorance of Epiphanius.
See Mosheim's General History of the Church, vol. i. p. 201.

[2] The treatment of the six bishops is specified by Sozomen (l. ii. c. 25);
but Athanasius himself, so copious on the subject of Arsenius and the
chalice, leaves this grave accusation without a reply.

[This is an error on Gibbon's part. Athanasius was summoned to
Nicomedia to answer the first list of accusations, and completely established
his innocence with respect to them. The affair of Arsenius was being
investigated when Constantine learned that Arsenius was alive, and immediately stopped the proceedings.—O. S.]

[3] Athanas. tom. i. p. 788 [tom. i. p. 147, ed. Bened.]. Socrates, l. i. c. 28.
Sozomen, l. ii. c. 25. The emperor, in his Epistle of Convocation (Euseb.
in Vit. Constant. l. iv. c. 42), seems to prejudge some members of the
clergy, and it was more than probable that the synod would apply those
reproaches to Athanasius.

the seeming patience of Athanasius, who expected the decisive
moment to produce Arsenius alive and unhurt in the midst of the
assembly.   The nature of the other charges did not admit of
such clear and satisfactory replies; yet, the archbishop was able
to prove that, in the village where he was accused of breaking a
consecrated chalice, neither church nor altar nor chalice could
really exist.   The Arians, who had secretly determined the guilt
and condemnation of their enemy, attempted, however, to disguise their injustice by the imitation of judicial forms: the synod
appointed an episcopal commission of six delegates to collect
evidence on the spot; and this measure, which was vigorously
opposed by the Egyptian bishops, opened new scenes of violence
and perjury.[1]   After the return of the deputies from Alexandria,
the majority of the council pronounced the final sentence of
degradation and exile against the primate of Egypt.   The decree,
expressed in the fiercest language of malice and revenge, was
communicated to the emperor and the catholic church; and the
bishops immediately resumed a mild and devout aspect, such as
became their holy pilgrimage to the Sepulchre of Christ.[2]

But the injustice of these ecclesiastical judges had not been
countenanced by the submission, or even by the presence, of
Athanasius.   He resolved to make a bold and dangerous experiment, whether the throne was inaccessible to the voice of truth;
and before the final sentence could be pronounced at Tyre, the
intrepid primate threw himself into a bark which was ready
to hoist sail for the Imperial city.   The request of a formal
audience might have been opposed or eluded; but Athanasius
concealed his arrival, watched the moment of Constantine's
return from an adjacent villa, and boldly encountered his angry
sovereign as he passed on horseback through the principal street
of Constantinople.   So strange an apparition excited his surprise
and indignation; and the guards were ordered to remove the
importunate suitor; but his resentment was subdued by involuntary respect; and the haughty spirit of the emperor was awed
by the courage and eloquence of a bishop who implored his
justice and awakened his conscience.[3]   Constantine listened to

---

[1] See, in particular, the second Apology of Athanasius (tom. i. p. 763-
808), and his Epistles to the Monks (p. 808-866 [tom. i. p. 271 sqq., ed.
Bened.]).   They are justified by original and authentic documents; but
they would inspire more confidence if he appeared less innocent, and his
enemies less absurd.

[2] Eusebius in Vit. Constantin. l. iv. c. 41-47.

[3] Athanas. tom. i. p. 804 [tom. i. p. 159, ed. Bened. 1777].   In a church
dedicated to St. Athanasius, this situation would afford a better subject
for a picture than most of the stories of miracles and martyrdoms.

the complaints of Athanasius with impartial and even gracious attention; the members of the synod of Tyre were summoned to justify their proceedings; and the arts of the Eusebian faction would have been confounded if they had not aggravated the guilt of the primate by the dexterous supposition of an unpardonable offence—a criminal design to intercept and detain the corn-fleet of Alexandria, which supplied the subsistence of the new capital.[1] The emperor was satisfied that the peace of Egypt would be secured by the absence of a popular leader; but he refused to fill the vacancy of the archiepiscopal throne; and the sentence which, after long hesitation, he pronounced, was that of a jealous ostracism rather than of an ignominious exile. In the remote province of Gaul, but in the hospitable court of Treves, Athanasius passed about twenty-eight months. The death of the emperor changed the face of public affairs; and, amidst the general indulgence of a young reign, the primate was restored to his country by an honourable edict of the younger Constantine, who expressed a deep sense of the innocence and merit of his venerable guest.[2]

The death of that prince exposed Athanasius to a second persecution; and the feeble Constantius, the sovereign of the East, soon became the secret accomplice of the Eusebians. Ninety bishops of that sect or faction assembled at Antioch under the specious pretence of dedicating the cathedral. They composed an ambiguous creed, which is faintly tinged with the colours of Semi-Arianism, and twenty-five canons, which still regulate the discipline of the orthodox Greeks.[3] It was decided, with some appearance of equity, that a bishop, deprived by a synod, should not resume his episcopal functions till he had been absolved by

[1] Athanas, tom. i. p. 729 [tom. i. p. 104, ed. Bened.]. Eunapius has related (in Vit. Sophist. p. 36, 37 [in Ædesio], edit. Commelin) a strange example of the cruelty and credulity of Constantine on a similar occasion. The eloquent Sopater, a Syrian philosopher, enjoyed his friendship, and provoked the resentment of Ablavius, his Prætorian præfect. The corn-fleet was detained for want of a south wind; the people of Constantinople were discontented; and Sopater was beheaded, on a charge that he had *bound* the winds by the power of magic. Suidas adds, that Constantine wished to prove, by this execution, that he had absolutely renounced the superstition of the Gentiles.

[2] In his return he saw Constantius twice—at Viminiacum, and at Cæsarea in Cappadocia (Athanas. tom. i. p. 676 [tom. i. p. 236, ed. Bened.]). Tillemont supposes that Constantine introduced him to the meeting of the three royal brothers in Pannonia. (Mémoires Ecclés. tom. viii. p. 69.)

[3] See Beveridge, Pandect. tom. i. p. 429-452, and tom. ii. Annotation. p. 182; Tillemont, Mém. Ecclés. tom. vi. p. 310-324. St. Hilary of Poitiers has mentioned this synod of Antioch with too much favour and respect. He reckons ninety-seven bishops.

the judgment of an equal synod; the law was immediately applied to the case of Athanasius; the council of Antioch pronounced, or rather confirmed, his degradation: a stranger, named Gregory, was seated on his throne; and Philagrius,[1] the præfect of Egypt, was instructed to support the new primate with the civil and military powers of the province. Oppressed by the conspiracy of the Asiatic prelates, Athanasius withdrew from Alexandria and passed three years [2] as an exile and a suppliant on the holy threshold of the Vatican.[3] By the assiduous study of the Latin language he soon qualified himself to negotiate with the western clergy; his decent flattery swayed and directed the haughty Julius: the Roman pontiff was persuaded to consider his appeal as the peculiar interest of the Apostolic see; and his innocence was unanimously declared in a council of fifty bishops of Italy. At the end of three years the primate was summoned to the court of Milan by the emperor Constans, who, in the indulgence of unlawful pleasures, still professed a lively regard for the orthodox faith. The cause of truth and justice was promoted by the influence of gold,[4] and the ministers of Constans advised their sovereign to require the convocation of an ecclesiastical assembly, which might act as the representatives of the catholic church. Ninety-four bishops of the West, seventy-six bishops of the East, encountered each other at Sardica, on the verge of the two empires, but in the dominions of the protector of Athanasius. Their debates soon degenerated into hostile alter-

---

[1] This magistrate, so odious to Athanasius, is praised by Gregory Nazianzen, tom. i. Orat. xxi. p. 390, 391 [ed. Par. 1630].

Sæpe premente Deo fert Deus alter opem.

For the credit of human nature, I am always pleased to discover some good qualities in those men whom party has represented as tyrants and monsters.

[2] The chronological difficulties which perplex the residence of Athanasius at Rome are strenuously agitated by Valesius (Observat. ad Calcem, tom. ii.; Hist. Eccles. l. i. c. 1-5) and Tillemont (Mém. Ecclés. tom. viii. p. 674, etc.). I have followed the simple hypothesis of Valesius, who allows only one journey after the intrusion of Gregory.

[3] I cannot forbear transcribing a judicious observation of Wetstein (Prolegomen. N. T. p. 19):—Si tamen Historiam Ecclesiasticam velimus consulere, patebit jam inde a seculo quarto, cum, ortis controversiis, ecclesiæ Græciæ doctores in duas partes scinderentur, ingenio, eloquentiâ, numero, tantum non æquales, eam partem quæ vincere cupiebat Romam confugisse, majestatemque pontificis comiter coluisse, eoque pacto oppressis per pontificem et episcopos Latinos adversariis prævaluisse, atque orthodoxiam in conciliis stabilivisse. Eam ob causam Athanasius, non sine comitatu, Romam petiit, pluresque annos ibi hæsit.

[4] Philostorgius, l. iii. c. 12. If any corruption was used to promote the interest of religion, an advocate of Athanasius might justify or excuse this questionable conduct by the example of Cato and Sidney, the former of whom is *said* to have given, and the latter to have received, a bribe in the cause of liberty.

cations; the Asiatics, apprehensive for their personal safety, retired to Philippopolis in Thrace; and the rival synods reciprocally hurled their spiritual thunders against their enemies, whom they piously condemned as the enemies of the true God. Their decrees were published and ratified in their respective provinces: and Athanasius, who in the West was revered as a saint, was exposed as a criminal to the abhorrence of the East.[1] The council of Sardica reveals the first symptoms of discord and schism between the Greek and Latin churches, which were separated by the accidental difference of faith and the permanent distinction of language.

During his second exile in the West, Athanasius was frequently admitted to the Imperial presence—at Capua, Lodi, Milan, Verona, Padua, Aquileia, and Treves. The bishop of the diocese usually assisted at these interviews; the master of the offices stood before the veil or curtain of the sacred apartment; and the uniform moderation of the primate might be attested by these respectable witnesses, to whose evidence he solemnly appeals.[2] Prudence would undoubtedly suggest the mild and respectful tone that became a subject and a bishop. In these familiar conferences with the sovereign of the West, Athanasius might lament the error of Constantius, but he boldly arraigned the guilt of his eunuchs and his Arian prelates; deplored the distress and danger of the catholic church; and excited Constans to emulate the zeal and glory of his father. The emperor declared his resolution of employing the troops and treasures of Europe in the orthodox cause; and signified, by a concise and peremptory epistle to his brother Constantius, that, unless he consented to the immediate restoration of Athanasius, he himself, with a fleet and army, would seat the archbishop on the throne of Alexandria.[3] But this religious war, so horrible to nature, was prevented by the timely compliance of Constantius; and the emperor of the East condescended to solicit a reconciliation with a subject whom he had injured. Athanasius waited

---

[1] The canon which allows appeals to the Roman pontiffs has almost raised the council of Sardica to the dignity of a general council, and its acts have been ignorantly or artfully confounded with those of the Nicene synod. See Tillemont, tom. viii. p. 689; and Geddes's Tracts, vol. ii. p. 419-460.

[2] As Athanasius dispersed secret invectives against Constantius (see the Epistle to the Monks) at the same time that he assured him of his profound respect, we might distrust the professions of the archbishop. Tom. i. p. 677.

[3] Notwithstanding the discreet silence of Athanasius and the manifest forgery of a letter inserted by Socrates, these menaces are proved by the unquestionable evidence of Lucifer of Cagliari, and even of Constantius himself. See Tillemont, tom. viii. p. 693.

with decent pride till he had received three successive epistles full of the strongest assurances of the protection, the favour, and the esteem of his sovereign; who invited him to resume his episcopal seat, and who added the humiliating precaution of engaging his principal ministers to attest the sincerity of his intentions. They were manifested in a still more public manner by the strict orders which were despatched into Egypt to recall the adherents of Athanasius, to restore their privileges, to proclaim their innocence, and to erase from the public registers the illegal proceedings which had been obtained during the prevalence of the Eusebian faction. After every satisfaction and security had been given which justice or even delicacy could require, the primate proceeded, by slow journeys, through the provinces of Thrace, Asia, and Syria; and his progress was marked by the abject homage of the Oriental bishops, who excited his contempt without deceiving his penetration.[1] At Antioch he saw the emperor Constantius; sustained, with modest firmness, the embraces and protestations of his master; and eluded the proposal of allowing the Arians a single church at Alexandria by claiming, in the other cities of the empire, a similar toleration for his own party; a reply which might have appeared just and moderate in the mouth of an independent prince. The entrance of the archbishop into his capital was a triumphal procession; absence and persecution had endeared him to the Alexandrians; his authority, which he exercised with rigour, was more firmly established; and his fame was diffused from Æthiopia to Britain, over the whole extent of the Christian world.[2]

But the subject who has reduced his prince to the necessity of dissembling can never expect a sincere and lasting forgiveness; and the tragic fate of Constans soon deprived Athanasius of a powerful and generous protector. The civil war between the assassin and the only surviving brother of Constans, which afflicted the empire above three years, secured an interval of repose to the catholic church; and the two contending parties

[1] I have always entertained some doubts concerning the retractation of Ursacius and Valens (Athanas. tom. i. p. 776 [tom. i. p. 139, ed. Bened. 1777]). Their epistles to Julius bishop of Rome, and to Athanasius himself, are of so different a cast from each other, that they cannot both be genuine: the one speaks the language of criminals who confess their guilt and infamy, the other of enemies, who solicit on equal terms an honourable reconciliation.

[2] The circumstances of his second return may be collected from Athanasius himself, tom. i. p. 769, and 822, 843 [tom. i. p. 283, ed. Bened.]. Socrates, l. ii. c. 15. Sozomen, l. iii. c. 19. Theodoret, l. ii. c. 11, 12. Philostorgius, l. iii. c. 12.

were desirous to conciliate the friendship of a bishop who, by the weight of his personal authority, might determine the fluctuating resolutions of an important province. He gave audience to the ambassadors of the tyrant, with whom he was afterwards accused of holding a secret correspondence; [1] and the emperor Constantius repeatedly assured his dearest father, the most reverend Athanasius, that, notwithstanding the malicious rumours which were circulated by their common enemies, he had inherited the sentiments, as well as the throne, of his deceased brother. [2] Gratitude and humanity would have disposed the primate of Egypt to deplore the untimely fate of Constans, and to abhor the guilt of Magnentius; but as he clearly understood that the apprehensions of Constantius were his only safeguard, the fervour of his prayers for the success of the righteous cause might perhaps be somewhat abated. The ruin of Athanasius was no longer contrived by the obscure malice of a few bigoted or angry bishops, who abused the authority of a credulous monarch. The monarch himself avowed the resolution, which he had so long suppressed, of avenging his private injuries; [3] and the first winter after his victory, which he passed at Arles, was employed against an enemy more odious to him than the vanquished tyrant of Gaul.

If the emperor had capriciously decreed the death of the most eminent and virtuous citizen of the republic, the cruel order would have been executed without hesitation by the ministers of open violence or of specious injustice. The caution, the delay, the difficulty with which he proceeded in the condemnation and punishment of a popular bishop, discovered to the world that the privileges of the church had already revived a sense of order and freedom in the Roman government. The sentence which was pronounced in the synod of Tyre, and subscribed by a large majority of the Eastern bishops, had never been expressly repealed; and as Athanasius had been once degraded from his episcopal dignity by the judgment of his brethren, every subsequent act might be considered as irregular,

---

[1] Athanasius (tom. i. p. 677, 678 [tom. i. p. 239, ed. Bened.]) defends his innocence by pathetic complaints, solemn assertions, and specious arguments. He admits that letters had been forged in his name, but he requests that his own secretaries and those of the tyrant may be examined, whether those letters had been written by the former or received by the latter.

[2] Athanas. tom. i. p. 825-844.

[3] Athanas. tom. i. p. 861. Theodoret, l. ii. c. 16. The emperor declared that he was more desirous to subdue Athanasius than he had been to vanquish Magnentius or Sylvanus.

and even criminal. But the memory of the firm and effectual support which the primate of Egypt had derived from the attachment of the Western church engaged Constantius to suspend the execution of the sentence till he had obtained the concurrence of the Latin bishops. Two years were consumed in ecclesiastical negotiations; and the important cause between the emperor and one of his subjects was solemnly debated, first in the synod of Arles, and afterwards in the great council of Milan,[1] which consisted of above three hundred bishops. Their integrity was gradually undermined by the arguments of the Arians, the dexterity of the eunuchs, and the pressing solicitations of a prince who gratified his revenge at the expense of his dignity, and exposed his own passions whilst he influenced those of the clergy. Corruption, the most infallible symptom of constitutional liberty, was successfully practised; honours, gifts, and immunities were offered and accepted as the price of an episcopal vote;[2] and the condemnation of the Alexandrian primate was artfully represented as the only measure which could restore the peace and union of the catholic church. The friends of Athanasius were not, however, wanting to their leader, or to their cause. With a manly spirit, which the sanctity of their character rendered less dangerous, they maintained, in public debate, and in private conference with the emperor, the eternal obligation of religion and justice. They declared that neither the hope of his favour, nor the fear of his displeasure, should prevail on them to join in the condemnation of an absent, an innocent, a respectable brother.[3] They affirmed, with apparent reason, that the illegal and obsolete decrees of the council of Tyre had long since been tacitly abolished by the Imperial edicts, the honourable re-establishment of the Archbishop of Alexandria, and the silence or recantation of his most clamorous

---

[1] The affairs of the council of Milan are so imperfectly and erroneously related by the Greek writers, that we must rejoice in the supply of some letters of Eusebius, extracted by Baronius from the archives of the church of Vercellæ, and of an old Life of Dionysius of Milan, published by Bollandus. See Baronius, A.D. 355, and Tillemont, tom. vii. p. 1415.

[2] The honours, presents, feasts, which seduced so many bishops, are mentioned with indignation by those who were too pure or too proud to accept them. " We combat " (says Hilary of Poitiers) " against Constantius the Antichrist, who strokes the belly instead of scourging the back; " qui non dorsa cædit, sed ventrem palpat. Hilarius contra Constant. c. 5, p. 1240.

[3] Something of this opposition is mentioned by Ammianus (xv. 7), who had a very dark and superficial knowledge of ecclesiastical history. Liberius . . . perseveranter renitebatur, nec visum hominem, nec auditum damnare, nefas ultimum sæpe exclamans; aperte scilicet recalcitrans Imperatoris arbitrio. Id enim ille Athanasio semper infestus, etc.

adversaries. They alleged that his innocence had been attested by the unanimous bishops of Egypt, and had been acknowledged in the councils of Rome and Sardica [1] by the impartial judgment of the Latin church. They deplored the hard condition of Athanasius, who, after enjoying so many years his seat, his reputation, and the seeming confidence of his sovereign, was again called upon to confute the most groundless and extravagant accusations. Their language was specious; their conduct was honourable: but in this long and obstinate contest, which fixed the eyes of the whole empire on a single bishop, the ecclesiastical factions were prepared to sacrifice truth and justice to the more interesting object of defending or removing the intrepid champion of the Nicene faith. The Arians still thought it prudent to disguise, in ambiguous language, their real sentiments and designs; but the orthodox bishops, armed with the favour of the people and the decrees of a general council, insisted on every occasion, and particularly at Milan, that their adversaries should purge themselves from the suspicion of heresy, before they presumed to arraign the conduct of the great Athanasius.[2]

But the voice of reason (if reason was indeed on the side of Athanasius) was silenced by the clamours of a factious or venal majority; and the councils of Arles and Milan were not dissolved till the archbishop of Alexandria had been solemnly condemned and deposed by the judgment of the Western, as well as of the Eastern, church. The bishops who had opposed were required to subscribe the sentence; and to unite in religious communion with the suspected leaders of the adverse party. A formulary of consent was transmitted by the messengers of state to the absent bishops: and all those who refused to submit their private opinion to the public and inspired wisdom of the councils of Arles and Milan were immediately banished by the emperor, who affected to execute the decrees of the catholic church. Among those prelates who led the honourable band of confessors and exiles, Liberius of Rome, Osius of Cordova, Paulinus of Treves, Dionysius of Milan, Eusebius of Vercellæ, Lucifer of Cagliari, and Hilary of Poitiers, may deserve to be particularly distinguished. The eminent station of Liberius, who governed

---

[1] More properly by the orthodox part of the council of Sardica. If the bishops of both parties had fairly voted, the division would have been 94 to 76. M. de Tillemont (see tom. viii. p. 1147-1158) is justly surprised that so small a majority should have proceeded so vigorously against their adversaries, the principal of whom they immediately deposed.

[2] Sulp. Severus, in Hist. Sacra, l. ii. p. 412.

the capital of the empire; the personal merit and long experience of the venerable Osius, who was revered as the favourite of the great Constantine, and the father of the Nicene faith, placed those prelates at the head of the Latin church: and their example, either of submission or resistance, would probably be imitated by the episcopal crowd. But the repeated attempts of the emperor to seduce or to intimidate the bishops of Rome and Cordova were for some time ineffectual. The Spaniard declared himself ready to suffer under Constantius, as he had suffered threescore years before under his grandfather Maximian. The Roman, in the presence of his sovereign, asserted the innocence of Athanasius, and his own freedom. When he was banished to Berǣa in Thrace, he sent back a large sum which had been offered for the accommodation of his journey; and insulted the court of Milan by the haughty remark, that the emperor and his eunuchs might want that gold to pay their soldiers and their bishops.[1] The resolution of Liberius and Osius was at length subdued by the hardships of exile and confinement. The Roman pontiff purchased his return by some criminal compliances; and afterwards expiated his guilt by a seasonable repentance. Persuasion and violence were employed to extort the reluctant signature of the decrepit bishop of Cordova, whose strength was broken, and whose faculties were perhaps impaired, by the weight of an hundred years; and the insolent triumph of the Arians provoked some of the orthodox party to treat with inhuman severity the character, or rather the memory, of an unfortunate old man, to whose former services Christianity itself was so deeply indebted.[2]

The fall of Liberius and Osius reflected a brighter lustre on the firmness of those bishops who still adhered, with unshaken fidelity, to the cause of Athanasius and religious truth. The ingenious malice of their enemies had deprived them of the benefit of mutual comfort and advice, separated those illustrious exiles into distant provinces, and carefully selected the most inhospitable spots of a great empire.[3] Yet they soon experi-

---

[1] The exile of Liberius is mentioned by Ammianus, xv. 7. See Theodoret, l. ii. c. 16.   Athanas. tom. i. p. 834-837 [tom. i. p. 161, ed. Bened.].   Hilar. Fragment. i.

[2] The life of Osius is collected by Tillemont (tom. vii. p. 524-561), who, in the most extravagant terms, first admires and then reprobates the bishop of Cordova.   In the midst of their lamentations on his fall, the prudence of Athanasius may be distinguished from the blind and intemperate zeal of Hilary.

[3] The confessors of the West were successively banished to the deserts of Arabia or Thebaïs, the lonely places of Mount Taurus, the wildest parts of

enced that the deserts of Libya, and the most barbarous tracts of Cappadocia, were less inhospitable than the residence of those cities in which an Arian bishop could satiate, without restraint, the exquisite rancour of theological hatred.[1] Their consolation was derived from the consciousness of rectitude and independence, from the applause, the visits, the letters, and the liberal alms of their adherents;[2] and from the satisfaction which they soon enjoyed of observing the intestine divisions of the adversaries of the Nicene faith. Such was the nice and capricious taste of the emperor Constantius, and so easily was he offended by the slightest deviation from his imaginary standard of Christian truth, that he persecuted, with equal zeal, those who defended the *consubstantiality*, those who asserted the *similar substance*, and those who denied the *likeness*, of the Son of God. Three bishops, degraded and banished for those adverse opinions, might possibly meet in the same place of exile; and, according to the difference of their temper, might either pity or insult the blind enthusiasm of their antagonists, whose present sufferings would never be compensated by future happiness.

The disgrace and exile of the orthodox bishops of the West were designed as so many preparatory steps to the ruin of Athanasius himself.[3] Six-and-twenty months had elapsed, during which the Imperial court secretly laboured, by the most insidious arts, to remove him from Alexandria, and to withdraw the allowance which supplied his popular liberality. But when the primate of Egypt, deserted and proscribed by the Latin church, was left destitute of any foreign support, Constantius despatched two of his secretaries with a verbal commission to announce and execute the order of his banishment. As the

Phrygia, which were in the possession of the impious Montanists, etc. When the heretic Aëtius was too favourably entertained at Mopsuestia in Cilicia, the place of his exile was changed, by the advice of Acacius, to Amblada, a district inhabited by savages, and infested by war and pestilence. Philostorg. l. v. c. 2.

[1] See the cruel treatment and strange obstinacy of Eusebius, in his own letters, published by Baronius, A.D. 356, No. 92-102.

[2] Cæterum exules satis constat, totius orbis studiis celebratos, pecuniasque eis in sumptum affatim congestas, legationibus quoque eos plebis catholicæ ex omnibus fere provinciis frequentatos. Sulp. Sever. Hist. Sacra, p. 414. Athanas. tom. i. p. 836, 840.

[3] Ample materials for the history of this third persecution of Athanasius may be found in his own works. See particularly his very able Apology to Constantius (tom. i. p. 673 [tom. i. p. 233 *sqq.* ed. Bened.]), his first Apology for his flight (p. 701 [tom. i. p. 253 *sqq.* ed. Bened.]), his prolix Epistle to the Solitaries (p. 808), and the original Protest of the People of Alexandria against the violences committed by Syrianus (p. 866 [p. 311, ed. Bened.]). Sozomen (l. iv. c. 9) has thrown into the narrative two or three luminous and important circumstances.

justice of the sentence was publicly avowed by the whole party, the only motive which could restrain Constantius from giving his messengers the sanction of a written mandate must be imputed to his doubt of the event; and to a sense of the danger to which he might expose the second city and the most fertile province of the empire, if the people should persist in the resolution of defending, by force of arms, the innocence of their spiritual father. Such extreme caution afforded Athanasius a specious pretence respectfully to dispute the truth of an order which he could not reconcile either with the equity or with the former declarations of his gracious master. The civil powers of Egypt found themselves inadequate to the task of persuading or compelling the primate to abdicate his episcopal throne; and they were obliged to conclude a treaty with the popular leaders of Alexandria, by which it was stipulated that all proceedings and all hostilities should be suspended till the emperor's pleasure had been more distinctly ascertained. By this seeming moderation the catholics were deceived into a false and fatal security; while the legions of the Upper Egypt, and of Libya, advanced, by secret orders and hasty marches, to besiege, or rather to surprise, a capital habituated to sedition, and inflamed by religious zeal.[1] The position of Alexandria, between the sea and the lake Mareotis, facilitated the approach and landing of the troops, who were introduced into the heart of the city before any effectual measures could be taken, either to shut the gates, or to occupy the important posts of defence. At the hour of midnight, twenty-three days after the signature of the treaty, Syrianus, duke of Egypt, at the head of five thousand soldiers, armed and prepared for an assault, unexpectedly invested the church of St. Theonas, where the archbishop, with a part of his clergy and people, performed their nocturnal devotions. The doors of the sacred edifice yielded to the impetuosity of the attack, which was accompanied with every horrid circumstance of tumult and bloodshed; but, as the bodies of the slain, and the fragments of military weapons, remained the next day an unexceptionable evidence in the possession of the catholics, the enterprise of Syrianus may be considered as a successful irruption rather than as an absolute conquest. The other churches of the city were profaned by similar outrages; and, during at

---

[1] Athanasius had lately sent for Antony and some of his chosen monks. They descended from their mountain, announced to the Alexandrians the sanctity of Athanasius, and were honourably conducted by the archbishop as far as the gates of the city. Athanas. tom. ii. p. 491, 492 [tom. i. p. 677 q. ed. Bened. 1777]. See likewise Rufinus, iii. 164, in Vit. Patr. p. 524.

least four months, Alexandria was exposed to the insults of a licentious army, stimulated by the ecclesiastics of an hostile faction. Many of the faithful were killed, who may deserve the name of martyrs if their deaths were neither provoked nor revenged; bishops and presbyters were treated with cruel ignominy; consecrated virgins were stripped naked, scourged, and violated; the houses of wealthy citizens were plundered; and, under the mask of religious zeal, lust, avarice, and private resentment were gratified with impunity, and even with applause. The Pagans of Alexandria, who still formed a numerous and discontented party, were easily persuaded to desert a bishop whom they feared and esteemed. The hopes of some peculiar favours, and the apprehension of being involved in the general penalties of rebellion, engaged them to promise their support to the destined successor of Athanasius, the famous George of Cappadocia. The usurper, after receiving the consecration of an Arian synod, was placed on the episcopal throne by the arms of Sebastian, who had been appointed count of Egypt for the execution of that important design. In the use, as well as in the acquisition, of power, the tyrant George disregarded the laws of religion, of justice, and of humanity; and the same scenes of violence and scandal which had been exhibited in the capital were repeated in more than ninety episcopal cities of Egypt. Encouraged by success, Constantius ventured to approve the conduct of his ministers. By a public and passionate epistle, the emperor congratulates the deliverance of Alexandria from a popular tyrant, who deluded his blind votaries by the magic of his eloquence; expatiates on the virtues and piety of the most reverend George, the elected bishop; and aspires, as the patron and benefactor of the city, to surpass the fame of Alexander himself. But he solemnly declares his unalterable resolution to pursue with fire and sword the seditious adherents of the wicked Athanasius, who, by flying from justice, has confessed his guilt, and escaped the ignominious death which he had so often deserved.[1]

Athanasius had indeed escaped from the most imminent dangers; and the adventures of that extraordinary man deserve and fix our attention. On the memorable night when the church of St. Theonas was invested by the troops of Syrianus, the archbishop, seated on his throne, expected, with calm and intrepid

---

[1] Athanas. tom. i. p. 694 [tom. i. p. 249, ed. Bened.]. The emperor, or his Arian secretaries, while they express their resentment, betray their fears and esteem of Athanasius.

dignity, the approach of death. While the public devotion was interrupted by shouts of rage and cries of terror, he animated his trembling congregation to express their religious confidence by chanting one of the psalms of David which celebrates the triumph of the God of Israel over the haughty and impious tyrant of Egypt. The doors were at length burst open: a cloud of arrows was discharged among the people; the soldiers, with drawn swords, rushed forwards into the sanctuary; and the dreadful gleam of their armour was reflected by the holy luminaries which burnt round the altar.[1] Athanasius still rejected the pious importunity of the monks and presbyters who were attached to his person; and nobly refused to desert his episcopal station till he had dismissed in safety the last of the congregation. The darkness and tumult of the night favoured the retreat of the archbishop; and though he was oppressed by the waves of an agitated multitude, though he was thrown to the ground, and left without sense or motion, he still recovered his undaunted courage, and eluded the eager search of the soldiers, who were instructed by their Arian guides that the head of Athanasius would be the most acceptable present to the emperor. From that moment the primate of Egypt disappeared from the eyes of his enemies, and remained above six years concealed in impenetrable obscurity.[2]

The despotic power of his implacable enemy filled the whole extent of the Roman world; and the exasperated monarch had endeavoured, by a very pressing epistle to the Christian princes of Æthiopia,[3] to exclude Athanasius from the most remote and

---

[1] These minute circumstances are curious, as they are literally transcribed from the protest which was publicly presented three days afterwards by the catholics of Alexandria. See Athanas. tom. i. p. 867 [tom. i. p. 311, ed. Bened. 1777].

[2] The Jansenists have often compared Athanasius and Arnauld, and have expatiated with pleasure on the faith and zeal, the merit and exile, of those celebrated doctors. This concealed parallel is very dexterously managed by the Abbé de la Bléterie, Vie de Jovien, tom. i. p. 130.

[3] [These princes were called Aeizanas and Saiazanas. Athanasius (Apol. ad Constantium, vol. i. p. 313) calls them the kings of Axum (οἱ ἐν Αὐξούμει τύραννοι). In the superscription of his letter, Constantius gives them no title, the words being Νικήτης Κονστάντιος μέγιστος σέβαστος 'Αιζανὰ καὶ Σαζανὰ. Mr. Salt (says Milman), in his first journey in Ethiopia in 1806, discovered in the ruins of Axum a long and very interesting inscription relating to these princes. It was erected to commemorate the victory of Aeizanas over the Bougaitæ. Aeizanas is styled king of the Axumites, the Homerites, of the Ethiopians, of Raeidan, of the Sabæites, of Silea, of Tiamo, of the Bougaites, and of Kaei. At this time the king of the Ethiopians reigned over the Homerites, the inhabitants of Yemen. He was not yet a Christian, but calls himself "the son of invincible Mars." (Salt's Travels. Cf. De Lacy, Annales des Voyages, xii. p. 53).—O. S.]

sequestered regions of the earth.　Counts, præfects, tribunes, whole armies, were successively employed to pursue a bishop and a fugitive; the vigilance of the civil and military powers was excited by the Imperial edicts; liberal rewards were promised to the man who should produce Athanasius, either alive or dead; and the most severe penalties were denounced against those who should dare to protect the public enemy.[1] But the deserts of Thebaïs were now peopled by a race of wild, yet submissive fanatics, who preferred the commands of their abbot to the laws of their sovereign.　The numerous disciples of Antony and Pachomius received the fugitive primate as their father, admired the patience and humility with which he conformed to their strictest institutions, collected every word which dropped from his lips as the genuine effusions of inspired wisdom; and persuaded themselves that their prayers, their fasts, and their vigils, were less meritorious than the zeal which they expressed, and the dangers which they braved, in the defence of truth and innocence.[2]　The monasteries of Egypt were seated in lonely and desolate places, on the summit of mountains, or in the islands of the Nile; and the sacred horn or trumpet of Tabenne was the well-known signal which assembled several thousand robust and determined monks, who, for the most part, had been the peasants of the adjacent country.　When their dark retreats were invaded by a military force which it was impossible to resist, they silently stretched out their necks to the executioner; and supported their national character, that tortures could never wrest from an Egyptian the confession of a secret which he was resolved not to disclose.[3]　The archbishop of Alexandria, for whose safety they eagerly devoted their lives, was lost among a uniform and well-disciplined multitude; and on the nearer approach of danger, he was swiftly removed, by their officious hands, from one place of concealment to another, till he reached the formidable deserts, which the gloomy and credulous temper of superstition had peopled with dæmons and savage monsters.　The retirement of Athanasius, which ended

---

[1] Hinc jam toto orbe profugus [agitur] Athanasius, nec ullus ei tutus ad latendum supererat locus.　Tribuni, Præfecti, Comites, exercitus quoque, ad pervestigandum eum moventur edictis Imperialibus; præmia delatoribus proponuntur, si quis eum vivum, si id minus, caput certe Athanasii detulisset.　Rufin. l. i. c. 18.

[2] Gregor. Nazianzen. tom. i. Orat. xxi. p. 384, 385.　See Tillemont, Mém. Ecclés. tom. vii. p. 176-410, 820-880.

[3] Et nulla tormentorum vis inveniri adhuc potuit, quæ obdurato illius tractûs latroni invito elicere potuit, ut nomen proprium dicat.　Ammian. xxii. 16, and Valesius ad locum.

only with the life of Constantius, was spent, for the most part, in the society of the monks, who faithfully served him as guards, as secretaries, and as messengers; but the importance of maintaining a more intimate connection with the catholic party tempted him, whenever the diligence of the pursuit was abated, to emerge from the desert, to introduce himself into Alexandria, and to trust his person to the discretion of his friends and adherents. His various adventures might have furnished the subject of a very entertaining romance. He was once secreted in a dry cistern, which he had scarcely left before he was betrayed by the treachery of a female slave;[1] and he was once concealed in a still more extraordinary asylum, the house of a virgin, only twenty years of age, and who was celebrated in the whole city for her exquisite beauty. At the hour of midnight, as she related the story many years afterwards, she was surprised by the appearance of the archbishop in a loose undress, who, advancing with hasty steps, conjured her to afford him the protection which he had been directed by a celestial vision to seek under her hospitable roof. The pious maid accepted and preserved the sacred pledge which was intrusted to her prudence and courage. Without imparting the secret to any one, she instantly conducted Athanasius into her most secret chamber, and watched over his safety with the tenderness of a friend and the assiduity of a servant. As long as the danger continued, she regularly supplied him with books and provisions, washed his feet, managed his correspondence, and dexterously concealed from the eye of suspicion this familiar and solitary intercourse between a saint whose character required the most unblemished chastity, and a female whose charms might excite the most dangerous emotions.[2] During the six years of persecution and exile, Athanasius repeated his visits to his fair and faithful companion; and the formal declaration, that he *saw* the councils of Rimini and Seleucia,[3] forces us to believe that he was secretly present at the time and place of their convocation. The advan-

---

[1] Rufin. l. i. c. 18. Sozomen, l. iv. c. 10. This and the following story will be rendered impossible if we suppose that Athanasius always inhabited the asylum which he accidentally or occasionally had used.

[2] Palladius (Hist. Lausiac. c. 136 in Vit. Patrum, p. 776 [p. 230, ed. Paris, Pallad. 1555]), the original author of this anecdote, had conversed with the damsel, who in her old age still remembered with pleasure so pious and honourable a connection. I cannot indulge the delicacy of Baronius, Valesius, Tillemont, etc., who almost reject a story so unworthy, as they deem it, of the gravity of ecclesiastical history.

[3] Athanas. tom. i. p. 869 [tom. . p. 572, ed. Bened. 1777]. I agree with Tillemont (tom. viii. p. 1197), that his expressions imply a personal, though perhaps secret, visit to the synods.

tage of personally negotiating with his friends, and of observing and improving the divisions of his enemies, might justify, in a prudent statesman, so bold and dangerous an enterprise: and Alexandria was connected by trade and navigation with every seaport of the Mediterranean. From the depth of his inaccessible retreat the intrepid primate waged an incessant and offensive war against the protector of the Arians; and his seasonable writings, which were diligently circulated and eagerly perused, contributed to unite and animate the orthodox party. In his public apologies, which he addressed to the emperor himself, he sometimes affected the praise of moderation; whilst at the same time, in secret and vehement invectives, he exposed Constantius as a weak and wicked prince, the executioner of his family, the tyrant of the republic, and the Antichrist of the church. In the height of his prosperity, the victorious monarch, who had chastised the rashness of Gallus, and suppressed the revolt of Sylvanus, who had taken the diadem from the head of Vetranio, and vanquished in the field the legions of Magnentius, received from an invisible hand a wound which he could neither heal nor revenge; and the son of Constantine was the first of the Christian princes who experienced the strength of those principles which, in the cause of religion, could resist the most violent exertions of the civil power.[1]

The persecution of Athanasius and of so many respectable bishops, who suffered for the truth of their opinions, or at least for the integrity of their conscience, was a just subject of indignation and discontent to all Christians, except those who were blindly devoted to the Arian faction. The people regretted the loss of their faithful pastors, whose banishment was usually followed by the intrusion of a stranger [2] into the episcopal chair, and loudly complained that the right of election was violated, and that they were condemned to obey a mercenary usurper, whose person was unknown and whose principles were suspected. The catholics might prove to the world that they were not in-

---

[1] The epistle of Athanasius to the monks is filled with reproaches, which the public must feel to be true (vol. i. p. 834, 856 [tom. i. p. 304, ed. Bened.]); and, in compliment to his readers, he has introduced the comparisons of Pharaoh, Ahab, Belshazzar, etc. The boldness of Hilary was attended with less danger, if he published his invective in Gaul after the revolt of Julian; but Lucifer sent his libels to Constantius, and almost challenged the reward of martyrdom. See Tillemont, tom. vii. p. 905.

[2] Athanasius (tom. i. p. 811) complains in general of this practice, which he afterwards exemplifies (p. 861 [tom. i. p. 307, ed. Bened.]) in the pretended election of Felix. Three eunuchs represented the Roman people, and three prelates, who followed the court, assumed the functions of the bishops of the Suburbicarian provinces.

volved in the guilt and heresy of their ecclesiastical governor, by publicly testifying their dissent, or by totally separating themselves from his communion. The first of these methods was invented at Antioch, and practised with such success that it was soon diffused over the Christian world. The doxology, or sacred hymn, which celebrates the *glory* of the Trinity, is susceptible of very nice, but material, inflections; and the substance of an orthodox or an heretical creed may be expressed by the difference of a disjunctive or a copulative particle. Alternate responses and a more regular psalmody [1] were introduced into the public service by Flavianus and Diodorus, two devout and active laymen, who were attached to the Nicene faith. Under their conduct a swarm of monks issued from the adjacent desert, bands of well-disciplined singers were stationed in the cathedral of Antioch, the Glory to the Father, AND the Son, AND the Holy Ghost [2] was triumphantly chanted by a full chorus of voices, and the catholics insulted, by the purity of their doctrine, the Arian prelate who had usurped the throne of the venerable Eustathius. The same zeal which inspired their songs prompted the more scrupulous members of the orthodox party to form separate assemblies, which were governed by the presbyters, till the death of their exiled bishop allowed the election and conse-cration of a new episcopal pastor.[3] The revolutions of the court multiplied the number of pretenders, and the same city was often disputed, under the reign of Constantius, by two, or three, or even four bishops, who exercised their spiritual jurisdiction over their respective followers, and alternately lost and regained

---

[1] Thomassin (Discipline de l'Eglise, tom. i. l. ii. c. 72, 73, p. 966-984) has collected many curious facts concerning the origin and progress of church-singing, both in the East and West.
[Arius seems to have been the first who availed himself of this means of impressing his doctrine on the popular ear. He composed songs for sailors, millers, and travellers, and set them to common airs, beguiling the ignorant by the sweetness of his music into the impiety of his doctrines. Arian singers used to parade the streets of Constantinople by night until Chrysostom arrayed against them a band of orthodox choristers.—O. S.]

[2] Philostorgius, l. iii. c. 13. Godefroy has examined this subject with singular accuracy (p. 147, etc.). There were three heterodox forms: " To the Father *by* the Son, *and* in the Holy Ghost; " " To the Father *and* the Son *in* the Holy Ghost; " and " To the Father *in* the Son *and* the Holy Ghost."

[3] After the exile of Eustathius, under the reign of Constantine, the rigid party of the orthodox formed a separation which afterwards degenerated into a schism, and lasted above fourscore years. See Tillemont, Mém. Ecclés. tom. vii. p. 35-54, 1137-1158, tom. viii. p. 573-632, 1314-1332. In many churches the Arians and Homoousians, who had renounced each other's *communion*, continued for some time to join in prayer. Philostorgius, l. iii. c. 14.

the temporal possessions of the church. The abuse of Christianity introduced into the Roman government new causes of tyranny and sedition; the bands of civil society were torn asunder by the fury of religious factions; and the obscure citizen, who might calmly have surveyed the elevation and fall of successive emperors, imagined and experienced that his own life and fortune were connected with the interests of a popular ecclesiastic. The example of the two capitals, Rome and Constantinople, may serve to represent the state of the empire and the temper of mankind under the reign of the sons of Constantine.

I. The Roman pontiff, as long as he maintained his station and his principles, was guarded by the warm attachment of a great people, and could reject with scorn the prayers, the menaces, and the oblations of an heretical prince. When the eunuchs had secretly pronounced the exile of Liberius, the well-grounded apprehension of a tumult engaged them to use the utmost precautions in the execution of the sentence. The capital was invested on every side, and the præfect was commanded to seize the person of the bishop, either by stratagem or by open force. The order was obeyed, and Liberius, with the greatest difficulty, at the hour of midnight, was swiftly conveyed beyond the reach of the Roman people before their consternation was turned into rage. As soon as they were informed of his banishment into Thrace, a general assembly was convened, and the clergy of Rome bound themselves, by a public and solemn oath, never to desert their bishop, never to acknowledge the usurper Felix, who, by the influence of the eunuchs, had been irregularly chosen and consecrated within the walls of a profane palace. At the end of two years their pious obstinacy subsisted entire and unshaken; and when Constantius visited Rome, he was assailed by the importunate solicitations of a people who had preserved, as the last remnant of their ancient freedom, the right of treating their sovereign with familiar insolence. The wives of many of the senators and most honourable citizens, after pressing their husbands to intercede in favour of Liberius, were advised to undertake a commission which in their hands would be less dangerous and might prove more successful. The emperor received with politeness these female deputies, whose wealth and dignity were displayed in the magnificence of their dress and ornaments; he admired their inflexible resolution of following their beloved pastor to the most distant regions of the earth, and consented that the two bishops, Liberius and Felix, should govern in peace their respective congregations. But the ideas of toleration were so repugnant to the practice, and even to the sentiments, of those times, that, when the answer of Constantius was publicly read in the Circus of Rome, so reasonable a project of accommodation was rejected with contempt and ridicule. The eager vehemence which animated the spectators in the decisive moment of a horse-race was now directed towards a different object, and the Circus resounded with the shout of thousands, who repeatedly exclaimed " One God, One Christ, One Bishop ! " The zeal of the Roman people in the cause of Liberius was not confined to words alone, and the dangerous and bloody sedition which they excited soon after the departure of Constantius determined that prince to accept the submission of the exiled prelate, and to restore him to the undivided dominion of the capital. After some ineffectual resistance, his rival was expelled from the city by the permission of the emperor and the power of the opposite faction; the adherents of Felix were inhumanly murdered in the streets, in the public places, in the baths, and even in the churches; and the face of Rome, upon the return of a Christian bishop, renewed the horrid image of the massacres of Marius and the proscriptions of Sylla.[1]

II. Notwithstanding the rapid increase of Christians under the reign of the Flavian family, Rome, Alexandria, and the other great cities of the empire, still contained a strong and powerful faction of Infidels, who envied the prosperity, and who ridiculed, even on their theatres, the theological disputes of the church. Constantinople alone enjoyed the advantage of being born and educated in the bosom of the faith. The capital of the East had never been polluted by the worship of idols, and the whole body of the people had deeply imbibed the opinions, the virtues, and the passions which distinguished the Christians of that age from the rest of mankind. After the death of Alexander the episcopal throne was disputed by Paul and Macedonius. By their zeal and abilities they both deserved the eminent station to which they aspired; and if the moral character of Macedonius was less exceptionable, his competitor had the advantage of a prior election and a more orthodox doctrine. His firm attachment to the Nicene creed, which has given Paul a place in the calendar among saints and martyrs, exposed him to the resentment of the Arians. In the space of fourteen years he was five times

---

[1] See, on this ecclesiastical revolution of Rome, Ammianus, xv. 7. Athanas. tom. i. p. 834, 861 [tom. i. p. 307, ed. Bened.]. Sozomen, l. iv. c. 15. Theodoret, l. ii. c. 17. Sulp. Sever. Hist. Sacra, l. ii. p. 413. Hieronym. Chron. Marcellin. et Faustin. Libell. p. 3, 4. Tillemont. Mém. Ecclés. tom. vi. p. 336.

driven from his throne, to which he was more frequently restored by the violence of the people than by the permission of the prince, and the power of Macedonius could be secured only by the death of his rival.   The unfortunate Paul was dragged in chains from the sandy deserts of Mesopotamia to the most desolate places of Mount Taurus,[1] confined in a dark and narrow dungeon, left six days without food, and at length strangled, by the order of Philip, one of the principal ministers of the emperor Constantius.[2] The first blood which stained the new capital was spilt in this ecclesiastical contest, and many persons were slain on both sides in the furious and obstinate seditions of the people.   The commission of enforcing a sentence of banishment against Paul had been intrusted to Hermogenes, the master-general of the cavalry, but the execution of it was fatal to himself.   The catholics rose in the defence of their bishop; the palace of Hermogenes was consumed; the first military officer of the empire was dragged by the heels through the streets of Constantinople, and, after he expired, his lifeless corpse was exposed to their wanton insults.[3] The fate of Hermogenes instructed Philip, the Prætorian præfect, to act with more precaution on a similar occasion.   In the most gentle and honourable terms he required the attendance of Paul in the baths of Zeuxippus, which had a private communication with the palace and the sea.   A vessel, which lay ready at the garden stairs, immediately hoisted sail, and, while the people were still ignorant of the meditated sacrilege, their bishop was already embarked on his voyage to Thessalonica.   They soon beheld, with surprise and indignation, the gates of the palace thrown open, and the usurper Macedonius seated by the side of the præfect on a lofty chariot, which was surrounded by troops of guards with drawn swords.   The military procession advanced towards the cathedral; the Arians and the catholics eagerly rushed to occupy that important post, and three thousand one

---

[1] Cucusus was the last stage of his life and sufferings.   The situation of that lonely town, on the confines of Cappadocia, Cilicia, and the Lesser Armenia, has occasioned some geographical perplexity; but we are directed to the true spot by the course of the Roman road from Cæsarea to Anazarbus.   See Cellarii Geograph. tom. ii. p. 213; Wesseling, ad Itinerar. p. 179, 703.

[2] Athanasius (tom. i. p. 703, 813, 814 [tom. i. p. 275, ed. Bened.]) affirms, in the most positive terms, that Paul was murdered; and appeals, not only to common fame, but even to the unsuspicious testimony of Philagrius, one of the Arian persecutors.   Yet he acknowledges that the heretics attributed to disease the death of the bishop of Constantinople.   Athanasius is servilely copied by Socrates (l. ii. c. 26); but Sozomen, who discovers a more liberal temper, presumes (l. iv. c. 2) to insinuate a prudent doubt.

[3] Ammianus (xiv. 10) refers to his own account of this tragic event.   But we no longer possess that part of his history.

hundred and fifty persons lost their lives in the confusion of the tumult. Macedonius, who was supported by a regular force, obtained a decisive victory, but his reign was disturbed by clamour and sedition, and the causes which appeared the least connected with the subject of dispute were sufficient to nourish and to kindle the flame of civil discord. As the chapel in which the body of the great Constantine had been deposited was in a ruinous condition, the bishop transported those venerable remains into the church of St. Acacius. This prudent and even pious measure was represented as a wicked profanation by the whole party which adhered to the Homoousian doctrine. The factions immediately flew to arms, the consecrated ground was used as their field of battle, and one of the ecclesiastical historians has observed, as a real fact, not as a figure of rhetoric, that the well before the church overflowed with a stream of blood which filled the porticoes and the adjacent courts. The writer who should impute these tumults solely to a religious principle would betray a very imperfect knowledge of human nature; yet it must be confessed that the motive which misled the sincerity of zeal, and the pretence which disguised the licentiousness of passion, suppressed the remorse which, in another cause, would have succeeded to the rage of the Christians of Constantinople.[1]

The cruel and arbitrary disposition of Constantius, which did not always require the provocations of guilt and resistance, was justly exasperated by the tumults of his capital and the criminal behaviour of a faction which opposed the authority and religion of their sovereign. The ordinary punishments of death, exile, and confiscation were inflicted with partial rigour, and the Greeks still revere the holy memory of two clerks, a reader and a subdeacon, who were accused of the murder of Hermogenes, and beheaded at the gates of Constantinople. By an edict of Constantius against the catholics, which has not been judged worthy of a place in the Theodosian code, those who refused to communicate with the Arian bishops, and particularly with Macedonius, were deprived of the immunities of ecclesiastics and of the rights of Christians; they were compelled to relinquish the possession of the churches, and were strictly prohibited from holding their assemblies within the walls of the city. The execution of this

[1] See Socrates, l. ii. c. 6, 7, 12, 13, 15, 16, 26, 27, 38; and Sozomen, l. iii. 3, 4, 7, 9, l. iv. c. ii. 21. The acts of St. Paul of Constantinople, of which Photius has made an abstract (Phot. Biblioth. p. 1419-1430), are an indifferent copy of these historians; but a modern Greek, who could write the Life of a saint without adding fables and miracles, is entitled to some commendation.

unjust law in the provinces of Thrace and Asia Minor was committed to the zeal of Macedonius; the civil and military powers were directed to obey his commands; and the cruelties exercised by this Semi-Arian tyrant in the support of the *Homoiousion* exceeded the commission and disgraced the reign of Constantius. The sacraments of the church were administered to the reluctant victims, who denied the vocation and abhorred the principles of Macedonius. The rites of baptism were conferred on women and children who, for that purpose, had been torn from the arms of their friends and parents; the mouths of the communicants were held open by a wooden engine while the consecrated bread was forced down their throat; the breasts of tender virgins were either burnt with red-hot egg-shells, or inhumanly compressed between sharp and heavy boards.[1] The Novatians of Constantinople and the adjacent country, by their firm attachment to the Homoousian standard, deserved to be confounded with the catholics themselves. Macedonius was informed that a large district of Paphlagonia was almost entirely inhabited by those sectaries. He resolved either to convert or to extirpate them, and, as he distrusted on this occasion the efficacy of an ecclesiastical mission, he commanded a body of four thousand legionaries to march against the rebels, and to reduce the territory of Mantinium[2] under his spiritual dominion. The Novatian peasants, animated by despair and religious fury, boldly encountered the invaders of their country, and, though many of the Paphlagonians were slain, the Roman legions were vanquished by an irregular multitude, armed only with scythes and axes, and, except a few who escaped by an ignominious flight, four thousand soldiers were left dead on the field of battle. The successor of Constantius has expressed, in a concise but lively manner, some of the theological calamities which afflicted the empire, and more especially the East, in the reign of a prince who was the slave of his own passions and of those of his eunuchs. "Many were imprisoned, and persecuted, and driven into exile.

---

[1] Socrates, l. ii. c. 27, 38. Sozomen, l. iv. c. 21. The principal assistants of Macedonius, in the work of persecution, were the two bishops of Nicomedia and Cyzicus, who were esteemed for their virtues, and especially for their charity. I cannot forbear reminding the reader that the difference between the *Homoousion* and *Homoiousion* is almost invisible to the nicest theological eye.

[2] We are ignorant of the precise situation of Mantinium. In speaking of these *four* bands of legionaries, Socrates, Sozomen, and the author of the Acts of St. Paul, use the indefinite terms of ἀριθμοί, φάλαγγες, τάγματα, which Nicephorus very properly translates *thousands*. Vales. ad Socrat. l. ii. c. 38.

Whole troops of those who are styled heretics were massacred, particularly at Cyzicus and at Samosata. In Paphlagonia, Bithynia, Galatia, and in many other provinces, towns and villages were laid waste and utterly destroyed." [1]

While the flames of the Arian controversy consumed the vitals of the empire, the African provinces were infested by their peculiar enemies, the savage fanatics who, under the name of *Circumcellions*, formed the strength and scandal of the Donatist party.[2] The severe execution of the laws of Constantine had excited a spirit of discontent and resistance; the strenuous efforts of his son Constans to restore the unity of the church exasperated the sentiments of mutual hatred which had first occasioned the separation; and the methods of force and corruption employed by the two Imperial commissioners, Paul and Macarius, furnished the schismatics with a specious contrast between the maxims of the apostles and the conduct of their pretended successors.[3] The peasants who inhabited the villages of Numidia and Mauritania were a ferocious race, who had been imperfectly reduced under the authority of the Roman laws, who were imperfectly converted to the Christian faith, but who were actuated by a blind and furious enthusiasm in the cause of their Donatist teachers. They indignantly supported the exile of their bishops, the demolition of their churches, and the interruption of their secret assemblies. The violence of the officers of justice, who were usually sustained by a military guard, was sometimes repelled with equal violence, and the blood of some popular ecclesiastics, which had been shed in the quarrel, in-

---

[1] Julian. Epistol. lii. p. 436, edit. Spanheim.

[2] See Optatus Milevitanus (particularly iii. 4), with the Donatist history by M. Dupin, and the original pieces at the end of his edition. The numerous circumstances which Augustin has mentioned, of the fury of the Circumcellions against others and against themselves, have been laboriously collected by Tillemont, Mém. Ecclés. tom. vi. p. 147-165; and he has often, though without design, exposed the injuries which had provoked those fanatics.

[3] It is amusing enough to observe the language of opposite parties when they speak of the same men and things. Gratus, bishop of Carthage, begins the acclamations of an orthodox synod, " Gratias Deo omnipotenti et Christo Jesu . . . qui imperavit religiosissimo Constanti Imperatori, ut votum gereret unitatis, et mitteret ministros sancti operis *famulos Dei* Paulum et Macarium." Monument. Vet. ad Calcem Optati, p. 313. Ecce subito," (says the Donatist author of the Passion of Marculus) " de Constantis regis tyrannicâ domo . . . pollutum Macarianæ persecutionis murmur increpuit, et *duabus bestiis* ad Africam missis, eodem scilicet Macario et Paulo, execrandum prorsus ac dirum ecclesiæ certamen indictum est; ut populus Christianus ad unionem cum traditoribus faciendam, nudatis militum gladiis et draconum præsentibus signis, et tubarum vocibus cogeretur." Monument. p. 304.

flamed their rude followers with an eager desire of revenging the death of these holy martyrs. By their own cruelty and rashness the ministers of persecution sometimes provoked their fate, and the guilt of an accidental tumult precipitated the criminals into despair and rebellion. Driven from their native villages, the Donatist peasants assembled in formidable gangs on the edge of the Gætulian desert, and readily exchanged the habits of labour for a life of idleness and rapine, which was consecrated by the name of religion, and faintly condemned by the doctors of the sect. The leaders of the Circumcellions assumed the title of captains of the saints; their principal weapon, as they were indifferently provided with swords and spears, was a huge and weighty club, which they termed an *Israelite,* and the well-known sound of " Praise be to God! " which they used as their cry of war, diffused consternation over the unarmed provinces of Africa. At first their depredations were coloured by the plea of necessity, but they soon exceeded the measure of subsistence, indulged without control their intemperance and avarice, burnt the villages which they had pillaged, and reigned the licentious tyrants of the open country. The occupations of husbandry and the administration of justice were interrupted; and, as the Circumcellions pretended to restore the primitive equality of mankind, and to reform the abuses of civil society, they opened a secure asylum for the slaves and debtors who flocked in crowds to their holy standard. When they were not resisted they usually contented themselves with plunder, but the slightest opposition provoked them to acts of violence and murder; and some catholic priests, who had imprudently signalised their zeal, were tortured by the fanatics with the most refined and wanton barbarity. The spirit of the Circumcellions was not always exerted against their defenceless enemies; they engaged, and sometimes defeated, the troops of the province, and in the bloody action of Bagai they attacked in the open field, but with unsuccessful valour, an advanced guard of the Imperial cavalry. The Donatists who were taken in arms received, and they soon deserved, the same treatment which might have been shown to the wild beasts of the desert. The captives died, without a murmur, either by the sword, the axe, or the fire; and the measures of retaliation were multiplied in a rapid proportion, which aggravated the horrors of rebellion and excluded the hope of mutual forgiveness. In the beginning of the present century the example of the Circumcellions has been renewed in the persecution, the boldness, the crimes, and the enthusiasm of the Camisards; and if the fanatics of Languedoc surpassed those of Numidia by their military achievements, the Africans maintained their fierce independence with more resolution and perseverance.[1]

Such disorders are the natural effects of religious tyranny; but the rage of the Donatists was inflamed by a frenzy of a very extraordinary kind; and which, if it really prevailed among them in so extravagant a degree, cannot surely be paralleled in any country or in any age. Many of these fanatics were possessed with the horror of life, and the desire of martyrdom; and they deemed it of little moment by what means, or by what hands, they perished, if their conduct was sanctified by the intention of devoting themselves to the glory of the true faith, and the hope of eternal happiness.[2] Sometimes they rudely disturbed the festivals, and profaned the temples of Paganism, with the design of exciting the most zealous of the idolaters to revenge the insulted honour of their gods. They sometimes forced their way into the courts of justice, and compelled the affrighted judge to give orders for their immediate execution. They frequently stopped travellers on the public highways, and obliged them to inflict the stroke of martyrdom, by the promise of a reward if they consented, and by the threat of instant death if they refused to grant so very singular a favour. When they were disappointed of every other resource, they announced the day on which, in the presence of their friends and brethren, they should cast themselves headlong from some lofty rock; and many precipices were shown which had acquired fame by the number of religious suicides. In the actions of these desperate enthusiasts, who were admired by one party as the martyrs of God, and abhorred by the other as the victims of Satan, an impartial philosopher may discover the influence and the last abuse of that inflexible spirit which was originally derived from the character and principles of the Jewish nation.

The simple narrative of the intestine divisions which distracted the peace and dishonoured the triumph of the church, will confirm the remark of a Pagan historian, and justify the complaint of a venerable bishop. The experience of Ammianus had convinced him that the enmity of the Christians towards

[1] The Histoire des Camisards, in 3 vols. 12mo., Villefranche, 1760, may be recommended as accurate and impartial. It requires some attention to discover the religion of the author.

[2] The Donatist suicides alleged in their justification the example of Razias, which is related in the 14th chapter of the second book of the Maccabees.

each other surpassed the fury of savage beasts against man;[1] and Gregory Nazianzen most pathetically laments that the kingdom of heaven was converted by discord into the image of chaos, of a nocturnal tempest, and of hell itself.[2] The fierce and partial writers of the times, ascribing *all* virtue to themselves, and imputing *all* guilt to their adversaries, have painted the battle of the angels and dæmons. Our calmer reason will reject such pure and perfect monsters of vice or sanctity, and will impute an equal, or at least an indiscriminate, measure of good and evil to the hostile sectaries, who assumed and bestowed the appellations of orthodox and heretics. They had been educated in the same religion and the same civil society. Their hopes and fears in the present, or in a future life, were balanced in the same proportion. On either side the error might be innocent, the faith sincere, the practice meritorious or corrupt. Their passions were excited by similar objects; and they might alternately abuse the favour of the court, or of the people. The metaphysical opinions of the Athanasians and the Arians could not influence their moral character; and they were alike actuated by the intolerant spirit which has been extracted from the pure and simple maxims of the Gospel.

A modern writer, who, with a just confidence, has prefixed to his own history the honourable epithets of political and philosophical,[3] accuses the timid prudence of Montesquieu, for neglecting to enumerate, among the causes of the decline of the empire, a law of Constantine, by which the exercise of the Pagan worship was absolutely suppressed, and a considerable part of his subjects was left destitute of priests, of temples, and of any public religion. The zeal of the philosophic historian for the rights of mankind has induced him to acquiesce in the ambiguous testimony of those ecclesiastics who have too lightly ascribed to their favourite hero the *merit* of a general persecution.[4] Instead of alleging this imaginary law, which would

---

[1] Nullas infestas hominibus bestias, ut sunt sibi ferales plerique Christianorum, expertus. Ammian. xxii. 5.

[2] Gregor. Nazianzen, Orat. i. p. 33. See Tillemont, tom. vi. p. 501, quarto edit.

[3] Histoire Politique et Philosophique des Etablissemens des Européens dans les deux Indes, tom. i. p. 9.

[4] According to Eusebius (in Vit. Constantin. l. ii. c. 45) the emperor prohibited, both in cities and in the country, τὰ μυσαρὰ . . . τῆς εἰδωλολατρείας; the abominable acts or parts of idolatry. Socrates (l. i. c. 18) and Sozomen (l. ii. c. 4, 5) have represented the conduct of Constantine with a just regard to truth and history, which has been neglected by Theodoret (l. v. c. 21) and Orosius (vii. 28). Tum deinde (says the latter) primus Constantinus *justo* ordine et *pio* vicem vertit edicto; siquidem statuit citra ullam hominum cædem, paganorum templa claudi.

have blazed in the front of the Imperial codes, we may safely appeal to the original epistle which Constantine addressed to the followers of the ancient religion, at a time when he no longer disguised his conversion, nor dreaded the rivals of his throne. He invites and exhorts, in the most pressing terms, the subjects of the Roman empire to imitate the example of their master; but he declares that those who still refuse to open their eyes to the celestial light may freely enjoy their temples and their fancied gods. A report that the ceremonies of Paganism were suppressed is formally contradicted by the emperor himself, who wisely assigns, as the principle of his moderation, the invincible force of habit, of prejudice, and of superstition.[1] Without violating the sanctity of his promise, without alarming the fears of the Pagans, the artful monarch advanced, by slow and cautious steps, to undermine the irregular and decayed fabric of polytheism. The partial acts of severity which he occasionally exercised, though they were secretly prompted by a Christian zeal, were coloured by the fairest pretences of justice and the public good; and while Constantine designed to ruin the foundations, he seemed to reform the abuses, of the ancient religion. After the example of the wisest of his predecessors, he condemned, under the most rigorous penalties, the occult and impious arts of divination, which excited the vain hopes, and sometimes the criminal attempts, of those who were discontented with their present condition. An ignominious silence was imposed on the oracles, which had been publicly convicted of fraud and falsehood; the effeminate priests of the Nile were abolished; and Constantine discharged the duties of a Roman censor, when he gave orders for the demolition of several temples of Phœnicia, in which every mode of prostitution was devoutly practised in the face of day, and to the honour of Venus.[2] The Imperial city of Constantinople was, in some measure, raised at the expense, and was adorned with the spoils, of the opulent temples of Greece and Asia; the sacred property was confiscated; the statues of gods and heroes were transported, with rude familiarity, among a people who considered them as objects, not of adoration, but of curiosity; the gold and silver were

---

[1] See Eusebius in Vit. Constantin. l. ii. c. 56, 60. In the sermon to the assembly of saints which the emperor pronounced when he was mature in years and piety, he declares to the idolaters (c. xi.) that they are permitted to offer sacrifices and to exercise every part of their religious worship.

[2] See Eusebius, in Vit. Constantin. l. iii. c. 54-58, and l. iv. c. 23, 25. These acts of authority may be compared with the suppression of the Bacchanals, and the demolition of the temple of Isis, by the magistrates of Pagan Rome.

restored to circulation; and the magistrates, the bishops, and the eunuchs, improved the fortunate occasion of gratifying, at once, their zeal, their avarice, and their resentment. But these depredations were confined to a small part of the Roman world; and the provinces had been long since accustomed to endure the same sacrilegious rapine, from the tyranny of princes and proconsuls who could not be suspected of any design to subvert the established religion.[1]

The sons of Constantine trod in the footsteps of their father with more zeal and with less discretion. The pretences of rapine and oppression were insensibly multiplied;[2] every indulgence was shown to the illegal behaviour of the Christians; every doubt was explained to the disadvantage of Paganism; and the demolition of the temples was celebrated as one of the auspicious events of the reign of Constans and Constantius.[3] The name of Constantius is prefixed to a concise law, which might have superseded the necessity of any future prohibitions. " It is our pleasure that in all places, and in all cities, the temples be immediately shut and carefully guarded, that none may have the power of offending. It is likewise our pleasure that all our subjects should abstain from sacrifices. If any one should be guilty of such an act, let him feel the sword of vengeance, and, after his execution, let his property be confiscated to the public use. We denounce the same penalties against the governors of the provinces, if they neglect to punish the criminals."[4]   But there is the strongest reason to believe

---

[1] Eusebius (in Vit. Constant. l. iii. c. 54) and Libanius (Orat. pro Templis, p. 9, 10, edit. Gothofred.) both mention the pious sacrilege of Constantine, which they viewed in very different lights. The latter expressly declares that " he made use of the sacred money, but made no alteration in the legal worship; the temples indeed were impoverished, but the sacred rites were performed there." Lardner's Jewish and Heathen Testimonies, vol. iv. p. 140.

[2] Ammianus (xxii. 4) speaks of some court eunuchs who were spoliis templorum pasti. Libanius says (Orat. pro Templ. p. 23) that the emperor often gave away a temple like a dog, or a horse, or a slave, or a gold cup: but the devout philosopher takes care to observe that these sacrilegious favourites very seldom prospered.

[3] See Gothofred. Cod. Theodos. tom. vi. p. 262.   Liban. Orat. Parental. c. x. in Fabric. Bibl. Græc. tom. vii. p. 235 [ed. Hamb. 1715].

[4] Placuit omnibus locis atque urbibus universis claudi protinus templa, et accessu vetitis omnibus licentiam delinquendi perditis abnegari. Volumus etiam cunctos a sacrificiis abstinere. Quod siquis aliquid forte hujusmodi perpetraverit, gladio [ultore] sternatur: facultates etiam perempti fisco decernimus vindicari: et similiter adfligi rectores provinciarum si facinora vindicare neglexerint. Cod. Theodos. l. xvi. tit. x. leg. 4. Chronology has discovered some contradiction in the date of this extravagant law; the only one, perhaps, by which the negligence of magistrates is punished by death and confiscation. M. de la Bastie (Mém. de l'Académie, tom. xv

that this formidable edict was either composed without being published, or was published without being executed. The evidence of facts, and the monuments which are still extant of brass and marble, continue to prove the public exercise of the Pagan worship during the whole reign of the sons of Constantine. In the East as well as in the West, in cities as well as in the country, a great number of temples were respected, or at least were spared; and the devout multitude still enjoyed the luxury of sacrifices, of festivals, and of processions, by the permission, or by the connivance, of the civil government. About four years after the supposed date of his bloody edict, Constantius visited the temples of Rome; and the decency of his behaviour is recommended by a Pagan orator as an example worthy of the imitation of succeeding princes. "That emperor," says Symmachus, "suffered the privileges of the vestal virgins to remain inviolate; he bestowed the sacerdotal dignities on the nobles of Rome, granted the customary allowance to defray the expenses of the public rites and sacrifices; and, though he had embraced a different religion, he never attempted to deprive the empire of the sacred worship of antiquity." [1] The senate still presumed to consecrate, by solemn decrees, the *divine* memory of their sovereigns; and Constantine himself was associated, after his death, to those gods whom he had renounced and insulted during his life. The title, the ensigns, the prerogatives, of SOVEREIGN PONTIFF, which had been instituted by Numa, and assumed by Augustus, were accepted, without hesitation, by seven Christian emperors, who were invested with a more absolute authority over the religion which they had deserted than over that which they professed.[2]

The divisions of Christianity suspended the ruin of *Paganism;* [3]

p. 98) conjectures, with a show of reason, that this was no more than the minutes of a law, the heads of an intended bill, which were found in Scriniis Memoriæ, among the papers of Constantius, and afterwards inserted, as a worthy model, in the Theodosian Code.

[1] Symmach. Epistol. x. 54 [p. 289, ed. Paris, 1604].

[2] The fourth Dissertation of M. de la Bastie, sur le Souverain Pontificat des Empereurs Romains (in the Mém. de l'Acad. tom. xv. 75-144), is a very learned and judicious performance, which explains the state, and proves the toleration, of Paganism from Constantine to Gratian. The assertion of Zosimus [iv. 36], that Gratian was the first who refused the pontifical robe, is confirmed beyond a doubt; and the murmurs of bigotry on that subject are almost silenced.

[3] As I have freely anticipated the use of *pagans* and paganism, I shall now trace the singular revolutions of those celebrated words. 1. Πάγη, in the Doric dialect, so familiar to the Italians, signifies a fountain; and the rural neighbourhood which frequented the same fountain derived the common appellation of *pagus* and *pagans* (Festus sub voce, and Servius ad

and the holy war against the infidels was less vigorously prosecuted by princes and bishops who were more immediately alarmed by the guilt and danger of domestic rebellion. The extirpation of *idolatry* [1] might have been justified by the established principles of intolerance: but the hostile sects, which alternately reigned in the Imperial court, were mutually apprehensive of alienating, and perhaps exasperating, the minds of a powerful, though declining faction. Every motive of authority and fashion, of interest and reason, now militated on the side of Christianity; but two or three generations elapsed before their victorious influence was universally felt. The religion which had so long and so lately been established in the Roman empire was still revered by a numerous people, less attached indeed to speculative opinion than to ancient custom. The honours of the state and army were indifferently bestowed on all the subjects of Constantine and Constantius; and a con-

---

Virgil. Georgic. ii. 382). 2. By an easy extension of the word, *pagan* and rural became almost synonymous (Plin. Hist. Natur. xxviii. 5); and the meaner rustics acquired that name, which has been corrupted into *peasants* in the modern languages of Europe. 3. The amazing increase of the military order introduced the necessity of a correlative term (Hume's Essays, vol. i. p. 555); and all the *people* who were not enlisted in the service of the prince were branded with the contemptuous epithet of pagans (Tacit. Hist. iii. 24, 43, 77. Juvenal. Satir. 16 [v. 32]. Tertullian de Pallio, c. 4). 4. The Christians were the soldiers of Christ; their adversaries who refused his *sacrament*, or military oath of baptism, might deserve the metaphorical name of pagans; and this popular reproach was introduced as early as the reign of Valentinian (A.D. 365) into Imperial laws (Cod. Theodos. l. xvi. tit. ii. leg. 18) and theological writings. 5. Christianity gradually filled the cities of the empire: the old religion, in the time of Prudentius (advers. Symmachum, l. i. [v. 575 *sqq.*] ad fin.) and Orosius (in Præfat. Hist.), retired and languished in obscure villages; and the word *pagans*, with its new signification, reverted to its primitive origin. 6. Since the worship of Jupiter and his family has expired, the vacant title of Pagans has been successively applied to all the idolaters and polytheists of the old and new world. 7. The Latin Christians bestowed it, without scruple, on their mortal enemies the Mahometans; and the purest *Unitarians* were branded with the unjust reproach of idolatry and paganism. See Gerard Vossius, Etymologicon Linguæ Latinæ, in his works, tom. i. p. 420; Godefroy's Commentary on the Theodosian Code, tom. vi. p. 250; and Ducange mediæ et infimæ Latinitat. Glossar.

[1] In the pure language of Ionia and Athens, Εἴδωλον and Λατρεία were ancient and familiar words. The former expressed a likeness, an apparition (Homer. Odys. xi. 602), a representation, an *image*, created either by fancy or art. The latter denoted any sort of *service* or slavery. The Jews of Egypt, who translated the Hebrew Scriptures, restrained the use of these words (Exod. xx. 4, 5) to the religious worship of an image. The peculiar idiom of the Hellenists, or Grecian Jews, has been adopted by the sacred and ecclesiastical writers; and the reproach of *idolatry* (Εἰδωλολατρεία) has stigmatised that visible and abject mode of superstition which some sects of Christianity should not hastily impute to the polytheists of Greece and Rome.

*L 435

siderable portion of knowledge and wealth and valour was still engaged in the service of polytheism. The superstition of the senator and of the peasant, of the poet and the philosopher, was derived from very different causes, but they met with equal devotion in the temples of the gods. Their zeal was insensibly provoked by the insulting triumph of a proscribed sect; and their hopes were revived by the well-grounded confidence that the presumptive heir of the empire, a young and valiant hero, who had delivered Gaul from the arms of the barbarians, had secretly embraced the religion of his ancestors.

CHAPTER XXII

Julian is declared Emperor by the Legions of Gaul—His March and Success—The Death of Constantius—Civil Administration of Julian

WHILE the Romans languished under the ignominious tyranny of eunuchs and bishops, the praises of Julian were repeated with transport in every part of the empire, except in the palace of Constantius. The barbarians of Germany had felt, and still dreaded, the arms of the young Cæsar; his soldiers were the companions of his victory; the grateful provincials enjoyed the blessings of his reign; but the favourites, who had opposed his elevation, were offended by his virtues; and they justly considered the friend of the people as the enemy of the court. As long as the fame of Julian was doubtful, the buffoons of the palace, who were skilled in the language of satire, tried the efficacy of those arts which they had so often practised with success. They easily discovered that his simplicity was not exempt from affectation: the ridiculous epithets of an hairy savage, of an ape invested with the purple, were applied to the dress and person of the philosophic warrior; and his modest despatches were stigmatised as the vain and elaborate fictions of a loquacious Greek, a speculative soldier, who had studied the art of war amidst the groves of the Academy.[1] The voice of

[1] Omnes qui plus poterant in palatio, adulandi professores jam docti, recte consulta, prospereque completa vertebant in deridiculum: talia sine modo strepentes insulse; in odium venit cum victoriis suis; capella, non homo; ut hirsutum Julianum carpentes, appellantesque loquacem talpam, et purpuratam simiam, et litterionem Græcum: et his congruentia plurima atque vernacula principi resonantes, audire hæc taliaque gestienti, virtutes ejus obruere verbis impudentibus conabantur, ut segnem incessentes et timidum et umbratilem, gestaque secus verbis comptioribus exornantem. Ammianus, xvii. 11.

malicious folly was at length silenced by the shouts of victory; the conqueror of the Franks and Alemanni could no longer be painted as an object of contempt; and the monarch himself was meanly ambitious of stealing from his lieutenant the honourable reward of his labours. In the letters crowned with laurel, which, according to ancient custom, were addressed to the provinces, the name of Julian was omitted. "Constantius had made his dispositions in person; *he* had signalised his valour in the foremost ranks; *his* military conduct had secured the victory; and the captive king of the barbarians was presented to *him* on the field of battle," from which he was at that time distant above forty days' journey.[1] So extravagant a fable was incapable, however, of deceiving the public credulity, or even of satisfying the pride of the emperor himself. Secretly conscious that the applause and favour of the Romans accompanied the rising fortunes of Julian, his discontented mind was prepared to receive the subtle poison of those artful sycophants who coloured their mischievous designs with the fairest appearances of truth and candour.[2] Instead of depreciating the merits of Julian, they acknowledged, and even exaggerated, his popular fame, superior talents, and important services. But they darkly insinuated that the virtues of the Cæsar might instantly be converted into the most dangerous crimes, if the inconstant multitude should prefer their inclinations to their duty; or if the general of a victorious army should be tempted from his allegiance by the hopes of revenge and independent greatness. The personal fears of Constantius were interpreted by his council as a laudable anxiety for the public safety; whilst in private, and perhaps in his own breast, he disguised, under the less odious appellation of fear, the sentiments of hatred and envy which he had secretly conceived for the inimitable virtues of Julian.

The apparent tranquillity of Gaul, and the imminent danger of the eastern provinces, offered a specious pretence for the design which was artfully concerted by the Imperial ministers. They resolved to disarm the Cæsar; to recall those faithful

---

[1] Ammian. xvi. 12 [*fin.*]. The orator Themistius (iv. p. 56, 57) believed whatever was contained in the Imperial letters, which were addressed to the senate of Constantinople. Aurelius Victor, who published his Abridgment in the last year of Constantius, ascribes the German victories to the *wisdom* of the emperor and the *fortune* of the Cæsar. Yet the historian, soon afterwards, was indebted to the favour or esteem of Julian for the honour of a brass statue, and the important offices of consular of the second Pannonia and præfect of the city. Ammian. xxi. 10.

[2] Callido nocendi artificio, accusatoriam diritatem laudum titulis peragebant. . . . Hæ voces fuerunt ad inflammanda odia probris omnibus potentiores. See Mamertin. in Actione Gratiarum in Vet. Panegyr. xi. 4, 5.

troops who guarded his person and dignity; and to employ, in a distant war against the Persian monarch, the hardy veterans who had vanquished, on the banks of the Rhine, the fiercest nations of Germany. While Julian used the laborious hours of his winter quarters at Paris in the administration of power, which, in his hands, was the exercise of virtue, he was surprised by the hasty arrival of a tribune and a notary, with positive orders from the emperor, which *they* were directed to execute, and *he* was commanded not to oppose. Constantius signified his pleasure that four entire legions—the Celtæ and Petulants, the Heruli and the Batavians—should be separated from the standard of Julian, under which they had acquired their fame and discipline; that in each of the remaining bands three hundred of the bravest youths should be selected; and that this numerous detachment, the strength of the Gallic army, should instantly begin their march, and exert their utmost diligence to arrive, before the opening of the campaign, on the frontiers of Persia.[1] The Cæsar foresaw and lamented the consequences of this fatal mandate. Most of the auxiliaries, who engaged their voluntary service, had stipulated that they should never be obliged to pass the Alps. The public faith of Rome, and the personal honour of Julian, had been pledged for the observance of this condition. Such an act of treachery and oppression would destroy the confidence, and excite the resentment, of the independent warriors of Germany, who considered truth as the noblest of their virtues, and freedom as the most valuable of their possessions. The legionaries, who enjoyed the title and privileges of Romans, were enlisted for the general defence of the republic; but those mercenary troops heard with cold indifference the antiquated names of the republic and of Rome. Attached, either from birth or long habit, to the climate and manners of Gaul, they loved and admired Julian; they despised, and perhaps hated, the emperor; they dreaded the laborious march, the Persian arrows, and the burning deserts of Asia. They claimed as their own the country which they had saved; and excused their want of spirit by pleading the sacred and more immediate duty of protecting their families and friends. The apprehensions of the Gauls were derived from the know-

[1] The minute interval which may be interposed between the *hieme adultâ* and the *primo vere* of Ammianus (xx. 1, 4), instead of allowing a sufficient space for a march of three thousand miles, would render the orders of Constantius as extravagant as they were unjust. The troops of Gaul could not have reached Syria till the end of autumn. The memory of Ammianus must have been inaccurate, and his language incorrect.

ledge of the impending and inevitable danger. As soon as the provinces were exhausted of their military strength, the Germans would violate a treaty which had been imposed on their fears; and notwithstanding the abilities and valour of Julian, the general of a nominal army, to whom the public calamities would be imputed, must find himself, after a vain resistance, either a prisoner in the camp of the barbarians, or a criminal in the palace of Constantius. If Julian complied with the orders which he had received he subscribed his own destruction, and that of a people who deserved his affection. But a positive refusal was an act of rebellion and a declaration of war. The inexorable jealousy of the emperor, the peremptory, and perhaps insidious, nature of his commands, left not any room for a fair apology or candid interpretation; and the dependent station of the Cæsar scarcely allowed him to pause or to deliberate. Solitude increased the perplexity of Julian; he could no longer apply to the faithful counsels of Sallust, who had been removed from his office by the judicious malice of the eunuchs: he could not even enforce his representations by the concurrence of the ministers, who would have been afraid or ashamed to approve the ruin of Gaul. The moment had been chosen when Lupicinus,[1] the general of the cavalry, was despatched into Britain, to repulse the inroads of the Scots and Picts; and Florentius was occupied at Vienne by the assessment of the tribute. The latter, a crafty and corrupt statesman, declining to assume a responsible part on this dangerous occasion, eluded the pressing and repeated invitations of Julian, who represented to him that in every important measure the presence of the præfect was indispensable in the council of the prince. In the meanwhile the Cæsar was oppressed by the rude and importunate solicitations of the Imperial messengers, who presumed to suggest that, if he expected the return of his ministers, he would charge himself with the guilt of the delay, and reserve for them the merit of the execution. Unable to resist, unwilling to comply, Julian expressed in the most serious terms his wish, and even his intention, of resigning the purple, which he could not preserve with honour, but which he could not abdicate with safety.

After a painful conflict, Julian was compelled to acknowledge

---

[1] Ammianus, xx. 1. The valour of Lupicinus and his military skill are acknowledged by the historian, who, in his affected language, accuses the general of exalting the horns of his pride, bellowing in a tragic tone, and exciting a doubt whether he was more cruel or avaricious. The danger from the Scots and Picts was so serious, that Julian himself had some thoughts of passing over into the island.

that obedience was the virtue of the most eminent subject, and
that the sovereign alone was entitled to judge of the public
welfare. He issued the necessary orders for carrying into execution the commands of Constantius; a part of the troops began
their march for the Alps; and the detachments from the several
garrisons moved towards their respective places of assembly.
They advanced with difficulty through the trembling and
affrighted crowds of provincials, who attempted to excite their
pity by silent despair or loud lamentations; while the wives of
the soldiers, holding their infants in their arms, accused the
desertion of their husbands in the mixed language of grief, of
tenderness, and of indignation. This scene of general distress
afflicted the humanity of the Cæsar; he granted a sufficient
number of post-waggons to transport the wives and families of
the soldiers,[1] endeavoured to alleviate the hardships which he
was constrained to inflict, and increased by the most laudable
arts his own popularity and the discontent of the exiled troops.
The grief of an armed multitude is soon converted into rage;
their licentious murmurs, which every hour were communicated
from tent to tent with more boldness and effect, prepared their
minds for the most daring acts of sedition; and by the connivance of their tribunes a seasonable libel was secretly dispersed,
which painted in lively colours the disgrace of the Cæsar, the
oppression of the Gallic army, and the feeble vices of the tyrant
of Asia. The servants of Constantius were astonished and
alarmed by the progress of this dangerous spirit. They pressed
the Cæsar to hasten the departure of the troops; but they
imprudently rejected the honest and judicious advice of Julian,
who proposed that they should not march through Paris, and
suggested the danger and temptation of a last interview.

As soon as the approach of the troops was announced, the
Cæsar went out to meet them, and ascended his tribunal, which
had been erected in a plain before the gates of the city. After
distinguishing the officers and soldiers who by their rank or
merit deserved a peculiar attention, Julian addressed himself in
a studied oration to the surrounding multitude: he celebrated
their exploits with grateful applause; encouraged them to
accept, with alacrity, the honour of serving under the eyes of a
powerful and liberal monarch; and admonished them that the
commands of Augustus required an instant and cheerful obedi-

---

[1] He granted them the permission of the *cursus clavularis*, or *clabularis*.
These post-waggons are often mentioned in the Code, and were supposed
to carry fifteen hundred pounds weight. See Vales. ad Ammian. xx. 4.

360 A.D.

ence. The soldiers, who were apprehensive of offending their
general by an indecent clamour, or of belying their sentiments
by false and venal acclamations, maintained an obstinate silence;
and, after a short pause, were dismissed to their quarters. The
principal officers were entertained by the Cæsar, who professed,
in the warmest language of friendship, his desire and his inability
to reward, according to their deserts, the brave companions of
his victories. They retired from the feast full of grief and perplexity; and lamented the hardship of their fate, which tore
them from their beloved general and their native country. The
only expedient which could prevent their separation was boldly
agitated and approved; the popular resentment was insensibly
moulded into a regular conspiracy; their just reasons of complaint were heightened by passion, and their passions were
inflamed by wine, as on the eve of their departure the troops
were indulged in licentious festivity. At the hour of midnight
the impetuous multitude, with swords, and bows, and torches
in their hands, rushed into the suburbs; encompassed the
palace;[1] and, careless of future dangers, pronounced the fatal
and irrevocable words, JULIAN AUGUSTUS! The prince, whose
anxious suspense was interrupted by their disorderly acclamations, secured the doors against their intrusion; and, as long as
it was in his power, secluded his person and dignity from the
accidents of a nocturnal tumult. At the dawn of day the
soldiers, whose zeal was irritated by opposition, forcibly entered
the palace, seized, with respectful violence, the object of their
choice, guarded Julian with drawn swords through the streets
of Paris, placed him on the tribunal, and with repeated shouts
saluted him as their emperor. Prudence as well as loyalty inculcated the propriety of resisting their treasonable designs, and

---

[1] Most probably the palace of the baths (*Thermarum*), of which a solid
and lofty hall still subsists in the *Rue de la Harpe*. The buildings covered
a considerable space of the modern quarter of the university; and the
gardens, under the Merovingian kings, communicated with the abbey of St.
Germain des Prez. By the injuries of time and the Normans this ancient
palace was reduced in the twelfth century to a maze of ruins, whose dark
recesses were the scene of licentious love.

> Explicat aula sinus montemque amplectitur alis;
> Multiplici latebrâ scelerum tersura ruborem.
> . . . . . . pereuntis sæpe pudoris
> Celatura nefas, Venerisque accommoda *furtis*.

(These lines are quoted from the Architrenius, l. iv. c. 8, a poetical work of
John de Hauteville, or Hanville, a monk of St. Alban's, about the year
1190. See Warton's History of English Poetry, vol. i. dissert. ii.) Yet
such *thefts* might be less pernicious to mankind than the theological disputes
of the Sorbonne, which have been since agitated on the same ground.
Bonamy, Mém. de l'Académie, tom. xv. p. 678-682.

of preparing for his oppressed virtue the excuse of violence. Addressing himself by turns to the multitude and to individuals, he sometimes implored their mercy, and sometimes expressed his indignation; conjured them not to sully the fame of their immortal victories; and ventured to promise that, if they would immediately return to their allegiance, he would undertake to obtain from the emperor not only a free and gracious pardon, but even the revocation of the orders which had excited their resentment. But the soldiers, who were conscious of their guilt, chose rather to depend on the gratitude of Julian than on the clemency of the emperor. Their zeal was insensibly turned into impatience, and their impatience into rage. The inflexible Cæsar sustained, till the third hour of the day, their prayers, their reproaches, and their menaces; nor did he yield till he had been repeatedly assured that, if he wished to live, he must consent to reign. He was exalted on a shield in the presence and amidst the unanimous acclamations of the troops; a rich military collar, which was offered by chance, supplied the want of a diadem;[1] the ceremony was concluded by the promise of a moderate donative;[2] and the new emperor, overwhelmed with real or affected grief, retired into the most secret recesses of his apartment.[3]

The grief of Julian could proceed only from his innocence; but his innocence must appear extremely doubtful[4] in the eyes of those who have learned to suspect the motives and the professions of princes. His lively and active mind was susceptible of the various impressions of hope and fear, of gratitude and revenge, of duty and of ambition, of the love of fame and of the fear of reproach. But it is impossible for us to calculate the

[1] Even in this tumultuous moment Julian attended to the forms of superstitious ceremony, and obstinately refused the inauspicious use of a female necklace, or a horse-collar, which the impatient soldiers would have employed in the room of a diadem.

[2] An equal proportion of gold and silver, five pieces of the former, one pound of the latter; the whole amounting to about five pounds ten shillings of our money.

[3] For the whole narrative of this revolt we may appeal to authentic and original materials; Julian himself (ad S. P. Q. Atheniensem, p. 282, 283, 284), Libanius (Orat. Parental. c. 44-48, in Fabricius Biblioth. Græc. tom. vii. p. 269-273), Ammianus (xx. 4), and Zosimus (l. iii. [c. 9], p. 151, 152, 153), who, in the reign of Julian, appears to follow the more respectable authority of Eunapius. With such guides we *might* neglect the abbreviators and ecclesiastical historians.

[4] Eutropius, a respectable witness, uses a doubtful expression, " consensu militum " (x. 15 [7]). Gregory Nazianzen, whose ignorance might excuse his fanaticism, directly charges the apostate with presumption, madness, and impious rebellion, αὐθάδεια, ἀπόνοια, ἀσέβεια. Orat. iii. p. 67.

respective weight and operation of these sentiments; or to ascertain the principles of action which might escape the observation, while they guided, or rather impelled, the steps of Julian himself. The discontent of the troops was produced by the malice of his enemies; their tumult was the natural effect of interest and of passion; and if Julian had tried to conceal a deep design under the appearances of chance, he must have employed the most consummate artifice without necessity, and probably without success. He solemnly declares, in the presence of Jupiter, of the Sun, of Mars, of Minerva, and of all the other deities, that till the close of the evening which preceded his elevation he was utterly ignorant of the designs of the soldiers;[1] and it may seem ungenerous to distrust the honour of a hero, and the truth of a philosopher. Yet the superstitious confidence that Constantius was the enemy, and that he himself was the favourite, of the gods, might prompt him to desire, to solicit, and even to hasten the auspicious moment of his reign, which was predestined to restore the ancient religion of mankind. When Julian had received the intelligence of the conspiracy, he resigned himself to a short slumber; and afterwards related to his friends that he had seen the Genius of the empire waiting with some impatience at his door, pressing for admittance, and reproaching his want of spirit and ambition.[2] Astonished and perplexed, he addressed his prayers to the great Jupiter, who immediately signified, by a clear and manifest omen, that he should submit to the will of heaven and of the army. The conduct which disclaims the ordinary maxims of reason excites our suspicion and eludes our inquiry. Whenever the spirit of fanaticism, at once so credulous and so crafty, has insinuated itself into a noble mind, it insensibly corrodes the vital principles of virtue and veracity.

To moderate the zeal of his party, to protect the persons of his enemies,[3] to defeat and to despise the secret enterprises

[1] Julian. ad S. P. Q. Athen. p. 284. The *devout* Abbé de la Blèterie (Vie de Julien, p. 159) is almost inclined to respect the *devout* protestations of a Pagan.

[2] Ammian. xx. 5, with the note of Lindenbrogius on the Genius of the empire. Julian himself, in a confidential letter to his friend and physician, Oribasius (Epist. xvii. p. 384), mentions another dream, to which, before the event, he gave credit; of a stately tree thrown to the ground, of a small plant striking a deep root into the earth. Even in his sleep the mind of the Cæsar must have been agitated by the hopes and fears of his fortune. Zosimus (l. iii. [c. 9] p. 155) relates a subsequent dream.

[3] The difficult situation of the prince of a rebellious army is finely described by Tacitus (Hist. i. 80-85). But Otho had much more guilt and much less abilities than Julian.]

which were formed against his life and dignity, were the cares
which employed the first days of the reign of the new emperor.
Although he was firmly resolved to maintain the station which he
had assumed, he was still desirous of saving his country from
the calamities of civil war, of declining a contest with the superior
forces of Constantius, and of preserving his own character from
the reproach of perfidy and ingratitude. Adorned with the
ensigns of military and imperial pomp, Julian showed himself in
the field of Mars to the soldiers, who glowed with ardent enthusiasm in the cause of their pupil, their leader, and their friend.
He recapitulated their victories, lamented their sufferings,
applauded their resolution, animated their hopes, and checked
their impetuosity; nor did he dismiss the assembly till he had
obtained a solemn promise from the troops that, if the emperor
of the East would subscribe an equitable treaty, they would
renounce any views of conquest, and satisfy themselves with the
tranquil possession of the Gallic provinces. On this foundation
he composed, in his own name, and in that of the army, a specious
and moderate epistle,[1] which was delivered to Pentadius, his
master of the offices, and to his chamberlain Eutherius; two
ambassadors whom he appointed to receive the answer and
observe the dispositions of Constantius. This epistle is inscribed
with the modest appellation of Cæsar; but Julian solicits in a
peremptory though respectful manner, the confirmation of the
title of Augustus. He acknowledges the irregularity of his own
election, while he justifies, in some measure, the resentment and
violence of the troops which had extorted his reluctant consent.
He allows the supremacy of his brother Constantius; and en-
gages to send him an annual present of Spanish horses, to recruit
his army with a select number of barbarian youths, and to accept
from his choice a Prætorian præfect of approved discretion and
fidelity. But he reserves for himself the nomination of his other
civil and military officers, with the troops, the revenue, and the
sovereignty of the provinces beyond the Alps. He admonishes
the emperor to consult the dictates of justice; to distrust the arts
of those venal flatterers who subsist only by the discord of princes;
and to embrace the offer of a fair and honourable treaty, equally
advantageous to the republic and to the house of Constantine.
In this negotiation Julian claimed no more than he had already
possessed. The delegated authority which he had long exercised

---

[1] To this ostensible epistle he added, says Ammianus, private letters,
objurgatorias et mordaces, which the historian had not seen, and would
not have published. Perhaps they never existed.

over the provinces of Gaul, Spain, and Britain, was still obeyed under a name more independent and august. The soldiers and the people rejoiced in a revolution which was not stained even with the blood of the guilty. Florentius was a fugitive; Lupicinus a prisoner. The persons who were disaffected to the new government were disarmed and secured; and the vacant offices were distributed, according to the recommendation of merit, by a prince who despised the intrigues of the palace and the clamours of the soldiers.[1]

The negotiations of peace were accompanied and supported by the most vigorous preparations for war. The army, which Julian held in readiness for immediate action, was recruited and augmented by the disorders of the times. The cruel persecution of the faction of Magnentius had filled Gaul with numerous bands of outlaws and robbers. They cheerfully accepted the offer of a general pardon from a prince whom they could trust, submitted to the restraints of military discipline, and retained only their implacable hatred to the person and government of Constantius.[2] As soon as the season of the year permitted Julian to take the field, he appeared at the head of his legions; threw a bridge over the Rhine in the neighbourhood of Cleves; and prepared to chastise the perfidy of the Attuarii, a tribe of Franks, who presumed that they might ravage with impunity the frontiers of a divided empire. The difficulty, as well as glory, of this enterprise consisted in a laborious march; and Julian had conquered, as soon as he could penetrate into, a country which former princes had considered as inaccessible. After he had given peace to the barbarians, the emperor carefully visited the fortifications along the Rhine from Cleves to Basel; surveyed, with peculiar attention, the territories which he had recovered from the hands of the Alemanni; passed through Besançon,[3] which had severely suffered from their fury; and fixed his head-quarters at Vienne for the ensuing winter. The barrier of Gaul was improved and strengthened with additional fortifications; and Julian entertained some hopes that the Germans, whom he had so often

---

[1] See the first transactions of his reign, in Julian ad S. P. Q. Athen. p. 285, 286. Ammianus, xx. 5, 8. Liban. Orat. Parent. c. 49, 50, p. 273-275.

[2] Liban. Orat. Parent. c. 50, p. 275, 276. A strange disorder, since it continued above seven years. In the factions of the Greek republics the exiles amounted to 20,000 persons; and Isocrates assures Philip that it would be easier to raise an army from the vagabonds than from the cities. See Hume's Essays, tom. i. p. 426, 427.

[3] Julian (Epist. xxxviii. p. 414) gives a short description of Vesontio, or Besançon; a rocky peninsula almost encircled by the river Doubs; once a magnificent city, filled with temples, etc., now reduced to a small town, emerging however from its ruins.

vanquished, might, in his absence, be restrained by the terror of his name. Vadomair [1] was the only prince of the Alemanni whom he esteemed or feared; and while the subtle barbarian affected to observe the faith of treaties, the progress of his arms threatened the state with an unseasonable and dangerous war. The policy of Julian condescended to surprise the prince of the Alemanni by his own arts: and Vadomair, who, in the character of a friend, had incautiously accepted an invitation from the Roman governors, was seized in the midst of the entertainment, and sent away prisoner into the heart of Spain. Before the barbarians were recovered from their amazement, the emperor appeared in arms on the banks of the Rhine, and, once more crossing the river, renewed the deep impressions of terror and respect which had been already made by four preceding expeditions.[2]

The ambassadors of Julian had been instructed to execute with the utmost diligence their important commission. But in their passage through Italy and Illyricum they were detained by the tedious and affected delays of the provincial governors; they were conducted by slow journeys from Constantinople to Cæsarea in Cappadocia; and when at length they were admitted to the presence of Constantius, they found that he had already conceived, from the despatches of his own officers, the most unfavourable opinion of the conduct of Julian and of the Gallic army. The letters were heard with impatience; the trembling messengers were dismissed with indignation and contempt; and the looks, the gestures, the furious language of the monarch, expressed the disorder of his soul. The domestic connection, which might have reconciled the brother and the husband of Helena, was recently dissolved by the death of that princess, whose pregnancy had been several times fruitless, and was at last fatal to herself.[3] The empress Eusebia had preserved, to the last

---

[1] Vadomair entered into the Roman service, and was promoted from a barbarian kingdom to the military rank of duke of Phœnicia. He still retained the same artful character (Ammian. xxi. 3); but, under the reign of Valens, he signalised his valour in the Armenian war (xxix. 1).

[2] Ammian. xx. 10, xxi. 3, 4. Zosimus, l. iii. [c. 10] p. 155.

[3] Her remains were sent to Rome, and interred near those of her sister Constantina, in the suburb of the *Via Nomentana*. Ammian. xxi. 1. Libanius has composed a very weak apology, to justify his hero from a very absurd charge of poisoning his wife, and rewarding her physician with his mother's jewels. (See the seventh of seventeen new orations, published at Venice 1754, from a MS. in St. Mark's library, p. 117-127.) Elpidius, the Prætorian præfect of the East, to whose evidence the accuser of Julian appeals, is arraigned by Libanius as *effeminate* and ungrateful; yet the religion of Elpidius is praised by Jerom (tom. i. p. 243), and his humanity by Ammianus (xxi. 6).

moment of her life, the warm, and even jealous, affection which she had conceived for Julian; and her mild influence might have moderated the resentment of a prince who, since her death, was abandoned to his own passions, and to the arts of his eunuchs. But the terror of a foreign invasion obliged him to suspend the punishment of a private enemy; he continued his march towards the confines of Persia, and thought it sufficient to signify the conditions which might entitle Julian and his guilty followers to the clemency of their offended sovereign. He required that the presumptuous Cæsar should expressly renounce the appellation and rank of Augustus which he had accepted from the rebels; that he should descend to his former station of a limited and dependent minister; that he should vest the powers of the state and army in the hands of those officers who were appointed by the Imperial court; and that he should trust his safety to the assurances of pardon, which were announced by Epictetus, a Gallic bishop, and one of the Arian favourites of Constantius. Several months were ineffectually consumed in a treaty which was negotiated at the distance of three thousand miles between Paris and Antioch; and, as soon as Julian perceived that his moderate and respectful behaviour served only to irritate the pride of an implacable adversary, he boldly resolved to commit his life and fortune to the chance of a civil war. He gave a public and military audience to the questor Leonas: the haughty epistle of Constantius was read to the attentive multitude; and Julian protested, with the most flattering deference, that he was ready to resign the title of Augustus, if he could obtain the consent of those whom he acknowledged as the authors of his elevation. The faint proposal was impetuously silenced; and the acclamations of " Julian Augustus, continue to reign, by the authority of the army, of the people, of the republic which you have saved," thundered at once from every part of the field, and terrified the pale ambassador of Constantius. A part of the letter was afterwards read, in which the emperor arraigned the ingratitude of Julian, whom he had invested with the honours of the purple; whom he had educated with so much care and tenderness; whom he had preserved in his infancy, when he was left a helpless orphan. " An orphan! " interrupted Julian, who justified his cause by indulging his passions, " does the assassin of my family reproach me that I was left an orphan? He urges me to revenge those injuries which I have long studied to forget." The assembly was dismissed; and Leonas, who with some difficulty had been protected from the popular fury, was sent back to his master with an epistle in which Julian expressed, in a strain of the most vehement eloquence, the sentiments of contempt, of hatred, and of resentment, which had been suppressed and embittered by the dissimulation of twenty years. After this message, which might be considered as a signal of irreconcilable war, Julian, who some weeks before had celebrated the Christian festival of the Epiphany,[1] made a public declaration that he committed the care of his safety to the IMMORTAL GODS; and thus publicly renounced the religion as well as the friendship of Constantius.[2]

The situation of Julian required a vigorous and immediate resolution. He had discovered from intercepted letters that his adversary, sacrificing the interest of the state to that of the monarch, had again excited the barbarians to invade the provinces of the West. The position of two magazines, one of them collected on the banks of the lake of Constance, the other formed at the foot of the Cottian Alps, seemed to indicate the march of two armies; and the size of those magazines, each of which consisted of six hundred thousand quarters of wheat, or rather flour,[3] was a threatening evidence of the strength and numbers of the enemy who prepared to surround him. But the Imperial legions were still in their distant quarters of Asia; the Danube was feebly guarded; and if Julian could occupy, by a sudden incursion, the important provinces of Illyricum, he might expect that a people of soldiers would resort to his standard, and that the rich mines of gold and silver would contribute to the expenses of the civil war. He proposed this bold enterprise to the assembly

---

[1] Feriarum die, quem celebrantes mense Januario, Christiani *Epiphania* dictitant, progressus, in eorum ecclesiam, solemniter numine orato discessit. Ammian. xxi. 2. Zonaras observes that it was on Christmas Day, and his assertion is not inconsistent; since the churches of Egypt, Asia, and perhaps Gaul, celebrated on the same day (the 6th of January) the nativity and the baptism of our Saviour. The Romans, as ignorant as their brethren of the real date of his birth, fixed the solemn festival to the 25th of December, the *Brumalia*, or winter solstice, when the Pagans annually celebrated the birth of the sun. See Bingham's Antiquities of the Christian Church, l. xx. c. 4; and Beausobre, Hist. Critique du Manichéisme, tom. ii. p. 690-700.

[2] The public and secret negotiations between Constantius and Julian must be extracted, with some caution, from Julian himself (Orat. ad S. P. Q. Athen. p. 286), Libanius (Orat. Parent. c. 51, p. 276), Ammianus (xx. 9), Zosimus (l. iii. [c. 9] p. 154), and even Zonaras (tom. ii. l. xiii. [c. 10] p. 20, 21, 22), who, on this occasion, appears to have possessed and used some valuable materials.

[3] Three hundred myriads, or three millions, of *medimni*, a corn-measure familiar to the Athenians, and which contained six Roman *modii*. Julian explains, like a soldier and a statesman, the danger of his situation, and the necessity and advantages of an offensive war (ad S. P. Q. Athen. p. 286, 287).

of the soldiers; inspired them with a just confidence in their general, and in themselves; and exhorted them to maintain their reputation of being terrible to the enemy, moderate to their fellow-citizens, and obedient to their officers. His spirited discourse was received with the loudest acclamations, and the same troops which had taken up arms against Constantius, when he summoned them to leave Gaul, now declared with alacrity that they would follow Julian to the farthest extremities of Europe or Asia. The oath of fidelity was administered; and the soldiers, clashing their shields, and pointing their drawn swords to their throats, devoted themselves, with horrid imprecations, to the service of a leader whom they celebrated as the deliverer of Gaul and the conqueror of the Germans.[1] This solemn engagement, which seemed to be dictated by affection rather than by duty, was singly opposed by Nebridius, who had been admitted to the office of Prætorian præfect. That faithful minister, alone and unassisted, asserted the rights of Constantius in the midst of an armed and angry multitude, to whose fury he had almost fallen an honourable, but useless sacrifice. After losing one of his hands by the stroke of a sword, he embraced the knees of the prince whom he had offended. Julian covered the præfect with his Imperial mantle, and protecting him from the zeal of his followers, dismissed him to his own house, with less respect than was perhaps due to the virtue of an enemy.[2] The high office of Nebridius was bestowed on Sallust; and the provinces of Gaul, which were now delivered from the intolerable oppression of taxes, enjoyed the mild and equitable administration of the friend of Julian, who was permitted to practise those virtues which he had instilled into the mind of his pupil.[3]

The hopes of Julian depended much less on the number of his troops than on the celerity of his motions. In the execution of a daring enterprise he availed himself of every precaution, as far as prudence could suggest; and where prudence could no longer accompany his steps, he trusted the event to valour and to fortune. In the neighbourhood of Basel he assembled and

---

[1] See his oration, and the behaviour of the troops, in Ammian. xxi. 5.

[2] He sternly refused his hand to the suppliant præfect, whom he sent into Tuscany (Ammian. xxi. 5). Libanius, with savage fury, insults Nebridius, applauds the soldiers, and almost censures the humanity of Julian (Orat. Parent. c. 53, p. 278).

[3] Ammian. xxi. 8. In this promotion Julian obeyed the law which he publicly imposed on himself. Neque civilis quisquam judex nec militaris [militiæ] rector, alio quodam præter merita suffragante, ad potiorem veniat gradum. (Ammian. xx. 5.) Absence did not weaken his regard for Sallust, with whose name (A.D. 363) he honoured the consulship.

divided his army.[1]   One body, which consisted of ten thousand
men, was directed, under the command of Nevitta, general of
the cavalry, to advance through the midland parts of Rhætia
and Noricum.   A similar division of troops, under the orders of
Jovius and Jovinus, prepared to follow the oblique course of the
highways through the Alps and the northern confines of Italy.
The instructions to the generals were conceived with energy and
precision: to hasten their march in close and compact columns,
which, according to the disposition of the ground, might readily
be changed into any order of battle; to secure themselves against
the surprises of the night by strong posts and vigilant guards;
to prevent resistance by their unexpected arrival; to elude
examination by their sudden departure; to spread the opinion
of their strength, and the terror of his name; and to join their
sovereign under the walls of Sirmium.   For himself Julian had
reserved a more difficult and extraordinary part.   He selected
three thousand brave and active volunteers, resolved, like their
leader, to cast behind them every hope of a retreat; at the head
of this faithful band he fearlessly plunged into the recesses of the
Marcian, or Black Forest, which conceals the sources of the
Danube;[2] and, for many days, the fate of Julian was unknown
to the world.   The secrecy of his march, his diligence, and
vigour, surmounted every obstacle; he forced his way over
mountains and morasses, occupied the bridges or swam the rivers,
pursued his direct course[3] without reflecting whether he traversed
the territory of the Romans or of the barbarians, and at length
emerged, between Ratisbon and Vienna, at the place where he
designed to embark his troops on the Danube.   By a well-
concerted stratagem he seized a fleet of light brigantines[4] as it
lay at anchor; secured a supply of coarse provisions sufficient

---

[1] Ammianus (xxi. 8) ascribes the same practice and the same motive to
Alexander the Great and other skilful generals.

[2] This wood was a part of the great Hercynian forest, which, in the time
of Cæsar, stretched away from the country of the Rauraci (Basel) into the
boundless regions of the North.   See Cluver. Germania Antiqua, l. iii. c. 47.

[3] Compare Libanius, Orat. Parent. c. 53. p. 278, 279, with Gregory
Nazianzen, Orat. iii. p. 68.   Even the saint admires the speed and secrecy
of this march.   A modern divine might apply to the progress of Julian the
lines which were originally designed for another apostate:—

———So eagerly the fiend,
O'er bog, or steep, through strait, rough, dense, or rare,
With head, hands, wings, or feet, pursues his way,
And swims, or sinks, or wades, or creeps, or flies.

[4] In that interval the *Notitia* places two or three fleets, the Lauriacensis
(at Lauriacum, or Lorch), the Arlapensis, the Maginensis; and mentions
five legions, or cohorts, of Liburnarii, who should be a sort of marines.
Sect. lviii. edit. Labb.

to satisfy the indelicate, but voracious, appetite of a Gallic army; and boldly committed himself to the stream of the Danube. The labours of his mariners, who plied their oars with incessant diligence, and the steady continuance of a favourable wind, carried his fleet above seven hundred miles in eleven days; [1] and he had already disembarked his troops at Bononia, only nineteen miles from Sirmium, before his enemies could receive any certain intelligence that he had left the banks of the Rhine. In the course of this long and rapid navigation, the mind of Julian was fixed on the object of his enterprise; and though he accepted the deputations of some cities, which hastened to claim the merit of an early submission, he passed before the hostile stations, which were placed along the river, without indulging the temptation of signalising an useless and ill-timed valour. The banks of the Danube were crowded on either side with spectators, who gazed on the military pomp, anticipated the importance of the event, and diffused through the adjacent country the fame of a young hero, who advanced with more than mortal speed at the head of the innumerable forces of the West. Lucilian, who, with the rank of general of the cavalry commanded the military powers of Illyricum, was alarmed and perplexed by the doubtful reports, which he could neither reject nor believe. He had taken some slow and irresolute measures for the purpose of collecting his troops, when he was surprised by Dagalaiphus, an active officer, whom Julian, as soon as he landed at Bononia, had pushed forwards with some light infantry. The captive general, uncertain of his life or death, was hastily thrown upon a horse, and conducted to the presence of Julian, who kindly raised him from the ground, and dispelled the terror and amazement which seemed to stupify his faculties. But Lucilian had no sooner recovered his spirits than he betrayed his want of discretion, by presuming to admonish his conqueror that he had rashly ventured, with a handful of men, to expose his person in the midst of his enemies. "Reserve for your master Constantius these timid remonstrances," replied Julian, with a smile of contempt; "when I gave you my purple to kiss, I received you not as a counsellor, but as a suppliant." Conscious that success alone could justify his attempt, and that boldness only could command success, he instantly advanced, at the head of three

---

[1] Zosimus alone (l. iii. [c. 10] p. 156) has specified this interesting circumstance. Mamertinus (in Panegyr. Vet. xi. [x.] 6, 7, 8), who accompanied Julian, as count of the sacred largesses, describes this voyage in a florid and picturesque manner, challenges Triptolemus and the Argonauts of Greece, etc.

thousand soldiers, to attack the strongest and most populous
city of the Illyrian provinces. As he entered the long suburb
of Sirmium, he was received by the joyful acclamations of the
army and people, who, crowned with flowers, and holding
lighted tapers in their hands, conducted their acknowledged
sovereign to his imperial residence. Two days were devoted
to the public joy, which was celebrated by the games of the
Circus; but, early on the morning of the third day, Julian
marched to occupy the narrow pass of Succi, in the defiles of
Mount Hæmus; which, almost in the midway between Sirmium
and Constantinople, separates the provinces of Thrace and Dacia,
by an abrupt descent towards the former, and a gentle declivity
on the side of the latter.[1] The defence of this important post
was intrusted to the brave Nevitta, who, as well as the generals
of the Italian division, successfully executed the plan of the
march and junction which their master had so ably conceived.[2]

The homage which Julian obtained from the fears or the
inclination of the people extended far beyond the immediate
effect of his arms.[3] The præfectures of Italy and Illyricum were
administered by Taurus and Florentius, who united that important office with the vain honours of the consulship; and, as
those magistrates had retired with precipitation to the court of
Asia, Julian, who could not always restrain the levity of his
temper, stigmatised their flight by adding, in all the Acts of the
Year, the epithet of *fugitive* to the names of the two consuls.
The provinces which had been deserted by their first magistrates
acknowledged the authority of an emperor who, conciliating the
qualities of a soldier with those of a philosopher, was equally
admired in the camps of the Danube and in the cities of Greece.
From his palace, or, more properly, from his headquarters of
Sirmium and Naissus, he distributed to the principal cities of
the empire a laboured apology for his own conduct; published
the secret despatches of Constantius; and solicited the judgment
of mankind between two competitors, the one of whom had

---

[1] The description of Ammianus, which might be supported by collateral
evidence, ascertains the precise situation of the *Angustiæ Succorum*, or
passes of *Succi*. M. d'Anville, from the trifling resemblance of names, has
placed them between Sardica and Naissus. For my own justification, I am
obliged to mention the *only* error which I have discovered in the maps or
writings of that admirable geographer.

[2] Whatever circumstances we may borrow elsewhere, Ammianus (xxi.
8, 9, 10) still supplies the series of the narrative.

[3] Ammian. xxi. 9, 10. Libanius, Orat. Parent. c. 54, p. 279, 280.
Zosimus, l. iii. [c. 10] p. 156, 157.

expelled, and the other had invited, the barbarians.[1] Julian, whose mind was deeply wounded by the reproach of ingratitude, aspired to maintain, by argument as well as by arms, the superior merits of his cause; and to excel not only in the arts of war, but in those of composition. His epistle to the senate and people of Athens [2] seems to have been dictated by an elegant enthusiasm, which prompted him to submit his actions and his motives to the degenerate Athenians of his own times, with the same humble deference as if he had been pleading in the days of Aristides before the tribunal of the Areopagus. His application to the senate of Rome, which was still permitted to bestow the titles of imperial power, was agreeable to the forms of the expiring republic. An assembly was summoned by Tertullus, præfect of the city; the epistle of Julian was read; and, as he appeared to be master of Italy, his claims were admitted without a dissenting voice. His oblique censure of the innovations of Constantine, and his passionate invective against the vices of Constantius, were heard with less satisfaction; and the senate, as if Julian had been present, unanimously exclaimed, " Respect, we beseech you, the author of your own fortune." [3] An artful expression, which, according to the chance of war, might be differently explained—as a manly reproof of the ingratitude of the usurper, or as a flattering confession that a single act of such benefit to the state ought to atone for all the failings of Constantius.

The intelligence of the march and rapid progress of Julian was speedily transmitted to his rival, who, by the retreat of Sapor, had obtained some respite from the Persian war. Disguising the anguish of his soul under the semblance of contempt, Constantius professed his intention of returning into Europe, and of giving chase to Julian; for he never spoke of

[1] Julian (ad S. P. Q. Athen. p. 286) positively asserts that he intercepted the letters of Constantius to the barbarians; and Libanius as positively affirms that he read them on his march to the troops and the cities. Yet Ammianus (xxi. 3) expresses himself with cool and candid hesitation, si famæ solius admittenda est fides. He specifies, however, an intercepted letter from Vadomair to Constantius, which supposes an intimate correspondence between them: " Cæsar tuus disciplinam non habet."

[2] Zosimus mentions his epistles to the Athenians, the Corinthians, and the Lacedæmonians. The substance was probably the same, though the address was properly varied. The epistle to the Athenians is still extant (p. 268-287), and has afforded much valuable information. It deserves the praises of the Abbé de la Blèterie (Préf. à l'Histoire de Jovien, p. 24, 25), and is one of the best manifestoes to be found in any language.

[3] Auctori tuo reverentiam rogamus. Ammian. xxi. 10. It is amusing enough to observe the secret conflicts of the senate between flattery and fear. See Tacit. Hist. i. 85.

this military expedition in any other light than that of a hunting party.[1] In the camp of Hierapolis, in Syria, he communicated this design to his army; slightly mentioned the guilt and rashness of the Cæsar; and ventured to assure them that, if the mutineers of Gaul presumed to meet them in the field, they would be unable to sustain the fire of their eyes and the irresistible weight of their shout of onset. The speech of the emperor was received with military applause; and Theodotus, the president of the council of Hierapolis, requested, with tears of adulation, that *his* city might be adorned with the head of the vanquished rebel.[2] A chosen detachment was despatched away in post-waggons, to secure, if it were yet possible, the pass of Succi; the recruits, the horses, the arms, and the magazines, which had been prepared against Sapor, were appropriated to the service of the civil war; and the domestic victories of Constantius inspired his partisans with the most sanguine assurances of success. The notary Gaudentius had occupied in his name the provinces of Africa; the subsistence of Rome was intercepted; and the distress of Julian was increased by an unexpected event, which might have been productive of fatal consequences. Julian had received the submission of two legions and a cohort of archers who were stationed at Sirmium; but he suspected, with reason, the fidelity of those troops which had been distinguished by the emperor; and it was thought expedient, under the pretence of the exposed state of the Gallic frontier, to dismiss them from the most important scene of action. They advanced, with reluctance, as far as the confines of Italy; but, as they dreaded the length of the way and the savage fierceness of the Germans, they resolved, by the instigation of one of their tribunes, to halt at Aquileia, and to erect the banners of Constantius on the walls of that impregnable city. The vigilance of Julian perceived at once the extent of the mischief, and the necessity of applying an immediate remedy. By his order, Jovinus led back a part of the army into Italy; and the siege of Aquileia was formed with diligence and prosecuted with vigour. But the legionaries, who seemed to have rejected the yoke of discipline, conducted the defence of the place with skill and perseverance; invited the rest of Italy to imitate the example of their courage

---

[1] Tanquam venaticiam prædam caperet: hoc enim ad leniendum suorum metum subinde prædicabat. Ammian. xxi. 7.

[2] See the speech and preparations in Ammianus, xxi. 13. The vile Theodotus afterwards implored and obtained his pardon from the merciful conqueror, who signified his wish of diminishing his enemies and increasing the number of his friends (xxii. 14).

and loyalty; and threatened the retreat of Julian, if he should be forced to yield to the superior numbers of the armies of the East.[1]

But the humanity of Julian was preserved from the cruel alternative which he pathetically laments of destroying or of being himself destroyed: and the seasonable death of Constantius delivered the Roman empire from the calamities of civil war. The approach of winter could not detain the monarch at Antioch; and his favourites durst not oppose his impatient desire of revenge. A slight fever, which was perhaps occasioned by the agitation of his spirits, was increased by the fatigues of the journey, and Constantius was obliged to halt at the little town of Mopsucrene, twelve miles beyond Tarsus, where he expired, after a short illness, in the forty-fifth year of his age, and the twenty-fourth of his reign.[2] His genuine character, which was composed of pride and weakness, of superstition and cruelty, has been fully displayed in the preceding narrative of civil and ecclesiastical events. The long abuse of power rendered him a considerable object in the eyes of his contemporaries; but, as personal merit can alone deserve the notice of posterity, the last of the sons of Constantine may be dismissed from the world with the remark that he inherited the defects, without the abilities, of his father. Before Constantius expired, he is said to have named Julian for his successor; nor does it seem improbable that his anxious concern for the fate of a young and tender wife, whom he left with child, may have prevailed in his last moments over the harsher passions of hatred and revenge. Eusebius and his guilty associates made a faint attempt to prolong the reign of the eunuchs by the election of another emperor; but their intrigues were rejected with disdain by an army which now abhorred the thought of civil discord; and two officers of rank were instantly despatched to assure Julian that every sword in the empire would be drawn for his service.

[1] Ammian. xxi. 7, 11, 12. He seems to describe, with superfluous labour, the operations of the siege of Aquileia, which on this occasion maintained its impregnable fame. Gregory Nazianzen (Orat. iii. p. 68) ascribes this accidental revolt to the wisdom of Constantius, whose assured victory he announces with some appearance of truth. Constantio, quem credebat proculdubio fore victorem: nemo enim omnium tunc ab hac constanti sententia discrepabat. Ammian. xxi. 7.

[2] His death and character are faithfully delineated by Ammianus (xxi. 14, 15, 16); and we are authorised to despise and detest the foolish calumny of Gregory (Orat. iii. p. 68), who accuses Julian of contriving the death of his benefactor. The private repentance of the emperor, that he had spared and promoted Julian (p. 69, and Orat. xxi. p. 389), is not improbable in itself, nor incompatible with the public verbal testament which prudential considerations might dictate in the last moments of his life.

The military designs of that prince, who had formed three different attacks against Thrace, were prevented by this fortunate event. Without shedding the blood of his fellow-citizens, he escaped the dangers of a doubtful conflict, and acquired the advantages of a complete victory. Impatient to visit the place of his birth and the new capital of the empire, he advanced from Naissus through the mountains of Hæmus and the cities of Thrace. When he reached Heraclea, at the distance of sixty miles, all Constantinople was poured forth to receive him; and he made his triumphal entry amidst the dutiful acclamations of the soldiers, the people, and the senate. An innumerable multitude pressed around him with eager respect, and were perhaps disappointed when they beheld the small stature and simple garb of a hero, whose inexperienced youth had vanquished the barbarians of Germany, and who had now traversed, in a successful career, the whole continent of Europe from the shores of the Atlantic to those of the Bosphorus.[1] A few days afterwards, when the remains of the deceased emperor were landed in the harbour, the subjects of Julian applauded the real or affected humanity of their sovereign. On foot, without his diadem, and clothed in a mourning habit, he accompanied the funeral as far as the church of the Holy Apostles, where the body was deposited: and if these marks of respect may be interpreted as a selfish tribute to the birth and dignity of his Imperial kinsman, the tears of Julian professed to the world that he had forgot the injuries, and remembered only the obligations, which he had received from Constantius.[2] As soon as the legions of Aquileia were assured of the death of the emperor, they opened the gates of the city, and, by the sacrifice of their guilty leaders, obtained an easy pardon from the prudence or lenity of Julian; who, in the thirty-second year of his age, acquired the undisputed possession of the Roman empire.[3]

[1] In describing the triumph of Julian, Ammianus (xxii. 1, 2) assumes the lofty tone of an orator or poet; while Libanius (Orat. Parent. c. 56, p. 281) sinks to the grave simplicity of an historian.

[2] The funeral of Constantius is described by Ammianus (xxi. 16), Gregory Nazianzen (Orat. iv. p. 119), Mamertinus (in Panegyr. Vet. xi. 27), Libanius (Orat. Parent. c. lvii. p. 283), and Philostorgius (l. vi. c. 6, with Godefroy's Dissertations, p. 265). These writers, and their followers, Pagans, Catholics, Arians, beheld with very different eyes both the dead and the living emperor.

[3] The day and year of the birth of Julian are not perfectly ascertained. The day is probably the sixth of November, and the year must be either 331 or 332. Tillemont, Hist. des Empereurs, tom. iv. p. 693. Ducange, Fam. Byzantin. p. 50. I have preferred the earlier date.

Philosophy had instructed Julian to compare the advantages of action and retirement; but the elevation of his birth and the accidents of his life never allowed him the freedom of choice. He might perhaps sincerely have preferred the groves of the Academy and the society of Athens; but he was constrained, at first by the will, and afterwards by the injustice of Constantius, to expose his person and fame to the dangers of Imperial greatness; and to make himself accountable to the world and to posterity for the happiness of millions.[1] Julian recollected with terror the observation of his master Plato,[2] that the government of our flocks and herds is always committed to beings of a superior species; and that the conduct of nations requires and deserves the celestial powers of the Gods or of the Genii. From this principle he justly concluded that the man who presumes to reign should aspire to the perfection of the divine nature; that he should purify his soul from her mortal and terrestrial part; that he should extinguish his appetites, enlighten his understanding, regulate his passions, and subdue the wild beast which, according to the lively metaphor of Aristotle,[3] seldom fails to ascend the throne of a despot. The throne of Julian, which the death of Constantius fixed on an independent basis, was the seat of reason, of virtue, and perhaps of vanity. He despised the honours, renounced the pleasures, and discharged with incessant diligence the duties of his exalted station: and there were few among his subjects who would have consented to relieve him from the weight of the diadem, had they been obliged to submit their time and their actions to the rigorous laws which their philosophic emperor imposed on himself. One of his most intimate friends,[4] who had often shared the frugal simplicity of his table, has remarked that his light and sparing

[1] Julian himself (p. 253-267) has expressed these philosophical ideas with much eloquence and some affectation, in a very elaborate epistle to Themistius. The Abbé de la Bléterie (tom. ii. p. 146-193), who has given an elegant translation, is inclined to believe that it was the celebrated Themistius, whose orations are still extant.

[2] Julian ad Themist. p. 258. Petavius (not. p. 95) observes that this passage is taken from the fourth book De Legibus; but either Julian quoted from memory, or his MSS. were different from ours. Xenophon opens the Cyropædia with a similar reflection.

[3] Ὁ δὲ ἄνθρωπον κελεύων ἄρχειν, προστίθησι καὶ θήριον. Aristot. ap. Julian. [in Epist. ad Themistium] p. 261. The MS. of Vossius, unsatisfied with the single beast, affords the stronger reading of θηρία, which the experience of despotism may warrant.

[4] Libanius (Orat. Parentalis, c. lxxxiv. lxxxv. p. 310, 311, 312) has given this interesting detail of the private life of Julian. He himself (in Misopogon, p. 350) mentions his vegetable diet, and upbraids the gross and sensual appetite of the people of Antioch.

diet (which was usually of the vegetable kind) left his mind and
body always free and active for the various and important
business of an author, a pontiff, a magistrate, a general, and a
prince. In one and the same day he gave audience to several
ambassadors, and wrote or dictated a great number of letters to
his generals, his civil magistrates, his private friends, and the
different cities of his dominions. He listened to the memorials
which had been received, considered the subject of the petitions,
and signified his intentions more rapidly than they could be
taken in shorthand by the diligence of his secretaries. He possessed such flexibility of thought, and such firmness of attention, that he could employ his hand to write, his ear to listen,
and his voice to dictate; and pursue at once three several
trains of ideas without hesitation, and without error. While
his ministers reposed, the prince flew with agility from one
labour to another; and, after a hasty dinner, retired into his
library till the public business which he had appointed for the
evening summoned him to interrupt the prosecution of his
studies. The supper of the emperor was still less substantial
than the former meal; his sleep was never clouded by the fumes
of indigestion; and, except in the short interval of a marriage
which was the effect of policy rather than love, the chaste Julian
never shared his bed with a female companion.[1] He was soon
awakened by the entrance of fresh secretaries, who had slept
the preceding day; and his servants were obliged to wait alternately, while their indefatigable master allowed himself scarcely
any other refreshment than the change of occupations. The
predecessors of Julian, his uncle, his brother, and his cousin,
indulged their puerile taste for the games of the Circus, under
the specious pretence of complying with the inclinations of the
people; and they frequently remained the greatest part of the
day as idle spectators, and as a part of the splendid spectacle,
till the ordinary round of twenty-four races [2] was completely
finished. On solemn festivals, Julian, who felt and professed

---

[1] Lectulus . . . Vestalium toris purior, is the praise which Mamertinus
(Panegyr. Vet. xi. [x.] 13) addresses to Julian himself. Libanius affirms,
in sober peremptory language, that Julian never knew a woman before his
marriage, or after the death of his wife (Orat. Parent. c. lxxxviii. p. 313).
The chastity of Julian is confirmed by the impartial testimony of Ammianus (xxv. 4), and the partial silence of the Christians. Yet Julian
ironically urges the reproach of the people of Antioch, that he *almost
always* (ὡς ἔπιπαν, in Misopogon, p. 345) lay alone. This suspicious expression is explained by the Abbé de la Bléterie (Hist. de Jovien, tom. ii. p. 103-
109) with candour and ingenuity.
[2] See Salmasius ad Sueton. in Claud. c. xxi. A twenty-fifth race, or

an unfashionable dislike to these frivolous amusements, condescended to appear in the Circus; and, after bestowing a careless glance on five or six of the races, he hastily withdrew with the impatience of a philosopher, who considered every moment as lost that was not devoted to the advantage of the public or the improvement of his own mind.[1] By this avarice of time he seemed to protract the short duration of his reign; and, if the dates were less securely ascertained, we should refuse to believe that only sixteen months elapsed between the death of Constantius and the departure of his successor for the Persian war. The actions of Julian can only be preserved by the care of the historian; but the portion of his voluminous writings which is still extant remains as a monument of the application, as well as of the genius, of the emperor. The Misopogon, the Cæsars, several of his orations, and his elaborate work against the Christian religion, were composed in the long nights of the two winters, the former of which he passed at Constantinople, and the latter at Antioch.

The reformation of the Imperial court was one of the first and most necessary acts of the government of Julian.[2] Soon after his entrance into the palace of Constantinople he had occasion for the service of a barber. An officer, magnificently dressed, immediately presented himself. "It is a barber," exclaimed the prince, with affected surprise, "that I want, and not a receiver-general of the finances."[3] He questioned the man concerning the profits of his employment, and was informed that, besides a large salary and some valuable perquisites, he enjoyed a daily allowance for twenty servants and as many horses. A thousand barbers, a thousand cupbearers, a thousand

missus, was added, to complete the number of one hundred chariots, four of which, the four colours, started each heat.

> Centum quadrijugos agitabo ad flumina currus.

It appears that they ran five or seven times round the *Meta* (Sueton. in Domitian. c. 4); and (from the measure of the Circus Maximus at Rome, the Hippodrome at Constantinople, etc.) it might be about a four-mile course.

[1] Julian, in Misopogon, p. 340. Julius Cæsar had offended the Roman people by reading his despatches during the actual race. Augustus indulged their taste, or his own, by his constant attention to the important business of the Circus, for which he professed the warmest inclination. Sueton. in August. c. xlv.

[2] The reformation of the palace is described by Ammianus (xxii. 4), Libanius (Orat. Parent. c. lxii. p. 288, etc.), Mamertinus (in Panegyr. Vet. xi. [x.] 11), Socrates (l. iii. c. 1), and Zonaras (tom. ii. l. xiii. [c. 12] p. 24).

[3] Ego non *rationalem* jussi sed tonsorem acciri. Zonaras uses the less natural image of a *senator*. Yet an officer of the finances, who was satiated with wealth, might desire and obtain the honours of the senate.

cooks, were distributed in the several offices of luxury; and the number of eunuchs could be compared only with the insects of a summer's day.[1] The monarch who resigned to his subjects the superiority of merit and virtue was distinguished by the oppressive magnificence of his dress, his table, his buildings, and his train. The stately palaces erected by Constantine and his sons were decorated with many-coloured marbles and ornaments of massy gold. The most exquisite dainties were procured to gratify their pride rather than their taste; birds of the most distant climates, fish from the most remote seas, fruits out of their natural season, winter roses, and summer snows.[2] The domestic crowd of the palace surpassed the expense of the legions; yet the smallest part of this costly multitude was subservient to the use, or even to the splendour, of the throne. The monarch was disgraced, and the people was injured, by the creation and sale of an infinite number of obscure and even titular employments; and the most worthless of mankind might purchase the privilege of being maintained, without the necessity of labour, from the public revenue. The waste of an enormous household, the increase of fees and perquisites, which were soon claimed as a lawful debt, and the bribes which they extorted from those who feared their enmity or solicited their favour, suddenly enriched these haughty menials. They abused their fortune, without considering their past or their future condition; and their rapine and venality could be equalled only by the extravagance of their dissipations. Their silken robes were embroidered with gold, their tables were served with delicacy and profusion; the houses which they built for their own use would have covered the farm of an ancient consul; and the most honourable citizens were obliged to dismount from their horses and respectfully to salute an eunuch whom they met on the public highway. The luxury of the palace excited the contempt and indignation of Julian, who usually slept on the ground, who yielded with reluctance to the indispensable calls of nature, and who placed his vanity not in emulating, but in despising the pomp of royalty.

---

[1] Μαγείρους μὲν χιλίους, κουρέας δὲ οὐκ ἐλάττους, οἰνοχόους δὲ πλείους, σμήνη τραπεζοποιῶν, εὐνούχους ὑπὲρ τὰς μυίας παρὰ τοῖς ποιμέσιν ἐν ἦρι, are the original words of Libanius, which I have faithfully quoted, lest I should be suspected of magnifying the abuses of the royal household.

[2] The expressions of Mamertinus [l. c.] are lively and forcible. Quin etiam prandiorum et cœnarum elaboratas magnitudines Respublica sentiebat; cum quæsitissimæ dapes non gustu, sed difficultatibus æstimarentur; miracula avium, longinqui maris pisces, alieni temporis poma, æstivæ nives, hibernæ rosæ.

By the total extirpation of a mischief which was magnified even beyond its real extent, he was impatient to relieve the distress and to appease the murmurs of the people, who support with less uneasiness the weight of taxes if they are convinced that the fruits of their industry are appropriated to the service of the state. But in the execution of this salutary work Julian is accused of proceeding with too much haste and inconsiderable severity. By a single edict he reduced the palace of Constantinople to an immense desert, and dismissed with ignominy the whole train of slaves and dependents,[1] without providing any just, or at least benevolent, exceptions for the age, the services, or the poverty of the faithful domestics of the Imperial family. Such indeed was the temper of Julian, who seldom recollected the fundamental maxim of Aristotle, that true virtue is placed at an equal distance between the opposite vices. The splendid and effeminate dress of the Asiatics, the curls and paint, the collars and bracelets, which had appeared so ridiculous in the person of Constantine, were consistently rejected by his philosophic successor. But, with the fopperies, Julian affected to renounce the decencies of dress; and seemed to value himself for his neglect of the laws of cleanliness. In a satirical performance, which was designed for the public eye, the emperor descants with pleasure, and even with pride, on the length of his nails and the inky blackness of his hands; protests that, although the greatest part of his body was covered with hair, the use of the razor was confined to his head alone; and celebrates with visible complacency the shaggy and *populous*[2] beard which he fondly cherished, after the example of the philosophers of Greece. Had Julian consulted the simple dictates of reason, the first magistrate of the Romans would have scorned the affectation of Diogenes, as well as that of Darius.

But the work of public reformation would have remained imperfect if Julian had only corrected the abuses, without

[1] Yet Julian himself was accused of bestowing whole towns on the eunuchs (Orat. vii. against Polyclet. p. 117-127). Libanius contents himself with a cold but positive denial of the fact, which seems indeed to belong more properly to Constantius. This charge, however, may allude to some unknown circumstance.

[2] In the Misopogon (p. 338, 339) he draws a very singular picture of himself, and the following words are strangely characteristic: αὐτὸς προσέθεικα τὸν βαθὺν τουτονὶ πώγωνα . . . ταῦτά τοι διαθέοντων ἀνέχομαι τῶν φθειρῶν ὥσπερ ἐν λοχμῇ τῶν θηρίων. The friends of the Abbé de la Bléterie adjured him, in the name of the French nation, not to translate this passage, so offensive to their delicacy (Hist. de Jovien, tom. ii. p. 94). Like him, I have contented myself with a transient allusion; but the little animal, which Julian *names*, is a beast familiar to man, and signifies love.

punishing the crimes, of his predecessor's reign. "We are now delivered," says he, in a familiar letter to one of his intimate friends, "we are now surprisingly delivered from the voracious jaws of the Hydra.[1] I do not mean to apply that epithet to my brother Constantius. He is no more; may the earth lie light on his head! But his artful and cruel favourites studied to deceive and exasperate a prince whose natural mildness cannot be praised without some efforts of adulation. It is not, however, my intention that even those men should be oppressed: they are accused, and they shall enjoy the benefit of a fair and impartial trial." To conduct this inquiry, Julian named six judges of the highest rank in the state and army, and, as he wished to escape the reproach of condemning his personal enemies, he fixed this extraordinary tribunal at Chalcedon, on the Asiatic side of the Bosphorus, and transferred to the commissioners an absolute power to pronounce and execute their final sentence, without delay and without appeal. The office of president was exercised by the venerable præfect of the East, a *second* Sallust,[2] whose virtues conciliated the esteem of Greek sophists and of Christian bishops. He was assisted by the eloquent Mamertinus,[3] one of the consuls elect, whose merit is loudly celebrated by the doubtful evidence of his own applause. But the civil wisdom of two magistrates was overbalanced by the ferocious violence of four generals, Nevitta, Agilo, Jovinus, and Arbetio. Arbetio, whom the public would have seen with less surprise at the bar than on the bench, was supposed to possess the secret of the commission; the armed and angry leaders of the Jovian and Herculian bands encompassed the tribunal, and the judges were alternately swayed by the laws of justice and by the clamours of faction.[4]

The chamberlain Eusebius, who had so long abused the favour of Constantius, expiated, by an ignominious death, the insolence,

---

[1] Julian, Epist. xxiii. p. 389. He uses the words πολυκέφαλον ὕδραν, in writing to his friend Hermogenes, who, like himself, was conversant with the Greek poets.

[2] The two Sallusts, the præfect of Gaul and the præfect of the East, must be carefully distinguished (Hist. des Empereurs, tom. iv. p. 696). I have used the surname of *Secundus* as a convenient epithet. The second Sallust extorted the esteem of the Christians themselves; and Gregory Nazianzen, who condemned his religion, has celebrated his virtues (Orat. iii. p. 90). See a curious note of the Abbé de la Blétérie, Vie de Julien, p. 363.

[3] Mamertinus praises the emperor (xi. [x.] 1) for bestowing the offices of treasurer and præfect on a man of wisdom, firmness, integrity, etc., like himself. Yet Ammianus ranks him (xxi. 1) among the ministers of Julian, quorum merita nôrat et fidem.

[4] The proceedings of this chamber of justice are related by Ammianus (xxii. 3) and praised by Libanius (Orat. Parent. c. 74, p. 299, 300).

the corruption, and cruelty of his servile reign. The executions of Paul and Apodemius (the former of whom was burnt alive) were accepted as an inadequate atonement by the widows and orphans of so many hundred Romans whom those legal tyrants had betrayed and murdered. But Justice herself (if we may use the pathetic expression of Ammianus [1]) appeared to weep over the fate of Ursulus, the treasurer of the empire, and his blood accused the ingratitude of Julian, whose distress had been seasonably relieved by the intrepid liberality of that honest minister. The rage of the soldiers, whom he had provoked by his indiscretion, was the cause and the excuse of his death; and the emperor, deeply wounded by his own reproaches and those of the public, offered some consolation to the family of Ursulus by the restitution of his confiscated fortunes. Before the end of the year in which they had been adorned with the ensigns of the prefecture and consulship,[2] Taurus and Florentius were reduced to implore the clemency of the inexorable tribunal of Chalcedon. The former was banished to Vercellæ in Italy, and a sentence of death was pronounced against the latter. A wise prince should have rewarded the crime of Taurus: the faithful minister, when he was no longer able to oppose the progress of a rebel, had taken refuge in the court of his benefactor and his lawful sovereign. But the guilt of Florentius justified the severity of the judges, and his escape served to display the magnanimity of Julian, who nobly checked the interested diligence of an informer, and refused to learn what place concealed the wretched fugitive from his just resentment.[3] Some months after the tribunal of Chalcedon had been dissolved, the prætorian vicegerent of Africa, the notary Gaudentius, and Artemius,[4] duke of Egypt, were executed at Antioch. Artemius had reigned the cruel and corrupt tyrant of a great province;

[1] Ursuli vero necem ipsa mihi videtur flêsse Justitia [Amm. l. c.]. Libanius, who imputes his death to the soldiers, attempts to criminate the count of the largesses.

[2] Such respect was still entertained for the venerable names of the commonwealth, that the public was surprised and scandalised to hear Taurus summoned as a criminal under the consulship of Ta rus. The summons of his colleague Florentius was probably delayed till the commencement of the ensuing year.

[3] Ammian. xxii. 7.

[4] For the guilt and punishment of Artemius, see Julian (Epist. x. p. 379) and Ammianus (xxii. 11, and Vales, ad loc.). The merit of Artemius, who demolished temples, and was put to death by an apostate, has tempted the Greek and Latin churches to honour him as a martyr. But as ecclesiastical history attests that he was not only a tyrant, but an Arian, it is not altogether easy to justify this indiscreet promotion. Tillemont, Mém. Ecclés. tom. vii. p. 1319.

Gaudentius had long practised the arts of calumny against the innocent, the virtuous, and even the person of Julian himself. Yet the circumstances of their trial and condemnation were so unskilfully managed that these wicked men obtained, in the public opinion, the glory of suffering for the obstinate loyalty with which they had supported the cause of Constantius. The rest of his servants were protected by a general act of oblivion, and they were left to enjoy with impunity the bribes which they had accepted either to defend the oppressed or to oppress the friendless. This measure, which, on the soundest principles of policy, may deserve our approbation, was executed in a manner which seemed to degrade the majesty of the throne. Julian was tormented by the importunities of a multitude, particularly of Egyptians, who loudly re-demanded the gifts which they had imprudently or illegally bestowed; he foresaw the endless prosecution of vexatious suits, and he engaged a promise, which ought always to have been sacred, that if they would repair to Chalcedon, he would meet them in person, to hear and determine their complaints. But as soon as they were landed, he issued an absolute order, which prohibited the watermen from transporting any Egyptian to Constantinople, and thus detained his disappointed clients on the Asiatic shore, till, their patience and money being utterly exhausted, they were obliged to return with indignant murmurs to their native country.[1]

The numerous army of spies, of agents, and informers enlisted by Constantius to secure the repose of one man, and to interrupt that of millions, was immediately disbanded by his generous successor. Julian was slow in his suspicions, and gentle in his punishments; and his contempt of treason was the result of judgment, of vanity, and of courage. Conscious of superior merit, he was persuaded that few among his subjects would dare to meet him in the field, to attempt his life, or even to seat themselves on his vacant throne. The philosopher could excuse the hasty sallies of discontent, and the hero could despise the ambitious projects which surpassed the fortune or the abilities of the rash conspirators. A citizen of Ancyra had prepared for his own use a purple garment, and this indiscreet action, which, under the reign of Constantius, would have been considered as a capital offence,[2] was reported to Julian by the officious impor-

---

[1] See Ammian. xxii. 6, and Vales. ad locum; and the Codex Theodosianus, l. ii. tit. xxix. leg. i.; and Godefroy's Commentary, tom. i. p. 218, ad locum.

[2] The president Montesquieu (Considérations sur la Grandeur, etc., des Romains, c. xiv. in his works, tom. iii. p. 448, 449) excuses this minute and absurd tyranny, by supposing that actions the most indifferent in our eyes

tunity of a private enemy. The monarch, after making some inquiry into the rank and character of his rival, despatched the informer with a present of a pair of purple slippers, to complete the magnificence of his Imperial habit. A more dangerous conspiracy was formed by ten of the domestic guards, who had resolved to assassinate Julian in the field of exercise near Antioch. Their intemperance revealed their guilt, and they were conducted in chains to the presence of their injured sovereign, who, after a lively representation of the wickedness and folly of their enterprise, instead of a death of torture, which they deserved and expected, pronounced a sentence of exile against the two principal offenders. The only instance in which Julian seemed to depart from his accustomed clemency was the execution of a rash youth, who, with a feeble hand, had aspired to seize the reins of empire. But that youth was the son of Marcellus, the general of cavalry, who, in the first campaign of the Gallic war, had deserted the standard of the Cæsar and the republic. Without appearing to indulge his personal resentment, Julian might easily confound the crime of the son and of the father; but he was reconciled by the distress of Marcellus, and the liberality of the emperor endeavoured to heal the wound which had been inflicted by the hand of justice.[1]

Julian was not insensible of the advantages of freedom.[2] From his studies he had imbibed the spirit of ancient sages and heroes; his life and fortunes had depended on the caprice of a tyrant; and, when he ascended the throne, his pride was sometimes mortified by the reflection that the slaves who would not dare to censure his defects were not worthy to applaud his virtues.[3] He sincerely abhorred the system of oriental despotism which Diocletian, Constantine, and the patient habits of fou score years, had established in the empire. A motive of superstition prevented the execution of the design which Julian had frequently meditated, of relieving his head from the weight of

might excite, in a Roman mind, the idea of guilt and danger. This strange apology is supported by a strange misapprehension of the English laws, "chez une nation . . . où il est défendu de boire à la santé d'une certaine personne."

[1] The clemency of Julian, and the conspiracy which was formed against his life at Antioch, are described by Ammianus (xxii. 9, 10, and Vales. ad loc.) and Libanius (Orat. Parent. c. 99, p. 323).

[2] According to some, says Aristotle (as he is quoted by Julian ad Themist. p. 261), the form of absolute government, the παμβασιλεια, is contrary to nature. Both the prince and the philosopher choose, however, to involve this eternal truth in artful and laboured obscurity.

[3] That sentiment is expressed almost in the words of Julian himself. Ammian. xxii. 10.

a costly diadem; [1] but he absolutely refused the title of *Dominus* or *Lord*,[2] a word which was grown so familiar to the ears of the Romans, that they no longer remembered its servile and humiliating origin. The office, or rather the name, of consul was cherished by a prince who contemplated with reverence the ruins of the republic; and the same behaviour which had been assumed by the prudence of Augustus was adopted by Julian from choice and inclination. On the calends of January, at break of day, the new consuls, Mamertinus and Nevitta, hastened to the palace to salute the emperor. As soon as he was informed of their approach, he leaped from his throne, eagerly advanced to meet them, and compelled the blushing magistrates to receive the demonstrations of his affected humility. From the palace they proceeded to the senate. The emperor, on foot, marched before their litters, and the gazing multitude admired the image of ancient times, or secretly blamed a conduct which, in their eyes, degraded the majesty of the purple.[3] But the behaviour of Julian was uniformly supported. During the games of the Circus, he had, imprudently or designedly, performed the manumission of a slave in the presence of the consul. The moment he was reminded that he had trespassed on the jurisdiction of *another* magistrate, he condemned himself to pay a fine of ten pounds of gold, and embraced this public occasion of declaring to the world that he was subject, like the rest of his fellow-citizens, to the laws,[4] and even to the forms, of the republic. The spirit of his administration, and his regard for the place of

---

[1] Libanius (Orat. Parent. c. 95, p. 320), who mentions the wish and design of Julian, insinuates in mysterious language (θεῶν οὔτω γνόντων . . . ἀλλ' ἦν ἀμείνων ὁ κωλύων) that the emperor was restrained by some particular revelation.

[2] Julian in Misopogon, p. 343. As he never abolished, by any public law, the proud appellations of *Despot*, or *Dominus*, they are still extant on his medals (Ducange, Fam. Byzantin. p. 38, 39); and the private displeasure which he affected to express only gave a different tone to the servility of the court. The Abbé de la Blétérie (Hist. de Jovien, tom. ii. p. 99-102) has curiously traced the origin and progress of the word *Dominus* under the Imperial government.

[3] Ammian. xxii. 7. The consul Mamertinus (in Panegyr. Vet. xi. [x.] 28, 29, 30) celebrates the auspicious day, like an eloquent slave, astonished and intoxicated by the condescension of his master.

[4] Personal satire was condemned by the laws of the twelve tables:—

> Si mala condiderit in quem quis carmina, jus est,
> Judiciumque——

Horat. Sat. ii. 1, 82.

Julian (in Misopogon, p. 337) owns himself subject to the law; and the Abbé de la Blétérie (Hist. de Jovien, tom. ii. p. 92) has eagerly embraced a declaration so agreeable to his own system, and indeed to the true spirit of the Imperial constitution.

his nativity, induced Julian to confer on the senate of Constantinople the same honours, privileges, and authority which were still enjoyed by the senate of ancient Rome.[1] A legal fiction was introduced and gradually established, that one half of the national council had migrated into the East, and the despotic successors of Julian, accepting the title of Senators, acknowledged themselves the members of a respectable body which was permitted to represent the majesty of the Roman name. From Constantinople the attention of the monarch was extended to the municipal senates of the provinces. He abolished, by repeated edicts, the unjust and pernicious exemptions which had withdrawn so many idle citizens from the service of their country; and by imposing an equal distribution of public duties, he restored the strength, the splendour, or, according to the glowing expression of Libanius,[2] the soul of the expiring cities of his empire. The venerable age of Greece excited the most tender compassion in the mind of Julian, which kindled into rapture when he recollected the gods, the heroes, and the men superior to heroes and to gods, who had bequeathed to the latest posterity the monuments of their genius or the example of their virtues. He relieved the distress and restored the beauty of the cities of Epirus and Peloponnesus.[3] Athens acknowledged him for her benefactor, Argos for her deliverer. The pride of Corinth, again rising from her ruins with the honours of a Roman colony, exacted a tribute from the adjacent republics for the purpose of defraying the games of the Isthmus, which were celebrated in the amphitheatre with the hunting of bears and panthers. From this tribute the cities of Elis, of Delphi, and of Argos, which had inherited from their remote ancestors the sacred office of perpetuating the Olympic, the Pythian, and the Nemean games, claimed a just exemption. The immunity of Elis and Delphi was respected by the Corinthians, but the poverty of Argos tempted the insolence of oppression, and the feeble complaints of its deputies were silenced by the decree of a provincial magis-

---

[1] Zosimus, l. iii. [c. 11] p. 158.

[2] Ἡ τῆς βουλῆς ἰσχὺς ψύχη πόλεως ἐστιν. See Libanius (Orat. Parent. c. 71, p. 296), Ammianus (xxii. 9), and the Theodosian Code (l. xii. tit. i. leg. 50-55) with Godefroy's Commentary (tom. iv. p. 390-402). Yet the whole subject of the *Curia*, notwithstanding very ample materials, still remains the most obscure in the legal history of the empire.

[3] Quæ paulo ante arida et siti anhelantia visebantur, ea nunc perlui, mundari, madere; Fora, Deambulacra, Gymnasia, lætis et gaudentibus populis frequentari; dies festos, et celebrari veteres, et novos in honorem principis consecrari (Mamertin. xi. [x.] 9). He particularly restored the city of Nicopolis, and the Actiac games, which had been instituted by Augustus.

trate, who seems to have consulted only the interest of the capital in which he resided. Seven years after this sentence Julian [1] allowed the cause to be referred to a superior tribunal, and his eloquence was interposed, most probably with success, in the defence of a city which had been the royal seat of Agamemnon,[2] and had given to Macedonia a race of kings and conquerors.[3]

The laborious administration of military and civil affairs, which were multiplied in proportion to the extent of the empire, exercised the abilities of Julian; but he frequently assumed the two characters of Orator [4] and of Judge,[5] which are almost unknown to the modern sovereigns of Europe. The arts of persuasion, so diligently cultivated by the first Cæsars, were neglected by the military ignorance and Asiatic pride of their successors, and, if they condescended to harangue the soldiers, whom they feared, they treated with silent disdain the senators, whom they despised. The assemblies of the senate, which Constantius had avoided, were considered by Julian as the place where he could exhibit with the most propriety the maxims of a republican and the talents of a rhetorician. He alternately practised, as in a school of declamation, the several modes of praise, of censure, of exhortation; and his friend Libanius has

[1] Julian, Epist. xxxv. p. 407-411. This epistle, which illustrates the declining age of Greece, is omitted by the Abbé de la Bléterie; and strangely disfigured by the Latin translator, who, by rendering ἀτέλεια, *tributum*, and ἰδιῶται, *populus*, directly contradicts the sense of the original.

[2] He reigned in Mycenæ, at the distance of fifty stadia, or six miles, from Argos: but those cities, which alternately flourished, are confounded by the Greek poets. Strabo, l. viii. p. 579, edit. Amstel. 1707 [p. 377, edit. Casaub.].

[3] Marsham, Canon. Chron. p. 421. This pedigree from Temenus and Hercules may be suspicious; yet it was allowed, after a strict inquiry by the judges of the Olympic games (Herodot. l. v. c. 22), at a time when the Macedonian kings were obscure and unpopular in Greece. When the Achæan league declared against Philip, it was thought decent that the deputies of Argos should retire (T. Liv. xxxii. 22).

[4] His eloquence is celebrated by Libanius (Orat. Parent. c. 75, 76, p. 300, 301), who distinctly mentions the orators of Homer. Socrates (l. iii. c. 1) has rashly asserted that Julian was the only prince since Julius Cæsar who harangued the senate. All the predecessors of Nero (Tacit. Annal. xiii. 3), and many of his successors, possessed the faculty of speaking in public; and it might be proved by various examples that they frequently exercised it in the senate.

[5] Ammianus (xxii. 10) has impartially stated the merits and defects of his judicial proceedings. Libanius (Orat. Parent. c. 90, 91, p. 315, etc.) has seen only the fair side; and his picture, if it flatters the person, expresses at least the duties of the judge. Gregory Nazianzen (Orat. iv. p. 120), who suppresses the virtues and exaggerates even the venial faults of the Apostate, triumphantly asks, Whether such a judge was fit to be seated between Minos and Rhadamanthus in the Elysian fields?

remarked that the study of Homer taught him to imitate the simple, concise style of Menelaus, the copiousness of Nestor, whose words descended like the flakes of a winter's snow, or the pathetic and forcible eloquence of Ulysses. The functions of a judge, which are sometimes incompatible with those of a prince, were exercised by Julian not only as a duty, but as an amusement; and although he might have trusted the integrity and discernment of his Prætorian præfects, he often placed himself by their side on the seat of judgment. The acute penetration of his mind was agreeably occupied in detecting and defeating the chicanery of the advocates, who laboured to disguise the truth of facts and to pervert the sense of the laws. He sometimes forgot the gravity of his station, asked indiscreet or unseasonable questions, and betrayed, by the loudness of his voice and the agitation of his body, the earnest vehemence with which he maintained his opinion against the judges, the advocates, and their clients. But his knowledge of his own temper prompted him to encourage, and even to solicit, the reproof of his friends and ministers: and whenever they ventured to oppose the irregular sallies of his passions, the spectators could observe the shame as well as the gratitude of their monarch. The decrees of Julian were almost always founded on the principles of justice, and he had the firmness to resist the two most dangerous temptations which assault the tribunal of a sovereign under the specious forms of compassion and equity. He decided the merits of the cause without weighing the circumstances of the parties; and the poor, whom he wished to relieve, were condemned to satisfy the just demands of a noble and wealthy adversary. He carefully distinguished the judge from the legislator;[1] and though he meditated a necessary reformation of the Roman jurisprudence, he pronounced sentence according to the strict and literal interpretation of those laws which the magistrates were bound to execute and the subjects to obey.

The generality of princes, if they were stripped of their purple and cast naked into the world, would immediately sink to the lowest rank of society, without a hope of emerging from their obscurity. But the personal merit of Julian was, in some measure, independent of his fortune. Whatever had been his choice of life, by the force of intrepid courage, lively wit, and

---

[1] Of the laws which Julian enacted in a reign of sixteen months, fifty-four have been admitted into the codes of Theodosius and Justinian. (Gothofred. Chron. Legum. p. 64-67.) The Abbé de la Blèterie (tom. ii. p. 329-336) has chosen one of these laws to give an idea of Julian's Latin style, which is forcible and elaborate, but less pure than his Greek.

intense application, he would have obtained, or at least he would
have deserved, the highest honours of his profession, and Julian
might have raised himself to the rank of minister or general of
the state in which he was born a private citizen. If the jealous
caprice of power had disappointed his expectations; if he had
prudently declined the paths of greatness, the employment of
the same talents in studious solitude would have placed beyond
the reach of kings his present happiness and his immortal fame.
When we inspect with minute, or perhaps malevolent, attention
the portrait of Julian, something seems wanting to the grace and
perfection of the whole figure. His genius was less powerful
and sublime than that of Cæsar, nor did he possess the consummate prudence of Augustus. The virtues of Trajan appear more
steady and natural, and the philosophy of Marcus is more simple
and consistent. Yet Julian sustained adversity with firmness,
and prosperity with moderation. After an interval of one
hundred and twenty years from the death of Alexander Severus,
the Romans beheld an emperor who made no distinction between
his duties and his pleasures, who laboured to relieve the distress
and to revive the spirit of his subjects, and who endeavoured
always to connect authority with merit, and happiness with
virtue. Even faction, and religious faction, was constrained
to acknowledge the superiority of his genius in peace as well as in
war, and to confess, with a sigh, that the apostate Julian was
a lover of his country, and that he deserved the empire of the
world.[1]

> [1] . . . Ductor fortissimus armis,
> Conditor et legum celeberrimus, ore manuque
> Consultor patriæ, sed non consultor habendæ
> Religionis, amans tercentûm millia Divûm.
> Perfidus ille Deo, quamvis non perfidus orbi.
> > Prudent. Apotheosis, 450, etc.

The consciousness of a generous sentiment seems to have raised the
Christian poet above his usual mediocrity.

CHAPTER XXIII

The Religion of Julian—Universal Toleration—He attempts to restore and reform the Pagan Worship—To rebuild the Temple of Jerusalem —His artful Persecution of the Christians—Mutual Zeal and Injustice

THE character of Apostate has injured the reputation of Julian; and the enthusiasm which clouded his virtues has exaggerated the real and apparent magnitude of his faults. Our partial ignorance may represent him as a philosophic monarch, who studied to protect, with an equal hand, the religious factions of the empire, and to allay the theological fever which had inflamed the minds of the people from the edicts of Diocletian to the exile of Athanasius. A more accurate view of the character and conduct of Julian will remove this favourable prepossession for a prince who did not escape the general contagion of the times. We enjoy the singular advantage of comparing the pictures which have been delineated by his fondest admirers and his implacable enemies. The actions of Julian are faithfully related by a judicious and candid historian, the impartial spectator of his life and death. The unanimous evidence of his contemporaries is confirmed by the public and private declarations of the emperor himself; and his various writings express the uniform tenor of his religious sentiments, which policy would have prompted him to dissemble rather than to affect. A devout and sincere attachment for the gods of Athens and Rome constituted the ruling passion of Julian;[1] the powers of an enlightened understanding were betrayed and corrupted by the influence of superstitious prejudice; and the phantoms which existed only in the mind of the emperor had a real and pernicious effect on the government of the empire. The vehement zeal of the Christians, who despised the worship, and overturned the altars, of those fabulous deities, engaged their votary in a state of irreconcilable hostility with a very numerous party of his subjects; and he was sometimes tempted, by the desire of victory or the shame of a repulse, to violate the laws of prudence, and

---

[1] I shall transcribe some of his own expressions from a short religious discourse which the Imperial pontiff composed to censure the bold impiety of a Cynic. Ἀλλ᾿ ὅμως οὕτω δή τι τοὺς θεοὺς πέφρικα, καὶ φιλῶ, καὶ σέβω, καὶ ἄζομαι, καὶ πάνθ᾿ ἁπλῶς τὰ τοιαῦτα πρὸς αὐτοὺς πάσχω, ὅσαπερ ἄν τις καὶ οἷα πρὸς ἀγαθοὺς δεσπότας, πρὸς διδασκάλους, πρὸς πατέρας, πρὸς κηδεμόνας. Orat. vii. p. 212. The variety and copiousness of the Greek tongue seems inadequate to the fervour of his devotion.

even of justice. The triumph of the party which he deserted and opposed has fixed a stain of infamy on the name of Julian; and the unsuccessful apostate has been overwhelmed with a torrent of pious invectives, of which the signal was given by the sonorous trumpet [1] of Gregory Nazianzen.[2] The interesting nature of the events which were crowded into the short reign of this active emperor deserves a just and circumstantial narrative. His motive, his counsels, and his actions, as far as they are connected with the history of religion, will be the subject of the present chapter.

The cause of his strange and fatal apostasy may be derived from the early period of his life when he was left an orphan in the hands of the murderers of his family. The names of Christ and of Constantius, the ideas of slavery and of religion, were soon associated in a youthful imagination, which was susceptible of the most lively impressions. The care of his infancy was intrusted to Eusebius, bishop of Nicomedia,[3] who was related to him on the side of his mother; and till Julian reached the twentieth year of his age, he received from his Christian preceptors the education not of a hero but of a saint. The emperor, less jealous of a heavenly than of an earthly crown, contented himself with the imperfect character of a catechumen, while he bestowed the advantages of baptism [4] on the nephews of Constantine.[5] They were even admitted to the inferior offices of the ecclesiastical order; and Julian publicly read the Holy

[1] The orator, with some eloquence, much enthusiasm, and more vanity, addresses his discourse to heaven and earth, to men and angels, to the living and the dead; and above all, to the great Constantius (εἰ τις αἰσθησις, an odd Pagan expression). He concludes with a bold assurance that he has erected a monument not less durable, and much more portable, than the Columns of Hercules. See Greg. Nazianzen, Orat. iii. p. 50, iv. p. 134.

[2] See this long invective, which has been injudiciously divided into two orations in Gregory's Works, tom. i. p. 49-134, Paris, 1630. It was published by Gregory and his friend Basil (iv. p. 133), about six months after the death of Julian, when his remains had been carried to Tarsus (iv. p. 120), but while Jovian was still on the throne (iii. p. 54, iv. p. 117). I have derived much assistance from a French version and remarks, printed at Lyons 1735.

[3] Nicomediæ ab Eusebio educatus Episcopo, quem genere longius contingebat (Ammian. xxii. 9). Julian never expresses any gratitude towards that Arian prelate; but he celebrates his preceptor, the eunuch Mardonius, and describes his mode of education, which inspired his pupil with a passionate admiration for the genius, and perhaps the religion, of Homer. Misopogon, p. 351, 352.

[4] Greg. Naz. iii. p. 70. He laboured to efface that holy mark in the blood, perhaps, of a Taurobolium. Baron. Annal. Eccles. A.D. 361, No. 3, 4.

[5] Julian himself (Epist. li. p. 434) assures the Alexandrians that he had been a Christian (he must mean a sincere one) till the twentieth year of his age.

Scriptures in the church of Nicomedia. The study of religion, which they assiduously cultivated, appeared to produce the fairest fruits of faith and devotion.[1] They prayed, they fasted, they distributed alms to the poor, gifts to the clergy, and oblations to the tombs of the martyrs; and the splendid monument of St. Mamas, at Cæsarea, was erected, or at least was undertaken, by the joint labour of Gallus and Julian.[2] They respectfully conversed with the bishops who were eminent for superior sanctity, and solicited the benediction of the monks and hermits who had introduced into Cappadocia the voluntary hardships of the ascetic life.[3] As the two princes advanced towards the years of manhood, they discovered, in their religious sentiments, the difference of their characters. The dull and obstinate understanding of Gallus embraced, with implicit zeal, the doctrines of Christianity, which never influenced his conduct, or moderated his passions. The mild disposition of the younger brother was less repugnant to the precepts of the Gospel; and his active curiosity might have been gratified by a theological system which explains the mysterious essence of the Deity, and opens the boundless prospect of invisible and future worlds. But the independent spirit of Julian refused to yield the passive and unresisting obedience which was required, in the name of religion, by the haughty ministers of the church. Their speculative opinions were imposed as positive laws, and guarded by the terrors of eternal punishments; but while they prescribed the rigid formulary of the thoughts, the words, and the actions of the young prince; whilst they silenced his objections, and severely checked the freedom of his inquiries, they secretly provoked his impatient genius to disclaim the authority of his ecclesiastical guides. He was educated in the Lesser Asia, amidst the scandals of the Arian controversy.[4] The fierce contests of the Eastern

---

[1] See his Christian, and even ecclesiastical education, in Gregory (iii. p. 58), Socrates (l. iii. c. 1), and Sozomen (l. v. c. 2). He escaped very narrowly from being a bishop, and perhaps a saiut.

[2] The share of the work which had been allotted to Gallus was prosecuted with vigour and success; but the earth obstinately rejected and subverted the structures which were imposed by the sacrilegious hand of Julian. Greg. iii. p. 59, 60, 61. Such a partial earthquake, attested by many living spectators, would form one of the clearest miracles in ecclesiastical story.

[3] The *philosopher* (Fragment. p. 288) ridicules the iron chains, etc., of these solitary fanatics (see Tillemont, Mém. Ecclés. tom. ix. p. 661, 662), who had forgot that man is by nature a gentle and social animal, ἀνθρώπου φύσει πολιτικοῦ ζώου καὶ ἡμέρου. The *Pagan* supposes that because they had renounced the gods, they were possessed and tormented by evil dæmons.

[4] See Julian apud Cyril. l. vi. p. 206, l. viii. p. 253, 262. "You perse-cute," says he, "those heretics who do not mourn the dead man precisely

bishops, the incessant alterations of their creeds, and the profane motives which appeared to actuate their conduct, insensibly strengthened the prejudice of Julian that they neither understood nor believed the religion for which they so fiercely contended. Instead of listening to the proofs of Christianity with that favourable attention which adds weight to the most respectable evidence, he heard with suspicion, and disputed with obstinacy and acuteness, the doctrines for which he already entertained an invincible aversion. Whenever the young princes were directed to compose declamations on the subject of the prevailing controversies, Julian always declared himself the advocate of Paganism, under the specious excuse that, in the defence of the weaker cause, his learning and ingenuity might be more advantageously exercised and displayed.

As soon as Gallus was invested with the honours of the purple, Julian was permitted to breathe the air of freedom, of literature, and of Paganism.[1] The crowd of sophists, who were attracted by the taste and liberality of their royal pupil, had formed a strict alliance between the learning and the religion of Greece; and the poems of Homer, instead of being admired as the original productions of human genius, were seriously ascribed to the heavenly inspiration of Apollo and the muses. The deities of Olympus, as they are painted by the immortal bard, imprint themselves on the minds which are the least addicted to superstitious credulity. Our familiar knowledge of their names and characters, their forms and attributes, *seems* to bestow on those airy beings a real and substantial existence; and the pleasing enchantment produces an imperfect and momentary assent of the imagination to those fables which are the most repugnant to our reason and experience. In the age of Julian every circumstance contributed to prolong and fortify the illusion—the magnificent temples of Greece and Asia; the works of those artists who had expressed, in painting or in sculpture, the divine conceptions of the poet; the pomp of festivals and sacrifices; the successful arts of divination; the popular traditions of oracles and prodigies; and the ancient practice of two thousand years. The weakness of polytheism was, in some measure, excused by the moderation of its claims; and the devotion of

in the way which you approve." He shows himself a tolerable theologian; but he maintains that the Christian Trinity is not derived from the doctrine of Paul, of Jesus, or of Moses.

[1] Libanius, Orat. Parentalis, c. 9, 10, p. 232, etc. Greg. Nazianzen, Orat. iii. p. 61. Eunap. Vit. Sophist. in Maximo, p. 88 *seqq.*, edit. Commelin. [1596].

the Pagans was not incompatible with the most licentious scepticism.[1] Instead of an indivisible and regular system, which occupies the whole extent of the believing mind, the mythology of the Greeks was composed of a thousand loose and flexible parts, and the servant of the gods was at liberty to define the degree and measure of his religious faith. The creed which Julian adopted for his own use was of the largest dimensions; and, by a strange contradiction, he disdained the salutary yoke of the Gospel, whilst he made a voluntary offering of his reason on the altars of Jupiter and Apollo. One of the orations of Julian is consecrated to the honour of Cybele, the mother of the gods, who required from her effeminate priests the bloody sacrifice so rashly performed by the madness of the Phrygian boy. The pious emperor condescends to relate, without a blush and without a smile, the voyage of the goddess from the shores of Pergamus to the mouth of the Tiber; and the stupendous miracle which convinced the senate and people of Rome that the lump of clay which their ambassadors had transported over the seas was endowed with life, and sentiment, and divine power.[2] For the truth of this prodigy he appeals to the public monuments of the city; and censures, with some acrimony, the sickly and affected taste of those men who impertinently derided the sacred traditions of their ancestors.[3]

But the devout philosopher, who sincerely embraced, and warmly encouraged, the superstition of the people, reserved for himself the privilege of a liberal interpretation, and silently withdrew from the foot of the altars into the sanctuary of the temple. The extravagance of the Grecian mythology proclaimed, with a clear and audible voice, that the pious inquirer, instead of being scandalised or satisfied with the literal sense, should

---

[1] A modern philosopher has ingeniously compared the different operation of theism and polytheism, with regard to the doubt or conviction which they produce in the human mind. See Hume's Essays, vol. ii. p. 444-457, in 8vo. edit. 1777.

[2] The Idæan mother landed in Italy about the end of the second Punic war. The miracle of Claudia, either virgin or matron, who cleared her fame by disgracing the graver modesty of the Roman ladies, is attested by a cloud of witnesses. Their evidence is collected by Drakenborch (ad Silium Italicum, xvii. 33); but we may observe that Livy (xxix. 14) slides over the transaction with discreet ambiguity.

[3] I cannot refrain from transcribing the emphatical words of Julian: ἐμοὶ δὲ δοκεῖ ταῖς πόλεσι πιστεύειν μᾶλλον τὰ τοιαῦτα, ἢ τουτοισὶ τοῖς κομψοῖς, ὧν τὸ ψυχάριον δριμὺ μὲν, ὑγιὲς δὲ οὐδὲ ἓν βλέπει. Orat. v. p. 161. Julian likewise declares his firm belief in the ancilia, the holy shields, which dropped from heaven on the Quirinal hill; and pities the strange blindness of the Christians, who preferred the cross to these celestial trophies. Apud Cyril. l. vi. p. 194.

diligently explore the occult wisdom, which had been disguised, by the prudence of antiquity, under the mask of folly and of fable.[1] The philosophers of the Platonic school,[2] Plotinus, Porphyry, and the divine Iamblichus, were admired as the most skilful masters of this allegorical science, which laboured to soften and harmonise the deformed features of Paganism. Julian himself, who was directed in the mysterious pursuit by Ædesius, the venerable successor of Iamblichus, aspired to the possession of a treasure which he esteemed, if we may credit his solemn asseverations, far above the empire of the world.[3] It was indeed a treasure which derived its value only from opinion; and every artist who flattered himself that he had extracted the precious ore from the surrounding dross claimed an equal right of stamping the name and figure the most agreeable to his peculiar fancy. The fable of Atys and Cybele had been already explained by Porphyry; but his labours served only to animate the pious industry of Julian, who invented and published his own allegory of that ancient and mystic tale. This freedom of interpretation, which might gratify the pride of the Platonists, exposed the vanity of their art. Without a tedious detail the modern reader could not form a just idea of the strange allusions, the forced etymologies, the solemn trifling, and the impenetrable obscurity of these sages, who professed to reveal the system of the universe. As the traditions of Pagan mythology were variously related, the sacred interpreters were at liberty to select the most convenient circumstances; and as they translated an arbitrary cipher, they could extract from *any* fable *any* sense which was adapted to their favourite system of religion and philosophy. The lascivious form of a naked Venus was tortured into the discovery of some moral precept, or some physical truth; and the castration of Atys explained the revolution of the sun between the tropics, or the separation of the human soul from vice and error.[4]

---

[1] See the principles of allegory, in Julian (Orat. vii. p. 216, 222). His reasoning is less absurd than that of some modern theologians, who assert that an extravagant or contradictory doctrine *must* be divine, since no man alive could have thought of inventing it.

[2] Eunapius has made these sophists the subject of a partial and fanatical history; and the learned Brucker (Hist. Philosoph. tom. ii. p. 217-303) has employed much labour to illustrate their obscure lives and incomprehensible doctrines.

[3] Julian, Orat. vii. p. 222. He swears with the most fervent and enthusiastic devotion; and trembles lest he should betray too much of these holy mysteries, which the profane might deride with an impious Sardonic laugh.

[4] See the fifth oration of Julian. But all the allegories which ever issued from the Platonic school are not worth the short poem of Catullus on the same extraordinary subject. The transition of Atys from the wildest

The theological system of Julian appears to have contained the sublime and important principles of natural religion. But as the faith which is not founded on revelation must remain destitute of any firm assurance, the disciple of Plato imprudently relapsed into the habits of vulgar superstition; and the popular and philosophic notion of the Deity seems to have been confounded in the practice, the writings, and even in the mind of Julian.[1] The pious emperor acknowledged and adored the Eternal Cause of the universe, to whom he ascribed all the perfections of an infinite nature, invisible to the eyes and inaccessible to the understanding of feeble mortals. The Supreme God had created, or rather, in the Platonic language, had generated, the gradual succession of dependent spirits, of gods, of dæmons, of heroes, and of men; and every being which derived its existence immediately from the First Cause received the inherent gift of immortality. That so precious an advantage might not be lavished upon unworthy objects, the Creator had intrusted to the skill and power of the inferior gods the office of forming the human body, and of arranging the beautiful harmony of the animal, the vegetable, and the mineral kingdoms. To the conduct of these divine ministers he delegated the temporal government of this lower world; but their imperfect administration is not exempt from discord or error. The earth and its inhabitants are divided among them, and the characters of Mars or Minerva, of Mercury or Venus, may be distinctly traced in the laws and manners of their peculiar votaries. As long as our immortal souls are confined in a mortal prison, it is our interest, as well as our duty, to solicit the favour, and to deprecate the wrath, of the powers of heaven; whose pride is gratified by the devotion of mankind, and whose grosser parts may be supposed to derive some nourishment from the fumes of sacrifice.[2] The inferior gods might sometimes condescend to animate the statues, and to inhabit the temples, which were dedicated to their honour. They might occasionally visit the earth, but the heavens were

enthusiasm to sober pathetic complaint for his irretrievable loss, must inspire a man with pity, an eunuch with despair.

[1] The true religion of Julian may be deduced from the Cæsars, p. 308, with Spanheim's notes and illustrations; from the fragments in Cyril, l. ii. p. 57, 58; and especially from the theological oration in Solem Regem, p. 130-158, addressed, in the confidence of friendship, to the præfect Sallust.

[2] Julian adopts this gross conception by ascribing it to his favourite Marcus Antoninus (Cæsares, p. 333. The Stoics and Platonists hesitated between the analogy of bodies and the purity of spirits; yet the gravest philosophers inclined to the whimsical fancy of Aristophanes and Lucian, that an unbelieving age might starve the immortal gods. See Observations de Spanheim, p. 284, 444, etc.

the proper throne and symbol of their glory. The invariable order of the sun, moon, and stars was hastily admitted by Julian as a proof of their *eternal* duration; and their eternity was a sufficient evidence that they were the workmanship, not of an inferior deity, but of the Omnipotent King. In the system of the Platonists the visible was a type of the invisible world. The celestial bodies, as they were informed by a divine spirit, might be considered as the objects the most worthy of religious worship. The SUN, whose genial influence pervades and sustains the universe, justly claimed the adoration of mankind, as the bright representative of the LOGOS, the lively, the rational, the beneficent image of the intellectual Father.[1]

In every age the absence of genuine inspiration is supplied by the strong illusions of enthusiasm and the mimic arts of imposture. If, in the time of Julian, these arts had been practised only by the Pagan priests, for the support of an expiring cause, some indulgence might perhaps be allowed to the interest and habits of the sacerdotal character. But it may appear a subject of surprise and scandal that the philosophers themselves should have contributed to abuse the superstitious credulity of mankind,[2] and that the Grecian mysteries should have been supported by the magic or theurgy of the modern Platonists. They arrogantly pretended to control the order of nature, to explore the secrets of futurity, to command the service of the inferior dæmons, to enjoy the view and conversation of the superior gods, and, by disengaging the soul from her material bands, to re-unite that immortal particle with the Infinite and Divine Spirit.

The devout and fearless curiosity of Julian tempted the philosophers with the hopes of an easy conquest, which, from the situation of their young proselyte, might be productive of the most important consequences.[3] Julian imbibed the first rudi-

---

[1] Ἥλιον λέγω, τὸ ζῶν ἄγαλμα καὶ ἔμψυχον, καὶ ἔννουν, καὶ ἀγαθοεργὸν τοῦ νοητοῦ πατρὸς. Julian, Epist. li. [p. 434]. In another place (apud Cyril. l. ii. p. 69) he calls the sun God, and the throne of God. Julian believed the Platonician Trinity; and only blames the Christians for preferring a mortal to an immortal *Logos*.

[2] The sophists of Eunapius perform as many miracles as the saints of the desert; and the only circumstance in their favour is, that they are of a less gloomy complexion. Instead of devils with horns and tails, Iamblichus evoked the genii of love, Eros and Anteros, from two adjacent fountains. Two beautiful boys issued from the water, fondly embraced him as their father, and retired at his command. P. 26, 27.

[3] The dexterous management of these sophists, who played their credulous pupil into each other's hands, is fairly told by Eunapius [in Maximo, p. 85 *seqq.*, ed. Commel.] with unsuspecting simplicity. The Abbé de la Blèterie understands, and neatly describes, the whole comedy. (Vie de Julien, p. 61-67.)

ments of the Platonic doctrines from the mouth of Ædesius, who had fixed at Pergamus his wandering and persecuted school. But as the declining strength of that venerable sage was unequal to the ardour, the diligence, the rapid conception of his pupil, two of his most learned disciples, Chrysanthes and Eusebius, supplied, at his own desire, the place of their aged master. These philosophers seem to have prepared and distributed their respective parts; and they artfully contrived, by dark hints and affected disputes, to excite the impatient hopes of the *aspirant* till they delivered him into the hands of their associate, Maximus, the boldest and most skilful master of the Theurgic science. By his hands Julian was secretly initiated at Ephesus, in the twentieth year of his age. His residence at Athens confirmed this unnatural alliance of philosophy and superstition. He obtained the privilege of a solemn initiation into the mysteries of Eleusis, which, amidst the general decay of the Grecian worship, still retained some vestiges of their primæval sanctity; and such was the zeal of Julian that he afterwards invited the Eleusinian pontiff to the court of Gaul, for the sole purpose of consummating, by mystic rites and sacrifices, the great work of his sanctification. As these ceremonies were performed in the depth of caverns and in the silence of the night, and as the inviolable secret of the mysteries was preserved by the discretion of the initiated, I shall not presume to describe the horrid sounds and fiery apparitions which were presented to the senses or the imagination of the credulous aspirant,[1] till the visions of comfort and knowledge broke upon him in a blaze of celestial light.[2] In the caverns of Ephesus and Eleusis the mind of Julian was penetrated with sincere, deep, and unalterable enthusiasm; though he might sometimes exhibit the vicissitudes of pious fraud and hypocrisy which may be observed, or at least suspected, in the characters of the most conscientious fanatics. From that moment he consecrated his life to the service of the gods; and while the occupations of war, of government, and of study seemed to claim the whole measure of his time, a stated portion of the

[1] When Julian, in a momentary panic, made the sign of the cross, the demons instantly disappeared (Greg. Naz. Orat. iii. p. 71). Gregory supposes that they were frightened, but the priests declared that they were indignant. The reader, according to the measure of his faith, will determine this profound question.

[2] A dark and distant view of the terrors and joys of initiation is shown by Dion Chrysostom, Themistius, Proclus, and Stobæus. The learned author of the Divine Legation has exhibited their words (vol. i. p. 239, 247, 248, 280, edit. 1765), which he dexterously or forcibly applies to his own hypothesis.

hours of the night was invariably reserved for the exercise of private devotion. The temperance which adorned the severe manners of the soldier and the philosopher was connected with some strict and frivolous rules of religious abstinence; and it was in honour of Pan or Mercury, of Hecate or Isis, that Julian, on particular days, denied himself the use of some particular food, which might have been offensive to his tutelar deities. By these voluntary fasts he prepared his senses and his understanding for the frequent and familiar visits with which he was honoured by the celestial powers. Notwithstanding the modest silence of Julian himself, we may learn from his faithful friend, the orator Libanius, that he lived in a perpetual intercourse with the gods and goddesses; that they descended upon earth to enjoy the conversation of their favourite hero; that they gently interrupted his slumbers by touching his hand or his hair; that they warned him of every impending danger, and conducted him, by their infallible wisdom, in every action of his life; and that he had acquired such an intimate knowledge of his heavenly guests, as readily to distinguish the voice of Jupiter from that of Minerva, and the form of Apollo from the figure of Hercules.[1] These sleeping or waking visions, the ordinary effects of abstinence and fanaticism, would almost degrade the emperor to the level of an Egyptian monk. But the useless lives of Antony or Pachomius were consumed in these vain occupations. Julian could break from the dream of superstition to arm himself for battle; and after vanquishing in the field the enemies of Rome, he calmly retired into his tent, to dictate the wise and salutary laws of an empire, or to indulge his genius in the elegant pursuits of literature and philosophy.

The important secret of the apostasy of Julian was intrusted to the fidelity of the *initiated*, with whom he was united by the sacred ties of friendship and religion.[2] The pleasing rumour was cautiously circulated among the adherents of the ancient worship; and his future greatness became the object of the hopes, the prayers, and the predictions of the Pagans in every province of the empire. From the zeal and virtues of their royal proselyte

---

[1] Julian's modesty confined him to obscure and occasional hints; but Libanius expatiates with pleasure on the fasts and visions of the religious hero. (Legat. ad. Julian. p. 157, and Orat. Parental. c. lxxxiii. p. 309, 310.)

[2] Libanius, Orat. Parent. c. x. p. 233, 234. Gallus had some reason to suspect the secret apostasy of his brother; and in a letter, which may be received as genuine, he exhorts Julian to adhere to the religion of their *ancestors*; an argument which, as it should seem, was not yet perfectly ripe. See Julian. Op. p. 454 [ed. Spanheim, Lips. 1696], and Hist. de Jovien, tom. ii. p. 141.

they fondly expected the cure of every evil and the restoration of every blessing; and instead of disapproving of the ardour of their pious wishes, Julian ingenuously confessed that he was ambitious to attain a situation in which he might be useful to his country and to his religion.   But this religion was viewed with an hostile eye by the successor of Constantine, whose capricious passions alternately saved and threatened the life of Julian. The arts of magic and divination were strictly prohibited under a despotic government which condescended to fear them; and if the Pagans were reluctantly indulged in the exercise of their superstition, the rank of Julian would have excepted him from the general toleration.   The apostate soon became the presumptive heir of the monarchy, and his death could alone have appeased the just apprehensions of the Christians.[1]   But the young prince, who aspired to the glory of a hero rather than of a martyr, consulted his safety by dissembling his religion; and the easy temper of polytheism permitted him to join in the public worship of a sect which he inwardly despised.   Libanius has considered the hypocrisy of his friend as a subject, not of censure, but of praise.   " As the statues of the gods," says that orator, " which have been defiled with filth are again placed in a magnificent temple, so the beauty of truth was seated in the mind of Julian after it had been purified from the errors and follies of his education.   His sentiments were changed; but as it would have been dangerous to have avowed his sentiments, his conduct still continued the same.   Very different from the ass in Æsop, who disguised himself with a lion's hide, our lion was obliged to conceal himself under the skin of an ass; and, while he embraced the dictates of reason, to obey the laws of prudence and necessity." [2]

The dissimulation of Julian lasted above ten years, from his secret initiation at Ephesus to the beginning of the civil war; when he declared himself at once the implacable enemy of Christ and of Constantius.   This state of constraint might contribute to strengthen his devotion; and as soon as he had satisfied the obligation of assisting, on solemn festivals, at the assemblies of the Christians, Julian returned, with the impatience of a lover, to burn his free and voluntary incense in the domestic chapels of Jupiter and Mercury.   But as every act of dissimulation must

---

[1] Gregory (iii. p. 50), with inhuman zeal, censures Constantius for sparing the infant apostate ($\kappa\acute{\alpha}\kappa\omega\varsigma$ $\sigma\acute{\omega}\theta\epsilon\nu\tau\alpha$).   His French translator (p. 265) cautiously observes that such expressions must not be prises à la lettre.

[2] Libanius, Orat. Parental. c. ix. p. 233.

be painful to an ingenuous spirit, the profession of Christianity
increased the aversion of Julian for a religion which oppressed
the freedom of his mind, and compelled him to hold a conduct
repugnant to the noblest attributes of human nature—sincerity
and courage.

The inclination of Julian might prefer the gods of Homer and
of the Scipios to the new faith which his uncle had established
in the Roman empire, and in which he himself had been sanctified
by the sacrament of baptism. But, as a philosopher, it was
incumbent on him to justify his dissent from Christianity, which
was supported by the number of its converts, by the chain of
prophecy, the splendour of miracles, and the weight of evidence.
The elaborate work [1] which he composed amidst the preparations
of the Persian war contained the substance of those arguments
which he had long revolved in his mind. Some fragments have
been transcribed and preserved by his adversary, the vehement
Cyril of Alexandria; [2] and they exhibit a very singular mixture
of wit and learning, of sophistry and fanaticism. The elegance
of the style and the rank of the author recommended his writings
to the public attention; [3] and in the impious list of the enemies
of Christianity the celebrated name of Porphyry was effaced by
the superior merit or reputation of Julian. The minds of the
faithful were either seduced, or scandalised, or alarmed; and the
Pagans, who sometimes presumed to engage in the unequal
dispute, derived, from the popular work of their Imperial missionary, an inexhaustible supply of fallacious objections. But
in the assiduous prosecution of these theological studies the
emperor of the Romans imbibed the illiberal prejudices and
passions of a polemic divine. He contracted an irrevocable
obligation to maintain and propagate his religious opinions; and
whilst he secretly applauded the strength and dexterity with
which he wielded the weapons of controversy, he was tempted

---

[1] Fabricius (Biblioth. Græc. l. v. c. viii. p. 88-90) and Lardner (Heathen
Testimonies, vol. iv. p. 44-47) have accurately compiled all that can now
be discovered of Julian's work against the Christians.

[2] About seventy years after the death of Julian he executed a task which
had been feebly attempted by Philip of Side, a prolix and contemptible
writer. Even the work of Cyril has not entirely satisfied the most favourable judges: and the Abbé de la Bléterie (Préface à l'Hist. de Jovien, p. 30,
32) wishes that some *théologien philosophe* (a strange centaur) would undertake the refutation of Julian.

[3] Libanius (Orat. Parental. c. lxxxvii. p. 313), who has been suspected of
assisting his friend, prefers this divine vindication (Orat. ix. in necem
Julian. p. 257, edit. Morel.) to the writings of Porphyry. His judgment
may be arraigned (Socrates, l. iii. c. 23), but Libanius cannot be accused of
flattery to a dead prince.

to distrust the sincerity, or to despise the understandings, of his antagonists, who could obstinately resist the force of reason and eloquence.

The Christians, who beheld with horror and indignation the apostasy of Julian, had much more to fear from his power than from his arguments. The Pagans, who were conscious of his fervent zeal, expected, perhaps with impatience, that the flames of persecution should be immediately kindled against the enemies of the gods; and that the ingenious malice of Julian would invent some cruel refinements of death and torture which had been unknown to the rude and inexperienced fury of his predecessors. But the hopes, as well as the fears, of the religious factions were apparently disappointed by the prudent humanity of a prince [1] who was careful of his own fame, of the public peace, and of the rights of mankind. Instructed by history aad reflection, Julian was persuaded that, if the diseases of the body may sometimes be cured by salutary violence, neither steel nor fire can eradicate the erroneous opinions of the mind. The reluctant victim may be dragged to the foot of the altar; but the heart still abhors and disclaims the sacrilegious act of the hand. Religious obstinacy is hardened and exasperated by oppression; and, as soon as the persecution subsides, those who have yielded are restored as penitents, and those who have resisted are honoured as saints and martyrs. If Julian adopted the unsuccessful cruelty of Diocletian and his colleagues, he was sensible that he should stain his memory with the name of tyrant, and add new glories to the catholic church, which had derived strength and increase from the severity of the Pagan magistrates. Actuated by these motives, and apprehensive of disturbing the repose of an unsettled reign, Julian surprised the world by an edict which was not unworthy of a statesman or a philosopher. He extended to all the inhabitants of the Roman world the benefits of a free and equal toleration; and the only hardship which he inflicted on the Christians was to deprive them of the power of tormenting their fellow-subjects, whom they stigmatised with the odious titles of idolaters and heretics. The Pagans received a gracious permission, or rather an express order, to open ALL their temples; [2]

[1] Libanius (Orat. Parent. c. lviii. p. 283, 284) has eloquently explained the tolerating principles and conduct of his Imperial friend. In a very remarkable epistle to the people of Bostra, Julian himself (Epist. lii. [p. 436]) professes his moderation, and betrays his zeal, which is acknowledged by Ammianus and exposed by Gregory. (Orat. iii. p. 72.)

[2] In Greece the temples of Minerva were opened by his express command, before the death of Constantius (Liban. Orat. Parent. c. 55, p. 280); and

and they were at once delivered from the oppressive laws and
arbitrary vexations which they had sustained under the reign
of Constantine and of his sons. At the same time, the bishops
and clergy who had been banished by the Arian monarch were
recalled from exile, and restored to their respective churches;
the Donatists, the Novatians, the Macedonians, the Eunomians,
and those who, with a more prosperous fortune, adhered to the
doctrine of the council of Nice. Julian, who understood and
derided their theological disputes, invited to the palace the
leaders of the hostile sects, that he might enjoy the agreeable
spectacle of their furious encounters. The clamour of controversy sometimes provoked the emperor to exclaim, " Hear me !
the Franks have heard me, and the Alemanni; " but he soon
discovered that he was now engaged with more obstinate and
implacable enemies; and though he exerted the powers of
oratory to persuade them to live in concord, or at least in peace,
he was perfectly satisfied, before he dismissed them from his
presence, that he had nothing to dread from the union of the
Christians. The impartial Ammianus has ascribed this affected
clemency to the desire of fomenting the intestine divisions of the
church; and the insidious design of undermining the foundations
of Christianity was inseparably connected with the zeal which
Julian professed to restore the ancient religion of the empire.[1]

As soon as he ascended the throne, he assumed, according to
the custom of his predecessors, the character of supreme pontiff;
not only as the most honourable title of Imperial greatness, but
as a sacred and important office, the duties of which he was
resolved to execute with pious diligence. As the business of
the state prevented the emperor from joining every day in the
public devotion of his subjects, he dedicated a domestic chapel to
his tutelar deity the Sun; his gardens were filled with statues
and altars of the gods; and each apartment of the palace displayed the appearance of a magnificent temple. Every morning he saluted the parent of light with a sacrifice; the blood of
another victim was shed at the moment when the Sun sunk

Julian declares himself a Pagan in his public manifesto to the Athenians.
This unquestionable evidence may correct the hasty assertion of Ammianus, who seems to suppose Constantinople to be the place where he discovered his attachment to the gods.

[1] Ammianus, xxii. 5. Sozomen, l. v. c. 5. Bestia moritur, tranquillitas
redit . . . omnes episcopi qui de propriis sedibus fuerant exterminati per
indulgentiam novi principis ad ecclesias redeunt. Jerom. adversus Luciferianos, tom. ii. p. 143 [tom. ii. p. 191, ed. Vallars.]. Optatus accuses the
Donatists for owing their safety to an apostate (l. ii. c. 16, p. 36, 37, edit.
Dupin).

below the horizon; and the Moon, the Stars, and the Genii of the night received their respective and seasonable honours from the indefatigable devotion of Julian. On solemn festivals he regularly visited the temple of the god or goddess to whom the day was peculiarly consecrated, and endeavoured to excite the religion of the magistrates and people by the example of his own zeal. Instead of maintaining the lofty state of a monarch, distinguished by the splendour of his purple, and encompassed by the golden shields of his guards, Julian solicited, with respectful eagerness, the meanest offices which contributed to the worship of the gods. Amidst the sacred but licentious crowd of priests, of inferior ministers, and of female dancers, who were dedicated to the service of the temple, it was the business of the emperor to bring the wood, to blow the fire, to handle the knife, to slaughter the victim, and, thrusting his bloody hands into the bowels of the expiring animal, to draw forth the heart or liver, and to read, with the consummate skill of an haruspex, the imaginary signs of future events. The wisest of the Pagans censured this extravagant superstition, which affected to despise the restraints of prudence and decency. Under the reign of a prince who practised the rigid maxims of economy, the expense of religious worship consumed a very large portion of the revenue; a constant supply of the scarcest and most beautiful birds was transported from distant climates, to bleed on the altars of the gods; an hundred oxen were frequently sacrificed by Julian on one and the same day; and it soon became a popular jest, that, if he should return with conquest from the Persian war, the breed of horned cattle must infallibly be extinguished. Yet this expense may appear inconsiderable, when it is compared with the splendid presents which were offered, either by the hand or by order of the emperor, to all the celebrated places of devotion in the Roman world; and with the sums allotted to repair and decorate the ancient temples, which had suffered the silent decay of time, or the recent injuries of Christian rapine. Encouraged by the example, the exhortations, the liberality of their pious sovereign, the cities and families resumed the practice of their neglected ceremonies. " Every part of the world," exclaims Libanius, with devout transport, " displayed the triumph of religion, and the grateful prospect of flaming altars, bleeding victims, the smoke of incense, and a solemn train of priests and prophets, without fear and without danger. The sound of prayer and of music was heard on the tops of the highest mountains; and the same ox afforded a sacrifice for the gods, and a supper for their joyous votaries." [1]

But the genius and power of Julian were unequal to the enterprise of restoring a religion which was destitute of theological principles, of moral precepts, and of ecclesiastical discipline; which rapidly hastened to decay and dissolution, and was not susceptible of any solid or consistent reformation. The jurisdiction of the supreme pontiff, more especially after that office had been united with the Imperial dignity, comprehended the whole extent of the Roman empire. Julian named for his vicars, in the several provinces, the priests and philosophers, whom he esteemed the best qualified to co-operate in the execution of his great design; and his pastoral letters,[2] if we may use that name, still represent a very curious sketch of his wishes and intentions. He directs that in every city the sacerdotal order should be composed, without any distinction of birth or fortune, of those persons who were the most conspicuous for their love of the gods and of men. " If they are guilty," continues he, " of any scandalous offence, they should be censured or degraded by the superior pontiff; but as long at they retain their rank, they are entitled to the respect of the magistrates and people. Their humility may be shown in the plainness of their domestic garb; their dignity, in the pomp of holy vestments. When they are summoned in their turn to officiate before the altar, they ought not, during the appointed number of days, to depart from the precincts of the temple; nor should a single day be suffered to elapse without the prayers and the sacrifice which they are obliged to offer for the prosperity of the state and of individuals. The exercise of their sacred functions requires an immaculate purity both of mind and body; and even when they are dismissed from the temple to the occupations of common life, it is incumbent on them to excel in decency and virtue the rest of their fellow-citizens. The priest of the gods should never be seen in theatres or taverns. His conversation should be chaste, his diet temperate, his friends of

[1] The restoration of the Pagan worship is described by Julian (Misopogon, p. 346), Libanius (Orat. Parent. c. 60, p. 286, 287, and Orat. Consular. ad Julian. p. 245, 246, edit. Morel.), Ammianus (xxii. 12), and Gregory Nazianzen (Orat. iv. p. 121). These writers agree in the essential, and even minute, facts; but the different lights in which they view the extreme devotion of Julian are expressive of the gradations of self-applause, passionate admiration, mild reproof, and partial invective.

[2] See Julian. Epistol. xlix. lxii. lxiii., and a long and curious fragment, without beginning or end (p. 288-305). The supreme pontiff derides the Mosaic history and the Christian discipline, prefers the Greek poets to the Hebrew prophets, and palliates, with the skill of a Jesuit, the *relative* worship of images.

honourable reputation; and if he sometimes visits the Forum
or the Palace, he should appear only as the advocate of those
who have vainly solicited either justice or mercy. His studies
should be suited to the sanctity of his profession. Licentious
tales, or comedies, or satires, must be banished from his library,
which ought solely to consist of historical and philosophical
writings; of history, which is founded in truth, and of philosophy,
which is connected with religion. The impious opinions of the
Epicureans and sceptics deserve his abhorrence and contempt; [1]
but he should diligently study the systems of Pythagoras, of
Plato, and of the Stoics, which unanimously teach that there *are*
gods; that the world is governed by their providence; that their
goodness is the source of every temporal blessing; and that they
have prepared for the human soul a future state of reward or
punishment." The Imperial pontiff inculcates, in the most
persuasive language, the duties of benevolence and hospitality;
exhorts his inferior clergy to recommend the universal practice of
those virtues; promises to assist their indigence from the public
treasury; and declares his resolution of establishing hospitals in
every city, where the poor should be received without any
invidious distinction of country or of religion. Julian beheld
with envy the wise and humane regulations of the church; and
he very frankly confesses his intention to deprive the Christians
of the applause, as well as advantage, which they had acquired
by the exclusive practice of charity and beneficence.[2] The same
spirit of imitation might dispose the emperor to adopt several
ecclesiastical institutions, the use and importance of which were
approved by the success of his enemies. But if these imaginary
plans of reformation had been realised, the forced and imperfect
copy would have been less beneficial to Paganism than honour-

[1] The exultation of Julian (p. 301) that these impious sects, and even their
writings, are extinguished, may be consistent enough with the sacerdotal
character; but it is unworthy of a philosopher to wish that any opinions
and arguments the most repugnant to his own should be concealed from
the knowledge of mankind.

[2] Yet he insinuates that the Christians, under the pretence of charity,
inveigled children from their religion and parents, conveyed them on shipboard, and devoted those victims to a life of poverty or servitude in a
remote country (p. 305). Had the charge been proved, it was his duty
not to complain but to punish.

[On this point of Julian's charge, that the Christians inveigled children
from their religion and parents to condemn them to a life of poverty in a
foreign land, Prof. Bury says, " It is very questionable whether Julian
meant to insinuate this charge. He compares the conduct of the Galileans
in looking after the poor for the sake of proselytising to that of kidnappers,
who inveigle children by giving them a cake, but the simile does not seem
to be applied literally to the Christians."—O. S.]

able to Christianity.[1] The Gentiles, who peaceably followed the customs of their ancestors, were rather surprised than pleased with the introduction of foreign manners; and, in the short period of his reign, Julian had frequent occasions to complain of the want of fervour of his own party.[2]

The enthusiasm of Julian prompted him to embrace the friends of Jupiter as his personal friends and brethren; and though he partially overlooked the merit of Christian constancy, he admired and rewarded the noble perseverance of those Gentiles who had preferred the favour of the gods to that of the emperor.[3] If they cultivated the literature as well as the religion of the Greeks, they acquired an additional claim to the friendship of Julian, who ranked the Muses in the number of his tutelar deities. In the religion which he had adopted, piety and learning were almost synonymous;[4] and a crowd of poets, of rhetoricians, and of philosophers, hastened to the Imperial court to occupy the vacant places of the bishops who had seduced the credulity of Constantius. His successor esteemed the ties of common initiation as far more sacred than those of consanguinity; he chose his favourites among the sages who were deeply skilled in the occult sciences of magic and divination, and every impostor who pretended to reveal the secrets of futurity was assured of enjoying the present hour in honour and affluence.[5] Among the philosophers, Maximus obtained the most eminent rank in the friendship of his royal disciple, who communicated, with unreserved confidence, his actions, his sentiments, and his religious designs, during the anxious suspense of the civil war.[6] As soon as Julian had taken possession of the palace of Constantinople,

[1] Gregory Nazianzen is facetious, ingenious, and argumentative (Orat. iii p. 101, 102, etc.). He ridicules the folly of such vain imitation; and amuses himself with inquiring what lessons, moral or theological, could be extracted from the Grecian fables.

[2] He accuses one of his pontiffs of a secret confederacy with the Christian bishops and presbyters (Epist. lxii). Ὁρῶν οὖν πολλὴν μὲν ὀλιγωρίαν οὖσαν ἡμῖν πρὸς τοὺς θεούς; and again, ἡμᾶς δὲ οὕτω ῥαθύμως, etc. Epist. lxiii.

[3] He praises the fidelity of Callixene, priestess of Ceres, who had been twice as constant as Penelope, and rewards her with the priesthood of the Phrygian goddess at Pessinus (Julian. Epist. xxi. [p. 389]). He applauds the firmness of Sopater of Hierapolis, who had been repeatedly pressed by Constantius and Gallus to *apostatise* (Epist. xxvii. p. 401).

[4] Ὁ δὲ νομίζων ἀδελφὰ λόγους τε καὶ θεῶν ἱερά. Orat. Parent. c. 77, p. 302. The same sentiment is frequently inculcated by Julian, Libanius, and the rest of their party.

[5] The curiosity and credulity of the emperor, who tried every mode of divination, are fairly exposed by Ammianus, xxii. 12.

[6] Julian. Epist. xxxviii. Three other epistles (xv. xvi. xxxix.), in the same style of friendship and confidence, are addressed to the philosopher Maximus.

he despatched an honourable and pressing invitation to Maximus, who then resided at Sardes in Lydia, with Chrysanthius, the associate of his art and studies. The prudent and superstitious Chrysanthius refused to undertake a journey which showed itself, according to the rules of divination, with the most threatening and malignant aspect; but his companion, whose fanaticism was of a bolder cast, persisted in his interrogations till he had extorted from the gods a seeming consent to his own wishes and those of the emperor. The journey of Maximus through the cities of Asia displayed the triumph of philosophic vanity, and the magistrates vied with each other in the honourable reception which they prepared for the friend of their sovereign. Julian was pronouncing an oration before the senate when he was informed of the arrival of Maximus. The emperor immediately interrupted his discourse, advanced to meet him, and, after a tender embrace, conducted him by the hand into the midst of the assembly, where he publicly acknowledged the benefits which he had derived from the instructions of the philosopher. Maximus,[1] who soon acquired the confidence, and influenced the councils, of Julian, was insensibly corrupted by the temptations of a court. His dress became more splendid, his demeanour more lofty, and he was exposed, under a succeeding reign, to a disgraceful inquiry into the means by which the disciple of Plato had accumulated, in the short duration of his favour, a very scandalous proportion of wealth. Of the other philosophers and sophists who were invited to the Imperial residence by the choice of Julian, or by the success of Maximus, few were able to preserve their innocence or their reputation.[2] The liberal gifts of money, lands, and houses were insufficient to satiate their rapacious avarice, and the indignation of the people was justly excited by the remembrance of their abject poverty and disinterested professions. The penetration of Julian could not always be deceived, but he was unwilling to despise the characters of those men whose talents deserved his esteem; he desired to escape the double reproach of imprudence and incon-

---

[1] Eunapius (in Maximo, p. 77, 78, 79, and in Chrysanthio, p. 147, 148 [p. 94 *sqq.* and 191 *sqq.*, ed. Comm.]) has minutely related these anecdotes, which he conceives to be the most important events of the age. Yet he fairly confesses the frailty of Maximus. His reception at Constantinople is described by Libanius (Orat. Parent. c. 76, p. 301) and Ammianus (xxii. 7).

[2] Chrysanthius, who had refused to quit Lydia, was created high-priest of the province. His cautious and temperate use of power secured him after the revolution: and he lived in peace; while Maximus, Priscus, etc., were persecuted by the Christian ministers. See the adventures of those fanatic sophists, collected by Brucker, tom. ii. p. 281-293.

stancy, and he was apprehensive of degrading, in the eyes of the profane, the honour of letters and of religion.[1]

The favour of Julian was almost equally divided between the Pagans who had firmly adhered to the worship of their ancestors, and the Christians who prudently embraced the religion of their sovereign. The acquisition of new proselytes [2] gratified the ruling passions of his soul, superstition and vanity; and he was heard to declare, with the enthusiasm of a missionary, that if he could render each individual richer than Midas, and every city greater than Babylon, he should not esteem himself the benefactor of mankind unless, at the same time, he could reclaim his subjects from their impious revolt against the immortal gods.[3] A prince, who had studied human nature, and who possessed the treasures of the Roman empire, could adapt his arguments, his promises, and his rewards to every order of Christians; [4] and the merit of a seasonable conversion was allowed to supply the defects of a candidate, or even to expiate the guilt of a criminal. As the army is the most forcible engine of absolute power, Julian applied himself, with peculiar diligence, to corrupt the religion of his troops, without whose hearty concurrence every measure must be dangerous and unsuccessful, and the natural temper of soldiers made this conquest as easy as it was important. The legions of Gaul devoted themselves to the faith, as well as to the fortunes, of their victorious leader; and even before the death of Constantius, he had the satisfaction of announcing to his friends that they assisted, with fervent devotion and voracious appetite, at the sacrifices, which were repeatedly offered in his camp, of whole hecatombs of fat oxen.[5] The

---

[1] See Libanius (Orat. Parent. c. 100, 101, p. 324, 325, 326) and Eunapius (Vit. Sophist. in Proæresio, p. 126 [p. 160, ed. Comm.]). Some students, whose expectations perhaps were groundless or extravagant, retired in disgust (Greg. Naz. Orat. iv. p. 120). It is strange that we should not be able to contradict the title of one of Tillemont's chapters (Hist. des Empereurs, tom. iv. p. 960), " La Cour de Julien est pleine de philosophes et de gens perdus."

[2] Under the reign of Louis XIV. his subjects of every rank aspired to the glorious title of *Convertisseur*, expressive of their zeal and success in making proselytes. The word and the idea are growing obsolete in France; may they never be introduced into England!

[3] See the strong expressions of Libanius, which were probably those of Julian himself (Orat. Parent. c. 59, p. 285).

[4] When Gregory Nazianzen (Orat. x. p. 167) is desirous to magnify the Christian firmness of his brother Cæsarius, physician to the Imperial court, he owns that Cæsarius disputed with a formidable adversary, πόλυν ἐν ὅπλοῖς, καὶ μέγαν ἐν λόγων δεινότητι. In his invectives he scarcely allows any share of wit or courage to the apostate.

[5] Julian. Epist. xxxviii. [p. 415]. Ammianus, xxii. 12. Adeo ut in dies pæne singulos milites carnis distentiore saginâ victitantes incultius, potusque

armies of the East, which had been trained under the standard of the cross and of Constantius, required a more artful and expensive mode of persuasion. On the days of solemn and public festivals the emperor received the homage, and rewarded the merit, of the troops. His throne of state was encircled with the military ensigns of Rome and the republic; the holy name of Christ was erased from the *Labarum*; and the symbols of war, of majesty, and of Pagan superstition were so dexterously blended that the faithful subject incurred the guilt of idolatry when he respectfully saluted the person or image of his sovereign. The soldiers passed successively in review, and each of them, before he received from the hand of Julian a liberal donative, proportioned to his rank and services, was required to cast a few grains of incense into the flame which burnt upon the altar. Some Christian confessors might resist, and others might repent; but the far greater number, allured by the prospect of gold and awed by the presence of the emperor, contracted the criminal engagement, and their future perseverance in the worship of the gods was enforced by every consideration of duty and of interest. By the frequent repetition of these arts, and at the expense of sums which would have purchased the service of half the nations of Scythia, Julian gradually acquired for his troops the imaginary protection of the gods, and for himself the firm and effectual support of the Roman legions.[1] It is indeed more than probable that the restoration and encouragement of Paganism revealed a multitude of pretended Christians, who, from motives of temporal advantage, had acquiesced in the religion of the former reign, and who afterwards returned, with the same flexibility of conscience, to the faith which was professed by the successors of Julian.

While the devout monarch incessantly laboured to restore and propagate the religion of his ancestors, he embraced the extraordinary design of rebuilding the temple of Jerusalem. In a public epistle [2] to the nation or community of the Jews dispersed

avidiate correpti, humeris imposi[t]i transeuntium per plateas, ex publicis ædibus . . . ad sua diversoria portarentur. The devout prince and the indignant historian describe the same scene; and in Illyricum or Antioch similar causes must have produced similar effects.

[1] Gregory (Orat. iii. p. 74. 75, 83-86) and Libanius (Orat. Parent. c. lxxxi. lxxxii. p. 307, 308), περὶ ταύτην τὴν σπουδήν, οὐκ ἀρνοῦμαι πλοῦτον ἀνηλῶσθαι μέγαν. The sophist owns and justifies the expense of these military conversions.

[2] Julian's epistle (xxv.) is addressed to the community of the Jews. Aldus (Venet. 1499) has branded it with an ἐι γνήσιος; but this stigma is justly removed by the subsequent editors, Petavius and Spanheim. The

through the provinces, he pities their misfortunes, condemns
their oppressors, praises their constancy, declares himself their
gracious protector, and expresses a pious hope that, after his
return from the Persian war, he may be permitted to pay his
grateful vows to the Almighty in his holy city of Jerusalem.
The blind superstition and abject slavery of those unfortunate
exiles must excite the contempt of a philosophic emperor, but
they deserved the friendship of Julian by their implacable hatred
of the Christian name.   The barren synagogue abhorred and
envied the fecundity of the rebellious church; the power of the
Jews was not equal to their malice, but their gravest rabbis
approved the private murder of an apostate,[1] and their seditious
clamours had often awakened the indolence of the Pagan magistrates.   Under the reign of Constantine, the Jews became the
subjects of their revolted children, nor was it long before they
experienced the bitterness of domestic tyranny.   The civil immunities which had been granted or confirmed by Severus were
gradually repealed by the Christian princes; and a rash tumult,
excited by the Jews of Palestine,[2] seemed to justify the lucrative
modes of oppression which were invented by the bishops and
eunuchs of the court of Constantius.   The Jewish patriarch,
who was still permitted to exercise a precarious jurisdiction, held
his residence at Tiberias,[3] and the neighbouring cities of Palestine
were filled with the remains of a people who fondly adhered to
the promised land.   But the edict of Hadrian was renewed and
enforced, and they viewed from afar the walls of the holy city,
which were profaned in their eyes by the triumph of the cross
and the devotion of the Christians.[4]

In the midst of a rocky and barren country the walls of Jerusalem [5] enclosed the two mountains of Sion and Acra within an

epistle is mentioned by Sozomen (l. v. c. 22), and the purport of it is confirmed by Gregory (Orat. iv. p. 111), and by Julian himself (Fragment.
p. 295).

[1] The Misnah denounced death against those who abandoned the foundation.   The judgment of zeal is explained by Marsham (Canon. Chron.
p. 161, 162, edit. fol. London, 1672) and Basnage (Hist. des Juifs, tom.
viii. p. 120).   Constantine made a law to protect Christian converts from
Judaism.   Cod. Theod. l. xvi. tit. viii. leg. 1. Godefroy, tom. vi. p. 215.

[2] Et interea (during the civil war of Magnentius) Judæorum seditio, qui
Patricium nefarie in regni speciem sustulerunt, oppressa.   Aurelius Victor,
in Constantio, c. xlii.   See Tillemont. Hist. des Empereurs, tom. iv. p. 379,
in 4to.

[3] The city and synagogue of Tiberias are curiously described by Reland,
Palestin. tom. ii. p. 1036-1042.

[4] Basnage has fully illustrated the state of the Jews under Constantine
and his successors (tom. viii. c. iv. p. 111-153).

[5] Reland (Palestin. l. i. p. 309, 390, l. iii. p. 838) describes, with learning
and perspicuity, Jerusalem and the face of the adjacent country.

oval figure of about three English miles.[1] Towards the south, the upper town and the fortress of David were erected on the lofty ascent of Mount Sion; on the north side, the buildings of the lower town covered the spacious summit of Mount Acra; and a part of the hill, distinguished by the name of Moriah, and levelled by human industry, was crowned with the stately temple of the Jewish nation. After the final destruction of the temple by the arms of Titus and Hadrian a ploughshare was drawn

[1] I have consulted a rare and curious treatise of M. d'Anville (sur l'Ancienne Jérusalem, Paris, 1747, p. 75). The circumference of the ancient city (Euseb. Preparat. Evangel. l. ix. c. 36) was 27 stadia, or 2550 *toises*. A plan taken on the spot assigns no more than 1980 for the modern town. The circuit is defined by natural landmarks, which cannot be mistaken or removed.

[With regard to this statement by Gibbon about the circumference of the ancient and modern cities of Jerusalem, Mr. Williams (Holy City, vol. i. p. 149), and Dr. Robinson (Bible Research in Palestine (vol. i. p. 467) agree that the account of Josephus (Bell. Jud. v. c. 4, sec. 8) of the circumference of the ancient city of Jerusalem, as 33 stadia or 3½ geographical miles, is correct. After its destruction by Titus, Jerusalem seems to have lain in ruins until the time of Hadrian, who rebuilt it under the name of Ælia Capitolina. The circumference of his walls was smaller, as part of Mount Zion was excluded. The walls of Hadrian (says Robinson) embraced about the same circumference as the modern city, or about 2⅓ geographical miles. This must have been its size when Julian attempted to rebuild the temple. Gibbon follows the plan of d'Anville, which is most inaccurate. Prof. Bury says in his note *in loc.*: " Josephus gives 33 stadia. Sir C. Wilson calculates not more than 25. The dimensions of the modern town are about 1000 yards from east to west, and the same from north to south. A map showing the various theories as to the line of the old walls is given in the book of Mr. T. H. Lewis, *The Holy Places of Jerusalem*, 1888." With regard to this matter the opinion of Principal George Adam Smith, D.D., LL.D., whose volume, issued in 1908 on " Jerusalem," has been regarded as the greatest contribution to the subject yet issued, will be considered as of prime value. He says in a letter to the editor with reference to the matter: " I have given all that is known on the circumference, size, etc., of ancient Jerusalem on pp. 438 ff. of vol. ii. Twenty-seven stadia is the estimate of Xenophon, the topographer in the first century, B.C., that is before Agrippa's or the third. A wall was built which formed the northern limit of the city during the siege by Titus. If Xenophon be right, then he included the suburb to the north which Agrippa's wall finally enclosed. The difficulty about Agrippa's wall is that there are rival themes both well supported as to its course. If, as I think most probable, it followed the line of the present north wall of the city, then 27 stadia are an approximately correct estimate for Jerusalem in Roman times, which I suppose is what Gibbon is describing—I am far from books here. But Josephus estimates the circumference after the third wall was built at 33 stadia (*Wars of the Jews*, v. iv. 2). This can be correct only if the third wall followed a line a good deal to the north of the present north wall. The other ancient estimates of 40 to 50 stadia are impossible. Even Josephus's 33 stadia would be difficult to make up unless we carried the third wall to a distance on the north which is hardly possible for it to have reached. On the whole, I think Gibbon's ' note ' may stand the 27 stadia, to my mind, are, on all the data we have at present, more probable than the 33 of Josephus.

" The modern city of Jerusalem, *i.e.*, the walled city (not counting the

over the consecrated ground, as a sign of perpetual interdiction.
Sion was deserted, and the vacant space of the lower city was
filled with the public and private edifices of the Ælian colony,
which spread themselves over the adjacent hill of Calvary.
The holy places were polluted with monuments of idolatry, and,
either from design or accident, a chapel was dedicated to Venus
on the spot which had been sanctified by the death and resurrection of Christ.[1] Almost three hundred years after those
stupendous events, the profane chapel of Venus was demolished
by the order of Constantine, and the removal of the earth and
stones revealed the holy sepulchre to the eyes of mankind. A
magnificent church was erected on that mystic ground by the
first Christian emperor, and the effects of his pious munificence
were extended to every spot which had been consecrated by the
footsteps of patriarchs, of prophets, and of the Son of God.[2]

The passionate desire of contemplating the original monuments
of their redemption attracted to Jerusalem a successive crowd
of pilgrims from the shores of the Atlantic Ocean and the most
distant countries of the East:[3] and their piety was authorised
by the example of the empress Helena, who appears to have
united the credulity of age with the warm feelings of a recent
conversion. Sages and heroes, who have visited the memorable

suburbs which have sprung up in the last twenty years, has stood at the
same size since Suleiman the Magnificent built the walls, *circa* 1540. I am
not sure of the exact length of the circumference, but it is about 12,500
feet. If we take the stadium at 582 feet, that is pretty near 21 stadia.
But such measurements depend on how they are taken; (1) exactly along
the course of the wall, following every bend; (2) roughly, on the general
direction of the walls; or (3) along the beds of the valleys at the foot of
the hills in which the walls stand. In the last case the estimate would, of
course, be considerably greater than in either of the two former."

Principal Smith goes into the matter in detail in his admirable volumes,
but there are one or two points in the above extract from his letter which
are not in the volume, and which go to throw further light upon this interesting, but decidedly vexed, question.—O. S.]

[1] See two curious passages in Jerom (tom. i. p. 102, tom. vi. p. 315), and
the ample details of Tillemont (Hist. des Empereurs, tom. i. p. 569, tom. ii.
p. 289, 294, 4to. edition).
[On the site of the " Holy Sepulchre," and for a summary of the controversy thereanent, read Robinson's *Travels in Palestine*, and Principal G.
A. Smith's *Jerusalem*.—O. S.]

[2] Eusebius in Vit. Constantin. l. iii. c. 25-47, 51-53. The emperor likewise
built churches at Bethlehem, the Mount of Olives, and the oak of Mambre.
The holy sepulchre is described by Sandys (Travels, p. 125-133), and
curiously delineated by Le Bruyn (Voyage au Levant, p. 288-296).

[3] The Itinerary from Bordeaux to Jerusalem was composed in the year
333, for the use of pilgrims; among whom Jerom (tom. i. p. 126) mentions
the Britons and the Indians. The causes of this superstitious fashion are
discussed in the learned and judicious preface of Wesseling (Itinerar. p.
537-545.

scenes of ancient wisdom or glory, have confessed the inspiration of the genius of the place;[1] and the Christian who knelt before the holy sepulchre ascribed his lively faith and his fervent devotion to the more immediate influence of the Divine Spirit. The zeal, perhaps the avarice, of the clergy of Jerusalem cherished and multiplied these beneficial visits. They fixed, by unquestionable tradition, the scene of each memorable event. They exhibited the instruments which had been used in the passion of Christ; the nails and the lance that had pierced his hands, his feet, and his side; the crown of thorns that was planted on his head; the pillar at which he was scourged; and, above all, they showed the cross on which he suffered, and which was dug out of the earth in the reign of those princes who inserted the symbol of Christianity in the banners of the Roman legions.[2] Such miracles as seemed necessary to account for its extraordinary preservation and seasonable discovery were gradually propagated without opposition. The custody of the *true cross*, which on Easter Sunday was solemnly exposed to the people, was intrusted to the bishop of Jerusalem; and he alone might gratify the curious devotion of the pilgrims by the gift of small pieces, which they enchased in gold or gems, and carried away in triumph to their respective countries. But as this gainful branch of commerce must soon have been annihilated, it was found convenient to suppose that the marvellous wood possessed a secret power of vegetation, and that its substance, though continually diminished, still remained entire and unimpaired.[3] It might perhaps have been expected that the influence of the place and

[1] Cicero (de Finibus, v. 1) has beautifully expressed the common sense of mankind.

[2] Baronius (Annal. Eccles. A.D. 326, No. 42-50) and Tillemont (Mém. Ecclés. tom. vii. p. 8-16) are the historians and champions of the miraculous *invention* of the cross, under the reign of Constantine. Their oldest witnesses are Paulinus, Sulpicius Severus, Rufinus, Ambrose, and perhaps Cyril of Jerusalem. The silence of Eusebius and the Bordeaux pilgrim, which satisfies those who think perplexes those who believe. See Jortin's sensible remarks, vol. ii. p. 238-248.

[The legend of the discovery of the cross by the pious Judas for the empress Helena is of very ancient date, and reaches us from three sources, Latin, Greek, and Syriac. The balance of evidence seems to indicate that the original legend regarding the discovery of the cross comes from a Syriac source, Mr. Rendal Harris having copied the oldest Greek version extant (of the eighth century) from a Sinai MS.—O. S.]

[3] This multiplication is asserted by Paulinus (Epist. xxxvi.; see Dupin. Bibliot. Ecclés. tom. iii. p. 149), who seems to have improved a rhetorical flourish of Cyril into a real fact. The same supernatural privilege must have been communicated to the Virgin's milk (Erasmi Opera, tom. i. p. 778, Lugd. Batav. 1703, in Colloq. de Peregrinat. Religionis ergo), saints' heads, etc., and other relics, which are repeated in so many different churches.

the belief of a perpetual miracle should have produced some salutary effects on the morals, as well as on the faith, of the people. Yet the most respectable of the ecclesiastical writers have been obliged to confess, not only that the streets of Jerusalem were filled with the incessant tumult of business and pleasure,[1] but that every species of vice—adultery, theft, idolatry, poisoning, murder—was familiar to the inhabitants of the holy city.[2] The wealth and pre-eminence of the church of Jerusalem excited the ambition of Arian as well as orthodox candidates; and the virtues of Cyril, who since his death has been honoured with the title of Saint, were displayed in the exercise, rather than in the acquisition, of his episcopal dignity.[3]

The vain and ambitious mind of Julian might aspire to restore the ancient glory of the temple of Jerusalem.[4] As the Christians were firmly persuaded that a sentence of everlasting destruction had been pronounced against the whole fabric of the Mosaic law, the Imperial sophist would have converted the success of his undertaking into a specious argument against the faith of prophecy and the truth of revelation.[5] He was displeased with the spiritual worship of the synogogue; but he approved the institutions of Moses, who had not disdained to adopt many of the rites and ceremonies of Egypt.[6] The local and national deity of the Jews was sincerely adored by a polytheist who desired only

[1] Jerom (tom. i. p. 103), who resided in the neighbouring village of Bethlehem, describes the vices of Jerusalem from his personal experience.

[2] Gregor. Nyssen. apud Wesseling, p. 539. The whole epistle, which condemns either the use or the abuse of religious pilgrimage, is painful to the catholic divines, while it is dear and familiar to our protestant polemics.

[3] He renounced his orthodox ordination, officiated as a deacon, and was re-ordained by the hands of the Arians. But Cyril afterwards changed with the times, and prudently conformed to the Nicene faith. Tillemont (Mém. Ecclés. tom. viii.), who treats his memory with tenderness and respect, has thrown his virtues into the text, and his faults into the notes, in decent obscurity, at the end of the volume.

[4] Imperii sui memoriam magnitudine operum gestiens propagare. Ammian. xxiii. 1. The temple of Jerusalem had been famous even among the Gentiles. They had many temples in each city (at Sichem five, at Gaza eight, at Rome four hundred and twenty-four); but the wealth and religion of the Jewish nation was centred in one spot.

[5] The secret intentions of Julian are revealed by the late bishop of Gloucester, the learned and dogmatic Warburton; who, with the authority of a theologian, prescribes the motives and conduct of the Supreme Being. The discourse entitled *Julian* (2nd edition, London, 1751) is strongly marked with all the peculiarities which are imputed to the Warburtonian school.

[6] I shelter myself behind Maimonides, Marsham, Spencer, Le Clerc, Warburton, etc., who have fairly derided the fears, the folly, and the falsehood of some superstitious divines. See Divine Legation, vol. iv. p. 25, etc.

to multiply the number of the gods;[1] and such was the appetite
of Julian for bloody sacrifice, that his emulation might be excited
by the piety of Solomon, who had offered at the feast of the dedication twenty-two thousand oxen and one hundred and twenty
thousand sheep.[2] These considerations might influence his
designs; but the prospect of an immediate and important advantage would not suffer the impatient monarch to expect the
remote and uncertain event of the Persian war. He resolved to
erect, without delay, on the commanding eminence of Moriah,
a stately temple, which might eclipse the splendour of the
church of the Resurrection on the adjacent hill of Calvary; to
establish an order of priests, whose interested zeal would detect
the arts and resist the ambition of their Christian rivals; and
to invite a numerous colony of Jews, whose stern fanaticism
would be always prepared to second, and even to anticipate,
the hostile measures of the Pagan government. Among the
friends of the emperor (if the names of emperor and of friend
are not incompatible) the first place was assigned, by Julian
himself, to the virtuous and learned Alypius.[3] The humanity
of Alypius was tempered by severe justice and manly fortitude;
and while he exercised his abilities in the civil administration of
Britain, he imitated, in his poetical compositions, the harmony
and softness of the odes of Sappho. This minister, to whom
Julian communicated, without reserve, his most careless levities
and his most serious counsels, received an extraordinary commission to restore, in its pristine beauty, the temple of Jerusalem;
and the diligence of Alypius required and obtained the strenuous
support of the governor of Palestine. At the call of their great
deliverer, the Jews from all the provinces of the empire assembled
on the holy mountain of their fathers; and their insolent triumph
alarmed and exasperated the Christian inhabitants of Jerusalem.
The desire of rebuilding the temple has in every age been the
ruling passion of the children of Israel. In this propitious
moment the men forgot their avarice, and the women their

---

[1] Julian (Fragment. p. 295) respectfully styles him μέγας θεός, and
mentions him elsewhere (Epist. lxiii.) with still higher reverence. He
doubly condemns the Christians, for believing and for renouncing the
religion of the Jews. Their Deity was a *true*, but not the *only*, God. Apud
Cyril. l. ix. p. 305, 306.

[2] 1 Kings viii. 63. 2 Chronicles vii. 5. Joseph. Antiquitat. Judaic. l
viii. c. 4 [§ 5], p. 431, edit. Havercamp. As the blood and smoke of so many
hecatombs might be inconvenient, Lightfoot, the Christian Rabbi, removes
them by a miracle. Le Clerc (ad loca) is bold enough to suspect the fidelity
of the numbers.

[3] Julian, Epist. xxix. xxx. [p. 402, *sqq.*] La Bléterie has neglected to
translate the second of these epistles.

delicacy; spades and pickaxes of silver were provided by the vanity of the rich, and the rubbish was transported in mantles of silk and purple.   Every purse was opened in liberal contributions, every hand claimed a share in the pious labour; and the commands of a great monarch were executed by the enthusiasm of a whole people.[1]

Yet, on this occasion, the joint efforts of power and enthusiasm were unsuccessful; and the ground of the Jewish temple, which is now covered by a Mahometan mosque,[2] still continued to exhibit the same edifying spectacle of ruin and desolation.   Perhaps the absence and death of the emperor, and the new maxims of a Christian reign, might explain the interruption of an arduous work, which was attempted only in the last six months of the life of Julian.[3]   But the Christians entertained a natural and pious expectation that in this memorable contest the honour of religion would be vindicated by some signal miracle.   An earthquake, a whirlwind, and a fiery eruption, which overturned and scattered the new foundations of the temple, are attested, with some variations, by contemporary and respectable evidence.[4] This public event is described by Ambrose,[5] bishop of Milan, in an epistle to the emperor Theodosius, which must provoke the severe animadversion of the Jews; by the eloquent Chrysostom,[6] who might appeal to the memory of the elder part of his congregation at Antioch; and by Gregory Nazianzen,[7] who published

---

[1] See the zeal and impatience of the Jews in Gregory Nazianzen (Orat. iv. p. 111) and Theodoret (l. iii. c. 20).

[2] Built by Omar, the second khalif, who died A.D. 644.   This great mosque covers the whole consecrated ground of the Jewish temple, and constitutes almost a square of 760 *toises*, or one Roman mile, in circumference.   See d'Anville, Jerusalem, p. 45.

[3] Ammianus records the consuls of the year 363, before he proceeds to mention the *thoughts* of Julian.   Templum . . . instaurare sumptibus *cogitabat* immodicis.   Warburton has a secret wish to anticipate the design; but he must have understood, from former examples, that the execution of such a work would have demanded many years.

[4] The subsequent witnesses, Socrates, Sozomen, Theodoret, Philostorgius, etc., add contradictions rather than authority.   Compare the objections of Basnage (Hist. des Juifs, tom. viii. p. 157-168) with Warburton's answers (Julian, p. 174-258).   The bishop has ingeniously explained the miraculous crosses which appeared on the garments of the spectators by a similar instance and the natural effects of lightning.

[5] Ambros. tom. ii. Epist. xl. p. 946, edit. Benedictin.   He composed this fanatic epistle (A.D. 388) to justify a bishop who had been condemned by the civil magistrate for burning a synagogue.

[6] Chrysostom, tom. i. p. 580, advers. Judæos et Gentes [c. 16], tom. ii. p. 574, de Sto. Babylâ [c. 22], edit. Montfaucon.   I have followed the common and natural supposition; but the learned Benedictine, who dates the composition of these sermons in the year 383, is confident they were never pronounced from the pulpit.

[7] Greg. Nazianzen, Orat. iv. p. 110-113.   Τὸ δὲ οὖν περιβόητον πᾶσι θαῦμα καὶ οὐδὲ τοῖς ἀθέοις αὐτοῖς ἀπιστούμενον, λέξων ἐρχόμαι.

'his account of the miracle before the expiration of the same year. The last of these writers has boldly declared that this preternatural event was not disputed by the infidels; and his assertion, strange as it may seem, is confirmed by the unexceptionable testimony of Ammianus Marcellinus.[1] The philosophic soldier, who loved the virtues without adopting the prejudices of his master, has recorded, in his judicious and candid history of his own times, the extraordinary obstacles which interrupted the restoration of the temple of Jerusalem. "Whilst Alypius, assisted by the governor of the province, urged with vigour and diligence the execution of the work, horrible balls of fire, breaking out near the foundations, with frequent and reiterated attacks, rendered the place, from time to time, inaccessible to the scorched and blasted workmen; and, the victorious element continuing in this manner obstinately and resolutely bent, as it were, to drive them to a distance, the undertaking was abandoned." Such authority should satisfy a believing, and must astonish an incredulous, mind. Yet a philosopher may still require the original evidence of impartial and intelligent spectators. At this important crisis any singular accident of nature would assume the appearance, and produce the effects, of a real prodigy. This glorious deliverance would be speedily improved and magnified by the pious art of the clergy of Jerusalem, and the active credulity of the Christian world; and, at the distance of twenty years, a Roman historian, careless of theological disputes, might adorn his work with the specious and splendid miracle.[2]

[1] Ammian, xxiii. 1. Cum itaque rei fortiter instaret Alypius, juvaretque provinciæ rector, metuendi globi flammarum prope fundamenta crebris assultibus erumpentes fecere locum exustis aliquoties operantibus inaccessum; hocque modo elemento destinatius repellente, cessavit inceptum. Warburton labours (p. 60-90) to extort a confession of the miracle from the mouths of Julian and Libanius, and to employ the evidence of a rabbi who lived in the fifteenth century. Such witnesses can only be received by a very favourable judge.

[2] Dr. Lardner, perhaps alone of the Christian critics, presumes to doubt the truth of this famous miracle (Jewish and Heathen Testimonies, vol. iv. p. 47-71). The silence of Jerom would lead to a suspicion that the same story which was celebrated at a distance might be despised on the spot.

[Michaelis would offer an explanation of the miracle of the balls of fire which drove the workmen from the site of the temple. It is based on a passage in Tacitus. That historian, speaking of Jerusalem, says, "The temple itself was a kind of citadel which had its own walls superior in their workmanship and construction to those of the city. The porticoes themselves which surrounded the temple were an excellent fortification. There was a fountain of constantly running water, subterranean excavations under the mountain, reservoirs and cisterns to collect the rain water." (Tacit. Hist. v. 12.) These excavations and reservoirs must have been very extensive. The latter furnished water during the whole siege to 1,100,000 people. As to the excavations, they were very considerable, and served

The restoration of the Jewish temple was secretly connected with the ruin of the Christian church. Julian still continued to maintain the freedom of religious worship, without distinguishing whether this universal toleration proceeded from his justice or his clemency. He affected to pity the unhappy Christians, who were mistaken in the most important object of their lives; but his pity was degraded by contempt, his contempt was embittered by hatred; and the sentiments of Julian were expressed in a style of sarcastic wit, which inflicts a deep and deadly wound whenever it issues from the mouth of a sovereign. As he was sensible that the Christians gloried in the name of their Redeemer, he countenanced, and perhaps enjoined, the use of the less honourable appellation of GALILÆANS.[1] He declared that, by the folly of the Galilæans, whom he describes as a sect of fanatics, contemptible to men and odious to the gods, the empire had been reduced to the brink of destruction; and he insinuates in a public edict that a frantic patient might sometimes be cured by salutary violence.[2] An ungenerous distinction was admitted into the mind and counsels of Julian, that, according to the difference

after and even before the return of the Jews from Babylon not only as magazines for oil, corn, and wine, but for the treasures laid up in the temple. When Jerusalem was on the point of being taken by Titus, the rebel chiefs, placing their last hopes in these vast subterranean caverns, formed a design of concealing themselves there and remaining during the conflagration of the city and until the Romans had returned. Many of them had not time to execute the design, but one of them, Simon the son of Gioras, having provided himself with food, descended into this retreat with some companions, and remained there until Titus had set out for Rome. Under the pressure of famine he issued forth on a sudden in the very place where the temple had stood, and appeared in the midst of the Roman guard. He was seized and sent to Rome, the hiding-place was searched, and many other fugitives in hiding were discovered. Now these passages were unquestionably a part of the first temple, and were built by Solomon's builders. In the centuries which elapsed between Solomon's reign and the fall of Jerusalem, gases would accumulate in the passages, and when the workmen of Julian's epoch approached the place to dig the foundations of the new temple, they would probably use torches to explore the passages, when the gases igniting would produce the explosions referred to.

But Dr. Hermann Adler, the Chief Rabbi, in the *Jewish Quarterly Review* for 1893 (p. 615 ff.) has proved that the whole story was a fiction of Gregory Nazianzen, from whose " Invective against Julian " it passed in Ambrose and other fathers, and that Julian's work was never commenced. See Dr. Adler's article.—O. S.]

[1] Greg. Naz. Orat. iii. p. 81. And this law was confirmed by the invariable practice of Julian himself. Warburton has justly observed (p. 35) that the Platonists believed in the mysterious virtue of words; and Julian's dislike for the name of Christ might proceed from superstition as well as from contempt.

[2] Fragment. Julian. p. 288. He derides the μωρία Γαλιλαίων (Epist. vii.), and so far loses sight of the principles of toleration as to wish (Epist. xlii. [p. 424]) ἄκοντας ἰᾶσθαι.

of their religious sentiments, one part of his subjects deserved his favour and friendship, while the other was entitled only to the common benefits that his justice could not refuse to an obedient people.[1] According to a principle pregnant with mischief and oppression, the emperor transferred to the pontiffs of his own religion the management of the liberal allowances from the public revenue which had been granted to the church by the piety of Constantine and his sons. The proud system of clerical honours and immunities, which had been constructed with so much art and labour, was levelled to the ground; the hopes of testamentary donations were intercepted by the rigour of the laws; and the priests of the Christian sect were confounded with the last and most ignominious class of the people. Such of these regulations as appeared necessary to check the ambition and avarice of the ecclesiastics were soon afterwards imitated by the wisdom of an orthodox prince. The peculiar distinctions which policy has bestowed, or superstition has lavished, on the sacerdotal order, *must* be confined to those priests who profess the religion of the state. But the will of the legislator was not exempt from prejudice and passion; and it was the object of the insidious policy of Julian to deprive the Christians of all the temporal honours and advantages which rendered them respectable in the eyes of the world.[2]

A just and severe censure has been inflicted on the law which prohibited the Christians from teaching the arts of grammar and rhetoric.[3] The motives alleged by the emperor to justify this partial and oppressive measure might command, during his lifetime, the silence of slaves and the applause of flatterers. Julian abuses the ambiguous meaning of a word which might be indifferently applied to the language and the religion of the GREEKS : he contemptuously observes that the men who exalt the merit of implicit faith are unfit to claim or to enjoy the advantages of science; and he vainly contends that, if they

---

[1] Οὐ γάρ μοι θέμις ἐστὶ κομιζέμεν ἢ ἐλεαίρειν
Ἀνέρας, οἵ κε θεοῖσιν ἀπέχθωντ᾽ ἀθανάτοισιν,

These two lines, which Julian has changed and perverted in the true spirit of a bigot (Epist. xlix. [p. 432]), are taken from the speech of Æolus, when he refuses to grant Ulysses a fresh supply of winds (Odyss. x. 73). Libanius (Orat. Parent. c. lix. p. 286) attempts to justify this partial behaviour by an apology, in which persecution peeps through the mask of candour.

[2] These laws, which affected the clergy, may be found in the slight hints of Julian himself (Epist. lii. [p. 433, *sqq.*]), in the vague declamations of Gregory (Orat. iii. p. 86, 87), and in the positive assertions of Sozomen (l. v. c. 5).

[3] Inclemens . . . perenni obruendum silentio. Ammian. xxii. 10, xxv. 5.

refuse to adore the gods of Homer and Demosthenes, they ought to content themselves with expounding Luke and Matthew in the churches of the Galilæans.[1]   In all the cities of the Roman world the education of the youth was intrusted to masters of grammar and rhetoric, who were elected by the magistrates, maintained at the public expense, and distinguished by many lucrative and honourable privileges.   The edict of Julian appears to have included the physicians, and professors of all the liberal arts; and the emperor, who reserved to himself the approbation of the candidates, was authorised by the laws to corrupt, or to punish, the religious constancy of the most learned of the Christians.[2]   As soon as the resignation of the more obstinate[3] teachers had established the unrivalled dominion of the Pagan sophists, Julian invited the rising generation to resort with freedom to the public schools, in a just confidence that their tender minds would receive the impressions of literature and idolatry.   If the greatest part of the Christian youth should be deterred by their own scruples, or by those of their parents, from accepting this dangerous mode of instruction, they must, at the same time, relinquish the benefits of a liberal education.   Julian had reason to expect that, in the space of a few years, the church would relapse into its primæval simplicity, and that the theologians, who possessed an adequate share of the learning and eloquence of the age, would be succeeded by a generation of blind and ignorant fanatics, incapable of defending the truth of their own principles, or of exposing the various follies of Polytheism.[4]

It was undoubtedly the wish and the design of Julian to deprive the Christians of the advantages of wealth, of knowledge, and

[1] The edict itself, which is still extant among the epistles of Julian (xlii. [p. 422]), may be compared with the loose invectives of Gregory (Orat. iii. p. 96). Tillemont (Mém. Ecclés. tom. vii. p. 1291-1294) has collected the seeming differences of ancients and moderns. They may be easily reconciled. The Christians were *directly* forbid to teach, they were *indirectly* forbid to learn; since they would not frequent the schools of the Pagans.

[2] Codex Theodos. l. xiii. tit. iii. de medicis et professoribus, leg. 5 (published the 17th of June, received, at Spoleto in Italy, the 29th of July, A.D. 363) with Godefroy's Illustrations, tom. v. p. 31.

[3] Orosius celebrates their disinterested resolution: Sicut a majoribus nostris compertum habemus, omnes ubique propemodum . . . officium quam fidem deserere maluerunt, vii. 30.   Proæresius, a Christian sophist, refused to accept the partial favour of the emperor.   Hieronym. in Chron. p. 185, edit. Scaliger [tom. viii. p. 805, ed. Vallars.].   Eunapius in Proæresio, p. 126 [p. 160, ed. Comm.].

[4] They had recourse to the expedient of composing books for their own schools.   Within a few months Apollinaris produced his Christian imitations of Homer (a sacred history in xxiv. books), Pindar, Euripides, and Menander; and Sozomen is satisfied that they equalled, or excelled, the originals.

of power; but the injustice of excluding them from all offices of trust and profit seems to have been the result of his general policy, rather than the immediate consequence of any positive law.[1] Superior merit might deserve and obtain some extraordinary exceptions; but the greater part of the Christian officers were gradually removed from their employments in the state, the army, and the provinces. The hopes of future candidates were extinguished by the declared partiality of a prince who maliciously reminded them that it was unlawful for a Christian to use the sword, either of justice or of war, and who studiously guarded the camp and the tribunals with the ensigns of idolatry. The powers of government were intrusted to the Pagans, who professed an ardent zeal for the religion of their ancestors; and as the choice of the emperor was often directed by the rules of divination, the favourites whom he preferred as the most agreeable to the gods did not always obtain the approbation of mankind.[2] Under the administration of their enemies, the Christians had much to suffer, and more to apprehend. The temper of Julian was averse to cruelty; and the care of his reputation, which was exposed to the eyes of the universe, restrained the philosophic monarch from violating the laws of justice and toleration which he himself had so recently established. But the provincial ministers of his authority were placed in a less conspicuous station. In the exercise of arbitrary power, they consulted the wishes, rather than the commands, of their sovereign; and ventured to exercise a secret and vexatious tyranny against the sectaries on whom they were not permitted to confer the honours of martyrdom. The emperor, who dissembled as long as possible his knowledge of the injustice that was exercised in his name, expressed his real sense of the conduct of his officers by gentle reproofs and substantial rewards.[3]

The most effectual instrument of oppression with which they were armed was the law that obliged the Christians to make full and ample satisfaction for the temples which they had destroyed under the preceding reign. The zeal of the triumphant church

---

[1] It was the instruction of Julian to his magistrates (Epist. vii.) προτιμᾶσ-θαι μέντοι τοὺς θεοσεβεῖς καὶ πάνυ φημὶ δεῖν. Sozomen (l. v. c. 18) and Socrates (l. iii. c. 13) must be reduced to the standard of Gregory (Orat. iii. p. 95), not less prone to exaggeration, but more restrained by the actual knowledge of his contemporary readers.

[2] Ψηφῷ θεῶν καὶ διδούς καὶ μὴ διδούς. Libanius, Orat. Parent. c. 88, p. 314.

[3] Greg. Naz. Orat. iii. p. 74, 91, 92. Socrates, l. iii. c. 14. Theodoret, l. iii. c. 6. Some drawback may however be allowed for the violence of *their* zeal. not less partial than the zeal of Julian.

had not always expected the sanction of the public authority; and the bishops, who were secure of impunity, had often marched at the head of their congregations to attack and demolish the fortresses of the prince of darkness. The consecrated lands, which had increased the patrimony of the sovereign or of the clergy, were clearly defined, and easily restored. But on these lands, and on the ruins of Pagan superstition, the Christians had frequently erected their own religious edifices: and as it was necessary to remove the church before the temple could be rebuilt, and justice and piety of the emperor were applauded by one party, while the other deplored and execrated his sacrilegious violence.[1] After the ground was cleared, the restitution of those stately structures which had been levelled with the dust, and of the precious ornaments which had been converted to Christian uses, swelled into a very large account of damages and debt. The authors of the injury had neither the ability nor the inclination to discharge this accumulated demand: and the impartial wisdom of a legislator would have been displayed in balancing the adverse claims and complaints by an equitable and temperate arbitration. But the whole empire, and particularly the East, was thrown into confusion by the rash edicts of Julian ; and the Pagan magistrates, inflamed by zeal and revenge, abused the rigorous privilege of the Roman law, which substitutes, in the place of his inadequate property, the person of the insolvent debtor. Under the preceding reign, Mark, bishop of Arethusa,[2] had laboured in the conversion of his people with arms more effectual than those of persuasion.[3] The magistrates required the full value of a temple which had been destroyed by his intolerant zeal; but as they were satisfied of his poverty, they desired only to bend his inflexible spirit to the promise of the slightest compensation. They apprehended the

---

[1] If we compare the gentle language of Libanius (Orat. Parent. c. 60, p. 286) with the passionate exclamations of Gregory (Orat. iii. p. 86, 87), we may find it difficult to persuade ourselves that the two orators are really describing the same events.

[2] Restan, or Arethusa, at the equal distance of sixteen miles between Emesa (*Homs*) and Epiphania (*Hamath*), was founded, or at least named, by Seleucus Nicator. Its peculiar era dates from the year of Rome 685, according to the medals of the city. In the decline of the Seleucides, Emesa and Arethusa were usurped by the Arab Sampsiceramus, whose posterity, the vassals of Rome, were not extinguished in the reign of Vespasian. See d'Anville's Maps and Géographie Ancienne, tom. ii. p. 134; Wesseling, Itineraria, p. 188; and Noris. Epoch. Syro-Macedon., p. 80, 481, 482.

[3] Sozomen, l. v. c. 10. It is surprising that Gregory and Theodoret should suppress a circumstance which, in their eyes, must have enhanced the religious merit of the confessor.

aged prelate, they inhumanly scourged him, they tore his beard; and his naked body, anointed with honey, was suspended, in a net, between heaven and earth, and exposed to the stings of insects and the rays of a Syrian sun.[1] From this lofty station, Mark still persisted to glory in his crime, and to insult the impotent rage of his persecutors. He was at length rescued from their hands, and dismissed to enjoy the honour of his divine triumph. The Arians celebrated the virtue of their pious confessor; the catholics ambitiously claimed his alliance;[2] and the Pagans, who might be susceptible of shame or remorse, were deterred from the repetition of such unavailing cruelty.[3] Julian spared his life: but if the bishop of Arethusa had saved the infancy of Julian,[4] posterity will condemn the ingratitude, instead of praising the clemency, of the emperor.

At the distance of five miles from Antioch, the Macedonian kings of Syria had consecrated to Apollo one of the most elegant places of devotion in the Pagan world.[5] A magnificent temple rose in honour of the god of light; and his colossal figure [6] almost filled the capacious sanctuary, which was enriched with gold and gems, and adorned by the skill of the Grecian artists. The deity was represented in a bending attitude, with a golden cup in his hand, pouring out a libation on the earth; as if he sup-

---

[1] The sufferings and constancy of Mark, which Gregory has so tragically painted (Orat. iii. p. 88-91), are confirmed by the unexceptionable and reluctant evidence of Libanius. Μάρκος ἐκεῖνος κρεμάμενος, καὶ μαστιγούμενος, καὶ τοῦ πώγωνος αὐτῷ τιλλομένου, πάντα ἐνεγκὼν ἀνδρείως, νῦν ἰσόθεός ἐστι ταῖς τιμαῖς, κἂν φανῇ που, περιμάχητος εὐθύς. Epist. 730, p. 350, 351. Edit. Wolf. Amstel. 1738.

[2] Περιμάχητος, certatim eum sibi (Christiani) vindicant. It is thus that La Croze and Wolfius (ad loc.) have explained a Greek word whose true signification had been mistaken by former interpreters, and even by Le Clerc (Bibliothèque Ancienne et Moderne, tom. iii. p. 371). Yet Tillemont is strangely puzzled to understand (Mém. Ecclés. tom. vii. p. 1309) *how* Gregory and Theodoret could mistake a Semi-Arian bishop for a saint.

[3] See the probable advice of Sallust (Greg. Nazianzen, Orat. iii. 90, 91). Libanius intercedes for a similar offender, lest they should find many *Marks*; yet he allows that, if Orion had secreted the consecrated wealth, he deserved to suffer the punishment of Marsyas—to be flayed alive (Epist. 730, p. 349-351).

[4] Gregory (Orat. iii. p. 90) is satisfied that, by saving the apostate, Mark had deserved still more than he had suffered.

[5] The grove and temple of Daphne are described by Strabo (l. xvi. p. 1089, 1090, edit. Amstel. 1707 [p. 750, ed. Casaub.]), Libanius (Nænia, p. 185-188; Antiochic. Orat. xi. p. 380, 381 [ed. Morell. 1627]), and Sozomen (l v. c. 19). Wesseling (Itinerar. p. 581) and Casaubon (ad Hist. August. p. 64) illustrate this curious subject.

[6] Simulacrum in eo Olympiaci Jovis imitamenti æquiparans magnitudinem. Ammian. xxii. 13. The Olympic Jupiter was sixty feet high, and his bulk was consequently equal to that of a thousand men. See a curious *Mémoire* of the Abbé Gedoyn (Académie des Inscriptions, tom. ix. p. 198.)

plicated the venerable mother to give to his arms the cold and
beauteous DAPHNE: for the spot was ennobled by fiction; and
the fancy of the Syrian poets had transported the amorous tale
from the banks of the Peneus to those of the Orontes. The
ancient rites of Greece were imitated by the royal colony of
Antioch. A stream of prophecy, which rivalled the truth and
reputation of the Delphic oracle, flowed from the *Castalian*
fountain of Daphne.[1] In the adjacent fields a stadium was built
by a special privilege,[2] which had been purchased from Elis;
the Olympic games were celebrated at the expense of the city;
and a revenue of thirty thousand pounds sterling was annually
applied to the public pleasures.[3] The perpetual resort of pilgrims
and spectators insensibly formed, in the neighbourhood of the
temple, the stately and populous village of Daphne, which
emulated the splendour, without acquiring the title, of a pro
vincial city. The temple and the village were deeply bosomed
in a thick grove of laurels and cypresses, which reached as far
as a circumference of ten miles, and formed in the most sultry
summers a cool and impenetrable shade. A thousand streams
of the purest water, issuing from every hill, preserved the verdure
of the earth and the temperature of the air; the senses were
gratified with harmonious sounds and aromatic odours; and the
peaceful grove was consecrated to health and joy, to luxury and
love. The vigorous youth pursued, like Apollo, the object of
his desires; and the blushing maid was warned, by the fate of
Daphne, to shun the folly of unseasonable coyness. The soldier
and the philosopher wisely avoided the temptation of this
sensual paradise;[4] where pleasure, assuming the character of

[1] Hadrian read the history of his future fortunes on a leaf dipped in the
Castalian stream; a trick which, according to the physician Vandale (de
Oraculis, p. 281, 282), might be easily performed by chemical preparations.
The emperor stopped the source of such dangerous knowledge, which was
again opened by the devout curiosity of Julian.

[2] It was purchased, A.D. 44, in the year 92 of the era of Antioch (Noris.
Epoch. Syro-Maced. p. 139-174) for the term of ninety Olympiads. But
the Olympic games of Antioch were not regularly celebrated till the reign of
Commodus. See the curious details in the Chronicle of John Malala (tom.
i. p. 291, 320, 372-381 [ed. Oxon.; p. 225, 248, and 283 *sqq.*, ed. Bonn.]), a
writer whose merit and authority are confined within the limits of his
native city.

[3] Fifteen talents of gold, bequeathed by Sosibius, who died in the reign
of Augustus. The theatrical merits of the Syrian cities, in the age of Constantine, are compared in the Expositio totius Mundi, p. 6 (Hudson, Geograph. Minor. tom. iii.).

[4] Avidio Cassio Syriacas legiones dedi luxuriâ diffluentes et *Daphnicis*
moribus. These are the words of the emperor Marcus Antoninus, in an
original letter preserved by his biographer in Hist. August. p. 41 [Vulcat.
Gallic. in Vitâ Avid. Cass. c. 6]. Cassius dismissed or punished every
soldier who was seen at Daphne.

religion, imperceptibly dissolved the firmness of manly virtue. But the groves of Daphne continued for many ages to enjoy the veneration of natives and strangers; the privileges of the holy ground were enlarged by the munificence of succeeding emperors; and every generation added new ornaments to the splendour of the temple.[1]

When Julian, on the day of the annual festival, hastened to adore the Apollo of Daphne, his devotion was raised to the highest pitch of eagerness and impatience. His lively imagination anticipated the grateful pomp of victims, of libations, and of incense; a long procession of youths and virgins, clothed in white robes, the symbol of their innocence; and the tumultuous concourse of an innumerable people. But the zeal of Antioch was diverted, since the reign of Christianity, into a different channel. Instead of hecatombs of fat oxen sacrificed by the tribes of a wealthy city to their tutelar deity, the emperor complains that he found only a single goose, provided at the expense of a priest, the pale and solitary inhabitant of this decayed temple.[2] The altar was deserted, the oracle had been reduced to silence, and the holy ground was profaned by the introduction of Christian and funereal rites. After Babylas[3] (a bishop of Antioch, who died in prison in the persecution of Decius) had rested near a century in his grave, his body, by the order of the Cæsar Gallus, was transported into the midst of the grove of Daphne. A magnificent church was erected over his remains; a portion of the sacred lands was usurped for the maintenance of the clergy, and for the burial of the Christians of Antioch, who were ambitious of lying at the feet of their bishop; and the priests of Apollo retired, with their affrighted and indignant votaries. As soon as another revolution seemed to restore the fortune of Paganism, the church of St. Babylas was demolished, and new buildings were added to the mouldering edifice which had been raised by the piety of Syrian kings. But the first and most serious care of Julian was to deliver his oppressed deity from the odious presence of the dead and living Christians, who had so

[1] Aliquantum agrorum Daphnensibus dedit (*Pompey*), quo lucus ibi spatiosior fieret; delectatus amœnitate loci et aquarum abundantiâ. Eutropius, vi. 14 [11]. Sextus Rufus, de Provinciis, c. 16.

[2] Julian (Misopogon, p. 361, 362) discovers his own character with that *naïveté*, that unconscious simplicity, which always constitutes genuine humour.

[3] Babylas is named by Eusebius in the succession of the bishops of Antioch (Hist. Eccles. l. vi. c. 29, 39). His triumph over two emperors (the first fabulous, the second historical) is diffusely celebrated by Chrysostom (tom. ii. p. 536-577, edit. Montfaucon). Tillemont (Mém. Ecclés. tom. iii. part ii. p. 287-302, 459-465) becomes almost a sceptic.

effectually suppressed the voice of fraud or enthusiasm.[1] The
scene of infection was purified, according to the forms of ancient
rituals; the bodies were decently removed; and the ministers of
the church were permitted to convey the remains of St. Babylas
to their former habitation within the walls of Antioch. The
modest behaviour which might have assuaged the jealousy of an
hostile government, was neglected on this occasion by the zeal
of the Christians. The lofty car that transported the relics of
Babylas was followed, and accompanied, and received, by an
innumerable multitude, who chanted, with thundering acclamations, the Psalms of David the most expressive of their contempt
for idols and idolaters. The return of the saint was a triumph;
and the triumph was an insult on the religion of the emperor, who
exerted his pride to dissemble his resentment. During the night
which terminated this indiscreet procession the temple of Daphne
was in flames; the statue of Apollo was consumed; and the walls
of the edifice were left a naked and awful monument of ruin. The
Christians of Antioch asserted, with religious confidence, that the
powerful intercession of St. Babylas had pointed the lightnings
of heaven against the devoted roof: but as Julian was reduced
to the alternative of believing either a crime or a miracle, he
chose, without hesitation, without evidence, but with some
colour of probability, to impute the fire of Daphne to the revenge
of the Galilæans.[2] Their offence, had it been sufficiently proved,
might have justified the retaliation, which was immediately
executed by the order of Julian, of shutting the doors, and con-
fiscating the wealth, of the cathedral of Antioch. To discover
the criminals who were guilty of the tumult, of the fire, or of
secreting the riches of the church, several ecclesiastics were tortured;[3] and a presbyter, of the name of Theodoret, was beheaded
by the sentence of the count of the East. But this hasty act
was blamed by the emperor, who lamented, with real or affected

---

[1] Ecclesiastical critics, particularly those who love relics, exult in the
confession of Julian (Misopogon, p. 361) and Libanius (Nænia, p. 185) that
Apollo was disturbed by the vicinity of *one* dead man. Yet Ammianus
(xxii. 12) clears and purifies the whole ground, according to the rites which
the Athenians formerly practised in the isle of Delos.

[2] Julian (in Misopogon, p. 361) rather insinuates than affirms their guilt.
Ammianus (xxii. 13) treats the imputation as *levissimus rumor*, and
relates the story with extraordinary candour.

[3] Quo tam atroci casû repente consumpto, ad id usque imperatoris ira
provexit, ut quæstiones agitari juberet solito acriores (yet Julian blames
the lenity of the magistrates of Antioch), et majorem ecclesiam Antiochiæ
claudi. [Amm. l. c.] This interdiction was performed with some circumstances of indignity and profanation: and the seasonable death of the
principal actor, Julian's uncle, is related with much superstitious complacency by the Abbé de la Bléterie, Vie de Julien, p. 362-369.

concern, that the imprudent zeal of his ministers would tarnish his reign with the disgrace of persecution.[1]

The zeal of the ministers of Julian was instantly checked by the frown of their sovereign; but when the father of his country declares himself the leader of a faction, the licence of popular fury cannot easily be restrained, nor consistently punished. Julian, in a public composition, applauds the devotion and loyalty of the holy cities of Syria, whose pious inhabitants had destroyed, at the first signal, the sepulchres of the Galilæans; and faintly complains that they had revenged the injuries of the gods with less moderation than he should have recommended.[2] This imperfect and reluctant confession may appear to confirm the ecclesiastical narratives—that in the cities of Gaza, Ascalon, Cæsarea, Heliopolis, etc., the Pagans abused, without prudence or remorse, the moment of their prosperity; that the unhappy objects of their cruelty were released from torture only by death; that, as their mangled bodies were dragged through the streets, they were pierced (such was the universal rage) by the spits of cooks, and the distaffs of enraged women; and that the entrails of Christian priests and virgins, after they had been tasted by those bloody fanatics, were mixed with barley, and contemptuously thrown to the unclean animals of the city.[3] Such scenes of religious madness exhibit the most contemptible and odious picture of human nature; but the massacre of Alexandria attracts still more attention, from the certainty of the fact, the rank of the victims, and the splendour of the capital of Egypt.

George,[4] from his parents or his education, surnamed the Cappadocian, was born at Epiphania in Cilicia, in a fuller's shop. From this obscure and servile origin he raised himself by the talents of a parasite; and the patrons whom he assiduously flattered procured for their worthless dependent a lucrative

[1] Besides the ecclesiastical historians, who are more or less to be suspected, we may allege the passion of St. Theodore, in the Acta Sincera of Ruinart, p. 591. The complaint of Julian gives it an original and authentic air.

[2] Julian. Misopogon, p. 361.

[3] See Gregory Nazianzen (Orat. iii. p. 87). Sozomen (l. v. c. 9) may be considered as an original, though not impartial, witness. He was a native of Gaza, and had conversed with the confessor Zeno, who, as bishop of Maiuma, lived to the age of an hundred (l. vii. c. 28). Philostorgius (l. vii. c. 4, with Godefroy's Dissertations, p. 284) adds some tragic circumstances of Christians who were *literally* sacrificed at the altars of the gods, etc.

[4] The life and death of George of Cappadocia are described by Ammianus (xxii. 11), Gregory Nazianzen (Orat. xxi. p. 382, 385, 389, 390), and Epiphanius (Hæres. lxxvi. [p. 912, ed. Paris, 1622]). The invectives of the two saints might not deserve much credit, unless they were confirmed by the testimony of the cool and impartial infidel.

commission, or contract, to supply the army with bacon. His employment was mean; he rendered it infamous. He accumulated wealth by the basest arts of fraud and corruption; but his malversations were so notorious, that George was compelled to escape from the pursuits of justice. After this disgrace, in which he appears to have saved his fortune at the expense of his honour, he embraced, with real or affected zeal, the profession of Arianism. From the love, or the ostentation, of learning, he collected a valuable library of history, rhetoric, philosophy, and theology; [1] and the choice of the prevailing faction promoted George of Cappadocia to the throne of Athanasius. The entrance of the new archbishop was that of a barbarian conqueror; and each moment of his reign was polluted by cruelty and avarice. The catholics of Alexandria and Egypt were abandoned to a tyrant, qualified by nature and education to exercise the office of persecution; but he oppressed with an impartial hand the various inhabitants of his extensive diocese. The primate of Egypt assumed the pomp and insolence of his lofty station; but he still betrayed the vices of his base and servile extraction. The merchants of Alexandria were impoverished by the unjust and almost universal monopoly, which he acquired, of nitre, salt, paper, funerals, etc.: and the spiritual father of a great people condescended to practise the vile and pernicious arts of an informer. The Alexandrians could never forget, nor forgive, the tax which he suggested on all the houses of the city, under an obsolete claim that the royal founder had conveyed to his successors, the Ptolemies and the Cæsars, the perpetual property of the soil. The Pagans, who had been flattered with the hopes of freedom and toleration, excited his devout avarice; and the rich temples of Alexandria were either pillaged or insulted by the haughty prelate, who exclaimed in a loud and threatening tone, " How long will these sepulchres be permitted to stand? " Under the reign of Constantius he was expelled by the fury, or rather by the justice, of the people; and it was not without a violent struggle that the civil and military powers of the state could restore his authority, and gratify his revenge. The messenger who proclaimed at Alexandria the accession of Julian

[1] After the massacre of George, the emperor Julian repeatedly sent orders to preserve the library for his own use, and to torture the slaves who might be suspected of secreting any books. He praises the merit of the collection, from whence he had borrowed and transcribed several manuscripts while he pursued his studies in Cappadocia. He could wish indeed that the works of the Galilæans might perish; but he requires an exact account even of those theological volumes, lest other treatises more valuable should be confounded in their loss. Julian. Epist. ix. xxxvi. [p. 377, 411].

announced the downfall of the archbishop. George, with two of his obsequious ministers, count Diodorus, and Dracontius, master of the mint, were ignominiously dragged in chains to the public prison. At the end of twenty-four days the prison was forced open by the rage of a superstitious multitude, impatient of the tedious forms of judicial proceedings. The enemies of gods and men expired under their cruel insults; the lifeless bodies of the archbishop and his associates were carried in triumph through the streets on the back of a camel; and the inactivity of the Athanasian party [1] was esteemed a shining example of evangelical patience. The remains of these guilty wretches were thrown into the sea; and the popular leaders of the tumult declared their resolution to disappoint the devotion of the Christians, and to intercept the future honours of these *martyrs*, who had been punished, like their predecessors, by the enemies of their religion.[2] The fears of the Pagans were just, and their precautions ineffectual. The meritorious death of the archbishop obliterated the memory of his life. The rival of Athanasius was dear and sacred to the Arians, and the seeming conversion of those sectaries introduced his worship into the bosom of the catholic church.[3] The odious stranger, disguising every circumstance of time and place, assumed the mask of a martyr, a saint, and a Christian hero; [4] and the infamous George of Cappadocia has been transformed [5] into the renowned St. George of England, the patron of arms, of chivalry, and of the garter.[6]

[1] Philostorgius, with cautious malice, insinuates their guilt, καὶ τὴν Ἀθανασίου γνώμην στρατηγῆσαι τῆς πράξεως, l. vii. c. 2. Godefroy, p. 267.

[2] Cineres projecit in mare, id metuens ut clamabat, ne, collectis supremis, ædes illis exstruerentur ut reliquis, qui deviare a religione compulsi, pertulere cruciabiles pœnas, adusque gloriosam mortem intemeratâ fide progressi, et nunc MARTYRES appellantur. Ammian. xxii. 11. Epiphanius proves to the Arians that George was not a martyr.

[3] Some Donatists (Optatus Milev. p. 60, 303, edit. Dupin; and Tillemont, Mém. Ecclés. tom. vi. p. 713, in 4to.) and Priscillianists (Tillemont, Mém. Ecclés. tom. viii. p. 517, in 4to.) have in like manner usurped the honours of catholic saints and martyrs.

[4] The saints of Cappadocia, Basil and the Gregories, were ignorant of their holy companion. Pope Gelasius (A.D. 494), the first catholic who acknowledges St. George, places him among the martyrs " qui Deo magis quam hominibus noti sunt." He rejects his Acts as the composition of heretics. Some, perhaps not the oldest, of the spurious Acts are still extant; and, through a cloud of fiction, we may yet distinguish the combat which St. George of Cappadocia sustained, in the presence of Queen *Alexandra*, against the *magician Athanasius*.

[5] This transformation is not given as absolutely certain, but as *extremely* probable. See the Longueruana, tom. i. p. 194.

[6] A curious history of the worship of St. George, from the sixth century (when he was already revered in Palestine, in Armenia, at Rome, and at

About the same time that Julian was informed of the tumult of Alexandria he received intelligence from Edessa that the proud and wealthy faction of the Arians had insulted the weakness of the Valentinians, and committed such disorders as ought not to be suffered with impunity in a well-regulated state. Without expecting the slow forms of justice, the exasperated prince directed his mandate to the magistrates of Edessa,[1] by which he confiscated the whole property of the church: the money was distributed among the soldiers; the lands were added to the domain; and this act of oppression was aggravated by the most ungenerous irony. " I show myself," says Julian, " the true friend of the Galilæans. Their *admirable* law has promised the kingdom of heaven to the poor; and they will advance with more diligence in the paths of virtue and salvation when they are relieved by my assistance from the load of temporal possessions. Take care," pursued the monarch, in a more serious tone, " take care how you provoke my patience and humanity. If these disorders continue, I will revenge on the magistrates the crimes of the people; and you will have reason to dread, not only con-fiscation and exile, but fire and the sword." The tumults of Alexandria were doubtless of a more bloody and dangerous nature: but a Christian bishop had fallen by the hands of the Pagans; and the public epistle of Julian affords a very lively proof of the partial spirit of his administration. His reproaches to the citizens of Alexandria are mingled with expressions of esteem and tenderness; and he laments that, on this occasion, they should have departed from the gentle and generous manners which attested their Grecian extraction. He gravely censures the offence which they had committed against the laws of justice and humanity; but he recapitulates, with visible complacency, the intolerable provocations which they had so long endured from the impious tyranny of George of Cappadocia. Julian admits the principle that a wise and vigorous government should chastise the insolence of the people; yet, in consideration of their founder Alexander, and of Serapis their tutelar deity, he grants a free and gracious pardon to the guilty city, for which he again feels the affection of a brother.[2]

Treves in Gaul), might be extracted from Dr. Heylin (History of St. George, and edition, London, 1633, in 4to. p. 429) and the Bollandists (Act. SS. Mens. April. tom. iii. p. 100-163). His fame and popularity in Europe, and especially in England, proceeded from the Crusades.

[1] Julian. Epist. xliii. [p. 424.]

[2] Julian. Epist. x. [p. 378.] He allowed his friends to assuage his anger. Ammian. xxii. 11.

After the tumult of Alexandria had subsided, Athanasius, amidst the public acclamations, seated himself on the throne from whence his unworthy competitor had been precipitated: and as the zeal of the archbishop was tempered with discretion, the exercise of his authority tended not to inflame, but to reconcile, the minds of the people. His pastoral labours were not confined to the narrow limits of Egypt. The state of the Christian world was present to his active and capacious mind; and the age, the merit, the reputation of Athanasius, enabled him to assume, in a moment of danger, the office of Ecclesiastical Dictator.[1] Three years were not yet elapsed since the majority of the bishops of the West had, ignorantly or reluctantly, subscribed the Confession of Rimini. They repented, they believed, but they dreaded the unseasonable rigour of their orthodox brethren; and if their pride was stronger than their faith, they might throw themselves into the arms of the Arians, to escape the indignity of a public penance, which must degrade them to the condition of obscure laymen. At the same time the domestic differences concerning the union and distinction of the divine persons were agitated with some heat among the catholic doctors; and the progress of this metaphysical controversy seemed to threaten a public and lasting division of the Greek and Latin churches. By the wisdom of a select synod, to which the name and presence of Athanasius gave the authority of a general council, the bishops who had unwarily deviated into error were admitted to the communion of the church, on the easy condition of subscribing the Nicene Creed, without any formal acknowledgment of their past fault, or any minute definition of their scholastic opinions. The advice of the primate of Egypt had already prepared the clergy of Gaul and Spain, of Italy and Greece, for the reception of this salutary measure; and, notwithstanding the opposition of some ardent spirits,[2] the fear of the common enemy promoted the peace and harmony of the Christians.[3]

[1] See Athanas. ad Rufin. tom. ii. p. 40, 41; and Greg. Nazianzen, Orat. xxi. p. 395, 396; who justly states the temperate zeal of the primate as much more meritorious than his prayers, his fasts, his persecutions, etc.

[2] I have not leisure to follow the blind obstinacy of Lucifer of Cagliari. See his adventures in Tillemont (Mém. Ecclés. tom. vii. p. 900-926); and observe how the colour of the narrative insensibly changes, as the confessor becomes a schismatic.

[3] Assensus est huic sententiæ Occidens, et, per tam necessarium concilium, Satanæ faucibus mundus ereptus. The lively and artful dialogue of Jerom against the Luciferians (tom. ii. p. 135-155 [tom. ii. p. 193, ed. Vallars.]) exhibits an original picture of the ecclesiastical policy of the times.

The skill and diligence of the primate of Egypt had improved the season of tranquillity before it was interrupted by the hostile edicts of the emperor.[1]   Julian, who despised the Christians, honoured Athanasius with his sincere and peculiar hatred. For his sake alone he introduced an arbitrary distinction, repugnant at least to the spirit of his former declarations.   He maintained that the Galilæans whom he had recalled from exile were not restored, by that general indulgence, to the possession of their respective churches; and he expressed his astonishment that a criminal, who had been repeatedly condemned by the judgment of the emperors, should dare to insult the majesty of the laws, and insolently usurp the archiepiscopal throne of Alexandria, without expecting the orders of his sovereign.   As a punishment for the imaginary offence, he again banished Athanasius from the city; and he was pleased to suppose that this act of justice would be highly agreeable to his pious subjects. The pressing solicitations of the people soon convinced him that the majority of the Alexandrians were Christians; and that the greatest part of the Christians were firmly attached to the cause of their oppressed primate.   But the knowledge of their sentiments, instead of persuading him to recall his decree, provoked him to extend to all Egypt the term of the exile of Athanasius.   The zeal of the multitude rendered Julian still more inexorable: he was alarmed by the danger of leaving at the head of a tumultuous city a daring and popular leader; and the language of his resentment discovers the opinion which he entertained of the courage and abilities of Athanasius.   The execution of the sentence was still delayed by the caution or negligence of Ecdicius, præfect of Egypt, who was at length awakened from his lethargy by a severe reprimand.   " Though you neglect," says Julian, " to write to me on any other subject, at least it is your duty to inform me of your conduct towards Athanasius, the enemy of the gods.   My intentions have been long since communicated to you.   I swear by the great Serapis, that unless, on the calends of December, Athanasius has departed from Alexandria, nay, from Egypt, the officers of your government shall pay a fine of one hundred pounds of gold.   You know my temper: I am slow to condemn, but I am still slower to forgive."

[1] Tillemont, who supposes that George was massacred in August, crowds the actions of Athanasius into a narrow space (Mém. Ecclés. tom. viii. p. 360).   An original fragment, published by the Marquis Maffei, from the old Chapter library of Verona (Osservazioni Letterarie, tom. iii. p. 60-92), affords many important dates, which are authenticated by the computation of Egyptian months.

This epistle was enforced by a short postscript written with the emperor's own hand. " The contempt that is shown for all the gods fills me with grief and indignation. There is nothing that I should see, nothing that I should hear, with more pleasure, than the expulsion of Athanasius from all Egypt. The abominable wretch! Under my reign, the baptism of several Grecian ladies of the highest rank has been the effect of his persecutions."[1] The death of Athanasius was not *expressly* commanded; but the præfect of Egypt understood that it was safer for him to exceed than to neglect the orders of an irritated master. The archbishop prudently retired to the monasteries of the Desert; eluded, with his usual dexterity, the snares of the enemy; and lived to triumph over the ashes of a prince who, in words of formidable import, had declared his wish that the whole venom of the Galilæan school were contained in the single person of Athanasius.[2]

I have endeavoured faithfully to represent the artful system by which Julian proposed to obtain the effects, without incurring the guilt or reproach, of persecution. But if the deadly spirit of fanaticism perverted the heart and understanding of a virtuous prince, it must, at the same time, be confessed, that the *real* sufferings of the Christians were inflamed and magnified by human passions and religious enthusiasm. The meekness and resignation which had distinguished the primitive disciples of the Gospel was the object of the applause, rather than of the imitation, of their successors. The Christians, who had now possessed above forty years the civil and ecclesiastical government of the empire, had contracted the insolent vices of prosperity,[3] and the habit of believing that the saints alone were entitled to reign over the earth. As soon as the enmity of Julian deprived the clergy of the privileges which had been conferred by the favour of Constantine, they complained of the most cruel oppression; and the free toleration of idolaters and heretics was a subject of grief and scandal to the orthodox party.[4] The acts of violence,

---

[1] Τὸν μιάρὸν, ὃς ἐτόλμησεν Ἑλληνίδας, ἐπ' ἐμοῦ, γυναῖκας τῶν ἐπισήμων βαπτίσαι, διώκεσθαι. [Julian. Ep. vi. p. 376.] I have preserved the ambiguous sense of the last word, the ambiguity of a tyrant who wished to find or to create guilt.

[2] The three epistles of Julian which explain his intentions and conduct with regard to Athanasius should be disposed in the following chronological order, xxvi. x. vi. See likewise Greg. Nazianzen, xxi. p. 393; Sozomen, l. v. c. 15; Socrates, l. iii. c. 14; Theodoret, l. iii. c. 9; and Tillemont, Mém. Ecclés. tom. viii. p. 361-368, who has used some materials prepared by the Bollandists.

[3] See the fair confession of Gregory (Orat. iii. p. 61, 62).

[4] Hear the furious and absurd complaint of Optatus (de Schismat. Donatist. l. ii. c. 16, 17).

which were no longer countenanced by the magistrates, were still committed by the zeal of the people. At Pessinus the altar of Cybele was overturned almost in the presence of the emperor; and in the city of Cæsarea, in Cappadocia, the temple of Fortune, the sole place of worship which had been left to the Pagans, was destroyed by the rage of a popular tumult. On these occasions, a prince who felt for the honour of the gods was not disposed to interrupt the course of justice; and his mind was still more deeply exasperated when he found that the fanatics, who had deserved and suffered the punishment of incendiaries, were rewarded with the honours of martyrdom.[1] The Christian subjects of Julian were assured of the hostile designs of their sovereign; and, to their jealous apprehension, every circumstance of his government might afford some grounds of discontent and suspicion. In the ordinary administration of the laws, the Christians, who formed so large a part of the people, must frequently be condemned; but their indulgent brethren, without examining the merits of the cause, presumed their innocence, allowed their claims, and imputed the severity of their judge to the partial malice of religious persecution.[2] These present hardships, intolerable as they might appear, were represented as a slight prelude of the impending calamities. The Christians considered Julian as a cruel and crafty tyrant, who suspended the execution of his revenge till he should return victorious from the Persian war. They expected that, as soon as he had triumphed over the foreign enemies of Rome, he would lay aside the irksome mask of dissimulation; that the amphitheatres would stream with the blood of hermits and bishops; and that the Christians who still persevered in the profession of the faith would be deprived of the common benefits of nature and society.[3] Every calumny[4] that could wound the reputation of

---

[1] Greg. Nazianzen, Orat. iii. p. 91, iv. p. 133. He praises the rioters of Cæsarea, τούτων δὲ τῶν μεγαλοφυῶν καὶ θερμῶν εἰς εὐσεβείαν. See Sozomen, l. v. 4, 11. Tillemont (Mém. Ecclés. tom. vii. p. 649, 650) owns that their behaviour was not dans l'ordre commun; but he is perfectly satisfied, as the great St. Basil always celebrated the festival of these blessed martyrs.

[2] Julian determined a lawsuit against the new Christian city at Maiuma, the port of Gaza; and his sentence, though it might be imputed to bigotry, was never reversed by his successors. Sozomen, l. v. c. 3. Reland, Palestin. tom. ii. p. 791.

[3] Gregory (Orat. iii. p. 93, 94, 95; Orat. iv. p. 114) pretends to speak from the information of Julian's confidants, whom Orosius (vii. 30) could not have seen.

[4] Gregory (Orat. iii. p. 91) charges the Apostate with secret sacrifices of boys and girls; and positively affirms that the dead bodies were thrown into the Orontes. See Theodoret, l. iii. c. 26, 27; and the equivocal candour of the Abbé de la Blétérie, Vie de Julien, p. 351, 352. Yet *con-*

the Apostate was credulously embraced by the fears and hatred of his adversaries; and their indiscreet clamours provoked the temper of a sovereign whom it was their duty to respect, and their interest to flatter. They still protested that prayers and tears were their only weapons against the impious tyrant, whose head they devoted to the justice of offended Heaven. But they insinuated, with sullen resolution, that their submission was no longer the effect of weakness; and that, in the imperfect state of human virtue, the patience which is founded on principle may be exhausted by persecution. It is impossible to determine how far the zeal of Julian would have prevailed over his good sense and humanity; but, if we seriously reflect on the strength and spirit of the church, we shall be convinced that, before the emperor could have extinguished the religion of Christ, he must have involved his country in the horrors of a civil war.[1]

CHAPTER XXIV

Residence of Julian at Antioch—His successful Expedition against the Persians—Passage of the Tigris—The Retreat and Death of Julian—Election of Jovian—He saves the Roman Army by a disgraceful Treaty

THE philosophical fable which Julian composed under the name of the CÆSARS [2] is one of the most agreeable and instructive productions of ancient wit.[3] During the freedom and equality of the days of the Saturnalia, Romulus prepared a feast for the

temporary malice could not impute to Julian the troops of martyrs, more especially in the West, which Baronius so greedily swallows, and Tillemont so faintly rejects (Mém. Ecclés. tom. vii. p. 1295-1315).

[1] The resignation of Gregory is truly edifying (Orat. iv. p. 123, 124). Yet, when an officer of Julian attempted to seize the church of Nazianzus, he would have lost his life if he had not yielded to the zeal of the bishop and people (Orat. xix. p. 308). See the reflections of Chrysostom, as they are alleged by Tillemont (Mém. Ecclés. tom. vii. p. 575).

[2] See this fable or satire, p. 306-336 of the Leipzig edition of Julian's works. The French version of the learned Ezekiel Spanheim (Paris, 1683) is coarse, languid, and correct; and his notes, proofs, illustrations, etc., are piled on each other till they form a mass of 557 close-printed quarto pages. The Abbé de la Bléterie (Vie de Jovien, tom. i. p. 241-393) has more happily expressed the spirit, as well as the sense, of the original, which he illustrates with some concise and curious notes.

[3] Spanheim (in his preface) has most learnedly discussed the etymology, origin, resemblance, and disagreement of the Greek *satyrs*, a dramatic piece, which was acted after the tragedy; and the Latin *satires* (from *Satura*), a *miscellaneous* composition, either in prose or verse. But the Cæsars of Julian are of such an original cast, that the critic is perplexed to which class he should ascribe them.

deities of Olympus, who had adopted him as a worthy associate, and for the Roman princes, who had reigned over his martial people and the vanquished nations of the earth. The immortals were placed in just order on their thrones of state, and the table of the Cæsars was spread below the moon, in the upper region of the air. The tyrants, who would have disgraced the society of gods and men, were thrown headlong, by the inexorable Nemesis, into the Tartarean abyss. The rest of the Cæsars successively advanced to their seats; and as they passed, the vices, the defects, the blemishes of their respective characters, were maliciously noticed by old Silenus, a laughing moralist, who disguised the wisdom of a philosopher under the mask of a Bacchanal.[1] As soon as the feast was ended, the voice of Mercury proclaimed the will of Jupiter, that a celestial crown should be the reward of superior merit. Julius Cæsar, Augustus, Trajan, and Marcus Antoninus, were selected as the most illustrious candidates; the effeminate Constantine [2] was not excluded from this honourable competition; and the great Alexander was invited to dispute the prize of glory with the Roman heroes. Each of the candidates was allowed to display the merit of his own exploits; but, in the judgment of the gods, the modest silence of Marcus pleaded more powerfully than the elaborate orations of his haughty rivals. When the judges of this awful contest proceeded to examine the heart and to scrutinise the springs of action, the superiority of the Imperial Stoic appeared still more decisive and conspicuous.[3] Alexander and Cæsar, Augustus, Trajan, and Constantine acknowledged, with a blush, that fame, or power, or pleasure, had been the important object of *their* labours; but the gods themselves beheld with reverence and love a virtuous mortal, who had practised on the throne the lessons of philosophy, and who, in a state of human imperfection, had aspired to imitate the moral attributes of the Deity. The value of this agreeable composition (the Cæsars of Julian) is enhanced by the rank of the author. A prince, who delineates with freedom the vices and virtues of his predecessors,

---

[1] This mixed character of Silenus is finely painted in the sixth eclogue of Virgil.

[2] Every impartial reader must perceive and condemn the partiality of Julian against his uncle Constantine and the Christian religion. On this occasion the interpreters are compelled, by a more sacred interest, to renounce their allegiance, and to desert the cause of their author.

[3] Julian was secretly inclined to prefer a Greek to a Roman. But when he seriously compared a hero with a philosopher, he was sensible that mankind had much greater obligations to Socrates than to Alexander (Orat. ad Themistium, p. 264).

subscribes, in every line, the censure or approbation of his own conduct.

In the cool moments of reflection, Julian preferred the useful and benevolent virtues of Antoninus; but his ambitious spirit was inflamed by the glory of Alexander, and he solicited, with equal ardour, the esteem of the wise and the applause of the multitude. In the season of life when the powers of the mind and body enjoy the most active vigour, the emperor, who was instructed by the experience and animated by the success of the German war, resolved to signalise his reign by some more splendid and memorable achievement. The ambassadors of the East, from the continent of India and the isle of Ceylon,[1] had respectfully saluted the Roman purple.[2] The nations of the West esteemed and dreaded the personal virtues of Julian both in peace and war. He despised the trophies of a Gothic victory,[3] and was satisfied that the rapacious barbarians of the Danube would be restrained from any future violation of the faith of treaties by the terror of his name and the additional fortifications with which he strengthened the Thracian and Illyrian frontiers. The successor of Cyrus and Artaxerxes was the only rival whom he deemed worthy of his arms, and he resolved, by the final conquest of Persia, to chastise the haughty nation which had so long resisted and insulted the majesty of Rome.[4] As soon as the Persian monarch was informed that the throne of Constantius

---

[1] Inde nationibus Indicis certatim cum donis optimates mittentibus . . . ab usque Divis et *Serendivis*. Ammian. xxii. 7. This island, to which the names of Taprobana, Serendib, and Ceylon, have been successively applied, manifests how imperfectly the seas and lands to the east of Cape Comorin were known to the Romans. 1. Under the reign of Claudius, a freedman, who farmed the customs of the Red Sea, was accidentally driven by the winds upon this strange and undiscovered coast: he conversed six months with the natives; and the king of Ceylon, who heard for the first time of the power and justice of Rome, was persuaded to send an embassy to the emperor (Plin. Hist. Nat. vi. 24). 2. The geographers (and even Ptolemy) have magnified above fifteen times the real size of this new world, which they extended as far as the equator, and the neighbourhood of China. [The name of Diva gens or Divorum regio was applied, according to M. Letronne, by the ancients to the whole eastern coast of the Indian peninsula from the Ganges to Ceylon.—O. S.]

[2] These embassies had been sent to Constantius. Ammianus, who unwarily deviates into gross flattery, must have forgotten the length of the way, and the short duration of the reign of Julian.

[3] Gothos sæpe fallaces et perfidos; hostes quærere se meliores aiebat: illis enim sufficere mercatores Galatas per quos ubique sine conditionis discrimine venumdantur. [Ammian. xxii. 7.] Within less than fifteen years these Gothic slaves threatened and subdued their masters.

[4] Alexander reminds his rival Cæsar, who depreciated the fame and merit of an Asiatic victory, that Crassus and Antony had felt the Persian arrows; and that the Romans, in a war of three hundred years, had not yet subdued the single province of Mesopotamia or Assyria (Cæsares, p. 324).

was filled by a prince of a very different character, he condescended to make some artful or perhaps sincere overtures towards a negotiation of peace. But the pride of Sapor was astonished by the firmness of Julian, who sternly declared that he would never consent to hold a peaceful conference among the flames and ruins of the cities of Mesopotamia, and who added, with a smile of contempt, that it was needless to treat by ambassadors, as he himself had determined to visit speedily the court of Persia. The impatience of the emperor urged the diligence of the military preparations. The generals were named, a formidable army was destined for this important service, and Julian, marching from Constantinople through the provinces of Asia Minor, arrived at Antioch about eight months after the death of his predecessor. His ardent desire to march into the heart of Persia was checked by the indispensable duty of regulating the state of the empire, by his zeal to revive the worship of the gods, and by the advice of his wisest friends, who represented the necessity of allowing the salutary interval of winter quarters to restore the exhausted strength of the legions of Gaul and the discipline and spirit of the Eastern troops. Julian was persuaded to fix, till the ensuing spring, his residence at Antioch, among a people maliciously disposed to deride the haste and to censure the delays of their sovereign.[1]

If Julian had flattered himself that his personal connection with the capital of the East would be productive of mutual satisfaction to the prince and people, he made a very false estimate of his own character and of the manners of Antioch.[2] The warmth of the climate disposed the natives to the most intemperate enjoyment of tranquillity and opulence, and the lively licentiousness of the Greeks was blended with the hereditary softness of the Syrians. Fashion was the only law, pleasure the only pursuit, and the splendour of dress and furniture was the only distinction of the citizens of Antioch. The arts of luxury were honoured, the serious and manly virtues were the subject of ridicule, and the contempt for female modesty and reverent age announced the universal corruption of the capital of the East. The love of spectacles was the taste, or rather passion, of the Syrians; the most skilful artists were procured

[1] The design of the Persian war is declared by Ammianus (xxii. 7, 12), Libanius (Orat. Parent. c. 79, 80, p. 305, 306 [Fabric. Bibl. Græc. ed. Hamb. 1715]), Zosimus (l. iii. [c. 11] p. 158), and Socrates (l. iii. c. 19).

[2] The Satire of Julian and the Homilies of St. Chrysostom exhibit the same picture of Antioch. The miniature which the Abbé de la Bléterie has copied from thence (Vie de Julien, p. 332) is elegant and correct.

from the adjacent cities;[1] a considerable share of the revenue
was devoted to the public amusements, and the magnificence of
the games of the theatre and circus was considered as the happiness and as the glory of Antioch. The rustic manners of a prince
who disdained such glory, and was insensible of such happiness,
soon disgusted the delicacy of his subjects, and the effeminate
Orientals could neither imitate nor admire the severe simplicity
which Julian always maintained and sometimes affected. The
days of festivity, consecrated by ancient custom to the honour
of the gods, were the only occasions in which Julian relaxed his
philosophic severity, and those festivals were the only days in
which the Syrians of Antioch could reject the allurements of
pleasure. The majority of the people supported the glory of the
Christian name, which had been first invented by their ancestors:[2]
they contented themselves with disobeying the moral precepts,
but they were scrupulously attached to the speculative doctrines,
of their religion. The church of Antioch was distracted by heresy
and schism; but the Arians and the Athanasians, the followers
of Meletius and those of Paulinus,[3] were actuated by the same
pious hatred of their common adversary.

The strongest prejudice was entertained against the character
of an apostate, the enemy and successor of a prince who had
engaged the affections of a very numerous sect, and the removal
of St. Babylas excited an implacable opposition to the person of
Julian. His subjects complained, with superstitious indignation, that famine had pursued the emperor's steps from Constantinople to Antioch, and the discontent of a hungry people
was exasperated by the injudicious attempt to relieve their
distress. The inclemency of the season had affected the harvests
of Syria, and the price of bread[4] in the markets of Antioch had

---

[1] Laodicea furnished charioteers; Tyre and Berytus, comedians;
Cæsarea, pantomimes; Heliopolis, singers; Gaza, gladiators; Ascalon,
wrestlers; and Castabala, rope-dancers. See the Expositio totius Mundi,
p. 6, in the third tome of Hudson's Minor Geographers.

[2] Χριστόν δὲ ἀγαπῶντες ἔχετε πολιοῦχον ἀντὶ τοῦ Διός. The people of
Antioch ingeniously professed their attachment to the *Chi* (Christ), and the
Kappa (Constantius). Julian in Misopogon, p. 357.

[3] The schism of Antioch, which lasted eighty-five years (A.D. 330-415),
was inflamed, while Julian resided in that city, by the indiscreet ordination
of Paulinus. See Tillemont. Mém. Ecclés. tom. vii. p. 803 of the quarto
edition (Paris, 1701, etc.), which henceforward I shall quote.

[4] Julian states three different proportions, of five, ten, or fifteen *modii* of
wheat, for one piece of gold, according to the degrees of plenty and scarcity
(in Misopogon, p. 369). From this fact, and from some collateral examples,
I conclude that, under the successors of Constantine, the moderate price of
wheat was about thirty-two shillings the English quarter, which is equal to
the average price of the sixty-four first years of the present century. See

naturally risen in proportion to the scarcity of corn. But the fair and reasonable proportion was soon violated by the rapacious arts of monopoly. In this unequal contest, in which the produce of the land is claimed by one party as his exclusive property, is used by another as a lucrative object of trade, and is required by a third for the daily and necessary support of life, all the profits of the intermediate agents are accumulated on the head of the defenceless consumers. The hardships of their situation were exaggerated and increased by their own impatience and anxiety, and the apprehension of a scarcity gradually produced the appearances of a famine. When the luxurious citizens of Antioch complained of the high price of poultry and fish, Julian publicly declared that a frugal city ought to be satisfied with a regular supply of wine, oil, and bread; but he acknowledged that it was the duty of a sovereign to provide for the subsistence of his people. With this salutary view the emperor ventured on a very dangerous and doubtful step, of fixing, by legal authority, the value of corn. He enacted that, in a time of scarcity, it should be sold at a price which had seldom been known in the most plentiful years; and that his own example might strengthen his laws, he sent into the market four hundred and twenty-two thousand *modii*, or measures, which were drawn by his order from the granaries of Hierapolis, of Chalcis, and even of Egypt. The consequences might have been foreseen, and were soon felt. The Imperial wheat was purchased by the rich merchants; the proprietors of land or of corn withheld from the city the accustomed supply; and the small quantities that appeared in the market were secretly sold at an advanced and illegal price. Julian still continued to applaud his own policy, treated the complaints of the people as a vain and ungrateful murmur, and convinced Antioch that he had inherited the obstinacy, though not the cruelty, of his brother Gallus.[1] The remonstrances of the municipal senate served only to exasperate his inflexible mind. He was persuaded, perhaps with truth, that the senators of Antioch, who possessed lands or were concerned

Arbuthnot's Tables of Coins, Weights, and Measures, p. 88, 89. Plin. Hist. Natur. xviii. 12. Mém. de l'Académie des Inscriptions, tom. xxviii. p. 718-721. Smith's Inquiry into the Nature and Causes of the Wealth of Nations, vol. i. p. 246. This last I am proud to quote, as the work of a sage and a friend.

[1] Nunquam a proposito declinabat, Galli similis fratris, licet incruentus. Ammian. xxii. 14. The ignorance of the most enlightened princes may claim some excuse; but we cannot be satisfied with Julian's own defence (in Misopogon, p. 368, 369), or the elaborate apology of Libanius (Orat. Parental. c. xcvii. p. 321).

in trade, had themselves contributed to the calamities of their country; and he imputed the disrespectful boldness which they assumed to the sense, not of public duty, but of private interest. The whole body, consisting of two hundred of the most noble and wealthy citizens, were sent, under a guard, from the palace to the prison; and though they were permitted, before the close of evening, to return to their respective houses,[1] the emperor himself could not obtain the forgiveness which he had so easily granted. The same grievances were still the subject of the same complaints, which were industriously circulated by the wit and levity of the Syrian Greeks. During the licentious days of the Saturnalia, the streets of the city resounded with insolent songs, which derided the laws, the religion, the personal conduct, and even the *beard*, of the conqueror; and the spirit of Antioch was manifested by the connivance of the magistrates and the applause of the multitude.[2] The disciple of Socrates was too deeply affected by these popular insults; but the monarch, endowed with quick sensibility and possessed of absolute power, refused his passions the gratification of revenge. A tyrant might have proscribed, without distinction, the lives and fortunes of the citizens of Antioch; and the unwarlike Syrians must have patiently submitted to the lust, the rapaciousness, and the cruelty of the faithful legions of Gaul. A milder sentence might have deprived the capital of the East of its honours and privileges, and the courtiers, perhaps the subjects of Julian, would have applauded an act of justice which asserted the dignity of the supreme magistrate of the republic.[3] But instead of abusing or exerting the authority of the state to revenge his personal injuries, Julian contented himself with an inoffensive mode of retaliation, which it would be in the power of few princes to employ. He had been insulted by satires and libels; in his turn he composed, under the title of the *Enemy of the Beard*, an ironical confession of his own faults, and a severe satire of the licentious and effeminate manners of Antioch. This Imperial reply was publicly exposed before the gates of the palace; and

---

[1] Their short and easy confinement is gently touched by Libanius (Orat. Parental. c. xcviii. p. 322, 323).

[2] Libanius (ad Antiochenos de Imperatoris ira, c. 17, 18, 19, in Fabricius, Biblioth. Græc. tom. vii. p. 221-223), like a skilful advocate, severely censures the folly of the people, who suffered for the crime of a few obscure and drunken wretches.

[3] Libanius (ad Antiochen. c. vii. p. 213) reminds Antioch of the recent chastisement of Cæsarea; and even Julian (in Misopogon, p. 355) insinuates how severely Tarentum had expiated the insult to the Roman ambassadors.

the MISOPOGON [1] still remains a singular monument of the resentment, the wit, the humanity, and the indiscretion of Julian.
Though he affected to laugh, he could not forgive.[2] His contempt was expressed, and his revenge might be gratified, by the
nomination of a governor [3] worthy only of such subjects; and
the emperor, for ever renouncing the ungrateful city, proclaimed
his resolution to pass the ensuing winter at Tarsus in Cilicia.[4]

Yet Antioch possessed one citizen whose genius and virtues
might atone, in the opinion of Julian, for the vice and folly of his
country. The sophist Libanius was born in the capital of the
East, he publicly professed the arts of rhetoric and declamation
at Nice, Nicomedia, Constantinople, Athens, and, during the
remainder of his life, at Antioch. His school was assiduously
frequented by the Grecian youth; his disciples, who sometimes
exceeded the number of eighty, celebrated their incomparable
master; and the jealousy of his rivals, who persecuted him from
one city to another, confirmed the favourable opinion which
Libanius ostentatiously displayed of his superior merit. The
preceptors of Julian had extorted a rash but solemn assurance
that he would never attend the lectures of their adversary; the
curiosity of the royal youth was checked and inflamed; he
secretly procured the writings of this dangerous sophist, and
gradually surpassed, in the perfect imitation of his style, the
most laborious of his domestic pupils.[5] When Julian ascended
the throne, he declared his impatience to embrace and reward
the Syrian sophist, who had preserved in a degenerate age the
Grecian purity of taste, of manners, and of religion. The
emperor's prepossession was increased and justified by the discreet pride of his favourite. Instead of pressing, with the fore-

---

[1] On the subject of the Misopogon, see Ammianus (xxii. 14), Libanius
(Orat. Parentalis, c. xcix. p. 323), Gregory Nazianzen (Orat. iv. p. 133 [ed.
Paris, 1609]), and the Chronicle of Antioch, by John Malala (tom. ii. p. 15,
16 [ed. Ox.; p. 328, ed. Bonn]). I have essential obligations to the translation and notes of the Abbé de la Bléterie (Vie de Jovien, tom. ii. p. 1-138).

[2] Ammianus [l. c.] very justly remarks, Coactus dissimulare pro tempore
irâ sufflabatur internâ. The elaborate irony of Julian at length bursts
forth into serious and direct invective.

[3] Ipse autem Antiochiam egressurus, Heliopoliten quendam Alexan-
drum Syriacæ jurisdictioni præfecit, turbulentum et sævum; dicebatque
non illum meruisse, sed Antiochensibus avaris et contumeliosis hujusmodi
judicem convenire. Ammian. xxiii. 2. Libanius (Epist. 722, p. 346, 347
[ed. Wolf. Amst. 1738]), who confesses to Julian himself that he had shared
the general discontent, pretends that Alexander was an useful, though
harsh, reformer of the manners and religion of Antioch.

[4] Julian, in Misopogon, p. 364. Ammian. xxiii. 2, and Valesius ad loc.
Libanius, in a professed oration, invites him to return to his loyal and
penitent city of Antioch.

[5] Libanius, Orat. Parent. c. vii. p. 230, 231.

most of the crowd, into the palace of Constantinople, Libanius calmly expected his arrival at Antioch, withdrew from court on the first symptoms of coldness and indifference, required a formal invitation for each visit, and taught his sovereign an important lesson, that he might command the obedience of a subject, but that he must deserve the attachment of a friend. The sophists of every age, despising or affecting to despise the accidental distinctions of birth and fortune,[1] reserve their esteem for the superior qualities of the mind, with which they themselves are so plentifully endowed. Julian might disdain the acclamations of a venal court who adored the Imperial purple; but he was deeply flattered by the praise, the admonition, the freedom, and the envy of an independent philosopher, who refused his favours, loved his person, celebrated his fame, and protected his memory. The voluminous writings of Libanius still exist; for the most part they are the vain and idle compositions of an orator who cultivated the science of words—the productions of a recluse student, whose mind, regardless of his contemporaries, was incessantly fixed on the Trojan war and the Athenian commonwealth. Yet the sophist of Antioch sometimes descended from this imaginary elevation; he entertained a various and elaborate correspondence;[2] he praised the virtues of his own times; he boldly arraigned the abuses of public and private life; and he eloquently pleaded the cause of Antioch against the just resentment of Julian and Theodosius. It is the common calamity of old age[3] to lose whatever might have rendered it desirable; but Libanius experienced the peculiar misfortune of surviving the religion and the sciences to which he had consecrated his genius. The friend of Julian was an indignant spectator of the triumph of Christianity, and his bigotry, which darkened the prospect of the visible world, did not inspire Libanius with any lively hopes of celestial glory and happiness.[4]

[1] Eunapius reports that Libanius refused the honorary rank of Prætorian præfect, as less illustrious than the title of Sophist (in Vit. Sophist. p. 135 [p. 175, ed. Comm.]). The critics have observed a similar sentiment in one of the epistles (xviii. [p. 7] ed. Wolf.) of Libanius himself.

[2] Near two thousand of his letters—a mode of composition in which Libanius was thought to excel—are still extant, and already published. The critics may praise their subtle and elegant brevity; yet Dr. Bentley (Dissertation upon Phalaris, p. 487) might justly though quaintly observe that " you feel, by the emptiness and deadness of them, that you converse with some dreaming pedant, with his elbow on his desk."

[3] His birth is assigned to the year 314. He mentions [Ep. 866] the seventy-sixth year of his age (A.D. 390), and seems to allude to some events of a still later date.

[4] Libanius has composed the vain, prolix, but curious narrative of his

The martial impatience of Julian urged him to take the field in the beginning of the spring, and he dismissed, with contempt and reproach, the senate of Antioch, who accompanied the emperor beyond the limits of their own territory, to which he was resolved never to return. After a laborious march of two days [1] he halted on the third at Berœa, or Aleppo, where he had the mortification of finding a senate almost entirely Christian, who received with cold and formal demonstrations of respect the eloquent sermon of the apostle of Paganism. The son of one of the most illustrious citizens of Berœa, who had embraced, either from interest or conscience, the religion of the emperor, was disinherited by his angry parent. The father and the son were invited to the Imperial table. Julian, placing himself between them, attempted without success to inculcate the lesson and example of toleration, supported, with affected calmness, the indiscreet zeal of the aged Christian, who seemed to forget the sentiments of nature and the duty of a subject, and at length, turning towards the afflicted youth, " Since you have lost a father," said he, " for my sake, it is incumbent on me to supply his place." [2] The emperor was received in a manner much more agreeable to his wishes at Batnæ, a small town pleasantly seated in a grove of cypresses, about twenty miles from the city of Hierapolis. The solemn rites of sacrifice were decently prepared by the inhabitants of Batnæ, who seemed attached to the worship of their tutelar deities, Apollo and Jupiter; but the serious piety of Julian was offended by the tumult of their applause, and he too clearly discerned that the smoke which arose from their altars was the incense of flattery rather than of devotion. The ancient and magnificent temple, which had sanctified for so many ages the city of Hierapolis,[3] no longer subsisted, and the consecrated

own life (tom. ii. p. 1-84, edit. Morell.), of which Eunapius (p. 130-135) has left a concise and unfavourable account. Among the moderns, Tillemont (Hist. des Empereurs, tom. iv. p. 571-576), Fabricius (Biblioth. Græc. tom. vii. p. 376-414), and Lardner (Heathen Testimonies, tom. iv. p. 127-163) have illustrated the character and writings of this famous sophist.

[1] From Antioch to Litarbe, in the territory of Chalcis, the road, over hills and through morasses, was extremely bad; and the loose stones were cemented only with sand (Julian, Epist. xxvii.). It is singular enough that the Romans should have neglected the great communication between Antioch and the Euphrates. See Wesseling, Itinerar. p. 190. Bergier, Hist. des Grands Chemins, tom. ii. p. 100.

[2] Julian alludes to this incident (Epist. xxvii.), which is more distinctly related by Theodoret (l. iii. c. 22). The intolerant spirit of the father is applauded by Tillemont (Hist. des Empereurs, tom. iv. p. 534), and even by La Bléterie (Vie de Julien, p. 413).

[3] See the curious treatise de Deâ Syriâ, inserted among the works of Lucian (tom. iii. p. 451-490, edit. Reitz.). The singular appellation of

wealth, which afforded a liberal maintenance to more than three hundred priests, might hasten its downfall. Yet Julian enjoyed the satisfaction of embracing a philosopher and a friend, whose religious firmness had withstood the pressing and repeated solicitations of Constantius and Gallus, as often as those princes lodged at his house in their passage through Hierapolis. In the hurry of military preparation, and the careless confidence of a familiar correspondence, the zeal of Julian appears to have been lively and uniform. He had now undertaken an important and difficult war, and the anxiety of the event rendered him still more attentive to observe and register the most trifling presages from which, according to the rules of divination, any knowledge of futurity could be derived.[1] He informed Libanius of his progress as far as Hierapolis by an elegant epistle,[2] which displays the facility of his genius and his tender friendship for the sophist of Antioch.

Hierapolis, situate almost on the banks of the Euphrates,[3] had been appointed for the general rendezvous of the Roman troops, who immediately passed the great river on a bridge of boats which was previously constructed.[4] If the inclinations of Julian had been similar to those of his predecessor, he might have wasted the active and important season of the year in the circus of Samosata or in the churches of Edessa. But as the war-like emperor, instead of Constantius, had chosen Alexander for his model, he advanced without delay to Carrhæ,[5] a very ancient city of Mesopotamia, at the distance of fourscore miles from

Ninus vetus (Ammian. xiv. 8) might induce a suspicion that Hierapolis had been the royal seat of the Assyrians.

[1] Julian (Epist. xxviii. [xxvii.]) kept a regular account of all the fortunate omens; but he suppresses the inauspicious signs, which Ammianus (xxiii. 2) has carefully recorded.

[2] Julian, Epist. xxvii. p. 399-402.

[3] I take the earliest opportunity of acknowledging my obligations to M. d'Anville for his recent geography of the Euphrates and Tigris (Paris, 1780, in 4to.), which particularly illustrates the expedition of Julian.

[Hierapolis was not situated on the banks of the Euphrates or even so near as to justify the expression " almost." It is about twenty-two miles from the river. It was also called Bambyce, which is the Hellenised form of its Syrian name Mabog, which the Arabs have converted into Manbedj. Cf. Smith's Dictionary of Greek and Roman Geography.—O. S.]

[4] There are three passages within a few miles of each other: 1. Zeugma, celebrated by the ancients; 2. Bir, frequented by the moderns; and, 3. The bridge of Menbigz [Manbedj] or Hierapolis, at the distance of four parasangs from the city.

[5] Haran, or Carrhæ, was the ancient residence of the Sabæans and of Abraham. See the Index Geographicus of Schultens (ad calcem Vit. Saladin.), a work from which I have obtained much *Oriental* knowledge concerning the ancient and modern geography of Syria and the adjacent countries.

Hierapolis. The temple of the Moon attracted the devotion of
Julian, but the halt of a few days was principally employed in
completing the immense preparations of the Persian war. The
secret of the expedition had hitherto remained in his own breast;
but as Carrhæ is the point of separation of the two great roads,
he could no longer conceal whether it was his design to attack
the dominions of Sapor on the side of the Tigris, or on that of the
Euphrates. The emperor detached an army of thirty thousand
men, under the command of his kinsman Procopius, and of
Sebastian, who had been duke of Egypt. They were ordered to
direct their march towards Nisibis, and to secure the frontier
from the desultory incursions of the enemy, before they attempted
the passage of the Tigris. Their subsequent operations were
left to the discretion of the generals; but Julian expected that,
after wasting with fire and sword the fertile districts of Media
and Adiabene, they might arrive under the walls of Ctesiphon
about the same time that he himself, advancing with equal steps
along the banks of the Euphrates, should besiege the capital of
the Persian monarchy. The success of this well-concerted plan
depended, in a great measure, on the powerful and ready assistance of the king of Armenia, who, without exposing the safety
of his own dominions, might detach an army of four thousand
horse and thousand twenty foot to the assistance of the Romans.[1]
But the feeble Arsaces Tiranus,[2] king of Armenia, had degenerated
still more shamefully than his father Chosroes from the manly
virtues of the great Tiridates; and as the pusillanimous monarch
was averse to any enterprise of danger and glory, he could disguise his timid indolence by the more decent excuses of religion
and gratitude. He expressed a pious attachment to the memory
of Constantius, from whose hands he had received in marriage
Olympias, the daughter of the præfect Ablavius; and the alliance
of a female who had been educated as the destined wife of the
emperor Constans exalted the dignity of a barbarian king.[3]

[1] See Xenophon, Cyropæd. l. iii. [c. 1, § 34] p. 189, edit. Hutchinson.
Artavasdes might have supplied Marc Antony with 16,000 horse, armed
and disciplined after the Parthian manner (Plutarch, in M. Antonio [c. 50],
tom v. p. 117).

[2] Moses of Chorene (Hist. Armeniac. l. iii. c. 11, p. 241 [ed. Whiston,
Lond. 1736]) fixes his accession (A.D. 354) to the 17th year of Constantius.
[According to the Armenian historians, Faustus of Byzantium, and
Mezrob, the biographer of the patriarch Narses, Tiranus, or Diran, the son
of Chosroes, had ceased to reign twenty-five years before, in A.D. 338, and
was succeeded by his son Arsaces. See Note 1 on chap. xviii. vol. ii. p. 158
—O. S.]

[3] Ammian. xx. 11. Athanasius (tom. i. p. 856) says, in general terms,
that Constantius gave his brother's widow τοῖς βαρβάροις, an expression
more suitable to a Roman than a Christian.

Tiranus professed the Christian religion; he reigned over a nation of Christians; and he was restrained, by every principle of conscience and interest, from contributing to the victory which would consummate the ruin of the church. The alienated mind of Tiranus was exasperated by the indiscretion of Julian, who treated the king of Armenia as *his* slave, and as the enemy of the gods. The haughty and threatening style of the Imperial mandates [1] awakened the secret indignation of a prince who, in the humiliating state of dependence, was still conscious of his royal descent from the Arsacides, the lords of the East, and the rivals of the Roman power.

The military dispositions of Julian were skilfully contrived to deceive the spies and to divert the attention of Sapor. The legions appeared to direct their march towards Nisibis and the Tigris. On a sudden they wheeled to the right, traversed the level and naked plain of Carrhæ, and reached, on the third day, the banks of the Euphrates, where the strong town of Nicephorium, or Callinicum, had been founded by the Macedonian kings. From thence the emperor pursued his march, above ninety miles, along the winding stream of the Euphrates, till at length, about one month after his departure from Antioch, he discovered the towers of Circesium, the extreme limit of the Roman dominions. The army of Julian, the most numerous that any of the Cæsars had ever led against Persia, consisted of sixty-five thousand effective and well-disciplined soldiers. The veteran bands of cavalry and infantry, of Romans and barbarians, had been selected from the different provinces, and a just preeminence of loyalty and valour was claimed by the hardy Gauls, who guarded the throne and person of their beloved prince. A formidable body of Scythian auxiliaries had been transported from another climate, and almost from another world, to invade a distant country of whose name and situation they were ignorant. The love of rapine and war allured to the Imperial standard several tribes of Saracens, or roving Arabs, whose service Julian had commanded, while he sternly refused the payment of the accustomed subsidies. The broad channel of the Euphrates [2] was crowded by a fleet of eleven hundred ships,

---

[1] Ammianus (xxiii 2) uses a word much too soft for the occasion, *monuerat.* Muratori (Fabricius, Bibliothec. Græc. tom. vii. p. 86) has published an epistle from Julian to the satrap Arsaces; fierce, vulgar, and (though it might deceive Sozomen, l. vi. c. 5 [c. 1]), most probably spurious. La Bléterie (Hist. de Jovien, tom. ii. p. 339) translates and rejects it.

[2] Latissimum flumen Euphraten artabat. Ammian. xxiii. 3. Somewhat higher, at the fords of Thapsacus, the river is four stadia, or 800 yards, almost half an English mile, broad (Xenophon, Anabasis, l. i. [c. 4

destined to attend the motions and to satisfy the wants of the Roman army.   The military strength of the fleet was composed of fifty armed galleys, and these were accompanied by an equal number of flat-bottomed boats, which might occasionally be connected into the form of temporary bridges.   The rest of the ships, partly constructed of timber and partly covered with raw hides, were laden with an almost inexhaustible supply of arms and engines, of utensils and provisions.   The vigilant humanity of Julian had embarked a very large magazine of vinegar and biscuit for the use of the soldiers, but he prohibited the indulgence of wine, and rigorously stopped a long string of superfluous camels that attempted to follow the rear of the army.   The river Chaboras falls into the Euphrates at Circesium,[1] and, as soon as the trumpet gave the signal of march, the Romans passed the little stream which separated two mighty and hostile empires. The custom of ancient discipline required a military oration, and Julian embraced every opportunity of displaying his eloquence. He animated the impatient and attentive legions by the example of the inflexible courage and glorious triumphs of their ancestors. He excited their resentment by a lively picture of the insolence of the Persians; and he exhorted them to imitate his firm resolution, either to extirpate that perfidious nation, or to devote his life in the cause of the republic.   The eloquence of Julian was enforced by a donative of one hundred and thirty pieces of silver to every soldier, and the bridge of the Chaboras was instantly cut away to convince the troops that they must place their hopes of safety in the success of their arms.   Yet the prudence of the emperor induced him to secure a remote frontier, perpetually exposed to the inroads of the hostile Arabs.   A detachment of four thousand men was left at Circesium, which completed, to the number of ten thousand, the regular garrison of that important fortress.[2]

From the moment that the Romans entered the enemy's

---

§ 11] p. 41, edit. Hutchinson, with Foster's Observations, p. 29, etc., in the second volume of Spelman's translation).   If the breadth of the Euphrates at Bir and Zeugma is no more than 130 yards (Voyages de Niebuhr, tom. ii. p. 335), the enormous difference must chiefly arise from the depth of the channel.

[1] Munimentum tutissimum et fabrè politum, cujus mœnia Abora (the Orientals aspirate Chaboras or Chabour) et Euphrates ambiunt flumina, velut spatium insulare fingentes.   Ammian. xxiii. 5.

[2] The enterprise and armament of Julian are described by himself (Epist. xxvii.), Ammianus Marcellinus (xxiii. 3, 4, 5), Libanius (Orat. Parent. c. 108, 109, p. 332, 333), Zosimus (l. iii. [c. 11] p. 160, 161, 162), Sozomen (l. vi. c. 1), and John Malala (tom. ii. p. 17 [ed. Ox.; p. 328, ed. Bonn]).

country,[1] the country of an active and artful enemy, the order of march was disposed in three columns.[2] The strength of the infantry, and consequently of the whole army, was placed in the centre, under the peculiar command of their master-general Victor. On the right, the brave Nevitta led a column of several legions along the banks of the Euphrates, and almost always in sight of the fleet. The left flank of the army was protected by the column of cavalry. Hormisdas and Arinthæus were appointed generals of the horse, and the singular adventures of Hormisdas [3] are not undeserving of our notice. He was a Persian prince, of the royal race of the Sassanides, who, in the troubles of the minority of Sapor, had escaped from prison to the hospitable court of the great Constantine. Hormisdas at first excited the compassion, and at length acquired the esteem, of his new masters; his valour and fidelity raised him to the military honours of the Roman service; and, though a Christian, he might indulge the secret satisfaction of convincing his ungrateful country that an oppressed subject may prove the most dangerous enemy. Such was the disposition of the three principal columns. The front and flanks of the army were covered by Lucilianus with a flying detachment of fifteen hundred light-armed soldiers, whose active vigilance observed the most distant signs, and conveyed the earliest notice of any hostile approach. Dagalaiphus, and Secundinus duke of Osrhoene, conducted the troops of the rear-guard; the baggage securely proceeded in the intervals of the columns; and the ranks, from a motive either of use or ostentation, were formed in such open order that the whole line of march extended almost ten miles. The ordinary post of Julian was at the head of the centre column, but, as he preferred the duties of a general to the state of a monarch, he rapidly moved, with a small escort of light cavalry, to the front, the rear, the flanks, wherever his presence could animate or protect the march of the Roman army. The country which

[1] Before he enters Persia, Ammianus copiously describes (xxiii. 6, p. 396-419, edit. Gronov. in 4to) the eighteen great satrapies or provinces (as far as the Seric or Chinese frontiers) which were subject to the Sassanides.

[2] Ammianus (xxiv. 1) and Zosimus (l. iii. [c. 14] p. 162, 163) have accurately expressed the order of march.

[3] The adventures of Hormisdas are related with some mixture of fable (Zosimus, l. ii. [c. 27] p. 100-102; Tillemont, Hist. des Empereurs, tom. iv. p. 198). It is almost impossible that he should be the brother (frater germanus) of an *eldest* and *posthumous* child; nor do I recollect that Ammianus ever gives him that title.

[Hormisdas could not be the brother of an elder and posthumous child as stated, but St. Martin suggests that possibly he was an elder brother by another mother who had several children.—O. S.]

they traversed from the Chaboras to the cultivated lands of
Assyria may be considered as a part of the desert of Arabia, a
dry and barren waste, which could never be improved by the
most powerful arts of human industry.   Julian marched over
the same ground which had been trod above seven hundred
years before by the footsteps of the younger Cyrus, and which
is described by one of the companions of his expedition, the sage
and heroic Xenophon.[1]   " The country was a plain throughout,
as even as the sea, and full of wormwood; and if any other kind
of shrubs or reeds grew there, they had all an aromatic smell, but
no trees could be seen.   Bustards and ostriches, antelopes and
wild asses,[2] appeared to be the only inhabitants of the desert,
and the fatigues of the march were alleviated by the amusements
of the chase."   The loose sand of the desert was frequently
raised by the wind into clouds of dust, and a great number of the
soldiers of Julian, with their tents, were suddenly thrown to the
ground by the violence of an unexpected hurricane.

The sandy plains of Mesopotamia were abandoned to the
antelopes and wild asses of the desert, but a variety of populous
towns and villages were pleasantly situated on the banks of the
Euphrates and in the islands which are occasionally formed by
that river.   The city of Anah, or Anatho,[3] the actual residence
of an Arabian emir, is composed of two long streets, which enclose,
within a natural fortification, a small island in the midst, and
two fruitful spots on either side, of the Euphrates.   The warlike
inhabitants of Anatho showed a disposition to stop the march
of a Roman emperor, till they were diverted from such fatal
presumption by the mild exhortations of Prince Hormisdas, and
the approaching terrors of the fleet and army.   They implored

[1] See the first book of the Anabasis [c. 5], p. 45, 46.   This pleasing work
is original and authentic.   Yet Xenophon's memory, perhaps many years
after the expedition, has sometimes betrayed him; and the distances
which he marks are often larger than either a soldier or a geographer will
allow.

[2] Mr. Spelman, the English translator of the Anabasis (vol. i. p. 51), confounds the antelope with the roebuck, and the wild ass with the zebra.

[3] See Voyages de Tavernier, part i. l. iii. p. 316, and more especially
Viaggi di Pietro della Valle, tom. i. lett. xvii. p. 671, etc.   He was ignorant
of the old name and condition of Anah.   Our blind travellers *seldom* possess
any previous knowledge of the countries which they visit.   Shaw and
Tournefort deserve an honourable exception.
[Anah was an important position for commerce in ancient times, and was
probably on the line of a caravan route.   It is mentioned in an ancient
Assyrian inscription under the name Anat, where it is described as stand-
ing in the middle of the Euphrates.   Cf. Layard's Nineveh and Babylon.
Zosimus (says Dr. W. Smith) does not mention Anah, but speaks of a town
in this neighbourhood called Phathusæ, which is probably the same place.
—O. S.]

and experienced the clemency of Julian, who transplanted the people to an advantageous settlement near Chalcis in Syria, and admitted Pusæus, the governor, to an honourable rank in his service and friendship.   But the impregnable fortress of Thilutha could scorn the menace of a siege, and the emperor was obliged to content himself with an insulting promise that, when he had subdued the interior provinces of Persia, Thilutha would no longer refuse to grace the triumph of the conqueror.   The inhabitants of the open towns, unable to resist and unwilling to yield, fled with precipitation, and their houses, filled with spoil and provisions, were occupied by the soldiers of Julian, who massacred, without remorse and without punishment, some defenceless women.   During the march the Surenas, or Persian general, and Malek Rodosaces, the renowned emir of the tribe of Gassan,[1] incessantly hovered round the army; every straggler was intercepted, every detachment was attacked, and the valiant Hormisdas escaped with some difficulty from their hands.   But the barbarians were finally repulsed, the country became every day less favourable to the operations of cavalry, and when the Romans arrived at Macepracta they perceived the ruins of the wall which had been constructed by the ancient kings of Assyria to secure their dominions from the incursions of the Medes. These preliminaries of the expedition of Julian appear to have employed about fifteen days, and we may compute near three hundred miles from the fortress of Circesium to the wall of Macepracta.[2]

The fertile province of Assyria,[3] which stretched beyond the Tigris, as far as the mountains of Media,[4] extended about four

[1] Famosi nominis latro, says Ammianus—a high encomium for an Arab. The tribe of Gassan had settled on the edge of Syria, and reigned some time in Damascus, under a dynasty of thirty-one kings or emirs, from the time of Pompey to that of the Khalif Omar.   D'Herbelot, Bibliothèque Orientale, p. 360. Pococke, Specimen Hist. Arabicæ, p. 75-78.   The name of Rodosaces does not appear in the list.

[Surenas. Gibbon does not seem to be aware, as St. Martin says, that this word is not a title but the name of a great Persian family.—O. S.]

[2] See Ammianus (xxiv. 1, 2), Libanius (Orat. Parental. c. 110, 111, p. 334), Zosimus (l. iii. [c. 15] p. 164-168).

[3] The description of Assyria is furnished by Herodotus (l. i. c. 192, etc.), who sometimes writes for children, and sometimes for philosophers; by Strabo (l. xvi. p. 1070-1082 [p. 736-746, ed. Casaub.]); and by Ammianus (l. xxiii. c. 6). The most useful of the modern travellers are Tavernier (part. i. l. ii. p. 226-258), Otter (tom. ii. p. 35-69, and 189-224), and Niebuhr (tom. ii. p. 172-288).   Yet I much regret that the *Irak Arabi* of Abulfeda has not been translated.

[4] Ammianus remarks that the primitive Assyria, which comprehended Ninus (Nineveh) and Arbela, had assumed the more recent and peculiar appellation of Adiabene; and he seems to fix Teredon, Vologesia, and Apollonia, as the *extreme* cities of the actual province of Assyria.

hundred miles from the ancient wall of Macepracta to the territory of Basra, where the united streams of the Euphrates and
Tigris discharge themselves into the Persian Gulf.[1] The whole
country might have claimed the peculiar name of Mesopotamia,
as the two rivers, which are never more distant than fifty,
approach, between Bagdad and Babylon, within twenty-five
miles of each other.   A multitude of artificial canals, dug without
much labour in a soft and yielding soil, connected the rivers and
intersected the plain of Assyria.   The uses of these artificial
canals were various and important.   They served to discharge
the superfluous waters from one river into the other at the season
of their respective inundations.   Subdividing themselves into
smaller and smaller branches, they refreshed the dry lands and
supplied the deficiency of rain.   They facilitated the intercourse
of peace and commerce, and, as the dams could be speedily
broke down, they armed the despair of the Assyrians with the
means of opposing a sudden deluge to the progress of an invading
army.   To the soil and climate of Assyria nature had denied
some of her choicest gifts—the vine, the olive, and the fig-tree;
but the food which supports the life of man, and particularly
wheat and barley, were produced with inexhaustible fertility,
and the husbandman, who committed his seed to the earth, was
frequently rewarded with an increase of two or even of three
hundred.   The face of the country was interspersed with groves
of innumerable palm-trees,[2] and the diligent natives celebrated,
either in verse or prose, the three hundred and sixty uses to
which the trunk, the branches, the leaves, the juice, and the
fruit were skilfully applied.   Several manufactures, especially
those of leather and linen, employed the industry of a numerous
people, and afforded valuable materials for foreign trade, which
appears, however, to have been conducted by the hands of
strangers.   Babylon had been converted into a royal park, but
near the ruins of the ancient capital new cities had successively
arisen, and the populousness of the country was displayed in
the multitude of towns and villages, which were built of bricks
dried in the sun and strongly cemented with bitumen, the

[1] The two rivers unite at Apamea, or Corna (one hundred miles from the
Persian Gulf), into the broad stream of the Pasitigris, or Shat-ul-Arab.
The Euphrates formerly reached the sea by a separate channel, which was
obstructed and diverted by the citizens of Orchoe, about twenty miles to
the south-east of modern Basra (D'Anville, in the Mémoires de l'Acad. des
Inscriptions, tom. xxx. p. 170-191).

[2] The learned Kæmpfer, as a botanist, an antiquary, and a traveller, has
exhausted (Amœnitat. Exoticæ, Fascicul. iv. p. 660-764) the whole subject
of palm-trees.

natural and peculiar production of the Babylonian soil. While the successors of Cyrus reigned over Asia, the province of Assyria alone maintained, during a third part of the year, the luxurious plenty of the table and household of the Great King. Four considerable villages were assigned for the subsistence of his Indian dogs; eight hundred stallions and sixteen thousand mares were constantly kept, at the expense of the country, for the royal stables; and as the daily tribute which was paid to the satrap amounted to one English bushel of silver, we may compute the annual revenue of Assyria at more than twelve hundred thousand pounds sterling.[1]

The fields of Assyria were devoted by Julian to the calamities of war; and the philosopher retaliated on a guiltless people the acts of rapine and cruelty which had been committed by their haughty master in the Roman provinces. The trembling Assyrians summoned the rivers to their assistance; and completed with their own hands the ruin of their country. The roads were rendered impracticable; a flood of waters was poured into the camp; and, during several days, the troops of Julian were obliged to contend with the most discouraging hardships. But every obstacle was surmounted by the perseverance of the legionaries, who were inured to toil as well as to danger, and who felt themselves animated by the spirit of their leader. The damage was gradually repaired; the waters were restored to their proper channels; whole groves of palm-trees were cut down and placed along the broken parts of the road; and the army passed over the broad and deeper canals on bridges of floating rafts, which were supported by the help of bladders. Two cities of Assyria presumed to resist the arms of a Roman emperor; and they both paid the severe penalty of their rashness. At the distance of fifty miles from the royal residence of Ctesiphon, Perisabor, or Anbar, held the second rank in the province: a city, large, populous, and well fortified, surrounded with a double wall, almost encompassed by a branch of the Euphrates, and defended by the valour of a numerous garrison. The ex-

---

[1] Assyria yielded to the Persian satrap an *artaba* of silver each day. The well-known proportion of weights and measures (see Bishop Hooper's elaborate Inquiry), the specific gravity of water and silver, and the value of that metal, will afford, after a short process, the annual revenue which I have stated. Yet the Great King received no more than 1000 Euboic, or Tyrian, talents (£252,000) from Assyria. The comparison of two passages in Herodotus (l. i. c. 192. l. iii. c. 89-96) reveals an important difference between the *gross* and the *net* revenue of Persia; the sums paid by the province, and the gold or silver deposited in the royal treasure. The monarch might annually save three millions six hundred thousand pounds, of the seventeen or eighteen millions raised upon the people.

hortations of Hormisdas were repulsed with contempt; and the ears of the Persian prince were wounded by a just reproach, that, unmindful of his royal birth, he conducted an army of strangers against his king and country. The Assyrians maintained their loyalty by a skilful as well as vigorous defence, till the lucky stroke of a battering-ram having opened a large breach by shattering one of the angles of the wall, they hastily retired into the fortifications of the interior citadel. The soldiers of Julian rushed impetuously into the town, and, after the full gratification of every military appetite, Perisabor was reduced to ashes; and the engines which assaulted the citadel were planted on the ruins of the smoking houses. The contest was continued by an incessant and mutual discharge of missile weapons; and the superiority which the Romans might derive from the mechanical powers of their balistæ and catapultæ was counterbalanced by the advantage of the ground on the side of the besieged. But as soon as an *Helepolis* had been constructed, which could engage on equal terms with the loftiest ramparts, the tremendous aspect of a moving turret, that would leave no hope of resistance or of mercy, terrified the defenders of the citadel into an humble submission; and the place was surrendered only two days after Julian first appeared under the walls of Perisabor. Two thousand five hundred persons of both sexes, the feeble remnant of a flourishing people, were permitted to retire: the plentiful magazines of corn, of arms, and of splendid furniture, were partly distributed among the troops and partly reserved for the public service; the useless stores were destroyed by fire or thrown into the stream of the Euphrates; and the fate of Amida was revenged by the total ruin of Perisabor.

The city, or rather fortress, of Maogamalcha, which was defended by sixteen large towers, a deep ditch, and two strong and solid walls of brick and bitumen, appears to have been constructed at the distance of eleven miles, as the safeguard of the capital of Persia. The emperor, apprehensive of leaving such an important fortress in his rear, immediately formed the siege of Maogamalcha; and the Roman army was distributed for that purpose into three divisions. Victor, at the head of the cavalry and of a detachment of heavy-armed foot, was ordered to clear the country as far as the banks of the Tigris and the suburbs of Ctesiphon. The conduct of the attack was assumed by Julian himself, who seemed to place his whole dependence in the military engines which he erected against the walls; while he secretly contrived a more efficacious method of introducing his troops into the heart of the city. Under the direction of Nevitta and Dagalaiphus, the trenches were opened at a considerable distance, and gradually prolonged as far as the edge of the ditch. The ditch was speedily filled with earth; and, by the incessant labour of the troops, a mine was carried under the foundations of the walls, and sustained at sufficient intervals by props of timber. Three chosen cohorts, advancing in a single file, silently explored the dark and dangerous passage; till their intrepid leader whispered back the intelligence that he was ready to issue from his confinement into the streets of the hostile city. Julian checked their ardour, that he might ensure their success; and immediately diverted the attention of the garrison by the tumult and clamour of a general assault. The Persians, who from their walls contemptuously beheld the progress of an impotent attack, celebrated with songs of triumph the glory of Sapor; and ventured to assure the emperor that he might ascend the starry mansion of Ormusd before he could hope to take the impregnable city of Maogamalcha. The city was already taken. History has recorded the name of a private soldier, the first who ascended from the mine into a deserted tower. The passage was widened by his companions, who pressed forwards with impatient valour. Fifteen hundred enemies were already in the midst of the city. The astonished garrison abandoned the walls, and their only hope of safety; the gates were instantly burst open; and the revenge of the soldier, unless it were suspended by lust or avarice, was satiated by an undistinguishing massacre. The governor, who had yielded on a promise of mercy, was burnt alive, a few days afterwards, on a charge of having uttered some disrespectful words against the honour of Prince Hormisdas. The fortifications were razed to the ground; and not a vestige was left that the city of Maogamalcha had ever existed. The neighbourhood of the capital of Persia was adorned with three stately palaces, laboriously enriched with every production that could gratify the luxury and pride of an Eastern monarch. The pleasant situation of the gardens along the banks of the Tigris was improved, according to the Persian taste, by the symmetry of flowers, fountains, and shady walks: and spacious parks were enclosed for the reception of the bears, lions, and wild boars, which were maintained at a considerable expense for the pleasure of the royal chase. The park-walls were broken down, the savage game was abandoned to the darts of the soldiers, and the palaces of Sapor were reduced to ashes, by the command of the Roman emperor. Julian, on this occasion, showed himself ignorant or careless of the laws of civility, which the prudence and refinement of polished ages have established between hostile princes. Yet these wanton ravages need not excite in our breasts any vehement emotions of pity or resentment. A simple, naked statue, finished by the hand of a Grecian artist, is of more genuine value than all these rude and costly monuments of barbaric labour; and, if we are more deeply affected by the ruin of a palace than by the conflagration of a cottage, our humanity must have formed a very erroneous estimate of the miseries of human life.[1]

Julian was an object of terror and hatred to the Persians; and the painters of that nation represented the invader of their country under the emblem of a furious lion, who vomited from his mouth a consuming fire.[2] To his friends and soldiers the philosophic hero appeared in a more amiable light; and his virtues were never more conspicuously displayed than in the last and most active period of his life. He practised, without effort, and almost without merit, the habitual qualities of temperance and sobriety. According to the dictates of that artificial wisdom which assumes an absolute dominion over the mind and body, he sternly refused himself the indulgence of the most natural appetites.[3] In the warm climate of Assyria, which solicited a luxurious people to the gratification of every sensual desire,[4] a youthful conqueror preserved his chastity pure and inviolate: nor was Julian ever tempted, even by a motive of curiosity, to visit his female captives of exquisite beauty,[5] who, instead of resisting his power, would have disputed with each other the honour of his embraces. With the same firmness that

[1] The operations of the Assyrian war are circumstantially related by Ammianus (xxiv. 2, 3, 4, 5), Libanius (Orat. Parent. c. 112-123, p. 335-347), Zosimus (l. iii. [c. 18] p. 168-180), and Gregory Nazianzen (Orat. iv. p. 113, 144). The *military* criticisms of the saint are devoutly copied by Tillemont, his faithful slave.

[2] Libanius de ulciscendâ Juliani nece, c. 13, p. 162 [in Fabric. Bibl. Græc. vol. vii.]

[3] The famous examples of Cyrus, Alexander, and Scipio, were acts of justice. Julian's chastity was voluntary, and, in his opinion, meritorious.

[4] Sallust (ap. Vet. Scholiast. Juvenal. Satir. i. 104) observes, that nihil corruptius moribus. The matrons and virgins of Babylon freely mingled with the men in licentious banquets: and as they felt the intoxication of wine and love, they gradually, and almost completely, threw aside the incumbrance of dress; ad ultimum ima corporum velamenta projiciunt. Q. Curtius. v. 1.

[5] Ex virginibus autem, quæ speciosæ sunt captæ, ut in Perside, ubi feminarum pulchritudo excellit, nec contrectare aliquam voluit nec videre. Ammian. xxiv. 4. The native race of Persians is small and ugly; but it has been improved by the perpetual mixture of Circassian blood (Herodot. l. iii. c. 97. Buffon, Hist. Naturelle, tom. iii. p. 420).

he resisted the allurements of love, he sustained the hardships of war. When the Romans marched through the flat and flooded country, their sovereign, on foot, at the head of his legions, shared their fatigues and animated their diligence. In every useful labour the hand of Julian was prompt and strenuous; and the Imperial purple was wet and dirty, as the coarse garment of the meanest soldier. The two sieges allowed him some remarkable opportunities of signalising his personal valour, which, in the improved state of the military art, can seldom be exerted by a prudent general. The emperor stood before the citadel of Perisabor, insensible of his extreme danger, and encouraged his troops to burst open the gates of iron, till he was almost overwhelmed under a cloud of missile weapons and huge stones that were directed against his person. As he examined the exterior fortifications of Maogamalcha, two Persians, devoting themselves for their country, suddenly rushed upon him with drawn scimitars: the emperor dexterously received their blows on his uplifted shield; and, with a steady and well-aimed thrust, laid one of his adversaries dead at his feet. The esteem of a prince who possesses the virtues which he approves is the noblest recompense of a deserving subject; and the authority which Julian derived from his personal merit enabled him to revive and enforce the rigour of ancient discipline. He punished with death, or ignominy, the misbehaviour of three troops of horse, who, in a skirmish with the Surenas, had lost their honour and one of their standards: and he distinguished with *obsidional*[1] crowns the valour of the foremost soldiers who had ascended into the city of Maogamalcha. After the siege of Perisabor the firmness of the emperor was exercised by the insolent avarice of the army, who loudly complained that their services were rewarded by a trifling donative of one hundred pieces of silver. His just indignation was expressed in the grave and manly language of a Roman. " Riches are the object of your desires; those riches are in the hands of the Persians; and the spoils of this fruitful country are proposed as the prize of your valour and discipline. Believe me," added Julian, " the Roman republic, which formerly possessed such immense treasures, is now reduced to want and wretchedness; since our princes have been persuaded, by weak and interested ministers, to purchase with gold the tranquillity of the barbarians. The revenue is exhausted; the

[1] Obsidionalibus coronis donati. Ammian. xxiv. 4. Either Julian or his historian were unskilful antiquaries. He should have given *mural* crowns. The *obsidional* were the reward of a general who had delivered a besieged city (Aulus Gellius, Noct. Attic. v. 6).

cities are ruined; the provinces are dispeopled. For myself, the only inheritance that I have received from my royal ancestors is a soul incapable of fear; and as long as I am convinced that every real advantage is seated in the mind, I shall not blush to acknowledge an honourable poverty, which in the days of ancient virtue was considered as the glory of Fabricius. That glory, and that virtue, may be your own, if you will listen to the voice of Heaven and of your leader. But if you will rashly persist, if you are determined to renew the shameful and mischievous examples of old seditions, proceed. As it becomes an emperor who has filled the first rank among men, I am prepared to die standing, and to despise a precarious life which every hour may depend on an accidental fever. If I have been found unworthy of the command, there are now among you (I speak it with pride and pleasure), there are many chiefs whose merit and experience are equal to the conduct of the most important war. Such has been the temper of my reign, that I can retire, without regret and without apprehension, to the obscurity of a private station." [1] The modest resolution of Julian was answered by the unanimous applause and cheerful obedience of the Romans, who declared their confidence of victory while they fought under the banners of their heroic prince. Their courage was kindled by his frequent and familiar asseverations (for such wishes were the oaths of Julian), " So may I reduce the Persians under the yoke!" " Thus may I restore the strength and splendour of the republic!" The love of fame was the ardent passion of his soul: but it was not before he trampled on the ruins of Maogamalcha that he allowed himself to say, " We have now provided some materials for the sophist of Antioch." [2]

The successful valour of Julian had triumphed over all the obstacles that opposed his march to the gates of Ctesiphon. But the reduction, or even the siege, of the capital of Persia was still at a distance: nor can the military conduct of the emperor be clearly apprehended without a knowledge of the country which was the theatre of his bold and skilful operations.[3]

---

[1] I give this speech as original and genuine. Ammianus might hear, could transcribe, and was incapable of inventing, it. I have used some slight freedoms, and conclude with the most forcible sentence.

[2] Ammian. xxiv. 3. Libanius, Orat. Parent. c. 122, p. 346.

[3] M. d'Anville (Mém. de l'Académie des Inscriptions, tom. xxviii. p. 246-259) has ascertained the true position and distance of Babylon, Seleucia, Ctesiphon, Bagdad, etc. The Roman traveller, Pietro della Valle (tom. i. lett. xvii. p. 650-780), seems to be the most intelligent spectator of that famous province. He is a gentleman and a scholar, but intolerably vain and prolix.

Twenty miles to the south of Bagdad, and on the eastern bank
of the Tigris, the curiosity of travellers has observed some ruins
of the palaces of Ctesiphon, which in the time of Julian was a
great and populous city. The name and glory of the adjacent
Seleucia were for ever extinguished; and the only remaining
quarter of that Greek colony had resumed, with the Assyrian
language and manners, the primitive appellation of Coche.
Coche was situate on the western side of the Tigris; but it was
naturally considered as a suburb of Ctesiphon, with which we
may suppose it to have been connected by a permanent bridge
of boats. The united parts contributed to form the common
epithet of Al Modain, THE CITIES, which the Orientals have
bestowed on the winter residence of the Sassanides; and the
whole circumference of the Persian capital was strongly fortified
by the waters of the river, by lofty walls, and by impracticable
morasses. Near the ruins of Seleucia the camp of Julian was
fixed, and secured by a ditch and rampart against the sallies of
the numerous and enterprising garrison of Coche. In this fruitful and pleasant country the Romans were plentifully supplied
with water and forage: and several forts, which might have
embarrassed the motions of the army, submitted, after some
resistance, to the efforts of their valour. The fleet passed from
the Euphrates into an artificial deviation of that river, which
pours a copious and navigable stream into the Tigris at a small
distance *below* the great city. If they had followed this royal
canal, which bore the name of Nahar-Malcha,[1] the intermediate
situation of Coche would have separated the fleet and army of
Julian; and the rash attempt of steering against the current of
the Tigris, and forcing their way through the midst of a hostile
capital, must have been attended with the total destruction of
the Roman navy. The prudence of the emperor foresaw the
danger, and provided the remedy. As he had minutely studied
the operations of Trajan in the same country, he soon recollected
that his warlike predecessor had dug a new and navigable canal,
which, leaving Coche on the right hand, conveyed the waters of
the Nahar-Malcha into the river Tigris at some distance *above*
the cities. From the information of the peasants Julian ascertained the vestiges of this ancient work, which were almost
obliterated by design or accident. By the indefatigable labour

---

[1] The Royal Canal (*Nahar-Malcha*) might be successively restored,
altered, divided, etc. (Cellarius, Geograph. Antiq. tom. ii. p. 453): and
these changes may serve to explain the seeming contradictions of antiquity.
In the time of Julian it must have fallen into the Euphrates *below* Ctesiphon.

of the soldiers a broad and deep channel was speedily prepared
for the reception of the Euphrates. A strong dyke was constructed to interrupt the ordinary current of the Nahar-Malcha:
a flood of waters rushed impetuously into their new bed; and
the Roman fleet, steering their triumphant course into the Tigris,
derided the vain and ineffectual barriers which the Persians of
Ctesiphon had erected to oppose their passage.

As it became necessary to transport the Roman army over the
Tigris, another labour presented itself, of less toil, but of more
danger, than the preceding expedition. The stream was broad
and rapid, the ascent steep and difficult; and the entrenchments
which had been formed on the ridge of the opposite bank were
lined with a numerous army of heavy cuirassiers, dexterous
archers, and huge elephants; who (according to the extravagant
hyperbole of Libanius) could trample with the same ease a field
of corn or a legion of Romans.[1] In the presence of such an
enemy the construction of a bridge was impracticable; and the
intrepid prince, who instantly seized the only possible expedient,
concealed his design, till the moment of execution, from the
knowledge of the barbarians, of his own troops, and even of his
generals themselves. Under the specious pretence of examining
the state of the magazines, fourscore vessels were gradually
unladen; and a select detachment, apparently destined for some
secret expedition, was ordered to stand to their arms on the first
signal. Julian disguised the silent anxiety of his own mind with
smiles of confidence and joy; and amused the hostile nations
with the spectacle of military games, which he insultingly celebrated under the walls of Coche. The day was consecrated to
pleasure; but, as soon as the hour of supper was past, the emperor
summoned the generals to his tent, and acquainted them that he
had fixed that night for the passage of the Tigris. They stood
in silent and respectful astonishment; but when the venerable
Sallust assumed the privilege of his age and experience, the rest
of the chiefs supported with freedom the weight of his prudent
remonstrances.[2] Julian contented himself with observing that
conquest and safety depended on the attempt; that, instead of
diminishing, the number of their enemies would be increased by
successive reinforcements; and that a longer delay would neither

---

[1] Καὶ μεγέθεσιν ἐλεφάντων, οἷς ἴσον ἔργον διὰ σταχύων ἐλθεῖν καὶ φάλαγγος.
[Or. Parent. c. 125.] Rien n'est beau que le vrai; a maxim which should
be inscribed on the desk of every rhetorician.

[2] Libanius alludes to the most powerful of the generals. I have ventured
to name *Sallust*. Ammianus [xxiv. 6] says, of all the leaders, quòd acri
metû territi duces concordi precatû fieri prohibere tentarent.

contract the breadth of the stream nor level the height of the bank. The signal was instantly given, and obeyed: the most impatient of the legionaries leaped into five vessels that lay nearest to the bank; and, as they plied their oars with intrepid diligence, they were lost after a few moments in the darkness of the night. A flame arose on the opposite side; and Julian, who too clearly understood that his foremost vessels in attempting to land had been fired by the enemy, dexterously converted their extreme danger into a presage of victory. "Our fellow-soldiers," he eagerly exclaimed, "are already masters of the bank: see— they make the appointed signal; let us hasten to emulate and assist their courage." The united and rapid motion of a great fleet broke the violence of the current, and they reached the eastern shore of the Tigris with sufficient speed to extinguish the flames and rescue their adventurous companions. The diffi- culties of a steep and lofty ascent were increased by the weight of armour and the darkness of the night. A shower of stones, darts, and fire was incessantly discharged on the heads of the assailants; who, after an arduous struggle, climbed the bank and stood victorious upon the rampart. As soon as they possessed a more equal field, Julian, who with his light infantry had led the attack,[1] darted through the ranks a skilful and experienced eye: his bravest soldiers, according to the precepts of Homer,[2] were distributed in the front and rear; and all the trumpets of the Imperial army sounded to battle. The Romans, after sending up a military shout, advanced in measured steps to the animating notes of martial music; launched their formidable javelins, and rushed forwards with drawn swords to deprive the barbarians, by a closer onset, of the advantage of their missile weapons. The whole engagement lasted above twelve hours; till the gradual retreat of the Persians was changed into a disorderly flight, of which the shameful example was given by the principal leaders and the Surenas himself. They were pursued to the gates of Ctesiphon; and the conquerors might have entered the dis- mayed city,[3] if their general, Victor, who was dangerously

[1] Hinc Imperator . . . (says Ammianus) ipse cum levis armaturæ auxiliis per prima postremaque discurrens, etc. Yet Zosimus, his friend, does not allow him to pass the river till two days after the battle.

[2] Secundum Homericam dispositionem. A similar disposition is ascribed to the wise Nestor, in the fourth book of the Iliad; and Homer was never absent from the mind of Julian.

[3] Persas terrore subito miscuerunt, versisque agminibus totius gentis, apertas Ctesiphontis portas victor miles intrâsset, ni major prædarum occasio fuisset, quam cura victoriæ (Sextus Rufus de Provinciis, c. 28). Their avarice might dispose them to hear the advice of Victor.

wounded with an arrow, had not conjured them to desist from a rash attempt, which must be fatal if it were not successful.   On *their* side the Romans acknowledged the loss of only seventy-five men; while they affirmed that the barbarians had left on the field of battle two thousand five hundred, or even six thousand, of their bravest soldiers.   The spoil was such as might be expected from the riches and luxury of an Oriental camp; large quantities of silver and gold, splendid arms and trappings, and beds and tables of massive silver.   The victorious emperor distributed, as the rewards of valour, some honourable gifts, civic, and mural, and naval crowns; which he, and perhaps he alone, esteemed more precious than the wealth of Asia.   A solemn sacrifice was offered to the god of war, but the appearances of the victims threatened the most inauspicious events; and Julian soon discovered, by less ambiguous signs, that he had now reached the term of his prosperity.[1]

On the second day after the battle the domestic guards, the Jovians and Herculians, and the remaining troops, which composed near two-thirds of the whole army, were securely wafted over the Tigris.[2]   While the Persians beheld from the walls of Ctesiphon the desolation of the adjacent country, Julian cast many an anxious look towards the North, in full expectation that, as he himself had victoriously penetrated to the capital of Sapor, the march and junction of his lieutenants, Sebastian and Procopius, would be executed with the same courage and diligence. His expectations were disappointed by the treachery of the Armenian king, who permitted, and most probably directed, the desertion of his auxiliary troops from the camp of the Romans;[3] and by the dissensions of the two generals, who were incapable of forming or executing any plan for the public service. When the emperor had relinquished the hope of this important reinforcement, he condescended to hold a council of war, and

---

[1] The labour of the canal, the passage of the Tigris, and the victory, are described by Ammianus (xxiv. 5, 6), Libanius (Orat. Parent. c. 124-128, p. 347-353), Greg. Nazianzen (Orat. iv. p. 115), Zosimus (l. iii. [c. 24, p. 159 *sqq.*] p. 181-183), and Sextus Rufus (de Provinciis, c. 28).

[2] The fleet and army were formed in three divisions, of which the first only had passed during the night (Ammian. xxiv. 6).   The πᾶσα δορυφορία, whom Zosimus transports on the third day (l. iii. [c. 26] p. 183), might consist of the protectors, among whom the historian Ammianus, and the future emperor Jovian, actually served; some *schools* of the *domestics ;* and perhaps the Jovians and Herculians, who often did duty as guards.

[3] Moses of Chorene (Hist. Armen. l. iii. c. 15, p. 246) supplies us with a national tradition and a spurious letter.   I have borrowed only the leading circumstance, which is consistent with truth, probability, and Libanius (Orat. Parent. c. 131, p. 355).

approved, after a full debate, the sentiment of those generals who dissuaded the siege of Ctesiphon, as a fruitless and pernicious undertaking. It is not easy for us to conceive by what arts of fortification a city thrice besieged and taken by the predecessors of Julian could be rendered impregnable against an army of sixty thousand Romans, commanded by a brave and experienced general, and abundantly supplied with ships, provisions, battering engines, and military stores. But we may rest assured, from the love of glory, and contempt of danger, which formed the character of Julian, that he was not discouraged by any trivial or imaginary obstacles.[1] At the very time when he declined the siege of Ctesiphon, he rejected, with obstinacy and disdain, the most flattering offers of a negotiation of peace. Sapor, who had been so long accustomed to the tardy ostentation of Constantius, was surprised by the intrepid diligence of his successor. As far as the confines of India and Scythia, the satraps of the distant provinces were ordered to assemble their troops, and to march, without delay, to the assistance of their monarch. But their preparations were dilatory, their motions slow; and before Sapor could lead an army into the field, he received the melancholy intelligence of the devastation of Assyria, the ruin of his palaces, and the slaughter of his bravest troops, who defended the passage of the Tigris. The pride of royalty was humbled in the dust; he took his repasts on the ground; and the disorder of his hair expressed the grief and anxiety of his mind. Perhaps he would not have refused to purchase, with one half of his kingdom, the safety of the remainder; and he would have gladly subscribed himself, in a treaty of peace, the faithful and dependent ally of the Roman conqueror. Under the pretence of private business, a minister of rank and confidence was secretly despatched to embrace the knees of Hormisdas, and to request, in the language of a suppliant, that he might be introduced into the presence of the emperor. The Sassanian prince, whether he listened to the voice of pride or humanity, whether he consulted the sentiments of his birth or the duties of his situation, was equally inclined to promote a salutary measure which would terminate the calamities of Persia, and secure the triumph of Rome. He was astonished by the inflexible firmness of a hero who remembered, most unfortunately for himself and for his

---

[1] Civitas inexpugnabilis, facinus audax et importunum. Ammianus, xxiv. 7. His fellow-soldier, Eutropius, turns aside from the difficulty: Assyriamque populatus, castra apud Ctesiphontem stativa aliquandiu habuit: remeansque victor, etc., x. 16 [8]. Zosimus is artful or ignorant, and Socrates inaccurate.

country, that Alexander had uniformly rejected the propositions of Darius. But as Julian was sensible that the hope of a safe and honourable peace might cool the ardour of his troops, he earnestly requested that Hormisdas would privately dismiss the minister of Sapor, and conceal this dangerous temptation from the knowledge of the camp.[1]

The honour, as well as interest, of Julian, forbade him to consume his time under the impregnable walls of Ctesiphon; and as often as he defied the barbarians, who defended the city, to meet him on the open plain, they prudently replied that, if he desired to exercise his valour, he might seek the army of the Great King. He felt the insult, and he accepted the advice. Instead of confining his servile march to the banks of the Euphrates and Tigris, he resolved to imitate the adventurous spirit of Alexander, and boldly to advance into the inland provinces, till he forced his rival to contend with him, perhaps in the plains of Arbela, for the empire of Asia. The magnanimity of Julian was applauded and betrayed by the arts of a noble Persian, who, in the cause of his country, had generously submitted to act a part full of danger, of falsehood, and of shame.[2] With a train of faithful followers he deserted to the Imperial camp; exposed, in a specious tale, the injuries which he had sustained; exaggerated the cruelty of Sapor, the discontent of the people, and the weakness of the monarchy; and confidently offered himself as the hostage and guide of the Roman march. The most rational grounds of suspicion were urged, without effect, by the wisdom and experience of Hormisdas; and the credulous Julian, receiving the traitor into his bosom, was persuaded to issue an hasty order, which, in the opinion of mankind, appeared to arraign his prudence and to endanger his safety. He destroyed in a single hour the whole navy, which had been transported above five hundred miles, at so great an expense of toil, of treasure, and of blood. Twelve, or, at the most, twenty-two, small vessels were saved, to accompany, on carriages, the march of the army, and to form occasional bridges for the passage of the rivers. A supply of twenty days'

---

[1] Libanius, Orat. Parent. c. 130, p. 354, c. 139, p. 361.　Socrates, l. iii. c. 21. The ecclesiastical historian imputes the refusal of peace to the advice of Maximus. Such advice was unworthy of a philosopher; but the philosopher was likewise a magician, who flattered the hopes and passions of his master.

[2] The arts of this new Zopyrus (Greg. Nazianzen, Orat. iv. p. 115, 116 [ed. Par. 1609]) may derive some credit from the testimony of two abbreviators (Sextus Rufus and Victor), and the casual hints of Libanius (Orat. Parent. c. 134, p. 357) and Ammianus (xxiv. 7). The course of genuine history is interrupted by a most unseasonable chasm in the text of Ammianus.

provisions was reserved for the use of the soldiers; and the rest of the magazines, with a fleet of eleven hundred vessels, which rode at anchor in the Tigris, were abandoned to the flames by the absolute command of the emperor. The Christian bishops, Gregory and Augustin, insult the madness of the apostate, who executed, with his own hands, the sentence of divine justice. Their authority, of less weight, perhaps, in a military question, is confirmed by the cool judgment of an experienced soldier, who was himself spectator of the conflagration, and who could not disapprove the reluctant murmurs of the troops.[1] Yet there are not wanting some specious, and perhaps solid, reasons, which might justify the resolution of Julian. The navigation of the Euphrates never ascended above Babylon, nor that of the Tigris above Opis.[2] The distance of the last-mentioned city from the Roman camp was not very considerable; and Julian must soon have renounced the vain and impracticable attempt of forcing upwards a great fleet against the stream of a rapid river,[3] which in several places was embarrassed by natural or artificial cataracts.[4] The power of sails and oars was insufficient; it became necessary to tow the ships against the current of the river; the strength of twenty thousand soldiers was exhausted in this tedious and servile labour; and if the Romans continued to march along the banks of the Tigris, they could only expect to return home without achieving any enterprise worthy of the genius or fortune of their leader. If, on the contrary, it was advisable to advance into the inland country, the destruction of the fleet and magazines was the only measure which could save that valuable prize from the hands of the numerous and active troops which might suddenly be poured from the gates of Ctesiphon. Had the arms of Julian been victorious, we should now admire the conduct as well as the courage of a hero who, by

[1] See Ammianus (xxiv. 7), Libanius (Orat. Parentalis, c. 132, 133, p. 356, 357), Zosimus (l. iii. [c. 26] p. 183), Zonaras (tom. ii. l. xiii. [c. 13] p. 26), Gregory (Orat. iv. p. 116), and Augustin (de Civitate Dei, l. iv. c. 29, l. v. c. 21). Of these Libanius alone attempts a faint apology for his hero; who, according to Ammianus, pronounced his own condemnation by a tardy and ineffectual attempt to extinguish the flames.

[2] Consult Herodotus (l. i. c. 194), Strabo (l. xvi. p. 1074 [p. 739, ed. Casaub.]), and Tavernier (part i. l. ii. p. 152).

[3] A celeritate Tigris incipit vocari, ita appellant Medi sagittam. Plin. Hist. Natur. vi. 31.

[4] One of these dykes, which produces an artificial cascade or cataract, is described by Tavernier (part i. l. ii. p. 226) and Thevenot (part ii. l. i. p. 193). The Persians, or Assyrians, laboured to interrupt the navigation of the river (Strabo, l. xvi. p. 1075 [p. 740]. D'Anville, l'Euphrate et le Tigre, p. 98, 99).

depriving his soldiers of the hopes of a retreat, left them only the alternative of death or conquest.[1]

The cumbersome train of artillery and waggons, which retards the operations of a modern army, was in a great measure unknown in the camps of the Romans.[2] Yet, in every age, the subsistence of sixty thousand men must have been one of the most important cares of a prudent general; and that subsistence could only be drawn from his own or from the enemy's country. Had it been possible for Julian to maintain a bridge of communication on the Tigris, and to preserve the conquered places of Assyria, a desolated province could not afford any large or regular supplies in a season of the year when the lands were covered by the inundation of the Euphrates,[3] and the unwholesome air was darkened with swarms of innumerable insects.[4] The appearance of the hostile country was far more inviting. The extensive region that lies between the river Tigris and the mountains of Media was filled with villages and towns; and the fertile soil, for the most part, was in a very improved state of cultivation. Julian might expect that a conqueror who possessed the two forcible instruments of persuasion, steel and gold, would easily procure a plentiful subsistence from the fears or avarice of the natives. But on the approach of the Romans this rich and smiling prospect was instantly blasted. Wherever they moved, the inhabitants deserted the open villages and took shelter in the fortified towns; the cattle was driven away; the grass and ripe corn were consumed with fire; and, as soon as the flames had subsided which interrupted the march of Julian, he beheld the melancholy face of a smoking and naked desert. This desperate but effectual method of defence can only be executed by the enthusiasm of a people who prefer their independence to their property; or by the rigour of an arbitrary government, which consults the public safety without submitting to their inclinations the liberty

[1] Recollect the successful and applauded rashness of Agathocles and Cortez, who burnt their ships on the coast of Africa and Mexico.

[2] See the judicious reflections of the author of the Essai sur la Tactique, tom. ii. p. 287-353, and the learned remarks of M. Guichardt, Nouveaux Mémoires Militaires, tom. i. p. 351-382, on the baggage and subsistence of the Roman armies.

[3] The Tigris rises to the south, the Euphrates to the north, of the Armenian mountains. The former overflows in March, the latter in July. These circumstances are well explained in the Geographical Dissertation of Foster, inserted in Spelman's Expedition of Cyrus, vol. ii. p. 26.

[4] Ammianus (xxiv. 8) describes, as he had felt, the inconveniency of the flood, the heat, and the insects. The lands of Assyria, oppressed by the Turks, and ravaged by the Curds or Arabs, yield an increase of ten, fifteen, and twenty fold, for the seed which is cast into the ground by the wretched and unskilful husbandmen. Voyages de Niebuhr, tom. ii. p. 279, 285.

of choice. On the present occasion the zeal and obedience of the Persians seconded the commands of Sapor; and the emperor was soon reduced to the scanty stock of provisions which continually wasted in his hands. Before they were entirely consumed he might still have reached the wealthy and unwarlike cities of Ecbatana or Susa by the effort of a rapid and well-directed march;[1] but he was deprived of this last resource by his ignorance of the roads and by the perfidy of his guides. The Romans wandered several days in the country to the eastward of Bagdad; the Persian deserter, who had artfully led them into the snare, escaped from their resentment; and his followers, as soon as they were put to the torture, confessed the secret of the conspiracy. The visionary conquests of Hyrcania and India, which had so long amused, now tormented, the mind of Julian. Conscious that his own imprudence was the cause of the public distress, he anxiously balanced the hopes of safety or success without obtaining a satisfactory answer either from gods or men. At length, as the only practicable measure, he embraced the resolution of directing his steps towards the banks of the Tigris, with the design of saving the army by a hasty march to the confines of Corduene, a fertile and friendly province, which acknowledged the sovereignty of Rome. The desponding troops obeyed the signal of the retreat, only seventy days after they had passed the Chaboras with the sanguine expectation of subverting the throne of Persia.[2]

As long as the Romans seemed to advance into the country, their march was observed and insulted from a distance by several bodies of Persian cavalry; who, showing themselves, sometimes in loose, and sometimes in closer order, faintly skirmished with the advanced guards. These detachments were, however, supported by a much greater force; and the heads of the columns were no sooner pointed towards the Tigris than a cloud of dust arose on the plain. The Romans, who now aspired only to the permission of a safe and speedy retreat, endeavoured to persuade themselves that this formidable appearance was occasioned by a troop of wild asses, or perhaps by the approach

[1] Isidore of Charax (Mansion, Parthic. p. 5, 6, in Hudson, Geograph. Minor. tom. ii.) reckons 129 schœni from Seleucia, and Thevenot (part i. l. i. ii. p. 209-245) 128 hours of march from Bagdad to Ecbatana, or Hamadan. These measures cannot exceed an ordinary parasang, or three Roman miles.

[2] The march of Julian from Ctesiphon is circumstantially, but not clearly, described by Ammianus (xxiv. 7, 8), Libanius (Orat. Parent. c. 134, p. 357), and Zosimus (l. iii. [c. 26] p. 183). The two last seem ignorant that their conqueror was retreating; and Libanius absurdly confines him to the banks of the Tigris.

of some friendly Arabs. They halted, pitched their tents, fortified their camp, passed the whole night in continual alarms; and discovered at the dawn of day that they were surrounded by an army of Persians. This army, which might be considered only as the van of the barbarians, was soon followed by the main body of cuirassiers, archers, and elephants, commanded by Meranes, a general of rank and reputation. He was accompanied by two of the king's sons and many of the principal satraps; and fame and expectation exaggerated the strength of the remaining powers, which slowly advanced under the conduct of Sapor himself. As the Romans continued their march, their long array, which was forced to bend or divide, according to the varieties of the ground, afforded frequent and favourable opportunities to their vigilant enemies. The Persians repeatedly charged with fury; they were repeatedly repulsed with firmness; and the action at Maronga, which almost deserved the name of a battle, was marked by a considerable loss of satraps and elephants, perhaps of equal value in the eyes of their monarch. These splendid advantages were not obtained without an adequate slaughter on the side of the Romans: several officers of distinction were either killed or wounded; and the emperor himself, who, on all occasions of danger, inspired and guided the valour of his troops, was obliged to expose his person and exert his abilities. The weight of offensive and defensive arms, which still constituted the strength and safety of the Romans, disabled them from making any long or effectual pursuit; and as the horsemen of the East were trained to dart their javelins and shoot their arrows at full speed, and in every possible direction,[1] the cavalry of Persia was never more formidable than in the moment of a rapid and disorderly flight. But the most certain and irreparable loss of the Romans was that of time. The hardy veterans, accustomed to the cold climate of Gaul and Germany, fainted under the sultry heat of an Assyrian summer; their vigour was exhausted by the incessant repetition of march and combat; and the progress of the army was suspended by the precautions of a slow and dangerous retreat in the presence of an active enemy. Every day, every hour, as the supply diminished, the value and price of subsistence increased in the Roman camp.[2]

[1] Chardin, the most judicious of modern travellers, describes (tom. iii. p. 57, 58, etc., edit. in 4to.) the education and dexterity of the Persian horsemen. Brissonius (de Regno Persico, p. 650, 661, etc.) has collected the testimonies of antiquity.

[2] In Mark Antony's retreat, an attic chœnix sold for fifty drachmæ, or, in other words, a pound of flour for twelve or fourteen shillings; barley

Julian, who always contented himself with such food as a hungry soldier would have disdained, distributed, for the use of the troops, the provisions of the Imperial household, and whatever could be spared from the sumpter-horses of the tribunes and generals. But this feeble relief served only to aggravate the sense of the public distress; and the Romans began to entertain the most gloomy apprehensions that, before they could reach the frontiers of the empire, they should all perish, either by famine or by the sword of the barbarians.[1]

While Julian struggled with the almost insuperable difficulties of his situation, the silent hours of the night were still devoted to study and contemplation. Whenever he closed his eyes in short and interrupted slumbers, his mind was agitated with painful anxiety: nor can it be thought surprising that the Genius of the empire should once more appear before him, covering with a funereal veil his head and his horn of abundance, and slowly retiring from the Imperial tent. The monarch started from his couch, and, stepping forth to refresh his wearied spirits with the coolness of the midnight air, he beheld a fiery meteor, which shot athwart the sky, and suddenly vanished. Julian was convinced that he had seen the menacing countenance of the god of war;[2] the council which he summoned, of Tuscan Haruspices,[3] unanimously pronounced that he should abstain from action; but, on this occasion, necessity and reason were more prevalent than superstition; and the trumpets sounded at the break of day. The army marched through a hilly country; and the hills had been secretly occupied by the Persians. Julian led the van with the skill and attention of a consummate general; he was alarmed by the intelligence that his rear was suddenly attacked. The heat of the weather had tempted him to lay

---

bread was sold for its weight in silver. It is impossible to peruse the interesting narrative of Plutarch (tom. v. p. 102-116 [c. 45]) without perceiving that Mark Antony and Julian were pursued by the same enemies and involved in the same distress.

[1] Ammian. xxiv. 8, xxv. 1. Zosimus, l. iii. [c. 27, seq.] p. 184, 185, 186. Libanius, Orat. Parent. c. 134, 135, p. 357, 358, 359. The sophist of Antioch appears ignorant that the troops were hungry.

[2] Ammian. xxv. 2. Julian had sworn in a passion, nunquam se Marti sacra facturum (xxiv. 6). Such whimsical quarrels were not uncommon between the gods and their insolent votaries; and even the prudent Augustus, after his fleet had been twice shipwrecked, excluded Neptune from the honours of public processions. See Hume's Philosophical Reflections. Essays, vol. ii. p. 418.

[3] They still retained the monopoly of the vain but lucrative science, which had been invented in Etruria; and professed to derive their knowledge of signs and omens from the ancient books of Tarquitius, a Tuscan sage.

aside his cuirass; but he snatched a shield from one of his
attendants, and hastened, with a sufficient reinforcement, to the
relief of the rear guard. A similar danger recalled the intrepid
prince to the defence of the front; and, as he galloped between
the columns, the centre of the left was attacked, and almost
overpowered, by a furious charge of the Persian cavalry and
elephants. This huge body was soon defeated by the well-
timed evolution of the light infantry, who aimed their weapons,
with dexterity and effect, against the backs of the horsemen,
and the legs of the elephants. The barbarians fled: and Julian,
who was foremost in every danger, animated the pursuit with
his voice and gestures. His trembling guards, scattered and
oppressed by the disorderly throng of friends and enemies,
reminded their fearless sovereign that he was without armour;
and conjured him to decline the fall of the impending ruin. As
they exclaimed,[1] a cloud of darts and arrows was discharged from
the flying squadrons; and a javelin, after razing the skin of
his arm, transpierced the ribs, and fixed in the inferior part of
the liver. Julian attempted to draw the deadly weapon from
his side; but his fingers were cut by the sharpness of the steel,
and he fell senseless from his horse. His guards flew to his
relief; and the wounded emperor was gently raised from the
ground, and conveyed out of the tumult of the battle into an
adjacent tent. The report of the melancholy event passed from
rank to rank; but the grief of the Romans inspired them with
invincible valour, and the desire of revenge. The bloody and
obstinate conflict was maintained by the two armies till they
were separated by the total darkness of the night. The Persians
derived some honour from the advantage which they obtained
against the left wing, where Anatolius, master of the offices,
was slain, and the præfect Sallust very narrowly escaped. But
the event of the day was adverse to the barbarians. They abandoned the field; their two generals, Meranes and Nohordates,[2]
fifty nobles or satraps, and a multitude of their bravest soldiers
[were slain]: and the success of the Romans, if Julian had
survived, might have been improved into a decisive and useful
victory.

The first words that Julian uttered, after his recovery from the

[1] Clamabant hinc inde *candidati* (see the note of Valesius) quos disjecerat
terror, ut fugientium molem tanquam ruinam male compositi culmin.s
declinaret. Ammian. xxv. 3.

[2] Sapor himself declared to the Romans that it was his practice to comfort the families of his deceased satraps by sending them, as a present, the
heads of the guards and officers who had not fallen by their master's side,
Libanius, de nece Julian. ulcis. c. xiii. p. 163.

fainting fit into which he had been thrown by loss of blood, were expressive of his martial spirit. He called for his horse and arms, and was impatient to rush into the battle. His remaining strength was exhausted by the painful effort; and the surgeons, who examined his wound, discovered the symptoms of approaching death. He employed the awful moments with the firm temper of a hero and a sage; the philosophers who had accompanied him in this fatal expedition compared the tent of Julian with the prison of Socrates; and the spectators, whom duty, or friendship, or curiosity, had assembled round his couch, listened with respectful grief to the funeral oration of their dying emperor.[1] " Friends and fellow-soldiers, the seasonable period of my departure is now arrived, and I discharge, with the cheerfulness of a ready debtor, the demands of nature. I have learned from philosophy how much the soul is more excellent than the body; and that the separation of the nobler substance should be the subject of joy, rather than of affliction. I have learned from religion that an early death has often been the reward of piety;[2] and I accept, as a favour of the gods, the mortal stroke that secures me from the danger of disgracing a character which has hitherto been supported by virtue and fortitude. I die without remorse, as I have lived without guilt. I am pleased to reflect on the innocence of my private life; and I can affirm with confidence that the supreme authority, that emanation of the Divine Power, has been preserved in my hands pure and immaculate. Detesting the corrupt and destructive maxims of despotism, I have considered the happiness of the people as the end of government. Submitting my actions to the laws of prudence, of justice, and of moderation, I have trusted the event to the care of Providence. Peace was the object of my counsels, as long as peace was consistent with the public welfare; but when the imperious voice of my country summoned me to arms, I exposed my person to the dangers of war, with the clear foreknowledge (which I had acquired from the art of divination) that I was destined to fall by the sword. I now offer my tribute of gratitude to the Eternal Being, who has not suffered me to

[1] The character and situation of Julian might countenance the suspicion that he had previously composed the elaborate oration, which Ammianus heard, and has transcribed. The version of the Abbé de la Bléterie is faithful and elegant. I have followed him in expressing the Platonic idea of emanations, which is darkly insinuated in the original.

[2] Herodotus (l. i. c. 31) has displayed that doctrine in an agreeable tale. Yet the Jupiter (in the 16th book of the Iliad), who laments with tears of blood the death of Sarpedon his son, had a very imperfect notion of happiness or glory beyond the grave.

perish by the cruelty of a tyrant, by the secret dagger of conspiracy, or by the slow tortures of lingering disease. He has
given me, in the midst of an honourable career, a splendid and
glorious departure from this world; and I hold it equally absurd,
equally base, to solicit, or to decline, the stroke of fate.—Thus
much I have attempted to say; but my strength fails me, and I
feel the approach of death.—I shall cautiously refrain from any
word that may tend to influence your suffrages in the election of
an emperor. My choice might be imprudent or injudicious; and
if it should not be ratified by the consent of the army, it might
be fatal to the person whom I should recommend. I shall only,
as a good citizen, express my hopes that the Romans may be
blessed with the government of a virtuous sovereign." After
this discourse, which Julian pronounced in a firm and gentle
tone of voice, he distributed, by a military testament,[1] the
remains of his private fortune; and making some inquiry why
Anatolius was not present, he understood, from the answer of
Sallust, that Anatolius was killed; and bewailed, with amiable
inconsistency, the loss of his friend. At the same time he re-
proved the immoderate grief of the spectators; and conjured
them not to disgrace, by unmanly tears, the fate of a prince who
in a few moments would be united with heaven and with the
stars.[2] The spectators were silent; and Julian entered into a
metaphysical argument with the philosophers Priscus and
Maximus on the nature of the soul. The efforts which he made,
of mind as well as body, most probably hastened his death.
His wound began to bleed with fresh violence: his respiration
was embarrassed by the swelling of the veins: he called for a
draught of cold water, and, as soon as he had drunk it, expired
without pain, about the hour of midnight. Such was the end
of that extraordinary man, in the thirty-second year of his
age, after a reign of one year and about eight months from the
death of Constantius. In his last moments he displayed, perhaps
with some ostentation, the love of virtue and of fame, which had
been the ruling passions of his life.[3]

---

[1] The soldiers who made their verbal or nuncupatory testaments upon
actual service (in procinctû) were exempted from the formalities of the
Roman law. See Heineccius (Antiquit. Jur. Roman. tom. i. p. 504) and
Montesquieu (Esprit des Loix, l. xxvii.).

[2] This union of the human soul with the divine etherial substance of the
universe is the ancient doctrine of Pythagoras and Plato, but it seems to
exclude any personal or conscious immortality. See Warburton's learned
and rational observations. Divine Legation, vol. ii. p. 199-216.

[3] The whole relation of the death of Julian is given by Ammianus (xxv.
3), an intelligent spectator. Libanius, who turns with horror from the

The triumph of Christianity, and the calamities of the empire, may, in some measure, be ascribed to Julian himself, who had neglected to secure the future execution of his designs by the timely and judicious nomination of an associate and successor. But the royal race of Constantius Chlorus was reduced to his own person; and if he entertained any serious thoughts of investing with the purple the most worthy among the Romans, he was diverted from his resolution by the difficulty of the choice, the jealousy of power, the fear of ingratitude, and the natural presumption of health, of youth, and of prosperity. His unexpected death left the empire without a master, and without an heir, in a state of perplexity and danger which, in the space of fourscore years, had never been experienced, since the election of Diocletian. In a government which had almost forgotten the distinction of pure and noble blood, the superiority of birth was of little moment; the claims of official rank were accidental and precarious; and the candidates who might aspire to ascend the vacant throne could be supported only by the consciousness of personal merit, or by the hopes of popular favour. But the situation of a famished army, encompassed on all sides by an host of barbarians, shortened the moments of grief and deliberation. In this scene of terror and distress, the body of the deceased prince, according to his own directions, was decently embalmed; and, at the dawn of day, the generals convened a military senate, at which the commanders of the legions, and the officers both of cavalry and infantry, were invited to assist. Three or four hours of the night had not passed away without some secret cabals; and when the election of an emperor was proposed, the spirit of faction began to agitate the assembly. Victor and Arinthæus collected the remains of the court of Constantius; the friends of Julian attached themselves to the Gallic chiefs Dagalaiphus and Nevitta; and the most fatal consequences might be apprehended from the discord of two factions, so opposite in their character and interest, in their maxims of government, and perhaps in their religious principles. The superior virtues of Sallust could alone reconcile their divisions and unite their suffrages; and the venerable præfect would immediately have been declared the successor of Julian, if he himself, with sincere and modest firmness, had not alleged his age and infirmities, so unequal to the weight of the diadem. The generals, who were

---

scene, has supplied some circumstances (Orat. Parental. c. 136-140, p. 359-362). The calumnies of Gregory, and the legends of more recent saints, may now be *silently* despised.

surprised and perplexed by his refusal, showed some disposition
to adopt the salutary advice of an inferior officer,[1] that they should
act as they would have acted in the absence of the emperor; that
they should exert their abilities to extricate the army from the
present distress; and, if they were fortunate enough to reach
the confines of Mesopotamia, they should proceed with united
and deliberate counsels in the election of a lawful sovereign.
While they debated, a few voices saluted Jovian, who was no
more than *first*[2] of the domestics, with the names of Emperor and
Augustus. The tumultuary acclamation was instantly repeated
by the guards who surrounded the tent, and passed, in a few
minutes, to the extremities of the line. The new prince, astonished
with his own fortune, was hastily invested with the Imperial
ornaments, and received an oath of fidelity from the generals,
whose favour and protection he so lately solicited. The strongest
recommendation of Jovian was the merit of his father, Count
Varronian, who enjoyed, in honourable retirement, the fruit of
his long services. In the obscure freedom of a private station,
the son indulged his taste for wine and women; yet he supported,
with credit, the character of a Christian[3] and a soldier. Without being conspicuous for any of the ambitious qualifications
which excite the admiration and envy of mankind, the comely
person of Jovian, his cheerful temper, and familiar wit, had gained
the affection of his fellow-soldiers; and the generals of both
parties acquiesced in a popular election which had not been conducted by the arts of their enemies. The pride of this unexpected elevation was moderated by the just apprehension that
the same day might terminate the life and reign of the new
emperor. The pressing voice of necessity was obeyed without
delay; and the first orders issued by Jovian, a few hours after
his predecessor had expired, were to prosecute a march which
could alone extricate the Romans from their actual distress.[4]

[1] Honoratior aliquis miles; perhaps Ammianus himself. The modest
and judicious historian describes the scene of the election, at which he was
undoubtedly present (xxv. 5).

[2] The *primus* or *primicerius* enjoyed the dignity of a senator; and,
though only a tribune, he ranked with the military dukes. Cod. Theodosian. l. vi. tit. xxiv. [leg. 11]. These privileges are perhaps more recent
than the time of Jovian.

[3] The ecclesiastical historians, Socrates (l. iii. c. 22), Sozomen (l. vi. c. 3),
and Theodoret (l. iv. c. 1), ascribe to Jovian the merit of a confessor under
the preceding reign, and piously suppose that he refused the purple till the
whole army unanimously exclaimed that they were Christians. Ammianus,
calmly pursuing his narrative, overthrows the legend by a single sentence.
Hostiis pro Joviano extisque inspectis, pronuntiatum est, etc. (xxv. 6).

[4] Ammianus (xxv. 10) has drawn from the life an impartial portrait of
Jovian, to which the younger Victor has added some remarkable strokes.

The esteem of an enemy is most sincerely expressed by his fears; and the degree of fear may be accurately measured by the joy with which he celebrates his deliverance. The welcome news of the death of Julian, which a deserter revealed to the camp of Sapor, inspired the desponding monarch with a sudden confidence of victory. He immediately detached the royal cavalry, perhaps the ten thousand *Immortals*,[1] to second and support the pursuit; and discharged the whole weight of his united forces on the rear-guard of the Romans. The rear-guard was thrown into disorder; the renowned legions, which derived their titles from Diocletian and his warlike colleague, were broke and trampled down by the elephants; and three tribunes lost their lives in attempting to stop the flight of their soldiers. The battle was at length restored by the persevering valour of the Romans; the Persians were repulsed with a great slaughter of men and elephants; and the army, after marching and fighting a long summer's day, arrived, in the evening, at Samara, on the banks of the Tigris, about one hundred miles above Ctesiphon.[2] On the ensuing day the barbarians, instead of harassing the march, attacked the camp of Jovian, which had been seated in a deep and sequestered valley. From the hills, the archers of Persia insulted and annoyed the wearied legionaries; and a body of cavalry, which had penetrated with desperate courage through the Prætorian gate, was cut in pieces, after a doubtful conflict, near the Imperial tent. In the succeeding night the camp of Carche was protected by the lofty dykes of the river; and the Roman army, though incessantly exposed to the vexatious pursuit of the Saracens, pitched their tents near the city of Dura [3] four days after the death of Julian. The Tigris was still on their left; their hopes and provisions were almost consumed; and the impatient soldiers, who had fondly persuaded

---

The Abbé de la Bléterie (Histoire de Jovien, tom. i. p. 1-238) has composed an elaborate history of his short reign—a work remarkably distinguished by elegance of style, critical disquisition, and religious prejudice.

[1] Regius equitatus. It appears from Procopius that the Immortals, so famous under Cyrus and his successors, were revived, if we may use that improper word, by the Sassanides. Brisson. de Regno Persico, p. 268, etc.

[2] The obscure villages of the inland country are irrecoverably lost; nor can we name the field of battle where Julian fell: but M. d'Anville has demonstrated the precise situation of Sumere, Carche, and Dura, along the banks of the Tigris (Géographie Ancienne, tom. ii. p. 248; l'Euphrate et le Tigre, p. 95, 97). In the ninth century, Sumere, or Samara, became, with a slight change of name, the royal residence of the khalifs of the house of Abbas.

[3] Dura was a fortified place in the wars of Antiochus against the rebels of Media and Persia (Polybius, l. v. c. 48, 52, p. 548, 552, edit. Casaubon, in 8vo.).

themselves that the frontiers of the empire were not far distant, requested their new sovereign that they might be permitted to hazard the passage of the river. With the assistance of his wisest officers, Jovian endeavoured to check their rashness, by representing that, if they possessed sufficient skill and vigour to stem the torrent of a deep and rapid stream, they would only deliver themselves naked and defenceless to the barbarians, who had occupied the opposite banks. Yielding at length to their clamorous importunities, he consented, with reluctance, that five hundred Gauls and Germans, accustomed from their infancy to the waters of the Rhine and Danube, should attempt the bold adventure, which might serve either as an encouragement or as a warning for the rest of the army. In the silence of the night they swam the Tigris, surprised an unguarded post of the enemy, and displayed at the dawn of day the signal of their resolution and fortune. The success of this trial disposed the emperor to listen to the promises of his architects, who proposed to construct a floating bridge of the inflated skins of sheep, oxen, and goats, covered with a floor of earth and fascines.[1] Two important days were spent in the ineffectual labour; and the Romans, who already endured the miseries of famine, cast a look of despair on the Tigris, and upon the barbarians, whose numbers and obstinacy increased with the distress of the Imperial army.[2]

In this hopeless situation, the fainting spirits of the Romans were revived by the sound of peace. The transient presumption of Sapor had vanished: he observed, with serious concern, that, in the repetition of doubtful combats, he had lost his most faithful and intrepid nobles, his bravest troops, and the greatest part of his train of elephants: and the experienced monarch feared to provoke the resistance of despair, the vicissitudes of fortune, and the unexhausted powers of the Roman empire, which might soon advance to relieve, or to revenge, the successor of Julian. The Surenas himself, accompanied by another satrap, appeared in the camp of Jovian,[3] and declared that the

---

[1] A similar expedient was proposed to the leaders of the ten thousand, and wisely rejected. Xenophon, Anabasis, l. iii..[c. v. §§ 9-11] p. 255, 256, 257. It appears from our modern travellers that rafts floating on bladders perform the trade and navigation of the Tigris.

[2] The first military acts of the reign of Jovian are related by Ammianus (xxv. 6), Libanius (Orat. Parent. c. 143, p. 364), and Zosimus (l. iii. [c. 30] p. 189, 190, 191). Though we may distrust the fairness of Libanius, the ocular testimony of Eutropius (uno a Persis atque altero proelio victus, x. 17 [9] must incline us to suspect that Ammianus has been too jealous of the honour of the Roman arms.

[3] Sextus Rufus (de Provinciis, c. 29) embraces a poor subterfuge of

clemency of his sovereign was not averse to signify the conditions on which he would consent to spare and to dismiss the Cæsar with the relics of his captive army. The hopes of safety subdued the firmness of the Romans; the emperor was compelled, by the advice of his council and the cries of the soldiers, to embrace the offer of peace; and the præfect Sallust was immediately sent, with the general Arinthæus, to understand the pleasure of the Great King. The crafty Persian delayed, under various pretences, the conclusion of the agreement; started difficulties, required explanations, suggested expedients, receded from his concessions, increased his demands, and wasted four days in the arts of negotiation, till he had consumed the stock of provisions which yet remained in the camp of the Romans. Had Jovian been capable of executing a bold and prudent measure, he would have continued his march with unremitting diligence; the progress of the treaty would have suspended the attacks of the barbarians; and, before the expiration of the fourth day, he might have safely reached the fruitful province of Corduene, at the distance only of one hundred miles.[1] The irresolute emperor, instead of breaking through the toils of the enemy, expected his fate with patient resignation; and accepted the humiliating conditions of peace which it was no longer in his power to refuse. The five provinces beyond the Tigris, which had been ceded by the grandfather of Sapor, were restored to the Persian monarchy. He acquired, by a single article, the impregnable city of Nisibis, which had sustained, in three successive sieges, the effort of his arms. Singara and the castle of the Moors, one of the strongest places of Mesopotamia, were likewise dismembered from the empire. It was considered as an indulgence that the inhabitants of those fortresses were permitted to retire with their effects; but the conqueror rigorously insisted that the Romans should for ever abandon the king and kingdom of Armenia. A peace, or rather a long truce, of thirty years, was stipulated between the hostile nations; the faith of the treaty was ratified by solemn oaths and religious ceremonies; and hostages of distinguished rank were reciprocally delivered to secure the performance of the conditions.[2]

national vanity. Tanta reverentia nominis Romani fuit, ut a Persis *primus* de pace sermo haberetur.

[1] It is presumptuous to controvert the opinion of Ammianus, a soldier and a spectator. Yet it is difficult to understand *how* the mountains of Corduene could extend over the plain of Assyria as low as the conflux of the Tigris and the Great Zab, or *how* an army of sixty thousand men could march one hundred miles in four days.

[2] The treaty of Dura is recorded with grief or indignation by Ammianus

The sophist of Antioch, who saw with indignation the sceptre of his hero in the feeble hand of a Christian successor, professes to admire the moderation of Sapor in contenting himself with so small a portion of the Roman empire. If he had stretched as far as the Euphrates the claims of his ambition, he might have been secure, says Libanius, of not meeting with a refusal. If he had fixed, as the boundary of Persia, the Orontes, the Cydnus, the Sangarius, or even the Thracian Bosphorus, flatterers would not have been wanting in the court of Jovian to convince the timid monarch that his remaining provinces would still afford the most ample gratifications of power and luxury.[1] Without adopting in its full force this malicious insinuation, we must acknowledge that the conclusion of so ignominious a treaty was facilitated by the private ambition of Jovian. The obscure domestic, exalted to the throne by fortune, rather than by merit, was impatient to escape from the hands of the Persians, that he might prevent the designs of Procopius, who commanded the army of Mesopotamia, and establish his doubtful reign over the legions and provinces which were still ignorant of the hasty and tumultuous choice of the camp beyond the Tigris.[2] In the neighbourhood of the same river, at no very considerable distance from the fatal station of Dura,[3] the ten thousand Greeks, without generals, or guides, or provisions, were abandoned, above twelve hundred miles from their native country, to the resentment of a victorious monarch. The difference of *their* conduct and success depended much more on their character than on their situation. Instead of tamely resigning themselves to the secret deliberations and private views of a single person, the united councils of the Greeks were inspired by the generous enthusiasm of a popular assembly, where the mind of each

---

(xxv. 7), Libanius (Orat. Parent. c. 142, p. 364), Zosimus (l. iii. [c. 31] p. 190, 191), Gregory Nazianzen (Orat. iv. p. 117, 118, who imputes the distress to Julian, the deliverance to Jovian), and Eutropius (x. 17 [9]). The last-mentioned writer, who was present in a military station, styles this peace necessariam quidem sed ignobilem.

[1] Libanius, Orat. Parent. c. 143, p. 364, 365.

[2] Conditionibus . . . dispendiosis Romanæ reipublicæ impositis . . . quibus cupidior regni quam gloriæ Jovianus, imperio rudis, adquievit. Sextus Rufus de Provinciis, c. 29. La Bléterie has expressed, in a long, direct oration, these specious considerations of public and private interest (Hist. de Jovien, tom. i. p. 39, etc.).

[3] The generals were murdered on the banks of the Zabatus (Anabasis, l. ii. [c. v. § 1] p. 156, l. iii. c. iii. § 6] p. 226), or Great Zab, a river of Assyria, 400 feet broad, which falls into the Tigris fourteen hours below Mosul. The error of the Greeks bestowed on the Great and Lesser Zab the names of the *Wolf* (Lycus) and the *Goat* (Capros). They created these animals to attend the *Tiger* of the East.

citizen is filled with the love of glory, the pride of freedom, and the contempt of death. Conscious of their superiority over the barbarians in arms and discipline, they disdained to yield, they refused to capitulate: every obstacle was surmounted by their patience, courage, and military skill; and the memorable retreat of the ten thousand exposed and insulted the weakness of the Persian monarchy.[1]

As the price of his disgraceful concessions, the emperor might perhaps have stipulated that the camp of the hungry Romans should be plentifully supplied,[2] and that they should be permitted to pass the Tigris on the bridge which was constructed by the hands of the Persians. But if Jovian presumed to solicit those equitable terms, they were sternly refused by the haughty tyrant of the East, whose clemency had pardoned the invaders of his country. The Saracens sometimes intercepted the stragglers on the march; but the generals and troops of Sapor respected the cessation of arms, and Jovian was suffered to explore the most convenient place for the passage of the river. The small vessels which had been saved from the conflagration of the fleet performed the most essential service. They first conveyed the emperor and his favourites, and afterwards transported, in many successive voyages, a great part of the army. But as every man was anxious for his personal safety and apprehensive of being left on the hostile shore, the soldiers, who were too impatient to wait the slow returns of the boats, boldly ventured themselves on light hurdles or inflated skins, and drawing after them their horses, attempted, with various success, to swim across the river. Many of these daring adventurers were swallowed by the waves; many others, who were carried along by the violence of the stream, fell an easy prey to the avarice or cruelty of the wild Arabs; and the loss which the army sustained in the passage of the Tigris was not inferior to the carnage of a day of battle. As soon as the Romans had landed on the western bank, they were delivered from the hostile pursuit of the barbarians; but in a laborious march of two hundred miles over the plains of Mesopotamia they endured the last extremities of thirst and hunger. They were obliged to traverse a sandy desert, which, in the extent of seventy miles, did not afford a

---

[1] The *Cyropædia* is vague and languid; the *Anabasis* circumstantial and animated. Such is the eternal difference between fiction and truth.

[2] According to Rufinus, an immediate supply of provisions was stipulated by the treaty, and Theodoret affirms that the obligation was faithfully discharged by the Persians. Such a fact is probable, but undoubtedly false. See Tillemont, Hist. des Empereurs, tom. iv. p. 702.

single blade of sweet grass nor a single spring of fresh water, and the rest of the inhospitable waste was untrod by the footsteps either of friends or enemies. Whenever a small measure of flour could be discovered in the camp, twenty pounds weight were greedily purchased with ten pieces of gold,[1] the beasts of burden were slaughtered and devoured, and the desert was strewed with the arms and baggage of the Roman soldiers, whose tattered garments and meagre countenances displayed their past sufferings and actual misery. A small convoy of provisions advanced to meet the army as far as the castle of Ur; and the supply was the more grateful, since it declared the fidelity of Sebastian and Procopius. At Thilsaphata [2] the emperor most graciously received the generals of Mesopotamia, and the remains of a once flourishing army at length reposed themselves under the walls of Nisibis. The messengers of Jovian had already proclaimed, in the language of flattery, his election, his treaty, and his return, and the new prince had taken the most effectual measures to secure the allegiance of the armies and provinces of Europe by placing the military command in the hands of those officers who, from motives of interest or inclination, would firmly support the cause of their benefactor.[3]

The friends of Julian had confidently announced the success of his expedition. They entertained a fond persuasion that the temples of the gods would be enriched with the spoils of the East; that Persia would be reduced to the humble state of a tributary province, governed by the laws and magistrates of Rome; that the barbarians would adopt the dress, and manners, and language of their conquerors; and that the youth of Ecbatana and Susa would study the art of rhetoric under Grecian masters.[4] The progress of the arms of Julian interrupted

[1] We may recollect some lines of Lucan (Pharsal. iv. 95), who describes a similar distress of Cæsar's army in Spain:—

> Sæva fames aderat ————
> Miles eget: toto censû non prodigus emit
> Exiguam Cererem. Proh lucri pallida tabes!
> Non deest prolato jejunus venditor auro.

See Guichardt (Nouveaux Mémoires Militaires, tom. i. p. 379-382). His analysis of the two campaigns in Spain and Africa is the noblest monument that has ever been raised to the fame of Cæsar.

[2] M. d'Anville (see his Maps, and l'Euphrate et le Tigre, p. 92, 93) traces their march, and assigns the true position of Hatra, Ur, and Thilsaphata, which Ammianus has mentioned. He does not complain of the Samiel, the deadly hot wind, which Thevenot (Voyages, part ii. l. i. p. 192) so much dreaded.

[3] The retreat of Jovian is described by Ammianus (xxv. 9), Libanius (Orat. Parent. c. 143, p. 365), and Zosimus (l. iii. [c. 33] p. 194).

[4] Libanius (Orat. Parent. c. 145, p. 366). Such were the natural hopes and wishes of a rhetorician.

his communication with the empire, and, from the moment that he passed the Tigris, his affectionate subjects were ignorant of the fate and fortunes of their prince. Their contemplation of fancied triumphs was disturbed by the melancholy rumour of his death, and they persisted to doubt, after they could no longer deny, the truth of that fatal event.[1] The messengers of Jovian promulgated the specious tale of a prudent and necessary peace; the voice of fame, louder and more sincere, revealed the disgrace of the emperor and the conditions of the ignominious treaty. The minds of the people were filled with astonishment and grief, with indignation and terror, when they were informed that the unworthy successor of Julian relinquished the five provinces which had been acquired by the victory of Galerius, and that he shamefully surrendered to the barbarians the important city of Nisibis, the firmest bulwark of the provinces of the East.[2] The deep and dangerous question, how far the public faith should be observed when it becomes incompatible with the public safety, was freely agitated in popular conversation, and some hopes were entertained that the emperor would redeem his pusillanimous behaviour by a splendid act of patriotic perfidy. The inflexible spirit of the Roman senate had always disclaimed the unequal conditions which were extorted from the distress of her captive armies; and, if it were necessary to satisfy the national honour by delivering the guilty general into the hands of the barbarians, the greatest part of the subjects of Jovian would have cheerfully acquiesced in the precedent of ancient times.[3]

But the emperor, whatever might be the limits of his constitutional authority, was the absolute master of the laws and arms of the state; and the same motives which had forced him to subscribe, now pressed him to execute the treaty of peace. He was impatient to secure an empire at the expense of a few provinces,

[1] The people of Carrhæ, a city devoted to Paganism, buried the inauspicious messenger under a pile of stones (Zosimus, l. iii. [c. 34] p. 196). Libanius, when he received the fatal intelligence, cast his eye on his sword; but he recollected that Plato had condemned suicide, and that he must live to compose the Panegyric of Julian (Libanius de Vitâ suâ, tom. ii. p. 45, 46 [ed. Morell. Paris. 1627]).

[2] Ammianus and Eutropius may be admitted as fair and credible witnesses of the public language and opinions. The people of Antioch reviled an ignominious peace which exposed them to the Persians on a naked and defenceless frontier (Excerpt. Valesiana, p. 845, ex Johanne Antiocheno.).

[3] The Abbé de la Blèterie (Hist. de Jovien, tom. i. p. 212-227), though a severe casuist, has pronounced that Jovian was not bound to execute his promise: since he *could not* dismember the empire, nor alienate, without their consent, the allegiance of his people. I have never found much delight or instruction in such political metaphysics.

and the respectable names of religion and honour concealed the
personal fears and the ambition of Jovian. Notwithstanding
the dutiful solicitations of the inhabitants, decency, as well as
prudence, forbade the emperor to lodge in the palace of Nisibis;
but the next morning after his arrival, Bineses, the ambassador
of Persia, entered the place, displayed from the citadel the
standard of the Great King, and proclaimed, in his name, the
cruel alternative of exile or servitude. The principal citizens
of Nisibis, who, till that fatal moment, had confided in the protection of their sovereign, threw themselves at his feet. They
conjured him not to abandon, or at least not to deliver, a faithful
colony to the rage of a barbarian tyrant, exasperated by the
three successive defeats which he had experienced under the
walls of Nisibis. They still possessed arms and courage to repel
the invaders of their country; they requested only the permission of using them in their own defence, and, as soon as they
had asserted their independence, they should implore the favour
of being again admitted into the rank of his subjects. Their
arguments, their eloquence, their tears, were ineffectual. Jovian
alleged, with some confusion, the sanctity of oaths; and as the
reluctance with which he accepted the present of a crown of gold
convinced the citizens of their hopeless condition, the advocate
Sylvanus was provoked to exclaim, " O emperor! may you thus
be crowned by all the cities of your dominions! " Jovian,
who in a few weeks had assumed the habits of a prince,[1] was
displeased with freedom, and offended with truth; and as he
reasonably supposed that the discontent of the people might
incline them to submit to the Persian government, he published
an edict, under pain of death, that they should leave the city
within the term of three days. Ammianus has delineated in
lively colours the scene of universal despair, which he seems to
have viewed with an eye of compassion.[2] The martial youth
deserted, with indignant grief, the walls which they had so
gloriously defended; the disconsolate mourner dropped a last
tear over the tomb of a son or husband, which must soon be
profaned by the rude hand of a barbarian master; and the aged
citizen kissed the threshold and clung to the doors of the house
where he had passed the cheerful and careless hours of infancy.
The highways were crowded with a trembling multitude; the

[1] At Nisibis he performed a *royal* act. A brave officer, his namesake,
who had been thought worthy of the purple, was dragged from supper,
thrown into a well, and stoned to death without any form of trial or
evidence of guilt. Ammian. xxv. 8.
[2] See xxv. 9, and Zosimus, l. iii. [c. 33] p. 194, 195.

distinctions of rank, and sex, and age, were lost in the general calamity. Every one strove to bear away some fragment from the wreck of his fortunes; and as they could not command the immediate service of an adequate number of horses or waggons, they were obliged to leave behind them the greatest part of their valuable effects. The savage insensibility of Jovian appears to have aggravated the hardships of these unhappy fugitives. They were seated, however, in a new-built quarter of Amida; and that rising city, with the reinforcement of a very considerable colony, soon recovered its former splendour and became the capital of Mesopotamia.[1] Similar orders were despatched by the emperor for the evacuation of Singara and the castle of the Moors, and for the restitution of the five provinces beyond the Tigris. Sapor enjoyed the glory and the fruits of his victory; and this ignominious peace has justly been considered as a memorable era in the decline and fall of the Roman empire. The predecessors of Jovian had sometimes relinquished the dominion of distant and unprofitable provinces; but, since the foundation of the city, the genius of Rome, the god Terminus, who guarded the boundaries of the republic, had never retired before the sword of a victorious enemy.[2]

After Jovian had performed those engagements which the voice of his people might have tempted him to violate, he hastened away from the scene of his disgrace, and proceeded with his whole court to enjoy the luxury of Antioch.[3] Without consulting the dictates of religious zeal, he was prompted, by humanity and gratitude, to bestow the last honours on the remains of his deceased sovereign;[4] and Procopius, who sincerely bewailed the loss of his kinsman, was removed from the command of the army, under the decent pretence of conducting the funeral. The corpse of Julian was transported from Nisibis to Tarsus, in a slow march of fifteen days, and, as it passed through the cities of the East, was saluted by the hostile factions with mournful lamentations and clamorous insults. The Pagans already placed their

---

[1] Chron. Paschal. p. 300 [tom. i. p. 554, ed. Bonn]. The ecclesiastical Notitiæ may be consulted.

[2] Zosimus, l. iii. [c. 32] p. 192, 193. Sextus Rufus de Provinciis, c. 29. Augustin de Civitat. Dei, l. iv. c. 29. This general position must be applied and interpreted with some caution.

[3] Ammianus, xxv. 10. Zosimus, l. iii. [c. 34] p. 196. He might be edax, et vino Venerique indulgens. But I agree with La Bléterie (tom. i. p. 148-154) in rejecting the foolish report of a Bacchanalian riot (ap. Suidam) celebrated at Antioch by the emperor, his *wife*, and a troop of concubines.

[4] The Abbé de la Bléterie (tom. i. p. 156, 209) handsomely exposes the brutal bigotry of Baronius, who would have thrown Julian to the dogs, ne cespititiâ quidem sepulturâ dignus.

beloved hero in the rank of those gods whose worship he had restored, while the invectives of the Christians pursued the soul of the apostate to hell, and his body to the grave.[1]   One party lamented the approaching ruin of their altars, the other celebrated the marvellous deliverance of the church.   The Christians applauded, in lofty and ambiguous strains, the stroke of divine vengeance which had been so long suspended over the guilty head of Julian.   They acknowledged that the death of the tyrant, at the instant he expired beyond the Tigris, was *revealed* to the saints of Egypt, Syria, and Cappadocia;[2] and instead of suffering him to fall by the Persian darts, their indiscretion ascribed the heroic deed to the obscure hand of some mortal or immortal champion of the faith.[3]   Such imprudent declarations were eagerly adopted by the malice or credulity of their adversaries,[4] who darkly insinuated or confidently asserted that the governors of the church had instigated and directed the fanaticism of a domestic assassin.[5]   Above sixteen years after the death of Julian, the charge was solemnly and vehemently urged in a public oration addressed by Libanius to the emperor Theodosius. His suspicions are unsupported by fact or argument, and we can only esteem the generous zeal of the sophist of Antioch for the cold and neglected ashes of his friend.[6]

[1] Compare the sophist and the saint (Libanius, Monod. tom. ii. p. 251, and Orat. Parent. c. 145, p. 367, c. 156, p. 377, with Gregory Nazianzen, Orat. iv. p. 125-132).   The Christian orator faintly mutters some exhortations to modesty and forgiveness: but he is well satisfied that the real sufferings of Julian will far exceed the fabulous torments of Ixion or Tantalus.

[2] Tillemont (Hist. des Empereurs, tom. iv. p. 549) has collected these visions.   Some saint or angel was observed to be absent in the night on a secret expedition, etc.

[3] Sozomen (l. vi. 2) applauds the Greek doctrine of *tyrannicide :* but the whole passage, which a Jesuit might have translated, is prudently suppressed by the president Cousin.

[4] Immediately after the death of Julian an uncertain rumour was scattered, telo cecidisse Romano.   It was carried by some deserters to the Persian camp; and the Romans were reproached as the assassins of the emperor by Sapor and his subjects (Ammian. xxv. 6; Libanius de ulciscendâ Juliani nece, c. xiii. p. 162, 163).   It was urged, as a decisive proof, that no Persian had appeared to claim the promised reward (Liban. Orat. Parent. c. 141, p. 363).   But the flying horseman who darted the fatal javelin might be ignorant of its effect, or he might be slain in the same action.   Ammianus neither feels nor inspires a suspicion.

[5] Ὅστις ἐντολὴν πληρῶν τῷ σφῶν αὐτῶν ἄρχοντι.   This dark and ambiguous expression may point to Athanasius, the first without a rival of the Christian clergy (Libanius de ulcis. Jul. nece, c. 5, p. 149.   La Blétérie, Hist. de Jovien, tom. i. p. 179).

[6] The orator (Fabricius, Biblioth. Græc. tom. vii. p. 145-179) scatters suspicions, demands an inquiry, and insinuates that proofs might still be obtained.   He ascribes the success of the Huns to the criminal neglect of revenging Julian's death.

It was an ancient custom in the funerals, as well as in the triumphs of the Romans, that the voice of praise should be corrected by that of satire and ridicule, and that, in the midst of the splendid pageants which displayed the glory of the living or of the dead, their imperfections should not be concealed from the eyes of the world.[1] This custom was practised in the funeral of Julian. The comedians, who resented his contempt and aversion for the theatre, exhibited, with the applause of a Christian audience, the lively and exaggerated representation of the faults and follies of the deceased emperor. His various character and singular manners afforded an ample scope for pleasantry and ridicule.[2] In the exercise of his uncommon talents he often descended below the majesty of his rank. Alexander was transformed into Diogenes—the philosopher was degraded into a priest. The purity of his virtue was sullied by excessive vanity; his superstition disturbed the peace and endangered the safety of a mighty empire; and his irregular sallies were the less entitled to indulgence, as they appeared to be the laborious efforts of art, or even of affectation. The remains of Julian were interred at Tarsus in Cilicia; but his stately tomb, which arose in that city on the banks of the cold and limpid Cydnus,[3] was displeasing to the faithful friends who loved and revered the memory of that extraordinary man. The philosopher expressed a very reasonable wish that the disciple of Plato might have reposed amidst the groves of the Academy,[4] while the soldier exclaimed, in bolder accents, that the ashes of Julian should have been mingled with those of Cæsar, in the field of Mars, and among the ancient monuments of Roman virtue.[5] The history of princes does not very frequently renew the example of a similar competition.

[1] At the funeral of Vespasian, the comedian who personated that frugal emperor anxiously inquired how much it cost?—Fourscore thousand pounds (centies).—Give me the tenth part of the sum, and throw my body into the Tiber. Sueton. in Vespasian. c. 19, with the notes of Casaubon and Gronovius.

[2] Gregory (Orat. iv. p. 119, 120 [ed. Paris, 1609; Orat. v. c. 16, 18, p. 157, seqq. ed. Bened. 1778]) compares this supposed ignominy and ridicule to the funeral honours of Constantius, whose body was chaunted over Mount Taurus by a choir of angels.

[3] Quintus Curtius, l. iii. c. 4. The luxuriancy of his descriptions has been often censured. Yet it was almost the duty of the historian to describe a river whose waters had nearly proved fatal to Alexander.

[4] Libanius, Orat. Parent. c. 156, p. 377. Yet he acknowledges with gratitude the liberality of the two royal brothers in decorating the tomb of Julian (de ulcis. Jul. nece, c. 7, p. 152).

[5] Cujus suprema et cineres, si qui tunc justè consuleret, non Cydnus videre deberet, quamvis gratissimus amnis et liquidus: sed ad perpetuandam gloriam recte factorum præterlambere Tiberis, intersecans urbem æternam, divorumque veterum monumenta præstringens. Ammian., xxv. 10.

CHAPTER XXV

The Government and Death of Jovian—Election of Valentinian, who associates his Brother Valens, and makes the final Division of the Eastern and Western Empires—Revolt of Procopius—Civil and Ecclesiastical Administration — Germany — Britain — Africa — The East—The Danube—Death of Valentinian—His two Sons, Gratian and Valentinian II., succeed to the Western Empire

THE death of Julian had left the public affairs of the empire in a very doubtful and dangerous situation. The Roman army was saved by an inglorious, perhaps a necessary, treaty;[1] and the first moments of peace were consecrated by the pious Jovian to restore the domestic tranquillity of the church and state. The indiscretion of his predecessor, instead of reconciling, had artfully fomented the religious war; and the balance which he affected to preserve between the hostile factions served only to perpetuate the contest by the vicissitudes of hope and fear, by the rival claims of ancient possession and actual favour. The Christians had forgotten the spirit of the Gospel, and the Pagans had imbibed the spirit of the church. In private families the sentiments of nature were extinguished by the blind fury of zeal and revenge; the majesty of the laws was violated or abused; the cities of the East were stained with blood; and the most implacable enemies of the Romans were in the bosom of their country. Jovian was educated in the profession of Christianity; and as he marched from Nisibis to Antioch, the banner of the Cross, the LABARUM of Constantine, which was again displayed at the head of the legions, announced to the people the faith of their new emperor. As soon as he ascended the throne he transmitted a circular epistle to all the governors of provinces, in which he confessed the divine truth and secured the legal establishment of the Christian religion. The insidious edicts of Julian were abolished, the ecclesiastical immunities were restored and enlarged, and Jovian condescended to lament that the distress of the times obliged him to diminish the measure of charitable distributions.[2] The Christians were unanimous in the loud and

[1] The medals of Jovian adorn him with victories, laurel crowns, and prostrate captives. Ducange, Famil. Byzantin. p. 52. Flattery is a foolish suicide; she destroys herself with her own hands.

[2] Jovian restored to the church τὸν ἀρχαῖον κόσμον; a forcible and comprehensive expression (Philostorgius, l. viii. c. 5, with Godefroy's Dissertations, p. 329. Sozomen, l. vi. c. 3). The new law which condemned the rape or marriage of nuns (Cod. Theod. l. ix. tit. xxv. leg. 2) is exaggerated by Sozomen, who supposes than an amorous glance, the adultery of the heart, was punished with death by the evangelic legislator.

sincere applause which they bestowed on the pious successor of
Julian; but they were still ignorant what creed or what synod he
would choose for the standard of orthodoxy, and the peace of
the church immediately revived those eager disputes which had
been suspended during the season of persecution. The episcopal
leaders of the contending sects, convinced from experience how
much their fate would depend on the earliest impressions that
were made on the mind of an untutored soldier, hastened to the
court of Edessa, or Antioch. The highways of the East were
crowded with Homoousian, and Arian, and Semi-Arian, and
Eunomian bishops, who struggled to outstrip each other in the
holy race; the apartments of the palace resounded with their
clamours, and the ears of the prince were assaulted, and perhaps
astonished, by the singular mixture of metaphysical argument
and passionate invective.[1] The moderation of Jovian, who
recommended concord and charity, and referred the disputants
to the sentence of a future council, was interpreted as a symptom
of indifference; but his attachment to the Nicene Creed was at
length discovered and declared by the reverence which he expressed for the *celestial*[2] virtues of the great Athanasius. The
intrepid veteran of the faith, at the age of seventy, had issued
from his retreat on the first intelligence of the tyrant's death.
The acclamations of the people seated him once more on the
archiepiscopal throne, and he wisely accepted or anticipated the
invitation of Jovian. The venerable figure of Athanasius, his
calm courage and insinuating eloquence, sustained the reputation which he had already acquired in the courts of four successive princes.[3] As soon as he had gained the confidence and
secured the faith of the Christian emperor, he returned in triumph
to his diocese, and continued, with mature counsels and un-
diminished vigour, to direct, ten years longer,[4] the ecclesiastical

---

[1] Compare Socrates, l. iii. c. 25, and Philostorgius, l. viii. c. 6, with Godefroy's Dissertations, p. 330.

[2] The word *celestial* faintly expresses the impious and extravagant flattery
of the emperor to the archbishop, τῆς πρὸς τὸν Θεὸν τῶν ὅλων ὁμοιώσεως.
(See the original epistle in Athanasius, tom. ii. p. 33.) Gregory Nazianzen
(Orat. xxi. p. 392) celebrates the friendship of Jovian and Athanasius.
The primate's journey was advised by the Egyptian monks (Tillemont,
Mém. Ecclés. tom. viii. p. 221).

[3] Athanasius, at the court of Antioch, is agreeably represented by La
Blèterie (Hist. de Jovien, tom. i. p. 121-148): he translates the singular
and original conferences of the emperor, the primate of Egypt, and the Arian
deputies. The Abbé is not satisfied with the coarse pleasantry of Jovian;
but his partiality for Athanasius assumes, in *his* eyes, the character of
justice.

[4] The true era of his death is perplexed with some difficulties (Tillemont,
Mém. Ecclés. tom. viii. p. 719-723). But the date (A.D. 373, May 2) which

government of Alexandria, Egypt, and the catholic church. Before his departure from Antioch, he assured Jovian that his orthodox devotion would be rewarded with a long and peaceful reign. Athanasius had reason to hope that he should be allowed either the merit of a successful prediction, or the excuse of a grateful though ineffectual prayer.[1]

The slightest force, when it is applied to assist and guide the natural descent of its object, operates with irresistible weight; and Jovian had the good fortune to embrace the religious opinions which were supported by the spirit of the times, and the zeal and numbers of the most powerful sect.[2] Under his reign Christianity obtained an easy and lasting victory; and as soon as the smile of royal patronage was withdrawn, the genius of Paganism, which had been fondly raised and cherished by the arts of Julian, sunk irrecoverably in the dust. In many cities the temples were shut or deserted; the philosophers, who had abused their transient favour, thought it prudent to shave their beards and disguise their profession; and the Christians rejoiced that they were now in a condition to forgive or to revenge the injuries which they had suffered under the preceding reign.[3] The consternation of the Pagan world was dispelled by a wise and gracious edict of toleration, in which Jovian explicitly declared that, although he should severely punish the sacrilegious rites of magic, his subjects might exercise, with freedom and safety, the ceremonies of the ancient worship. The memory of this law has been preserved by the orator Themistius, who was deputed by the senate of Constantinople to express their loyal devotion for the new emperor. Themistius expatiates on the clemency of the Divine Nature, the facility of human error, the rights of conscience, and the independence of the mind, and, with some eloquence, inculcates the principles of philosophical toleration, whose aid Superstition herself, in the hour of her distress, is not ashamed to implore. He justly observes that in the recent

seems the most consistent with history and reason is ratified by his authentic Life (Maffei, Osservazioni Letterarie, tom. iii. p. 81).

[1] See the observations of Valesius and Jortin (Remarks on Ecclesiastical History, vol. iv. p. 38) on the original letter of Athanasius, which is preserved by Theodoret (l. iv. c. 3). In some MSS. this indiscreet promise is omitted; perhaps by the Catholics, jealous of the prophetic fame of their leader.

[2] Athanasius (apud Theodoret, l. iv. c. 3) magnifies the number of the orthodox, who composed the whole world, πάρεξ ὀλίγων τῶν τὰ Ἀρείου φρονούντων. This assertion was verified in the space of thirty or forty years.

[3] Socrates, l. iii. c. 24. Gregory Nazianzen (Orat. iv. p. 131) and Libanius (Orat. Parentalis, c. 148, p. 369) express the living sentiments of their respective factions.

changes both religions had been alternately disgraced by the seeming acquisition of worthless proselytes, of those votaries of the reigning purple who could pass, without a reason and without a blush, from the church to the temple, and from the altars of Jupiter to the sacred table of the Christians.[1]

In the space of seven months the Roman troops, who were now returned to Antioch, had performed a march of fifteen hundred miles, in which they had endured all the hardships of war, of famine, and of climate. Notwithstanding their services, their fatigues, and the approach of winter, the timid and impatient Jovian allowed only to the men and horses a respite of six weeks. The emperor could not sustain the indiscreet and malicious raillery of the people of Antioch.[2] He was impatient to possess the palace of Constantinople, and to prevent the ambition of some competitor who might occupy the vacant allegiance of Europe; but he soon received the grateful intelligence that his authority was acknowledged from the Thracian Bosphorus to the Atlantic ocean. By the first letters which he despatched from the camp of Mesopotamia, he had delegated the military command of Gaul and Illyricum to Malarich, a brave and faithful officer of the nation of the Franks, and to his father-in-law, Count Lucillian, who had formerly distinguished his courage and conduct in the defence of Nisibis. Malarich had declined an office to which he thought himself unequal, and Lucillian was massacred at Rheims, in an accidental mutiny of the Batavian cohorts.[3] But the moderation of Jovinus, master-general of the cavalry, who forgave the intention of his disgrace, soon appeased the tumult and confirmed the uncertain minds of the soldiers. The oath of fidelity was administered and taken with loyal acclamations, and the deputies of the Western armies [4] saluted their new sovereign as he descended from Mount Taurus to the city of

---

[1] Themistius, Orat. v. p. 63-71, edit. Harduin, Paris, 1684. The Abbé de la Bléterie judiciously remarks (Hist. de Jovien, tom. i. p. 199) that Sozomen has forgot the general toleration; and Themistius the establishment of the Catholic religion. Each of them turned away from the object which he disliked, and wished to suppress the part of the edict the least honourable, in his opinion, to the emperor Jovian.

[2] Οἱ δὲ Ἀντιοχεῖς οὐχ ἡδέως διέκειντο πρὸς αὐτόν· ἀλλ' ἐπέσκωπτον αὐτὸν ᾠδαῖς καὶ παρῳδίαις καὶ τοῖς καλουμένοις φαμώσσοις (famosis libellis). Johan. Antiochen. in Excerpt. Valesian. p. 845. The libels of Antioch may be admitted on very slight evidence.

[3] Compare Ammianus (xxv. 10), who omits the name of the Batavians, with Zosimus (l. iii. [c. 35] p. 197), who removes the scene of action from Rheims to Sirmium.

[4] Quos capita scholarum ordo castrensis appellat. Ammian. xxv. 10, and Vales. ad locum.

Tyana, in Cappadocia. From Tyana he continued his hasty march to Ancyra, capital of the province of Galatia, where Jovian assumed, with his infant son, the name and ensigns of the consulship.[1] Dadastana,[2] an obscure town, almost at an equal distance between Ancyra and Nice, was marked for the fatal term of his journey and his life. After indulging himself with a plentiful, perhaps an intemperate supper, he retired to rest, and the next morning the emperor Jovian was found dead in his bed. The cause of this sudden death was variously understood. By some it was ascribed to the consequences of an indigestion, occasioned either by the quantity of the wine or the quality of the mushrooms which he had swallowed in the evening. According to others, he was suffocated in his sleep by the vapour of charcoal, which extracted from the walls of the apartment the unwholesome moisture of the fresh plaster.[3] But the want of a regular inquiry into the death of a prince whose reign and person were soon forgotten appears to have been the only circumstance which countenanced the malicious whispers of poison and domestic guilt.[4] The body of Jovian was sent to Constantinople to be interred with his predecessors, and the sad procession was met on the road by his wife Charito, the daughter of Count Lucillian, who still wept the recent death of her father, and was hastening to dry her tears in the embraces of an Imperial husband. Her disappointment and grief were embittered by the anxiety of maternal tenderness. Six weeks before the death of Jovian, his infant son had been placed in the curule chair, adorned with the title of *Nobilissimus* and the vain ensigns of the consulship. Unconscious of his fortune, the royal youth, who from his grandfather assumed the name of Varronian, was reminded only by the jealousy of the government that he was

---

[1] Cujus vagitus, pertinaciter reluctantis, ne in curuli sellâ veheretur ex more, id quod mox accidit portendebat. [Amm. l. c.] Augustus and his successors respectfully solicited a dispensation of age for the sons or nephews whom they raised to the consulship. But the curule chair of the first Brutus had never been dishonoured by an infant.

[2] The Itinerary of Antoninus fixes Dadastana 125 Roman miles from Nice, 117 from Ancyra (Wesseling, Itinerar. p. 142). The pilgrim of Bordeaux, by omitting some stages, reduces the whole space from 242 to 181 miles. Wesseling, p. 574.

[3] See Ammianus (xxv. 10), Eutropius (x. 18 [9]), who might likewise be present; Jerom (tom. i. p. 26 [tom. i. p. 341 ed. Vallars.] ad Heliodorum), Orosius (vii. 31), Sozomen (l. vi. c. 6), Zosimus (l. iii. [c. 35] p. 197, 198), and Zonaras (tom. ii. l. xiii. [c. 14] p. 28, 29). We cannot expect a perfect agreement, and we shall not discuss minute differences.

[4] Ammianus, unmindful of his usual candour and good sense, compares the death of the harmless Jovian to that of the second Africanus, who had excited the fears and resentment of the popular faction.

the son of an emperor. Sixteen years afterwards he was still
alive; but he had already been deprived of an eye, and his
afflicted mother expected, every hour, that the innocent victim
would be torn from her arms, to appease with his blood the suspicions of the reigning prince.[1]

After the death of Jovian the throne of the Roman world
remained ten days[2] without a master. The ministers and
generals still continued to meet in council, to exercise their
respective functions, to maintain the public order, and peaceably
to conduct the army to the city of Nice in Bithynia, which was
chosen for the place of the election.[3] In a solemn assembly of
the civil and military powers of the empire, the diadem was again
unanimously offered to the præfect Sallust. He enjoyed the
glory of a second refusal; and, when the virtues of the father
were alleged in favour of the son, the præfect, with the firmness
of a disinterested patriot, declared to the electors that the feeble
age of the one, and the inexperienced youth of the other,
were equally incapable of the laborious duties of government.
Several candidates were proposed, and, after weighing the objections of character or situation, they were successively rejected:
but as soon as the name of Valentinian was pronounced, the
merit of that officer united the suffrages of the whole assembly,
and obtained the sincere approbation of Sallust himself.
Valentinian[4] was the son of Count Gratian, a native of Cibalis,

[1] Chrysostom, tom. i. p. 336-349, edit. Montfaucon. The Christian
orator attempts to comfort a widow by the examples of illustrious misfortunes; and observes, that, of nine emperors (including the Cæsar Gallus)
who had reigned in his time, only two (Constantine and Constantius) died
a natural death. Such vague consolations have never wiped away a single
tear.

[2] Ten days appear scarcely sufficient for the march and election. But
it may be observed—1. That the generals might command the expeditious
use of the public posts for themselves, their attendants, and messengers.
2. That the troops, for the ease of the cities, marched in many divisions;
and that the head of the column might arrive at Nice when the rear halted
at Ancyra.

[3] Ammianus, xxvi. 1; Zosimus, l. iii. [c. 36] p. 198; Philostorgius, l. viii.
c. 8; and Godefroy, Dissertat. p. 334. Philostorgius, who appears to have
obtained some curious and authentic intelligence, ascribes the choice of
Valentinian to the præfect Sallust, the master-general Arintheus, Dagalaiphus count of the domestics, and the patrician Datianus, whose pressing
recommendations from Ancyra had a weighty influence in the election.

[4] Ammianus (xxx. 7, 9) and the younger Victor [Epit. c. 45] have
furnished the portrait of Valentinian, which naturally precedes and illustrates the history of his reign.

[Symmachus, in a fragment of an oration, describes Valentinian as born
among the snows of Illyria, and habituated to military labour amid the

in Pannonia, who from an obscure condition had raised himself,
by matchless strength and dexterity, to the military commands
of Africa and Britain, from which he retired with an ample
fortune and suspicious integrity. The rank and services of
Gratian contributed, however, to smooth the first steps of the
promotion of his son, and afforded him an early opportunity of
displaying those solid and useful qualifications which raised his
character above the ordinary level of his fellow-soldiers. The
person of Valentinian was tall, graceful, and majestic. His
manly countenance, deeply marked with the impression of sense
and spirit, inspired his friends with awe, and his enemies with
fear; and, to second the efforts of his undaunted courage, the
son of Gratian had inherited the advantages of a strong and
healthy constitution. By the habits of chastity and temperance,
which restrain the appetites and invigorate the faculties, Valentinian preserved his own and the public esteem. The avocations
of a military life had diverted his youth from the elegant pursuits
of literature; he was ignorant of the Greek language and the arts
of rhetoric; but, as the mind of the orator was never disconcerted
by timid perplexity, he was able, as often as the occasion
prompted him, to deliver his decided sentiments with bold and
ready elocution. The laws of martial discipline were the only
laws that he had studied, and he was soon distinguished by the
laborious diligence and inflexible severity with which he discharged and enforced the duties of the camp. In the time of
Julian he provoked the danger of disgrace by the contempt
which he publicly expressed for the reigning religion;[1] and it
should seem, from his subsequent conduct, that the indiscreet

heat and dust of Libya. The following is a table of the members of the
family to which Valentinian belonged:—

Gratianus

Marina or Severa = Valentinianus I. = Justina,   Valens,
                   Imp. b. 321   widow of   Imp. b. 329
                   d. 375   Magnentius   d. 378

   Gratianus,   Valentinianus II.
   Imp. b. 359, d. 383.   Imp. b. 371
   m. (1) Constantia, dau. d. 392
   of Constantius II.; (2) Læta   —O. S.]

[1] At Antioch, where he was obliged to attend the emperor to the temple,
he struck a priest who had presumed to purify him with lustral water
(Sozomen, l. vi. c. 6. Theodoret, l. iii. c. 16). Such public defiance might
become Valentinian; but it could leave no room for the unworthy delation
of the philosopher Maximus, which supposes some more private offence
(Zosimus, l. iv. [c. 2] p. 200, 201).

and unseasonable freedom of Valentinian was the effect of military spirit rather than of Christian zeal. He was pardoned, however, and still employed by a prince who esteemed his merit,[1] and in the various events of the Persian war he improved the reputation which he had already acquired on the banks of the Rhine. The celerity and success with which he executed an important commission recommended him to the favour of Jovian, and to the honourable command of the second *school*, or company, of Targeteers of the domestic guards. In the march from Antioch he had reached his quarters at Ancyra, when he was unexpectedly summoned, without guilt and without intrigue, to assume, in the forty-third year of his age, the absolute government of the Roman empire.

The invitation of the ministers and generals at Nice was of little moment, unless it were confirmed by the voice of the army. The aged Sallust, who had long observed the irregular fluctuations of popular assemblies, proposed, under pain of death, that none of those persons whose rank in the service might excite a party in their favour, should appear in public on the day of the inauguration. Yet such was the prevalence of ancient superstition, that a whole day was voluntarily added to this dangerous interval because it happened to be the intercalation of the Bissextile.[2] At length, when the hour was supposed to be propitious, Valentinian showed himself from a lofty tribunal; the judicious choice was applauded, and the new prince was solemnly invested with the diadem and the purple, amidst the acclamations of the troops, who were disposed in martial order round the tribunal. But when he stretched forth his hand to address the armed multitude, a busy whisper was accidentally started in the ranks, and insensibly swelled into a loud and imperious clamour, that he should name, without delay, a colleague in the empire. The intrepid calmness of Valentinian obtained silence

---

[1] Socrates, l. iv. A previous exile to Melitene, or Thebais (the first might be possible), is interposed by Sozomen (l. vi. c. 6) and Philostorgius (l. vii. c. 7, with Godefroy's Dissertations, p. 293).

[2] Ammianus, in a long, because unseasonable, digression (xxvi. 1, and Valesius ad locum), rashly supposes that he understands an astronomical question, of which his readers are ignorant. It is treated with more judgment and propriety by Censorinus (de Die Natali, c. 20), and Macrobius (Saturnal. l. i. c. 12-16). The appellation of *Bissextile*, which marks the inauspicious year (Augustin. ad Januarium, Epist. 119), is derived from the *repetition* of the *sixth* day of the calends of March.

[There is an error in this note of Gibbon's. It should read, " The repetition of the sixth day before the kalends of March, for both the 24th and 25th of February in leap-year, were styled ' A.D. VI. Kal. Mart.,' the former being termed ' *posteriorem* ' and the latter ' *priorem.*' "—O. S.]

and commanded respect, and he thus addressed the assembly:
" A few minutes since it was in *your* power, fellow-soldiers, to
have left me in the obscurity of a private station. Judging
from the testimony of my past life that I deserved to reign, you
have placed me on the throne. It is now *my* duty to consult
the safety and interest of the republic. The weight of the
universe is undoubtedly too great for the hands of a feeble
mortal. I am conscious of the limits of my abilities and the
uncertainty of my life, and, far from declining, I am anxious
to solicit, the assistance of a worthy colleague. But, where
discord may be fatal, the choice of a faithful friend requires
mature and serious deliberation. That deliberation shall be
my care. Let *your* conduct be dutiful and consistent. Retire
to your quarters; refresh your minds and bodies; and expect
the accustomed donative on the accession of a new emperor." [1]
The astonished troops, with a mixture of pride, of satisfaction,
and of terror, confessed the voice of their master. Their angry
clamours subsided into silent reverence, and Valentinian, encompassed with the eagles of the legions and the various banners
of the cavalry and infantry, was conducted in warlike pomp to
the palace of Nice. As he was sensible, however, of the importance of preventing some rash declaration of the soldiers, he consulted the assembly of the chiefs, and their real sentiments were
concisely expressed by the generous freedom of Dagalaiphus.
" Most excellent prince," said that officer, " if you consider only
your family, you have a brother; if you love the republic, look
round for the most deserving of the Romans." [2] The emperor,
who suppressed his displeasure without altering his intention,
slowly proceeded from Nice to Nicomedia and Constantinople.
In one of the suburbs of that capital,[3] thirty days after his own
elevation, he bestowed the title of Augustus on his brother
Valens: and as the boldest patriots were convinced that their
opposition, without being serviceable to their country, would be
fatal to themselves, the declaration of his absolute will was

---

[1] Valentinian's first speech is full in Ammianus (xxvi. 2); concise and
sententious in Philostorgius (l. viii. c. 8).

[2] Si tuos amas, Imperator optime, habes fratrem; si Rempublicam,
quære quem vestias. Ammian. xxvi. 4. In the division of the empire,
Valentinian retained that sincere counsellor for himself (c. 6).

[3] In suburbano, Ammian. xxvi. 4. The famous *Hebdomon*, or field of
Mars, was distant from Constantinople either seven stadia or seven miles.
See Valesius and his brother, ad loc.; and Ducange, Const. l. ii. p. 140, 141,
172, 173.

[Symmachus praises the liberality of Valentinian in raising his brother
Valens at once to the rank of Augustus, and not after the slow and proba-
tionary stages of the Cæsar.—O. S.]

received with silent submission. Valens was now in the thirty-sixth year of his age, but his abilities had never been exercised in any employment, military or civil, and his character had not inspired the world with any sanguine expectations. He possessed, however, one quality which recommended him to Valentinian, and preserved the domestic peace of the empire: a devout and grateful attachment to his benefactor, whose superiority of genius, as well as of authority, Valens humbly and cheerfully acknowledged in every action of his life.[1]

Before Valentinian divided the provinces, he reformed the administration of the empire. All ranks of subjects who had been injured or oppressed under the reign of Julian were invited to support their public accusations. The silence of mankind attested the spotless integrity of the præfect Sallust,[2] and his own pressing solicitations that he might be permitted to retire from the business of the state were rejected by Valentinian with the most honourable expressions of friendship and esteem. But among the favourites of the late emperor there were many who had abused his credulity or superstition, and who could no longer hope to be protected either by favour or justice.[3] The greater part of the ministers of the palace and the governors of the provinces were removed from their respective stations, yet the eminent merit of some officers was distinguished from the obnoxious crowd, and, notwithstanding the opposite clamours of zeal and resentment, the whole proceedings of this delicate inquiry appear to have been conducted with a reasonable share of wisdom and moderation.[4] The festivity of a new reign received a short and suspicious interruption from the sudden illness of the two princes, but as soon as their health was restored they left Constantinople in the beginning of the spring. In the castle or palace of Mediana, only three miles from Naissus, they executed the solemn and final division of the Roman empire.[5] Valentinian bestowed on his brother the rich præfecture of the *East*, from the Lower Danube to the confines of Persia; whilst

---

[1] Participem quidem legitimæ potestatis; sed in modum apparitoris morigerum, ut progrediens aperiet textus. Ammian. xxvi. 4.

[2] Notwithstanding the evidence of Zonaras, Suidas, and the Paschal Chronicle, M. de Tillemont (Hist. des Empereurs, tom. v. p. 671) *wishes* to disbelieve these stories si avantageuses à un payen.

[3] Eunapius celebrates and exaggerates the sufferings of Maximus (p. 82, 83 [p. 102, ed. Comm.]); yet he allows that this sophist or magician, the guilty favourite of Julian, and the personal enemy of Valentinian, was dismissed on the payment of a small fine.

[4] The loose assertions of a general disgrace (Zosimus, l. iv. [c. 2] p. 201) are detected and refuted by Tillemont (tom. v. p. 21).

[5] Ammianus, xxvi. 5.

he reserved for his immediate government the warlike præfectures of *Illyricum, Italy,* and *Gaul,* from the extremity of Greece to the Caledonian rampart, and from the rampart of Caledonia to the foot of Mount Atlas. The provincial administration remained on its former basis, but a double supply of generals and magistrates was required for two councils and two courts; the division was made with a just regard to their peculiar merit and situation, and seven master-generals were soon created either of the cavalry or infantry. When this important business had been amicably transacted, Valentinian and Valens embraced for the last time. The emperor of the West established his temporary residence at Milan, and the emperor of the East returned to Constantinople to assume the dominion of fifty provinces, of whose language he was totally ignorant.[1]

The tranquillity of the East was soon disturbed by rebellion, and the throne of Valens was threatened by the daring attempts of a rival whose affinity to the emperor Julian [2] was his sole merit, and had been his only crime. Procopius had been hastily promoted from the obscure station of a tribune and a notary to the joint command of the army of Mesopotamia; the public opinion already named him as the successor of a prince who was destitute of natural heirs; and a vain rumour was propagated by his friends or his enemies, that Julian, before the altar of the Moon at Carrhæ, had privately invested Procopius with the Imperial purple.[3] He endeavoured, by his dutiful and submissive behaviour, to disarm the jealousy of Jovian, resigned without a contest his military command, and retired, with his wife and family, to cultivate the ample patrimony which he possessed in the province of Cappadocia. These useful and innocent occupations were interrupted by the appearance of an officer with a band of soldiers, who, in the name of his new sovereigns, Valentinian and Valens, was despatched to conduct the unfortunate Procopius either to a perpetual prison or an

---

[1] Ammianus says, in general terms, subagrestis ingenii, nec bellicis nec liberalibus studiis eruditus. Ammian. xxxi. 14. The orator Themistius, with the genuine impertinence of a Greek, wished for the first time to speak the Latin language, the dialect of his sovereign, τὴν διάλεκτον κρατοῦσαν. Orat. vi. p. 71.

[2] The uncertain degree of alliance, or consanguinity, is expressed by the words ἀνέψιος, cognatus, consobrinus (see Valesius ad Ammian. xxiii. 3). The mother of Procopius might be a sister of Basilina and Count Julian, the mother and uncle of the Apostate. Ducange, Fam. Byzantin. p. 49.

[3] Ammian. xxiii. 3, xxvi. 6. He mentions the report with much hesitation: susurravit obscurior fama; nemo enim dicti auctor exstitit verus. It serves, however, to mark that Procopius was a Pagan. Yet his religion does not appear to have promoted, or obstructed, his pretensions.

ignominious death. His presence of mind procured him a longer respite and a more splendid fate. Without presuming to dispute the royal mandate, he requested the indulgence of a few moments to embrace his weeping family, and, while the vigilance of his guards was relaxed by a plentiful entertainment, he dexterously escaped to the sea-coast of the Euxine, from whence he passed over to the country of Bosphorus. In that sequestered region he remained many months, exposed to the hardships of exile, of solitude, and of want; his melancholy temper brooding over his misfortunes, and his mind agitated by the just apprehension that, if any accident should discover his name, the faithless barbarians would violate, without much scruple, the laws of hospitality. In a moment of impatience and despair, Procopius embarked in a merchant-vessel which made sail for Constantinople, and boldly aspired to the rank of a sovereign because he was not allowed to enjoy the security of a subject. At first he lurked in the villages of Bithynia, continually changing his habitation and his disguise.[1] By degrees he ventured into the capital, trusted his life and fortune to the fidelity of two friends, a senator and an eunuch, and conceived some hopes of success from the intelligence which he obtained of the actual state of public affairs. The body of the people was infected with a spirit of discontent: they regretted the justice and the abilities of Sallust, who had been imprudently dismissed from the præfecture of the East. They despised the character of Valens, which was rude without vigour, and feeble without mildness. They dreaded the influence of his father-in-law, the patrician Petronius, a cruel and rapacious minister, who rigorously exacted all the arrears of tribute that might remain unpaid since the reign of the emperor Aurelian. The circumstances were propitious to the designs of an usurper. The hostile measures of the Persians required the presence of Valens in Syria; from the Danube to the Euphrates the troops were in motion, and the capital was occasionally filled with the soldiers who passed or repassed the Thracian Bosphorus. Two cohorts of Gauls were persuaded to listen to the secret proposals of the conspirators, which were recommended by the promise of a liberal donative; and as they still revered the memory of Julian, they easily consented to support the hereditary claim of his proscribed kinsman. At the dawn of day they were drawn up

[1] One of his retreats was a country-house of Eunomius, the heretic. The master was absent, innocent, ignorant; yet he narrowly escaped a sentence of death, and was banished into the remote parts of Mauritania (Philostorg. l. ix. c. 5, 8, and Godefroy's Dissert. p. 369-378).

near the baths of Anastasia, and Procopius, clothed in a purple garment more suitable to a player than to a monarch, appeared, as if he rose from the dead, in the midst of Constantinople. The soldiers, who were prepared for his reception, saluted their trembling prince with shouts of joy and vows of fidelity. Their numbers were soon increased by a sturdy band of peasants collected from the adjacent country, and Procopius, shielded by the arms of his adherents, was successively conducted to the tribunal, the senate, and the palace. During the first moments of his tumultuous reign he was astonished and terrified by the gloomy silence of the people, who were either ignorant of the cause or apprehensive of the event. But his military strength was superior to any actual resistance; the malcontents flocked to the standard of rebellion; the poor were excited by the hopes, and the rich were intimidated by the fear, of a general pillage; and the obstinate credulity of the multitude was once more deceived by the promised advantages of a revolution. The magistrates were seized, the prisons and arsenals broke open, the gates and the entrance of the harbour were diligently occupied, and, in a few hours, Procopius became the absolute, though precarious, master of the Imperial city. The usurper improved this unexpected success with some degree of courage and dexterity. He artfully propagated the rumours and opinions the most favourable to his interest, while he deluded the populace by giving audience to the frequent but imaginary ambassadors of distant nations. The large bodies of troops stationed in the cities of Thrace and the fortresses of the Lower Danube were gradually involved in the guilt of rebellion, and the Gothic princes consented to supply the sovereign of Constantinople with the formidable strength of several thousand auxiliaries. His generals passed the Bosphorus, and subdued, without an effort, the unarmed but wealthy provinces of Bithynia and Asia. After an honourable defence the city and island of Cyzicus yielded to his power, the renowned legions of the Jovians and Herculians embraced the cause of the usurper whom they were ordered to crush, and, as the veterans were continually augmented with new levies, he soon appeared at the head of an army whose valour, as well as numbers, were not unequal to the greatness of the contest. The son of Hormisdas,[1] a youth of spirit and

---

[1] Hormisdæ maturo juveni Hormisdæ regalis illius filio, potestatem Proconsulis detulit; et civilia, more veterum, et bella, recturo. Ammian. xxvi. 8. The Persian prince escaped with honour and safety, and was afterwards (A.D. 380) restored to the same extraordinary office of proconsul of Bithynia (Tillemont, Hist. des Empereurs, tom. v. p. 204). I am ignorant

ability, condescended to draw his sword against the lawful emperor of the East, and the Persian prince was immediately invested with the ancient and extraordinary powers of a Roman proconsul. The alliance of Faustina, the widow of the emperor Constantius, who intrusted herself and her daughter to the hands of the usurper, added dignity and reputation to his cause. The princess Constantia, who was then about five years of age, accompanied, in a litter, the monarch of the army. She was shown to the multitude in the arms of her adopted father, and, as often as she passed through the ranks, the tenderness of the soldiers was inflamed into martial fury:[1] they recollected the glories of the house of Constantine, and they declared, with loyal acclamation, that they would shed the last drop of their blood in the defence of the royal infant.[2]

In the meanwhile Valentinian was alarmed and perplexed by the doubtful intelligence of the revolt of the East. The difficulties of a German war forced him to confine his immediate care to the safety of his own dominions; and, as every channel of communication was stopped or corrupted, he listened, with doubtful anxiety, to the rumours which were industriously spread that the defeat and death of Valens had left Procopius sole master of the Eastern provinces. Valens was not dead; but on the news of the rebellion, which he received at Cæsarea, he basely despaired of his life and fortune, proposed to negotiate with the usurper, and discovered his secret inclination to abdicate the Imperial purple. The timid monarch was saved from disgrace and ruin by the firmness of his ministers, and their abilities soon decided in his favour the event of the civil war. In a season of tranquillity Sallust had resigned without a murmur, but, as soon as the public safety was attacked, he ambitiously solicited the pre-eminence of toil and danger, and the restoration of that virtuous minister to the præfecture of the East was the first step which indicated the repentance of Valens, and satisfied the minds of the people. The reign of Procopius was apparently supported by powerful armies and obedient provinces. But many of the principal officers, military as well as civil, had been urged, either by motives of duty or interest, to withdraw them-

whether the race of Sassan was propagated. I find (A.D. 514) a pope Hormisdas; but he was a native of Frusino, in Italy (Pagi. Brev. Pontific. tom. i. p. 247).

[1] The infant rebel was afterwards the wife of the emperor Gratian, but she died young and childless. See Ducange, Fam. Byzantin. p. 48, 59.

[2] Sequimini culminis summi prosapiam, was the language of Procopius, who affected to despise the obscure birth and fortuitous election of the upstart Pannonian. Ammian. xxvi. 7.

selves from the guilty scene, or to watch the moment of betraying
and deserting the cause of the usurper. Lupicinus advanced
by hasty marches to bring the legions of Syria to the aid of
Valens. Arintheus, who in strength, beauty, and valour excelled
all the heroes of the age, attacked with a small troop a superior
body of the rebels. When he beheld the faces of the soldiers
who had served under his banner, he commanded them, with a
loud voice, to seize and deliver up their pretended leader, and
such was the ascendant of his genius that this extraordinary
order was instantly obeyed.[1] Arbetio, a respectable veteran of
the great Constantine, who had been distinguished by the
honours of the consulship, was persuaded to leave his retirement,
and once more to conduct an army into the field. In the heat
of action, calmly taking off his helmet, he showed his grey hairs
and venerable countenance, saluted the soldiers of Procopius
by the endearing names of children and companions, and exhorted them no longer to support the desperate cause of a contemptible tyrant, but to follow their old commander, who had
so often led them to honour and victory. In the two engagements of Thyatira [2] and Nacolia the unfortunate Procopius was
deserted by his troops, who were seduced by the instructions
and example of their perfidious officers. After wandering some
time among the woods and mountains of Phrygia, he was
betrayed by his desponding followers, conducted to the Imperial
camp, and immediately beheaded. He suffered the ordinary
fate of an unsuccessful usurper, but the acts of cruelty which
were exercised by the conqueror, under the forms of legal
justice, excited the pity and indignation of mankind.[3]

[1] Et dedignatus hominem superare certamine despicabilem, auctoritatis
et celsi fiduciâ corporis, ipsis hostibus jussit, suum vincire rectorem: atque
ita turmarum antesignanus umbratilis comprensus suorum manibus. The
strength and beauty of Arintheus, the new Hercules, are celebrated by St.
Basil, who supposes that God had created him as an inimitable model of
the human species. The painters and sculptors could not express his
figure: the historians appeared fabulous when they related his exploits
(Ammian. xxvi. [c. 8] and Vales. ad loc.).

[2] The same field of battle is placed by Ammianus in Lycia, and by
Zosimus at Thyatira, which are at the distance of 150 miles from each other.
But Thyatira alluitur Lyco (Plin. Hist. Natur. v. 31; Cellarius, Geograph.
Antiq. tom. ii. p. 79): and the transcribers might easily convert an obscure
river into a well-known province.

[Ammianus (xxvi. 9) and Zosimus (iv. 25) both place the last battle at
Nacolia in Phrygia. Ammianus altogether omits the former battle at
Thyatira. Procopius was on his march towards Lycia.—O. S.]

[3] The adventures, usurpation, and fall of Procopius, are related, in a
regular series, by Ammianus (xxvi. 6, 7, 8, 9, 10) and Zosimus (l. iv. [c. 4
seq.] p. 203-210). They often illustrate, and seldom contradict, each
other. Themistius (Orat. vii. p. 91, 92) adds some base panegyric; and
Eunapius (p. 83, 64 [p. 104, ed. Comm.]) some malicious satire.

Such indeed are the common and natural fruits of despotism and rebellion. But the inquisition into the crime of magic, which, under the reign of the two brothers, was so rigorously prosecuted both at Rome and Antioch, was interpreted as the fatal symptom, either of the displeasure of Heaven or of the depravity of mankind.[1] Let us not hesitate to indulge a liberal pride that, in the present age, the enlightened part of Europe has abolished[2] a cruel and odious prejudice, which reigned in every climate of the globe and adhered to every system of religious opinions.[3] The nations and the sects of the Roman world admitted, with equal credulity and similar abhorrence, the reality of that infernal art[4] which was able to control the eternal order of the planets and the voluntary operations of the human mind. They dreaded the mysterious power of spells and incantations, of potent herbs and execrable rites, which could extinguish or recall life, inflame the passions of the soul, blast the works of creation, and extort from the reluctant dæmons the secrets of futurity. They believed, with the wildest inconsistency, that this preternatural dominion of the air, of earth, and of hell was exercised, from the vilest motives of malice or gain, by some wrinkled hags and itinerant sorcerers, who passed

---

[1] Libanius de ulciscend. Julian. nece, c. ix. [x.] p. 158, 159. The sophist deplores the public frenzy, but he does not (after their deaths) impeach the justice of the emperors.

[Milman, in his edition referring to this note, says, " This infamous inquisition into sorcery and witchcraft has been of greater influence on human affairs than is commonly supposed. The persecution against philosophers and their libraries was carried on with such fury that from this time (A.D. 374) the names of the Gentile philosophers became almost extinct, and the Christian philosophy and religion, particularly in the East, established their ascendancy. Besides vast heaps of MSS. publicly destroyed throughout the East, men of learning burned their whole libraries lest some fatal volume should expose them to the malice of the informers and the extreme penalty of the law."—O. S.]

[2] The French and English lawyers of the present age allow the *theory*, and deny the *practice*, of witchcraft (Denisart, Recueil de Décisions de Jurisprudence, au mot *Sorciers*, tom. iv. p. 553. Blackstone's Commentaries, vol. iv. p. 60). As private reason always prevents, or outstrips, public wisdom, the president Montesquieu (Esprit des Loix, l. xii. c. 5, 6) rejects the *existence* of magic.

[3] See Œuvres de Bayle, tom. iii. p. 567-589. The sceptic of Rotterdam exhibits, according to his custom, a strange medley of loose knowledge and lively wit.

[4] The Pagans distinguished between good and bad magic, the Theurgic and the Goetic (Hist. de l'Académie, etc., tom. vii. p. 25). But they could not have defended this obscure distinction against the acute logic of Bayle. In the Jewish and Christian system, *all* demons are infernal spirits; and *all* commerce with them is idolatry, apostasy, etc., which deserves death and damnation.

their obscure lives in penury and contempt.[1]   The arts of magic were equally condemned by the public opinion and by the laws of Rome, but, as they tended to gratify the most imperious passions of the heart of man, they were continually proscribed and continually practised.[2]   An imaginary cause is capable of producing the most serious and mischievous effects.   The dark predictions of the death of an emperor or the success of a conspiracy were calculated only to stimulate the hopes of ambition and to dissolve the ties of fidelity, and the intentional guilt of magic was aggravated by the actual crimes of treason and sacrilege.[3]   Such vain terrors disturbed the peace of society and the happiness of individuals, and the harmless flame which insensibly melted a waxen image might derive a powerful and pernicious energy from the affrighted fancy of the person whom it was maliciously designed to represent.[4]   From the infusion of those herbs which were supposed to possess a supernatural influence it was an easy step to the use of more substantial poison, and the folly of mankind sometimes became the instrument and the mask of the most atrocious crimes.   As soon as the zeal of informers was encouraged by the ministers of Valens and Valentinian, they could not refuse to listen to another charge too frequently mingled in the scenes of domestic guilt, a charge of a softer and less malignant nature, for which the pious though excessive rigour of Constantine had recently decreed the punish-

---

[1] The Canidia of Horace (Carm. l. v. Od. 5 [Epod. 5], with Dacier's and Sanadon's illustrations) is a vulgar witch.   The Erichtho of Lucan (Pharsal. vi. 430-827) is tedious, disgusting, but sometimes sublime.   She chides the delay of the Furies; and threatens, with tremendous obscurity, to pronounce their real names; to reveal the true infernal countenance of Hecate; to invoke the secret powers that lie *below* hell, etc.

[2] Genus hominum potentibus infidum, sperantibus fallax, quod in civitate nostrâ et vetabitur semper et retinebitur.   Tacit. Hist. i. 22.   See Augustin, de Civitate Dei, l. viii. c. 19, and the Theodosian Code, l. ix. tit. xvi. with Godefroy's Commentary.

[3] The persecution of Antioch was occasioned by a criminal consultation. The twenty-four letters of the alphabet were arranged round a magic tripod: and a dancing ring, which had been placed in the centre, pointed to the four first letters in the name of the future emperor, Θ. Ε. Ο. Δ. Theodorus (perhaps with many others, who owned the fatal syllables) was executed.   Theodosius succeeded.   Lardner (Heathen Testimonies, vol. iv. p. 353-372) has copiously and fairly examined this dark transaction of the reign of Valens.

[4]   Limus ut hic durescit, et hæc ut cera liquescit
    Uno eodemque igni ————————   Virgil. Bucolic. viii. 80.
  Devovet absentes, simulacraque cerea figit.
        Ovid. in Epist. Hypsil. ad Jason. 91 [Ep. vi.].
Such vain incantations could affect the mind, and increase the disease, of Germanicus.   Tacit. Annal. ii. 69.

ment of death.[1] This deadly and incoherent mixture of treason
and magic, of poison and adultery, afforded infinite gradations of
guilt and innocence, of excuse and aggravation, which in these
proceedings appear to have been confounded by the angry or
corrupt passions of the judges. They easily discovered that the
degree of their industry and discernment was estimated by the
Imperial court according to the number of executions that were
furnished from their respective tribunals. It was not without
extreme reluctance that they pronounced a sentence of acquittal,
but they eagerly admitted such evidence as was stained with
perjury or procured by torture to prove the most improbable
charges against the most respectable characters. The progress
of the inquiry continually opened new subjects of criminal prosecution; the audacious informer, whose falsehood was detected,
retired with impunity; but the wretched victim who discovered
his real or pretended accomplices was seldom permitted to receive
the price of his infamy. From the extremity of Italy and Asia
the young and the aged were dragged in chains to the tribunals
of Rome and Antioch. Senators, matrons, and philosophers
expired in ignominious and cruel tortures. The soldiers who
were appointed to guard the prisons declared, with a murmur of
pity and indignation, that their numbers were insufficient to
oppose the flight or resistance of the multitude of captives. The
wealthiest families were ruined by fines and confiscations; the
most innocent citizens trembled for their safety; and we may
form some notion of the magnitude of the evil from the extravagant assertion of an ancient writer, that in the obnoxious
provinces the prisoners, the exiles, and the fugitives formed the
greatest part of the inhabitants.[2]

When Tacitus describes the deaths of the innocent and illustrious Romans who were sacrificed to the cruelty of the first
Cæsars, the art of the historian, or the merit of the sufferers,
excites in our breasts the most lively sensations of terror, of
admiration, and of pity. The coarse and undistinguishing pencil
of Ammianus has delineated his bloody figures with tedious and
disgusting accuracy. But as our attention is no longer engaged

[1] See Heineccius Antiquitat. Juris Roman. tom. ii. p. 353, etc. Cod.
Theodosian. l. ix. tit. 7, with Godefroy's Commentary.
[2] The cruel persecution of Rome and Antioch is described, and most
probably exaggerated, by Ammianus (xxviii. 1, xxix. 1, 2) and Zosimus (l.
iv. [c. 13] p. 216-218). The philosopher Maximus, with some justice, was
involved in the charge of magic (Eunapius in Vit. Sophist. p. 88, 89 [p. 110,
ed. Comm.]); and young Chrysostom, who had accidentally found one
of the proscribed books, gave himself up for lost. (Tillemont, Hist. des
Empereurs, tom. v. p. 340).

by the contrast of freedom and servitude, of recent greatness
and of actual misery, we should turn with horror from the frequent executions which disgraced, both at Rome and Antioch,
the reign of the two brothers.[1] Valens was of a timid,[2] and
Valentinian of a choleric, disposition.[3] An anxious regard to his
personal safety was the ruling principle of the administration
of Valens. In the condition of a subject, he had kissed, with
trembling awe, the hand of the oppressor; and when he ascended
the throne, he reasonably expected that the same fears which
had subdued his own mind would secure the patient submission
of his people. The favourites of Valens obtained, by the privilege of rapine and confiscation, the wealth which his economy
would have refused.[4] They urged, with persuasive eloquence,
that, in all cases of treason, suspicion is equivalent to proof;
that the power supposes the intention of mischief; *that* the intention is not less criminal than the act; and *that* a subject no
longer deserves to live, if his life may threaten the safety, or disturb the repose, of his sovereign. The judgment of Valentinian
was sometimes deceived, and his confidence abused; but he
would have silenced the informers with a contemptuous smile,
had they presumed to alarm his fortitude by the sound of danger.
They praised his inflexible love of justice; and, in the pursuit of
justice, the emperor was easily tempted to consider clemency
as a weakness, and passion as a virtue. As long as he wrestled
with his equals in the bold competition of an active and ambitious
life, Valentinian was seldom injured, and never insulted, with
impunity: if his prudence was arraigned, his spirit was
applauded; and the proudest and most powerful generals were
apprehensive of provoking the resentment of a fearless soldier.
After he became master of the world, he unfortunately forgot
that, where no resistance can be made, no courage can be exerted;
and instead of consulting the dictates of reason and magna-

---

[1] Consult the six last books of Ammianus, and more particularly the
portraits of the two royal brothers (xxx. 8, 9, xxxi. 14). Tillemont has
collected (tom. v. p. 12-18, p. 127-133) from all antiquity their virtues and
vices.

[2] The younger Victor asserts that he was valde timidus [Epit. c. 46]; yet
he behaved, as almost every man would do, with decent resolution at the
head of an army. The same historian attempts to prove that his anger
was harmless. Ammianus observes, with more candour and judgment,
incidentia crimina ad contemptam vel læsam principis amplitudinem
trahens, in sanguinem sæviebat [xxxi. 14].

[3] Cum esset in acerbitatem naturæ calore propensior . . . pœnas per
ignes augebat et gladios. Ammian. xxx. 8. See xxvii. 7.

[4] I have transferred the reproach of avarice from Valens to his servants.
Avarice more properly belongs to ministers than to kings, in whom that
passion is commonly extinguished by absolute possession.

nimity, he indulged the furious emotions of his temper, at a time when they were disgraceful to himself, and fatal to the defenceless objects of his displeasure. In the government of his household, or of his empire, slight, or even imaginary offences—a hasty word, a casual omission, an involuntary delay—were chastised by a sentence of immediate death. The expressions which issued the most readily from the mouth of the emperor of the West were, " Strike off his head; "—" Burn him alive; "—" Let him be beaten with clubs till he expires; " [1] and his most favoured ministers soon understood that, by a rash attempt to dispute or suspend the execution of his sanguinary commands, they might involve themselves in the guilt and punishment of disobedience. The repeated gratification of this savage justice hardened the mind of Valentinian against pity and remorse; and the sallies of passion were confirmed by the habits of cruelty.[2] He could behold with calm satisfaction the convulsive agonies of torture and death: he reserved his friendship for those faithful servants whose temper was the most congenial to his own. The merit of Maximin, who had slaughtered the noblest families of Rome, was rewarded with the royal approbation, and the præfecture of Gaul. Two fierce and enormous bears, distinguished by the appellations of *Innocence* and *Mica Aurea*, could alone deserve to share the favour of Maximin. The cages of those trusty guards were always placed near the bedchamber of Valentinian, who frequently amused his eyes with the grateful spectacle of seeing them tear and devour the bleeding limbs of the malefactors who were abandoned to their rage. Their diet and exercises were carefully inspected by the Roman emperor; and when *Innocence* had earned her discharge, by a long course of meritorious service, the faithful animal was again restored to the freedom of her native woods.[3]

But in the calmer moments of reflection, when the mind of Valens was not agitated by fear, or that of Valentinian by rage,

---

[1] He sometimes expressed a sentence of death with a tone of pleasantry: " Abi, Comes, et muta ei caput, qui sibi mutari provinciam cupit." A boy, who had slipped too hastily a Spartan hound; an armourer, who had made a polished cuirass that wanted some grains of the legitimate weight, etc., were the victims of his fury.

[2] The innocents of Milan were an agent and three apparitors, whom Valentinian condemned for signifying a legal summons. Ammianus (xxvii. 7) strangely supposes that all who had been unjustly executed were worshipped as martyrs by the Christians. His impartial silence does not allow us to believe that the great chamberlain Rhodanus was burnt alive for an act of oppression (Chron. Paschal. p. 302 [tom. i. p. 558, ed. Bonn]).

[3] Ut bene meritam in silvas jussit abire *Innoxiam*. Ammian. xxix. 3, and Valesius ad locum.

the tyrant resumed the sentiments, or at least the conduct, of the father of his country. The dispassionate judgment of the Western emperor could clearly perceive, and accurately pursue, his own and the public interest; and the sovereign of the East, who imitated with equal docility the various examples which he received from his elder brother, was sometimes guided by the wisdom and virtue of the præfect Sallust. Both princes invariably retained, in the purple, the chaste and temperate simplicity which had adorned their private life; and, under their reign, the pleasures of the court never cost the people a blush or a sigh. They gradually reformed many of the abuses of the times of Constantius; judiciously adopted and improved the designs of Julian and his successor; and displayed a style and spirit of legislation which might inspire posterity with the most favourable opinion of their character and government. It is not from the master of *Innocence* that we should expect the tender regard for the welfare of his subjects which prompted Valentinian to condemn the exposition of new-born infants,[1] and to establish fourteen skilful physicians, with stipends and privileges, in the fourteen quarters of Rome. The good sense of an illiterate soldier founded an useful and liberal institution for the education of youth, and the support of declining science.[2] It was his intention that the arts of rhetoric and grammar should be taught, in the Greek and Latin languages, in the metropolis of every province; and as the size and dignity of the school was usually proportioned to the importance of the city, the academies of Rome and Constantinople claimed a just and singular pre-eminence. The fragments of the literary edicts of Valentinian imperfectly represent the school of Constantinople, which was gradually improved by subsequent regulations. That school consisted of thirty-one professors in different branches of learning. One philosopher and two lawyers; five sophists and ten grammarians for the Greek, and three orators and ten grammarians for the Latin tongue; besides seven scribes, or, as they

---

[1] See the Code of Justinian, l. viii. tit. lii. leg. 2. Unusquisque sobolem suam nutriat. Quod si exponendam putaverit animadversioni quæ constituta est subjacebit. For the present I shall not interfere in the dispute between Noodt and Binkershoek, how far or how long this unnatural practice had been condemned or abolished by law, philosophy, and the more civilised state of society.

[2] These salutary institutions are explained in the Theodosian Code, l. xiii. tit. iii. *De Professoribus et Medicis ;* and l. xiv. tit. ix. *De Studiis liberalibus Urbis Romæ.* Besides our usual guide (Godefroy), we may consult Giannone (Istoria di Napoli, tom. i. p. 105-111), who has treated the interesting subject with the zeal and curiosity of a man of letters who studies his domestic history.

were then styled, antiquarians, whose laborious pens supplied the public library with fair and correct copies of the classic writers. The rule of conduct which was prescribed to the students is the more curious, as it affords the first outlines of the form and discipline of a modern university. It was required that they should bring proper certificates from the magistrates of their native province. Their names, professions, and places of abode, were regularly entered in a public register. The studious youth were severely prohibited from wasting their time in feasts or in the theatre; and the term of their education was limited to the age of twenty. The præfect of the city was empowered to chastise the idle and refractory by stripes or expulsion; and he was directed to make an annual report to the master of the offices, that the knowledge and abilities of the scholars might be usefully applied to the public service. The institutions of Valentinian contributed to secure the benefits of peace and plenty; and the cities were guarded by the establishment of the *Defensors*;[1] freely elected as the tribunes and advocates of the people, to support their rights, and to expose their grievances, before the tribunals of the civil magistrates, or even at the foot of the Imperial throne. The finances were diligently administered by two princes who had been so long accustomed to the rigid economy of a private fortune; but in the receipt and application of the revenue, a discerning eye might observe some difference between the government of the East and of the West. Valens was persuaded that royal liberality can be supplied only by public oppression, and his ambition never aspired to secure, by their actual distress, the future strength and prosperity of his people. Instead of increasing the weight of taxes, which in the space of forty years had been gradually doubled, he reduced, in the first years of his reign, one-fourth of the tribute of the East.[2] Valentinian appears to have been less attentive and less anxious to relieve the burthens of his people. He might reform the abuses of the fiscal administration; but he exacted, without scruple, a very large share of the private property; as he was convinced that the revenues which supported the luxury of individuals would

[1] Cod. Theodos. l. i. tit. xi. with Godefroy's *Paratitlon*, which diligently gleans from the rest of the code.

[2] Three lines of Ammianus (xxxi. 14) countenance a whole oration of Themistius (viii. p. 101-120), full of adulation, pedantry, and commonplace morality. The eloquent M. Thomas (tom. i. p. 366-396) has amused himself with celebrating the virtues and genius of Themistius, who was not unworthy of the age in which he lived.

be much more advantageously employed for the defence and improvement of the state. The subjects of the East, who enjoyed the present benefit, applauded the indulgence of their prince. The solid, but less splendid, merit of Valentinian was felt and acknowledged by the subsequent generation.[1]

But the most honourable circumstance of the character of Valentinian is the firm and temperate impartiality which he uniformly preserved in an age of religious contention. His strong sense, unenlightened, but uncorrupted, by study, declined, with respectful indifference, the subtle questions of theological debate. The government of the *Earth* claimed his vigilance, and satisfied his ambition; and while he remembered that he was the disciple of the church, he never forgot that he was the sovereign of the clergy. Under the reign of an apostate, he had signalised his zeal for the honour of Christianity: he allowed to his subjects the privilege which he had assumed for himself; and they might accept with gratitude and confidence the general toleration which was granted by a prince addicted to passion, but incapable of fear or of disguise.[2] The Pagans, the Jews, and all the various sects which acknowledged the divine authority of Christ, were protected by the laws from arbitrary power or popular insult; nor was any mode of worship prohibited by Valentinian, except those secret and criminal practices which abused the name of religion for the dark purposes of vice and disorder. The art of magic, as it was more cruelly punished, was more strictly proscribed: but the emperor admitted a formal distinction to protect the ancient methods of divination, which were approved by the senate and exercised by the Tuscan haruspices. He had condemned, with the consent of the most rational Pagans, the licence of nocturnal sacrifices; but he immediately admitted the petition of Prætextatus, proconsul of Achaia, who represented that the life of the Greeks would become dreary and comfortless if they were deprived of the invaluable blessing of the Eleusinian mysteries.[3] Philosophy alone can

---

[1] Zosimus, l. iv. [c. 3] p. 202. Ammian. xxx. 9. His reformation of costly abuses might entitle him to the praise of, in provinciales admodum parcus, tributorum ubique molliens sarcinas. By some his frugality was styled avarice (Jerom. Chron. p. 186 [tom. viii. p. 809, ed. Vallars.]).

[2] Testes sunt leges a me in exordio Imperii mei datæ; quibus unicuique quod animo imbibisset colendi libera facultas tributa est. Cod. Theodos. l. ix. tit. xvi. leg. 9. To this declaration of Valentinian we may add the various testimonies of Ammianus (xxx. 9). Zosimus (l. iv. [c. 3] p. 204). and Sozomen (l. vi. c. 7, 21). Baronius would naturally blame such rational toleration (Annal. Eccles. A.D. 370, No. 129-132, A.D. 376, No. 3, 4).

[3] [The Eleusenian mysteries continued to be celebrated during the whole of the second half of the fourth century (says Smith) till they were put an

boast (and perhaps it is no more than the boast of philosophy)
that her gentle hand is able to eradicate from the human mind
the latent and deadly principle of fanaticism.   But this truce of
twelve years, which was inforced by the wise and vigorous
government of Valentinian, by suspending the repetition of
mutual injuries, contributed to soften the manners, and abate
the prejudices, of the religious factions.

The friend of toleration was unfortunately placed at a distance
from the scene of the fiercest controversies.   As soon as the
Christians of the West had extricated themselves from the snares
of the creed of Rimini, they happily relapsed into the slumber of
orthodoxy; and the small remains of the Arian party, that still
subsisted at Sirmium or Milan, might be considered rather as
objects of contempt than of resentment.   But in the provinces
of the East, from the Euxine to the extremity of Thebais, the
strength and numbers of the hostile factions were more equally
balanced; and this equality, instead of recommending the
counsels of peace, served only to perpetuate the horrors of
religious war.   The monks and bishops supported their arguments by invectives; and their invectives were sometimes
followed by blows.   Athanasius still reigned at Alexandria; the
thrones of Constantinople and Antioch were occupied by Arian
prelates; and every episcopal vacancy was the occasion of a
popular tumult.   The Homoousians were fortified by the reconciliation of fifty-nine Macedonian, or Semi-Arian, bishops; but
their secret reluctance to embrace the divinity of the Holy Ghost
clouded the splendour of the triumph; and the declaration of
Valens, who, in the first years of his reign, had imitated the
impartial conduct of his brother, was an important victory on
the side of Arianism.   The two brothers had passed their private
life in the condition of catechumens; but the piety of Valens
prompted him to solicit the sacrament of baptism before he
exposed his person to the dangers of a Gothic war.   He naturally
addressed himself to Eudoxus,[1] bishop of the Imperial city; and
if the ignorant monarch was instructed by that Arian pastor in
the principles of heterodox theology, his misfortune, rather than
his guilt, was the inevitable consequence of his erroneous choice.

end to by the destruction of the temple at Eleusis, and by the devastation
of Greece in the invasion of the Goths under Alaric in 395.   Cf. Eunapius
in Vitâ Maximi; Fallmerayer, Geschichte Moreas, i. p. 119 ff.—O. S.]

[1] Eudoxus was of a mild and timid disposition.   When he baptised
Valens (A.D. 367) he must have been extremely old, since he had studied
theology fifty-five years before, under Lucian, a learned and pious martyr.
Philostorg. l. ii. c 14-16, l. iv. c. 4, with Godefroy, p. 82, 206, and Tillemont,
Mém. Ecclés. tom. v. p. 474-480, etc.

Whatever had been the determination of the emperor, he must have offended a numerous party of his Christian subjects; as the leaders both of the Homoousians and of the Arians believed that, if they were not suffered to reign, they were most cruelly injured and oppressed. After he had taken this decisive step, it was extremely difficult for him to preserve either the virtue, or the reputation, of impartiality. He never aspired, like Constantius, to the fame of a profound theologian; but, as he had received with simplicity and respect the tenets of Eudoxus, Valens resigned his conscience to the direction of his ecclesiastical guides, and promoted by the influence of his authority the re-union of the *Athanasian heretics* to the body of the catholic church. At first he pitied their blindness; by degrees he was provoked at their obstinacy; and he insensibly hated those sectaries to whom he was an object of hatred.[1] The feeble mind of Valens was always swayed by the persons with whom he familiarly conversed; and the exile or imprisonment of a private citizen are the favours the most readily granted in a despotic court. Such punishments were frequently inflicted on the leaders of the Homoousian party; and the misfortune of fourscore ecclesiastics of Constantinople, who, perhaps accidentally, were burnt on shipboard, was imputed to the cruel and premeditated malice of the emperor and his Arian ministers. In every contest the catholics (if we may anticipate that name) were obliged to pay the penalty of their own faults, and of those of their adversaries. In every election the claims of the Arian candidate obtained the preference; and if they were opposed by the majority of the people, he was usually supported by the authority of the civil magistrate, or even by the terrors of a military force. The enemies of Athanasius attempted to disturb the last years of his venerable age; and his temporary retreat to his father's sepulchre has been celebrated as a fifth exile. But the zeal of a great people, who instantly flew to arms, intimidated the præfect: and the archbishop was permitted to end his life in peace and in glory, after a reign of forty-seven years. The death of Athanasius was the signal of the persecution of Egypt; and the Pagan minister of Valens, who forcibly seated the worthless Lucius on the archiepiscopal throne, purchased the favour of the reigning party by the blood and sufferings of their Christian brethren. The free toleration of the heathen and Jewish worship was bitterly lamented, as a circumstance

---

[1] Gregory Nazianzen (Orat. xxv. p. 432) insults the persecuting spirit of the Arians, as an infallible symptom of error and heresy.

which aggravated the misery of the catholics, and the guilt of the impious tyrant of the East.[1]

The triumph of the orthodox party has left a deep stain of persecution on the memory of Valens; and the character of a prince who derived his virtues, as well as his vices, from a feeble understanding and a pusillanimous temper, scarcely deserves the labour of an apology. Yet candour may discover some reasons to suspect that the ecclesiastical ministers of Valens often exceeded the orders, or even the intentions, of their master; and that the real measure of facts has been very liberally magnified by the vehement declamation and easy credulity of his antagonists.[2]   1. The silence of Valentinian may suggest a probable argument that the partial severities which were exercised in the name and provinces of his colleague amounted only to some obscure and inconsiderable deviations from the established system of religious toleration; and the judicious historian, who has praised the equal temper of the elder brother, has not thought himself obliged to contrast the tranquillity of the West with the cruel persecution of the East.[3]   2. Whatever credit may be allowed to vague and distant reports, the character, or at least the behaviour, of Valens may be most distinctly seen in his personal transactions with the eloquent Basil, archbishop of Cæsarea, who had succeeded Athanasius in the management of the Trinitarian cause.[4]   The circumstantial narrative has been composed by the friends and admirers of Basil; and as soon as we have stripped away a thick coat of rhetoric and miracle, we shall be astonished by the unexpected mildness of the Arian tyrant, who admired the firmness of his character, or was apprehensive, if he employed violence, of a general revolt in the province of Cappadocia. The archbishop, who asserted, with

[1] This sketch of the ecclesiastical government of Valens is drawn from Socrates (l. iv.), Sozomen (l. vi.), Theodoret (l. iv.), and the immense compilations of Tillemont (particularly tom. vi. viii. and ix.).

[2] Dr. Jortin (Remarks on Ecclesiastical History, vol. iv. p. 78) has already conceived and intimated the same suspicion.

[3] This reflection is so obvious and forcible, that Orosius (l. vii. c. 32, 33) delays the persecution till after the death of Valentinian. Socrates, on the other hand, supposes (l. iii. [iv.] c. 32) that it was appeased by a philosophical oration which Themistius pronounced in the year 374 (Orat. xii. p. 154, in Latin only). Such contradictions diminish the evidence and reduce the term of the persecution of Valens.

[4] Tillemont, whom I follow and abridge, has extracted (Mém. Ecclés. tom. viii. p. 153-167) the most authentic circumstances from the Panegyrics of the two Gregories; the brother and the friend of Basil. The letters of Basil himself (Dupin, Bibliothèque Ecclésiastique, tom. ii. p. 155-180) do not present the image of a very lively persecution.

inflexible pride,[1] the truth of his opinions and the dignity of his rank, was left in the free possession of his conscience and his throne. The emperor devoutly assisted at the solemn service of the cathedral;. and, instead of a sentence of banishment, subscribed the donation of a valuable estate for the use of an hospital which Basil had lately founded in the neighbourhood of Cæsarea.[2] 3. I am not able to discover that any law (such as Theodosius afterwards enacted against the Arians) was published by Valens against the Athanasian sectaries; and the edict which excited the most violent clamours may not appear so extremely reprehensible. The emperor had observed that several of his subjects, gratifying their lazy disposition under the pretence of religion, had associated themselves with the monks of Egypt; and he directed the count of the East to drag them from their solitude, and to compel those deserters of society to accept the fair alternative of renouncing their temporal possessions, or of discharging the public duties of men and citizens.[3] The ministers of Valens seem to have extended the sense of this penal statute, since they claimed a right of enlisting the young and able-bodied monks in the Imperial armies. A detachment of cavalry and infantry, consisting of three thousand men, marched from Alexandria into the adjacent desert of Nitria,[4] which was peopled by five thousand monks. The soldiers were conducted by Arian priests; and it is reported that a considerable slaughter was made in the monasteries which disobeyed the commands of their sovereign.[5]

The strict regulations which have been framed by the wisdom

[1] Basilius Cæsariensis episcopus Cappadociæ clarus habetur . . . qui multa continentiæ et ingenii bona uno superbiæ malo perdidit [Chron. Ann. 2392, tom. viii. p. 816, ed. Vallars.]. This irreverent passage is perfectly in the style and character of St. Jerom. It does not appear in Scaliger's edition of his Chronicle; but Isaac Vossius found it in some old MSS. which had not been reformed by the monks.

[2] This noble and charitable foundation (almost a new city) surpassed in merit, if not in greatness, the pyramids, or the walls of Babylon. It was principally intended for the reception of lepers (Greg. Nazianzen, Orat. xx. p. 439).

[3] Cod. Theodos. l. xii. tit. i. leg. 63. Godefroy (tom. iv. p. 409-413) performs the duty of a commentator and advocate. Tillemont (Mém. Ecclés. tom. viii. p. 808) *supposes* a second law to excuse his orthodox friends, who had misrepresented the edict of Valens, and suppressed the liberty of choice.

[4] See D'Anville, Description de l'Egypte, p. 74. Hereafter I shall consider the monastic institutions.

[5] Socrates, l. iv. c. 24, 25. Orosius, l. vii. c. 33. Jerom. in Chron. p. 189 [tom. viii. p. 816, ed. Vallars.], and tom. ii. p. 212. The monks of Egypt performed many miracles, which prove the truth of their faith. Right, says Jortin (Remarks, vol. iv. p. 79), but what proves the truth of those miracles?

of modern legislators to restrain the wealth and avarice of the clergy may be originally deduced from the example of the emperor Valentinian. His edict,[1] addressed to Damasus, bishop of Rome, was publicly read in the churches of the city. He admonished the ecclesiastics and monks not to frequent the houses of widows and virgins; and menaced their disobedience with the animadversion of the civil judge. The director was no longer permitted to receive any gift, or legacy, or inheritance, from the liberality of his spiritual daughter: every testament contrary to this edict was declared null and void: and the illegal donation was confiscated for the use of the treasury. By a subsequent regulation it should seem that the same provisions were extended to nuns and bishops; and that all persons of the ecclesiastical order were rendered incapable of receiving any testamentary gifts, and strictly confined to the natural and legal rights of inheritance. As the guardian of domestic happiness and virtue, Valentinian applied this severe remedy to the growing evil. In the capital of the empire the females of noble and opulent houses possessed a very ample share of independent property; and many of those devout females had embraced the doctrines of Christianity, not only with the cold assent of the understanding, but with the warmth of affection, and perhaps with the eagerness of fashion. They sacrificed the pleasures of dress and luxury; and renounced, for the praise of chastity, the soft endearments of conjugal society. Some ecclesiastic, of real or apparent sanctity, was chosen to direct their timorous conscience, and to amuse the vacant tenderness of their heart: and the unbounded confidence which they hastily bestowed was often abused by knaves and enthusiasts, who hastened from the extremities of the East, to enjoy, on a splendid theatre, the privileges of the monastic profession. By their contempt of the world, they insensibly acquired its most desirable advantages; the lively attachment, perhaps, of a young and beautiful woman, the delicate plenty of an opulent household, and the respectful homage of the slaves, the freedmen, and the clients of a senatorial family. The immense fortunes of the Roman ladies were gradually consumed in lavish alms and expensive pilgrimages; and the artful monk, who had assigned himself the first, or possibly the sole place, in the testament of his spiritual

---

[1] Cod. Theodos. l. xvi. tit. ii. leg. 20. Godefroy (tom. vi. p. 49), after the example of Baronius, impartially collects all that the fathers have said on the subject of this important law; whose spirit was long afterwards revived by the emperor Frederic II., Edward I. of England, and other Christian princes who reigned after the twelfth century.

daughter, still presumed to declare, with the smooth face of hypocrisy, that *he* was only the instrument of charity, and the steward of the poor. The lucrative, but disgraceful, trade,[1] which was exercised by the clergy to defraud the expectations of the natural heirs, had provoked the indignation of a superstitious age: and two of the most respectable of the Latin fathers very honestly confess that the ignominious edict of Valentinian was just and necessary; and that the Christian priests had deserved to lose a privilege which was still enjoyed by comedians, charioteers, and the ministers of idols. But the wisdom and authority of the legislator are seldom victorious in a contest with the vigilant dexterity of private interest: and Jerom, or Ambrose, might patiently acquiesce in the justice of an ineffectual or salutary law. If the ecclesiastics were checked in the pursuit of personal emolument, they would exert a more laudable industry to increase the wealth of the church; and dignify their covetousness with the specious names of piety and patriotism.[2]

Damasus, bishop of Rome, who was constrained to stigmatise the avarice of his clergy by the publication of the law of Valentinian, had the good sense, or the good fortune, to engage in his service the zeal and abilities of the learned Jerom; and the grateful saint has celebrated the merit and purity of a very ambiguous character.[3] But the splendid vices of the church of Rome, under the reign of Valentinian and Damasus, have been curiously observed by the historian Ammianus, who delivers his impartial sense in these expressive words:—" The præfecture of Juventius was accompanied with peace and plenty, but the tranquillity of his government was soon disturbed by a bloody sedition of the distracted people. The ardour of Damasus and Ursinus to seize

---

[1] The expressions which I have used are temperate and feeble, if compared with the vehement invectives of Jerom (tom. i. p. 13, 45, 144, etc. [tom. i. p. 259, etc., ed. Vallars.]). In *his* turn he was reproached with the guilt which he imputed to his brother monks: and the *Sceleratus*, the *Versipellis*, was publicly accused as the lover of the widow Paula (tom. ii. p. 363). He undoubtedly possessed the affections both of the mother and the daughter; but he declares that he never abused his influence to any selfish or sensual purpose.

[2] Pudet dicere, sacerdotes idolorum, mimi et aurigæ, et scorta, hæreditates capiunt: solis *clericis* ac *monachis* hâc [hoc] lege prohibetur. Et non prohibetur a persecutoribus, sed a principibus Christianis. Nec de lege queror; sed doleo cur *meruerimus* hanc legem. Jerom (tom. i. p. 13 [tom. i. p. 258, ed. Vallars.]) discreetly insinuates the secret policy of his patron Damasus.

[3] Three words of Jerom, *sanctæ memoriæ Damasus* (tom. ii. p. 109 [Ep. ad Pammachium. tom. i. p. 228, ed. Vallars.]), wash away all his stains, and blind the devout eyes of Tillemont (Mém. Ecclés. tom. viii. p. 386-424).

the episcopal seat surpassed the ordinary measure of human ambition. They contended with the rage of party; the quarrel was maintained by the wounds and death of their followers; and the præfect, unable to resist or to appease the tumult, was constrained by superior violence to retire into the suburbs. Damasus prevailed: the well-disputed victory remained on the side of his faction; one hundred and thirty-seven dead bodies [1] were found in the *Basilica* of Sicininus,[2] where the Christians hold their religious assemblies; and it was long before the angry minds of the people resumed their accustomed tranquillity. When I consider the splendour of the capital, I am not astonished that so valuable a prize should inflame the desires of ambitious men, and produce the fiercest and most obstinate contests. The successful candidate is secure that he will be enriched by the offerings of matrons;[3] that, as soon as his dress is composed with becoming care and elegance, he may proceed in his chariot through the streets of Rome;[4] and that the sumptuousness of the Imperial table will not equal the profuse and delicate entertainments provided by the taste and at the expense of the Roman pontiffs. How much more rationally (continues the honest Pagan) would those pontiffs consult their true happiness, if, instead of alleging the greatness of the city as an excuse for their manners, they would imitate the exemplary life of some provincial bishops, whose temperance and sobriety, whose mean apparel and downcast looks, recommend their pure and modest virtue to the Deity and his true worshippers!"[5] The schism of Damasus and Ursinus was extinguished by the exile of the latter; and the wisdom of the præfect Prætextatus[6] restored

---

[1] Jerom himself is forced to allow, crudelissimæ interfectiones diversi sexûs perpetratæ (in Chron. p. 186 [tom. viii. p. 809, ed. Vallars.]). But an original *libel* or petition of two presbyters of the adverse party has unaccountably escaped. They affirm that the doors of the basilica were burnt, and that the roof was untiled; that Damasus marched at the head of his own clergy, gravediggers, charioteers, and hired gladiators; that none of *his* party were killed, but that one hundred and sixty dead bodies were found. This petition is published by the P. Sirmond, in the first volume of his works.

[2] The *Basilica* of Sicininus, or Liberius, is probably the church of Sancta Maria Maggiore, on the Esquiline hill. Baronius, A.D. 367, No. 3; and Donatus, Roma Antiqua et Nova, l. iv. c. 3, p. 462.

[3] The enemies of Damasus styled him *Auriscalpius Matronarum*, the ladies' ear-scratcher.

[4] Gregory Nazianzen (Orat. xxxii. p. 526) describes the pride and luxury of the prelates who reigned in the Imperial cities; their gilt car, fiery steeds, numerous train, etc. The crowd gave way as to a wild beast.

[5] Ammian. xxvii. 3. Perpetuo Numini, *verisque* ejus cultoribus. The incomparable pliancy of a polytheist!

[6] Ammianus, who makes a fair report of his præfecture (xxvii. 9), styles

the tranquillity of the city. Prætextatus was a philosophic Pagan, a man of learning, of taste, and politeness; who disguised a reproach in the form of a jest, when he assured Damasus that if he could obtain the bishopric of Rome, he himself would immediately embrace the Christian religion.[1] This lively picture of the wealth and luxury of the popes in the fourth century becomes the more curious as it represents the intermediate degree between the humble poverty of the apostolic fisherman and the royal state of a temporal prince whose dominions extend from the confines of Naples to the banks of the Po.

When the suffrage of the generals and of the army committed the sceptre of the Roman empire to the hands of Valentinian, his reputation in arms, his military skill and experience, and his rigid attachment to the forms as well as spirit of ancient discipline, were the principal motives of their judicious choice. The eagerness of the troops, who pressed him to nominate his colleague, was justified by the dangerous situation of public affairs; and Valentinian himself was conscious that the abilities of the most active mind were unequal to the defence of the distant frontiers of an invaded monarchy. As soon as the death of Julian had relieved the barbarians from the terror of his name, the most sanguine hopes of rapine and conquest excited the nations of the East, of the North, and of the South. Their inroads were often vexatious, and sometimes formidable; but, during the twelve years of the reign of Valentinian, his firmness and vigilance protected his own dominions; and his powerful genius seemed to inspire and direct the feeble counsels of his brother. Perhaps the method of annals would more forcibly express the urgent and divided cares of the two emperors; but the attention of the reader, likewise, would be distracted by a tedious and desultory narrative. A separate view of the five great theatres of war— I. Germany; II. Britain; III. Africa; IV. The East; and V. The Danube—will impress a more distinct image of the

---

him præclaræ indolis, gravitatisque, senator (xxii. 7, and Vales. ad loc.). A curious inscription (Gruter MCII. No. 2) records, in two columns, his religious and civil honours. In one line he was Pontiff of the Sun and of Vesta, Augur, Quindecemvir, Hierophant, etc., etc. In the other, 1. Quæstor candidatus, more probably titular. 2. Prætor. 3. Corrector of Tuscany and Umbria. 4. Consular of Lusitania. 5. Proconsul of Achaia. 6. Præfect of Rome. 7. Prætorian præfect of Italy. 8. Of Illyricum. 9. Consul elect; but he died before the begining of the year 385. See Tillemont, Hist. des Empereurs, tom. v. p. 241, 736.

[1] Facite me Romanæ urbis episcopum, et ero protinus Christianus (Jerom, tom. ii. p. 165 [contra Joann. Ierosol. tom. ii. p. 415, ed. Vallars.]). It is more than probable that Damasus would not have purchased his conversion at such a price.

military state of the empire under the reigns of Valentinian
and Valens.

I. The ambassadors of the Alemanni had been offended by
the harsh and haughty behaviour of Ursacius, master of the
offices;[1] who, by an act of unseasonable parsimony, had
diminished the value, as well as the quantity, of the presents to
which they were entitled, either from custom or treaty, on the
accession of a new emperor. They expressed, and they communicated to their countrymen, their strong sense of the
national affront. The irascible minds of the chiefs were exasperated by the suspicion of contempt; and the martial youth
crowded to their standard. Before Valentinian could pass the
Alps, the villages of Gaul were in flames: before his general
Dagalaiphus could encounter the Alemanni, they had secured
the captives and the spoil in the forests of Germany. In the
beginning of the ensuing year the military force of the whole
nation, in deep and solid columns, broke through the barrier of
the Rhine during the severity of a northern winter. Two Roman
counts were defeated and mortally wounded; and the standard
of the Heruli and Batavians fell into the hands of the conquerors,
who displayed, with insulting shouts and menaces, the trophy
of their victory.

The standard was recovered; but the Batavians had not
redeemed the shame of their disgrace and flight in the eyes
of their severe judge. It was the opinion of Valentinian that
his soldiers must learn to fear their commander before they
could cease to fear the enemy. The troops were solemnly
assembled; and the trembling Batavians were enclosed within
the circle of the Imperial army. Valentinian then ascended his
tribunal; and, as if he disdained to punish cowardice with death,
he inflicted a stain of indelible ignominy on the officers whose
misconduct and pusillanimity were found to be the first occasion
of the defeat. The Batavians were degraded from their rank,
stripped of their arms, and condemned to be sold for slaves to
the highest bidder. At this tremendous sentence the troops
fell prostrate on the ground, deprecated the indignation of their
sovereign, and protested that if he would indulge them in another
trial, they would approve themselves not unworthy of the name
of Romans, and of his soldiers. Valentinian, with affected
reluctance, yielded to their entreaties: the Batavians resumed
their arms; and, with their arms, the invincible resolution of

---

[1] Ammian. xxvi. 5. Valesius adds a long and good note on the master
of the offices.

wiping away their disgrace in the blood of the Alemanni.[1] The principal command was declined by Dagalaiphus; and that experienced general, who had represented, perhaps with too much prudence, the extreme difficulties of the undertaking, had the mortification, before the end of the campaign, of seeing his rival Jovinus convert those difficulties into a decisive advantage over the scattered forces of the barbarians. At the head of a well-disciplined army of cavalry, infantry, and light troops, Jovinus advanced, with cautious and rapid steps, to Scarponna,[2] in the territory of Metz, where he surprised a large division of the Alemanni before they had time to run to their arms; and flushed his soldiers with the confidence of an easy and bloodless victory. Another division, or rather army, of the enemy, after the cruel and wanton devastation of the adjacent country, reposed themselves on the shady banks of the Moselle.[2] Jovinus, who had viewed the ground with the eye of a general, made his silent approach through a deep and woody vale, till he could distinctly perceive the indolent security of the Germans. Some were bathing their huge limbs in the river; others were combing their long and flaxen hair; others again were swallowing large draughts of rich and delicious wine. On a sudden they heard the sound of the Roman trumpet; they saw the enemy in their camp. Astonishment produced disorder; disorder was followed by flight and dismay; and the confused multitude of the bravest warriors was pierced by the swords and javelins of the legionaries and auxiliaries. The fugitives escaped to the third, and most considerable, camp in the Catalaunian plains, near Châlons in Champagne: the straggling detachments were hastily recalled to their standard; and the barbarian chiefs, alarmed and admonished by the fate of their companions, prepared to encounter in a decisive battle the victorious forces of the lieutenant of Valentinian. The bloody and obstinate conflict lasted a whole summer's day, with equal valour and with alternate success. The Romans at length prevailed, with the loss of about twelve hundred men. Six thousand of the Alemanni were slain, four thousand were wounded; and the brave Jovinus, after chasing the flying remnant of their host as far as the banks of the Rhine,

---

[1] Ammian. xxvii. 1. Zosimus, l. iv. [c. 9] p. 208. The disgrace of the Batavians is suppressed by the contemporary soldier, from a regard for military honour, which could not affect a Greek rhetorician of the succeeding age.

[2] See D'Anville, Notice de l'Ancienne Gaule, p. 587. The name of the Moselle, which is not specified by Ammianus, is clearly understood by Mascou (Hist. of the Ancient Germans, vii. 2).

returned to Paris, to receive the applause of his sovereign, and the ensigns of the consulship for the ensuing year.[1] The triumph of the Romans was indeed sullied by their treatment of the captive king, whom they hung on a gibbet, without the knowledge of their indignant general. This disgraceful act of cruelty, which might be imputed to the fury of the troops, was followed by the deliberate murder of Withicab, the son of Vadomair, a German prince, of a weak and sickly constitution, but of a daring and formidable spirit. The domestic assassin was instigated and protected by the Romans;[2] and the violation of the laws of humanity and justice betrayed their secret apprehension of the weakness of the declining empire. The use of the dagger is seldom adopted in public councils, as long as they retain any confidence in the power of the sword.

While the Alemanni appeared to be humbled by their recent calamities, the pride of Valentinian was mortified by the unexpected surprisal of Moguntiacum, or Mentz, the principal city of the Upper Germany. In the unsuspicious moment of a Christian festival, Rando, a bold and artful chieftain, who had long meditated his attempt, suddenly passed the Rhine, entered the defenceless town, and retired with a multitude of captives of either sex. Valentinian resolved to execute severe vengeance on the whole body of the nation. Count Sebastian, with the bands of Italy and Illyricum, was ordered to invade their country, most probably on the side of Rhætia. The emperor in person, accompanied by his son Gratian, passed the Rhine at the head of a formidable army, which was supported on both flanks by Jovinus and Severus, the two masters-general of the cavalry and infantry of the West. The Alemanni, unable to prevent the devastation of their villages, fixed their camp on a lofty and almost inaccessible mountain in the modern duchy of Wirtemberg, and resolutely expected the approach of the Romans. The life of Valentinian was exposed to imminent danger by the intrepid curiosity with which he persisted to explore some secret and unguarded path. A troop of barbarians suddenly rose from their ambuscade; and the emperor, who vigorously spurred his horse down a steep and slippery descent, was obliged to leave behind him his armour-bearer, and his helmet magnificently enriched with gold and precious stones. At the signal of the general assault, the Roman troops

[1] The battles are described by Ammianus (xxvii. 2) and by Zosimus (l. iv. [c. 9] p. 209), who supposes Valentinian to have been present.
[2] Studio solicitante nostrorum, occubuit. Ammian. xxvii. 10.

encompassed and ascended the mountain of Solicinium on three different sides. Every step which they gained increased their ardour, and abated the resistance of the enemy: and after their united forces had occupied the summit of the hill, they impetuously urged the barbarians down the northern descent, where Count Sebastian was posted to intercept their retreat. After this signal victory Valentinian returned to his winter quarters at Trèves, where he indulged the public joy by the exhibition of splendid and triumphal games.[1] But the wise monarch, instead of aspiring to the conquest of Germany, confined his attention to the important and laborious defence of the Gallic frontier, against an enemy whose strength was renewed by a stream of daring volunteers, which incessantly flowed from the most distant tribes of the North.[2] The banks of the Rhine, from its source to the straits of the ocean, were closely planted with strong castles and convenient towers; new works and new arms were invented by the ingenuity of a prince who was skilled in the mechanical arts; and his numerous levies of Roman and barbarian youth were severely trained in all the exercises of war. The progress of the work, which was sometimes opposed by modest representations and sometimes by hostile attempts, secured the tranquillity of Gaul during the nine subsequent years of the administration of Valentinian.[3]

[1] The expedition of Valentinian is related by Ammianus (xxvii. 10); and celebrated by Ausonius (Mosell. 421, etc.), who foolishly supposes that the Romans were ignorant of the sources of the Danube.
[Dr. William Smith points out that Ausonius merely says that " they are not recorded in Roman history."—O. S.]

[2] Immanis enim natio, jam inde ab incunabulis primis varietate casuum imminuta; ita sæpius adolescit, ut fuisse longis sæculis æstimetur intacta. Ammian. xxviii. 5. The Count de Buat (Hist. des Peuples de l'Europe, tom. vi. p. 370), ascribes the fecundity of the Alemanni to their easy adoption of strangers.
[Guizot cites the following passage from Malthus as throwing light on this point of the extraordinary fecundity of the Alemanni, as shown by the fact that while the birth-rate of Rome was decreasing, that of the Germans was increasing beyond all precedent. Malthus asks, " What northern reservoir supplied this incessant stream of daring adventurers? Montesquieu's solution of the problem will, I think, hardly be admitted. (Grandeur et Decadence des Romains, c. 16, p. 187). The whole difficulty is at once removed if we apply to the German nations, at that time, a fact which is so generally known to have occurred in America, and suppose that, when not checked by wars and famine, they increased at a rate which would double their numbers in twenty-five or thirty years. The propriety, nay, even the necessity of applying this rate of increase to the inhabitants of ancient Germany, will strikingly appear from that valuable picture of their manners which has been left us by Tacitus." [Tac. Germania, section De Moribus Germanorum, c. 16-20.—O.S.]

[3] Ammian. xxviii. 2. Zosimus, l. iv. [c. 16] p. 214. The younger Victor mentions the mechanical genius of Valentinian: nova arma meditari; fingere terrâ seu limo simulacra. [Epit. c. 45.]

That prudent emperor, who diligently practised the wise maxims of Diocletian, was studious to foment and excite the intestine divisions of the tribes of Germany. About the middle of the fourth century, the countries, perhaps of Lusace and Thuringia, on either side of the Elbe, were occupied by the vague dominion of the BURGUNDIANS, a warlike and numerous people of the Vandal race,[1] whose obscure name insensibly swelled into a powerful kingdom, and has finally settled on a flourishing province. The most remarkable circumstance in the ancient manners of the Burgundians appears to have been the difference of their civil and ecclesiastical constitution. The appellation of *Hendinos* was given to the king or general, and the title of *Sinistus* to the high-priest of the nation. The person of the priest was sacred, and his dignity perpetual; but the temporal government was held by a very precarious tenure. If the events of war accused the courage or conduct of the king, he was immediately deposed; and the injustice of his subjects made him responsible for the fertility of the earth and the regularity of the seasons, which seemed to fall more properly within the sacerdotal department.[2] The disputed possession of some salt-pits[3] engaged the Alemanni and the Burgundians in frequent contests: the latter were easily tempted by the secret solicitations and liberal offers of the emperor; and their fabulous descent from the Roman soldiers who had formerly been left to garrison the fortresses of Drusus was admitted with mutual credulity, as it was conducive to mutual interest.[4] An army of fourscore thousand Burgundians soon appeared on the banks of the Rhine, and impatiently required the support and subsidies which

---

[1] Bellicosos et pubis immensæ viribus affluentes; et ideo metuendos finitimis universis. Ammian. xxviii. 5.
[Pliny thought the Burgundians to be a pure Vandalic race. In reality they were cognate in blood and speech to both the Vandals and the Goths. —O. S.]

[2] I am always apt to suspect historians and travellers of improving extraordinary facts into general laws. Ammianus ascribes a similar custom to Egypt; and the Chinese have imputed it to the Ta-tsin, or Roman empire (De Guignes, Hist. des Huns, tom. ii. part i. p. 79).

[3] Salinarum finiumque causâ Alemannis sæpe jurgabant. Ammian. xxviii. 5. Possibly they disputed the possession of the *Sala*, a river which produced salt, and which had been the object of ancient contention. Tacit. Annal. xiii. 57, and Lipsius ad loc.

[4] Jam inde temporibus priscis sobolem se esse Romanam Burgundii sciunt: and the vague tradition gradually assumed a more regular form (Oros. l. vii. c. 32). It is annihilated by the decisive authority of Pliny, who composed the History of Drusus, and served in Germany (Plin. Secund. Epist. iii. 5), within sixty years after the death of that hero. *Germanorum genera* quinque; Vindili. quorum pars *Burgundiones*, etc. (Hist. Natur. iv. 28).

Valentinian had promised; but they were amused with excuses and delays, till at length, after a fruitless expectation, they were compelled to retire. The arms and fortifications of the Gallic frontier checked the fury of their just resentment; and their massacre of the captives served to embitter the hereditary feud of the Burgundians and the Alemanni. The inconstancy of a wise prince may perhaps be explained by some alteration of circumstances; and perhaps it was the original design of Valentinian to intimidate rather than to destroy; as the balance of power would have been equally overturned by the extirpation of either of the German nations. Among the princes of the Alemanni, Macrianus, who, with a Roman name, had assumed the arts of a soldier and a statesman, deserved his hatred and esteem. The emperor himself, with a light and unincumbered band, condescended to pass the Rhine, marched fifty miles into the country, and would infallibly have seized the object of his pursuit, if his judicious measures had not been defeated by the impatience of the troops. Macrianus was afterwards admitted to the honour of a personal conference with the emperor; and the favours which he received fixed him, till the hour of his death, a steady and sincere friend of the republic.[1]

The land was covered by the fortifications of Valentinian; but the sea-coast of Gaul and Britain was exposed to the depredations of the Saxons. That celebrated name, in which we have a dear and domestic interest, escaped the notice of Tacitus; and in the maps of Ptolemy it faintly marks the narrow neck of the Cimbric peninsula, and three small islands towards the mouth of the Elbe.[2] This contracted territory, the present duchy of Schleswig, or perhaps of Holstein, was incapable of pouring forth the inexhaustible swarms of Saxons who reigned over the ocean, who filled the British island with their language, their laws, and their colonies, and who so long defended the liberty of the North against the arms of Charlemagne.[3] The solution of this diffi-

[1] The wars and negotiations relative to the Burgundians and Alemanni are distinctly related by Ammianus Marcellinus.(xxviii. 5, xxix. 4, xxx. 3). Orosius (l. vii. c. 32), and the Chronicles of Jerom and Cassiodorus, fix some dates and add some circumstances.

[2] Ἐπὶ τὸν αὐχένα τῆς Κιμβρικῆς Χερσονήσου, Σάξονες. At the northern extremity of the peninsula (the Cimbric promontory of Pliny, iv. 27) Ptolemy fixes the remnant of the *Cimbri*. He fills the interval between the *Saxons* and the Cimbri with six obscure tribes, who were united, as early as the sixth century, under the national appellation of *Danes*. See Cluver German. Antiq. l. iii. c. 21, 22, 23.

[3] M. d'Anville (Etablissement des Etats de l'Europe, etc., p. 19-26) has marked the extensive limits of the Saxony of Charlemagne.

[Latham proposes another solution of this Saxon problem. He suggests culty is easily derived from the similar manners and loose constitution of the tribes of Germany, which were blended with each other by the slightest accidents of war or friendship. The situation of the native Saxons disposed them to embrace the hazardous professions of fishermen and pirates; and the success of their first adventures would naturally excite the emulation of their bravest countrymen, who were impatient of the gloomy solitude of their woods and mountains. Every tide might float down the Elbe whole fleets of canoes, filled with hardy and intrepid associates, who aspired to behold the unbounded prospect of the ocean, and to taste the wealth and luxury of unknown worlds. It should seem probable, however, that the most numerous auxiliaries of the Saxons were furnished by the nations who dwelt along the shores of the Baltic. They possessed arms and ships, the art of navigation, and the habits of naval war; but the difficulty of issuing through the northern Columns of Hercules [1] (which during several months of the year are obstructed with ice) confined their skill and courage within the limits of a spacious lake. The rumour of the successful armaments which sailed from the mouth of the Elbe would soon provoke them to cross the narrow isthmus of Schleswig, and to launch their vessels on the great sea. The various troops of pirates and adventurers who fought under the same standard were insensibly united in a permanent society, at first of rapine, and afterwards of government. A military confederation was

that the term " Saxon " was a general appellation given by the Celts of Britain to the Germans of the sea-coast and the water-systems of the Lower Rhine, Weser, Lower Elbe, and Eyder, to Low Germans on the Rhine, to Frisians and Saxons on the Elbe, and to North Frisians on the Eyder. He observes that Saxon was a word like Greek, *i.e.* a term which in the language of the Hellenes was so very special, partial, and unimportant, as to have been practically a foreign term, or at least anything but a native name, whilst in that of the Romans it was one of general and widely extended import. Hence, *mutatis mutandis*, it is the insignificant Saxones of the neck of the Cimbric Chersonese, and the three Saxon islands first mentioned by Ptolemy, who are the analogues of the equally unimportant Græci of Epirus; and these it was whose name eventually comprised populations as different as the Angles and the Saxons of Saxony, even as the word Græcus in the mouth of a Roman comprised Dorians, Æolians, Macedonians, Athenians, Rhodians, etc. In this way the name was German, but its extended import was Celtic and Roman. Cf. Latham. Germania of Tacitus, Epilegomena, p. cxv. ff., also Morris, Outlines of English Accidence, pp. 3-10.—O. S.]

[1] The fleet of Drusus had failed in their attempt to pass, or even to approach, the *Sound* (styled, from an obvious resemblance, the Columns of Hercules), and the naval enterprise was never resumed (Tacit. de Moribus German. c. 34). The knowledge which the Romans acquired of the naval powers of the Baltic (c. 44, 45) was obtained by their land journeys in search of amber.

gradually moulded into a national body by the gentle operation
of marriage and consanguinity; and the adjacent tribes, who
solicited the alliance, accepted the name and laws of the Saxons.
If the fact were not established by the most unquestionable
evidence, we should appear to abuse the credulity of our readers
by the description of the vessels in which the Saxon pirates
ventured to sport in the waves of the German Ocean, the British
Channel, and the Bay of Biscay. The keel of their large flat-
bottomed boats was framed of light timber, but the sides and
upper works consisted only of wicker, with a covering of strong
hides.[1] In the course of their slow and distant navigations they
must always have been exposed to the danger, and very frequently to the misfortune, of shipwreck; and the naval annals
of the Saxons were undoubtedly filled with the accounts of the
losses which they sustained on the coasts of Britain and Gaul.
But the daring spirit of the pirates braved the perils both of the
sea and of the shore: their skill was confirmed by the habits of
enterprise; the meanest of their mariners was alike capable of
handling an oar, of rearing a sail, or of conducting a vessel; and
the Saxons rejoiced in the appearance of a tempest, which concealed their design, and dispersed the fleets of the enemy.[2]
After they had acquired an accurate knowledge of the maritime
provinces of the West they extended the scene of their depredations, and the most sequestered places had no reason to presume
on their security. The Saxon boats drew so little water that they

---

[1] Quin et Aremoricus piratam *Saxona* tractus
     Sperabat; cui pelle salum sulcare Britannum
     Ludus; et assuto glaucum mare findere lembo.
                         Sidon. in Panegyr. Avit. 369.
The genius of Cæsar imitated, for a particular service, these rude, but light
vessels, which were likewise used by the natives of Britain (Comment. de
Bell. Civil. i. 54, and Guichardt, Nouveaux Mémoires Militaires, tom. ii.
p. 41, 42). The British vessels would now astonish the genius of Cæsar.
  [2] The best original account of the Saxon pirates may be found in Sidonius
Apollinaris (l. viii. Epist. 6, p. 223, edit. Sirmond), and the best commentary in the Abbé du Bos (Hist. Critique de la Monarchie Françoise, etc.,
tom. i. l. i. c. 16, p. 148-155. See likewise p. 77, 78).
  [With regard to the Saxon inroads, it would appear that they were
settled at this time on the coast of Gaul, since the Notitia (Imp. Occid. c.
36), which must have been drawn up at this period (according to Dr. W.
Smith) or shortly after, the " Littus Saxonicum " is mentioned as part of
the Armorican limit. In the " Notitia " the settlement is named Gran-
nona, of which the site is uncertain, but subsequently we find the Saxons
permanently settled near Bayeux. In the " Notitia " (c. 25, Imp. Occid.
the " Littus Saxonicum per Britannias " is also mentioned, which goes to
show that the Saxons were settled in our island earlier than is usually
supposed, probably at the same time as their brethren on the opposite
coast of Gaul. Cf. Kemble, *The Saxons in England*, vol. i. p. 13; Pal-
grave, *Rise and Progress of the English Commonwealth* vol. i. p. 384.—O. S.]

could easily proceed fourscore or an hundred miles up the great rivers; their weight was so inconsiderable that they were transported on waggons from one river to another; and the pirates who had entered the mouth of the Seine or of the Rhine might descend, with the rapid stream of the Rhone, into the Mediterranean. Under the reign of Valentinian the maritime provinces of Gaul were afflicted by the Saxons: a military count was stationed for the defence of the sea-coast, or Armorican limit; and that officer, who found his strength or his abilities unequal to the task, implored the assistance of Severus, master-general of the infantry. The Saxons, surrounded and outnumbered, were forced to relinquish their spoil, and to yield a select band of their tall and robust youth to serve in the Imperial armies. They stipulated only a safe and honourable retreat; and the condition was readily granted by the Roman general, who meditated an act of perfidy,[1] imprudent as it was inhuman, while a Saxon remained alive and in arms to revenge the fate of his countrymen. The premature eagerness of the infantry, who were secretly posted in a deep valley, betrayed the ambuscade; and they would perhaps have fallen the victims of their own treachery, if a large body of cuirassiers, alarmed by the noise of the combat, had not hastily advanced to extricate their companions, and to overwhelm the undaunted valour of the Saxons. Some of the prisoners were saved from the edge of the sword to shed their blood in the amphitheatre; and the orator Symmachus complains that twenty-nine of those desperate savages, by strangling themselves with their own hands, had disappointed the amusement of the public. Yet the polite and philosophic citizens of Rome were impressed with the deepest horror when they were informed that the Saxons consecrated to the gods the tithe of their *human* spoil; and that they ascertained by lot the objects of the barbarous sacrifice.[2]

II. The fabulous colonies of Egyptians and Trojans, of Scandinavians and Spaniards, which flattered the pride and amused the credulity of our rude ancestors, have insensibly vanished in the light of science and philosophy.[3] The present age is

[1] Ammian. (xxviii. 5) justifies this breach of faith to pirates and robbers; and Orosius (l. vii. c. 32) more clearly expresses their real guilt; virtute atque agilitate terribiles.

[2] Symmachus (l. ii. Epist. 46) still presumes to mention the sacred names of Socrates and philosophy. Sidonius, bishop of Clermont, might condemn (l. viii. Epist. 6), with *less* inconsistency, the human sacrifices of the Saxons.

[3] In the beginning of the last century the learned Camden was obliged to undermine with respectful scepticism, the romance of *Brutus* the

satisfied with the simple and rational opinion that the islands of Great Britain and Ireland were gradually peopled from the adjacent continent of Gaul. From the coast of Kent, to the extremity of Caithness and Ulster, the memory of a Celtic origin was distinctly preserved in the perpetual resemblance of language, of religion, and of manners: and the peculiar characters of the British tribes might be naturally ascribed to the influence of accidental and local circumstances.[1]   The Roman province was reduced to the state of civilised and peaceful servitude: the rights of savage freedom were contracted to the narrow limits of Caledonia.   The inhabitants of that northern region were divided, as early as the reign of Constantine, between the two great tribes of the SCOTS and of the PICTS,[2] who have since experienced a very different fortune.   The power, and almost the memory, of the Picts have been extinguished by their successful rivals; and the Scots, after maintaining for ages the dignity of an indpendent kingdom, have multiplied, by an equal and voluntary union, the honours of the English name.   The hand of nature had contributed to mark the ancient distinction of the Scots and Picts.   The former were the men of the hills, and the latter those of the plain.   The eastern coast of Caledonia may be considered as a level and fertile country, which, even in a rude state of tillage, was capable of producing a considerable quantity of corn; and the epithet of *cruitnich*, or wheat-eaters, expressed the contempt or envy of the carnivorous highlander.

Trojan, who is now buried in silent oblivion, with *Scota*, the daughter of Pharaoh, and her numerous progeny.   Yet I am informed that some champions of the *Milesian colony* may still be found among the original natives of Ireland.   A people dissatisfied with their present condition grasp at any visions of their past or future glory.

[1] Tacitus, or rather his father-in-law Agricola, might remark the German or Spanish complexion of some British tribes.   But it was their sober, deliberate opinion: " In universum tamen æstimanti Gallos vicinum solum occupâsse credibile est   Eorum sacra deprehendas · · · sermo haud multum diversus " (in Vit. Agricol. c. xi.).   Cæsar had observed their common religion (Comment. de Bello Gallico, vi. 13); and in his time the emigration from the Belgic Gaul was a recent, or at least an historical event (v. 12). Camden, the British Strabo, has modestly ascertained our genuine antiquities (Britannia, vol. i. Introduction, p. ii.-xxxi.).

[2] In the dark and doubtful paths of Caledonian antiquity, I have chosen for my guides two learned and ingenious Highlanders, whose birth and education had peculiarly qualified for that office.   See Critical Dissertations on the Origin, Antiquities, etc., of the Caledonians, by Dr. John Macpherson, London, 1768, in 4to.; and Introduction to the History of Great Britain and Ireland, by James Macpherson, Esq., London, 1773, in 4to. third edit.   Dr. Macpherson was a minister in the Isle of Skye: and it is a circumstance honourable for the present age, that a work replete with erudition and criticism should have been composed in the most remote of the Hebrides.

The cultivation of the earth might introduce a more accurate separation of property, and the habits of a sedentary life; but the love of arms and rapine was still the ruling passion of the Picts; and their warriors, who stripped themselves for a day of battle, were distinguished, in the eyes of the Romans, by the strange fashion of painting their naked bodies with gaudy colours and fantastic figures. The western part of Caledonia irregularly rises into wild and barren hills, which scarcely repay the toil of the husbandman, and are most profitably used for the pasture of cattle. The highlanders were condemned to the occupations of shepherds and hunters; and as they seldom were fixed to any permanent habitation, they acquired the expressive name of Scots, which, in the Celtic tongue, is said to be equivalent to that of *wanderers*, or *vagrants*. The inhabitants of a barren land were urged to seek a fresh supply of food in the waters. The deep lakes and bays which intersect their country are plentifully stored with fish; and they gradually ventured to cast their nets in the waves of the ocean. The vicinity of the Hebrides, so profusely scattered along the western coast of Scotland, tempted their curiosity and improved their skill; and they acquired, by slow degrees, the art, or rather the habit, of managing their boats in a tempestuous sea, and of steering their nocturnal course by the light of the well-known stars. The two bold headlands of Caledonia almost touch the shores of a spacious island, which obtained, from its luxuriant vegetation, the epithet of *Green ;* and has preserved, with a slight alteration, the name of Erin, or Ierne, or Ireland. It is *probable* that in some remote period of antiquity the fertile plains of Ulster received a colony of hungry Scots; and that the strangers of the North, who had dared to encounter the arms of the legions, spread their conquests over the savage and unwarlike natives of a solitary island. It is *certain* that, in the declining age of the Roman empire, Caledonia, Ireland, and the Isle of Man were inhabited by the Scots, and that the kindred tribes, who were often associated in military enterprise, were deeply affected by the various accidents of their mutual fortunes. They long cherished the lively tradition of their common name and origin: and the missionaries of the Isle of Saints, who diffused the light of Christianity over North Britain, established the vain opinion that their Irish countrymen were the natural, as well as spiritual, fathers of the Scottish race. The loose and obscure tradition has been preserved by the venerable Bede, who scattered some rays of light over the darkness of the eighth century. On this slight foundation a huge

superstructure of fable was gradually reared by the bards and
the monks; two orders of men who equally abused the privilege
of fiction. The Scottish nation, with mistaken pride, adopted
their Irish genealogy: and the annals of a long line of imaginary
kings have been adorned by the fancy of Boethius and the
classic elegance of Buchanan.[1]

Six years after the death of Constantine the destructive inroads
of the Scots and Picts required the presence of his youngest
son, who reigned in the Western empire. Constans visited his
British dominions: but we may form some estimate of the
importance of his achievements by the language of panegyric,
which celebrates only his triumph over the elements, or, in other
words, the good fortune of a safe and easy passage from the port
of Boulogne to the harbour of Sandwich.[2] The calamities which
the afflicted provincials continued to experience from foreign

---

[1] The Irish descent of the Scots has been revived, in the last moments of
its decay, and strenuously supported, by the Rev. Mr. Whitaker (Hist. of
Manchester, vol. i. p. 430, 431; and Genuine History of the Britons
asserted, etc., p. 154-293). Yet he acknowledges, 1. *That* the Scots of
Ammianus Marcellinus (A.D. 340) were already settled in Caledonia, and
that the Roman authors do not afford any hints of their emigration from
another country. 2. *That all* the accounts of such emigrations, which
have been asserted or received, by Irish bards, Scotch historians, or
English antiquaries (Buchanan, Camden, Usher, Stillingfleet, etc.), are
totally fabulous. 3. *That* three of the Irish tribes, which are mentioned
by Ptolemy (A.D. 150), were of Caledonian extraction. 4. *That* a younger
branch of Caledonian princes, of the house of Fingal, acquired and possessed
the monarchy of Ireland. After these concessions, the remaining difference
between Mr. Whitaker and his adversaries is minute and obscure. The
genuine history, which he produces, of a Fergus, the cousin of Ossian, who
was transplanted (A.D. 320) from Ireland to Caledonia, is built on a con-
jectural supplement to the Erse poetry, and the feeble evidence of Richard
of Cirencester, a monk of the fourteenth century. The lively spirit of the
learned and ingenious antiquarian has tempted him to forget the nature of
a question which he so *vehemently* debates, and so *absolutely* decides.
[The origin of the Picts and Scots has been a vexed question for the past
120 years. With respect to the Scots, it is now generally admitted that
they belonged to the same race as the inhabitants of Ireland, being indeed
emigrants from the north-east of Ireland, and are to all intents and purposes represented by the Gaels of the present day. The Picts are now
generally believed to be closely allied to the Kelts and the Welsh. They
were probably those ancient Caledonian tribes which inhabited the far
north of Scotland, and were the remains of an older emigration from
Gaul. Both Professor Rhys and Professor Bury have fallen into error
here. Cf. Skene, *Celtic Scotland*, vol. i., also Hume Brown's *History of
Scotland*, vol. i. chaps. i.-iii.; Andrew Lang's *History of Scotland*, vol. i.
chaps. i.-v. The Picts are more akin to the Welsh, the Cornish and the
Armoricans than to the Gaels proper.—O. S.]
[2] Hieme tumentes ac sævientes undas calcâstis Oceani sub remis
vestris; . . . insperatum imperatoris faciem Britannus expavit. Julius
Firmicus Maternus de Errore Profan. Relig. p. 464 [p. 59, ed. Lugd. B.
1672] edit. Gronov. ad calcem Minuc. Fel. See Tillemont (Hist. des
Empereurs, tom. iv. p. 336).

war and domestic tyranny were aggravated by the feeble and corrupt administration of the eunuchs of Constantius; and the transient relief which they might obtain from the virtues of Julian was soon lost by the absence and death of their bene-factor. The sums of gold and silver which had been painfully collected, or liberally transmitted, for the payment of the troops, were intercepted by the avarice of the commanders; discharges, or, at least, exemptions, from the military service, were publicly sold; the distress of the soldiers, who were injuriously deprived of their legal and scanty subsistence, provoked them to frequent desertion; the nerves of discipline were relaxed, and the high-ways were infested with robbers.[1] The oppression of the good and the impunity of the wicked equally contributed to diffuse through the island a spirit of discontent and revolt; and every ambitious subject, every desperate exile, might entertain a reasonable hope of subverting the weak and distracted govern-ment of Britain. The hostile tribes of the North, who detested the pride and power of the King of the World, suspended their domestic feuds; and the barbarians of the land and sea, the Scots, the Picts, and the Saxons, spread themselves, with rapid and irresistible fury, from the wall of Antoninus to the shores of Kent. Every production of art and nature, every object of convenience or luxury, which they were incapable of creating by labour or procuring by trade, was accumulated in the rich and fruitful province of Britain.[2] A philosopher may deplore the eternal discord of the human race, but he will confess that the desire of spoil is a more rational provocation than the vanity of conquest. From the age of Constantine to that of the Plan-tagenets this rapacious spirit continued to instigate the poor and hardy Caledonians: but the same people whose generous humanity seems to inspire the songs of Ossian was disgraced by a savage ignorance of the virtues of peace and of the laws of war. Their southern neighbours have felt, and perhaps exag-gerated, the cruel depredations of the Scots and Picts;[3] and a

[1] Libanius, Orat. Parent. c. xxxix. p. 264. This curious passage has escaped the diligence of our British antiquaries.

[2] The Caledonians praised and coveted the gold, the steeds, the lights, etc., of the *stranger*. See Dr. Blair's Dissertation on Ossian, vol. ii. p. 343; and Mr. Macpherson's Introduction, p. 242-286.

[3] Lord Lyttelton has circumstantially related (History of Henry II. vol. i. p. 182), and Sir David Dalrymple has slightly mentioned (Annals of Scotland, vol. i. p. 69), a barbarous inroad of the Scots, at a time (A.D. 1137) when law, religion, and society must have softened their primitive manners.

valiant tribe of Caledonia, the Attacotti,[1] the enemies, and afterwards the soldiers, of Valentinian, are accused by an eye-witness of delighting in the taste of human flesh. When they hunted the woods for prey, it is said that they attacked the shepherd rather than his flock; and that they curiously selected the most delicate and brawny parts both of males and females, which they prepared for their horrid repasts.[2] If in the neighbourhood of the commercial and literary town of Glasgow a race of cannibals has really existed, we may contemplate in the period of the Scottish history the opposite extremes of savage and civilised life. Such reflections tend to enlarge the circle of our ideas, and to encourage the pleasing hope that New Zealand may produce in some future age the Hume of the Southern Hemisphere.

Every messenger who escaped across the British Channel conveyed the most melancholy and alarming tidings to the ears of Valentinian, and the emperor was soon informed that the two military commanders of the province had been surprised and cut off by the barbarians. Severus, count of the domestics, was hastily despatched, and as suddenly recalled, by the court of Trèves. The representations of Jovinus served only to indicate the greatness of the evil, and, after a long and serious consultation, the defence, or rather the recovery, of Britain was intrusted to the abilities of the brave Theodosius. The exploits of that general, the father of a line of emperors, have been celebrated, with peculiar complacency, by the writers of the age; but his real merit deserved their applause, and his nomination was received, by the army and province, as a sure presage of approaching victory. He seized the favourable moment of navigation, and securely landed the numerous and veteran bands of the Heruli and Batavians, the Jovians and the Victors. In his march from Sandwich to London, Theodosius defeated several parties of the barbarians, released a multitude of captives, and, after distributing to his soldiers a small portion of the spoil, established the fame of disinterested justice by the restitution of the remainder to the rightful proprietors. The citizens of

---

[1] Attacotti bellicosa hominum natio. Ammian. xxvii. 8. Camden (Introduct. p. clii.) has restored their true name in the text of Jerom. The bands of Attacotti which Jerom had seen in Gaul were afterwards stationed in Italy and Illyricum (Notitia, S. viii. xxxix. xl.).

[2] Cum ipse adolescentulus in Galliâ viderim Attacottos (or ·Scotos) gentem Brittannicam humanis vesci carnibus; et cum per silvas porcorum greges, et armentorum pecudumque reperiant, pastorum *nates* et feminarum *papillas* solere abscindere; et has solas ciborum delicias arbitrari. Such is the evidence of Jerom (tom. ii. p. 75 [adv. Jovinianum, l. ii. tom. ii. p. 335, ed. Vallars.]), whose veracity I find no reason to question.

London, who had almost despaired of their safety, threw open their gates, and, as soon as Theodosius had obtained from the court of Trèves the important aid of a military lieutenant and a civil governor, he executed with wisdom and vigour the laborious task of the deliverance of Britain. The vagrant soldiers were recalled to their standard, an edict of amnesty dispelled the public apprehensions, and his cheerful example alleviated the rigour of martial discipline. The scattered and desultory warfare of the barbarians, who infested the land and sea, deprived him of the glory of a signal victory; but the prudent spirit and consummate art of the Roman general were displayed in the operations of two campaigns, which successively rescued every part of the province from the hands of a cruel and rapacious enemy. The splendour of the cities and the security of the fortifications were diligently restored by the paternal care of Theodosius, who with a strong hand confined the trembling Caledonians to the northern angle of the island, and perpetuated, by the name and settlement of the new province of *Valentia*, the glories of the reign of Valentinian.[1] The voice of poetry and panegyric may add, perhaps with some degree of truth, that the unknown regions of Thule were stained with the blood of the Picts, that the oars of Theodosius dashed the waves of the Hyperborean ocean, and that the distant Orkneys were the scene of his naval victory over the Saxon pirates.[2] He left the province with a fair as well as splendid reputation, and was immediately promoted to the rank of master-general of the cavalry by a prince who could applaud, without envy, the merit of his servants. In the important station of the Upper Danube, the conqueror of Britain checked and defeated the armies of the Alemanni, before he was chosen to suppress the revolt of Africa.

III. The prince who refuses to be the judge, instructs his people to consider him as the accomplice of his ministers. The military

[1] Ammianus has concisely represented (xx. 1, xxvi. 4, xxvii. 8, xxviii. 3) the whole series of the British war.

[2] Horrescit . . . ratibus . . . impervia Thule.
  Ille . . . nec falso nomine Pictos
 Edomuit. Scotumque vago mucrone secutus
 Fregit Hyperboreas remis audacibus undas.
     Claudian, in iii. Cons. Honorii, ver. 53, etc.
   ———Maduerunt Saxone fuso
 Orcades: incaluit Pictorum sanguine Thule.
 Scotorum cumulos flevit glacialis Ierne.
      In iv. Cons. Hon. ver. 31, etc.
See likewise Pacatus (in Panegyr. Vet. xii. 5). But it is not easy to appreciate the intrinsic value of flattery and metaphor. Compare the *British* victories of Bolanus (Statius, Silv. v. 2) with his real character (Tacit. in Vit. Agricol. c. 16).

command of Africa had been long exercised by Count Romanus,
and his abilities were not inadequate to his station; but as sordid
interest was the sole motive of his conduct, he acted on most
occasions as if he had been the enemy of the province, and the
friend of the barbarians of the desert. The three flourishing
cities of Oea, Leptis, and Sabrata, which, under the name of
Tripoli, had long constituted a federal union,[1] were obliged, for
the first time, to shut their gates against a hostile invasion;
several of their most honourable citizens were surprised and
massacred, the villages and even the suburbs were pillaged, and
the vines and fruit-trees of that rich territory were extirpated
by the malicious savages of Gætulia. The unhappy provincials
implored the protection of Romanus; but they soon found that
their military governor was not less cruel and rapacious than the
barbarians. As they were incapable of furnishing the four
thousand camels and the exorbitant present which he required
before he would march to the assistance of Tripoli, his demand
was equivalent to a refusal, and he might justly be accused
as the author of the public calamity. In the annual assembly
of the three cities, they nominated two deputies to lay at the
feet of Valentinian the customary offering of a gold victory, and
to accompany this tribute of duty, rather than of gratitude, with
their humble complaint that they were ruined by the enemy
and betrayed by their governor. If the severity of Valentinian
had been rightly directed, it would have fallen on the guilty
head of Romanus. But the count, long exercised in the arts of
corruption, had despatched a swift and trusty messenger to
secure the venal friendship of Remigius, master of the offices.
The wisdom of the imperial council was deceived by artifice, and
their honest indignation was cooled by delay. At length, when
the repetition of complaint had been justified by the repetition
of public misfortunes, the notary Palladius was sent from the
court of Trèves to examine the state of Africa and the conduct
of Romanus. The rigid impartiality of Palladius was easily
disarmed; he was tempted to reserve for himself a part of the
public treasure which he brought with him for the payment of
the troops, and, from the moment that he was conscious of his
own guilt, he could no longer refuse to attest the innocence and

---

[1] Ammianus frequently mentions their concilium annuum, legitimum,
etc. Leptis and Sabrata are long since ruined; but the city of Oea, the
native country of Apuleius, still flourishes under the provincial denomination of *Tripoli*. See Cellarius (Geograph. Antiqua, tom. ii. part ii. p. 81),
D'Anville (Géographie Ancienne, tom. iii. p. 71, 72), and Marmol (Afrique,
tom. ii. p. 562).

merit of the count. The charge of the Tripolitans was declared
to be false and frivolous, and Palladius himself was sent back
from Trèves to Africa with a special commission to discover and
prosecute the authors of this impious conspiracy against the
representatives of the sovereign. His inquiries were managed
with so much dexterity and success, that he compelled the
citizens of Leptis, who had sustained a recent siege of eight days,
to contradict the truth of their own decrees and to censure the
behaviour of their own deputies. A bloody sentence was pronounced, without hesitation, by the rash and headstrong cruelty
of Valentinian. The president of Tripoli, who had presumed
to pity the distress of the province, was publicly executed at
Utica; four distinguished citizens were put to death as the
accomplices of the imaginary fraud, and the tongues of two
others were cut out by the express order of the emperor.
Romanus, elated by impunity and irritated by resistance, was
still continued in the military command, till the Africans were
provoked, by his avarice, to join the rebellious standard of
Firmus, the Moor.[1]

His father Nabal was one of the richest and most powerful
of the Moorish princes who acknowledged the supremacy of
Rome. But as he left, either by his wives or concubines, a very
numerous posterity, the wealthy inheritance was eagerly disputed, and Zamma, one of his sons, was slain in a domestic
quarrel by his brother Firmus. The implacable zeal with which
Romanus prosecuted the legal revenge of this murder could be
ascribed only to a motive of avarice or personal hatred; but on
this occasion his claims were just, his influence was weighty,
and Firmus clearly understood that he must either present his
neck to the executioner, or appeal from the sentence of the
Imperial consistory to his sword and to the people.[2] He was
received as the deliverer of his country, and, as soon as it appeared

---

[1] Ammian. xxviii. 6. Tillemont (Hist. des Empereurs, tom. v. p. 25,
676) has discussed the chronological difficulties of the history of Count
Romanus.

[2] The chronology of Ammianus is loose and obscure; and Orosius (l. vii. c.
33, p. 551, edit. Havercamp.) seems to place the revolt of Firmus after the
deaths of Valentinian and Valens. Tillemont (Hist. des Emp. tom. v.
p. 691) endeavours to pick his way. The patient and sure-footed mule of
the Alps may be trusted in the most slippery paths.

[Gibbon has erred here through misunderstanding Orosius. What the
latter does say is that Theodosius was sent by Valentinian against Firmus
the Moor. The revolt was suppressed either in 373 according to Reiche
and Sièvers, or in 374 according to Cagnat. The war was much longer
protracted than Gibbon's account would lead us to suppose. Only after
Igmazen had been more than once severely defeated did he consent to give
up the person of the man who had sought his protection.—O. S.]

that Romanus was formidable only to a submissive province, the tyrant of Africa became the object of universal contempt. The ruin of Cæsarea, which was plundered and burnt by the licentious barbarians, convinced the refractory cities of the danger of resistance; the power of Firmus was established, at least in the provinces of Mauritania and Numidia, and it seemed to be his only doubt whether he should assume the diadem of a Moorish king or the purple of a Roman emperor. But the imprudent and unhappy Africans soon discovered that, in this rash insurrection, they had not sufficiently consulted their own strength or the abilities of their leader. Before he could procure any certain intelligence that the emperor of the West had fixed the choice of a general, or that a fleet of transports was collected at the mouth of the Rhone, he was suddenly informed that the great Theodosius, with a small band of veterans, had landed near Igilgilis, or Gigeri, on the African coast, and the timid usurper sunk under the ascendant of virtue and military genius. Though Firmus possessed arms and treasures, his despair of victory immediately reduced him to the use of those arts which, in the same country and in a similar situation, had formerly been practised by the crafty Jugurtha. He attempted to deceive, by an apparent submission, the vigilance of the Roman general, to seduce the fidelity of his troops, and to protract the duration of the war by successively engaging the independent tribes of Africa to espouse his quarrel or to protect his flight. Theodosius imitated the example and obtained the success of his predecessor Metellus. When Firmus, in the character of a suppliant, accused his own rashness and humbly solicited the clemency of the emperor, the lieutenant of Valentinian received and dismissed him with a friendly embrace; but he diligently required the useful and substantial pledges of a sincere repentance, nor could he be persuaded, by the assurances of peace, to suspend for an instant the operations of an active war. A dark conspiracy was detected by the penetration of Theodosius, and he satisfied, without much reluctance, the public indignation which he had secretly excited. Several of the guilty accomplices of Firmus were abandoned, according to ancient custom, to the tumult of a military execution; many more, by the amputation of both their hands, continued to exhibit an instructive spectacle of horror; the hatred of the rebels was accompanied with fear, and the fear of the Roman soldiers was mingled with respectful admiration. Amidst the boundless plains of Gætulia and the innumerable valleys of Mount Atlas, it was impossible to prevent the escape of Firmus; and if the usurper could have tired the patience of his antagonist, he would have secured his person in the depth of some remote solitude, and expected the hopes of a future revolution. He was subdued by the perseverance of Theodosius, who had formed an inflexible determination that the war should end only by the death of the tyrant, and that every nation of Africa which presumed to support his cause should be involved in his ruin. At the head of a small body of troops, which seldom exceeded three thousand five hundred men, the Roman general advanced with a steady prudence, devoid of rashness or of fear, into the heart of a country where he was sometimes attacked by armies of twenty thousand Moors. The boldness of his charge dismayed the irregular barbarians; they were disconcerted by his seasonable and orderly retreats; they were continually baffled by the unknown resources of the military art; and they felt and confessed the just superiority which was assumed by the leader of a civilised nation. When Theodosius entered the extensive dominions of Igmazen, king of the Isaflenses, the haughty savage required, in words of defiance, his name and the object of his expedition. " I am," replied the stern and disdainful count, " I am the general of Valentinian, the lord of the world, who has sent me hither to pursue and punish a desperate robber. Deliver him instantly into my hands; and be assured, that, if thou dost not obey the commands of my invincible sovereign, thou and the people over whom thou reignest shall be utterly extirpated." As soon as Igmazen was satisfied that his enemy had strength and resolution to execute the fatal menace, he consented to purchase a necessary peace by the sacrifice of a guilty fugitive. The guards that were placed to secure the person of Firmus deprived him of the hopes of escape, and the Moorish tyrant, after wine had extinguished the sense of danger, disappointed the insulting triumph of the Romans by strangling himself in the night. His dead body, the only present which Igmazen could offer to the conqueror, was carelessly thrown upon a camel; and Theodosius, leading back his victorious troops to Sitifi, was saluted by the warmest acclamations of joy and loyalty.[1]

Africa had been lost by the vices of Romanus; it was restored by the virtues of Theodosius; and our curiosity may be usefully directed to the inquiry of the respective treatment which the two

---

[1] Ammian. xxix. 5. The text of this long chapter (fifteen quarto pages) is broken and corrupted; and the narrative is perplexed by the want of chronological and geographical landmarks.

generals received from the Imperial court. The authority of
Count Romanus had been suspended by the master-general of
the cavalry, and he was committed to safe and honourable
custody till the end of the war. His crimes were proved by the
most authentic evidence, and the public expected, with some
impatience, the decree of severe justice. But the partial and
powerful favour of Mellobaudes encouraged him to challenge his
legal judges, to obtain repeated delays for the purpose of procuring a crowd of friendly witnesses, and, finally, to cover his
guilty conduct by the additional guilt of fraud and forgery.
About the same time the restorer of Britain and Africa, on a
vague suspicion that his name and services were superior to the
rank of a subject, was ignominiously beheaded at Carthage.
Valentinian no longer reigned; and the death of Theodosius, as
well as the impunity of Romanus, may justly be imputed to the
arts of the ministers who abused the confidence and deceived
the inexperienced youth of his sons.[1]

If the geographical accuracy of Ammianus had been fortunately bestowed on the British exploits of Theodosius, we should
have traced, with eager curiosity, the distinct and domestic
footsteps of his march. But the tedious enumeration of the unknown and uninteresting tribes of Africa may be reduced to the
general remark, that they were all of the swarthy race of the
Moors; that they inhabited the back settlements of the Mauri-
tanian and Numidian provinces, the country, as they have since
been termed by the Arabs, of dates and of locusts;[2] and that, as
the Roman power declined in Africa, the boundary of civilised
manners and cultivated land was insensibly contracted. Beyond
the utmost limits of the Moors, the vast and inhospitable desert
of the South extends above a thousand miles to the banks of the
Niger. The ancients, who had a very faint and imperfect knowledge of the great peninsula of Africa, were sometimes tempted to
believe that the torrid zone must ever remain destitute of inhabitants;[3] and they sometimes amused their fancy by filling the
vacant space with headless men, or rather monsters,[4] with

[1] Ammian. xxviii. 4. Orosius, l. vii. c. 33, p. 551, 552. Jerom. in Chron.
p. 187.

[2] Leo Africanus (in the Viaggi di Ramusio, tom. i. fol. 78-83) has traced
a curious picture of the people and the country, which are more minutely
described in the Afrique de Marmol, tom. iii. p. 1-54.

[3] This uninhabitable zone was gradually reduced, by the improvements
of ancient geography, from forty-five to twenty-four, or even sixteen
degrees of latitude. See a learned and judicious note of Dr. Robertson,
Hist. of America, vol. i. p. 426.

[4] Intra, si credere libet, vix jam homines et magis semiferi . . . Blem-
myes, Satyri, etc. Pomponius Mela, i. 4, p. 26, edit. Voss. in 8vo. Pliny

horned and cloven-footed satyrs,[1] with fabulous centaurs,[2] and with human pigmies, who waged a bold and doubtful warfare against the cranes.[3] Carthage would have trembled at the strange intelligence that the countries on either side of the equator were filled with innumerable nations who differed only in their colour from the ordinary appearance of the human species; and the subjects of the Roman empire might have anxiously expected that the swarms of barbarians which issued from the North would soon be encountered from the South by new swarms of barbarians, equally fierce and equally formidable. These gloomy terrors would indeed have been dispelled by a more intimate acquaintance with the character of their African enemies. The inaction of the negroes does not seem to be the effect either of their virtue or of their pusillanimity. They indulge, like the rest of mankind, their passions and appetites, and the adjacent tribes are engaged in frequent acts of hostility.[4] But their rude ignorance has never invented any effectual weapons of defence or of destruction; they appear incapable of forming any extensive plans of government or conquest; and the obvious inferiority of their mental faculties has been discovered and abused by the nations of the temperate zone. Sixty thousand blacks are annually embarked from the coast of Guinea, never to return to their native country; but they are embarked in chains;[5] and this constant emigration, which in

philosophically explains (vi. 35) the irregularities of nature, which he had *credulously* admitted (v. 8).

[1] If the satyr was the orang-outang, the great human ape (Buffon, Hist. Nat. tom. xiv. p. 43, etc.), one of that species might actually be shown alive at Alexandria in the reign of Constantine. Yet some difficulty will still remain about the conversation which St. Anthony held with one of these pious savages in the desert of Thebais (Jerom. in Vit. Paul. Eremit. tom. i. p. 238).

[2] St. Anthony likewise met one of *these* monsters, whose existence was seriously asserted by the emperor Claudius. The public laughed; but his præfect of Egypt had the address to send an artful preparation, the embalmed corpse of an *Hippocentaur*, which was preserved almost a century afterwards in the Imperial palace. See Pliny (Hist. Natur. vii. 3), and the judicious observations of Fréret (Mémoires de l'Acad. tom. vii. p. 321, etc.).

[3] The fable of the pigmies is as old as Homer (Iliad, iii. 6). The pigmies of India and Æthiopia were (trispithami) twenty-seven inches high. Every spring their cavalry (mounted on rams and goats) marched in battle array to destroy the cranes' eggs, aliter (says Pliny) futuris gregibus non resisti. Their houses were built of mud, feathers, and egg-shells. See Pliny (vi. 35, vii. 2) and Strabo (l. ii. p. 121 [p. 70, ed. Casaub.]).

[4] The third and fourth volumes of the valuable Histoire des Voyages describe the present state of the negroes. The nations of the sea-coast have been polished by European commerce, and those of the inland country have been improved by Moorish colonies.

[5] Histoire Philosophique et Politique, etc., tom. iv. p. 102

the space of two centuries might have furnished armies to over-
run the globe, accuses the guilt of Europe and the weakness of
Africa.

IV. The ignominious treaty which saved the army of Jovian had
been faithfully executed on the side of the Romans; and as they
had solemnly renounced the sovereignty and alliance of Armenia
and Iberia, those tributary kingdoms were exposed, without
protection, to the arms of the Persian monarch.[1] Sapor entered
the Armenian territories at the head of a formidable host of
cuirassiers, of archers, and of mercenary foot; but it was the
invariable practice of Sapor to mix war and negotiation, and to
consider falsehood and perjury as the most powerful instruments
of regal policy. He affected to praise the prudent and moderate
conduct of the king of Armenia; and the unsuspicious Tiranus
was persuaded, by the repeated assurances of insidious friendship, to deliver his person into the hands of a faithless and cruel
enemy. In the midst of a splendid entertainment, he was bound
in chains of silver, as an honour due to the blood of the Arsacides;
and, after a short confinement in the Tower of Oblivion at
Ecbatana, he was released from the miseries of life, either by his
own dagger or by that of an assassin. The kingdom of Armenia
was reduced to the state of a Persian province; the administration was shared between a distinguished satrap and a favourite
eunuch; and Sapor marched, without delay, to subdue the
martial spirit of the Iberians. Sauromaces, who reigned in that
country by the permission of the emperors, was expelled by a
superior force, and, as an insult on the majesty of Rome, the
king of kings placed a diadem on the head of his abject vassal
Aspacuras. The city of Artogerassa[2] was the only place of

---

[1] The evidence of Ammianus is original and decisive (xxvii. 12). Moses
of Chorene (l. iii. c. 17, p. 249, and c. 34, p. 269) and Procopius (de Bell.
Persico, l. i. c. 5, p. 17, edit. Louvre [tom. i. p. 29, ed. Bonn]) have been
consulted; but those historians, who confound distinct facts, repeat the
same events, and introduce strange stories, must be used with diffidence
and caution.

[2] Perhaps Artagera, or Ardis, under whose walls Caius, the grandson of
Augustus, was wounded. This fortress was situate above Amida, near
one of the sources of the Tigris. See D'Anville, Géographie Ancienne,
tom. ii. p. 106.

[According to St. Martin, Sapor, though supported by the two apostate
Armenian princes, Meroujan, the Ardzronnian and Vahan, the Mami-
gonian, was gallantly resisted by Arsaces, and his brave though impious
wife, Pharandsem. Sapor's troops were defeated by Vasag, the high con-
stable of the kingdom. But after four years' courageous defence of his
kingdom, Arsaces was abandoned by his nobles and obliged to accept the
perfidious hospitality of Sapor. Arsaces was blinded and imprisoned in
the Castle of Aniush (" The Castle of Oblivion ") in Susiana; his brave
general, Vasag, was flayed alive, his skin stuffed and placed near the king

Armenia which presumed to resist the effort of his arms. The treasure deposited in that strong fortress tempted the avarice of Sapor; but the danger of Olympias, the wife or widow of the Armenian king, excited the public compassion and animated the desperate valour of her subjects and soldiers. The Persians were surprised and repulsed under the walls of Artogerassa by a bold and well-concerted sally of the besieged. But the forces of Sapor were continually renewed and increased; the hopeless courage of the garrison was exhausted; the strength of the walls yielded to the assault; and the proud conqueror, after wasting the rebellious city with fire and sword, led away captive an unfortunate queen, who, in a more auspicious hour, had been the destined bride of the son of Constantine.[1] Yet if Sapor already triumphed in the easy conquest of two dependent kingdoms, he soon felt that a country is unsubdued as long as the minds of the people are actuated by an hostile and contumacious spirit. The satraps, whom he was obliged to trust, embraced the first opportunity of regaining the affection of their countrymen, and of signalising their immortal hatred to the Persian name. Since the conversion of the Armenians and Iberians, those nations considered the Christians as the favourites, and the Magians as the adversaries, of the Supreme Being; the influence of the clergy over a superstitious people was uniformly exerted in the cause of Rome; and as long as the successors of Constantine disputed with those of Artaxerxes the sovereignty of the intermediate provinces, the religious connection always threw a decisive advantage into the scale of the empire. A numerous and active party acknowledged Para, the son of Tiranus, as the lawful sovereign of Armenia, and his title to the throne was deeply rooted in the hereditary succession of five hundred years. By the unanimous consent of the Iberians, the country was equally divided between the rival princes; and Aspacuras, who owed his diadem to the choice of Sapor, was obliged to declare that his regard for his children, who were detained as hostages by the tyrant, was the only consideration which prevented him from openly renouncing the alliance of Persia. The emperor Valens, who respected the obligations of the treaty, and who was apprehensive of involving the East in

in his lonely prison. It was not till many years after (A.D. 371) that Arsaces stabbed himself, in a paroxysm of excitement at his restoration to royal honours.—O. S.]

[1] Tillemont (Hist. des Empereurs, tom. v. p. 701) proves from chronolog that Olympias must have been the mother of Para

a dangerous war, ventured, with slow and cautious measures, to support the Roman party in the kingdoms of Iberia and Armenia. Twelve legions established the authority of Sauromaces on the banks of the Cyrus. The Euphrates was protected by the valour of Arintheus. A powerful army, under the command of Count Trajan, and of Vadomair king of the Alemanni, fixed their camp on the confines of Armenia. But they were strictly enjoined not to commit the first hostilities, which might be understood as a breach of the treaty; and such was the implicit obedience of the Roman general, that they retreated, with exemplary patience, under a shower of Persian arrows, till they had clearly acquired a just title to an honourable and legitimate victory. Yet these appearances of war insensibly subsided in a vain and tedious negotiation. The contending parties supported their claims by mutual reproaches of perfidy and ambition; and it should seem that the original treaty was expressed in very obscure terms, since they were reduced to the necessity of making their inconclusive appeal to the partial testimony of the generals of the two nations who had assisted at the negotiations.[1] The invasion of the Goths and Huns, which soon afterwards shook the foundations of the Roman empire, exposed the provinces of Asia to the arms of Sapor. But the declining age, and perhaps the infirmities of the monarch, suggested new maxims of tranquillity and moderation. His death, which happened in the full maturity of a reign of seventy years, changed in a moment the court and councils of Persia, and their attention was most probably engaged by domestic troubles and the distant efforts of a Carmanian war.[2] The remembrance of ancient injuries was lost in the enjoyment of peace. The kingdoms of Armenia and Iberia were permitted, by the mutual though tacit consent of both empires, to resume their doubtful neutrality. In the first years of the reign of Theodosius, a Persian embassy arrived at Constantinople to excuse the unjustifiable measures of the former reign, and to offer, as the tribute of friendship, or even of

---

[1] Ammianus (xxvii. 12, xxix. 1, xxx. 1, 2) has described the events, without the dates, of the Persian war. Moses of Chorene (Hist. Armen. l. iii. c. 28, p. 261, c. 31, p. 266, c. 35, p. 271) affords some additional facts; but it is extremely difficult to separate truth from fable.

[2] Artaxerxes was the successor and brother (*the cousin-german*) of the great Sapor, and the guardian of his son Sapor III. (Agathias, l. iv. [c. 26] p. 136, edit. Louvre [p. 263, ed. Bonn.]). See the Universal History, vol. xi. p. 86, 161. The authors of that unequal work have compiled the Sassanian dynasty with erudition and diligence; but it is a preposterous arrangement to divide the Roman and Oriental accounts into two distinct histories.

respect, a splendid present of gems, of silk, and of Indian elephants.[1]

In the general picture of the affairs of the East under the reign of Valens, the adventures of Para form one of the most striking and singular objects. The noble youth, by the persuasion of his mother Olympias, had escaped through the Persian host that besieged Artogerassa, and implored the protection of the emperor of the East. By his timid councils, Para was alternately supported, and recalled, and restored, and betrayed. The hopes of the Armenians were sometimes raised by the presence of their natural sovereign, and the ministers of Valens were satisfied that they preserved the integrity of the public faith, if their vassal was not suffered to assume the diadem and title of King. But they soon repented of their own rashness. They were confounded by the reproaches and threats of the Persian monarch. They found reason to distrust the cruel and inconstant temper of Para himself, who sacrificed, to the slightest suspicions, the lives of his most faithful servants, and held a secret and disgraceful correspondence with the assassin of his father and the enemy of his country. Under the specious pretence of consulting with the emperor on the subject of their common interest, Para was persuaded to descend from the mountains of Armenia, where his party was in arms, and to trust his independence and safety to the discretion of a perfidious court. The king of Armenia, for such he appeared in his own eyes and in those of his nation, was received with due honours by the governors of the provinces through which he passed; but when he arrived at Tarsus in Cilicia, his progress was stopped under various pretences, his motions were watched with respectful vigilance, and he gradually discovered that he was a prisoner in the hands of the Romans. Para suppressed his indignation, dissembled his fears, and, after secretly preparing his escape, mounted on horseback with three hundred of his faithful followers. The officer stationed at the door of his appartment immediately communicated his flight to the consular of Cilicia, who overtook him in the suburbs, and endeavoured, without success, to dissuade him from prosecuting his rash and dangerous design. A legion was ordered to pursue the royal fugitive; but the pursuit of infantry could not be very alarming to a body of light cavalry; and upon the first cloud of arrows that was dis-

---

[1] Pacatus in Panegyr. Vet. xii. 22; and Orosius, l. vii. c. 34. Ictumque tum fœdus est, quo universus Oriens usque ad nunc (A.D. 416) tranquillissime fruitur.

charged into the air, they retreated with precipitation to the gates of Tarsus. After an incessant march of two days and two nights, Para and his Armenians reached the banks of the Euphrates; but the passage of the river, which they were obliged to swim, was attended with some delay and some loss. The country was alarmed, and the two roads, which were only separated by an interval of three miles, had been occupied by a thousand archers on horseback, under the command of a count and a tribune. Para must have yielded to superior force, if the accidental arrival of a friendly traveller had not revealed the danger and the means of escape. A dark and almost impervious path securely conveyed the Armenian troops through the thicket; and Para had left behind him the count and the tribune, while they patiently expected his approach along the public highways. They returned to the Imperial court to excuse their want of diligence or success: and seriously alleged that the king of Armenia, who was a skilful magician, had transformed himself and his followers, and passed before their eyes under a borrowed shape. After his return to his native kingdom, Para still continued to profess himself the friend and ally of the Romans: but the Romans had injured him too deeply ever to forgive, and the secret sentence of his death was signed in the council of Valens. The execution of the bloody deed was committed to the subtle prudence of Count Trajan, and he had the merit of insinuating himself into the confidence of the credulous prince, that he might find an opportunity of stabbing him to the heart. Para was invited to a Roman banquet, which had been prepared with all the pomp and sensuality of the East; the hall resounded with cheerful music, and the company was already heated with wine, when the count retired for an instant, drew his sword, and gave the signal of the murder. A robust and desperate barbarian instantly rushed on the king of Armenia, and though he bravely defended his life with the first weapon that chance offered to his hand, the table of the Imperial general was stained with the royal blood of a guest and an ally. Such were the weak and wicked maxims of the Roman administration, that, to attain a doubtful object of political interest, the laws of nations, and the sacred rights of hospitality, were inhumanly violated in the face of the world.[1]

[1] See in Ammianus (xxx. 1) the adventures of Para. Moses of Chorene calls him Tiridates; and tells a long and not improbable story of his son Gnelus, who afterwards made himself popular in Armenia, and provoked the jealousy of the reigning king (l. iii. c. 21, etc., p. 253, etc.).

[There is a serious error here. Para is not the same as Tiridates. The

V. During a peaceful interval of thirty years, the Romans secured their frontiers, and the Goths extended their dominions. The victories of the great Hermanric,[1] king of the Ostrogoths, and the most noble of the race of the Amali, have been compared, by the enthusiasm of his countrymen, to the exploits of Alexander: with this singular, and almost incredible, difference, that the martial spirit of the Gothic hero, instead of being supported by the vigour of youth, was displayed with glory and success in the extreme period of human life, between the age of fourscore and one hundred and ten years. The independent tribes were persuaded, or compelled, to acknowledge the king of the Ostrogoths as the sovereign of the Gothic nation: the chiefs of the Visigoths, or Thervingi, renounced the royal title, and assumed the more humble appellation of *Judges ;* and, among those judges, Athanaric, Fritigern, and Alavivus were the most illustrious, by their personal merit, as well as by their vicinity to the Roman provinces. These domestic conquests, which increased the military power of Hermanric, enlarged his ambitious designs. He invaded the adjacent countries of the North, and twelve considerable nations, whose names and limits cannot be accurately defined, successively yielded to the superiority of the Gothic arms.[2] The Heruli, who inhabited the marshy lands near the lake Mæotis, were renowned for their strength and agility; and the assistance of their light infantry was eagerly solicited, and highly esteemed, in all the wars of the barbarians. But the active spirit of the Heruli was subdued by the slow and steady perseverance of the Goths; and, after a bloody action, in which the king was slain, the remains of that warlike tribe became an useful accession to the camp of Hermanric. He then marched against the Venedi; unskilled in the use of arms, and formidable only by their numbers, which filled the wide extent of the plains of modern Poland. The victorious Goths, who were not inferior in numbers, prevailed in the contest, by the decisive advantages of exercise and discipline. After the submission of the Venedi, the conqueror advanced, without resistance, as far as latter was the father of Gnel, first husband of Pharandsem, the future wife of Arsaces and the mother of Para.—O. S.]

[1] The concise account of the reign and conquests of Hermanric seems to be one of the valuable fragments which Jornandes (c. 23) borrowed from the Gothic histories of Ablavius, or Cassiodorus.

[2] M. de Buat (Hist. des Peuples de l'Europe, tom. vi. p. 311-329) investigates, with more industry than success, the nations subdued by the arms of Hermanric. He denies the existence of the *Vasinobroncæ*, on account of the immoderate length of their name. Yet the French envoy to Ratisbon, or Dresden, must have traversed the country of the *Mediomatrici*.

the confines of the Æstii,[1] an ancient people, whose name is still preserved in the province of Esthonia. Those distant inhabitants of the Baltic coast were supported by the labours of agriculture, enriched by the trade of amber, and consecrated by the peculiar worship of the Mother of the Gods. But the scarcity of iron obliged the Æstian warriors to content themselves with wooden clubs; and the reduction of that wealthy country is ascribed to the prudence, rather than to the arms, of Hermanric. His dominions, which extended from the Danube to the Baltic, included the native seats, and the recent acquisitions, of the Goths; and he reigned over the greatest part of Germany and Scythia with the authority of a conqueror, and sometimes with the cruelty of a tyrant. But he reigned over a part of the globe incapable of perpetuating and adorning the glory of its heroes. The name of Hermanric is almost buried in oblivion; his exploits are imperfectly known: and the Romans themselves appeared unconscious of the progress of an aspiring power which threatened the liberty of the North and the peace of the empire.[2]

The Goths had contracted an hereditary attachment for the Imperial house of Constantine, of whose power and liberality they had received so many signal proofs. They respected the public peace; and if an hostile band sometimes presumed to pass the Roman limit, their irregular conduct was candidly ascribed to the ungovernable spirit of the barbarian youth. Their contempt for two new and obscure princes, who had been raised to the throne by a popular election, inspired the Goths with bolder hopes; and, while they agitated some design of marching their confederate force under the national standard,[3] they were easily tempted to embrace the party of Procopius, and to foment, by their dangerous aid, the civil discord of the Romans. The public treaty might stipulate no more than ten thousand auxiliaries; but the design was so zealously adopted by the chiefs of the Visigoths, that the army which passed the Danube amounted to the number of thirty thousand men.[4] They marched with the

---

[1] The edition of Grotius (Jornandes, p. 642) exhibits the name of *Æstri*. But reason and the Ambrosian MS. have restored the *Æstii*, whose manners and situation are expressed by the pencil of Tacitus (Germania, c. 45).

[2] Ammianus (xxxi. 3) observes, in general terms, Ermenrichi . . . bellicosissimi Regis, et per multa variaque fortiter facta, vicinis gentibus formidati, etc.

[3] Valens . . . docetur relationibus Ducum, gentem Gothorum, eâ tempestate intactam ideoque sævissimam, conspirantem in unum, ad pervadenda parari collimitia Thraciarum. Ammian. xxvi. 6.

[4] M. de Buat (Hist. des Peuples de l'Europe, tom. vi. p. 332) has curiously ascertained the real number of these auxiliaries. The 3000 of Ammianus, and the 10,000 of Zosimus, were only the first divisions of the Gothic army.

proud confidence that their invincible valour would decide the fate of the Roman empire; and the provinces of Thrace groaned under the weight of the barbarians, who displayed the insolence of masters, and the licentiousness of enemies. But the intemperance which gratified their appetites retarded their progress; and before the Goths could receive any certain intelligence of the defeat and death of Procopius, they perceived, by the hostile state of the country, that the civil and military powers were resumed by his successful rival. A chain of posts and fortifications, skilfully disposed by Valens, or the generals of Valens, resisted their march, prevented their retreat, and intercepted their subsistence. The fierceness of the barbarians was tamed and suspended by hunger; they indignantly threw down their arms at the feet of the conqueror, who offered them food and chains: the numerous captives were distributed in all the cities of the East; and the provincials, who were soon familiarised with their savage appearance, ventured, by degrees, to measure their own strength with these formidable adversaries, whose name had so long been the object of their terror. The king of Scythia (and Hermanric alone could deserve so lofty a title) was grieved and exasperated by this national calamity. His ambassadors loudly complained, at the court of Valens, of the infraction of the ancient and solemn alliance which had so long subsisted between the Romans and the Goths. They alleged that they had fulfilled the duty of allies, by assisting the kinsman and successor of the emperor Julian; they required the immediate restitution of the noble captives; and they urged a very singular claim, that the Gothic generals, marching in arms, and in hostile array, were entitled to the sacred character and privileges of ambassadors. The decent, but peremptory, refusal of these extravagant demands was signified to the barbarians by Victor, master-general of the cavalry, who expressed, with force and dignity, the just complaints of the emperor of the East.[1] The negotiation was interrupted, and the manly exhortations of Valentinian encouraged his timid brother to vindicate the insulted majesty of the empire.[2]

---

[1] The march and subsequent negotiation are described in the Fragments of Eunapius (Excerpt. Legat. p. 18, edit. Louvre [p. 47, ed. Bonn]). The provincials, who afterwards became familiar with the barbarians, found that their strength was more apparent than real. They were tall of stature, but their legs were clumsy and their shoulders were narrow.

[2] Valens enim, ut consulto placuerat fratri, cujus regebatur arbitrio, arma concussit in Gothos ratione justâ permotus. Ammianus (xxvii. 4) then proceeds to describe, not the country of the Goths, but the peaceful and obedient province of Thrace, which was not affected by the war.

The splendour and magnitude of this Gothic war are celebrated by a contemporary historian: [1] but the events scarcely deserve the attention of posterity, except as the preliminary steps of the approaching decline and fall of the empire. Instead of leading the nations of Germany and Scythia to the banks of the Danube, or even to the gates of Constantinople, the aged monarch of the Goths resigned to the brave Athanaric the danger and glory of a defensive war, against an enemy who wielded with a feeble hand the powers of a mighty state. A bridge of boats was established upon the Danube, the presence of Valens animated his troops, and his ignorance of the art of war was compensated by personal bravery, and a wise deference to the advice of Victor and Arintheus, his masters-general of the cavalry and infantry. The operations of the campaign were conducted by their skill and experience; but they found it impossible to drive the Visigoths from their strong posts in the mountains, and the devastation of the plains obliged the Romans themselves to repass the Danube on the approach of winter. The incessant rains, which swelled the waters of the river, produced a tacit suspension of arms, and confined the emperor Valens, during the whole course of the ensuing summer, to his camp of Marcianopolis. The third year of the war was more favourable to the Romans, and more pernicious to the Goths. The interruption of trade deprived the barbarians of the objects of luxury, which they already confounded with the necessaries of life; and the desolation of a very extensive tract of country threatened them with the horrors of famine. Athanaric was provoked, or compelled, to risk a battle, which he lost, in the plains; and the pursuit was rendered more bloody by the cruel precaution of the victorious generals, who had promised a large reward for the head of every Goth that was brought into the Imperial camp. The submission of the barbarians appeased the resentment of Valens and his council: the emperor listened with satisfaction to the flattering and eloquent remonstrance of the senate of Constantinople, which assumed, for the first time, a share in the public deliberations; and the same generals, Victor and Arintheus, who had successfully directed the conduct of the war, were empowered to regulate the conditions of peace. The freedom of trade which the Goths had hitherto enjoyed was restricted to two cities on the Danube; the rashness of their

---

[1] Eunapius, in Excerpt. Legat. p. 18, 19 [p. 47, 48, ed. Bonn]. The Greek sophist must have considered as *one* and the *same* war, the whole series of Gothic history till the victories and peace of Theodosius.

leaders was severely punished by the suppression of their pensions and subsidies; and the exception, which was stipulated in favour of Athanaric alone, was more advantageous than honourable to the Judge of the Visigoths. Athanaric, who, on this occasion, appears to have consulted his private interest, without expecting the orders of his sovereign, supported his own dignity, and that of his tribe, in the personal interview which was proposed by the ministers of Valens. He persisted in his declaration that it was impossible for him, without incurring the guilt of perjury, ever to set his foot on the territory of the empire; and it is more than probable that his regard for the sanctity of an oath was confirmed by the recent and fatal examples of Roman treachery. The Danube, which separated the dominions of the two independent nations, was chosen for the scene of the conference. The emperor of the East, and the Judge of the Visigoths, accompanied by an equal number of armed followers, advanced in their respective barges to the middle of the stream. After the ratification of the treaty, and the delivery of hostages, Valens returned in triumph to Constantinople, and the Goths remained in a state of tranquillity about six years, till they were violently impelled against the Roman empire by an innumerable host of Scythians, who appeared to issue from the frozen regions of the North.[1]

The emperor of the West, who had resigned to his brother the command of the Lower Danube, reserved for his immediate care the defence of the Rhætian and Illyrian provinces, which spread so many hundred miles along the greatest of the European rivers. The active policy of Valentinian was continually employed in adding new fortifications to the security of the frontier: but the abuse of this policy provoked the just resentment of the barbarians. The Quadi complained that the ground for an intended fortress had been marked out on their territories, and their complaints were urged with so much reason and moderation, that Equitius, master-general of Illyricum, consented to suspend the prosecution of the work till he should be more clearly informed of the will of his sovereign. This fair occasion of injuring a rival, and of advancing the fortune of his son, was eagerly embraced by the inhuman Maximin, the præfect, or rather

[1] The Gothic war is described by Ammianus (xxvii. 5), Zosimus (l. iv. [c. 10] p. 211-214), and Themistius (Orat. x. p. 129-141). The orator Themistius was sent from the senate of Constantinople to congratulate the victorious emperor; and his servile eloquence compares Valens *on* the Danube to Achilles *in* the Scamander. Jornandes forgets a war peculiar to the *Visi*-Goths, and inglorious to the Gothic name (Mascou's Hist. of the Germans, vii. 3).

tyrant, of Gaul. The passions of Valentinian were impatient of control, and he credulously listened to the assurances of his favourite, that, if the government of Valeria, and the direction of the work, were intrusted to the zeal of his son Marcellinus, the emperor should no longer be importuned with the audacious remonstrances of the barbarians. The subjects of Rome, and the natives of Germany, were insulted by the arrogance of a young and worthless minister, who considered his rapid elevation as the proof and reward of his superior merit. He affected, however, to receive the modest application of Gabinius, king of the Quadi, with some attention and regard; but this artful civility concealed a dark and bloody design, and the credulous prince was persuaded to accept the pressing invitation of Marcellinus. I am at a loss how to vary the narrative of similar crimes; or how to relate that, in the course of the same year, but in remote parts of the empire, the inhospitable table of two Imperial generals was stained with the royal blood of two guests and allies, inhumanly murdered by their order, and in their presence. The fate of Gabinius, and of Para, was the same: but the cruel death of their sovereign was resented in a very different manner by the servile temper of the Armenians and the free and daring spirit of the Germans. The Quadi were much declined from that formidable power which, in the time of Marcus Antoninus, had spread terror to the gates of Rome. But they still possessed arms and courage; their courage was animated by despair, and they obtained the usual reinforcement of the cavalry of their Sarmatian allies. So improvident was the assassin Marcellinus, that he chose the moment when the bravest veterans had been drawn away to suppress the revolt of Firmus, and the whole province was exposed, with a very feeble defence, to the rage of the exasperated barbarians. They invaded Pannonia in the season of harvest, unmercifully destroyed every object of plunder which they could not easily transport, and either disregarded or demolished the empty fortifications. The princess Constantia, the daughter of the emperor Constantius, and the granddaughter of the great Constantine, very narrowly escaped. That royal maid, who had innocently supported the revolt of Procopius, was now the destined wife of the heir of the Western empire. She traversed the peaceful province with a splendid and unarmed train. Her person was saved from danger, and the republic from disgrace, by the active zeal of Messalla, governor of the provinces. As soon as he was informed that the village where she stopped only to dine was almost encompassed by the barbarians, he hastily placed her in his own chariot, and drove full speed till he reached the gates of Sirmium, which were at the distance of six-and-twenty miles. Even Sirmium might not have been secure if the Quadi and Sarmatians had diligently advanced during the general consternation of the magistrates and people. Their delay allowed Probus, the Prætorian præfect, sufficient time to recover his own spirits and to revive the courage of the citizens. He skilfully directed their strenuous efforts to repair and strengthen the decayed fortifications, and procured the season-able and effectual assistance of a company of archers to protect the capital of the Illyrian provinces. Disappointed in their attempts against the walls of Sirmium, the indignant barbarians turned their arms against the master-general of the frontier, to whom they unjustly attributed the murder of their king. Equitius could bring into the field no more than two legions, but they contained the veteran strength of the Mæsian and Pan-nonian bands. The obstinacy with which they disputed the vain honours of rank and precedency was the cause of their destruction, and, while they acted with separate forces and divided councils, they were surprised and slaughtered by the active vigour of the Sarmatian horse. The success of this invasion provoked the emulation of the bordering tribes, and the province of Mæsia would infallibly have been lost if young Theodosius, the duke or military commander of the frontier, had not signalised, in the defeat of the public enemy, an intrepid genius worthy of his illustrious father and of his future greatness.[1]

The mind of Valentinian, who then resided at Trèves, was deeply affected by the calamities of Illyricum, but the lateness of the season suspended the execution of his designs till the ensuing spring. He marched in person, with a considerable part of the forces of Gaul, from the banks of the Moselle; and to the suppliant ambassadors of the Sarmatians, who met him on the way, he returned a doubtful answer, that as soon as he reached the scene of action he should examine and pronounce. When he arrived at Sirmium he gave audience to the deputies of the Illyrian provinces, who loudly congratulated their own felicity under the auspicious government of Probus, his Prætorian præfect.[2] Valentinian, who was flattered by these demonstra-

---

[1] Ammianus (xxix. 6) and Zosimus (l. iv. [c. 16] p. 219, 220) carefully mark the origin and progress of the Quadic and Sarmatian war.

[2] Ammianus (xxx. 5), who acknowledges the merit, has censured, with becoming asperity, the oppressive administration of Petronius Probus. When Jerom translated and continued the Chronicle of Eusebius (A.D. 380; see Tillemont, Mém. Ecclés. tom. xii. p. 53, 626), he expressed the truth,

tions of their loyalty and gratitude, imprudently asked the
deputy of Epirus, a Cynic philosopher of intrepid sincerity,[1]
whether he was freely sent by the wishes of the province?
"With tears and groans am I sent (replied Iphicles) by a reluctant people." The emperor paused, but the impunity of his
ministers established the pernicious maxim that they might
oppress his subjects without injuring his service. A strict
inquiry into their conduct would have relieved the public discontent. The severe condemnation of the murder of Gabinius
was the only measure which could restore the confidence of the
Germans, and vindicate the honour of the Roman name. But
the haughty monarch was incapable of the magnanimity which
dares to acknowledge a fault. He forgot the provocation,
remembered only the injury, and advanced into the country of
the Quadi with an insatiate thirst of blood and revenge. The
extreme devastation and promiscuous massacre of a savage war
were justified in the eyes of the emperor, and perhaps in those
of the world, by the cruel equity of retaliation;[2] and such was
the discipline of the Romans, and the consternation of the enemy,
that Valentinian repassed the Danube without the loss of a single
man. As he had resolved to complete the destruction of the
Quadi by a second campaign, he fixed his winter-quarters at
Bregetio, on the Danube, near the Hungarian city of Presburg.
While the operations of war were suspended by the severity of
the weather, the Quadi made an humble attempt to deprecate
the wrath of their conqueror, and, at the earnest persuasion of
Equitius, their ambassadors were introduced into the Imperial
council. They approached the throne with bended bodies and
dejected countenances, and, without daring to complain of the
murder of their king, they affirmed, with solemn oaths, that the
late invasion was the crime of some irregular robbers, which the
public council of the nation condemned and abhorred. The

---

or at least the public opinion of his country, in the following words:
"Probus P. P. Illyrici iniquissimis tributorum exactionibus, ante provin-
cias quas regebat, quam a Barbaris vastarentur, *erasit.*" (Chron. edit.
Scaliger, p. 187; Animadvers. p. 259.) The saint afterwards formed an
intimate and tender friendship with the widow of Probus; and the name of
Count Equitius, with less propriety, but without much injustice, has been
substituted in the text.

[1] Julian (Orat. vi. p. 198) represents his friend Iphicles as a man of virtue
and merit, who had made himself ridiculous and unhappy by adopting the
extravagant dress and manners of the Cynics.

[2] Ammian. xxx. 5. Jerom, who exaggerates the misfortune of Valentinian, refuses him even this last consolation of revenge. Vastato genitali
solo, et *inultam* patriam derelinquens (tom. i. p. 26 [Ep. ad Heliodor. tom.
i. p. 341, ed. Vallars.]).

answer of the emperor left them but little to hope from his clemency or compassion. He reviled, in the most intemperate language, their baseness, their ingratitude, their insolence. His eyes, his voice, his colour, his gestures, expressed the violence of his ungoverned fury; and while his whole frame was agitated with convulsive passion a large blood-vessel suddenly burst in his body, and Valentinian fell speechless into the arms of his attendants. Their pious care immediately concealed his situation from the crowd, but in a few minutes the emperor of the West expired in an agony of pain, retaining his senses till the last, and struggling, without success, to declare his intentions to the generals and ministers who surrounded the royal couch. Valentinian was about fifty-four years of age, and he wanted only one hundred days to accomplish the twelve years of his reign.[1]

The polygamy of Valentinian is seriously attested by an ecclesiastical historian.[2] "The empress Severa (I relate the fable) admitted into her familiar society the lovely Justina, the daughter of an Italian governor; her admiration of those naked charms, which she had often seen in the bath, was expressed with such lavish and imprudent praise that the emperor was tempted to introduce a second wife into his bed; and his public edict extended to all the subjects of the empire the same domestic privilege which he had assumed for himself." But we may be assured, from the evidence of reason as well as history, that the two marriages of Valentinian with Severa and with Justina were *successively* contracted, and that he used the ancient permission of divorce, which was still allowed by the laws, though it was condemned by the church. Severa was the mother of Gratian, who seemed to unite every claim which could entitle him to the undoubted succession of the Western empire. He was the eldest son of a monarch whose glorious reign had confirmed the free and honourable choice of his fellow-soldiers. Before he had attained the ninth year of his age the royal youth received from the hands of his indulgent father the purple robe

---

[1] See, on the death of Valentinian, Ammianus (xxx. 6), Zosimus (l. iv. [c. 17] p. 221), Victor (in Epitom. [c. 45]), Socrates (l. iv. c. 31), and Jerom (in Chron. p. 187 [tom viii. p. 815, ed. Vallars.], and tom. i. p. 26, ad Heliodor. [tom. i. p. 341, ed. Vallars.]). There is much variety of circumstances among them; and Ammianus is so eloquent that he writes nonsense.

[2] Socrates (l. iv. c. 31) is the only original witness of this foolish story, so repugnant to the laws and manners of the Romans, that it scarcely deserved the formal and elaborate dissertation of M. Bonamy (Mém. de l'Académie, tom. xxx. p. 394-405). Yet I would preserve the natural circumstance of the bath, instead of following Zosimus, who represents Justina as an old woman, the widow of Magnentius.

and diadem, with the title of Augustus; the election was solemnly ratified by the consent and applause of the armies of Gaul,[1] and the name of Gratian was added to the names of Valentinian and Valens in all the legal transactions of the Roman government. By his marriage with the grand-daughter of Constantine, the son of Valentinian acquired all the hereditary rights of the Flavian family, which, in a series of three Imperial generations, were sanctified by time, religion, and the reverence of the people. At the death of his father the royal youth was in the seventeenth year of his age, and his virtues already justified the favourable opinion of the army and people. But Gratian resided, without apprehension, in the palace of Trèves, whilst at the distance of many hundred miles Valentinian suddenly expired in the camp of Bregetio. The passions which had been so long suppressed by the presence of a master immediately revived in the Imperial council, and the ambitious design of reigning in the name of an infant was artfully executed by Mellobaudes and Equitius, who commanded the attachment of the Illyrian and Italian bands. They contrived the most honourable pretences to remove the popular leaders and the troops of Gaul, who might have asserted the claims of the lawful successor; they suggested the necessity of extinguishing the hopes of foreign and domestic enemies by a bold and decisive measure. The empress Justina, who had been left in a palace about one hundred miles from Bregetio, was respectfully invited to appear in the camp with the son of the deceased emperor. On the sixth day after the death of Valentinian, the infant prince of the same name, who was only four years old, was shown, in the arms of his mother, to the legions, and solemnly invested, by military acclamation, with the titles and ensigns of supreme power. The impending dangers of a civil war were seasonably prevented by the wise and moderate conduct of the emperor Gratian. He cheerfully accepted the choice of the army, declared that he should always consider the son of Justina as a brother, not as a rival, and advised the empress, with her son Valentinian, to fix their residence at Milan, in the fair and peaceful province of Italy, while he assumed the more arduous command of the countries beyond the Alps. Gratian dissembled his resentment till he could safely punish or disgrace the authors of the conspiracy; and though he uniformly behaved with tenderness and regard to his infant col-

---

[1] Ammianus (xxvii. 6) describes the form of this military election, and *august* investiture. Valentinian does not appear to have consulted, or even informed, the senate of Rome.

league, he gradually confounded, in the administration of the Western empire, the office of a guardian with the authority of a sovereign. The government of the Roman world was exercised in the united names of Valens and his two nephews; but the feeble emperor of the East, who succeeded to the rank of his elder brother, never obtained any weight or influence in the councils of the West.[1]

---

[1] Ammianus, xxx. 10. Zosimus, l. iv. [c. 19] p. 222, 223. Tillemont has proved (Hist. des Empereurs, tom. v. p. 707-709) that Gratian *reigned* in Italy, Africa, and Illyricum. I have endeavoured to express his authority over his brother's dominions, as he used it, in an ambiguous style.

EVERYMAN'S LIBRARY

A Selected List

In each of the thirteen classifications in this list (except BIO-GRAPHY) the volumes are arranged alphabetically under the authors' names, but Anthologies, etc., are listed under titles. Where authors appear in more than one section, a cross-reference is given. The number at the end of each item is the number of the volume in the series.

EVERYMAN'S LIBRARY

BIOGRAPHY

CLASSICAL

ESSAYS AND BELLES-LETTRES

2

FICTION

HISTORY

ORATORY

PHILOSOPHY AND THEOLOGY

POETRY AND DRAMA

REFERENCE

The following volumes in this section are now in the special edition of
Everyman's Reference Library:

ROMANCE

SCIENCE

TRAVEL AND TOPOGRAPHY

FOR YOUNG PEOPLE

EVERYMAN'S LIBRARY was founded in 1906, and for all the changes and chances in the book world during its long life the series stands strong to-day as the most comprehensive, inexpensive collection of books of classic measure. It is, indeed, still what its publisher intended it to be. J. M. Dent conceived it as a library arranged to cover the whole field of English literature, including translations of the ancient classics and outstanding foreign works; a series to make widely available those great books which appeal, as he says in his Memoirs, 'to every kind of reader: the worker, the student, the cultured man, the child, the man, and the woman.' The aim and scope of the series was crystallized in the title *Everyman's Library*, a title which has justified itself by the worldwide sales, totalling in 1953 some forty millions.

There were, of course, already in being in 1906 other popular series of reprints, but none on the scale proposed for *Everyman*. 155 volumes were published in three batches in the Library's first year; they comprised a balanced selection from many branches of literature and set the standard on which the Library has been built up. By early 1915 the 733rd volume had been issued; and, in spite of the interruptions of two world wars and their aftermath, the 994th volume was published in 1953. The founder-publisher aimed at a library of a thousand volumes, and that goal will surely be achieved before the jubilee of the Library in 1956.

A rough and ready pointer to the representative character of the Library is the number of volumes in each of the broad classifications into which the Library is divided—Biography has some 80 volumes; the Greek and Latin classics, about 40; Essays and Belles-lettres, 100; Fiction, 300; History, 80; Poetry and Drama, 100; Romance, 30; Science, 25; Religion and Philosophy, 60; Travel and Topography, 45; For Young People, 65. (The reference section is now being published separately as Everyman's Reference Library.) Most of but not all these volumes are in print now; some absent ones are works which changing taste has ruled out; but the classified sections of the Library are maintained in the original proportions, and to-day there are available in the Library the works of some five hundred authors of all times and all lands, the honoured names that stand for great literature. Moreover, many 'temporarily out of print' volumes are now being reinstated.

In March 1953 a fresh development of the Library began; new volumes and all new issues of established volumes in *Everyman's Library* are now in the larger size of crown octavo (except the volumes in the Young People's Section). The larger volumes have new title-pages, bindings, and wrappers, and the text pages have generous margins. Ninety volumes in this improved format will have been issued within one year of its inauguration.

Editorially the Library is under constant survey; all volumes are re-examined and brought up to date, with new introductions, annotations, and additional matter, wherever desirable; often a completely new translation or newly edited text is substituted when transferring an old volume to the new format, such as the new editions of *Pepys's Diary*, *Caesar's War Commentaries*, and *The Anglo-Saxon Chronicle*.

The new larger volumes are in keeping with the reader's own collection in his home, for which the Library is planned, and they are also in the suitable size for the shelves of all public, institutional, university, and school libraries. Many important works in *Everyman's Library* are unobtainable in any other edition, and they are as essential to the comprehensiveness of the Library as are the masterpieces of fiction, some of which are in one *Everyman* volume of anything up to 800 or 900 pages. The new *Everyman's Library* in crown octavo is published at two prices (except in the U.S.A.), according to the length and nature of the work; volumes in red binding and wrapper are at one price and those in blue at a slightly higher price.

This development entails no break in the continuity of the Library; there are at this date nearly 600 volumes in the original format, and they will be obtainable in the old size and at the old price until they are reissued in the new. Four times a year the Publishers issue a prospectus of the volumes to be issued in the larger format during the next three months: this will be sent free to all applicants. A descriptive catalogue of all volumes is also freely available, the annotations giving the year of birth and death of the author, the date of first publication of the work, and a brief description of, or details of the contents of, the last revised *Everyman's Library* edition.

J. M. DENT & SONS LTD.